WEBSTER'S
NEW W◯RLD®

Pocket French Dictionary

WILEY

Wiley Publishing, Inc.

Webster's New World® Pocket French Dictionary

Published by:

Wiley Publishing, Inc.

111 River Street

Hoboken, NJ 07030-5774

www.wiley.com

For general information on our other products and services or to obtain technical support, please contact our Customer Care Department within the U.S. at 800-762-2974, outside the U.S. at 317-572-3993, or fax 317-572-4002.

ISBN: 0-7645-5620-7

Cataloging-in-Publication Data available from the Library of Congress.

Designed and typeset by Chambers Harrap Publishers Ltd, Edinburgh.

Manufactured in the United States of America.

10 9 8 7 6 5 4 3 2 1

Contents

Contents

Preface

Based on the text of *Harrap's Micro French Dictionary*, this dictionary has been revised and expanded and benefits from a new, easy-to-read design. With more than 25,000 words and expressions and a focus on American English, it is an accurate, reliable tool for learners of French.

With around 1,500 new words and phrases added to this edition, the dictionary provides a wide-ranging selection of the most useful and up-to-date vocabulary of French and English, including terms from the ever-expanding fields of information technology and telecommunications. The syllabification of all English headwords has been included in this edition, providing the user with extra help.

The dictionary has been designed to allow the user easy navigation through the entries. Different senses of the headword are shown by source-language indicating material in brackets, as in **chance** *(luck)* hasard *m*; *(opportunity)* chances *fpl*. Further contextualizing material is provided by target-language indicators which are given after the translation in cases where the sense of the translation is ambiguous, eg **scrapbook** album *m (pour collages etc)*. Finally, source-language labels such as *Grammar, Sports, Cartes, Échecs* and so on are provided for items belonging to specific domains of vocabulary.

Further clarity is provided by English phrasal verbs (such as **go ahead**), many French pronominal verbs (such as **se laver**) and the most common English compound nouns (such as **heat wave**) all being presented as separate entries.

The different grammatical divisions of an entry (such as noun, verb and so on) are easily identified by bold numbers **1, 2, 3** and so on. Similarly, sense divisions within longer entries are clearly indicated by a ▪ symbol.

The dictionary also benefits from several space-saving devices. A headword is represented by its first letter when it appears as an example within the entry, for example **on the h.** in the entry **horizon**. In addition, a slash (/) within an entry is used both to separate non-interchangeable parts of a phrase matched exactly in English and in French, such as **qui/quoi encore?** who/what else? and to show productive expressions such as **how many apples/etc?** combien de pommes/*etc*?.

French grammar notes

In French, the feminine of an adjective is formed, when regular, by adding **e** to the masculine form (eg grand, grande; carré, carrée; fin, fine). If the masculine already ends in **e**, the feminine is the same as the masculine (eg utile). Both regular and irregular feminine forms of adjectives (eg généreux, généreuse; léger, légère; doux, douce) are given on the French-English side of the dictionary. On the English-French side, French adjectives are shown in the masculine, but highly irregular feminine forms (eg frais, fraîche; faux, fausse) have also been included to help the user.

To form the plural of a French noun or adjective **s** is usually added to the singular (eg arbre, arbres; taxi, taxis; petit, petits). The plural form of a noun ending in **s, x** or **z** (eg pois, croix, nez) is the same as that of the singular. Plurals of nouns and adjectives which do not follow these general rules (eg where **x** or **aux** is added in the plural, or where there is a highly irregular plural such as œil, yeux) are listed in the French section. Also included are the plurals of French compounds where the formation of the plural involves a change other than the addition of final **s** (eg chou-fleur, choux-fleurs; arc-en-ciel, arcs-en-ciel). The irregular plurals of French nouns (and irregular masculine plurals of French adjectives) are listed on the French-English side (eg cerveau, -x; général, -aux). Included on the English-French side, to help the user, are the plurals of French nouns (and adjectives) ending in **al, eu** and **au** where **s**, and not the usual **x**, forms the plural (eg pneu, pneus; naval, navals) and of those nouns in **ail** and **ou** where the plural is formed with **x**, and not the usual **s** (eg travail, travaux; chou, choux).

Pronunciation of French

Table of phonetic symbols

Vowels

[i] vite, cygne, sortie
[e] été, donner, légal
[ɛ] elle, mais, père, prêt
[a] chat, fameux, toit [twa]
[ɑ] pas, âge, tâche
[ɔ] donne, fort, album
[o] dos, chaud, peau, dôme
[u] tout, cour, roue, goût

[y] cru, sûr, rue
[ø] feu, meule, nœud
[ï] œuf, jeune, cueillir [kœjir]
[ə] le, refaire, entre
[ɛ̃] vin, plein, faim, saint
[ɑ̃] enfant, temps, paon
[ɔ̃] mon, nombre, honte
[œ̃] lundi, humble, un

Consonants

[p] pain, absolu, taper, frapper
[b] beau, abbé, robe
[t] table, nette, vite
[d] donner, sud, raide
[k] camp, képi, qui, taxe [taks],
     accès [aksɛ]
[g] garde, guerre, second,
     exister [ɛgziste]
[f] feu, siffler, phase
[v] voir, trouver, wagon
[s] son, cire, ça, chasse, nation
[z] cousin, zéro, rose
[ʃ] chose, hache, schéma
[ʒ] gilet, jeter, âge
[l] lait, facile, elle

[r] rare, rhume, sortir, barreau
[m] mon, flamme, aimer
[n] né, canne, animal
[ɲ] campagne, agneau
[ŋ] jogging

Semi-consonants

[j] piano, voyage, fille, yeux
[w] ouest, noir [nwar], tramway
[ɥ] muet, lui, huile

Abbreviations

adjective	*adj*	adjectif
abbreviation	*abbr, abrév*	abréviation
adverb	*adv*	adverbe
article	*art*	article
auxiliary	*aux*	auxiliaire
Canadian	*Can*	canadien
conjunction	*conj*	conjonction
definite	*def, déf*	défini
demonstrative	*dem, dém*	démonstratif
et cetera	*etc*	et cetera
feminine	*f*	féminin
familiar	*Fam*	familier
feminine plural	*fpl*	féminin pluriel
French	*Fr*	français
indefinite	*indef, indéf*	indéfini
interjection	*int*	interjection
invariable	*inv*	invariable
masculine	*m*	masculin
masculine and feminine	*mf*	masculin et féminin
masculine plural	*mpl*	masculin pluriel
noun	*n*	nom
plural	*pl*	pluriel
possessive	*poss*	possessif
past participle	*pp*	participe passé
preposition	*prep, prép*	préposition
present participle	*pres p*	participe présent
pronoun	*pron*	pronom
	qch	quelque chose
	qn	quelqu'un
registered trademark	®	marque déposée
relative	*rel*	relatif
singular	*sing*	singulier
somebody	*sb*	
something	*sth*	
United States	*US*	États-Unis
auxiliary verb	*v aux*	verbe auxiliare
intransitive verb	*vi*	verbe intransitif
pronominal verb	*vpr*	verbe pronominal
transitive verb	*vt*	verbe transitif
transitive and intransitive verb	*vti*	verbe transitif et intransitif

A

a (*before vowel or mute h* **an**) *indef art* un, une; **a man** un homme; **an apple** une pomme; **two dollars a pound** deux dollars la livre; **30 miles an hour** 50 km à l'heure; **he's a doctor** il est médecin; **twice a month** deux fois par mois.

a·ban·don *vt* abandonner.

ab·bey abbaye *f*.

ab·bre·vi·a·tion abréviation *f*.

a·bil·i·ty capacité *f* (**to do** pour faire); **to the best of my a.** de mon mieux.

a·ble *adj* capable; **to be a. to do** être capable de faire, pouvoir faire; **to be a. to swim/drive** savoir nager/conduire.

a·ble-bod·ied *adj* robuste.

ab·nor·mal *adj* anormal.

a·board 1 *adv* (*on ship*) à bord; **all a.** (*on train*) en voiture. **2** *prep* **a. the ship** à bord du navire; **a. the train** dans le train.

a·bol·ish *vt* supprimer.

a·bor·tion avortement *m*; **to have an a.** se faire avorter.

a·bout 1 *adv* (*approximately*) à peu près, environ; (**at**) **a. two o'clock** vers deux heures; **out and a.** (*after illness*) sur pied; **up and a.** (*out of bed*) levé, debout. **2** *prep* (*concerning*) au sujet de; **to talk a.** parler de; **a book a.** un livre sur; **what's it (all) a.?** de quoi s'agit-il?; **what** *or* **how a. me?** et moi?; **what** *or* **how a. a drink?** que dirais-tu de prendre un verre? ■ (*+ infinitive*) **a. to do** sur le point de faire.

a·bove 1 *adv* au-dessus; **from a.** d'en haut; **floor a.** étage *m* supérieur. **2** *prep* au-dessus de; **a. all** par-dessus tout; **he's a. me** (*in rank*) c'est mon supérieur.

a·bove-men·tioned *adj* susmentionné.

a·breast *adv* **four a.** par rangs de quatre; **to keep a. of** se tenir au courant de.

a·broad *adv* à l'étranger; **from a.** de l'étranger.

a·brupt *adj* (*sudden, rude*) brusque.

ab·scess abcès *m*.

ab·sence absence *f*.

ab·sent *adj* absent (**from** de).

ab·sent-mind·ed *adj* distrait.

ab·so·lute *adj* absolu; (*coward etc*) parfait.

ab·so·lute·ly *adv* absolument.

ab·sorb *vt* (*liquid*) absorber; **absorbed in one's work** absorbé dans *or* par son travail.

ab·surd *adj* absurde.

a·buse 1 *n* abus *m* (**of** de); (*of child etc*) mauvais traitements *mpl*; (*insults*) injures *fpl*. **2** *vt* (*use badly or wrongly*) abuser de; (*ill-treat*) maltraiter; (*insult*) injurier.

a·bu·sive *adj* grossier.

ac·a·dem·ic 1 *adj* (*year, diploma etc*) universitaire. **2** *n* (*teacher*) universitaire *mf*.

ac·cel·er·ate *vi* (*in vehicle*) accélérer.

ac·cel·er·a·tor accélérateur *m*.

ac·cent accent *m*.

ac·cept *vt* accepter.

ac·cept·a·ble *adj* acceptable.

ac·cess accès *m* (**to sth** à qch; **to sb** auprès de qn).

ac·ces·si·ble *adj* accessible.

ac·ces·so·ries *npl* (*objects*) accessoires *mpl*.

ac·ci·dent accident *m*; **by a.** (*without meaning to*) accidentellement; (*by chance*) par hasard.

ac·ci·den·tal *adj* accidentel.

ac·ci·den·tal·ly *adv* accidentellement.

ac·com·mo·date *vt* (*of house*) loger; (*oblige*) rendre service à.

ac·com·mo·da·tion(s) logement *m*

ac·com·pa·ny *vt* accompagner.

ac·com·plish *vt* accomplir; *(aim)* réaliser.

ac·cord of my own a. volontairement.

ac·cor·dance in a. with conformément à.

ac·cord·ing·ly *adv* en conséquence.

ac·cord·ing to *prep* selon.

ac·cor·di·on accordéon *m*.

ac·count *(with bank or firm)* compte *m*; *(report)* compte rendu *m*; accounts *(of firm)* comptabilité *f*; to take into a. tenir compte de; on a. of à cause de.

ac·count·ant comptable *mf*.

▸**account for** *vt (explain)* expliquer; *(represent)* représenter.

ac·count·ing comptabilité *f*.

ac·cu·mu·late 1 *vt* accumuler. 2 *vi* s'accumuler.

ac·cu·rate *adj* exact, précis.

ac·cu·rate·ly *adv* avec précision.

ac·cu·sa·tion accusation *f*.

ac·cuse *vt* accuser *(of* de).

ac·cused the a. l'accusé, -ée *mf*.

ac·cus·tomed *adj* habitué *(to sth* à qch; *to doing* à faire); to get a. to s'habituer à.

ace *(card, person)* as *m*.

ache 1 *n* douleur *f*; to have an a. in one's arm avoir mal au bras. 2 *vi* faire mal; my head aches ma tête me fait mal; I'm aching all over j'ai mal partout.

a·chieve *vt* réaliser; *(success, result)* obtenir; *(victory)* remporter.

a·chieve·ment *(success)* réussite *f*.

ach·ing *adj* douloureux.

ac·id *adj & n* acide *(m)*.

ac·knowl·edge *vt* reconnaître *(as* pour); to a. *(receipt of)* accuser réception de.

ac·ne acné *f*.

a·corn gland *m*.

ac·quaint *vt* to be acquainted with sb connaître qn; we are acquainted on se connaît.

ac·quain·tance connaissance *f*.

ac·quire *vt* acquérir.

a·cre acre *f (= 0,4 hectare)*.

ac·ro·bat acrobate *mf*.

ac·ro·bat·ic *adj* acrobatique.

a·cross *adv & prep (from side to side (of))* d'un côté à l'autre *(de)*; *(on the other side (of))* de l'autre côté *(de)*; *(so as to cross, diagonally)* en travers *(de)*; to be half a mile a. *(wide)* avoir un kilomètre de large; to walk *or* go a. *(street)* traverser.

a·cryl·ic acrylique *m*; a. sweater/ *etc* pull *m/etc* en acrylique.

act 1 *n (deed, part of play)* acte *m*; *(in circus)* numéro *m*; caught in the a. pris sur le fait. 2 *vt (role in play or film)* jouer. 3 *vi (do sth, behave)* agir; to a. as *(secretary etc)* faire office de; *(of object)* servir de.

▸**act for** *vt* représenter.

ac·tion action *f*; *(military)* combat *m*; to take a. prendre des mesures; to put into a. *(plan)* exécuter; out of a. hors d'usage; *(person)* hors *(de)* combat.

ac·tive *adj* actif; *(interest, dislike)* vif. 2 *n Grammar* actif *m*.

ac·tiv·i·ty activité *f*; *(in street)* animation *f*.

▸**act (up)on** *vt (affect)* agir sur; *(advice)* suivre.

ac·tor acteur *m*.

ac·tress actrice *f*.

ac·tu·al *adj* réel; the a. book le livre même.

ac·tu·al·ly *adv (truly)* réellement; *(in fact)* en réalité.

a·cute *adj* aigu *(f -uë)*; *(emotion)* vif; *(shortage)* grave.

AD *abbr (anno Domini)* après Jésus-Christ.

ad *Fam* pub *f*; *(private, in newspaper)* annonce *f*, want ad petite annonce.

a·dapt *vt* adapter *(to* à); to a. *(oneself)* s'adapter.

a·dapt·a·ble *adj (person)* souple.

a·dap·ter, a·dap·tor (plug) prise f multiple.

add vt ajouter (**to** à; **that** que); (total) additionner.

ad·dict TV a. fana mf de la télé; **drug a.** drogué, -ée mf.

ad·dict·ed adj **to be a. to** (TV) se passionner pour; **a. to alcohol** alcoolique; **to be a. to cocaine** avoir une dépendance à la cocaïne, être cocaïnomane.

ad·dic·tion drug a. toxicomanie f.

▶**add in** vt (include) inclure.

ad·di·tion addition f; **in a.** de plus; **in a. to** en plus de.

ad·di·tion·al adj supplémentaire.

ad·di·tive additif m.

ad·dress 1 n (on letter etc) adresse f; (speech) allocution f. 2 vt (person) s'adresser à; (audience) parler devant; (letter) mettre l'adresse sur.

▶**add to** vt (increase) augmenter.

▶**add together** vt (numbers) additionner.

▶**add up** 1 vt (numbers) additionner. **2** vi **to a. up to** (total) s'élever à; (mean) signifier; (represent) constituer.

ad·e·noids npl végétations fpl (adénoïdes).

ad·e·quate adj (quantity etc) suffisant; (acceptable) convenable; (person) compétent.

ad·e·quate·ly adv suffisamment; convenablement.

▶**ad·here to** vt adhérer à; (decision, rule) s'en tenir à.

ad·he·sive adj & n adhésif (m).

ad·ja·cent adj (building, angle) adjacent (**to** à).

ad·jec·tive adjectif m.

ad·just vt (machine) régler; (salaries) ajuster; **to a. (oneself) to** s'adapter à.

ad·just·a·ble adj (seat) réglable.

ad·just·ment réglage m; (of person) adaptation f.

ad lib vi improviser.

ad·min·is·ter vt administrer.

ad·min·is·tra·tion administration f; (government) gouvernement m.

ad·min·is·tra·tive adj administratif.

ad·min·is·tra·tor directeur, -trice mf, administrateur, -trice mf.

ad·mi·ral amiral m.

ad·mi·ra·tion admiration f.

ad·mire vt admirer (**for** pour; **for doing** de faire).

ad·mis·sion (to movies etc) entrée f; **a. charge** prix m d'entrée.

ad·mit vt (let in) laisser entrer, admettre; (acknowledge) reconnaître, admettre (**that** que).

ad·mit·tance entrée f; **'no a.'** 'entrée interdite'.

▶**admit to** vt (confess) avouer.

ad·o·les·cent adolescent, -ente mf.

a·dopt vt (child, attitude) adopter.

a·dopt·ed adj (child) adoptif.

a·dop·tion adoption f.

a·dor·a·ble adj adorable.

a·dore vt adorer (**doing** faire).

a·dult 1 n adulte mf. 2 adj (animal etc) adulte; **a. class/film/etc** classe f/film m/etc pour adultes.

ad·vance 1 n (movement, money) avance f; **advances** (sexual) avances fpl; **in a.** à l'avance, d'avance. 2 adj (payment) anticipé; **a. reservation** réservation f. 3 vt (put forward, lend) avancer. 4 vi (go forward, progress) avancer.

ad·vanced adj avancé; (studies, level) supérieur; (course) de niveau supérieur.

ad·van·tage avantage m (**over** sur); **to take a. of** profiter de; (person) exploiter.

ad·ven·ture aventure f.

ad·ven·tur·ous adj aventureux.

ad·verb adverbe m.

ad·ver·tise 1 vt (commercially) faire de la publicité pour; (pri-

vately) passer une annonce pour vendre; (*make known*) annoncer. **2** *vi* faire de la publicité; (*privately*) passer une annonce (**for** pour trouver).

ad·ver·tise·ment publicité *f*; (*private, in newspaper*) annonce *f*; (*poster*) affiche *f*; **classified a.** petite annonce.

ad·vice conseil(s) *m(pl)*; **a piece of a.** un conseil.

ad·vis·a·ble *adj* (*wise*) prudent (to do de faire).

ad·vise *vt* conseiller; (*recommend*) recommander; **to a. sb to do** conseiller à qn de faire.

▸ **advise against** *vt* déconseiller.

ad·vis·er conseiller, -ère *mf*.

ad·vo·cate 1 *n* (*supporter*) défenseur *m*. **2** *vt* préconiser.

aer·i·al antenne *f*.

aer·o·bics *npl* aérobic *m*.

aer·o·sol aérosol *m*.

aes·thet·ic *adj* esthétique.

af·fair affaire *f*; (*love*) a. liaison *f*.

af·fect *vt* (*concern, move*) toucher, affecter; (*harm*) nuire à.

af·fec·tion affection *f* (**for** pour).

af·fec·tion·ate *adj* affectueux.

af·flu·ent *adj* riche.

af·ford *vt* (*be able to pay for*) avoir les moyens d'acheter; (*time*) pouvoir trouver.

af·ford·a·ble *adj* (*price etc*) abordable.

a·float *adv* (*ship, swimmer, business*) à flot.

a·fraid *adj* **to be a.** avoir peur (**of**, to de); **he's a. (that) she may be sick** il a peur qu'elle (ne) soit malade; **I'm a. he's out** (*I regret to say*) je regrette, il est sorti.

Af·ri·can 1 *n* Africain, -aine *mf*. **2** *adj* africain.

af·ter 1 *adv* après; **the month a.** le mois suivant. **2** *prep* après; **a. all** après tout; **a. eating** après avoir mangé; **a. you!** je vous en prie!; **ten to. four** quatre heures dix; **to**

be a. sth/sb (*seek*) chercher qch/qn. **3** *conj* après que.

af·ter·ef·fects *npl* suites *fpl*.

af·ter·noon après-midi *m* or *f inv*; **in the a.** l'après-midi; **good a.!** (*hello*) bonjour!

af·ter·noons *adv* l'après-midi.

af·ter·shave après-rasage *m*.

af·ter·ward(s) *adv* après, plus tard.

a·gain *adv* de nouveau, encore une fois; **never a.** plus jamais; **a. and a., time and (time) a.** bien des fois, maintes fois.

a·gainst *prep* contre; **a. the law** illégal.

age 1 *n* âge *m*; (*old*) a. vieillesse *f*; **the Middle Ages** le Moyen Âge; **five years of a.** âgé de cinq ans; **under a.** trop jeune. **2** *vti* vieillir.

aged *adj* a. ten âgé de dix ans.

a·gen·cy (*office*) agence *f*.

a·gen·da ordre *m* du jour.

a·gent agent *m*; (*dealer*) concessionnaire *mf*.

ag·gra·vate *vt* (*make worse*) aggraver; (*annoy*) Fam exaspérer.

ag·gra·va·tion (*annoyance*) ennui(s) *m(pl)*.

ag·gres·sion agression *f*.

ag·gres·sive *adj* agressif.

ag·ile *adj* agile.

ag·i·tat·ed *adj* agité.

a·go *adv* **a year a.** il y a un an; **how long a.?** il y a combien de temps (de cela)?

ag·o·ny to be in a. souffrir horriblement.

a·gree 1 *vi* (*come to an agreement*) se mettre d'accord; (*be in agreement*) être d'accord (**with** avec); (*of facts, dates*) concorder; *Grammar* s'accorder; **to a. to sth/to doing** consentir à qch/à faire; **it doesn't a. with me** (*food, climate*) ça ne me réussit pas. **2** *vt* **to a. to do** accepter de faire; **to a. that** admettre que.

a·gree·a·ble *adj* (*pleasant*) agréable.

a·greed *adj (time, place)* convenu; **we are a.** nous sommes d'accord; **a.!** entendu!

a·gree·ment accord *m*; **in a. with** d'accord avec; **to reach an a.** tomber d'accord.

▸**agree (up)on** *vt* convenir de.

ag·ri·cul·tur·al *adj* agricole.

ag·ri·cul·ture agriculture *f.*

a·head *adv (in space)* en avant; *(leading)* en tête; *(in the future)* dans l'avenir; **a. (of time)** en avance (sur l'horaire); **to be one hour a.** avoir une heure d'avance *(of* sur); **a. of** *(space)* devant; *(time)* en avance sur; **straight a.** *(to walk)* tout droit; *(to look)* droit devant soi.

aid aide *f, (device)* accessoire *m,* support *m*; **with the a. of** *(a stick etc)* à l'aide de; **in a. of** *(charity)* au profit de.

AIDS *abrev (acquired immune deficiency syndrome)* SIDA *m.*

aim 1 *n* but *m*; **with the a. of** dans le but de. 2 *vt (gun)* braquer (at sur); **aimed at children/***etc (product)* destiné aux enfants/*etc.* 3 *vi* viser; **to a. at sb** viser qn; **to a. to do** *or* **at doing** avoir l'intention de faire.

air 1 *n* air *m*; **in the open a.** en plein air; **by a.** *(to travel, send)* par avion; **(up) in(to) the a.** en l'air. 2 *adj (raid, base)* aérien. 3 *vt (room)* aérer.

air-con·di·tioned *adj* climatisé.

air con·di·tion·ing climatisation *f.*

air·craft *inv* avion(s) *m(pl).*

air·craft car·ri·er porte-avions *m inv.*

air·fare prix *m* du billet d'avion.

air force armée *f* de l'air.

air·line ligne *f* aérienne.

air·line tick·et billet *m* d'avion.

air·mail poste *f* aérienne; **by a.** par avion.

air·plane avion *m.*

air·port aéroport *m.*

air·sick·ness mal *m* de l'air.

air ter·mi·nal aérogare *f.*

air·tight *adj* hermétique.

air traf·fic con·trol·ler aiguilleur *m* du ciel.

aisle *(walkway in plane, theater)* allée *f, (in church)* nef *f* latérale; *(row of seats)* rangée *f, (section of supermarket)* rayon *m.*

a·jar *adj (door)* entrouvert.

a·larm 1 *n (warning, device in house or car)* alarme *f, (mechanism)* sonnerie *f* (d'alarme); **a. (clock)** réveil *m.* 2 *vt* alarmer.

al·bum *(book, record)* album *m.*

al·co·hol alcool *m.*

al·co·hol·ic 1 *adj (drink)* alcoolisé. 2 *n (person)* alcoolique *mf.*

a·lert *adj (watching carefully)* vigilant.

al·ge·bra algèbre *f.*

a·li·as 1 *n (pl* aliases) nom *m* d'emprunt. 2 *adv* alias.

al·i·bi alibi *m.*

a·li·en étranger, -ère *mf.*

a·light *adj (fire)* allumé; **to set a.** mettre le feu à.

a·like 1 *adj (people, things)* semblables; **to look** *or* **be a.** se ressembler. 2 *adv* de la même manière.

a·live *adj* vivant, en vie.

all 1 *adj* tout, toute, *pl* tous, toutes; **a. day** toute la journée; **a. (the) men** tous les hommes. 2 *pron* tous *mpl,* toutes *fpl; (everything)* tout; **my sisters are a. here** toutes mes sœurs sont ici; **he ate it a., he ate a. of it** il a tout mangé; **a. (that) he has** tout ce qu'il a; **a. of us** nous tous; **in a., a. told** en tout; **a. but** *(almost)* presque; **if there's any wind at a.** s'il y a le moindre vent; **not at a.** pas du tout; *(after 'thank you')* pas de quoi. 3 *adv* tout seul; **six a.** *Sport* six buts partout.

al·le·giance fidélité *f* (**to** à).

al·ler·gic *adj* allergique (**to** à).

al·ley ruelle *f, (in park)* allée *f.*

al·li·ance alliance *f.*

al·lied *adj (country)* allié; *(matters)* lié.

al·li·ga·tor alligator *m*.

al·lo·cate *vt* allouer (**to** à); *(distribute)* répartir.

al·lot·ment *(land)* lopin *m* de terre *(loué pour la culture)*.

all-out *adj (effort)* énergique.

al·low *vt* permettre; *(give)* accorder; *(as discount)* déduire; **to a. sb to do** permettre à qn de faire; **you're not allowed to go on** vous interdit de partir.

al·low·ance allocation *f*, *(for travel, housing, food)* indemnité *f*, *(for duty-free goods)* tolérance *f*, *(for children)* argent *m* de poche; **to make allowances for sb** être indulgent envers qn.

▶ **allow for** *vt* tenir compte de.

all-pur·pose *adj (tool)* universel.

all-right 1 *adj (satisfactory)* bien *inv*; *(unharmed)* sain et sauf; *(undamaged)* intact; *(without worries)* tranquille; **it's a.** ça va; **I'm a.** *(healthy)* je vais bien. **2** *adv (well)* bien; **a.!** *(agreement)* d'accord!; **I got your letter a.** *(emphatic)* j'ai bien reçu votre lettre.

all-round *adj* complet.

al·ly allié, -ée *mf*.

al·mond amande *f*.

al·most *adv* presque; **he a. fell**/*etc* il a failli tomber/*etc*.

a·lone *adj & adv* seul; **to leave a.** *(person)* laisser tranquille; *(thing)* ne pas toucher à.

a·long 1 *prep* **(all)** a. *(tout)* le long de; **to go** *or* **walk a.** *(street)* passer par; **a. with** avec. **2** *adv* **all a.** *(time)* dès le début.

a·long·side *prep & adv* à côté (de).

a·loud *adv* à haute voix.

al·pha·bet alphabet *m*.

al·pha·bet·i·cal *adj* alphabétique.

Alps *npl* **the A.** les Alpes *fpl*.

al·read·y *adv* déjà.

al·right *adv Fam* = **all-right**.

al·so *adv* aussi.

al·tar autel *m*.

al·ter 1 *vt* changer; *(clothing)* retoucher. **2** *vi* changer.

al·ter·a·tion changement *m*; *(of clothing)* retouche *f*.

al·ter·nate 1 *adj* alterné; **on a. days** tous les deux jours. **2** *vi* alterner (**with** avec).

al·ter·na·tive 1 *adj (other)* autre. **2** *n* alternative *f*.

al·ter·na·tive·ly *adv* comme alternative.

al·though *adv* bien que (+ subjunctive).

al·to·geth·er *adv (completely)* tout à fait; *(on the whole)* somme toute; **how much a.?** combien en tout?

a·lu·mi·num aluminium *m*.

al·ways *adv* toujours.

am *see* **be**.

a.m. *adv* du matin.

am·a·teur 1 *n* amateur *m*. **2** *adj* **a.** *painter*/*etc* peintre/*etc* amateur.

a·maze *vt* étonner.

a·mazed *adj* stupéfait (**at sth** de qch; **at seeing** de voir); *(filled with wonder)* émerveillé.

a·maz·ing *adj* stupéfiant; *(incredible)* extraordinaire.

am·bas·sa·dor ambassadeur *m*; *(woman)* ambassadrice *f*.

am·ber **a.** *(light)* *(of traffic signal)* (feu *m*) orange *m*.

am·big·u·ous *adj* ambigu (*f* -uë).

am·bi·tion ambition *f*.

am·bi·tious *adj* ambitieux.

am·bu·lance ambulance *f*.

am·bu·lance driv·er ambulancier, -ière *mf*.

a·mend *vt (text)* modifier; *(law)* amender.

A·mer·i·can 1 *n* Américain, -aine *mf*. **2** *adj* américain.

a·mid(st) *prep* au milieu de, parmi.

am·mu·ni·tion munitions *fpl*.

a·mong(st) prep parmi, entre; **a. the crowd/books** parmi la foule/ les livres; **a. themselves/friends** entre eux/amis.

a·mount quantité f; (sum of money) somme f; (total of bill etc) montant m.

▸ **amount to** vt s'élever à; (mean) signifier; (represent) représenter.

am·ple adj (enough) largement assez de; **you have a. time** tu as largement le temps.

am·pli·fi·er amplificateur m.

am·pu·tate vt amputer.

a·muse vt amuser.

a·muse·ment amusement m.

a·mus·ing adj amusant.

an see a.

a·nal·y·sis, pl -ses analyse f.

an·a·lyst analyste mf; (psychoanalyst) (psych)analyste mf.

an·a·lyze vt analyser.

an·ar·chy anarchie f.

a·nat·o·my anatomie f.

an·ces·tor ancêtre m.

an·chor ancre f.

an·chored adj ancré.

an·cho·vy anchois m.

an·cient adj ancien; (pre-medieval) antique.

and conj et; **two hundred a. two** deux cent deux; **better a. better** de mieux en mieux; **go a. see** va voir.

an·es·thet·ic anesthésie f, (substance) anesthésique m; **general a.** anesthésie générale.

an·gel ange m.

an·ger colère f.

an·gle angle m; **at an a.** en biais.

an·gler pêcheur, -euse mf à la ligne.

an·gri·ly adv (to speak etc) avec colère.

an·gry adj fâché; (letter) indigné; **to get a.** se fâcher (**with** contre).

an·i·mal n & adj animal (m).

an·kle cheville f.

an·kle sock socquette f.

an·nex (building) annexe f.

an·ni·ver·sa·ry (of event) anniversaire m.

an·nounce vt annoncer; (birth, marriage) faire part de.

an·nounce·ment (statement) annonce f, (notice) avis m.

an·nounc·er (on TV) speaker m, speakerine f.

an·noy vt (inconvenience) ennuyer; (irritate) agacer.

an·noyed adj fâché; **to get a.** se fâcher (**with** contre).

an·noy·ing adj ennuyeux.

an·nu·al 1 adj annuel. **2** n (book) annuaire m.

an·nu·al·ly adv annuellement.

a·non·y·mous adj anonyme.

an·oth·er adj & pron un(e) autre; **a. man** un autre homme; **a. month** (additional) encore un mois; **a. ten** encore dix; **one a.** l'un(e) l'autre, pl les un(e)s les autres; **they love one a.** ils s'aiment (l'un l'autre).

an·swer 1 n réponse f, (to problem) solution f (**to** de). **2** vt (person, question, phone) répondre à; (prayer, wish) exaucer; **to a. the door** ouvrir la porte. **3** vi répondre.

▸ **answer back** vt répondre à.

▸ **answer for** vt répondre de.

an·swer·ing ma·chine répondeur m.

ant fourmi f.

an·te·lope antilope f.

an·ten·na antenne f.

an·them national **a.** hymne m national.

an·thol·o·gy recueil m.

an·ti- prefix anti-.

an·ti·bi·ot·ic antibiotique m.

an·ti·bod·y anticorps m.

an·tic·i·pate vt (foresee) prévoir; (expect) s'attendre à.

an·tic·i·pa·tion in a. of en prévision de.

an·tics npl singeries fpl.

an·ti·freeze antigel m.

an·ti·his·ta·mine antihistaminique m.

an·tique 1 *adj (furniture etc)* ancien. **2** *n* antiquité *f*.

an·tique deal·er antiquaire *mf*.

an·tique shop magasin *m* d'antiquités.

an·ti·sep·tic *adj & n* antiseptique *(m)*.

anx·i·e·ty *(worry)* inquiétude *f*, *(fear)* anxiété *f*.

anx·ious *adj (worried)* inquiet *(about* de, pour); *(afraid)* anxieux; *(eager)* impatient *(to do* de faire).

anx·ious·ly *adv (to wait)* impatiemment.

an·y 1 *adj (with question)* du, de la, des; **do you have a. milk/tickets?** avez-vous du lait/des billets? ▪ *(negative)* de; **he hasn't got a. milk/tickets** il n'a pas de lait/de billets. ▪ *(no matter which)* n'importe quel; *(every)* tout; **in a. case, at a. rate** de toute façon. **2** *pron (no matter which one)* n'importe lequel; *(somebody)* quelqu'un; **if a. of you** si l'un d'entre vous. ▪ *(quantity)* en; **do you have a.?** en as-tu? **3** *adv* **(not) a. happier/etc** (pas) plus heureux/*etc*; **I don't see him a. more** je ne le vois plus; **a. more tea?** encore du thé?; **a. better?** c'est mieux?

an·y·bod·y *pron (somebody)* quelqu'un; **do you see a.?** vois-tu quelqu'un? ▪ *(negative)* personne; **he doesn't know a.** il ne connaît personne. ▪ *(no matter who)* n'importe qui.

an·y·how *adv (at any rate)* de toute façon; *(badly)* n'importe comment.

an·y·one *pron* = **anybody**.

an·y·place *adv* = **anywhere**.

an·y·thing *pron (something)* quelque chose. ▪ *(negative)* rien; **he doesn't do a.** il ne fait rien. ▪ *(everything)* tout; **a. you like** *(tout)* ce que tu veux. ▪ *(no matter what)* **a. (at all)** n'importe quoi.

an·y·way *adv (at any rate)* de toute façon.

an·y·where *adv (no matter where)* n'importe où. ▪ *(everywhere)* partout; **a. you go** partout où vous allez; **a. you like** là où tu veux. ▪ *(negative)* nulle part; **he doesn't go a.** il ne va nulle part.

a·part *adv* **we kept them a.** *(separate)* on les tenait séparés; **with legs a.** les jambes écartées; **they are three feet a.** ils se trouvent à un mètre l'un de l'autre; **a. from** *(except for)* à part.

a·part·ment appartement *m*; **a. house** *or* **building** immeuble *m* (d'habitation).

ape singe *m*.

a·pé·ri·tif apéritif *m*.

a·pol·o·get·ic *adj* **to be a.** s'excuser *(about* de).

a·pol·o·gize *vi* s'excuser *(for* de); **to a. to sb** faire ses excuses à qn *(for* pour).

a·pol·o·gy excuses *fpl*.

a·pos·tro·phe apostrophe *f*.

ap·pall *vt* consterner.

ap·pall·ing *adj* épouvantable.

ap·pa·ra·tus appareil *m*; *(in gym)* agrès *mpl*.

ap·par·el vêtements *mpl*.

ap·par·ent *adj* apparent; **it's a. that** il est évident que.

ap·par·ent·ly *adv* apparemment.

ap·peal[1] *(charm)* attrait *m*; *(interest)* intérêt *m*.

ap·peal[2] **1** *n (in court)* appel *m*. **2** *vi* faire appel.

▶ **appeal to** *vt (attract)* plaire à; *(interest)* intéresser.

ap·pear *vi (become visible)* apparaître; *(present oneself)* se présenter; *(seem, be published)* paraître; *(in court)* comparaître; **it appears that** il semble que *(+ subjunctive or indicative)*.

ap·pear·ance *(act)* apparition *f*, *(look)* apparence *f*.

ap·pen·di·ci·tis appendicite *f*.

ap·pen·dix, *pl* -**ixes** *or* -**ices** *(in book, body)* appendice *m*.

ap·pe·tite appétit *m*.

ap·pe·tiz·ing *adj* appétissant.

ap·plaud *vti* (clap) applaudir.

ap·plause applaudissements *mpl*.

ap·ple pomme *f*; **cooking a.** pomme *f* à cuire; **a. pie** tarte *f* aux pommes.

ap·pli·ance appareil *m*.

ap·pli·ca·ble *adj* applicable (**to** à).

ap·pli·cant candidat, -ate *mf* (**for** à).

ap·pli·ca·tion (for job) candidature *f*, (for membership) demande *f* d'adhésion; **a. (form)** (for job) formulaire *m* de candidature.

ap·ply 1 *vt* appliquer; (brake) appuyer sur; **to a. oneself** to s'appliquer à. 2 *vi* (be relevant) s'appliquer (**to** à).

▸**apply for** *vt* (job) poser sa candidature à.

ap·point *vt* (person) nommer (**to sth** à qch; **to do** pour faire).

ap·point·ment nomination *f*, (meeting) rendez-vous *m inv*.

ap·point·ment book agenda *m*.

ap·prais·al évaluation *f*.

ap·praise *vt* évaluer.

ap·pre·ci·ate *vt* (enjoy, value) apprécier; (understand) comprendre; (be grateful for) être reconnaissant de.

ap·pre·ci·a·tion (gratitude) reconnaissance *f*.

ap·pren·tice apprenti, -ie *mf*.

ap·pren·tice·ship apprentissage *m*.

ap·proach 1 *vt* (person, door etc) s'approcher de; (age, result, town) approcher de; (subject) aborder. 2 *vi* (of person, vehicle) s'approcher; (of date) approcher. 3 *n* (method) façon *f* de s'y prendre.

ap·pro·pri·ate *adj* convenable.

ap·prov·al approbation *f*, **on a.** (goods) à l'essai.

▸**ap·prove of** *vt* (conduct etc) approuver; **I don't a. of him** il ne me

plaît pas; **I a. of his going** je trouve bon qu'il y aille.

ap·prox·i·mate *adj* approximatif.

ap·prox·i·mate·ly *adv* à peu près.

a·pri·cot abricot *m*.

A·pril avril *m*.

a·pron tablier *m*.

apt *adj* (remark, reply) juste, convenable; **to be a.** to avoir tendance à.

ap·ti·tude aptitude *f* (**for** à, pour).

a·quar·i·um aquarium *m*.

Ar·ab *adj* & *n* arabe (*mf*).

Ar·a·bic *adj* & *n* (language) arabe (*m*); **A. numerals** chiffres *mpl* arabes.

ar·bi·trar·y *adj* arbitraire.

arc (of circle) arc *m*.

arch (of bridge) arche *f*, (of building) voûte *f*.

arch·er archer *m*.

arch·er·y tir *m* à l'arc.

ar·chi·tect architecte *mf*.

ar·chi·tec·ture architecture *f*.

Arc·tic the A. l'Arctique *f*.

are see **be.**

ar·e·a (in geometry) superficie *f*, (of country) région *f*, (of town) quartier *m*; **parking a.** aire *f* de stationnement.

ar·e·a code (phone number) indicatif *m*.

a·re·na arène *f*.

ar·gue 1 *vi* (quarrel) se disputer (**with** avec; **about** au sujet de); (reason) raisonner (**with** avec, **about** sur). 2 *vt* **to a. that** (maintain) soutenir que.

ar·gu·ment (quarrel) dispute *f*, (reasoning) argument *m*; **to have an a.** se disputer.

a·rise* *vi* (of problem, opportunity) se présenter; (result) résulter (**from** de).

a·rith·me·tic arithmétique *f*.

arm 1 *n* bras *m*; (weapon) arme *f*. 2 *vt* armer (**with** de).

arm·band brassard *m*.

arm·chair fauteuil *m*.

ar·mor *(of knight)* armure *f; (of tank etc)* blindage *m*.

ar·mored *adj (car etc)* blindé.

arm·pit aisselle *f*.

ar·my 1 *n* armée *f*. **2** *adj* militaire.

a·round 1 *prep* autour de; *(approximately)* environ. **2** *adv* autour; **a. here** par ici; **he's still a.** il est encore là; **there's a lot of flu a.** il y a pas mal de grippes dans l'air; **there's a rumor going a.** il y a un bruit qui court; **up and a.** *(after illness)* sur pied.

a·rouse *vt* éveiller.

ar·range *vt* arranger; *(time, meeting)* fixer; **to a. to do** s'arranger pour faire.

ar·range·ment *(layout, agreement)* arrangement *m*; **arrangements** préparatifs *mpl; (plans)* projets *mpl*.

ar·rears *npl* **in a.** en retard dans ses paiements.

ar·rest 1 *vt* arrêter. **2** *n* arrestation *f*; **under a.** en état d'arrestation.

ar·ri·val arrivée *f*.

ar·rive *vi* arriver.

ar·row flèche *f*.

art *n*; **work of a.** œuvre *f* d'art.

ar·ter·y artère *f*.

ar·thri·tis arthrite *f*.

ar·ti·cle *(object, in newspaper, in grammar)* article *m*.

ar·tic·u·late[1] *adj (speech)* clair; *(person)* qui s'exprime clairement.

ar·tic·u·late[2] *vti* articuler.

ar·ti·fi·cial *adj* artificiel.

art·ist *(actor, painter etc)* artiste *mf*.

ar·tis·tic *adj* artistique; *(person)* artiste.

as *adv & conj (manner etc)* comme; **as you like** comme tu veux; **as much or as hard as I can** (au)tant que je peux; **as (it) is** *(to leave sth)* comme ça, tel quel; **as if, as though** comme si. ▪ *(comparison)* **as tall as you** aussi grand que vous; **as white as a sheet** blanc comme un linge; **as much or as hard as you** autant que vous; **twice as big as** deux fois plus grand que. ▪ *(though)* **(as) smart as he is** si intelligent qu'il soit. ▪ *(capacity)* **as a teacher** comme professeur; **to act as a father** agir en père. ▪ *(reason)* puisque; **as it's late** puisqu'il est tard. ▪ *(time)* **as I was leaving** comme je partais; **as he slept** pendant qu'il dormait; **as from, as of** *(time)* à partir de. ▪ *(concerning)* **as for that** quant à cela. ▪ *(+ infinitive)* **so as to** de manière à; **so stupid as to** assez bête pour.

asap *abbr (as soon as possible)* le plut tôt possible.

as·cer·tain *vt* établir, déterminer.

ash cendre *f*.

a·shamed *adj* **to be a.** avoir honte *(of* de).

a·shore *adv* **to go a.** débarquer.

ash·tray cendrier *m*.

A·sian 1 *n* Asiatique *mf*. **2** *adj* asiatique.

a·side *adv* de côté; **a. from** en dehors de.

ask 1 *vt* demander; *(a question)* poser; *(invite)* inviter; **to a. sb (for) sth** demander qch à qn; **to a. sb to do** demander à qn de faire. **2** *vi* demander; **to a. for sth/sb** demander qch/qn; **to a. about sth** se renseigner sur qch; **to a. about sb** demander des nouvelles de qn; **to a. sb about** interroger qn sur.

a·sleep *adj* **to be a.** dormir; **to fall a.** s'endormir.

as·par·a·gus asperges *fpl*.

as·pect aspect *m*.

as·pi·rin aspirine *f*.

as·sault 1 *n (crime)* agression *f*. **2** *vt (attack)* agresser.

as·sem·ble 1 *vt* assembler; *(people)* rassembler; *(machine)* monter. **2** *vi* se rassembler.

as·sem·bly *(meeting)* assemblée *f, (in school)* rassemblement *m*.

as·sert vt affirmer; **to a. oneself** s'affirmer; **to a. one's rights** faire valoir ses droits.

as·sess vt (estimate) évaluer; (decide amount of) fixer le montant de.

as·set (advantage) atout m; **assets** (of business) actif m.

as·sign vt (give) attribuer (**to** à).

as·sign·ment (task) mission f.

as·sist vti aider (**in doing, to do** à faire).

as·sis·tance aide f; **to be of a. to sb** aider qn.

as·sis·tant 1 n assistant, -ante mf; (in shop) vendeur, -euse mf. 2 adj adjoint.

as·so·ci·ate 1 vt associer; **associated with sth/sb** associé à qch/avec qn. 2 n & adj associé, -ée (mf).

as·so·ci·a·tion association f.

as·sort·ed adj variés; (foods) assortis.

as·sort·ment assortiment m.

as·sume vt (suppose) présumer (**that** que); (take on) prendre; (responsibility, role) assumer.

as·sur·ance assurance f.

as·sure vt assurer (**sb that** à qn que; **sb of** qn de).

as·ter·isk astérisque m.

asth·ma asthme m.

asth·mat·ic adj & n asthmatique (mf).

a·ston·ish vt étonner; **to be astonished** s'étonner (**at sth** de qch).

a·ston·ish·ing adj étonnant.

a·stray adv **to go a.** s'égarer.

as·trol·o·gy astrologie f.

as·tro·naut astronaute mf.

as·tron·o·my astronomie f.

a·sy·lum asile m; **to seek a.** chercher asile; (mental) a. asile m (d'aliénés).

at prep à; **at work** au travail; **at six** (o'clock) à six heures. ▪ chez; **at the doctor's** chez le médecin. ▪ en; **at sea** en mer. ▪ contre; **angry at** fâché contre. ▪ sur; **to shoot at** tirer sur. ▪ de; **to laugh at** rire de. ▪ (au)près de; **at the window** (au-)près de la fenêtre. ▪ par; **six at a time** six par six.

ath·lete athlète mf.

ath·let·ic adj athlétique.

ath·let·ics npl athlétisme m.

At·lan·tic 1 adj atlantique. 2 n **the A.** l'Atlantique m.

at·las atlas m.

at·mos·phere atmosphère f.

at·om atome m.

a·tom·ic adj (bomb etc) atomique.

at·tach vt attacher (**to** à); (document) joindre (**to** à); **attached to** (fond of) attaché à.

at·ta·ché case attaché-case m, mallette f.

at·tach·ment (tool) accessoire m; (to e-mail) fichier m joint.

at·tack 1 n attaque f. 2 vti attaquer.

at·tack·er agresseur m.

at·tain vt (aim) atteindre; (goal, ambition) réaliser; (rank) parvenir à.

at·tempt 1 n tentative f; **to make an a. to** tenter de. 2 vt tenter; (task) entreprendre; **to a. to do** tenter de faire.

at·tend 1 vt (meeting etc) assister à; (course) suivre; (school, church) aller à. 2 vi assister.

at·ten·dance présence f (**at** à); (school) a. scolarité f.

at·ten·dant employé, -ée mf; (in gas station) pompiste mf; (in museum) gardien, -ienne mf.

▸ **attend to** vt (customer, task) s'occuper de.

at·ten·tion attention f; **to pay a.** faire attention (**to** à).

at·ten·tive adj attentif (**to** à).

at·tic grenier m.

at·ti·tude attitude f.

at·tor·ney avocat m.

at·tract vt attirer.

at·trac·tion (charm) attrait m.

at·trac·tive adj (price, offer etc) intéressant; (person) attirant, séduisant.

at·trib·ute 1 n (quality) attribut m. **2** vt attribuer (**to**) à.

auc·tion (off) vt vendre (aux enchères).

auc·tion·eer commissaire-priseur m.

au·di·ble adj perceptible.

au·di·ence (of speaker, musician) auditoire m; (in theater) spectateurs mpl; (of radio broadcast) auditeurs mpl. **TV a.** téléspectateurs mpl.

au·di·o adj audio inv.

au·di·o·vi·su·al adj audiovisuel.

au·dit 1 n audit m. **2** vt vérifier.

Au·gust août m.

aunt tante f.

aunt·ie, aunt·y Fam tata f.

au pair 1 adv au pair. **2** n au p. **(girl)** jeune fille f au pair.

Aus·tra·li·an 1 n Australien, -ienne mf. **2** adj australien.

Aus·tri·an 1 n Autrichien, -ienne mf. **2** adj autrichien.

au·then·tic adj authentique.

au·thor auteur m.

au·thor·i·ty autorité f; (permission) autorisation f (**to do** à faire).

au·thor·i·za·tion autorisation f (**to do** à faire).

au·to·bi·og·ra·phy autobiographie f.

au·to·graph 1 n autographe m. **2** vt dédicacer (**for** à).

au·to·mat·ic adj automatique.

au·to·mat·i·cal·ly adv automatiquement.

au·to·mo·bile auto(mobile) f.

au·ton·o·mous adj autonome.

au·tumn automne m.

aux·il·ia·ry adj & n a. (verb) (verbe m) auxiliaire m.

a·vail·a·bil·i·ty disponibilité f.

a·vail·a·ble adj disponible; **a. to all** accessible à tous.

av·a·lanche avalanche f.

av·e·nue avenue f.

av·er·age 1 n moyenne f; **on a.** en moyenne. **2** adj moyen.

a·vi·a·tion aviation f.

av·o·ca·do, pl -os avocat m.

a·void vt éviter; **to a. doing** éviter de faire.

a·void·a·ble adj évitable.

a·wake 1 vi* se réveiller. **2** adj éveillé; **to keep sb a.** empêcher qn de dormir; **he's (still) a.** il ne dort pas (encore).

a·ward 1 vt (money, prize) attribuer. **2** n (prize) prix m; (scholarship) bourse f; **awards ceremony** distribution f des prix.

a·ware adj **a. of** (conscious) conscient de; (informed) au courant de; **to become a. of** prendre conscience de.

a·way adv (distant) loin; **far a.** au loin; **3 miles a.** à 5km (de distance); **to play a.** (of team) jouer à l'extérieur. ■ (in time) **ten days a.** dans dix jours. ■ (absent) parti. ■ (continuously) **to work/talk/etc** sans relâche.

aw·ful adj affreux; (terrifying) épouvantable; **an a. lot of** Fam un nombre incroyable de.

aw·ful·ly adv (very) Fam affreusement.

awk·ward adj (clumsy) maladroit; (difficult) difficile; (tool) peu commode; (time) inopportun.

awn·ing (over shop) store m.

ax 1 n hache f. **2** vt (job etc) supprimer.

ax·is, pl -es axe m.

ax·le essieu m.

B

BA abbr = **Bachelor of Arts**.

ba·by bébé m; **b. boy** petit garçon m; **b. girl** petite fille f.

ba·by car·riage landau m (pl -aus).

ba·by clothes vêtements *mpl* de bébé.

ba·by·sit *vi* garder les enfants.

ba·by·sit·ter baby-sitter *mf*.

bach·e·lor célibataire *m*; **B. of Arts/of Science** licencié, -ée *mf* ès lettres/ès sciences.

back[1] **1** *n* dos *m*; *(of chair)* dossier *m*; *(of hand)* revers *m*; *(of house)* derrière *m*, arrière *m*; *(of room)* fond *m*; *(of vehicle)* arrière *m*; *(of page)* verso *m*; **at the b. of the book** à la fin du livre; **b. to front** devant derrière; **in b. of** derrière. **2** *adj* arrière *inv*; de derrière; **b. door** porte *f* de derrière; **b. tooth** molaire *f*. **3** *adv (behind)* en arrière; **to come b.** revenir; **he's b.** il est de retour, il est revenu.

back[2] *vt (support)* appuyer; *(with money)* financer; *(horse etc)* parier sur.

back·ache mal *m* de dos; **to have a b.** avoir mal au dos.

back·fire *vi (of vehicle)* pétarader.

back·ground fond *m*; *(events)* antécédents *mpl*; *(education)* formation *f*; *(environment)* milieu *m*; **b. music** musique *f* de fond.

back·ing *(aid)* soutien *m*; *(material)* support *m*.

back·log *(of work)* arriéré *m*.

▸ **back out** *vi (withdraw)* se retirer.

back·pack sac *m* à dos.

back·side *(buttocks) Fam* derrière *m*.

back·stage *adv* dans les coulisses.

▸ **back up** *vt (support)* appuyer qn.

back·ward *adj (retarded)* arriéré; *(glance)* en arrière.

back·wards *adv* en arrière; *(to walk)* à reculons; *(to put on garment)* à l'envers.

back·yard jardin *m*.

ba·con bacon *m*.

bac·te·ri·a *npl* bactéries *fpl*.

bad *adj* mauvais; *(wicked)* méchant; *(accident, wound)* grave;

(arm, leg) malade; *(pain)* violent; **to feel b.** *(ill)* se sentir mal; **things are b.** ça va mal; **not b.!** pas mal!

badge *(of plastic)* badge *m*; *(of metal)* pin's *m*; *(of policeman etc)* plaque *f*.

badg·er blaireau *m*.

bad·ly *adv* mal; *(hurt)* grièvement; **b. affected** très touché; **to want b.** avoir grande envie de.

bad-man·nered *adj* mal élevé.

bad·min·ton badminton *m*.

bad-tem·pered *adj* grincheux.

baf·fle *vt* déconcerter.

bag sac *m*; *(baggage)* valises *fpl*; *(under eyes)* poches *fpl*.

bag·gage bagages *mpl*.

bag·gage check consigne *f*.

bag·gy *adj (out of shape)* déformé; *(by design)* large.

bag·pipes *npl* cornemuse *f*.

bail *(in court)* caution *f*; **on b.** en liberté provisoire.

bait amorce *f*, appât *m*.

bake *vt* faire (au four). **2** *vi (of cook) (make cakes)* faire de la pâtisserie; *(make bread)* faire du pain; *(of cake etc)* cuire (au four).

baked beans *npl* haricots *mpl* blancs (à la tomate).

bak·er boulanger, -ère *mf*.

bak·er·y boulangerie *f*.

bal·ance 1 *n* équilibre *m*; *(of account)* solde *m*; *(remainder)* reste *m*; **to lose one's b.** perdre l'équilibre. **2** *vt* tenir en équilibre (**on** sur); *(account)* équilibrer. **3** *vi (of person)* se tenir en équilibre; *(of accounts)* être en équilibre.

bal·ance sheet bilan *m*.

bald *adj* chauve.

bald-head·ed *adj* chauve.

bald·ness calvitie *f*.

ball[1] *(round object)* balle *f*; *(inflated) (for sports)* ballon *m*; *(of string, wool)* pelote *f*; *(any round shape)* boule *f*; *(of meat or fish)* boulette *f*; **on the b.** *Fam (alert)* éveillé; *(efficient)* au point.

ball² (*dance*) bal *m* (*pl* bals).
bal·le·ri·na ballerine *f*.
bal·let ballet *m*.
bal·loon ballon *m*.
bal·lot (*voting*) scrutin *m*.
ball·park stade *m* de base-ball.
ball·point stylo *m* à bille, bic® *m*.
ball·room salle *f* de danse.
ban 1 *n* interdiction *f*. 2 *vt* interdire (**sb from doing** à qn de faire); (*exclude*) exclure (**from** de).
ba·nan·a banane *f*.
band (*strip*) bande *f*; (*musicians*) (petit) orchestre *m*; (*pop group*) groupe *m*; **rubber b.** élastique *m*.
band·age *n* bandage *m*.
▸ **bandage up** *vt* (*arm, wound*) bander.
Band-Aid® pansement *m* adhésif.
bang 1 *n* coup *m* (violent); (*of door*) claquement *m*. 2 *vt* cogner; (*door*) (faire) claquer. 3 *vi* cogner; (*of door*) claquer.
▸ **bang down** *vt* (*lid*) rabattre (violemment).
▸ **bang into** *vt* heurter.
ban·gle bracelet *m* (rigide).
bangs *npl* (*of hair*) frange *f*.
ban·is·ter(s) *n(pl)* rampe *f* (d'escalier).
bank (*of river*) bord *m*; (*for money*) banque *f*.
bank ac·count compte *m* en banque.
bank·er banquier *m*.
bank·ing (*activity*) la banque.
▸ **bank on** *vt* compter sur.
bank·rupt *adj* **to go b.** faire faillite.
bank·rupt·cy faillite *f*.
ban·ner (*at rallies, on two poles*) banderole *f*.
bar 1 *n* barre *f*; (*of gold*) lingot *m*; (*of chocolate*) tablette *f*; (*on window*) barreau *m*; (*pub, counter*) bar *m*. 2 *vt* (*way*) bloquer; (*prohibit*) interdire (**sb from doing** à qn de faire); (*exclude*) exclure (**from** de).
bar·be·cue barbecue *m*.

barbed *adj* **b. wire** fil *m* de fer barbelé.
bar·ber coiffeur *m*.
bare *adj* nu; (*tree*) dénudé; **with his b. hands** mains nues.
bare·foot *adv* nu-pieds.
bare·ly *adv* (*scarcely*) à peine.
bar·gain 1 *n* (*deal*) marché *m*; **a b.** (*cheap buy*) une affaire; **b. price** prix *m* exceptionnel. 2 *vi* négocier.
▸ **bargain for** *vt* (*expect*) s'attendre à.
barge chaland *m*.
▸ **barge in** *vi* (*enter a room*) faire irruption; (*interrupt sb*) interrompre.
bark 1 *n* (*of tree*) écorce *f*. 2 *vi* (*of dog*) aboyer.
bark·ing aboiements *mpl*.
bar·ley orge *f*.
bar·maid serveuse *f* de bar.
bar·man barman *m*.
barn (*for crops*) grange *f*.
ba·rom·e·ter baromètre *m*.
bar·racks *npl* caserne *f*.
bar·rage (*barrier*) barrage *m*.
bar·rel (*cask*) tonneau *m*; (*of oil*) baril *m*; (*of gun*) canon *m*.
bar·ren *adj* stérile.
bar·rette barrette *f*.
bar·ri·cade 1 *n* barricade *f*. 2 *vt* barricader.
bar·ri·er barrière *f*.
bar·tend·er barman *m*.
base 1 *n* base *f*; (*of tree, lamp*) pied *m*. 2 *vt* baser.
base·ball base-ball *m*.
base·board plinthe *f*.
base·ment sous-sol *m*.
bash 1 *n* (*bang*) coup *m*. 2 *vt* (*hit*) cogner.
▸ **bash up** *vt* **to b. sb up** tabasser qn.
ba·sic 1 *adj* essentiel, de base; (*elementary*) élémentaire; (*pay*) de base. 2 *n* **the basics** l'essentiel *m*.
ba·si·cal·ly *adv* au fond.
ba·sin bassin *m*; (*sink*) lavabo *m*.
ba·sis (*of agreement etc*) bases *fpl*; **on the b. of** d'après; **on that b.** dans

ces conditions; **on a weekly b.**
chaque semaine.

bask *vi* se chauffer.

bas·ket panier *m*; *(for bread, laundry, litter)* corbeille *f*.

bass 1 *n (singer)* basse *f*; *(notes)*
graves *mpl*; **b. drum** grosse caisse
f; **b. (guitar)** *(guitare f)* basse *f*. 2
adj grave, bas, *f* (basse).

bat 1 *n (animal)* chauve-souris *f*;
Sports batte *f*. 2 *vt* **she didn't b. an
eyelid** elle n'a pas sourcillé.

batch *(of people)* groupe *m*; *(of letters)* paquet *m*; *(of papers)* liasse *f*.

bath 1 *n* bain *m*; *(tub)* baignoire *f*; **to
take a b.** prendre un bain. 2 *vt*
baigner.

bathe 1 *vt* baigner. 2 *vi (swim)* se
baigner; *(take a bath)* prendre un
bain. 3 *n* bain *m* (de mer).

bath·ing suit maillot *m* de bain.

bath·robe robe *f* de chambre.

bath·room salle *f* de bain(s); *(toilet)* toilettes *fpl*.

bath·tub baignoire *f*.

bat·ter 1 *n* pâte *f* à frire. 2 *vt (baby)*
martyriser.

▸**bat·ter down** *vt (door)* défoncer.

bat·tered *adj (car)* cabossé.

bat·ter·y batterie *f*; *(in radio, appliance)* pile *f*.

bat·tle 1 *n* bataille *f*; *(struggle)* lutte
f. 2 *vi* se battre.

bat·tle·ship cuirassé *m*.

bawl (out) *vti* beugler; **to b. sb
out** *Fam* engueuler qn.

bay *(part of coastline)* baie *f*; *(for
loading)* aire *f*.

BC *abbr (before Christ)* avant Jésus-
Christ.

be* *vi* être; **she's a doctor** elle est
médecin; **it's 3 o'clock** il est trois
heures. ▪ avoir; **to be hot/right/
lucky** avoir chaud/raison/de la
chance; **he's 20** il a 20 ans; **to be 7
feet high** avoir 2 mètres de haut. ▪
(health) aller; **how are you?**
comment vas-tu? ▪ *(go, come)* **I've
been to see her** je suis allé *or* j'ai

été la voir; **he's (already) been here**
il est (déjà) venu. ▪ *(weather, calculations)* faire; **it's sunny** il fait
beau; **2 and 2 are 4** 2 et 2 font 4. ▪
(cost) faire; **how much is it?** ça fait
combien? ▪ *(auxiliary)* **I am/was
doing** je fais/faisais; **he was killed**
il a été tué; **I've been waiting (for)
two hours** j'attends depuis deux
heures; **isn't it?, aren't you?**/*etc*
n'est-ce pas?, non? ▪ *(+ infinitive)*
he is to come *(must)* il doit venir. ▪
there is *or* **are** il y a; *(pointing)* voilà!; **here is** *or* **are** voici.

beach plage *f*.

bea·con balise *f*.

bead perle *f*; *(of sweat)* goutte *f*;
(string of) beads collier *m*.

beak bec *m*.

beak·er *(for drinking)* gobelet *m*;
(in laboratory) vase *m* à bec.

beam *(of wood)* poutre *f*; *(of light)*
rayon *m*; *(of headlight)* faisceau *m*.

beam·ing *adj (radiant)* radieux.

bean haricot *m*; *(of coffee)* grain *m*;
(broad) b. fève *f*.

bean·sprouts *npl* germes *mpl* de
soja.

bear[1] *(animal)* ours *m*.

bear[2]***** 1 *vt (carry, show)* porter;
(endure) supporter; *(responsibility)*
assumer; **to b. in mind** tenir compte de. 2 *vi* **to b. left/right** tourner à
gauche/droite.

bear·a·ble *adj* supportable.

beard barbe *f*.

beard·ed *adj* barbu.

bear·ing *(relevance)* relation *f* (**on**
avec); **to get one's bearings**
s'orienter.

▸**bear out** *vt* corroborer.

beast bête *f*; *(person)* brute *f*.

beast·ly *adj (bad)* *Fam* vilain.

beat 1 *n (of heart, drum)* battement
m; *(of policeman)* ronde *f*. 2 *vt**
battre.

▸**beat down** 1 *vt (door)* défoncer. 2
vi (of rain) tomber à verse; *(of sun)*
taper.

beat·ing *(blows, defeat)* raclée *f.*

▸ **beat off** *vt* repousser.

▸ **beat up** *vt* tabasser.

beau·ti·ful *adj* (très) beau *(f* belle).

beau·ty *(quality, woman)* beauté *f.*

beau·ty mark *(on skin)* grain *m* de beauté.

beau·ty par·lor institut *m* de beauté.

beau·ty spot *(on skin)* grain *m* de beauté.

bea·ver castor *m.*

be·cause *conj* parce que; **b. of** à cause de.

be·come* *vi* devenir; **to b. a painter** devenir peintre; **what has b. of her?** qu'est-elle devenue?

bed lit *m;* **to go to b.** (se) coucher; **in b.** couché; **to get out of b.** se lever; **b. and breakfast** chambre *f* avec petit déjeuner.

bed·clothes *npl* couvertures *fpl* et draps *mpl.*

bed·room chambre *f* à coucher.

bed·side chevet *m;* **b. lamp/book** lampe *f*/livre *m* de chevet.

bed·time heure *f* de coucher.

bee abeille *f.*

beech *(tree, wood)* hêtre *m.*

beef bœuf *m.*

bee·hive ruche *f.*

been *pp de* be.

beep 1 *n* bip *m;* *(on answering machine)* bip *m* sonore. **2** *vt* biper.

beep·er récepteur *m* d'appels, bip *m.*

beer bière *f;* **b. glass** chope *f.*

beet betterave *f (potagère).*

bee·tle scarabée *m.*

be·fore 1 *adv* avant; *(already)* déjà; *(in front)* devant; **the day b.** la veille. **2** *prep (time)* avant; *(place)* devant; **the year b. last** il y a deux ans. **3** *conj* avant que (+ ne + subjunctive), avant de (+ infinitive); **b. he goes** avant qu'il (ne) parte; **b. going** avant de partir.

be·friend *vt* prendre en amitié, se prendre d'amitié pour.

beg 1 *vt* **to b. (for)** solliciter; *(bread, money)* mendier; **to b. sb to do** supplier qn de faire. **2** *vi* mendier.

beg·gar mendiant, -ante *mf.*

be·gin* 1 *vt* commencer; *(campaign)* lancer; **to b. doing** *or* **to do** commencer *or* se mettre à faire. **2** *vi* commencer (**with** par; **by doing** par faire); **to b. with** *(first)* d'abord.

be·gin·ner débutant, -ante *mf.*

be·gin·ning commencement *m,* début *m.*

be·grudge *vt (envy)* envier (**sb sth** qch à qn); **to b. doing sth** faire qch à contrecœur.

be·half on b. of *(to act)* pour le compte de; *(to call, write)* de la part de.

be·have *vi* se conduire; *(of machine)* fonctionner; **to b. (oneself)** se tenir bien; *(of child)* être sage.

be·hav·ior conduite *f.*

be·hind 1 *prep* derrière; *(in making progress)* en retard sur. **2** *adv* derrière; *(late)* en retard. **3** *n (buttocks) Fam* derrière *m.*

beige *adj & n* beige *(m).*

belch 1 *vi* faire un renvoi. **2** *n* renvoi *m.*

Bel·gian 1 *n* Belge *mf.* **2** *adj* belge.

be·lief croyance *f* (**in** en); *(trust)* confiance *f,* foi *f; (opinion)* opinion *f.*

be·liev·a·ble *adj* croyable.

be·lieve *vti* croire (**in sth** à qch; **in God** en Dieu; **I b. so** je crois que oui; **to b. in doing** croire qu'il faut faire.

be·liev·er *(religious)* croyant, -ante *mf.*

be·lit·tle *vt* dénigrer.

bell cloche *f; (small)* clochette *f; (in phone)* sonnerie *f; (on door, bicycle)* sonnette *f.*

bell·boy groom *m.*

bel·ly ventre *m;* **b. button** *Fam* nombril *m.*

bel·ly·ache mal *m* au ventre.

be·long *vi* appartenir (**to** à); **to b. to** (*club*) être membre de.

be·long·ings *npl* affaires *fpl*.

be·low 1 *prep* au-dessous de. **2** *adv* en dessous.

belt ceinture *f*; (*in machine*) courroie *f*.

belt·way périphérique *m*.

bench (*seat*) banc *m*; (*work table*) établi *m*.

bend 1 *n* courbe *f*; (*in river*) coude *m*; (*in road*) virage *m*; (*of arm, knee*) pli *m*. **2** *vt* courber; (*leg, arm*) plier. **3** *vi* (*of road*) tourner.

bend (down) *vi* se baisser.

bend (over) *vi* se pencher.

be·neath 1 *prep* au-dessous de. **2** *adv* (au-)dessous.

ben·e·fi·cial *adj* bénéfique.

ben·e·fit 1 *n* avantage *m*; (*money*) allocation *f*; **child b.** allocations familiales; **for your (own) b.** pour vous. **2** *vt* faire du bien à; (*be useful to*) profiter à. **3** *vi* **you'll b. from it** ça vous fera du bien.

bent *adj* (*nail*) tordu; **b. on doing** résolu à faire.

be·reave·ment deuil *m*.

ber·ry baie *f*.

ber·serk *adj* **to go b.** devenir fou.

berth (*in ship, train*) couchette *f*.

be·side *prep* à côté de; **that's b. the point** ça n'a rien à voir.

be·sides 1 *prep* en plus de; (*except*) excepté. **2** *adv* de plus; (*moreover*) d'ailleurs.

best 1 *adj* meilleur (**in** de); **the b. part of** (*most*) la plus grande partie de. **2** *n* **the b.** le meilleur, la meilleure; **at b.** au mieux; **to do one's b.** faire de son mieux; **to make the b. of** s'accommoder de. **3** *adv* (the) **b.** (*to play, sing etc*) le mieux; **the b. loved** le plus aimé.

best man (*at wedding*) garçon *m* d'honneur.

best·sell·er best-seller *m*.

bet 1 *n* pari *m*. **2** *vti* parier (**on** sur; **that** que).

be·tray *vt* trahir.

be·tray·al trahison *f*.

bet·ter 1 *adj* meilleur (**than** que); **she's (much) b.** (*in health*) elle va (beaucoup) mieux; **that's b.** c'est mieux; **to get b.** (*recover*) se remettre; (*improve*) s'améliorer; **it's b. to go** il vaut mieux partir. **2** *adv* mieux; **I had b. go** il vaut mieux que je parte. **3** *vt* **to b. oneself** améliorer sa condition.

betting pari(s) *m(pl)*.

be·tween 1 *prep* entre; **in b. sth and sth/two things** entre qch et qch/deux choses. **2** *adv* **in b.** au milieu; (*time*) dans l'intervalle.

bev·er·age boisson *f*.

be·ware *vi* **to b. of** se méfier de; **b.!** méfiez-vous!

be·wil·der *vt* dérouter.

be·yond 1 *prep* au-delà de; (*reach, doubt*) hors de; **b. my means** au dessus de mes moyens; **it's b. me** ça me dépasse. **2** *adv* au-delà.

bi·as penchant *m* (**towards** pour); (*prejudice*) préjugé *m*.

bi·as(s)ed *adj* partial; **to be b. against** avoir des préjugés contre.

bib (*baby's*) bavoir *m*.

Bi·ble bible *f*; **the B.** la Bible.

bi·cy·cle bicyclette *f*.

bid* *vt* (*money*) offrir. **2** *vi* faire une offre (**for** pour). **3** *n* (*at auction*) offre *f*; (*for job*) tentative *f*.

big *adj* grand, gros (*f* grosse); (*in age, generous*) grand; (*in bulk, amount*) gros; **b. deal!** *Fam* (bon) et alors!

big·head *Fam* (*conceited*) prétentieux, -euse *mf*; (*boasting*) vantard, -arde *mf*.

big·shot *Fam* gros bonnet *m*.

bike *Fam* vélo *m*.

bike path *Fam* piste *f* cyclable.

bi·ki·ni deux-pièces *m inv*; **b. briefs** mini-slip *m*.

bile bile *f*.

bi·lin·gual *adj* bilingue.

bill 1 *n* (*invoice*) facture *f*, note *f*; (*in*

restaurant) addition *f*; *(in hotel)* note *f*; *(money)* billet *m*; *(proposed law)* projet *m* de loi. **2** *vt* to b. sb envoyer la facture à qn.

bill·board panneau *m* d'affichage.

bill·fold portefeuille *m*.

bil·liards *npl* (jeu *m* de) billiard *m*.

bil·lion milliard *m*.

bin boîte *f*, *(for trash)* poubelle *f*.

bind *vt** lier; *(book)* relier.

bind·er *(for papers)* classeur *m*.

bind·ing *(of book)* reliure *f*.

bin·go loto *m*.

bin·oc·u·lars *npl* jumelles *fpl*.

bi·o·log·i·cal *adj* biologique.

bi·ol·o·gy biologie *f*.

birch (silver) b. *(tree)* bouleau *m*.

bird oiseau *m*; *(fowl)* volaille *f*; **b.'s-eye view** vue *f* d'ensemble.

birth naissance *f*; **to give b. to** donner naissance à.

birth cer·tif·i·cate acte *m* de naissance.

birth·day anniversaire *m*; **happy b.!** bon anniversaire!

birth·mark tache *f* de naissance.

bis·cuit petit pain *m*.

bish·op évêque *m*.

bit morceau *m*; **a b.** *(a little)* un peu; **quite a b.** *(very)* très; *(a lot)* beaucoup; **not a b.** pas du tout; **b. by b.** petit à petit.

bitch 1 *n* *(dog)* chienne *f*; *(spiteful woman)* Fam garce *f*. **2** *vi* to b. (about) Fam *(criticize)* déblatérer (contre).

bite 1 *n* *(wound)* morsure *f*, *(from insect)* piqûre *f*, **a b. to eat** quelque chose à manger. **2** *vti** mordre; **to b. one's nails** se ronger les ongles.

bit·ter *adj* amer; *(cold, wind)* glacial; *(conflict)* violent.

bit·ter·ness amertume *f*, *(of conflict)* violence *f*.

bi·zarre *adj* bizarre.

black 1 *adj* noir; **b. eye** œil *m* poché; **to give sb a b. eye** pocher l'œil à qn; **b. and blue** *(bruised)*

couvert de bleus. **2** *n* *(color)* noir *m*; *(person)* Noir, -e *mf*.

black·ber·ry mûre *f*.

black·bird merle *m*.

black·board tableau *m* (noir); **on the b.** au tableau.

black·cur·rant cassis *m*.

black·list 1 *n* liste *f* noire. **2** *vt* mettre sur la liste noire.

black·mail 1 *n* chantage *m*. **2** *vt* faire chanter.

black·mail·er maître chanteur *m*.

▶ **black out** *vi* *(faint)* s'évanouir.

black·out panne *f* d'électricité; *(fainting fit)* syncope *f*.

blad·der vessie *f*.

blade lame *f*, *(of grass)* brin *m*.

blame 1 *vt* accuser; **to b. sb for sth** reprocher qch à qn; **you're to b.** c'est ta faute. **2** *n* faute *f*.

blame·less *adj* irréprochable.

bland *adj* *(food)* fade.

blank 1 *adj* *(paper, page)* blanc *(f* blanche); *(check)* en blanc. **2** *adj* & *n* b. *(space)* blanc *m*.

blan·ket couverture *f*.

blare (out) *vi* *(of radio)* beugler; *(of music)* retentir.

blast 1 *n* explosion *f*, *(air from explosion)* souffle *m*. **2** *int* Fam zut!

blast·ed *adj* Fam fichu.

blast·off *(of spacecraft)* mise *f* à feu.

blaze 1 *n* *(fire)* flamme *f*, *(large)* incendie *m*. **2** *vi* *(of fire)* flamber; *(of sun)* flamboyer.

blaz·er blazer *m*.

blaz·ing *adj* en feu; *(sun)* brûlant.

bleach *(household)* eau *f* de Javel.

bleak *adj* morne.

bleed* *vti* saigner.

blem·ish *(fault)* défaut *m*; *(mark)* tache *f*.

blend 1 *n* mélange *m*. **2** *vt* mélanger. **3** *vi* se mélanger.

blend·er *(for food)* mixer *m*.

bless *vt* bénir; **b. you!** *(after sneeze)* à tes souhaits!

bless·ing bénédiction f, (benefit) bienfait m.

blew pt de blow¹.

blind 1 adj aveugle; **b. person** aveugle mf. **2** n (on window) store m; **the b.** les aveugles mpl.

blind·fold 1 n bandeau m. **2** vt bander les yeux à.

blind·ly adv aveuglément.

blind·ness cécité f.

blink 1 vi (of person) cligner des yeux; (of eyes) cligner. **2** n clignement m.

bliss félicité f.

blis·ter (on skin) ampoule f.

bliz·zard tempête f de neige.

bloat vt gonfler.

blob goutte f, (of ink) tache f.

block 1 n (of stone) bloc m; (of buildings) pâté m (de maisons); (child's toy) cube m. **2** vt (obstruct) bloquer.

block·age obstruction f.

▸**block off** vt (road) barrer.

▸**block up** vt (pipe, hole) bloquer.

blond adj & n blond (m).

blonde adj & n blonde (f).

blood sang m; **b. donor** donneur, -euse mf de sang; **b. group** groupe m sanguin; **b. pressure** tension f (artérielle); **to have high b. pressure** avoir de la tension.

blood·shed effusion f de sang.

blood·shot adj (eye) injecté de sang.

blood·y adj sanglant.

bloom 1 n fleur f, **in b.** en fleur(s). **2** vi fleurir.

blos·som 1 n fleur(s) f(pl). **2** vi fleurir.

blot tache f.

blotch·y adj couvert de taches.

blot·ting pa·per buvard m.

blouse chemisier m.

blow¹* **1** vt (of wind) pousser (un navire), chasser (la pluie); (of person) (smoke) souffler; (bubbles) faire; (trumpet) souffler dans; **to b. one's nose** se moucher; **to b. a** whistle siffler. **2** vi (of wind, person) souffler.

blow² (with fist, tool etc) coup m.

▸**blow away 1** vt (of wind) emporter. **2** vi (of hat, newspaper etc) s'envoler.

▸**blow down, blow over 1** vt (chimney etc) faire tomber. **2** vi tomber.

blow-dry brushing m.

blow-dry·er sèche-cheveux m.

▸**blow off 1** vt (hat etc) emporter. **2** vi s'envoler.

▸**blow out** (candle) souffler.

blow·torch chalumeau m.

▸**blow up 1** vt (building) faire sauter; (tire, balloon) gonfler. **2** vi exploser.

blue 1 adj bleu (mpl bleus). **2** n bleu m (pl bleus).

blue·ber·ry myrtille f.

blue·print bleu m; (plan) plan m, projet m.

bluff 1 vti bluffer. **2** n bluff m.

blun·der 1 n (mistake) bévue f. **2** vi faire une bévue.

blunt adj (edge) émoussé; (person, speech) franc, brusque.

blur 1 n tache f floue. **2** vt rendre flou.

blurred adj flou.

blush vi rougir (with de).

blus·ter·y adj (weather) de grand vent.

board¹1 n (piece of wood) planche f, (for notices) tableau m; (cardboard) carton m; **b. (of directors)** conseil m d'administration; **on b.** (ship, aircraft) à bord (de). **2** vt monter à bord de; (bus, train) monter dans.

board² (food) pension f, **room and b.** pension f (complète).

board·er pensionnaire mf.

board·ing (of passengers) embarquement m.

board·ing house pension f (de famille).

board·ing school pensionnat m.

board·walk promenade f (de planches).

boast vi se vanter (**about, of** de).

boat bateau m; (small) barque f, canot m; (liner) paquebot m.

bob·by pin pince f à cheveux.

bob·by socks, bob·by sox npl socquettes fpl (de fille).

bod·i·ly adj (need) physique.

bod·y corps m; (institution) organisme m.

bod·y·guard garde m du corps.

bod·y·work carrosserie f.

bogged down adj **to get b.** s'enliser.

bo·gus adj faux (f fausse).

boil[1] (pimple) furoncle m.

boil[2] **1** n **to come to the b.** bouillir. **2** vt faire bouillir. **3** vi bouillir.

boiled adj bouilli; (potato) à l'eau; **b. egg** œuf m à la coque; **hard-b. egg** œuf m dur.

boil·er chaudière f.

boil·ing adj **b. (hot)** bouillant; **it's b. (hot)** (weather) il fait une chaleur infernale.

▶ **boil over** vi (of milk) déborder.

▶ **boil up** vt faire bouillir.

bold adj hardi.

bold·ness hardiesse f.

bolt 1 n (on door) verrou m; (for nut) boulon m. **2** vt (of door) fermer au verrou. **3** vi (dash) se précipiter.

bomb 1 n bombe f. **2** vt bombarder.

bomb·er (aircraft) bombardier m.

bomb·ing bombardement m.

bond (link) lien m; (investment certificate) bon m.

bone os m; (of fish) arête f.

bon·fire (celebration) feu m de joie; (for dead leaves) feu m (de jardin).

bon·net (hat) bonnet m; (of car) capot m.

bo·nus prime f.

bon·y adj (thin) osseux; (fish) plein d'arêtes.

boo 1 vti siffler. **2** n **boos** sifflets mpl.

boo·by-trap vt piéger.

book 1 n livre m; (of tickets) carnet m; (exercise) **b.** cahier m (de brouillon); **books** (accounts) comptes mpl. **2** vt (room etc) réserver.

book·case bibliothèque f.

booked up adj (hotel) complet.

book·ing réservation f.

book·keep·er comptable mf.

book·keep·ing comptabilité f.

book·let (pamphlet) brochure f.

book·mak·er bookmaker m.

book·sell·er libraire mf.

book·shelf rayon m.

book·store librairie f.

boom (economic) expansion f.

boost vt (increase) augmenter; (product) faire de la réclame pour; (economy) stimuler.

boot (footwear) botte f; (ankle) **b.** bottillon m; **to get the b.** Fam être mis à la porte; (Denver) **b.** (on car) sabot m (de Denver).

booth (for phone) cabine f.

▶ **boot out** vt mettre à la porte.

booze Fam **1** n alcool m. **2** vi picoler.

bor·der (of country) frontière f; (edge) bord m.

bor·der (on) vt (country) toucher à.

bor·der·line case cas m limite.

bore vt ennuyer; **to be bored** s'ennuyer. **2** n (person) raseur, -euse mf; (thing) ennui m.

bore·dom ennui m.

bor·ing adj ennuyeux.

born adj né; **to be b.** naître; **he was b.** il est né.

bor·ough municipalité f.

bor·row vt emprunter (**from** à).

boss patron, -onne mf, chef m.

▶ **boss around** vt donner des ordres à.

boss·y adj Fam autoritaire.

botch (up) vt (ruin) bâcler.

both 1 adj les deux. **2** pron tous/toutes (les) deux; **b. of us** nous deux. **3** adv (at the same time) à la fois; **b. you and I** vous et moi.

both·er 1 vt (annoy, worry) ennuyer; (disturb) déranger; (pester) importuner; **to b. doing** or **to do se donner la peine de faire**; **I can't be bothered** je n'en ai pas envie. **2** n (trouble) ennui m; (effort) peine f; (inconvenience) dérangement m.

▸ **bother about** vt (worry about) se préoccuper de.

bot·tle bouteille f, (small) flacon m; (for baby) biberon m; **hot-water b.** bouillotte f.

bot·tle o·pen·er ouvre-bouteilles m inv.

bot·tom 1 n (of sea, box) fond m; (of page, hill) bas m; (buttocks) Fam derrière m; **to be at the b. of the class** être le dernier de la classe. **2** adj (part, shelf) inférieur, du bas; **b. floor** rez-de-chaussée m.

boul·der rocher m.

bounce 1 vi (of ball) rebondir; (of check) Fam être sans provision. **2** vt faire rebondir. **3** n (re)bond m.

bound adj **b. to do** (obliged) obligé de faire; (certain) sûr de faire; **it's b. to happen/snow**/etc ça arrivera/il neigera/etc sûrement; **b. for** en route pour.

bound·a·ry limite f.

bounds npl **out of b.** (place) interdit.

bou·quet (of flowers) bouquet m.

bou·tique boutique f (de mode).

bow¹ (weapon) arc m; (knot) nœud m.

bow² **1** n révérence f; (nod) salut m. **2** vi s'incliner (**to** devant); (nod) incliner la tête (**to** devant).

bow·els npl intestins mpl.

bowl (for food) bol m; (for sugar) sucrier m; (for salad) saladier m; (for fruit) coupe f.

bowl·ing (tenpin) **b.** bowling m.

bowl·ing al·ley bowling m.

bow tie nœud m papillon.

box 1 n boîte f, (large) caisse f. **2** vi (of boxer) boxer.

box·er boxeur m.

box·er shorts caleçon m.

▸ **box in** vt (enclose) enfermer.

box·ing boxe f; **b. ring** ring m.

box of·fice guichet m (pour spectacles).

boy garçon m; **American b.** jeune Américain m; **oh b.!** mon Dieu!

boy·cott 1 vt boycotter. **2** n boycottage m.

boy·friend petit ami m.

bra soutien-gorge m.

brace·let bracelet m.

brack·et (in typography) crochet m; (for shelf etc) équerre f.

brag vi se vanter (**about, of** de).

brag·ging vantardise f.

braid 1 n (of hair) tresse f. **2** vt tresser.

brain cerveau m; **to have brains** avoir de l'intelligence.

brain·storm (brilliant idea) idée f géniale.

brain·wash vt faire un lavage de cerveau à.

brain·y adj Fam intelligent.

brake 1 n frein m. **2** vi freiner.

brake light (signal m de) stop m.

branch branche f, (of road) embranchement m; (of store, office) succursale f.

▸ **branch off** vi (of road) bifurquer.

▸ **branch out** vi (of firm, person) étendre ses activités (**into** à).

brand (trademark) marque f.

brand-new adj tout neuf (f toute neuve).

bran·dy cognac m.

brass cuivre m.

brave adj courageux, brave.

brav·er·y courage m.

brawl bagarre f.

brawn·y adj musclé.

bread inv pain m; **loaf of b.** pain m; **(slice** or **piece of) b. and butter** tartine f.

bread·box coffre m à pain.

bread·crumb miette f (de pain); **breadcrumbs** (in cooking) chapelure f.

breadth largeur f.

bread·win·ner soutien m de famille.

break 1 vt* casser; (into pieces) briser; (silence, spell) rompre; (strike, heart, ice) briser; (sports record) battre; (law) violer; (one's word, promise) manquer à; (journey) interrompre; (news) révéler (**to** à). **2** vi (se) casser; (into pieces) se briser; se rompre; (of news) éclater; (stop work) faire la pause. **3** n cassure f, (in bone) fracture f, (with person, group) rupture f, (in journey) interruption f, (rest) repos m; (in activity, for tea etc) pause f, (in school) récréation f, **a lucky b.** une chance.

break·a·ble adj fragile.

▸ **break away** vi se détacher.

▸ **break down 1** vt (door) enfoncer. **2** vi (of vehicle, machine) tomber en panne; (of talks) échouer; (collapse) (of person) s'effondrer.

break·down (of vehicle, machine) panne f, (in talks) rupture f, (nervous) dépression f.

break·fast petit déjeuner m.

▸ **break in 1** vi (of burglar) entrer par effraction. **2** vt (door) enfoncer; (vehicle) roder.

break-in cambriolage m.

▸ **break into** vt (house) cambrioler; (safe) forcer.

▸ **break loose** vi s'échapper.

▸ **break off 1** vt détacher; (relations) rompre. **2** vi se détacher; (stop) s'arrêter; **to b. off with sb** rompre avec qn.

▸ **break out** vi (of war, fire) éclater; (escape) s'échapper.

break·through percée f, découverte f.

▸ **break up 1** vt mettre en morceaux; (fight) mettre fin à. **2** vi (of group) se disperser; (of marriage) se briser.

break-up (of marriage) rupture f.

breast sein m; (of chicken) blanc m.

breast·feed vt allaiter.

breast·stroke brasse f.

breath haleine f, souffle m; **out of b.** (tout) essoufflé.

Breath·a·lyz·er® alcootest® m.

breathe vti respirer; **to b. in** aspirer; **to b. out** expirer.

breath·ing respiration f, **b. space** moment m de repos.

breath·tak·ing adj époustouflant.

breed 1 vt* (animals) élever. **2** vi (of animals) se reproduire. **3** n race f.

breed·er éleveur, -euse mf.

breed·ing (of animals) élevage m; (good manners) éducation f, **b. ground** foyer m, terrain m propice.

breeze brise f.

breez·y adj (weather) frais.

brew vi (storm) se préparer; (of tea) infuser; **something is brewing** il se prépare quelque chose.

brew·er·y brasserie f.

bribe 1 n pot-de-vin m. **2** vt (person) acheter.

brick brique f.

brick·lay·er maçon m.

bride mariée f, **the b. and groom** les mariés mpl.

bride·groom marié m.

brides·maid demoiselle f d'honneur.

bridge pont m.

brief 1 adj bref (f brève). **2** vt (inform) mettre au courant (**on** de). **3** n briefs (underpants) slip m.

brief·case serviette f.

brief·ing instructions fpl.

brief·ly adv (quickly) en vitesse.

bright 1 adj brillant; (weather, room) clair; (clever) intelligent; (idea) génial. **2** adv **b. and early** de bonne heure.

bright·en (up) 1 vt (room) égayer. **2** vi (of weather) s'éclaircir.

bright·ly adv avec éclat.

bright·ness éclat m.

bril·liance éclat m; (of person) grande intelligence f.

bril·liant *adj* *(light)* éclatant; *(clever)* brillant.

bring* *vt (person, vehicle)* amener; *(thing)* apporter; *(to cause)* amener; **to b. to an end** mettre fin à; **to b. to mind** rappeler.

▸ **bring about** *vt* provoquer.

▸ **bring along** *vt (object)* emporter; *(person)* emmener.

▸ **bring around** *vt* ranimer.

▸ **bring back** *vt (person)* ramener; *(object)* rapporter; *(memories)* rappeler.

▸ **bring down** *vt (object)* descendre; *(overthrow)* faire tomber; *(reduce)* réduire.

▸ **bring in** *vt (object)* rentrer; *(person)* faire entrer; *(introduce)* introduire.

▸ **bring out** *vt (object)* sortir; *(person)* faire sortir; *(meaning)* faire ressortir; *(book)* publier; *(product)* lancer.

▸ **bring to** *vt* ranimer.

▸ **bring together** *vt (reconcile)* réconcilier.

▸ **bring up** *vt (object)* monter; *(child)* élever; *(subject)* mentionner.

brink bord *m*.

brisk *adj* vif.

brisk·ly *adv (to walk)* vite.

bris·tle poil *m*.

Brit·ish 1 *adj* britannique. **2** *n* **the B.** les Britanniques *mpl*.

Brit·ish Isles îles *fpl* Britanniques.

Brit·on Britannique *mf*.

brit·tle *adj* fragile.

broad *adj (wide)* large; *(outline)* général; **in b. daylight** en plein jour.

broad·cast 1 *vt** diffuser, retransmettre. **2** *n* émission *f*.

broad·en *vt* élargir.

broc·co·li *inv* brocolis *mpl*.

bro·chure brochure *f*.

broke 1 *pt de* **break**. **2** *adj (penniless)* fauché.

bro·ken *pp de* **break**.

bro·ken-down *adj (machine)* délingué.

bron·chi·tis bronchite *f*.

bronze bronze *m*.

brooch broche *f*.

brood 1 *n* couvée *f*. **2** *vi* méditer tristement (**over** sur).

brook ruisseau *m*.

broom balai *m*.

broom·stick manche *m* à balai.

broth·er frère *m*.

broth·er-in-law, *pl* brothers-in-law beau-frère *m*.

brought *pt & pp de* **bring**.

brow *(forehead)* front *m*; *(eyebrow)* sourcil *m*; *(of hill)* sommet *m*.

brown 1 *adj* marron; *(hair)* châtain; *(tanned)* bronzé. **2** *n* marron *m*.

brown·ie brownie *m*.

browse *vi (in bookstore)* feuilleter des livres; *(in store)* regarder.

bruise 1 *vt* **to b. one's knee/***etc* se faire un bleu au genou/*etc*. **2** *n* bleu *m* (*pl* bleus), contusion *f*.

bruised *adj* couvert de bleus.

brunch brunch *m*.

bru·nette brunette *f*.

brush 1 *n* brosse *f*, *(for painting)* pinceau *m*. **2** *vt (teeth, hair)* (se) brosser.

▸ **brush aside** *vt* écarter.

▸ **brush away, brush off** *vt* enlever.

▸ **brush up (on)** *vt (language)* se remettre à.

bru·tal *adj* brutal.

bru·tal·i·ty brutalité *f*.

brute brute *f*.

BS *abbr* = **Bachelor of Science**.

bub·ble 1 *n* bulle *f*. **2** *vi* bouillonner.

▸ **bubble over** *vi* déborder.

buck *Fam* dollar *m*.

buck·et seau *m*.

buck·le 1 *n* boucle *f*. **2** *vt* boucler. **3** *vti (warp)* voiler.

▸ **buck up 1** *vt (person)* remonter le moral à. **2** *vi (become livelier)* reprendre du poil de la bête.

bud 1 n (of tree) bourgeon m; (of flower) bouton m. **2** vi (of tree) bourgeonner; (of flower) pousser des boutons.

Bud·dhist adj & n bouddhiste (mf).

bud·dy Fam copain, -ine mf.

budge vi bouger.

budg·et budget m.

▸ **budget for** vt inscrire au budget.

buf·fa·lo, pl -oes or -os buffle m; (American) b. bison m.

buff·er (device) tampon m; (in computer) tampon, mémoire f intermédiaire.

buf·fet (table, meal) buffet m.

bug¹ punaise f; (any insect) bestiole f; (germ) microbe m, virus m; (in machine) défaut m; (in computer program) erreur f, (listening device) micro m clandestin.

bug² vt (annoy) Fam embêter.

bu·gle clairon m.

build 1 n (of person) carrure f. **2** vt* construire; (house) construire, bâtir.

build·er maçon m; (contractor) entrepreneur m.

build·ing bâtiment m; (of apartments, offices) immeuble m.

▸ **build up 1** vt (increase) augmenter; (collection) constituer; (business) monter; (speed) prendre. **2** vt (of tension, pressure) augmenter.

built-in adj (closet) encastré; (part of machine) incorporé.

built-up a·re·a agglomération f.

bulb (of plant) oignon m; (of lamp) ampoule f.

bulge renflement m.

bulge (out) vi se renfler.

bulg·ing adj renflé.

bulk inv grosseur f; **the b. of** (most) la majeure partie de.

bulk·y adj gros (f grosse).

bull taureau m.

bull·dog bouledogue m.

bull·doz·er bulldozer m.

bul·let boule f (de révolver etc).

bul·le·tin bulletin m.

bul·le·tin board tableau m d'affichage.

bul·let·proof adj (vest) pareballes inv; (car) blindé.

bull·fight corrida f.

bul·ly 1 n (grosse) brute f. **2** vt brutaliser.

bum Fam (tramp) clochard, -arde mf; (good-for-nothing) propre mf à rien.

bum·ble·bee bourdon m.

bump 1 vt (of car) heurter; **to b. one's head/knee** se cogner la tête/le genou. **2** n (impact) choc m; (jerk) cahot m; (on road, body) bosse f.

bump·er pare-chocs m inv.

▸ **bump into** vt se cogner contre; (of car) rentrer dans; (meet) tomber sur.

bump·y adj (road, ride) cahoteux.

bun (roll) petit pain m au lait.

bunch (of flowers) bouquet m; (of keys) trousseau m; (of people) bande f, **b. of grapes** grappe f de raisin.

bun·dle 1 n paquet m; (of papers) liasse f. **2** vt (put) fourrer; (push) pousser (into dans).

▸ **bundle up** vi (dress warmly) se couvrir.

bun·ga·low bungalow m.

bunk couchette f, **b. beds** lits mpl superposés.

bun·ny Fam Jeannot m lapin.

buoy bouée f.

bur·den 1 n fardeau m; (of tax) poids m. **2** vt accabler (with de).

bu·reau, pl bureaux (office) service m, office m; (chest of drawers) commode f.

bu·reau·cra·cy bureaucratie f.

bu·reau·crat bureaucrate mf.

burg·er hamburger m.

bur·glar cambrioleur, -euse mf.

bur·glar a·larm alarme f antivol.

bur·glar·ize vt cambrioler.

bur·gla·ry cambriolage m.

bur·gle vt cambrioler.

bur·i·al enterrement m.

burn 1 n brûlure f. **2** vti* brûler; **burnt alive** brûlé vif.

▸**burn down 1** vt détruire par le feu. **2** vi être détruit par le feu.

burn·er (of stove) brûleur m.

burn·ing adj en feu; (fire, light) allumé.

burp 1 n rot m. **2** vi roter.

burst 1 n (of laughter) éclat m; (of thunder) coup m. **2** vi* (with force) éclater; (of bubble, balloon, boil, tire) crever.

burst·ing adj (full) plein à craquer.

▸**burst into** vt (room) faire irruption dans; **to b. into tears** fondre en larmes.

▸**burst out** vi **to b. out laughing** éclater de rire.

bur·y vt enterrer; (hide) enfouir; (plunge, absorb) plonger.

bus (auto)bus m; (long-distance) (auto)car m.

bush buisson m.

bush·y adj broussailleux.

busi·ness 1 n affaires fpl, commerce m; (shop) commerce m; (task, concern, matter) affaire f; **on b.** pour affaires; **it's your b. to…** c'est à vous de…; **that's none of your b.!, mind your own b.!** ça ne vous regarde pas! **2** adj commercial; (meeting, trip) d'affaires; **b. hours** heures fpl de bureau; **b. card** carte f de visite.

busi·ness·man, pl -men homme m d'affaires.

busi·ness·wom·an, pl -women femme f d'affaires.

bus shel·ter abribus m.

bus sta·tion gare f routière.

bus stop arrêt m d'autobus.

bust 1 n (sculpture) buste m; (woman's breasts) poitrine f. **2** adj **to go b.** Fam (bankrupt) faire faillite.

bus·tle 1 vi s'affairer. **2** n activité f.

bus·tling adj (street, town) bruyant.

bus·y adj occupé (**doing** à faire); (active) actif; (day) chargé; (street) animé; (phone) occupé; **to be b. doing** (in the process of) être en train de faire; **b. signal** sonnerie f occupé.

bus·y·bod·y **to be a b.** Fam faire la mouche du coche.

but 1 conj mais. **2** prep (except) sauf; **b. for that/him** sans cela/lui. **3** adv (only) seulement.

butch·er boucher, -ère mf; **b.'s shop** boucherie f.

but·ler maître m d'hôtel.

butt (of cigarette) mégot m; (buttocks) Fam cul m.

but·ter 1 n beurre m. **2** vt beurrer.

but·ter·cup bouton-d'or m.

but·ter·fly papillon m.

▸**butt in** vi interrompre.

but·tock fesse f.

but·ton bouton m; (of phone etc) touche f; (bearing slogan) pin's m.

button (up) vt (garment) boutonner.

but·ton·hole boutonnière f.

buy 1 vt* acheter (**from sb** à qn; **for sb** à or pour qn). **2** n **a good b.** une bonne affaire.

buy·er acheteur, -euse mf.

buzz 1 vi bourdonner. **2** n bourdonnement m.

▸**buzz off** vi Fam décamper.

by 1 prep (agent, manner) par; **hit/ etc by** frappé/etc par; **surrounded/ etc by** entouré/etc de; **by doing** en faisant; **by sea** par mer; **by car** en voiture; **by bicycle** à bicyclette; **by day** de jour; **by oneself** tout seul. ■ (next to) à côté de; (near) près de; **by the lake** au bord du lac. ■ (before in time) avant; **by Monday** avant lundi; **by now** à cette heure-ci. ■ (amount) à; **by weight** au poids; **paid by the hour** payé à l'heure. **2** adv **close by** tout près;

to go by, pass by passer; **by and large** en gros.

bye(-bye)! *int Fam* salut!

by·pass 1 *n* (of highway) bretelle *f* (de contournement); (heart surgery) pontage *m*. **2** *vt* contourner.

by·stand·er spectateur, -trice *mf*.

C

cab taxi *m*.

cab·bage chou *m* (*pl* choux).

cab·in (on ship) cabine *f*; (hut) cabane *f*.

cab·i·net¹ armoire *f*; (for display) vitrine *f*; **(filing) c.** classeur *m* (de bureau).

cab·i·net² (in politics) gouvernement *m*; **c. meeting** conseil *m* des ministres.

ca·ble câble *m*; **c. television** la télévision par câble.

ca·ble car téléphérique *m*; (on tracks) funiculaire *m*.

cac·tus, *pl* -ti *or* -tuses cactus *m*.

caf·e·te·ri·a cafétéria *f*.

caf·feine caféine *f*.

cage cage *f*.

cake gâteau *m*.

cal·cu·late *vti* calculer.

cal·cu·la·tion calcul *m*.

cal·cu·la·tor calculatrice *f*.

cal·en·dar calendrier *m*.

calf, *pl* calves (animal) veau *m*; (part of leg) mollet *m*.

call 1 *n* appel *m*; (shout) cri *m*; (visit) visite *f*; **(telephone) c.** communication *f*; **to make a c.** (phone) téléphoner (**to** à). **2** *vt* appeler; (shout) crier; (attention) attirer (**to** sur); **he's called David** il s'appelle David; **to c. a meeting** convoquer une assemblée; **to c. sb a liar/etc** qualifier

qn de menteur/etc. **3** *vi* appeler; (cry out) crier; (visit) passer.

▶ **call back** *vti* rappeler.

call·er visiteur, -euse *mf*; (on phone) correspondant, -ante *mf*.

▶ **call for** *vt* (require) demander; (summon) appeler; (collect) passer prendre.

▶ **call in** *vt* (into room etc) faire entrer.

call·ing card (for telephone) télécarte *f*.

▶ **call off** *vt* (cancel) annuler.

▶ **call on** *vt* (visit) passer voir; **to c. on sb to do** inviter qn à faire; (urge) presser qn de faire.

▶ **call out 1** *vt* (shout) crier; (doctor) appeler. **2** *vi* crier; **to c. out for** demander à haute voix.

▶ **call up** *vt* (phone) appeler.

calm 1 *adj* calme; **keep c.!** du calme! **2** *n* calme *m*. **3** *vt* calmer.

▶ **calm down 1** *vi* se calmer. **2** *vt* calmer.

calm·ly *adv* calmement.

cal·o·rie calorie *f*.

cam·cord·er caméscope *m*.

came *pt de* come.

cam·el chameau *m*.

cam·er·a appareil photo *m*; **(TV or film) c.** caméra *f*.

camp camp *m*.

camp (out) *vi* camper.

cam·paign campagne *f*.

camp·er (person) campeur, -euse *mf*; (recreational vehicle) camping-car *m*; (trailer) caravane *f*.

camp·fire feu *m* de camp.

camp·ing camping *m*; **c. site** camping *m*.

camp·site camping *m*.

cam·pus campus *m*, complexe *m* universitaire.

can¹ *v aux* (*pt* could) pouvoir; (know how to) savoir; **he couldn't help me** il ne pouvait pas m'aider; **she c. swim** elle sait nager; **you could be wrong** (possibility) tu as peut-être tort; **he can't be old**

(probability) il ne doit pas être vieux; **c. I come in?** puis-je entrer?

can² *(for food)* boîte f; *(for drinks)* cannette f.

Ca·na·di·an 1 n Canadien, -ienne mf. **2** adj canadien.

ca·nal canal m.

ca·nar·y canari m.

can·cel vt *(flight, appointment etc)* annuler; *(goods, taxi)* décommander; *(train)* supprimer.

can·cel·la·tion *(of flight, appointment etc)* annulation f; *(of train)* suppression f.

can·cer cancer m.

can·did adj franc *(f* franche).

can·di·date candidat, -ate mf.

can·dle bougie f; *(in church)* cierge m.

can·dle·stick bougeoir m; *(tall)* chandelier m.

can·dy bonbon(s) m(pl).

candystore confiserie f.

cane 1 n *(stick)* canne f; *(for punishing sb)* baguette f. **2** vt *(punish)* fouetter.

can·na·bis *(drug)* haschisch m.

canned adj en boîte; **c. food** conserves fpl.

can·ni·bal cannibale mf.

ca·noe canoë m.

ca·noe·ing **to go c.** faire du canoë.

canola colza m.

can·o·pen·er ouvre-boîtes m inv.

can·o·py *(hood of baby carriage)* capote f; *(small roof)* auvent m.

can·ta·loup(e) *(melon)* cantaloup m.

can·teen *(place)* cantine f; *(flask)* gourde f.

can·vas toile f.

can·yon canyon m.

cap *(hat)* casquette f; *(for shower)* bonnet m; *(of soldier)* képi m; *(of bottle, tube)* bouchon m; *(of milk or beer bottle)* capsule f; *(of pen)* capuchon m; *(of child's gun)* amorce f.

ca·pa·bil·i·ty capacité f.

ca·pa·ble adj *(person)* capable (**of** sth de qch; **of doing** de faire).

ca·pac·i·ty *(of container)* capacité f, *(ability)* aptitude f; **in my c. as** en ma qualité de.

cape *(cloak)* cape f; *(of cyclist)* pèlerine f.

cap·i·tal *(money)* capital m; **c.** (**city**) capitale f; **c.** (**letter**) majuscule f.

cap·size vti chavirer.

cap·sule capsule f.

cap·tain capitaine m.

cap·ture vt *(of person, town)* prendre.

car voiture f, auto f; *(of train)* wagon m; **c. radio** autoradio m.

car·a·mel caramel m.

car·a·van caravane f; *(horse-drawn)* roulotte f.

car·bon carbone m; **c. copy** double m (au carbone).

car·bon pa·per *(papier m)* carbone m.

car·bu·re·tor carburateur m.

card carte f; *(cardboard)* carton m; (**index**) **c.** fiche f; **to play cards** jouer aux cartes.

card·board carton m.

car·di·gan gilet m.

car·di·nal adj *(number, point)* cardinal.

card in·dex fichier m.

care 1 vi *(like)* aimer; **would you c. to try?** aimeriez-vous essayer?; **I don't c.** ça m'est égal; **who cares?** qu'est-ce que ça fait? **2** n *(attention)* soin(s) m(pl); *(protection)* garde f; *(anxiety)* souci m; **to take c. not to do** faire attention à ne pas faire; **to take c. to do** veiller à faire; **to take c. of** s'occuper de; *(keep safely)* garder (**for sb** pour qn); *(sick person)* prendre soin de; **to take c. of oneself** *(manage)* se débrouiller; *(keep healthy)* faire bien attention à soi.

▶ **care about** vt se soucier de.

ca·reer carrière f.

▸ **care for** vt (want) avoir envie de; **to c. for sb** (look after) s'occuper de qn; (sick person) soigner qn; (like) avoir de la sympathie pour qn; **I don't c. for it** je n'aime pas beaucoup ça.

care·free adj insouciant.

care·ful adj (exact, thorough) soigneux (**about** de); (cautious) prudent; **to be c. of** or **with** faire attention à.

care·ful·ly adv avec soin; (cautiously) prudemment.

care·giv·er (professional) aide mf à domicile; (relative) = personne s'occupant d'un parent malade ou âgé.

care·less adj négligent; (absent-minded) étourdi.

care·tak·er gardien, -ienne mf.

car fer·ry ferry-boat m.

car·go, pl -os cargaison f.

car·ing adj (loving) aimant; (understanding) très humain.

car·na·tion œillet m.

car·ni·val carnaval m (pl -als).

car·ol chant m (de Noël).

carp (fish) carpe f.

car·pen·ter charpentier m; (for light woodwork) menuisier m.

car·pen·try charpenterie f; menuiserie f.

car·pet tapis m; (fitted) moquette f.

car·pet·ing (wall-to-wall) c. moquette f.

car·pet sweep·er balai m mécanique.

car·riage (of train, horse-drawn) voiture f.

car·ri·er (company) entreprise f de transport; (of disease) porteur, -euse mf.

car·rot carotte f.

car·ry vt porter; (goods) transporter; (sell) stocker; (in calculation) retenir.

▸ **carry away** vt emporter; **to get carried away** (excited) s'emballer.

▸ **carry back** vt rapporter; (person) ramener.

▸ **carry off** vt emporter; (prize) remporter; **to c. it off** réussir.

▸ **carry on 1** vt continuer; (conduct) diriger; (sustain) soutenir. **2** vi continuer (**doing** à faire).

▸ **carry out** vt (plan, order, promise) exécuter; (repair, reform) effectuer; (duty) accomplir; (meal) emporter.

▸ **carry through** vt (plan) mener à bien.

cart (horse-drawn) charrette f; (in supermarket) caddie® m, (serving) c. table f roulante.

cart (a·round) vt Fam trimbal(l)er.

▸ **cart away** vt emporter.

car·ton (box) carton m; (of milk etc) brique f; (of cigarettes) cartouche f, (of cream) pot m.

car·toon dessin m (humoristique); (film) dessin m animé; (strip) c. bande f dessinée.

car·tridge cartouche f.

carve vt tailler (**out of** dans); (initials etc) graver.

carve (up) vt (meat) découper.

car wash (machine) lave-auto m.

case¹ (instance, in hospital) cas m; (in court) affaire f; **in any c.** en tout cas; **in c. it rains** pour le cas où il pleuvrait; **in c. of** en cas de; (just) **in c.** à tout hasard.

case² (bag) valise f, (crate) caisse f, (for pen, glasses, camera, cigarettes) étui m; (for jewels) coffret m.

cash 1 n argent m; **to pay (in) c.** payer en espèces. **2** vt **to c. a check** encaisser un chèque; (of bank) payer un chèque.

cash·box caisse f.

cash·ier caissier, -ière mf.

cash ma·chine distributeur m de billets.

cash price prix m (au) comptant.

cash re·gis·ter caisse f enregistreuse.

ca·si·no, pl -os casino m.

cas·se·role cocotte f; *(stew)* ragoût m en cocotte.

cas·sette *(audio, video)* cassette f; *(film)* cartouche f.

cas·sette play·er lecteur m de cassettes.

cas·sette re·cord·er magnétophone m à cassettes.

cast¹ *(actors)* acteurs mpl; *(list of actors)* distribution f; *(for broken bone)* plâtre m.

cast²∗ vt jeter; *(light, shadow)* projeter; *(doubt)* exprimer; **to c. a vote** voter.

cast-i·ron adj *(pan)* en fonte; *(alibi)* inattaquable, en béton.

cas·tle château m; *Chess* tour f.

cas·tor *(wheel)* roulette f.

ca·su·al adj *(remark)* fait en passant; *(stroll)* sans but; *(offhand)* désinvolte; *(worker)* temporaire; *(work)* irrégulier; **c. clothes** vêtements mpl sport.

ca·su·al·ty *(dead)* mort m, morte f; *(wounded)* blessé, -ée mf.

cat chat m; *(female)* chatte f; **c. food** pâtée f.

cat·a·log catalogue m.

cat·a·pult catapulte f.

ca·tas·tro·phe catastrophe f.

catch¹ 1 vt *(ball, thief, illness, train etc)* attraper; *(grab, surprise)* prendre; *(understand)* saisir; *(attention)* attirer; *(on nail etc)* accrocher (**on** à); *(finger etc)* se prendre (**in** dans); **to c. fire** prendre feu; **to c. one's breath** *(rest)* reprendre haleine. 2 vi **her skirt (got) caught in the door** sa jupe s'est prise dans la porte; **to c. on fire** prendre feu. 3 n *(trick)* piège m; *(on door)* loquet m.

catch·ing adj contagieux.

▶**catch on** vi *(become popular)* prendre; *(understand)* saisir.

▶**catch out** vt prendre en défaut.

▶**catch up** 1 vt **to c. sb up** rattraper qn. 2 vi se rattraper; **to c. up with sb** rattraper qn.

cat·e·go·ry catégorie f.

▶**cater for** or **to** vt *(need, taste)* satisfaire.

cat·er·pil·lar chenille f.

ca·the·dral cathédrale f.

Cath·o·lic adj & n catholique *(mf)*.

cau·li·flow·er chou-fleur m.

cause 1 n cause f. 2 vt causer; **to c. sth to move/etc** faire bouger/etc qch.

cau·tion *(care)* prudence f; *(warning)* avertissement m.

cau·tious adj prudent.

cau·tious·ly adv prudemment.

cave caverne f.

▶**cave in** vi *(fall in)* s'effondrer.

cav·i·ty cavité f.

CD abbr *(compact disc)* CD m.

cease vti cesser (**doing** de faire).

cease-fire cessez-le-feu m inv.

ceil·ing plafond m.

cel·e·brate 1 vt fêter; *(mass)* célébrer. 2 vi faire la fête.

cel·e·bra·tion fête f.

ce·leb·ri·ty *(person)* célébrité f.

cel·er·y céleri m.

cell cellule f.

cel·lar cave f.

cel·lo·phane® cellophane f.

cell·phone *(téléphone m)* portable m.

ce·ment 1 n ciment m. 2 vt cimenter.

ce·ment mix·er bétonnière f.

cem·e·ter·y cimetière m.

cen·sus recensement m.

cent *(coin)* cent m.

cen·ter 1 n centre m. 2 vt centrer.

cen·ti·grade adj centigrade.

cen·ti·me·ter centimètre m.

cen·ti·pede mille-pattes m inv.

cen·tral adj central.

cen·tral·ize vt centraliser.

cen·tu·ry siècle m.

ce·ram·ic adj *(tile)* de céramique.

ce·re·al céréale f.

cer·e·mo·ny cérémonie f.

cer·tain adj *(sure, particular)* certain; **she's c. to come** c'est certain qu'elle viendra; **I'm not c. what to**

do je ne sais pas très bien ce qu'il faut faire; **to be c. of sth/that** être certain de qch/que; **to make c. of** (fact) s'assurer de; (seat etc) s'assurer.

cer·tain·ly adv certainement; (yes) bien sûr.

cer·tain·ty certitude f.

cer·tif·i·cate certificat m; (from university) diplôme m.

cer·ti·fied adj certifié, agréé; **C. Public Accountant** expert-comptable m.

cer·ti·fy vt (document etc) certifier.

chain (of rings, mountains) chaîne f.

chain (up) vt (dog) mettre à l'attache; (person) enchaîner.

chain saw tronçonneuse f.

chain store magasin m à succursales multiples.

chair chaise f, (armchair) fauteuil m.

chair lift télésiège m.

chair·man, pl -men président, -ente mf.

cha·let chalet m.

chalk 1 n craie f. 2 vti écrire à la craie.

chal·lenge 1 n défi m; (task) challenge m, gageure f. 2 vt défier (**sb to do** qn de faire); (dispute) contester.

chal·leng·ing adj (job) exigeant.

cham·ber **c. of commerce** chambre f de commerce.

cham·ois (leather) peau f de chamois.

cham·pagne champagne m.

cham·pi·on champion, -onne mf.

cham·pi·on·ship championnat m.

chance 1 n (luck) hasard m; (possibility) chances fpl; (opportunity) occasion f; **by c.** par hasard. 2 vt to **c. it** risquer le coup.

chan·cel·lor (head of state, in embassy) chancelier m.

chan·de·lier lustre m.

change 1 n changement m; (money) monnaie f; **for a c.** pour changer; **it makes a c. from** ça change de; **a c. of clothes** des vêtements de rechange. 2 vt changer; (exchange) échanger (**for** contre); (money) changer; **to c. trains/one's skirt/etc** changer de train/de jupe/etc; **to c. the subject** changer de sujet. 3 vi changer; (change clothes) se changer.

change·a·ble adj changeant.

▸ **change over** vi passer (**from** de; **to** à).

change·o·ver passage m (**from** de; **to** à).

chang·ing room vestiaire m.

chan·nel (on television) chaîne f; (for inquiry etc) voie f; **the English C.** la Manche; **to go through the normal channels** passer par la voie normale.

chant 1 vt (slogan) scander. 2 vi (of demonstrators) scander des slogans.

cha·os chaos m.

cha·ot·ic adj sens dessus dessous.

chap·el chapelle f.

chapped adj gercé.

chap·ter chapitre m.

char vt carboniser; (scorch) brûler légèrement.

char·ac·ter caractère m; (in book, film) personnage m; (strange person) numéro m.

char·ac·ter·is·tic adj & n caractéristique (f).

charge¹ 1 n (cost) prix m; **charges** (expenses) frais mpl; **there's a c. (for it)** c'est payant; **free of c.** gratuit. 2 vt (amount) demander (**for** pour); (person) faire payer.

charge² 1 n (in court) accusation f; (care) garde f, **to take c. of** prendre en charge; **to be in c. of** (child) avoir la garde de; (office) être responsable de. 2 vt (battery, soldiers) charger; (accuse) accuser (**with** de). 3 vi (rush) se précipiter.

char·i·ty *(society)* fondation *f* charitable; **to give to c.** faire la charité.

charm 1 *n* charme *m*; *(trinket)* amulette *f.* **2** *vt* charmer.

charm·ing *adj* charmant.

chart *(map)* carte *f*; *(graph)* graphique *m*; **(pop) charts** hit-parade *m*.

char·ter 1 *n (of institution)* statuts *mpl.* **2** *vt (plane, boat)* affréter.

char·ter flight charter *m.*

chase 1 *n* poursuite *f.* **2** *vt* poursuivre.

▸ **chase after** *vt* courir après, poursuivre.

▸ **chase away** *or* **off** *vt* chasser.

chasm abîme *m*, gouffre *m.*

chas·sis *(of vehicle)* châssis *m.*

chat 1 *n* petite conversation *f*; **to have a c.** bavarder. **2** *vi* causer.

chat·ter *vi (of person)* bavarder; **his teeth are chattering** il claque des dents. **2** *n* bavardage *m.*

chat·ter·box bavard, -arde *mf.*

chat·ty *adj* bavard.

chauf·feur chauffeur *m.*

cheap 1 *adj* bon marché *inv*; *(rate)* réduit; *(worthless)* sans valeur; **cheaper** meilleur marché. **2** *adv (to buy)* (à) bon marché.

cheap·ly *adv* (à) bon marché.

cheat 1 *vt* tromper; **to c. sb out of sth** escroquer qch à qn. **2** *vi (at games etc)* tricher.

cheat·er tricheur, -euse *mf.*

check 1 *vt (examine)* vérifier; *(inspect)* contrôler; *(stop)* arrêter; *(baggage)* mettre à la consigne. **2** *vi* vérifier. **3** *n* vérification *f*, *(inspection)* contrôle *m*; Chess échec *m*; *(mark)* croix *f*; *(receipt)* reçu *m*; *(bill in restaurant)* addition *f*, *(in banking)* chèque *m.*

check·book carnet *m* de chèques.

checked, checkered *adj* à carreaux.

check·ers *npl* jeu *m* de dames.

check-in enregistrement *m* (des bagages).

▸ **check in 1** *vt (luggage)* enregistrer. **2** *vi (at hotel)* signer le registre; *(arrive)* arriver; *(at airport)* se présenter (à l'enregistrement).

check·ing ac·count compte *m* courant.

▸ **check·mate** Chess échec et mat *m.*

▸ **check off** *vt (names on list etc)* cocher.

▸ **check on** *vt* vérifier.

check·out *(in supermarket)* caisse *f.*

▸ **check out 1** *vt* confirmer. **2** *vi (at hotel)* régler la note.

check·up bilan *m* de santé.

▸ **check up** *vi* vérifier.

ched·dar *(cheese)* cheddar *m.*

cheek joue *f*, *(impudence)* culot *m.*

cheek·y *adj* effronté.

cheer 1 *n* **cheers** acclamations *fpl*; **cheers!** *Fam* à votre santé! **2** *vt (applaud)* acclamer. **3** *vi* applaudir.

cheer·ful *adj* gai.

cheer·ing acclamations *fpl.*

▸ **cheer up 1** *vt* donner du courage à; *(amuse)* égayer. **2** *vi* prendre courage; *(become happier)* s'égayer; **c. up!** (du) courage!

cheese fromage *m.*

cheese·burg·er cheeseburger *m.*

cheese·cake tarte *f* au fromage blanc, cheesecake *m.*

chef *(cook)* chef *m.*

chem·i·cal 1 *adj* chimique. **2** *n* produit *m* chimique.

chem·ist chimiste *mf.*

chem·is·try chimie *f.*

cher·ry cerise *f.*

cher·ry bran·dy cherry *m.*

chess échecs *mpl.*

chess·board échiquier *m.*

chest *(part of body)* poitrine *f*, *(box)* coffre *m*; **c. of drawers** commode *f.*

chest·nut châtaigne *f.*

chew *vt* **to c. (up)** mâcher. **2** *vi* mastiquer.

chew·ing gum chewing-gum *m.*

chick poussin *m*.

chick·en 1 *n* poulet *m*. **2** *adj (cowardly)* Fam froussard.

▸ **chicken out** *vi Fam* se dégonfler.

chick·en·pox varicelle *f*.

chick·pea pois *m* chiche.

chic·o·ry *(for salad)* endive *f*.

chief 1 *n* chef *m*; **in c.** en chef. **2** *adj* principal.

chief·ly *adv* principalement.

chil·blain engelure *f*.

child, *pl* **children** enfant *mf*.

child care *(for working parents)* crèches *fpl* et garderies *fpl*.

child·hood enfance *f*.

child·ish *adj* puéril.

chil·i, *pl* **-ies** piment *m* (de Cayenne).

chill 1 *n* froid *m*; *(illness)* refroidissement *m*; **to catch a c.** prendre froid. **2** *vt (wine, melon)* faire rafraîchir; *(meat)* réfrigérer.

chilled *adj (wine)* frais.

chill·y *adj* froid; **it's c.** il fait (un peu) froid.

chime *vi (of clock)* sonner.

chim·ney cheminée *f*.

chim·ney·pot tuyau *m* de cheminée.

chim·pan·zee chimpanzé *m*.

chin menton *m*.

chi·na 1 *n inv* porcelaine *f*. **2** *adj* en porcelaine.

Chi·nese 1 *n inv* Chinois, -oise *(mf)*; *(language)* chinois *m*. **2** *adj* chinois.

chip 1 *vt (cup etc)* ébrécher; *(paint)* écailler. **2** *n (break)* ébréchure *f*; *(microchip)* puce *f*, *(counter)* jeton *m*; *(potato)* **chips** chips *mpl*.

chi·ro·po·dist pédicure *mf*.

chis·el ciseau *m*.

chives ciboulette *f*.

chock-a-block *adj Fam* archiplein.

choc·o·late 1 *n* chocolat *m*; **milk c.** chocolat *m* au lait; **bittersweet c.** chocolat *m* à croquer. **2** *adj (cake)* au chocolat.

choice choix *m*.

choir chœur *m*.

choke 1 *vt (person)* étrangler; *(clog)* boucher. **2** *vi* s'étrangler (**on** avec).

cho·les·ter·ol cholestérol *m*.

choose* 1 *vt* choisir; **to c. to do** *(decide)* juger bon de faire. **2** *vi* choisir.

choos·(e)y *adj* difficile.

chop 1 *n (of lamb, pork)* côtelette *f*. **2** *vt* couper (à la hache); *(food)* hacher.

▸ **chop down** *vt (tree)* abattre.

▸ **chop off** *vt (branch, finger etc)* couper.

chop·per hachoir *m*.

chop·sticks *npl* baguettes *fpl*.

▸ **chop up** *vt* couper en morceaux.

chord *(in music)* accord *m*.

chore travail *m (routinier)*; *(unpleasant)* corvée *f*; **chores** travaux *mpl* ménagers.

cho·rus *(of song)* refrain *m*.

chris·ten *vt* baptiser.

chris·ten·ing baptême *m*.

Chris·tian *adj & n* chrétien, -ienne *(mf)*.

Christ·mas 1 *n* Noël *m*; **Merry C.** Joyeux Noël; **C. Eve** la veille de Noël. **2** *adj* de Noël.

chrome chrome *m*.

chron·ic *adj* chronique.

chry·san·the·mum chrysanthème *m*.

chub·by *adj* potelé.

chuck *vt Fam (throw)* jeter; *(job etc)* laisser tomber.

chuck (out) *vt (old clothes etc)* Fam balancer.

chum Fam copain *m*, copine *f*.

chunk (gros) morceau *m*.

church église *f*.

chute *(for refuse)* vide-ordures *m inv*; *(in pool)* toboggan *m*.

ci·der cidre *m*.

ci·gar cigare *m*.

cig·a·rette cigarette *f*.

cig·a·rette butt mégot *m*.

cig·a·rette light·er briquet *m*.

cin·e·ma cinéma *m*.

cin·na·mon cannelle *f*.

cir·cle 1 *n* cercle *m*; **circles** *(political etc)* milieux *mpl*. 2 *vt* faire le tour de; *(word)* encadrer. 3 *vi (of aircraft etc)* décrire des cercles.

cir·cuit *(electrical path, in sports etc)* circuit *m*.

cir·cu·lar 1 *adj* circulaire. 2 *n (letter)* circulaire *f*, *(advertisement)* prospectus *m*.

cir·cu·late *vi (of blood etc)* circuler. 2 *vt (pass around)* faire circuler.

cir·cu·la·tion *(of newspaper)* tirage *m*.

cir·cum·fer·ence circonférence *f*.

cir·cum·stance circonstance *f*, **in** *or* **under no circumstances** en aucun cas.

cir·cus cirque *m*.

cite *vt (quote)* citer.

cit·i·zen citoyen, -enne *mf*, *(of town)* habitant, -ante *mf*.

cit·y *(grande)* ville *f*.

cit·y coun·cil conseil *m* municipal.

cit·y hall hôtel *m* de ville.

civ·ic *adj (authority, building)* municipal; *(duty, rights)* civique.

civ·il *adj* civil.

ci·vil·ian *adj & n* civil, -ile *(mf)*.

civ·i·li·za·tion civilization *f*.

civ·il ser·vant fonctionnaire *mf*.

civ·il ser·vice fonction *f* publique.

claim 1 *vt* réclamer; **to c. that** prétendre que. 2 *n (demand)* revendication *f*, *(statement)* affirmation *f*, *(right)* droit *m* (**to** à); *(insurance)* **c.** demande *f* d'indemnité.

clam *(shellfish)* palourde *f*.

clap *vti* applaudir; **to c. (one's hands)** battre des mains.

clap·ping applaudissements *mpl*.

clar·i·fy *vt* clarifier.

clar·i·net clarinette *f*.

clash 1 *vi (of plates)* s'entrechoquer; *(of interests)* se heurter; *(of colors)* jurer (**with** avec); *(of people)* se bagarrer; *(coincide)* tomber en même temps (**with** que). 2 *n (noise)* choc *m*; *(of interests)* conflit *m*.

clasp 1 *vt* serrer. 2 *n (fastener)* fermoir *m*; *(of belt)* boucle *f*.

class 1 *n* classe *f*, *(lesson)* cours *m*. 2 *vt* classer.

clas·sic 1 *adj* classique. 2 *n (work etc)* classique *m*.

clas·si·cal *adj* classique.

clas·si·fy *vt* classer.

class·mate camarade *mf* de classe.

class·room *(salle f de)* classe *f*.

clause *(in sentence)* proposition *f*.

claw griffe *f*, *(of lobster)* pince *f*.

clay argile *f*.

clean 1 *adj (not dirty)* propre; *(clearcut)* net *(f* nette*)*. 2 *adv (utterly)* complètement; *(to break, cut)* net. 3 *vt* nettoyer; *(wash)* laver; *(wipe)* essuyer. 4 *vi* faire le nettoyage.

clean cop·y copie *f* au propre.

clean·er *(dry)* **c.** teinturier, -ière *mf*.

clean·ing nettoyage *m*; *(housework)* ménage *m*.

clean·ing wom·an femme *f* de ménage.

clean·ly *adv (to break, cut)* net.

▸ **clean out** *vt (room etc)* nettoyer; *(empty)* vider.

cleans·ing cream crème *f* démaquillante.

▸ **clean up** 1 *vt* nettoyer. 2 *vi* faire le nettoyage.

clear 1 *adj (sky, outline, sound, thought etc)* clair; *(glass)* transparent; *(road)* libre; *(profit)* net; *(obvious)* évident, clair; **to be c. of** *(free of)* être libre de; **to make oneself c.** se faire comprendre; **to keep** *or* **steer c. of** se tenir à l'écart de; **to get c. of** s'éloigner de. 3 *vt (path, table)* débarrasser; *(fence)* franchir; *(accused person)* disculper; *(check)* faire passer (sur un compte); *(through customs)* dédouaner; **to c. one's throat** s'éclaircir la gorge. **4** *vi (of weather)* s'éclaircir; *(of fog)* se dissiper.

clear·ance *(sale)* soldes *mpl*; *(space)* dégagement *m*.

▸ **clear away** *vt (remove)* enlever.

clear-cut *adj* net *(f* nette).

clear·ing *(in wood)* clairière *f*.

clear·ly *adv* clairement; *(obviously)* évidemment.

▸ **clear out 1** *vt* vider; *(clean)* nettoyer; *(remove)* enlever. **2** *vi (go) Fam* décamper.

▸ **clear up 1** *vt (room)* ranger; *(mystery)* éclaircir. **2** *vi (tidy)* ranger.

cleat *(sports shoe)* crampon *m*.

clem·en·tine clémentine *f*.

clench *vt (fist)* serrer.

cler·gy clergé *m*.

cler·i·cal *adj (job)* d'employé; *(work)* de bureau.

clerk employé, -ée *mf (de bureau)*; *(in store)* vendeur, -euse *mf*.

clev·er *adj* intelligent; *(smart)* astucieux; *(skillful)* habile; *(machine, book etc)* ingénieux.

click 1 *n* déclic *m*. **2** *vi (of machine etc)* faire un déclic.

cli·ent client, -ente *mf*.

cliff falaise *f*.

cli·mate climat *m*.

cli·max point *m* culminant.

climb (o·ver) *vt (wall)* escalader.

climb (up) 1 *vt (stairs, steps)* monter; *(hill, mountain)* gravir; *(tree, ladder)* monter à. **2** *vi* monter.

▸ **climb down 1** *vt (wall, tree, hill)* descendre de. **2** *vi* descendre *(* from de*)*.

climb·er *(mountaineer)* alpiniste *mf*.

cling* *vi* se cramponner; *(stick)* adhérer *(* to à*)*.

clin·ic *(private)* clinique *f*; *(public)* centre *m* médical.

clip 1 *vt* couper; *(hedge)* tailler;

(ticket) poinçonner; *(attach)* attacher. **2** *n (paper)* trombone *m*; *(of brooch, of cyclist, for hair)* pince *f*.

▸ **clip on** *vt* attacher *(* to à*)*.

clip·pers *npl (for hair)* tondeuse *f*; *(for nails)* coupe-ongles *m inv*.

clip·ping *(newspaper article)* coupure *f*.

cloak *(grande)* cape *f*.

cloak·room vestiaire *m*.

clock horloge *f*; *(small)* pendule *f*; **around the c.** vingt-quatre heures sur vingt-quatre.

clock·wise *adv* dans le sens des aiguilles d'une montre.

close¹ 1 *adj (place, relative etc)* proche *(* to de*)*; *(collaboration, connection)* étroit; *(friend)* intime; *(atmosphere)* lourd. **2** *adv* **c. (by)** *(tout)* près; **c. to** près de; **c. behind** juste derrière.

close² 1 *n (end)* fin *f*. **2** *vt (door, shop etc)* fermer; *(road)* barrer; *(deal)* conclure. **3** *vi* se fermer; *(of shop)* fermer.

closed *adj* fermé; **c.-circuit television** télévision *f* en circuit fermé.

▸ **close down** *vti* fermer *(* définitivement*)*.

▸ **close in** *vi* approcher.

close·ly *adv (to follow, guard)* de près; *(to listen)* attentivement.

clos·et *(for linens, clothes etc)* placard *m*; *(for clothing only)* penderie *f*.

▸ **close up 1** *vt* fermer. **2** *vi (of shopkeeper)* fermer; *(of line of people)* se rapprocher.

clos·ing time heure *f* de fermeture.

clo·sure fermeture *f*.

clot 1 *n (of blood)* caillot *m*. **2** *vi* se coaguler.

cloth tissu *m*; *(for dusting)* chiffon *m*; *(for dishes)* torchon *m*; *(tablecloth)* nappe *f*.

clothes *npl* vêtements *mpl*; **to put one's c. on** s'habiller.

clothes brush brosse *f* à habits.

clothes·line corde *f* à linge.

clothes·pin pince *f* à linge.

cloth·ing vêtements *mpl*; **an arti·cle of c.** un vêtement.

cloth·ing store magasin *m* d'habillement.

cloud nuage *m*.

▶ **cloud over** *vi (of sky)* se couvrir.

cloud·y *adj (weather)* couvert.

clove c. **of garlic** gousse *f* d'ail.

clown clown *m*.

club *(society, stick for golf)* club *m*; **club(s)** *(at cards)* trèfle *m*.

club so·da eau *f* gazeuse.

clue indice *m*; *(of crossword)* définition *f*; **I don't have a c.** *Fam* je n'en ai pas la moindre idée.

clum·sy *adj* maladroit; *(tool)* peu commode.

clunk·er *(car) Fam* tacot *m*.

clus·ter **1** *n* groupe *m*. **2** *vi* se grouper.

clutch **1** *vt (hold)* serrer; *(grasp)* saisir. **2** *n (in vehicle)* embrayage *m*; *(pedal)* pédale *f* d'embrayage.

▶ **clutter up** *vt (room etc)* encombrer (**with** de).

cm *abbr (centimeter)* cm.

Co *abbr (company)* Cie.

coach **1** *n (part of train)* voiture *f*; *(bus)* autocar *m*. **2** *vt (pupil)* donner des leçons *(particulières)* à.

coal charbon *m*.

coal·mine mine *f* de charbon.

coarse *adj (person, fabric)* grossier.

coast côte *f*.

coat **1** *n* manteau *m*; *(jacket)* veste *f*; *(of animal)* pelage *m*; *(of paint)* couche *f*. **2** *vt* couvrir (**with** de).

coat·hang·er cintre *m*.

coat·ing couche *f*.

cob corn on the c. épi *m* de maïs.

cob·bled *adj* pavé.

cob·web toile *f* d'araignée.

co·caine cocaïne *f*.

cock *(fowl)* coq *m*.

cock·le *(shellfish)* coque *f*.

cock·pit poste *m* de pilotage.

cock·roach *(insect)* cafard *m*.

cock·tail cocktail *m*; **fruit c.** macédoine *f* (de fruits); **shrimp c.** crevettes *fpl* à la mayonnaise.

cock·tail par·ty cocktail *m*.

co·coa cacao *m*.

co·co·nut noix *f* de coco.

cod morue *f*.

code code *m*.

cod·liv·er oil huile *f* de foie de morue.

co·ed·u·ca·tion·al *adj (school etc)* mixte.

cof·fee café *m*; **c. with milk** café *m* au lait; *(in restaurant)* café *(m)* crème *m*.

cof·fee bar café *m*.

cof·fee break pause-café *f*.

cof·fee·pot cafetière *f*.

cof·fee ta·ble table *f* basse.

cof·fin cercueil *m*.

co·gnac cognac *m*.

co·her·ent *adj* cohérent.

coil **1** *n (of wire, rope etc)* rouleau *m*. **2** *vt* enrouler.

coin pièce *f* (de monnaie).

coin bank tirelire *f*.

co·in·cide *vi* coïncider (**with** avec).

co·in·ci·dence coïncidence *f*.

coke *(Coca-Cola®)* coca *m*.

col·an·der passoire *f*.

cold **1** *n* froid *m*; *(illness)* rhume *m*; **to catch c.** prendre froid. **2** *adj* froid; **to be** *or* **feel c.** avoir froid; **my hands are c.** j'ai froid aux mains; **it's c.** *(of weather)* il fait froid; **to get c.** *(of weather)* se refroidir; *(of food)* refroidir.

cold cuts assiette *f* anglaise.

cold·ness froideur *f*.

cole·slaw salade *f* de chou cru.

col·lab·o·rate *vi* collaborer (**on** à).

col·lab·o·ra·tion collaboration *f*.

col·lapse **1** *vi (of person, building)* s'effondrer. **2** *n* effondrement *m*.

col·lar col *m*; *(of dog)* collier *m*.

col·lar·bone clavicule *f*.

col·league collègue *mf*.

col·lect 1 *vt* (pick up) ramasser; (gather) rassembler; (taxes) percevoir; (rent) encaisser; (stamps etc) collectionner; (fetch) (passer) prendre; **to c. (money)** (in street, church) quêter. **2** *vi* (of dust) s'accumuler. **3** *adv* **to call c.** téléphoner en PCV.

col·lec·tion (group of objects) collection *f*, (of poems etc) recueil *m*; (of mail) levée *f*.

col·lec·tor (of stamps etc) collectionneur, -euse *mf*.

col·lege université *f*.

col·lide *vi* entrer en collision (**with** avec).

col·li·sion collision *f*.

col·lo·qui·al *adj* familier.

co·logne eau *f* de Cologne.

co·lon Grammar deux-points *m inv*.

colo·nel colonel *m*.

co·lo·ni·al *adj* colonial.

col·o·ny colonie *f*.

col·or 1 *n* couleur *f*. **2** *adj* (photo, TV set) en couleurs. **3** *vt* colorer.

col·or (in) *vt* (drawing) colorier.

col·ored *adj* (pencil) de couleur.

col·or·ful *adj* coloré; (person) pittoresque.

col·or·ing book album *m* de coloriages.

col·umn colonne *f*, (newspaper feature) chronique *f*.

co·ma coma *m*; **in a c.** dans le coma.

comb 1 *n* peigne *m*. **2** *vt* **to c. one's hair** se peigner.

com·bi·na·tion combinaison *f*.

com·bine 1 *vt* joindre (**with** à); **our combined efforts achieved a result** en joignant nos efforts nous avons obtenu un résultat. **2** *vi* s'unir.

come* *vi* venir (**from** de; **to** à); **to c. first** (in race) arriver premier; (in exam) être le premier; **to c. close to doing** faillir faire.

▸**come about** *vi* (happen) se faire, arriver.

▸**come across** *vt* (thing, person) tomber sur.

▸**come along** *vi* venir (**with** avec); (progress) avancer; **c. along!** allons!

▸**come apart** *vi* (of two objects) se séparer.

▸**come around** *vi* (visit) venir; (of date) revenir; (regain consciousness) revenir à soi.

▸**come away** *vi* (leave, come off) partir.

come·back to make a c. faire un come-back.

▸**come back** *vi* revenir; (return home) rentrer.

▸**come by** *vt* obtenir; (find) trouver.

co·me·di·an (actor *m*) comique *m*, actrice *f* comique.

▸**come down** *vi* descendre; (of rain, price) tomber.

▸**come down with** *vt* attraper.

com·e·dy comédie *f*.

▸**come for** *vt* venir chercher.

▸**come forward** *vi* s'avancer; (volunteer) se présenter; **to c. forward with sth** offrir qch.

▸**come in** *vi* entrer; (of tide) monter; (of train) arriver.

▸**come into** *vt* (room etc) entrer dans; (money) hériter de.

▸**come off 1** *vi* (of button etc) se détacher; (succeed) réussir. **2** *vt* (fall from) tomber de; (get down from) descendre de.

▸**come on** *vi* (progress) avancer; **c. on!** (reproving, encouraging) allons!, allez!

▸**come out** *vi* sortir; (of sun, book) paraître; (of stain) partir.

▸**come over 1** *vi* (visit) venir. **2** *vt* (of feeling) saisir.

▸**come through 1** *vi* (survive) s'en tirer. **2** *vt* (crisis etc) se tirer indemne de.

▸**come to 1** *vt* (amount to) revenir à; (a decision) parvenir à. **2** *vi* (regain consciousness) revenir à soi.

▸**come under** *vt (heading)* être classé sous; *(sb's influence)* tomber sous.

▸**come up** *vi (rise)* monter; *(of plant)* sortir; *(of question, job)* se présenter.

▸**come up against** *vt (wall, problem)* se heurter à.

▸**come up to** *vt (reach)* arriver jusqu'à.

▸**come up with** *vt (idea, money)* trouver.

com·fort 1 *n* confort *m*; *(consolation)* réconfort *m*. **2** *vt* consoler.

com·fort·a·ble *adj (chair etc)* confortable; *(rich)* aisé; **he's c.** *(in chair etc)* il est à l'aise; **make yourself c.** mets-toi à l'aise.

com·fort·er *(quilt)* édredon *m*, couette *f*.

com·ic 1 *adj* comique. **2** *n (magazine)* bande *f* dessinée.

com·ings *npl* **c. and goings** allées *fpl* et venues.

com·ma virgule *f*.

com·mand 1 *vt (order)* commander (**sb to do** à qn de faire). **2** *n (order)* ordre *m*; *(mastery)* maîtrise *f* (**of** de); **to be in c. (of)** *(army etc)* commander; *(situation)* être maître (de).

com·mand·er commandant *m*.

com·mem·o·rate *vt* commémorer.

com·mence *vti* commencer (**doing** à faire).

com·ment commentaire *m*.

com·men·ta·ry commentaire *m*; **(live) c.** reportage *m*.

com·men·ta·tor reporter *m*.

▸**comment on** *vt (event etc)* commenter.

com·merce commerce *m*.

com·mer·cial 1 *adj* commercial. **2** *n* **commercial(s)** *(on television)* publicité *f*.

com·mis·sion *(fee, group)* commission *f*.

com·mit *vt (crime)* commettre; **to c. suicide** se suicider.

com·mit·ment *(promise)* engagement *m*.

com·mit·tee comité *m*.

com·mod·i·ty produit *m*.

com·mon *adj (shared, frequent etc)* commun; **in c. (shared)** en commun (**with** avec); **in c. with** *(like)* comme.

com·mon·ly *adv (generally)* en général.

com·mon·place *adj* banal (*mpl* banals).

com·mon room salle *f* commune.

com·mon sense sens *m* commun.

com·mo·tion agitation *f*.

com·mu·nal *adj (bathroom etc)* commun.

com·mu·ni·cate *vti* communiquer.

com·mu·ni·ca·tion communication *f*.

com·mun·ion communion *f*.

com·mu·ni·ty communauté *f*.

com·mu·ni·ty cen·ter centre *m* socio-culturel.

com·mute *vi* faire la navette (**to work** pour se rendre à son travail).

com·mut·er banlieusard, -arde *mf*.

com·mut·ing trajets *mpl* journaliers.

com·pact 1 *adj* compact. **2** *n (for face powder)* poudrier *m*.

com·pact disc *or* **disk** disque *m* compact.

com·pan·ion compagnon *m*.

com·pa·ny *(being with others, firm)* compagnie *f*; *(guests)* invités, -ées *mfpl*; **to keep sb c.** tenir compagnie à qn.

com·pa·ra·ble *adj* comparable (**to, with** à).

com·pa·ra·tive·ly *adv* relativement.

com·pare *vt* comparer (**with, to** à); **compared to** *or* **with** en comparaison de.

com·par·i·son comparaison *f* (**with** avec).

com·part·ment compartiment *m.*

com·pass *(for direction)* boussole *f; (on ship)* compas *m;* **(pair of) compasses** *(for drawing etc)* compas *m.*

com·pat·i·ble *adj* compatible.

com·pel *vt* forcer, contraindre (**to do** à faire).

com·pen·sate 1 *vt* **to c. sb** dédommager qn (**for** de). **2** *vi* compenser (**for sth** qch).

com·pen·sa·tion dédommagement *m.*

com·pete *vi (take part)* concourir (**in** à; **for** pour); **to c. (with sb)** rivaliser (avec qn); *(in business)* faire concurrence (à qn).

com·pe·tent *adj* compétent (**to do** pour faire).

com·pe·tent·ly *adv* avec compétence.

com·pe·ti·tion *(rivalry)* compétition *f;* **a c.** *(contest)* un concours; *(in sports)* une compétition.

com·pet·i·tive *adj (price etc)* compétitif; *(person)* aimant la compétition.

com·pet·i·tor concurrent, -ente *mf.*

com·pile *vt (dictionary)* rédiger; *(list)* dresser.

com·plain *vi* se plaindre (**of, about** de; **that** que).

com·plaint plainte *f; (in shop etc)* réclamation *f; (illness)* maladie *f.*

com·ple·ment 1 *n* complément *m.* **2** *vt* compléter.

com·plete 1 *adj (total)* complet; *(finished)* achevé; **a c. idiot** un parfait imbécile. **2** *vt* compléter; *(finish)* achever; *(a form)* remplir.

com·plete·ly *adv* complètement.

com·plex 1 *adj* complexe. **2** *n (feeling, buildings)* complexe *m.*

com·plex·ion *(of face)* teint *m.*

com·pli·cate *vt* compliquer.

com·pli·cat·ed *adj* compliqué.

com·pli·ca·tion complication *f.*

com·pli·ment compliment *m.*

com·pli·men·ta·ry *adj (praising)* flatteur; *(free)* gratuit.

com·ply *vi* obéir (**with** à).

com·pose *vt* composer; **to c. oneself** se calmer.

com·posed *adj* calme.

com·pos·er compositeur, -trice *mf.*

com·po·si·tion *(school essay)* rédaction *f.*

com·pound *(substance, word)* composé *m.*

com·pre·hen·sive *adj* complet; *(insurance)* tous risques.

com·prise *vt* comprendre.

com·pro·mise compromis *m.*

com·pul·sive *adj (smoker etc)* invétéré; **c. liar** mythomane *mf.*

com·pul·so·ry *adj* obligatoire.

com·put·er ordinateur *m;* **c. technician** informaticien, -enne *mf.*

com·put·er·ized *adj* informatisé.

com·put·er sci·ence informatique *f.*

com·put·ing informatique *f.*

con *vt (deceive) Fam* escroquer.

con·ceal *vt* dissimuler (**from sb** à qn); *(plan)* tenir secret.

con·cede *vt* concéder (**to** à).

con·ceit·ed *adj* vaniteux.

con·ceiv·a·ble *adj* concevable.

con·ceive *vti* concevoir.

con·cen·trate 1 *vt* concentrer. **2** *vi* se concentrer (**on** sur); **to c. on doing** s'appliquer à faire.

con·cen·tra·tion concentration *f.*

con·cern 1 *vt* concerner; **to be concerned with/about** s'occuper de/s'inquiéter de. **2** *n (matter)* affaire *f, (anxiety)* inquiétude *f; his c. for* son souci de; *(business)* **c.** entreprise *f.*

con·cerned *adj (anxious)* inquiet.

con·cern·ing *prep* en ce qui concerne.

con·cert concert *m.*

con·ces·sion concession *f*.

con·cise *adj* concis.

con·clude 1 *vt* conclure; **to c. that** conclure que. **2** *vi* se terminer (**with** par); *(of speaker)* conclure.

con·clu·sion conclusion *f*.

con·crete 1 *n* béton *m*. **2** *adj* en béton; *(real)* concret.

con·demn *vt* condamner (**to** à).

con·den·sa·tion *(mist)* buée *f*.

con·di·tion condition *f*; **on c. that one does** se faire, à condition de faire, à condition que l'on fasse.

con·di·tion·er (hair) c. après-shampooing *m*.

con·do, *pl* **-os** *abbr* = **condominium**.

con·dom préservatif *m*.

con·do·min·i·um *(building)* copropriété *f*, *(apartment)* appartement *m* dans une copropriété.

con·duct 1 *n* conduite *f*. **2** *vt* conduire; *(orchestra)* diriger.

con·duct·ed tour excursion *f* accompagnée.

con·duc·tor *(of orchestra)* chef *m* d'orchestre; *(on bus)* receveur, -euse *mf*; *(on train)* chef *m* de train.

cone cône *m*; *(of ice cream)* cornet *m*.

con·fer 1 *vt (title)* conférer, accorder (**on** à). **2** *vi (discuss)* se consulter (**on, about** sur).

con·fer·ence conférence *f*, *(scientific, etc)* congrès *m*.

con·fess 1 *vt* avouer (**that** que). **2** *vi* **to c.** *(to)* avouer.

con·fes·sion aveu(x) *m(pl)*.

con·fet·ti confettis *mpl*.

con·fi·dence *(trust)* confiance *f*, *(self-)c.* confiance *f* en soi; **in c.** en confidence.

con·fi·dent *adj* sûr; *(self-)c.* sûr de soi.

con·fi·den·tial *adj* confidentiel *m*.

confi·dent·ly *adv* avec confiance.

con·fine *vt* limiter (**to** à); **to c. one-self to doing** se limiter à faire.

con·fined *adj (space)* réduit; **c. to bed** cloué au lit.

con·firm *vt* confirmer (**that** que).

con·fir·ma·tion confirmation *f*.

con·firmed *adj (bachelor)* endurci.

con·fis·cate *vt* confisquer (**from sb** à qn).

con·flict 1 *n* conflit *m*. **2** *vi* être en contradiction (**with** avec).

con·flict·ing *adj (views etc)* contradictoires; *(dates)* incompatibles.

con·form *vi (of person)* se conformer (**to** à).

con·front *vt (problems, danger)* faire face à; **to c. sb** *(be face to face with)* se trouver en face de qn; *(oppose)* affronter qn.

con·fron·ta·tion confrontation *f*.

con·fuse *vt (make unsure)* embrouiller; **to c. with** *(mistake for)* confondre avec.

con·fused *adj (situation)* confus; **to be c.** *(of person)* s'y perdre; **to get c.** s'embrouiller.

con·fus·ing *adj* déroutant.

con·fu·sion confusion *f*.

con·gest·ed *adj (street)* encombré.

con·ges·tion *(traffic)* encombrement(s) *m(pl)*.

con·grat·u·late *vt* féliciter (**sb on sth** qn de qch).

con·grat·u·la·tions félicitations *fpl* (**on** pour).

con·gre·gate *vi* se rassembler.

con·gress congrès *m*; **C.** *(political body)* le Congrès.

Con·gress·man, *pl* **-men** membre *m* du Congrès.

con·ju·gate *vt (verb)* conjuguer.

con·ju·ga·tion conjugaison *f*.

con·junc·tion *Grammar* conjonction *f*.

con·jur·er prestidigitateur, -trice *mf*.

con·jur·ing trick tour *m* de prestidigitation.

con man *Fam* escroc *m*.

con·nect 1 *vt* relier (**with, to** à); *(telephone etc)* brancher; **to c. sb with sb** *(by phone)* mettre qn en communication avec qn. **2** *vi* **to c. with** *(of train, bus)* assurer la correspondance avec.

con·nect·ed *adj (facts)* liés; **to be c. with** *(have dealings with, relate to)* être lié à.

con·nec·tion *(link)* rapport *m* (**with** avec); *(train etc)* correspondance *f*; *(phone call)* communication *f*; **connections** *(contacts)* relations *fpl*; **in c. with** à propos de.

con·quer *vt (country)* conquérir; *(enemy, habit)* vaincre.

con·quest conquête *f*.

con·science conscience *f*.

con·sci·en·tious *adj* consciencieux.

con·scious *adj (awake)* conscient; **c. of sth** *(aware)* conscient de qch; **to be c. of doing** avoir conscience de faire.

con·sen·sus consensus *m*.

con·sent 1 *vi* consentir (**to** à). **2** *n* consentement *m*.

con·se·quence *(result)* conséquence *f*.

con·se·quent·ly *adv* par conséquent.

con·ser·va·tion *(of energy)* économies *fpl*, d'énergie; *(of nature)* protection *f* de l'environnement.

con·ser·va·tive *adj & n* conservateur, -trice *(mf)*.

con·ser·va·to·ry *(room)* véranda *f*.

con·serve *vt* **to c. energy** faire des économies d'énergie.

con·sid·er *vt* considérer (**that** que); *(take into account)* tenir compte de; **to c. doing** envisager de faire.

con·sid·er·a·ble *adj (large)* considérable; *(much)* beaucoup de.

con·sid·er·ate *adj* plein d'égards (**to** pour).

con·sid·er·a·tion considération *f*; **to take into c.** prendre en considération.

con·sid·er·ing *prep* compte tenu de.

con·sign·ment *(goods)* arrivage *m*.

con·sis·ten·cy consistance *f*.

con·sis·tent *adj (unchanging)* constant; *(ideas)* logique; **c. with** compatible avec.

con·sis·tent·ly *adv (always)* constamment.

▶ **con·sist in** *vt* consister dans; **to c. in doing** consister à faire.

▶ **con·sist of** *vt* consister en.

con·so·la·tion consolation *f*, **c. prize** lot *m* de consolation.

con·sole¹ *vt* consoler.

con·sole² *(control desk)* console *f*.

con·so·nant consonne *f*.

con·spic·u·ous *adj* visible; *(striking)* remarquable.

con·spir·a·cy conspiration *f*.

con·stant *adj (frequent)* incessant; *(unchanging)* constant.

con·stant·ly *adv* constamment.

con·sti·pat·ed *adj* constipé.

con·sti·tu·tion constitution *f*.

con·straint contrainte *f*.

con·struct *vt* construire.

con·struc·tion construction *f*; **under c.** en construction.

con·struc·tive *adj* constructif.

con·sul consul *m*.

con·su·late consulat *m*.

con·sult 1 *vt* consulter. **2** *vi* **to c. with** discuter avec.

con·sul·tant *(doctor)* spécialiste *mf*; *(financial, legal)* expert-conseil *m*.

con·sul·ta·tion consultation *f*.

con·sult·ing firm cabinet *m* d'experts-conseils.

con·sume *vt (food, supplies)* consommer.

con·sum·er consommateur, -trice *mf*.

con·sump·tion consommation *f* (of de).

con·tact 1 *n* contact *m*; *(person)* contact *m*, relation *f*; **in c. with** en contact avec. **2** *vt* contacter.

con·tact lens·es lentilles *fpl or* verres *mpl* de contact.

con·ta·gious *adj* contagieux.

con·tain *vt* contenir.

con·tain·er récipient *m*; *(for goods)* conteneur *m*.

con·tem·po·rar·y *adj & n* contemporain, -aine *(mf)*.

con·tempt mépris *m*.

▶**con·tend with** *vt (problem)* faire face à; *(person)* avoir affaire à.

con·tent¹ *adj* satisfait *(with* de).

con·tent² *(of text etc)* contenu *m*; **contents** *(of container)* contenu *m*; **(table of) contents** *(of book)* table *f* des matières.

con·tent·ed *adj* satisfait.

con·test concours *m*; *(fight)* lutte *f*.

con·tes·tant concurrent, -ente *mf*, *(in fight)* adversaire *mf*.

con·text contexte *m*.

con·ti·nent continent *m*.

con·ti·nen·tal *adj* continental; **c. breakfast** petit déjeuner *m* à la française.

con·tin·u·al *adj* continuel.

con·tin·u·al·ly *adv* continuellement.

con·tin·ue 1 *vt* continuer *(to do or doing* à *or* de faire); **to c. (with)** *(work etc)* poursuivre; *(resume)* reprendre. **2** *vi* continuer; *(resume)* reprendre.

con·tin·u·ous *adj* continu.

con·tin·u·ous·ly *adv* sans interruption.

con·tra·cep·tion contraception *f*.

con·tra·cep·tive *adj & n* contraceptif *(m)*.

con·tract contrat *m*.

con·trac·tor entrepreneur *m*.

con·tra·dict *vt* contredire.

con·tra·dic·tion contradiction *f*.

con·trar·y 1 *adv* **c. to** contrairement à. **2** *n* **on the c.** au contraire.

con·trast contraste *m*; **in c. to** par opposition à.

con·trast·ing *adj (colors, opinions)* opposés.

con·trib·ute 1 *vt* donner *(to* à); *(article)* écrire *(to* pour); **to c. money to** contribuer à. **2** *vi* **to c. to** contribuer à; *(publication)* collaborer à.

con·tri·bu·tion contribution *f*; *(to fund etc)* cotisation(s) *f(pl)*.

con·trive *vt* **to c. to do** trouver moyen de faire.

con·trived *adj* artificiel.

con·trol 1 *vt (organization)* diriger; *(traffic)* régler; *(prices, quality, situation, emotion)* contrôler; **to c. oneself** se côntroler. **2** *n* autorité *f* *(over* sur); *(over prices, quality)* contrôle *m*; **controls** *(of train etc)* commandes *fpl*; *(of TV set etc)* boutons *mpl*; **everything is under c.** tout est en ordre; **in c. of** maître de; **to lose c. of** perdre le contrôle de.

con·trol tow·er tour *f* de contrôle.

con·va·lesce *vi* être en convalescence.

con·va·les·cence convalescence *f*.

conva·les·cent home maison *f* de convalescence.

con·ven·ience commodité *f*; **c. foods** plats *mpl* tout préparés; **(public) conveniences** toilettes *fpl*.

con·ven·ient *adj* commode; *(well-situated)* bien situé *(to shopping/etc* par rapport aux magasins/etc); *(moment)* convenable; **to be c. (for)** *(suit)* convenir (à).

con·vent couvent *m*.

con·ver·sa·tion conversation *f*.

con·verse *vi* s'entretenir *(with* avec).

con·ver·sion conversion *f*; *(of building)* aménagement *m*.

con·vert vt convertir (**into** en; **to** à); (building) aménager (**into** en).

con·vert·i·ble (car) (voiture f) décapotable f.

con·vey vt (goods, people) transporter; (sound, message) transmettre; (idea) communiquer.

con·vey·or belt tapis m roulant.

con·vict vt déclarer coupable.

con·vic·tion (for crime) condamnation f; (belief) conviction f.

con·vince vt convaincre (**of** de).

con·vinc·ing adj convaincant.

con·voy (cars) convoi m.

cook 1 vt (food) (faire) cuire. **2** vi (of food) cuire; (of person) faire la cuisine. **3** n cuisinier, -ière mf.

cook·book livre m de cuisine.

cook·ie biscuit m.

cook·ing cuisine f.

cook·ing ap·ple pomme f à cuire.

cool 1 adj (weather, place, drink etc) frais (f fraîche); (manner) calme; (unfriendly) froid; **to keep sth c.** tenir qch au frais; **to c.** (of evening) fraîcheur f; **to lose one's c.** perdre son sang-froid.

cool (down) 1 vi (of angry person) se calmer; (of hot liquid) refroidir. **2** vt refroidir.

cool·er (for food) glacière f.

cool·head·ed adj calme.

cool·ness fraîcheur f; (unfriendliness) froideur f.

▸**cool off** vi (refresh oneself) se rafraîchir.

co·op appartement m en copropriété.

co·op·er·ate vi coopérer (**in** à; **with** avec).

co·op·er·a·tion coopération f.

▸**coop up** vt (person) enfermer.

co·or·di·nate 1 vt coordonner. **2** n **coordinates** (clothes) coordonnés mpl.

cop (policeman) Fam flic m.

cope vi **to c. with** s'occuper de; (problem) faire face à; **(to be able) to c.** (savoir) se débrouiller.

cop·per (metal) cuivre m.

cop·y 1 n copie f; (of book, magazine etc) exemplaire m. **2** vti copier.

▸**copy out** or **down** vt (address etc) (re)copier.

cord cordon m; (electrical) cordon m électrique.

cor·dial (fruit) c. sirop m.

▸**cor·don off** vt (of police etc) interdire l'accès de.

cor·du·roy velours m côtelé; **corduroys** pantalon m en velours (côtelé).

core (of apple etc) trognon m.

cork liège m; (for bottle) bouchon m.

cork (up) vt (bottle) boucher.

cork·screw tire-bouchon m.

corn maïs m; (on foot) cor m.

corn·bread pain m à la farine de maïs.

corned beef corned-beef m.

cor·ner 1 n coin m; (bend in road) virage m. **2** vt (person in corridor etc) coincer; (market) monopoliser.

corn·flakes céréales fpl.

corn·starch fécule f de maïs.

corn·y adj (joke) rebattu.

cor·o·nar·y infarctus m.

cor·po·ral caporal(-chef) m.

corps inv corps m.

corpse cadavre m.

cor·rect 1 adj exact, correct; (proper) correct; **he's c.** (right) il a raison. **2** vt corriger.

cor·rec·tion correction f.

cor·rect·ly adv correctement.

cor·re·spond correspondre (**to, with** à); (by letter) correspondre (**with** avec).

cor·re·spon·dence correspondance f; **c. course** cours m par correspondance.

cor·re·spond·ing adj (matching) correspondant.

cor·ri·dor couloir m.

cor·ru·gat·ed adj **c. iron** tôle f ondulée.

cor·rupt adj corrompu.

cor·rup·tion corruption f.

cos·met·ic produit m de beauté.

cost 1 vti coûter; **how much does it c.?** ça coûte combien? **2** n prix m; **at all costs** à tout prix.

cost·ly adj coûteux.

cos·tume costume m.

cos·tume ball bal m masqué.

cos·tume jew·el·ry bijoux mpl de fantaisie.

cot lit m d'enfant; (camp bed) lit m de camp.

cot·tage petite maison f de campagne; (thatched) c. chaumière f.

cot·tage cheese fromage m blanc (maigre).

cot·ton coton m; (yarn) fil m (de coton); **c. wool** coton m hydrophile.

couch canapé m.

cou·chette (on train) couchette f.

cough 1 n toux f; **c. syrup** sirop m contre la toux. **2** vi tousser.

cough up 1 vt (blood) cracher. **2** vti (pay) Fam casquer.

could see **can**[1].

coun·cil conseil m; (city) c. conseil m municipal, municipalité f.

coun·cil·man (city) c. conseiller m municipal.

coun·sel·ing aide f psychologique.

count[1] **1** vt compter. **2** vi (calculate, be important) compter. **3** n **he's lost c. of the books he has** il ne sait plus combien il a livres.

count[2] (title) comte m.

count·down compte m à rebours.

coun·ter (in shop, bar etc) comptoir m; (in bank etc) guichet m; (in games) jeton m.

coun·ter- prefix contre-.

coun·ter·at·tack contre-attaque f.

coun·ter·clock·wise adj & adv dans le sens inverse des aiguilles d'une montre.

coun·ter·part (thing) équivalent m; (person) homologue mf.

▸ **count in** vt inclure.

▸ **count on** vt (rely on) compter sur; **to c. on doing** compter faire.

▸ **count out** vt exclure; (money) compter.

coun·try pays m; (regarded with affection) patrie f; (opposed to town) campagne f; **c. house** maison f de campagne.

coun·try·side campagne f.

coun·ty comté m.

coup coup m d'état.

cou·ple (of people) couple m; **a c. of** deux ou trois; (a few) quelques.

cou·pon (voucher) bon m.

cour·age courage m.

cou·ra·geous adj courageux.

cou·ri·er (messenger) messager m.

course 1 n (duration, movement) cours m; **c.** (of action) ligne f de conduite; (option) parti m; **in the c. of** au cours de. ▪ (lessons) cours m; **c. of lectures** série f de conférences. ▪ **c.** (of treatment) traitement m. ▪ (of meal) plat m; **first c.** entrée f. ▪ (golf) c. terrain m de golf. **2** adv **of c.!** bien sûr!; **of c. not!** bien sûr que non!

court (of king etc, for trials) cour f; (tennis) c. court m (de tennis); **to take sb to c.** poursuivre qn en justice.

cour·te·ous adj poli.

cour·te·sy politesse f, courtoisie f.

court·room salle f du tribunal.

court·yard cour f.

cous·in cousin, -ine mf.

▸ **cov·er 1** n (lid) couvercle m; (of book) couverture f; (for furniture etc) housse f; **the covers** (on bed) les couvertures fpl et les draps mpl; **to take c.** se mettre à l'abri. **2** vt couvrir (**with** de); (insure) assurer.

cov·er·age couverture f.

cov·er·alls bleu m (de travail).

cov·er charge (in restaurant) couvert m.

cov·er·ing (wrapping) enveloppe f; (layer) couche f.

cov·er let·ter lettre *f* jointe (à un document); *(seeking job)* lettre *f* de motivation.
▸ **cover over** *vt (floor etc)* recouvrir.
▸ **cover up 1** *vt* recouvrir; *(truth, tracks)* dissimuler; *(scandal)* étouffer. **2** *vi (wrap up)* se couvrir.
▸ **cover up for** *vt* couvrir.
cow vache *f*.
cow·ard lâche *mf*.
cow·ard·ice lâcheté *f*.
cow·ard·ly *adj* lâche.
cow·boy cow-boy *m*.
co·zy *adj* douillet.
CPA *abbr* = **Certified Public Accountant**
crab crabe *m*.
crack 1 *n* fente *f*; *(in glass, china, bone)* fêlure *f*; *(noise)* craquement *m*; *(of whip)* claquement *m*; *(joke) Fam* plaisanterie *f*. **2** *vt (glass, ice)* fêler; *(nut)* casser; *(whip)* faire claquer; *(joke)* lancer. **3** *vi* se fêler; *(of branch, wood)* craquer; **to get cracking** *(get to work) Fam* s'y mettre.
crack·er *(biscuit)* biscuit *m (salé)*.
crack·pot *Fam* cinglé, -ée *mf*.
▸ **crack up** *vi (mentally) Fam* craquer.
cra·dle berceau *m*.
craft *(skill)* art *m*; *(job)* métier *m (artisanal)*.
crafts·man, *pl* **-men** artisan *m*.
craft·y *adj* astucieux.
cram 1 *vt* **to c. into** *(force)* fourrer dans; **to c. with** *(fill)* bourrer de. **2** *vi* **to c. into** *(of people)* s'entasser dans; **to c. (for an exam)** banchoter.
cramp *(muscle pain)* crampe *f* (**in** à).
cramped *adj* à l'étroit.
crane *(machine)* grue *f*.
crank¹ *(handle)* manivelle *f*.
crank² *Fam (person)* excentrique *mf*.
crash 1 *n* accident *m*; *(of firm)* faillite *f*; *(noise)* fracas *m*. **2** *int (of fall-*

en object) patatras! **3** *vt (car)* avoir un accident avec; **to c. one's car into** faire rentrer sa voiture dans. **4** *vi (of car, plane)* s'écraser; **to c. into** rentrer dans.
crash course cours *m* intensif.
crash di·et régime *m* intensif.
▸ **crash down** *vi (fall)* tomber; *(break)* se casser.
crash hel·met casque *m* (anti-choc).
crash-land *vi* atterrir en catastrophe.
crash land·ing atterrissage *m* en catastrophe.
crate caisse *f*.
crav·ing désir *m* (**for** de).
crawl 1 *vi* ramper; *(of child)* marcher à quatre pattes; *(of vehicle)* avancer au pas; **to be crawling with** grouiller de. **2** *n (swimming stroke)* crawl *m*.
cray·on crayon *m* de couleur *(en cire)*.
craze manie *f* (**for** de).
cra·zy *adj* fou *(f* folle); **c. about sth** fana de qch; **c. about sb** fou de qn.
creak *vi (of hinge)* grincer.
cream crème *f*; **c. cake** gâteau *m* à la crème.
cream cheese fromage *m* blanc.
cream·y *adj* crémeux.
crease 1 *vt (wrinkle)* froisser. **2** *vi* se froisser. **3** *n (in trousers)* pli *m*.
cre·ate *vt* créer; *(impression, noise)* faire.
cre·a·tion création *f*.
cre·a·tive *adj* créatif.
crea·ture animal *m*; *(person)* créature *f*.
crèche *(nursery)* crèche *f*.
cred·i·bil·i·ty crédibilité *f*.
cred·i·ble *adj* croyable; *(politician etc)* crédible.
cred·it 1 *n (financial)* crédit *m*; *(merit)* mérite *m*; *(from university)* unité *f* de valeur; **to be a c. to** faire honneur à; **on c.** à crédit; **my account shows a c. balance of** mon

compte est créditeur de. **2** *vt (of bank)* créditer (**sb with sth** qn de qch).

cred·it card carte *f* de crédit.

cred·it terms facilités *fpl* de paiement.

cred·it·wor·thy *adj* solvable.

creek *(stream)* ruisseau *m*.

creep* *vi* ramper; *(silently)* se glisser; *(slowly)* avancer lentement.

creep·y *adj (causing fear) Fam* terrifiant.

cre·mate *vt* incinérer.

cre·ma·tion crémation *f*.

cre·ma·to·ri·um, cre·ma·-to·ry crématorium *m*.

crêpe pa·per papier *m* crépon.

cress cresson *m*.

crest *(of wave etc)* crête *f*; *(of hill)* sommet *m*.

crew *(of ship, plane)* équipage *m*.

crew cut *(coupe f en)* brosse *f*.

crib *(cot)* lit *m* d'enfant; *(list of answers)* pompe *f*, anti-sèche *f*.

crick·et *(insect)* grillon *m*.

crime crime *m*; *(not serious)* délit *m*; *(criminal practice)* criminalité *f*.

crim·i·nal *adj & n* criminel, -elle *(mf)*.

cri·sis, *pl* **-ses** crise *f*.

crisp *adj (cookie)* croustillant; *(apple)* croquant.

cri·te·ri·on, *pl* **criteria** critère *m*.

crit·ic critique *m*.

crit·i·cal *adj* critique.

crit·i·cal·ly *adv (ill)* gravement.

crit·i·cism critique *f*.

crit·i·cize *vti* critiquer.

cro·chet 1 *vt* faire au crochet. **2** *vi* faire du crochet. **3** *n* (travail *m* au) crochet *m*.

croc·o·dile crocodile *m*.

cro·cus crocus *m*.

crook *(thief)* escroc *m*.

crook·ed *adj (stick)* courbé; *(path)* tortueux; *(hat, picture)* de travers.

crop *(harvest)* récolte *f*; *(produce)* culture *f*.

▶ **crop up** *vi* se présenter.

cro·quet croquet *m*.

cross¹ 1 *n* croix *f*; **a c. between** *(animal)* un croisement entre *or* de. **2** *vt (street, room etc)* traverser; *(barrier)* franchir; *(legs)* croiser. **3** *vi (of paths)* se croiser.

cross² *adj (angry)* fâché (**with** contre).

cross-coun·try race cross (-country) *m*.

cross-eyed *adj* qui louche.

cross·ing *(by ship)* traversée *f*.

▶ **cross off** *or* **out** *vt (word, name etc)* rayer.

▶ **cross over** *vti* traverser.

cross-ref·er·ence renvoi *m*.

cross·roads carrefour *m*.

cross-sec·tion coupe *f* transversale; *(sample)* échantillon *n*.

cross·walk passage *m* clouté.

cross·word (puz·zle) mots *mpl* croisés.

crouch (down) *vi* s'accroupir.

crow corbeau *m*.

crow·bar levier *m*, pied *m* de biche.

crowd foule *f*; *(particular group)* bande *f*.

crowd·ed *adj* plein (**with** de).

▶ **crowd into** *vt (of people)* s'entasser dans.

▶ **crowd round** *vt* se presser autour de.

crown couronne *f*.

cru·cial *adj* crucial.

crude *adj (manners, language)* grossier; *(work)* rudimentaire.

cru·el *adj* cruel.

cru·el·ty cruauté *f*; **an act of c.** une cruauté.

cru·et petit flacon *m*; *(for oil and vinegar)* huilier *m*.

cruise 1 *vi (of ship)* croiser; *(of car)* rouler; *(of plane)* voler. **2** *n* croisière *f*; **to take a c.** faire une croisière.

crumb miette *f*.

crum·ble 1 *vt (bread)* émietter. **2** *vi (in small pieces)* s'effriter; *(of* *bread)* s'émietter; *(become ruined)* tomber en ruine.

crum·bly *adj* friable.

crum·my *adj Fam* moche.

crum·ple *vt* froisser.

crunch *vt (food)* croquer.

crunch·y *adj (apple etc)* croquant; *(bread, cookie)* croustillant.

crush 1 *n (crowd)* cohue *f, (rush)* bousculade *f.* **2** *vt* écraser; *(clothes)* froisser; *(cram)* entasser (**into** dans).

crust croûte *f.*

crust·y *adj (bread)* croustillant.

crutch *(of invalid)* béquille *f.*

cry 1 *n (shout)* cri *m;* **to have a c.** *Fam* pleurer. **2** *vi* pleurer; *(shout)* pousser un cri.

cry·ing *(weeping)* pleurs *mpl.*

▸ **cry off** *vi* se décommander.

▸ **cry out 1** *vi* pousser un cri; *(exclaim)* s'écrier. **2** *vt* crier.

▸ **cry out for** *vt* demander (à grands cris); **to be crying out for sth** avoir grand besoin de qch.

▸ **cry over** *vt* pleurer (sur).

crys·tal cristal *m.*

cub *(scout)* louveteau *m.*

cube cube *m, (of meat etc)* dé *m.*

cu·bic *adj (metre etc)* cube.

cu·bi·cle *(in office building)* box *m.*

cuck·oo *(bird)* coucou *m.*

cu·cum·ber concombre *m.*

cud·dle 1 *vt (hug)* serrer; *(caress)* câliner. **2** *vi* se serrer. **3** *vt* caresse *f.*

▸ **cuddle up to** *vt* se serrer contre.

cud·dly *adj* câlin; *(toy)* doux *(f* douce).

cue *(in theatre)* réplique *f, (signal)* signal *m.*

cuff *(of shirt)* poignet *m; (of trousers)* revers *m.*

cuff link bouton *m* de manchette.

cul-de-sac impasse *f.*

cul·prit coupable *mf.*

cult culte *m;* **c. film** film *m* culte.

cul·ti·vate *vt* cultiver.

cul·ti·vat·ed *adj* cultivé.

cul·tur·al *adj* culturel.

cul·ture culture *f.*

cul·tured *adj* cultivé.

cum·ber·some *adj* encombrant.

cun·ning 1 *adj* astucieux. **2** *n* astuce *f.*

cup tasse *f, (prize)* coupe *f.*

cup·board armoire *f, (built-in)* placard *m.*

cup·cake petit gâteau *m.*

cup·ful tasse *f.*

cur·a·ble *adj* guérissable.

curb bord *m* du trottoir.

cure 1 *vt* guérir *(qn)* *(of* de). **2** *n* remède *m (for* contre); **rest c.** cure *f* de repos.

cu·ri·os·i·ty curiosité *f.*

cu·ri·ous *adj (odd)* curieux; *(inquisitive)* curieux *(about* de).

curl 1 *vti (hair)* boucler. **2** *n* boucle *f.*

curl·er bigoudi *m.*

▸ **curl up** *vi* se pelotonner.

curl·y *adj (hair)* bouclé.

cur·rant *(dried grape)* raisin *m* de Corinthe.

cur·ren·cy monnaie *f, (foreign)* devises *fpl* (étrangères).

cur·rent 1 *adj* actuel; *(opinion)* courant; *(year)* courant. **2** *n (of river, electric)* courant *m.*

cur·rent af·fairs questions *fpl* d'actualité.

cur·rent·ly *adv* actuellement.

cur·ric·u·lum programme *m (scolaire).*

cur·ry curry *m.*

curse *vi (swear)* jurer.

cur·sor *(of computer)* curseur *m.*

cur·tain rideau *m.*

curt·s(e)y 1 *n* révérence *f.* **2** *vi* faire une révérence.

curve 1 *n* courbe *f, (in road)* virage *m.* **2** *vi* se courber; *(of road)* faire une courbe.

cush·ion coussin *m.*

cus·tard crème *f* anglaise; *(when set)* crème *f* renversée.

cus·to·dy garde *f.*

cus·tom coutume f; (customers) clientèle f.

cus·tom·ar·y adj habituel.

cus·tom·er client, -ente mf.

cus·tom·er ser·vice service m après-vente.

cus·toms la douane; **c. (duty)** droits mpl de douane; **c. officer** douanier m.

cut 1 n (mark) coupure f; (stroke) coup m; (of clothes, hair) coupe f; (in salary, prices etc) réduction f; (of meat) morceau m. **2** vt* couper; (meat) découper; (glass, tree) tailler; (salary etc) réduire; **to c. open** ouvrir (au couteau etc). **3** vi (of person, scissors) couper; **to c. in line** passer avant son tour.

▸ **cut away** vt (remove) enlever.

cut·back réduction f.

▸ **cut back (on)** vti réduire.

▸ **cut down** vt (tree) abattre; (reduce) réduire.

▸ **cut down on** vt réduire.

cute adj Fam (pretty) mignon (f mignonne).

▸ **cut into** vt (cake) entamer.

cut·ler·y couverts mpl.

cut·let côtelette f.

▸ **cut off** vt (remove; (isolate) isoler.

▸ **cut out 1** vi (of engine) caler. **2** vt (article) découper; (remove) enlever; **to c. out drinking** s'arrêter de boire; **c. it out!** Fam ça suffit!; **c. out to be a doctor/etc** fait pour être médecin/etc.

cut·out (picture) découpage m.

cut·ting 1 n (from newspaper) coupure m; (plant) bouture f. **2** adj (wind, remark) cinglant.

▸ **cut up** vt couper (en morceaux).

cy·cle 1 n (bicycle) bicyclette f; (series, period) cycle m. **2** vi aller à bicyclette (to à).

cy·cling cyclisme m.

cy·clist cycliste mf.

cyl·in·der cylindre m.

cym·bal cymbale f.

cyn·i·cal adj cynique.

D

dab vt (wound) tamponner; **to d. sth on sth** appliquer qch sur qch.

Da·cron® tergal® m.

dad·dy Fam papa m.

daf·fo·dil jonquille f.

daft adj Fam idiot, bête.

dai·ly 1 adj quotidien. **2** adv quotidiennement. **3** n **d. (paper)** quotidien m.

dair·y adj (product) laitier.

dai·sy pâquerette f.

dam barrage m.

dam·age 1 n dégâts mpl, (harm) préjudice m. **2** vt (spoil) abîmer; (harm) nuire à.

dam·ag·ing adj préjudiciable.

damn Fam **1** int **d. (it)!** merde!; **d. him!** qu'il aille au diable! **2** adj (awful) fichu. **3** adv (very) vachement.

damp 1 adj humide. **2** n humidité f.

damp·en vt humecter.

damp·ness humidité f.

dance 1 n danse f; (social event) bal m (pl bals). **2** vti danser.

dance hall salle f de danse.

danc·er danseur, -euse mf.

danc·ing danse f.

dan·de·li·on pissenlit m.

dan·druff pellicules fpl.

Dane Danois, -oise mf.

dan·ger danger m (**to** pour); **in d.** en danger; **to be in d. of falling/etc** risquer de tomber/etc.

dan·ger·ous adj dangereux (**to** pour).

Dan·ish 1 adj danois. **2** n (language) danois m.

dare vt oser (do faire); **to d. sb to do** défier qn de faire.

dar·ing adj audacieux.

dark 1 adj obscur, noir; (color, eyes) foncé; (skin, hair) brun; **it's d.** il fait nuit *or* noir; **d. glasses** lunettes *fpl* noires. **2** *n* noir *m*, obscurité *f*.

dark-haired *adj* aux cheveux bruns.

dark·ness obscurité *f*, noir *m*.

dark-skinned *adj* brun.

dar·ling (my) d. (mon) chéri, (ma) chérie.

dart fléchette *f*; **darts** (*game*) fléchettes *fpl*.

dart·board cible *f*.

dash 1 *vi* se précipiter. **2** *n* (*stroke*) trait *m*.

▶**dash away** *or* **off** *vi* partir en vitesse.

dash·board tableau *m* de bord.

da·ta *npl* données *fpl*.

dat·a bank banque *f* de données.

dat·a pro·cess·ing informatique *f*.

date¹ 1 *n* (*time*) date *f*; (*meeting*) *Fam* rendez-vous *m inv* (galant); (*person*) *Fam* copain, -ine *mf*; **up to d.** moderne; (*information*) à jour; (*well-informed*) au courant (**on** de); **out of d.** (*old-fashioned*) démodé; (*expired*) périmé. **2** *vt* (*letter etc*) dater; (*girl, boy*) *Fam* sortir avec.

date² (*fruit*) datte *f*.

dat·ed *adj* démodé.

date stamp (*tampon m*) dateur *m*; (*mark*) cachet *m*.

daugh·ter fille *f*.

daugh·ter-in-law, *pl* **daughters-in-law** belle-fille *f*.

daw·dle *vi* traîner.

dawn aube *f*.

day jour *m*; (*whole day long*) journée *f*; **all d. (long)** toute la journée; **the following** *or* **next d.** le lendemain; **the day before** la veille; **the d. before yesterday** avant-hier; **the d. after tomorrow** après-demain.

day·break point *m* du jour.

day·care (*for ages 3 and below*) crèche *f*; (*for older children*) garderie *f*.

day·light (lumière *f* du) jour *m*.

day·time journée *f*, jour *m*.

dead 1 *adj* mort; (*battery*) à plat. **2** *adv* (*completely*) absolument; (*very*) très.

dead-end (*street*) impasse *f*.

dead·line date *f* limite; (*time*) heure *f* limite.

dead·ly 1 *adj* mortel; **d. weapon** arme *f* meurtrière. **2** *adv* (*extremely*) mortellement.

deaf *adj* sourd; **d. and dumb** sourd-muet (*f* sourde-muette).

deaf·ness surdité *f*.

deal¹ **a good** *or* **great d.** (a lot) beaucoup (**of** de).

deal² *n* (*in business*) marché *m*, affaire *f*; **it's a d.** d'accord. **2** *vi** (*trade*) traiter (**with sb** avec qn); **to d. in** faire le commerce de; **to d. with sb** s'occuper de; (*concern*) traiter de. **3** *vt* (*cards*) donner.

deal·er marchand, -ande *mf* (**in** de); (*agent*) dépositaire *mf*; (*for cars*) concessionnaire *mf*.

deal·ings *npl* relations *fpl* (**with** avec); (*in business*) transactions *fpl*.

dear 1 *adj* (*loved, expensive*) cher; **D. Sir** (*in letter*) Monsieur; **oh d.!** oh là là! **2** *n* **(my) d.** (*darling*) (mon) chéri, (ma) chérie; (*friend*) mon cher, ma chère.

death mort *f*.

death cer·tif·i·cate acte *m* de décès.

de·bate 1 *vti* discuter. **2** *n* débat *m*, discussion *f*.

deb·it 1 *n* débit *m*; **my account shows a d. balance of** mon compte est débiteur de. **2** *vt* débiter (**sb with sth** qn de qch).

debt dette *f*; **to be in d.** avoir des dettes.

debt·or débiteur, -trice *mf*.

de·but début *m*; **to make one's d.** faire ses débuts.

dec·ade décennie *f*.

de·caf·fein·at·ed *adj* décaféiné.

de·cal décalcomanie f.

de·cay (of tooth) carie(s) f(pl).

de·ceive vti tromper.

De·cem·ber décembre m.

de·cent adj (respectable) convenable, décent; (good) Fam bon; (kind) Fam gentil.

de·cep·tion tromperie f.

de·cide 1 vt (question etc) décider; to d. to do décider de faire; to d. that décider que. 2 vi (make decisions) décider (on de); (make up one's mind) se décider (on doing à faire); (choose) se décider (on pour).

dec·i·mal 1 adj d. point virgule f. 2 n décimale f.

de·ci·sion décision f.

de·ci·sive adj décisif; (victory) net (f nette).

deck (of ship) pont m; (of cards) jeu m; (of house) terrasse f.

deck·chair transat m.

de·clare vt déclarer (that que); (verdict, result) proclamer.

de·cline 1 vi (become less) (of popularity etc) être en baisse. 2 vt (invitation) refuser.

dec·o·rate vt (cake, house, soldier) décorer (with de); (hat, skirt etc) orner (with de); (paint etc) peindre (et tapisser).

dec·o·ra·tion décoration f.

dec·o·ra·tive adj décoratif.

dec·o·ra·tor peintre m décorateur; (interior) d. décorateur, -trice mf.

de·crease 1 vti diminuer. 2 n diminution f (in de).

de·cree 1 n (by court) jugement m. 2 vt décréter.

ded·i·cate vt consacrer (to à); (book) dédier (to à).

ded·i·cat·ed adj (teacher etc) consciencieux.

de·duct vt déduire (from de); (from wage, account) prélever (from sur).

de·duc·tion déduction f.

deed action f, acte m; (document) acte m (notarié).

deep adj profond; (voice) grave; to be 20 feet/etc d. avoir six mètres/ etc de profondeur; the d. end (in pool) le grand bain.

deep-freeze 1 vt surgeler. 2 n congélateur m.

deer inv cerf m.

de·fault by d. par défaut; to win by d. gagner par forfait.

de·feat 1 vt battre. 2 n défaite f.

de·fect défaut m.

de·fec·tive adj défectueux.

de·fend vt défendre.

de·fen·dant (accused) prévenu, -ue mf.

de·fense défense f.

de·fen·sive 1 adj défensif; to be d. être sur la défensive. 2 n to be on the d. être sur la défensive.

de·fi·ant adj (tone, attitude) de défi; (person) rebelle.

de·fi·cien·cy manque m; (of vitamins etc) carence f.

de·fi·cient adj insuffisant; to be d. in manquer de.

def·i·cit déficit m.

de·fine vt définir.

def·i·nite adj (date, plan) précis; (reply, improvement) net (f nette); (order, offer) ferme; (certain) certain; d. article Grammar article m défini.

def·i·nite·ly adv certainement; (considerably) nettement; (to say) catégoriquement.

def·i·ni·tion définition f.

de·formed adj (body) difforme.

de·frost vt (fridge) dégivrer; (food) décongeler.

de·fy vt défier (qn); to d. sb to do défier qn de faire.

de·gen·er·ate vi dégénérer (into en).

de·gree (angle, temperature) degré m; (from university) diplôme m; (Bachelor's) licence f, (Master's) maîtrise f, (PhD) doctorat m; to such a d. à tel point (that que).

de·ice vt (car window etc) dégivrer.

de·ic·er (substance) dégivreur m.

de·ject·ed adj abattu.

de·lay 1 vt retarder; (payment) différer. **2** vi (be slow) tarder (doing à faire); (linger) s'attarder. **3** n retard m; (waiting period) délai m; without d. sans tarder.

del·e·gate 1 vt déléguer (to à). **2** n délégué, -ée mf.

del·e·ga·tion délégation f.

de·lete vt rayer.

de·lib·er·ate adj (intentional) intentionnel.

de·liber·ate·ly adv (intentionally) exprès.

del·i·ca·cy (food) mets m délicat.

del·i·cate adj délicat.

del·i·ca·tes·sen traiteur m, épicerie f fine.

de·li·cious adj délicieux.

de·light 1 n délice m; to take d. in sth/in doing se délecter de qch/à faire. **2** vt réjouir. **3** vi to d. in doing se délecter à faire.

de·light·ed adj ravi (with sth de qch; to do de faire; that que).

de·light·ful adj charmant; (meal) délicieux.

de·lin·quent délinquant, -ante mf.

de·liv·er vt (goods etc) livrer; (letters) distribuer; (hand over) remettre (to à); (speech) prononcer; (warning) lancer.

de·liv·er·y livraison f, (of letters) distribution f, (hand over) remise f, (birth) accouchement m.

de·lude vt tromper; to d. oneself se faire des illusions.

de·lu·sion illusion f.

de·luxe adj de luxe.

de·mand 1 vt exiger (sth from sb qch de qn); (rights, more pay) revendiquer; to d. that exiger que. **2** n exigence f, (claim) revendication f, (for goods) demande f, in great d. très demandé.

de·mand·ing adj exigeant.

dem·o Fam (demonstration) manif f, d. tape cassette f de démonstration.

de·moc·ra·cy démocratie f.

dem·o·crat·ic adj démocratique; (person) démocrate.

de·mol·ish vt démolir.

dem·o·li·tion démolition f.

de·mon démon m.

dem·on·strate 1 vt démontrer; (machine) faire une démonstration de. **2** vi manifester.

dem·on·stra·tion démonstration f, (protest) manifestation f.

de·mon·stra·tive adj & n Grammar démonstratif (m).

dem·on·stra·tor (protester) manifestant, -ante mf.

de·mor·al·ize vt démoraliser.

den tanière f.

de·ni·al (of rumor) démenti m.

den·im (toile f de) coton m.

de·nounce vt (person, injustice etc) dénoncer (to à).

dense adj dense; (stupid) Fam lourd, bête.

dent 1 n (in car etc) bosse f. **2** vt cabosser.

den·tal adj dentaire.

den·tist dentiste mf.

den·tures npl dentier m.

de·ny vt nier (doing avoir fait; that que); (rumor) démentir; to d. sb sth refuser qch à qn.

de·o·dor·ant déodorant m.

de·part vi partir; (deviate) s'écarter (from de).

de·part·ment département m; (in office) service m; (in shop) rayon m; (of government) = ministère m; D. of State Ministère des Affaires Etrangères.

de·part·ment store grand magasin m.

de·par·ture départ m; a d. from (rule) un écart par rapport à.

de·pend vi dépendre (on, upon de); to d. (up)on (rely on) compter sur (for sth pour qch).

de·pend·a·ble *adj* sûr.

de·pen·dant personne *f* à charge.

de·pen·dent *adj* dépendant; **to be d. on sth** dépendre de qch.

de·pict *vt (describe)* dépeindre; *(in pictures)* représenter.

de·plor·a·ble *adj* déplorable.

de·plore *vt* déplorer.

de·pos·it 1 *vt* déposer; **to d.** *(check)* verser (**to one's account** sur son compte). **2** *n* dépôt *m*; *(part payment)* acompte *m*, arrhes *fpl*; *(against damage)* caution *f*, *(on bottle)* consigne *f*.

de·pot *(railroad station)* gare *f*; **bus d.** gare *f* routière.

de·press *vt (discourage)* déprimer.

de·pressed *adj* déprimé; **to get d.** se décourager.

de·pres·sion dépression *f*.

de·prive *vt* priver (**of** de).

de·prived *adj (child etc)* déshérité.

depth profondeur *f*.

dep·u·ty *(replacement)* remplaçant, -ante *mf*; *(assistant)* adjoint, -ointe *mf*.

de·rail·ment déraillement *m*.

der·e·lict *adj* abandonné.

de·rive *vt* **to d. from sth** *(pleasure etc)* tirer de qch; **to be derived from** *(of word etc)* dériver de.

de·scend 1 *vi* descendre (**from** de). **2** *vt (stairs)* descendre.

de·scen·dant descendant, -ante *mf*.

▶**descend upon** *vt (of tourists)* envahir.

de·scent *(of aircraft etc)* descente *f*.

de·scribe *vt* décrire.

de·scrip·tion description *f*; *(on passport)* signalement *m*; **of every d.** de toutes sortes.

des·ert[1] désert *m*; **d. island** île *f* déserte.

de·sert[2] *vt* abandonner.

de·sert·ed *adj (place)* désert.

de·serve *vt* mériter (**to do** de faire).

de·sign 1 *vt (car etc)* dessiner; **designed to do/for sb** conçu pour faire/pour qn; **well designed** bien conçu. **2** *n (pattern)* motif *m*; *(sketch)* plan *m*, dessin *m*; *(type of dress or car)* modèle *m*.

des·ig·nate *vt* désigner.

de·sign·er dessinateur, -trice *mf*.

de·sign·er clothes vêtements *mpl* griffés.

de·sir·a·ble *adj* désirable.

de·sire 1 *n* désir *m*; **I have no d. to** je n'ai aucune envie de. **2** *vt* désirer (**to do** faire).

desk *(in school)* pupitre *m*; *(in office)* bureau *m*; *(in shop)* caisse *f*; **(reception) d.** réception *f*.

desk clerk *(in hotel)* réceptionniste *mf*.

desk·top bureau *m*; **d. publishing** publication *f* assistée par ordinateur.

de·spair 1 *n* désespoir *m*; **to be in d.** être au désespoir. **2** *vi* désespérer (**of sb** de qn; **of doing** de faire).

des·per·ate *adj* désespéré; **to be d. for** avoir désespérément besoin de; *(cigarette, baby)* mourir d'envie d'avoir.

des·pi·ca·ble *adj* méprisable.

de·spise *vt* mépriser.

de·spite *prep* malgré.

des·sert dessert *m*.

des·sert·spoon cuillère *f* à dessert.

des·ti·na·tion destination *f*.

des·ti·tute *adj* indigent.

de·stroy *vt* détruire.

de·struc·tion destruction *f*.

de·struc·tive *adj* destructeur.

de·tach *vt* détacher (**from** de).

de·tach·a·ble *adj (lining)* amovible.

de·tached house maison *f* individuelle.

de·tail détail *m*; **in d.** en détail.

de·tailed *adj* détaillé.

de·tain vt retenir; (prisoner) détenir.

de·tect (find) découvrir; (see, hear) distinguer.

de·tec·tive inspecteur m de police; (private) détective m.

de·tec·tor détecteur m.

de·ten·tion (school punishment) retenue f.

de·ter vt to d. sb dissuader qn (from doing de faire; from sth de qch).

de·ter·gent détergent m.

de·te·ri·o·rate vi se détériorer.

de·te·ri·o·ration détérioration f.

de·ter·mi·na·tion (intention) ferme intention f.

de·ter·mine vt déterminer; (price) fixer.

de·ter·mined adj déterminé; d. to do or on doing décidé à faire.

de·ter·rent to be a d. être dissuasif.

de·test vt détester (doing faire).

de·tour déviation f.

dev·as·tat·ing adj (news, results) accablant.

de·vel·op 1 vt développer; (area, land) mettre en valeur; (habit, illness) contracter. **2** vi se développer.

▶ **develop into** vt devenir.

de·vel·op·ment développement m; housing d. lotissement m; (large) grand ensemble m; a (new) d. (in situation) un fait nouveau.

de·vi·ate vi dévier (from de).

de·vice dispositif m; left to one's own devices livré à soi-même.

dev·il diable m; what/where/why the d.? que/où/pourquoi diable?

de·vise vt (a plan) combiner; (invent) inventer.

de·vote vt consacrer (to à).

de·vot·ed adj dévoué.

de·vo·tion dévouement m (to sb à qn).

dew rosée f.

di·a·be·tes diabète m.

di·a·bet·ic diabétique mf.

di·ag·nose vt diagnostiquer.

di·ag·no·sis, pl -oses diagnostic m.

di·ag·o·nal 1 adj diagonal. **2** n d. (line) diagonale f.

di·ag·o·nal·ly adv en diagonale.

di·a·gram schéma m.

di·al 1 n cadran m. **2** vt (phone number) faire; (person) appeler.

di·a·lect dialecte m.

di·al tone tonalité f.

di·a·log dialogue m.

di·am·e·ter diamètre m.

di·a·mond diamant m; (shape) losange m; Baseball terrain m; diamond(s) Cards carreau m; d. necklace collier m de diamants.

di·a·per couche f.

di·ar·rhe·a diarrhée f.

di·a·ry journal m (intime).

dice 1 n inv dé m (à jouer). **2** vt (food) couper en dés.

dic·tate vti dicter (to à).

dic·ta·tion dictée f.

dic·tion·ar·y dictionnaire m.

did pt de **do**.

die* vi mourir (of, from de); to be dying to do mourir d'envie de faire; to be dying for sth avoir une envie folle de qch.

▶ **die away** vi (of noise) mourir.

▶ **die down** vi (of storm) se calmer.

▶ **die out** vi (of custom) mourir.

die·sel adj & n (engine) (moteur m) diesel m; d. (oil) gazole m.

di·et 1 n (to lose weight) régime m; (usual food) alimentation f; to go on a d. faire un régime. **2** vi suivre un régime.

dif·fer vi différer (from de); (disagree) ne pas être d'accord (from avec).

dif·fer·ence différence f (in de); d. (of opinion) différend m; it makes no d. ça n'a pas d'importance; it makes no d. to me ça m'est égal.

dif·fer·ent adj différent (from, to de); (another) autre; (various) divers.

differ·ent·ly *adv* autrement (from, to que).

dif·fi·cult *adj* difficile (to do à faire); **it's d. for us to** il nous est difficile de.

dif·fi·cul·ty difficulté *f*; **to have d. doing** avoir du mal à faire.

dig* 1 *vt (ground)* bêcher; *(hole)* creuser. 2 *vi* creuser.

di·gest *vti* digérer.

di·ges·tion digestion *f*.

dig·ger *(machine)* pelleteuse *f*.

dig·it *(number)* chiffre *m*.

dig·i·tal *adj* numérique.

dig·ni·ty dignité *f*.

▸ **dig out** *vt (from ground)* déterrer; *(accident victim)* dégager; *(find)* dénicher.

▸ **dig up** *vt (from ground)* déterrer; *(weed)* arracher; *(earth)* retourner; *(street)* piocher.

di·lap·i·dat·ed *adj* délabré.

di·lem·ma dilemme *f*.

di·lute *vt* diluer.

dim 1 *adj (light)* faible; *(room)* sombre; *(memory, outline)* vague; *(person)* stupide. 2 *vt (light)* baisser; **to d. one's headlights** se mettre en code.

dime *(pièce f de)* dix cents *mpl*; **d. store** magasin *m* à prix unique.

di·men·sion dimension *f*.

di·min·ish *vti* diminuer.

dimmed head·lights codes *mpl*.

din vacarme *m*.

dine *vi* dîner (**on** de).

▸ **dine out** *vi* dîner en ville.

din·er dîneur, -euse *mf*; *(restaurant)* petit restaurant *m*.

din·ghy petit canot *m*; **(rubber) d.** canot *m* pneumatique.

din·gy *adj (room etc)* minable; *(color)* terne.

din·ing car wagon-restaurant *m*.

din·ing room salle *f* à manger.

din·ner dîner *m*; *(lunch)* déjeuner *m*; **to have d.** dîner.

din·ner jack·et smoking *m*.

din·ner par·ty dîner *m* (à la maison).

din·ner ser·vice *or* **set** service *m* de table.

di·no·saur dinosaure *m*.

dip 1 *vt* plonger. 2 *vi (of road)* plonger; **to d. into** *(pocket, savings)* puiser dans. 3 *n (in road)* petit creux *m*; **to go for a d.** *(swim)* faire trempette.

diph·thong diphtongue *f*.

di·plo·ma diplôme *m*.

dip·lo·mat diplomate *mf*.

dip·lo·mat·ic *adj Pol* diplomatique; *(tactful)* diplomate.

di·rect 1 *adj* direct. 2 *adv* directement. 3 *vt* diriger; *(remark)* adresser (**to** à); **to d. sb to** *(place)* indiquer à qn le chemin de.

di·rec·tion direction *f*; **directions (for use)** mode *m* d'emploi; **in the opposite d.** en sens inverse.

di·rect·ly 1 *adv* directement; *(at once)* tout de suite. 2 *conj* aussitôt que (+ *indicative*).

di·rec·tor directeur, -trice *mf*; *(board member in firm)* administrateur, -trice *mf*; *(of film)* metteur *m* en scène.

di·rec·to·ry (telephone) d. annuaire *m* (téléphonique).

di·rec·to·ry as·sis·tance renseignements *mpl*.

dirt saleté *f*; *(earth)* terre *f*; **d. cheap** *Fam* très bon marché.

dirt·y 1 *adj* sale; *(job)* salissant; *(word)* grossier; **to get d.** se salir; **to get sth d.** salir qch; **a d. joke** une histoire cochonne. 2 *vt* salir.

dis- *prefix* dé-, dés-.

dis·a·bil·i·ty infirmité *f*.

dis·a·bled 1 *adj* handicapé. 2 *n* **the d.** les handicapés *mpl*.

dis·ad·van·tage désavantage *m*.

dis·a·gree *vi* ne pas être d'accord (**with** avec); **to d. with sb** *(of food etc)* ne pas réussir à qn.

dis·a·gree·a·ble *adj* désagréable.

dis·a·gree·ment désaccord m; (quarrel) différend m.

dis·ap·pear vi disparaître.

dis·ap·pear·ance disparition f.

dis·ap·point vt décevoir; I'm disappointed with it ça m'a déçu.

dis·ap·point·ing adj décevant.

dis·ap·point·ment déception f.

dis·ap·prov·al désapprobation f.

dis·ap·prove vi to d. of sb/sth désapprouver qn/qch; I d. je suis contre.

dis·arm vt désarmer.

dis·as·ter désastre m.

dis·as·trous adj désastreux.

dis·card vt se débarrasser de.

dis·charge vt (patient, employee) renvoyer; (soldier) libérer.

dis·ci·pline 1 n discipline f. 2 vt discipliner; (punish) punir.

disc jock·ey disc-jockey m.

dis·close vt révéler.

dis·co, pl -os disco f.

dis·com·fort douleur f; I have d. in my wrist mon poignet me gêne.

dis·con·nect vt détacher; (unplug) débrancher; (wires) déconnecter; (gas, telephone) couper.

dis·con·tent·ed adj mécontent.

dis·con·tin·ued adj (article) qui ne se fait plus.

dis·co·theque (club) discothèque f.

dis·count (on article) remise f, réduction f; at a d. à prix réduit.

dis·count store solderie f.

dis·cour·age vt décourager; to get discouraged se décourager.

dis·cov·er vt découvrir (that que).

dis·cov·er·y découverte f.

dis·creet adj discret.

dis·crim·i·nate vi to d. against faire de la discrimination contre.

dis·crim·i·na·tion (against sb) discrimination f.

dis·cuss vt discuter de; (plan, question, price) discuter.

dis·cus·sion discussion f.

dis·ease maladie f.

dis·em·bark vti débarquer.

dis·fig·ured adj défiguré.

dis·grace 1 n (shame) honte f (to à). 2 vt déshonorer.

dis·grace·ful adj honteux.

dis·guise 1 vt déguiser (as en). 2 n déguisement m; in d. déguisé.

dis·gust 1 n dégoût m (for, at, with de); in d. dégoûté. 2 vt dégoûter.

dis·gust·ed adj dégoûté (at, by, with de); d. with sb (annoyed) fâché contre qn.

dis·gust·ing adj dégoûtant.

dish (container, food) plat m; the dishes la vaisselle; to do the dishes faire la vaisselle.

dish·cloth (for washing) lavette f; (for drying) torchon m.

di·shev·eled adj débraillé.

dis·hon·est adj malhonnête.

dis·hon·es·ty malhonnêteté f.

▸ **dish out** or **up** vt (food) servir.

dish towel torchon m.

dish·wash·er (machine) lave-vaisselle m inv.

dis·il·lu·sioned adj déçu (with de).

dis·in·cen·tive mesure f dissuasive.

dis·in·fect vt désinfecter.

dis·in·fec·tant désinfectant m.

disk disque m.

dis·like 1 vt ne pas aimer (doing faire); to have a d. for, of pour); to take a d. to sb/sth prendre qn/qch en grippe.

dis·lo·cate vt (limb) démettre.

dis·mal adj morne.

dis·man·tle vt (machine) démonter.

dis·may vt consterner.

dis·miss vt (from job) renvoyer (from de).

dis·miss·al renvoi m.

dis·o·be·di·ence désobéissance f.

dis·o·be·di·ent adj désobéissant.

dis·o·bey 1 vt désobéir à. **2** vi désobéir.

dis·or·der (confusion) désordre m; (illness) troubles mpl.

dis·or·gan·ized adj désorganisé.

dis·patch vt expédier; (troops, messenger) envoyer.

dis·pel vt dissiper.

dis·pens·er (device) distributeur m; **cash d.** distributeur m de billets.

dis·perse 1 vt disperser. **2** vi se disperser.

dis·play 1 vt montrer; (notice, electronic data) afficher; (painting, goods) exposer; (courage etc) faire preuve de. **2** n (in shop) étalage m; (of data) affichage m; **on d.** exposé.

dis·pleased adj mécontent (**with** de).

dis·pos·a·ble adj (plate etc) à jeter, jetable.

dis·pos·al **at the d. of** à la disposition de.

dis·pose vi **to d. of** (get rid of) se débarrasser de; (sell) vendre.

dis·pute 1 n (quarrel) dispute f; (industrial) conflit m. **2** vt contester.

dis·qual·i·fy vt rendre inapte (**from** à); (in sport) disqualifier.

dis·re·gard vt ne tenir aucun compte de.

dis·re·spect·ful adj irrespectueux.

dis·rupt vt (traffic, class etc) perturber; (plan etc) déranger.

dis·rup·tion perturbation f; (of plan etc) dérangement m.

dis·rup·tive adj (child) turbulent.

dis·sat·is·fac·tion mécontentement m.

dis·sat·is·fied adj mécontent (**with** de).

dis·sent 1 n désaccord m. **2** vi être en désaccord (**from** avec).

dis·solve 1 vt dissoudre. **2** vi se dissoudre.

dis·suade vt dissuader (**from doing** de faire).

dis·tance distance f; **in the d.** au loin; **from a d.** de loin; **it's within walking d.** on peut y aller à pied; **to keep one's d.** garder ses distances.

dis·tant adj éloigné; (reserved) distant.

dis·taste aversion f (**for** pour).

dis·taste·ful adj désagréable.

dis·tinct adj (voice, light) distinct; (difference, improvement) net (f nette); (different) distinct (**from** de).

dis·tinc·tion distinction f; (at graduation) **with d.** avec mention f.

dis·tinc·tive adj distinctif.

dis·tinct·ly adv distinctement; (definitely) sensiblement.

dis·tin·guish vti distinguer (**from** de; **between** entre).

dis·tin·guished adj distingué.

dis·tort vt déformer.

dis·tract vt distraire (**from** de).

dis·trac·tion distraction f.

dis·tress (pain) douleur f; (anguish) détresse f; **in d.** (ship) en détresse.

dis·tress·ing adj affligeant.

dis·trib·ute vt distribuer; (spread evenly) répartir.

dis·tri·bu·tion distribution f.

dis·trib·u·tor (in car) distributeur m; (of goods) concessionnaire mf.

dis·trict région f; (of town) quartier m; **d. attorney** = procureur m (de la République).

dis·trust vt se méfier de.

dis·turb vt (sleep) troubler; (papers, belongings) déranger; **to d. sb** (bother) déranger qn; (worry) troubler qn.

dis·tur·bance (noise) tapage m; **disturbances** (riots) troubles mpl.

dis·turb·ing adj (worrying) inquiétant.

ditch fossé m.

dit·to *adv* idem.

di·van divan *m*.

dive* 1 *vi* plonger; *(rush)* se précipiter. **2** *n (of swimmer, goalkeeper)* plongeon *m*; *(of aircraft)* piqué *m*.

div·er plongeur, -euse *mf*.

di·ver·sion *(on road)* déviation *f*; *(distraction)* diversion *f*.

di·vert *vt (traffic)* dévier; *(aircraft)* dérouter.

di·vide *vt* diviser **(into** en**)**; *(share out)* partager; *(separate)* séparer **(from** de**)**.

▸**divide off** *vt* séparer **(from sth de** qch**)**.

▸**divide up** *vt (share out)* partager.

di·vid·ed high·way route *f* à quatre voies.

div·i·dend dividende *m*.

div·ing plongée *f* sous-marine.

diving board plongeoir *m*.

di·vi·sion division *f*.

di·vorce 1 *n* divorce *m*. **2** *vt (husband, wife)* divorcer d'avec.

di·vorced *adj* divorcé **(from** d'avec**)**; **to get d.** divorcer.

DIY *abbr (do-it-yourself)* bricolage *m*.

diz·zi·ness vertige *m*.

diz·zy *adj* **to be** *or* **feel d.** avoir le vertige; **to make sb (feel) d.** donner le vertige à qn.

DJ *abbr* = **disc jockey.**

do* 1 *v aux* **do you know?** savez-vous?, est-ce que vous savez?; **I do not** *or* **don't see** je ne vois pas; **he did say so** *(emphasis)* il l'a bien dit; **do stay** reste donc; **you know him, don't you?** tu le connais, n'est-ce pas?; **neither do I** moi non plus; **so do I** moi aussi. **2** *vt* faire; **what does she do?** *(in general)*, **what is she doing?** *(now)* qu'est-ce qu'elle fait?; **what have you done (with)…?** qu'as-tu fait (de)…?; **well done** *(congratulations)* bravo!; *(steak)* bien cuit; **to do sb out of sth** escroquer qch à qn; **he's done for** *Fam* il est fichu. **3** *vi (get along)* aller; *(suit)*

faire l'affaire; *(be enough)* suffire; *(finish)* finir; **how do you do?** *(introduction)* enchanté!; **he did well** *or* **right to leave** il a bien fait de partir; **do as I do** fais comme moi; **to have to do with** *(relate to)* avoir à voir avec; *(concern)* concerner.

▸**do away with** *vt* supprimer.

dock 1 *n (for ship)* dock *m*. **2** *vi (at pier)* se mettre à quai.

dock·er docker *m*.

dock·yard chantier *m* naval.

doc·tor médecin *m*; *(academic)* docteur *m*.

doc·tor·ate doctorat *m*.

doc·trine doctrine *f*.

doc·u·ment document *m*.

doc·u·men·ta·ry *(film)* documentaire *m*.

dodge 1 *vt* esquiver; *(pursuer)* échapper à; *(tax)* éviter de payer. **2** *vi* **to d. through** *(crowd)* se faufiler dans.

does *see* **do.**

dog chien *m*; *(female)* chienne *f*; **d. food** pâtée *f*.

dog·gy bag *(in restaurant)* petit sac *m* pour emporter les restes.

dog·house niche *f*.

dog tags plaque *f* d'identité.

do·ing **that's your d.** c'est toi qui es fait ça.

do-it-your·self 1 *n* bricolage *m*. **2** *adj (store, book)* de bricolage.

doll poupée *f*.

dol·lar dollar *m*.

doll·house maison *f* de poupée.

dol·phin dauphin *m*.

do·main domaine *m*; **d. name** nom *m* de domaine.

dome dôme *m*.

do·mes·tic *adj* domestique; *(trade, flight)* intérieur.

dom·i·nant *adj* dominant; *(person)* dominateur.

dom·i·nate *vti* dominer.

dom·i·no domino *m*; **dominoes** *(game)* dominos *mpl*.

do·nate 1 vt faire don de; (blood) donner. **2** vi donner.

do·na·tion don m.

done pp de **do**.

don·key âne m.

do·nor (to charity) donateur, -trice mf; (of organ, blood) donneur, -euse mf.

door porte f.

door·bell sonnette f.

door·knob poignée f de porte.

door·knock·er marteau m.

door·man, pl -men (of hotel) portier m.

door·mat paillasson m.

door·step seuil m.

door·stop butoir m (de porte).

door·way in the d. dans l'encadrement de la porte.

► **do over** vt (redecorate) refaire.

dope (drugs) Fam drogue f.

dor·mi·to·ry dortoir m; (at university) résidence f (universitaire).

dos·age (amount) dose f.

dose dose f.

dot point m.

dot·ted line pointillé m.

dou·ble 1 adj double; **a d. bed** un grand lit; **a d. room** une chambre pour deux personnes. **2** adv (twice) deux fois, le double; (to fold) en deux. **3** n double m. **4** vti doubler.

► **double back** vi (of person) revenir en arrière.

dou·ble-breast·ed adj (jacket) croisé.

dou·ble-cross vt trahir, doubler.

dou·ble-deck·er (bus) autobus m à impériale.

dou·ble-glaz·ing double vitrage m.

► **double up** vi (with pain, laughter) être plié en deux.

doubt 1 n doute m; **no d.** (probably) sans doute. **2** vt douter de; **to d. whether** or **that** or **if** douter que (+ subjunctive).

doubt·ful adj to be d. (about sth) avoir des doutes (sur qch); **it's d.**

whether or **that** or **if** ce n'est pas sûr que (+ subjunctive).

doubt·less adj sans doute.

dough pâte f, (money) Fam fric m.

dough·nut beignet m (rond).

► **do up** vt (coat, button) boutonner; (zipper) fermer; (house) refaire, décorer; (goods) emballer.

dove colombe f.

► **do with** vt I could do with that j'aimerais bien ça.

► **do without** vt se passer de.

down 1 adv en bas; (to the ground) par terre; (of curtain, temperature) baissé; (in writing) inscrit; (out of bed) descendu; **to come** or **go d.** descendre; **d. there** or **here** en bas; **d. with flu** grippé; **to feel d.** avoir le cafard. **2** prep (at bottom of) en bas de; (from top to bottom of) du haut en bas de; (along) le long de; **to go d.** (hill, street, stairs) descendre.

down-and-out adj to be d. être sur le pavé.

down·fall chute f.

down·hill adv to go d. descendre; (of sick person, business) aller de plus en plus mal.

down pay·ment acompte m, arrhes fpl.

down·fall chute f.

down·pour averse f.

down·right 1 adj (rogue etc) véritable; (refusal) catégorique. **2** adv (rude etc) franchement.

down·stairs 1 adj (room, neighbors) d'en bas. **2** adv en bas; **to come** or **go d.** descendre l'escalier.

down-to-earth adj terre-à-terre.

down·town adj au centreville; **d. Chicago** le centre de Chicago.

down·ward(s) adv vers le bas.

doze 1 n petit somme m. **2** vi sommeiller.

doz·en douzaine f; **a d.** (books etc) une douzaine de.

► **doze off** vi s'assoupir.

Dr abbr (Doctor) Docteur.

drab adj terne; (weather) gris.

draft courant *m* d'air.

draft beer bière *f* pression.

draft·y *adj* (*room*) plein de courants d'air.

drag *vti* traîner.

▶ **drag along** *vt* (en)traîner.

▶ **drag away** arracher (**from** à).

▶ **drag on** *or* **out** *vi* (*last a long time*) se prolonger, s'éterniser.

drag·on dragon *m*.

drain 1 *n* (*sewer*) égout *m*; (*outside house*) puisard *m*; (*in street*) bouche *f* d'égout. **2** *vt* (*tank*) vider; (*vegetables*) égoutter.

drain (*liquid*) faire écouler. **2** *vi* (*of liquid*) s'écouler.

drain·board paillasse *f*.

drainer (*board*) paillasse *f*, (*rack, basket*) égouttoir *m*.

drain·pipe tuyau *m* d'évacuation.

dra·ma (*event*) drame *m*; (*dramatic art*) théâtre *m*.

dra·mat·ic *adj* dramatique; (*very great, striking*) spectaculaire.

dra·mat·i·cal·ly *adv* (*to change etc*) de façon spectaculaire.

drapes *npl* (*heavy curtains*) rideaux *mpl*.

dras·tic *adj* radical.

dras·ti·cal·ly *adv* radicalement.

draw¹* 1 *n* (*in sports, games*) match *m* nul. **2** *vt** (*pull*) tirer; (*attract*) attirer.

draw²* *vt* (*picture*) dessiner; (*circle*) tracer. **2** *vi* dessiner.

draw·back inconvénient *m*.

draw·er tiroir *m*.

draw·ing dessin *m*.

draw·ing room salon *m*.

▶ **draw near** *vi* s'approcher; (*of time*) approcher.

▶ **draw near to** *vt* s'approcher de; (*of time*) approcher de.

▶ **draw on** (*savings*) puiser dans.

▶ **draw up 1** (*list, plan*) dresser. **2** *vi* (*of vehicle*) s'arrêter.

dread 1 *vt* (*exam etc*) appréhender; **to d. doing** appréhender de faire. **2** *n* crainte *f*.

dread·ful *adj* épouvantable; (*child*) insupportable; (*ill*) malade.

dread·ful·ly *adv* terriblement; **to be d. sorry** regretter infiniment.

dream 1 *vi** rêver (**of** *or* **of going** de faire). **2** *vt* rêver (**that** que). **3** *n* rêve *m*; **to have a d.** faire un rêve (**about** de); **a d. house**/*etc* une maison/*etc* de rêve.

▶ **dream up** *vt* imaginer.

drea·ry *adj* (*gloomy*) morne; (*boring*) ennuyeux.

drench *vt* tremper; **to get drenched** se faire tremper.

dress 1 *n* (*woman's*) robe *f*; (*style of dressing*) tenue *f*. **2** *vt* (*person*) habiller; (*wound*) panser; **to get dressed** s'habiller. **3** *vi* s'habiller.

dress·er (*furniture*) coiffeuse *f*.

dress·mak·er couturière *f*.

▶ **dress up** *vi* (*smartly*) bien s'habiller; (*in disguise*) se déguiser (**as** en).

drew *pt de* **draw¹,²**.

drib·ble 1 *vi* (*of liquids*) couler lentement. **2** *vti* (*in sports*) dribbler.

dried *adj* (*fruit*) sec (*f* sèche); (*flowers*) séché.

drift *vi* être emporté par le vent *or* le courant, dériver.

drill 1 *n* (*tool*) perceuse *f*, (*bit*) mèche *f*, (*dentist's*) roulette *f*. **2** *vt* (*hole*) percer.

drink 1 *n* boisson *f*, (*glass of sth*) verre *m*; **to give sb a d.** donner (quelque chose) à boire à qn. **2** *vt** boire (**out of** dans); **to d. to sb** boire à la santé de qn.

drink·a·ble *adj* potable; (*not unpleasant*) buvable.

▶ **drink down** *vt* boire.

drink·ing wa·ter eau *f* potable.

▶ **drink up 1** *vt* boire. **2** *vi* finir son verre.

drip 1 *vi* dégouliner; (*of laundry, vegetables*) s'égoutter; (*of faucet*) fuir. **2** *vt* (*paint etc*) laisser couler. **3** *n* goutte *f*, (*fool*) *Fam* nouille *f*.

drip-dry *adj* (*shirt etc*) sans repassage.

drip·ping *adj & adv* **d. (wet)** dégoulinant.

drive 1 *n* promenade *f* en voiture; *(energy)* énergie *f*, *(road to house)* allée *f*; **an hour's d.** une heure de voiture; **four-wheel d. (vehicle)** quatre-quatre *m*. **2** *vt* (vehicle, train, passenger)* conduire; *(machine)* actionner; *(chase away)* chasser; **to d. sb to do** pousser qn à faire; **to d. sb mad** *or* **crazy** rendre qn fou. **3** *vi (drive a car)* conduire; *(go by car)* rouler.

▸**drive along** *vi (in car)* rouler.
▸**drive away 1** *vt (chase)* chasser. **2** *vi* partir (en voiture).
▸**drive back 1** *vt (enemy)* repousser; *(passenger)* ramener (en voiture). **2** *vi* revenir (en voiture).
▸**drive in** *vt (nail)* enfoncer.

driv·el idioties *fpl.*

▸**drive off** *vi* partir (en voiture).
▸**drive on** *vi (in car)* continuer.
▸**drive out** *vt (chase away)* chasser.

driv·er conducteur, -trice *mf*; **(train** *or* **engine) d.** mécanicien *m*; **she's a good d.** elle conduit bien.

driv·er's li·cense permis *m* de conduire.

▸**drive up** *vi* arriver (en voiture).

driv·ing conduite *f.*

driv·ing les·son leçon *f* de conduite.

driv·ing school auto-école *f.*

driv·ing test examen *m* du permis de conduire.

driz·zle 1 *n* bruine *f.* **2** *vi* bruiner.

drool *vi* baver.

droop *vi (of flower)* se faner.

drop 1 *n (of liquid)* goutte *f*; *(fall)* baisse *f* (**in** de). **2** *vt* laisser tomber; *(price, voice)* baisser; *(passenger, goods from vehicle)* déposer; *(put)* mettre; *(leave out)* omettre; **to d. a line to** écrire un mot à. **3** *vi* tomber; *(of price)* baisser.

▸**drop back** *or* **behind** *vi* rester en arrière.

▸**drop in** *vi (visit)* passer (**to sb's house** chez qn).
▸**drop off 1** *vi (fall asleep)* s'endormir; *(fall off)* tomber; *(of sales)* diminuer. **2** *vt (passenger)* déposer.
▸**drop out** *vi (withdraw)* se retirer.

drought sécheresse *f.*

drown 1 *vi* se noyer. **2** *vt* **to d. one-self, to be drowned** se noyer.

drows·y *adj* **to be** *or* **feel d.** avoir sommeil.

drug 1 *n* médicament *m*; *(narcotic)* stupéfiant *m*; **drugs** *(narcotics in general)* la drogue; **to be on drugs, to take drugs** se droguer. **2** *vt* droguer (qn).

drug ad·dict drogué, -ée *mf.*

drug deal·er trafiquant *m* de drogue.

drug·gist pharmacien, -ienne *mf.*

drug·store drugstore *m.*

drum tambour *m*; *(for oil)* bidon *m*; **the drums** *(in pop or jazz group)* la batterie.

drum·mer (joueur, -euse *mf* de) tambour *m*; *(in pop or jazz group)* batteur *m.*

drum·stick baguette *f* (de tambour); *(of chicken)* pilon *m.*

drunk *(pp de drink)* **1** *adj* ivre; **to get d.** s'enivrer; **d. driving** conduite *f* en état d'ivresse. **2** *n* ivrogne *mf.*

drunk·ard ivrogne *mf.*

dry 1 *adj* sec *(f* sèche); *(well, river)* à sec; *(day)* sans pluie; *(book)* aride; **to feel** *or* **be d.** *(thirsty)* avoir soif. **2** *vt* sécher; *(by wiping)* essuyer.

dry-clean *vt* nettoyer à sec.

dry clean·er teinturier, -ière *mf.*

dry clean·ing nettoyage *m* à sec.

dry·er séchoir *m*; *(helmet-style for hair)* casque *m*; *(for laundry)* sèche-linge *m.*

▸**dry off** *vt* sécher.
▸**dry up 1** *vt* sécher. **2** *vi* sécher; *(dry the dishes)* essuyer la vaisselle.

du·al *adj* double.

dub *vt (film)* doubler.

du·bi·ous *adj* douteux; **I'm d.**

about going je me demande si je dois y aller.

duch·ess duchesse f.

duck 1 n canard m. **2** vi se baisser (vivement).

due adj (money) dû (f due) (**to** à); (rent, bill) à payer; **to fall d.** échoir; **he's d. (to arrive)** il doit arriver; **in d. course** en temps utile; (finally) à la longue; **d. to** dû à; (because of) à cause de.

du·el duel m.

duf·fel coat, duf·fle coat duffel-coat m.

duke duc m.

dull adj (boring) ennuyeux; (color) terne; (weather) maussade; (sound, ache) sourde.

dull·ness (of life, town) monotonie f.

du·ly adv (properly) dûment; (as expected) commme prévu.

dumb adj muet (f muette); (stupid) idiot.

dum·my (for clothes) mannequin m; (person) Fam idiot m.

dump 1 vt (garbage) déposer. **2** n (dull town) Fam trou m; (garbage) **d.** tas m d'ordures; (place) dépôt m d'ordures; (room) dépotoir m.

dump truck camion m à benne basculante.

du·plex (apartment) duplex m.

du·pli·cate double m; **in d.** en deux exemplaires; **a d. copy** une copie en double.

du·ra·ble adj (material) résistant.

du·ra·tion durée f.

dur·ing prep pendant.

dusk crépuscule m.

dust 1 n poussière f. **2** vt (furniture etc) essuyer (la poussière de). **3** vi faire la poussière.

dust cloth chiffon m (à poussière).

dust jack·et (for book) jaquette f.

dust·y adj poussiéreux.

Dutch 1 adj hollandais, néerlandais. **2** n (language) hollandais m,

néerlandais m; **the D.** les Hollandais mpl, les Néerlandais mpl.

Dutch·man, pl **-men** Hollandais m, Néerlandais m.

Dutch·wom·an, pl **-women** Hollandaise f, Néerlandaise f.

du·ty devoir m; (tax) droit m; **duties** (responsibilities) fonctions fpl; **on d.** (policeman, teacher) de service; (doctor) de garde; **off d.** libre.

du·ty-free adj (goods, shop) hors-taxe inv.

du·vet couette f.

DVD abbr (digital versatile disk, digital video disk) DVD m; **D. player** lecteur m (de) DVD.

dwarf nain m, naine f.

dye 1 n teinture f. **2** vt teindre; **to d. green** teindre en vert.

dy·nam·ic adj dynamique.

dy·na·mite dynamite f.

dy·na·mo, pl **-os** dynamo f.

dys·lex·ic adj & n dyslexique (mf).

E

each 1 adj chaque. **2** pron e. (one) chacun, -une; **e. other** l'un(e) l'autre, pl les un(e)s les autres; **e. of us** chacun, -une d'entre nous.

ea·ger adj impatient (**to do** de faire); (enthusiastic) plein d'enthousiasme; **to be e. to do** (want) tenir (beaucoup) à faire.

ea·ger·ly adv avec enthousiasme; (to await) impatience.

ea·ger·ness impatience f (**to do** de faire).

ea·gle aigle m.

ear oreille f.

ear·ache mal m d'oreille; **to have an e.** avoir mal à l'oreille.

ear·ly 1 adj (first) premier; (age) jeune; **it's e.** (on clock) il est tôt; (re-

ferring to meeting) c'est tôt; **it's too e. to get up** il est trop tôt pour se lever; **to be e.** *(ahead of time)* être en avance; **to have an e. meal/ night** manger/se coucher de bonne heure; **in e. summer** au début de l'été. **2** *adv* tôt, de bonne heure; *(ahead of time)* en avance; **as e. as possible** le plus tôt possible; **earlier (on)** plus tôt.

earn *vt* gagner; *(interest)* rapporter.

ear·nest 1 *adj* sérieux, -euse. **2** *n* **in e.** sérieusement.

earn·ings *npl (wages)* rémunérations *fpl.*

ear·phones *npl* casque *m.*

ear·plug boule *f* Quies®.

ear·ring boucle *f* d'oreille.

earth *(world, ground)* terre *f*; **where/what on e.?** où/que diable?

earth·quake tremblement *m* de terre.

ease 1 *n* facilité *f*; **with e.** facilement; **(ill) at e.** (mal) à l'aise. **2** *vt (pain)* soulager; *(mind)* calmer.

ease (off *or* **up)** *vi (become less)* diminuer; *(of pain)* se calmer; *(not work so hard)* se relâcher.

ea·sel chevalet *m.*

▸ **ease off** *vti* enlever doucement.

eas·i·ly *adv* facilement; **e. the best**/*etc* de loin le meilleur/*etc.*

east 1 *n* est *m*; **(to the) e. of** à l'est de. **2** *adj (coast)* est *inv*; *(wind)* d'est. **3** *adv* à l'est.

east·bound *adj* en direction de l'est.

Eas·ter Pâques *m sing or fpl*; **Happy E.!** joyeuses Pâques!

east·ern *adj (coast)* est *inv*; **E. Europe** Europe *f* de l'Est.

east·ward(s) *adj & adv* vers l'est.

eas·y 1 *adj* facile; *(life)* tranquille; **it's e. to do** c'est facile à faire. **2** *adv* doucement; **go e. on** *(sugar etc)* vas-y doucement avec; *(person)* ne sois pas trop dur avec; **take it e.** calme-toi; *(rest)* repose-toi; *(work less)* ne te fatigue pas.

eas·y chair fauteuil *m.*

eas·y·go·ing *adj (carefree)* insouciant; *(easy to get along with)* facile à vivre.

eat* 1 *vt* manger; *(meal)* prendre. **2** *vi* manger.

eat·er big e. gros mangeur *m*, grosse mangeuse *f.*

▸ **eat out** *vi* manger dehors.

▸ **eat up** *vt (finish)* finir.

ec·cen·tric *adj & n* excentrique *(mf).*

ech·o, *pl* **-oes 1** *n* écho *m*. **2** *vi* the explosion/*etc* echoed l'écho de l'explosion/*etc* se répercuta.

ec·o·nom·ic *adj* économique; *(profitable)* rentable.

ec·o·nom·i·cal *adj* économique.

e·con·o·mize *vti* économiser (**on** sur).

e·con·o·my class *(on aircraft)* classe *f* touriste.

edge bord *m*; *(of forest)* lisière *f*; *(of town)* abords *mpl*; *(of page)* marge *f*; *(of knife)* tranchant *m*; **on e.** énervé; *(nerves)* tendu.

▸ **edge forward** *vi* avancer doucement.

ed·i·ble *adj* comestible; *(not unpleasant)* mangeable.

ed·it *vt (newspaper)* diriger; *(article)* mettre au point; *(film)* monter; *(text)* éditer; *(compile)* rédiger.

e·di·tion édition *f.*

ed·i·tor *(of newspaper)* rédacteur *m* en chef; *(compiler)* rédacteur, -trice *mf.*

ed·i·to·ri·al e. staff rédaction *f.*

ed·u·cate *vt* éduquer; *(pupil, mind)* former.

ed·u·cat·ed *adj* **(well-)e.** instruit.

ed·u·ca·tion éducation *f*; *(teaching, training)* formation *f.*

ed·u·ca·tion·al *adj (establishment)* d'enseignement; *(game)* éducatif.

eel anguille *f.*

ef·fect effet *m* (**on** sur); **to put into e.** mettre en application; **to come**

into e., to take e. (of law) entrer en vigueur; **to take e.** (of drug) agir; **to have an e.** (of medicine) faire de l'effet.

ef·fec·tive adj (efficient) efficace; (striking) frappant.

ef·fec·tive·ly adv efficacement; (in fact) effectivement.

ef·fi·cien·cy efficacité f, (of machine) performances fpl.

ef·fi·cient adj efficace; (machine) performant.

ef·fi·cient·ly adv efficacement; **to work e.** (of machine) bien fonctionner.

ef·fort effort m; **to make an e.** faire un effort (**to** pour); **it isn't worth the e.** ça ne or n'en vaut pas la peine.

e.g. abbr par exemple.

egg œuf m.

egg·cup coquetier m.

egg·plant aubergine f.

egg tim·er sablier m.

e·go amour-propre m; **to have an enormous e.** être imbu de soi-même.

E·gyp·tian 1 n Égyptien, -ienne mf. **2** adj égyptien, -ienne.

ei·der·down édredon m.

eight adj & n huit (m).

eight·een adj & n dix-huit (m).

eighth adj & n huitième (mf).

eight·y adj & n quatre-vingts (m); **e.-one** quatre-vingt-un.

ei·ther 1 adj & pron (one or other) l'un(e) ou l'autre; (with negative) ni l'un(e) ni l'autre; (each) chaque; **on e. side** de chaque côté. **2** adv **she can't swim e.** elle ne sait pas nager non plus; **I don't e.** (ni) moi non plus. **3** conj **e…or** ou (bien)…ou (bien); (with negative) ni…ni.

e·lab·o·rate 1 vt (work out) élaborer; (explain) décrire en détail. **2** vi donner des détails; **to e. on sth** développer qch. **3** adj (meal, system) élaboré; (pattern, design) compliqué; (style, costume) recherché.

e·las·tic adj & n élastique (m).

el·bow 1 n coude m. **2** vt **to e. one's way** se frayer un chemin (à coups de coude) (**through** à travers).

eld·er adj & n (of two people) aîné, -ée (mf).

eld·er·ly adj âgé.

eld·est adj & n aîné, -ée (mf); **his or her e. brother** l'aîné de ses frères.

e·lect vt élire (qn) (**to** à).

e·lec·tion 1 n élection f. **2** adj (campaign) électoral; (day, results) du scrutin.

e·lec·tor·ate électorat m.

e·lec·tric adj électrique; **e. blanket** couverture f chauffante; **e. chair** chaise f électrique; **e. shock** décharge f électrique.

e·lec·tri·cal adj éléctrique.

e·lec·tri·cian électricien m.

e·lec·tri·cian's tape chatterton m.

e·lec·tric·i·ty électricité f.

e·lec·tro·cute vt électrocuter.

e·lec·tron·ic adj électronique.

e·lec·tron·ics électronique f.

el·e·gance élégance f.

el·e·gant adj élégant.

el·e·gant·ly adv avec élégance.

el·e·ment élément m; (of heater) résistance f.

el·e·men·ta·ry adj élémentaire; (school) primaire.

el·e·phant éléphant m.

el·e·va·tor ascenseur m.

el·ev·en adj & n onze (m).

el·ev·enth adj & n onzième (mf).

el·i·gi·ble adj (for post) admissible (**for** à); **to be e. for** (entitled to) avoir droit à.

e·lim·i·nate vt supprimer; (applicant, possibility) éliminer.

e·lite élite f.

else adv d'autre; **everybody e.** tous les autres; **somebody/nobody/ nothing e.** quelqu'un/personne/ rien d'autre; **something e.** autre chose; **anything e.?** encore quelque chose? **somewhere** e. ailleurs; **how** e.? de quelle autre façon?; **or** e. ou bien.

else·where adv ailleurs.

e·lude vt (of word, name) échapper à (qn).

e-mail 1 n courrier m électronique. **2** vt envoyer un courrier électronique à.

em·bark vi (s')embarquer.

▸ **em·bark on** vt (start) commencer.

em·bar·rass vt embarrasser.

em·bar·rass·ing adj embarrassant.

em·bar·rass·ment embarras m.

em·bas·sy ambassade f.

em·blem emblème m.

em·brace 1 vt (hug) étreindre. **2** vi s'étreindre. **3** n étreinte f.

em·broi·der vt (cloth) broder.

em·broi·der·y broderie f.

em·bry·o embryon m.

em·er·ald émeraude f.

e·merge vi apparaître (**from** de); (from hole) sortir; (of truth, from water) émerger.

e·mer·gen·cy 1 n urgence f; **in an** e. en cas d'urgence. **2** adj (measure) d'urgence; (exit, brake) de secours; e. **room** salle f des urgences; e. **landing** atterrissage m forcé.

em·i·grate vi émigrer.

e·mo·tion (strength of feeling) émotion f; (joy, love etc) sentiment m.

e·mo·tion·al adj (person, reaction) émotif; (story) émouvant.

em·per·or empereur m.

em·pha·sis (in word or phrase) accent m; **to lay** or **put** e. **on** mettre l'accent sur.

em·pha·size vt souligner (**that** que).

em·pire empire m.

em·ploy vt employer.

em·ploy·ee employé, -ée mf.

em·ploy·er patron, -onne mf.

em·ploy·ment emploi m; **place of** e. lieu m de travail.

em·ploy·ment a·gen·cy bureau m de placement.

emp·ty 1 adj vide; (stomach) creux; (threat, promise) vain; **to return** e.**-handed** revenir les mains vides. **2** vi (of building, tank etc) se vider.

emp·ty (out) vt (box, liquid etc) vider; (vehicle) décharger; (objects in box etc) sortir (**from** de).

e·mul·sion émulsion f.

en·a·ble vt **to** e. **sb to do** permettre à qn de faire.

en·chant·ing adj charmant, enchanteur (f -eresse).

en·close vt (send with letter) joindre (**in, with** à); (fence off) clôturer.

en·closed adj (space) clos; (receipt etc) ci-joint.

en·clo·sure (in letter) pièce f jointe; (place) enceinte f.

en·coun·ter 1 vt rencontrer. **2** n rencontre f.

en·cour·age vt encourager (**to do** à faire).

en·cour·age·ment encouragement m.

en·cy·clo·pe·di·a encyclopédie f.

end 1 n (of street, box etc) bout m; (of meeting, month, book etc) fin f; (purpose) fin f, but m; at an e. (discussion etc) fini; (patience) à bout; **in the** e. à la fin; **to come to an** e. prendre fin; **to put an** e. **to, bring to an** e. mettre fin à; **no** e. **of** Fam beaucoup de; **for days on** e. pendant des jours et des jours. **2** vt finir (**with** par); (rumor) mettre fin à. **3** vi finir; **to** e. **in failure** se solder par un échec.

en·dan·ger vt mettre en danger.

end·ing fin f; (of word) terminaison f.

en·dive (curly) chicorée f; (smooth) endive f.

end·less adj interminable.

en·dorse vt (check) endosser; (action) approuver.

en·dorse·ment (signature) aval m; (backing) appui m; (on check) endossement m.

▶**end up** vi to e. up doing finir par faire; **to e. up in** (place) se retrouver à; **he ended up in prison/a doctor** il a fini en prison/par devenir médecin.

en·dur·ance endurance f.

en·dure vt supporter (**doing** de faire).

en·e·my n & adj ennemi, -ie (mf).

en·er·get·ic adj énergique.

en·er·gy 1 n énergie f. **2** adj (crisis, resources etc) énergétique.

en·force vt (law) faire respecter.

en·gaged adj e. (to be married) fiancé; **to get e.** se fiancer.

en·gage·ment (to marry) fiançailles fpl; (meeting) rendez-vous m inv; **e. ring** bague f de fiançailles.

en·gine (of vehicle) moteur m; (of train) locomotive f; (of jet) réacteur m.

en·gi·neer ingénieur m; (repairer) dépanneur, -euse mf.

en·gi·neer·ing ingénierie f, génie m.

Eng·lish 1 adj anglais; (teacher) d'anglais; **the E. Channel** la Manche. **2** n (language) anglais m; **the E.** les Anglais mpl.

Eng·lish·man, pl **-men** Anglais m.

Eng·lish-speak·ing adj anglophone.

Eng·lish·wom·an, pl **-women** Anglaise f.

en·grave vt graver.

en·grav·ing gravure f.

en·joy vt aimer (**doing** faire); (meal) apprécier; **to e. the evening** passer une bonne soirée; **to e. one-self** s'amuser; **to e. being in Paris** se plaire à Paris.

en·joy·a·ble adj agréable.

en·joy·ment plaisir m.

en·large vt agrandir.

en·light·en vt éclairer (**sb on** or **about sth** qn sur qch).

en·list 1 vt (recruit) engager; (supporter) recruter; (support, help) s'assurer. **2** vi (in the army) s'engager.

e·nor·mous adj énorme.

e·nor·mous·ly adv (very much) énormément; (very) extrêmement.

e·nough 1 adj & n assez (de); **e. time/cups/etc** assez de temps/de tasses/etc; **to have e. to live on** avoir de quoi vivre; **e. to drink** assez à boire; **to have had e.** en avoir assez de; **that's e.** ça suffit. **2** adv assez; **big/good/etc e.** assez grand/bon/etc (**to** pour).

en·quire vi = inquire.

en·quir·y n = inquiry.

en·roll vi s'inscrire (**in, for** à).

en·roll·ment inscription f.

en·sure vt assurer; **to e. that** s'assurer que.

en·tail vt supposer.

en·ter 1 vt (room, vehicle etc) entrer dans; (university) s'inscrire à; (race, competition) s'inscrire pour; (write down) inscrire (**in** dans); **to e. sb/sth in** (competition) présenter qn/qch à; **it didn't e. my head** or **mind** ça ne m'est pas venu à l'esprit. **2** vi entrer.

▶**enter into** vt (conversation) entrer en; (career) entrer dans; (agreement) conclure.

en·ter·prise (undertaking, firm) entreprise f; (spirit) initiative f.

en·ter·pris·ing adj plein d'initiative.

en·ter·tain 1 vt amuser; (guest) recevoir. **2** vi (receive guests) recevoir.

en·ter·tain·er artiste mf.

en·ter·tain·ing adj amusant.

en·ter·tain·ment amusement m; (show) spectacle m.

en·thu·si·asm enthousiasme m.

en·thu·si·ast enthousiaste mf;

jazz/*etc* e. passionné, -ée *mf* de jazz/*etc*.

en·thu·si·as·tic *adj* enthousiaste; (*golfer etc*) passionné; **to be e. about** (*hobby*) être passionné de; (*gift*) être emballé par; **to get e.** s'emballer (**about** pour).

en·thu·si·as·ti·cal·ly *adv* avec enthousiasme.

en·tire *adj* entier.

en·tire·ly *adv* tout à fait.

en·ti·tle *vt* to e. sb to do donner à qn le droit de faire; **to e. sb to sth** donner à qn (le) droit à qch.

en·ti·tled *adj* **to be e. to do** avoir le droit de faire; **to be e. to sth** avoir droit à qch.

en·trance entrée *f* (**to** de); (*to university*) admission *f* (**to** à); **e. exam** examen *m* d'entrée.

en·trant (*in race*) concurrent, -ente *mf*, (*for exam*) candidat, -ate *mf*.

en·try (*way in, action*) entrée *f*; (*bookkeeping item*) écriture *f*; (*dictionary term*) entrée *f*, (*in competition*) objet *m* (*or* œuvre *f or* projet *m*) soumis au jury; **'no e.'** (*doorway*) 'entrée interdite'; (*road sign*) 'sens interdit'.

en·try form feuille *f* d'inscription.

en·ve·lope enveloppe *f*.

en·vi·ous *adj* envieux (**of sth** de qch); **e. of sb** jaloux de qn.

en·vi·ron·ment milieu *m*; (*natural*) environnement *m*.

en·vi·ron·men·tal *adj* du milieu; (*natural*) de l'environnement; (*group*) écologiste; (*issue*) écologique, lié à l'environnement.

en·vis·age, en·vi·sion *vt* (*imagine*) envisager; (*foresee*) prévoir.

en·vy 1 *n* envie *f*. **2** *vt* envier (**sb sth** qch à qn).

ep·i·dem·ic épidémie *f*.

ep·i·sode épisode *m*.

e·qual 1 *adj* égal (**to** à); **to be e. to** (*number*) égaler; **she's e. to** (*task*) elle est à la hauteur de. **2** *n* (*person*) égal, -ale *mf*.

e·qual·i·ty égalité *f*.

e·qual·ize *vi* (*score*) égaliser.

e·qual·ly *adv* également; (*to divide*) en parts égales.

e·qua·tion équation *f*.

e·qua·tor équateur *m*.

e·quip *vt* équiper (**with** de); (**well-) equipped with** pourvu de; (**well-) equipped to do** compétent pour faire.

e·quip·ment équipement (*m*).

e·quiv·a·lent *adj* & *n* équivalent (*m*).

e·ra époque *f*, (*historical, geological*) ère *f*.

e·rase *vt* effacer.

e·ras·er gomme *f*.

e·rect 1 *adj* (*upright*) (bien) droit. **2** *vt* construire; (*statue etc*) ériger; (*scaffolding, tent*) monter.

e·ro·sion érosion *f*.

er·rand commission *f*.

er·rat·ic *adj* (*service, machine etc*) capricieux; (*person*) lunatique.

er·ror erreur *f*; **to do sth in e.** faire qch par erreur.

e·rupt *vi* (*volcano*) entrer en éruption; (*war, violence*) éclater.

e·rup·tion (*of volcano*) éruption *f*, (*of violence*) flambée *f*.

es·ca·la·tor escalier *m* roulant.

es·cape 1 *vi* s'échapper; **to e. from** (*person*) échapper à; (*place*) s'échapper de. **2** *vt* (*death*) échapper à; (*punishment*) éviter; **her name escapes me** son nom m'échappe. **3** *n* (*of gas*) fuite *f*, (*of person*) évasion *f*.

es·cort 1 *n* (*soldiers etc*) escorte *f*. **2** *vt* escorter.

Es·ki·mo, *pl* -os Esquimau, -aude *mf*.

es·pe·cial·ly *adv* (*tout*) spécialement; **e. as** d'autant plus que.

es·pres·so, *pl* -os (*café m*) express *m inv*.

es·say (*at school*) rédaction *f*.

es·sen·tial *adj* essentiel.

es·sen·tial·ly *adv* essentiellement.

es·tab·lish vt établir.

es·tab·lished adj (company) solide; (fact) reconnu; (reputation) établi.

es·tab·lish·ment (institution, firm) établissement m.

es·tate (land) terre(s) f(pl); (property after death) succession f.

es·ti·mate 1 vt estimer (that que). **2** n évaluation f; (price for work to be done) devis m.

etch·ing eau-forte f.

e·ter·nal adj éternel.

eth·ics (study) éthique f; (principles) morale f; (of profession) déontologie f.

et·i·quette bienséances fpl.

Euro- prefix euro-.

Eu·ro·pe·an 1 adj européen, -éenne. **2** n Européen, -éenne.

Eu·ro·pe·an Un·ion Union f européenne.

e·vac·u·ate vt évacuer.

e·vade vt éviter; (pursuer, tax) échapper à; (law, question) éluder.

e·val·u·ate vt évaluer (at à).

e·vap·o·rat·ed milk lait m concentré.

eve on the e. of à la veille de.

e·ven 1 adj (flat) uni; (equal) égal; (regular) régulier; (number) pair; to get e. with sb se venger de qn; we're e. nous sommes quittes; (in score) nous sommes à égalité; to break e. (financially) s'y retrouver. **2** adv même; e. better/more encore mieux/plus; e. if or though même si; e. so quand même.

eve·ning soir m; (whole evening, event) soirée f; in the e. le soir; at seven in the e. à sept heures du soir; every Tuesday e. tous les mardis soir; all e. (long) toute la soirée.

eve·ning dress tenue f de soirée.

eve·ning gown robe f du soir.

e·ven·ly adv de manière égale; (regularly) régulièrement.

▸ **even out** or **up** vt égaliser.

e·vent événement m; (in sport)

épreuve f; in the e. of death en cas de décès; in any e. en tout cas.

e·ven·tu·al adj final.

e·ven·tu·al·ly adv finalement; (some day or other) un jour ou l'autre.

ev·er adv jamais; more than e. plus que jamais; nothing e. jamais rien; hardly e. presque jamais; the first e. le tout premier; e. since (that event etc) depuis; e. since then depuis lors; for e. pour toujours; (continually) sans cesse; e. so happy/etc vraiment heureux/etc; why e. not? et pourquoi pas?

eve·ry adj chaque; e. one chacun, -une; e. single one tous or toutes (sans exception); e. other day tous les deux jours; e. so often, e. now and then de temps en temps.

eve·ry·bod·y pron tout le monde; e. in turn chacun or chacune à son tour.

eve·ry·day adj (life) de tous les jours; (ordinary) banal (mpl banals); in e. use d'usage courant.

eve·ry·one pron = **everybody**.

eve·ry·place adv = **everywhere**.

eve·ry·thing pron tout; e. I have tout ce que j'ai.

eve·ry·where adv partout; e. she goes où qu'elle aille.

ev·i·dence preuve(s) f(pl); (given by witness etc) témoignage m; e. of (wear etc) des signes mpl de.

ev·i·dent adj évident (that que).

ev·i·dent·ly adv évidemment; (apparently) apparemment.

e·vil 1 adj (influence, person) malfaisant; (deed, system) mauvais. **2** n mal m.

e·voke vt évoquer.

ewe brebis f.

ex- prefix ex-; **ex-wife** ex-femme f.

ex·act adj exact; to be e. about sth préciser qch.

ex·act·ly adv exactement.

ex·ag·ger·ate vti exagérer.

ex·ag·ger·a·tion exagération f.

ex·am examen m.

ex·am·i·na·tion (in school etc) examen m.

ex·am·ine vt examiner; (accounts, luggage) vérifier; (passport) contrôler; (question) interroger.

ex·am·in·er examinateur, -trice mf.

ex·am·ple exemple m; **for e.** par example; **to set an e.** donner l'exemple (**to** à).

ex·ceed vt dépasser.

ex·cel vi **to e. in sth** être excellent en qch.

ex·cel·lent adj excellent.

ex·cept prep sauf, excepté; **e. for** à part; **e. that** sauf que.

ex·cep·tion exception f; **with the e. of** à l'exception de.

ex·cep·tion·al adj exceptionnel.

ex·cep·tion·al·ly adv exceptionnellement.

ex·cerpt extrait m.

ex·cess 1 n excès m; (surplus) excédent m. **2** adj **e. fare** supplément m (de billet); **e. luggage** or **baggage** excédent m de bagages.

ex·ces·sive adj excessif.

ex·ces·sive·ly adv (too, too much) excessivement; (very) extrêmement.

ex·change 1 vt échanger (**for** contre). **2** n échange m; (of foreign currencies) change m; (telephone) **e. central** m (téléphonique); **in e.** en échange (**for** de).

ex·cite vt (enthuse) passionner.

ex·cit·ed adj (happy) surexcité; (nervous) énervé; **to get e.** (nervous, enthusiastic) s'exciter; **to be e. about** (new car etc) se réjouir de.

ex·cite·ment agitation f, (emotion) vive émotion f.

ex·cit·ing adj (book etc) passionnant.

ex·claim vti s'exclamer (**that** que).

ex·cla·ma·tion point point m d'exclamation.

ex·clude vt exclure (**from** de).

ex·clu·sive adj exclusif; (club) fermé; **e. of wine/etc** vin/etc non compris.

ex·cur·sion excursion f.

ex·cuse 1 vt excuser (**sb for doing** qn d'avoir fait, qn de faire); (exempt) dispenser (**from** de). **2** n excuse f.

ex·e·cute vt (criminal) exécuter.

ex·e·cu·tion exécution f.

ex·ec·u·tive 1 adj (job) de cadre; (car, plane) de direction. **2** n (person) cadre m; **senior e.** cadre m supérieur; **junior e.** jeune cadre m; **sales e.** cadre m commercial.

ex·empt 1 adj dispensé (**from** de). **2** vt dispenser (**from** de).

ex·emp·tion dispense f.

ex·ert vt exercer; **to e. oneself** (physically) se dépenser; **don't e. yourself!** ne te fatigue pas!

ex·er·tion effort m.

ex·haust 1 vt épuiser. **2** n **e. (pipe)** tuyau m d'échappement.

ex·haust·ed adj épuisé; **to become e.** s'épuiser.

ex·haust·ing adj épuisant.

ex·hib·it 1 vt (put on display) exposer. **2** n objet m exposé.

ex·hi·bi·tion exposition f.

ex·hib·i·tor exposant, -ante mf.

ex·ile 1 n (banishment) exil m; (person) exilé, -ée m f. **2** vt exiler.

ex·ist vi exister; (live) vivre (**on** de).

ex·is·tence existence f; **to be in e.** exister.

ex·ist·ing adj (situation) actuel.

ex·it sortie f.

ex·or·bi·tant adj exorbitant.

ex·pand 1 vt (trade, ideas) développer; (production) augmenter; (gas, metal) dilater. **2** vi se développer; (of production) augmenter; (of gas, metal) se dilater.

ex·panse étendue f.

ex·pan·sion (of trade etc) développement m.

ex·pect vt s'attendre à; (think)

penser (**that** que); *(suppose)* supposer (**that** que); *(await)* attendre; **to e. sth from sb/sth** attendre qch de qn/qch; **to e. to do** compter faire; **to e. that** s'attendre à ce que (+ *subjunctive)*; **I e. you to come** *(want)* je compte sur votre présence; **it was expected** c'était prévu; **she's expecting (a baby)** elle attend un bébé.

ex·pec·ta·tion attente *f.*

ex·pe·di·tion expédition *f.*

ex·pel *vt (from school)* renvoyer.

ex·pen·di·ture *(money)* dépenses *fpl.*

ex·pense frais *mpl*; **business expenses** frais *mpl* généraux; **at sb's e.** aux dépens de qn.

ex·pen·sive *adj* cher.

ex·pe·ri·ence 1 *n* expérience *f*; **he's had e. of driving** il a déjà conduit. **2** *vt* connaître; *(difficulty)* éprouver.

ex·pe·ri·enced *adj* expérimenté; **to be e. in** s'y connaître en.

ex·per·i·ment 1 *n* expérience *f.* **2** *vi* faire une expérience *or* des expériences.

ex·pert expert *m* (**on, in** en); **e. advice** le conseil d'un expert.

ex·per·tise compétence *f* (**in** en).

ex·pi·ra·tion date date *f* d'expiration.

ex·pire *vi* expirer.

ex·pired *adj (ticket, passport etc)* périmé.

ex·plain *vt* expliquer (**to** à; **that** que).

▶ **explain away** *vt* justifier.

ex·pla·na·tion explication *f.*

ex·plic·it *adj* explicite.

ex·plode *vi* exploser.

ex·ploi·ta·tion exploration *f.*

ex·plore *vt* explorer; *(causes etc)* examiner.

ex·plor·er explorateur, -trice *mf.*

ex·plo·sion explosif *m.*

ex·port 1 *n* exportation *f.* **2** *vt* exporter; **from** de).

ex·pose *vt* exposer (**to** à); *(plot etc)* révéler; *(crook etc)* démasquer.

ex·press 1 *vt* exprimer; **to e. oneself** s'exprimer. **2** *adj (letter, delivery)* exprès *inv*; *(train)* rapide. **3** *adv (send)* par express *or* Chronopost®. **4** *n (train)* rapide *m.*

ex·pres·sion *(phrase, look)* expression *f.*

ex·press·way autoroute *f.*

ex·tend 1 *vt (arm, business)* étendre; *(line, visit)* prolonger (**by** de); *(house)* agrandir; *(time limit)* reculer. **2** *vi* s'étendre (**to** jusqu'à); *(in time)* se prolonger.

ex·ten·sion *(for table)* rallonge *f*; *(to building)* agrandissement(s) *m(pl)*; *(of phone)* appareil *m* supplémentaire; *(of office phone)* poste *m*; **e. cord** rallonge *f.*

ex·ten·sive *adj* étendu; *(repairs, damage)* important.

ex·ten·sive·ly *adv (very much)* énormément, considérablement.

ex·tent *(scope)* étendue *f*; *(size)* importance *f*; **to a large/certain e.** dans une large/certaine mesure; **to such an e. that** à tel point que.

ex·te·ri·or *adj & n* extérieur *(m).*

ex·ter·nal *adj* extérieur; **for e. use** *(medicine)* à usage externe.

ex·tin·guish·er *(fire)* **e.** extincteur *m.*

ex·tra 1 *adj* supplémentaire; **one e. glass** un verre de *or* en plus; **to be e.** *(spare)* être en trop; *(cost more)* être en supplément; **e. charge** *or* **portion** supplément *m.* **2** *adv* **to pay e.** payer un supplément; **wine costs** *or* **is 50 euros e.** il y a un supplément de 50 euros pour le vin. **3** *n (perk)* à-côté *m*; **extras** *(expenses)* frais *mpl* supplémentaires.

ex·tra- *prefix* extra-.

ex·tract 1 *vt* extraire (**from** de). **2** *n* extrait *m.*

ex·tra·cur·ric·u·lar adj extrascolaire.

ex·traor·di·nar·y adj extraordinaire.

ex·tra·spe·cial adj (occasion) très spécial.

ex·trav·a·gant adj (wasteful with money) dépensier.

ex·treme 1 adj extrême; (danger, poverty) très grand. **2** n extrême m.

ex·treme·ly adv extrêmement.

eye œil m (pl yeux); **to keep an e. on** surveiller; **to lay** or **set eyes on** voir; **to take one's eyes off sb/sth** quitter qn/qch des yeux.

eye·brow sourcil m.

eye·glass·es npl lunettes fpl.

eye·lash cil m.

eye·lid paupière f.

eye·lin·er eye-liner m.

eye shad·ow fard m à paupières.

eye·sight vue f.

F

fab·ric tissu m, étoffe f.

fab·u·lous adj (wonderful) Fam formidable.

face 1 n (of person) visage m, figure f; (of clock) cadran m; **f. down** face contre terre; (thing) tourné à l'envers; (look in the face) **f. to f.** face à face; **to make faces** faire des grimaces. **2** vt (danger, problem etc) faire face à; (accept) accepter; (look in the face) regarder (qn) bien en face; (be opposite) être en face de; (of window) donner sur; **faced with** (problem) confronté à; **he can't f. leaving** il n'a pas le courage de partir. **3** vi (of house) être orienté (**north**/etc au nord/etc); (be turned) être tourné (**towards** vers).

face·cloth gant m de toilette.

▸ **face up to** vt (danger, problem) faire face à; (fact) accepter.

fa·cil·i·tate vt faciliter.

fa·cil·i·ties npl (for sports, cooking etc) équipements mpl; (in harbor, airport) installations fpl.

fact fait m; **as a matter of f., in f.** en fait.

fac·tor facteur m.

fac·to·ry usine f.

fac·tu·al adj basé sur les faits.

fade vi (of flower) se faner; (of light) baisser; (of color) passer; (of fabric) se décolorer.

fade (a·way) vi (of sound) s'affaiblir.

fail 1 vi échouer; (of business) faire faillite; (of health, sight) baisser; (of brakes) lâcher. **2** vt (exam) rater, échouer à; (candidate) refuser, recaler; **to f. to do** (forget) manquer de faire; (not be able) ne pas arriver à faire. **3** n **without f.** à coup sûr.

failed adj (attempt, poet) manqué.

fail·ing 1 n défaut m. **2** prep **f. that** à défaut.

fail·ure échec m; (of business) faillite f; (person) raté, -ée mf; **f. to do** incapacité f de faire.

faint 1 adj faible; (color) pâle; **I haven't got the faintest idea** je n'en ai pas la moindre idée; **to feel f.** se trouver mal. **2** vi s'évanouir.

faint·ly adv faiblement; (slightly) légèrement.

fair¹ (for trade) foire f; (for entertainment) fête f foraine, kermesse f; (for charity) fête f.

fair² adj (just) juste; (game, fight) loyal; **f. enough!** très bien! ■ (rather good) passable; (weather) beau; (price) raisonnable; **a f. amount (of)** pas mal (de).

fair³ adj (hair, person) blond.

fair-haired adj blond.

fair·ly adv (to treat) équitablement; (rather) assez.

fair·ness justice f; (of person) impartialité f.

fair play fair-play *m inv.*
fair-sized *adj* assez grand.
fair·y fée *f*; **f. tale** *or* **story** conte *m* de fées.
faith foi *f*; **to have f. in sb** avoir confiance en qn.
faith·ful *adj* fidèle (**to** à).
fake 1 *n* faux *m*; *(person)* imposteur *m*. **2** *vt (document etc)* falsifier. **3** *vi* faire semblant. **4** *adj* faux (*f* fausse).
fall 1 *n* chute *f*; *(in price etc)* baisse *f* (**in** de); *(season)* automne *m*. **2** *vi** tomber; **to f. off** *or* **out of** *or* **down sth** tomber de qch; **to f. over** *(chair)* tomber en butant contre; *(balcony)* tomber de; **to f. ill** tomber malade.
▸ **fall apart** *vi (of machine)* tomber en morceaux; *(of group)* se défaire.
▸ **fall back on** *vt (as last resort)* se rabattre sur.
▸ **fall behind** *vi* rester en arrière; *(in work, payments)* prendre du retard.
▸ **fall down** *vi* tomber; *(of building)* s'effondrer.
▸ **fall for** *vt* tomber amoureux de; *(trick)* se laisser prendre à.
▸ **fall in** *vi (collapse)* s'écrouler.
▸ **fall off** *vi (come off)* se détacher; *(of numbers)* diminuer.
▸ **fall out** *vi (quarrel)* se brouiller (**with** avec).
▸ **fall over** *vi* tomber; *(of table, vase)* se renverser.
▸ **fall through** *vi (of plan)* tomber à l'eau.
false *adj* faux (*f* fausse).
fame renommée *f*.
fa·mil·iar *adj* familier (**to** à); **f. with sb** *(too friendly)* familier avec qn; **to be f. with** *(know)* connaître.
fa·mil·iar·i·ty familiarité *f* (**with** avec).
fam·i·ly famille *f*.
fa·mous *adj* célèbre (**for** pour).
fan¹ *(held in hand)* éventail *m*; *(mechanical)* ventilateur *m*.
fan² *(of person)* fan *m*; *(of team etc)* supporter *m*; **to be a jazz/sports f.** être passionné de jazz/de sport.

fan·cy 1 *n* **I took a f. to it** j'en ai eu envie. **2** *adj (hat, button etc)* fantaisie *inv*. **3** *int* **f. (that)!** tiens (donc)!
fan·tas·tic *adj* fantastique.
fan·ta·sy *(dream)* fantasme *m*; *(imagination)* fantaisie *f*.
far 1 *adv (distance)* loin; **f. bigger/** *etc* beaucoup plus grand/*etc* (**than** que); **how f. is it to?** combien y a-t-il d'ici là?; **so f.** *(time)* jusqu'ici; **as f. as** *(place)* jusqu'à; **as f. as I know** autant que je sache; **as f. as I'm concerned** en ce qui me concerne; **f. from** doing loin de faire; **f. away** *or* **off** au loin; **by f.** de loin. **2** *adj (side, end)* autre.
far·a·way *adj (country)* lointain.
farce farce *f*.
fare *(price)* prix *m* du billet.
fare·well *int* adieu.
far-fetched *adj* tiré par les cheveux.
farm 1 *n* ferme *f*. **2** *adj (worker, produce)* agricole; **f. land** terres *fpl* cultivées. **3** *vt* cultiver.
farm·er fermier, -ière *mf*.
farm·house ferme *f*.
farm·ing agriculture *f*.
farm·yard basse-cour *f*, cour *f* de ferme.
far-off *adj* lointain.
far-reach·ing *adj* de grande portée.
far·ther *adv* plus loin; **to get f. away** s'éloigner.
far·thest 1 *adj* le plus éloigné. **2** *adv* le plus loin.
fas·ci·nate *vt* fasciner.
fas·ci·nat·ing *adj* fascinant.
fas·ci·na·tion fascination *f*.
fash·ion *(style in clothes)* mode *f*; *(manner)* façon *f*; **in f.** à la mode; **out of f.** démodé.
fash·ion·a·ble *adj* à la mode; *(place)* chic *inv*.
fash·ion show présentation *f* de collections.
fast 1 *adj* rapide; **to be f.** *(of clock)*

avancer (**by** de). **2** *adv* (*quickly*) vite; **f. asleep** profondément endormi.

fas·ten *vt* attacher (**to** à); (*door, window*) fermer (bien).

fas·ten·er (*clip*) attache *f*; (*of garment*) fermeture *f*; (*of bag*) fermoir *m*; (*hook*) agrafe *f*.

fat 1 *n* graisse *f*; (*on meat*) gras *m*. **2** *adj* gras (*f* grasse); (*cheek, salary*) gros (*f* grosse); **to get f.** grossir.

fa·tal *adj* mortel; (*mistake etc*) fatal (*mpl* fatals).

fate destin *m*, sort *m*.

fa·ther père *m*.

fa·ther-in-law, *pl* **fathers-in-law** beau-père *m*.

fa·tigue fatigue *f*.

fat·ten·ing *adj* (*food*) qui fait grossir.

fat·ty *adj* (*food*) gras (*f* grasse).

fau·cet (*tap*) robinet *m*.

fault faute *f*, (*defect*) défaut *m*; (*mistake*) erreur *f*; **it's your f.** c'est ta faute; **to find f.** (**with**) critiquer.

fault·y *adj* défectueux.

fa·vor 1 *n* (*act of kindness*) service *m*; **to do sb a f.** rendre service à qn; **to be in f. of** (*support*) être pour; (*prefer*) préférer. **2** *vt* (*encourage*) favoriser; (*prefer*) préférer.

fa·vor·a·ble *adj* favorable (**to** à).

fa·vor·ite *adj & n* favori, -ite *mf*, préféré, -ée *mf*.

fax 1 *n* (*machine*) télécopieur *m*, fax *m*; (*message*) télécopie *f*, fax *m*. **2** *vt* (*message*) faxer; **to f. sb** envoyer une télécopie *or* un fax à qn.

fear 1 *n* crainte *f*, peur *f*; **for f. of doing** de peur de faire. **2** *vt* craindre.

fear·ful *adj* (*person*) apeuré; (*noise, pain*) épouvantable.

fear·less *adj* intrépide.

feast festin *m*.

feat exploit *m*.

feath·er plume *f*.

fea·ture (*of face, person*) trait *m*; (*of thing, place*) caractéristique *f*.

Feb·ru·ar·y février *m*.

fed·er·al *adj* fédéral.

fed up *adj* **to be f. up** *Fam* en avoir marre (**with** de).

fee prix *m*; **fee(s)** (*professional*) honoraires *mpl*; (*for registration*) droits *mpl*; **school** *or* **tuition fees** frais *mpl* de scolarité.

fee·ble *adj* faible.

feed* *vt* donner à manger à; (*breast-feed*) allaiter; (*bottle-feed*) donner le biberon à (*un bébé*).

feed·back réaction(s) *f(pl)*.

feel 1 *n* toucher *m*; (*feeling*) sensation *f*. **2** *vt** (*be aware of*) sentir; (*experience*) éprouver; (*touch*) tâter; **to f. that** avoir l'impression que. **3** *vi* (*tired, old etc*) se sentir; **I f. hot/sleepy/etc** j'ai chaud/sommeil/*etc*; **she feels better** elle va mieux; **to f. like sth** (*want*) avoir envie de qch.

▶ **feel around** *vi* tâtonner; (*in pocket etc*) fouiller.

feel·ing sentiment *m*; (*physical*) sensation *f*.

▶ **feel up to** *vt* être en forme pour.

feet *see* **foot.**

fell *pt of* **fall.**

fel·low (*man*) type *m*.

fel·o·ny crime *m*.

felt¹ *pt & pp of* **feel.**

felt² feutre *m*.

felt-tip (pen) (crayon *m*) feutre *m*.

fe·male 1 *adj* (*voice etc*) féminin; (*animal*) femelle; **f. student** étudiante *f*. **2** *n* femme *f*; (*animal*) femelle *f*.

fem·i·nine *adj* féminin.

fence 1 *n* barrière *f*; (*in race*) obstacle *m*. **2** *vi* (*with sword*) faire de l'escrime.

fence (in) *vt* (*land*) clôturer.

fenc·ing (*sport*) escrime *f*.

fend *vi* **to f. for oneself** se débrouiller.

fend·er (*on car*) aile *f*.

fern fougère *f*.

fe·ro·cious *adj* féroce.

fer·ry ferry-boat *m*; *(small, for river)* bac *m*.

fer·tile *adj (land)* fertile.

fer·til·iz·er engrais *m*.

fes·ti·val festival *m (pl* -als*)*.

fes·tiv·i·ties *npl* festivités *fpl*.

fetch[1] *vt (bring)* amener *(qn)*; *(object)* apporter; **to (go and) f.** aller chercher.

fetch[2] *vt (be sold for)* rapporter.

fête fête *f*.

feud **1** *n* querelle *f*. **2** *vi* se quereller, se disputer.

fe·ver fièvre *f*; **to have a f.** avoir de la fièvre.

fe·ver·ish *adj* fiévreux.

few *adj & pron* peu (de); **f. towns/etc** peu de villes/*etc*; **a f. towns/etc** quelques villes/*etc*; **f. of them** peu d'entre eux; **a f.** quelques-un(e)s (**of** de); **a f. of us** quelques-uns d'entre nous; **quite a f., a good f.** bon nombre (de); **a f. more books/etc** encore quelques livres/*etc*; **every f. days** tous les trois ou quatre jours.

few·er *adj & pron* moins (de) (**than** que).

fi·an·cé(e) fiancé, -ée *mf*.

fi·ber fibre *f*.

fi·ber·board *(bois)* aggloméré *m*.

fic·tion (works of) *f*. romans *mpl*.

fid·dle *(dishonest act)* Fam combine *f*.

▶**fiddle (around) with** *vt (pen etc)* tripoter; *(cars etc)* bricoler.

fidg·et *vi* gigoter.

field champ *m*; *(for sports)* terrain *m*.

fierce *adj* féroce; *(attack)* furieux.

fif·teen *adj & n* quinze *(m)*.

fif·teenth *adj & n* quinzième *(mf)*.

fifth *adj & n* cinquième *(mf)*.

fif·ti·eth *adj & n* cinquantième *(mf)*.

fif·ty *adj & n* cinquante *(m)*.

fig figue *f*.

fight **1** *n* bagarre *f*, *Boxing* combat *m*; *(struggle)* lutte *f*, *(quarrel)* dispute *f*. **2** *vi** se battre (**against** contre); *(struggle)* lutter (**for** pour); *(quarrel)* se disputer. **3** *vt* se battre avec *(qn)*.

▶**fight back** *vi* se défendre.

fight·er *(determined person)* battant, -ante *mf*.

▶**fight off** *vt (attacker)* repousser; *(disease)* résister à.

▶**fight over** *vt* se disputer.

fig·ure[1] *(numeral)* chiffre *m*; *(price)* prix *m*; *(of woman)* ligne *f*; *(diagram, person)* figure *f*.

fig·ure[2] *vt* to f. that *(guess)* penser que.

▶**figure on doing** *vt* compter faire.

▶**figure out** *vt* arriver à comprendre; *(problem)* résoudre.

file *(tool)* lime *f*; *(folder, information)* dossier *m*; *(computer data)* fichier *m*; **in single f.** en file.

file (a·way) *vt (document)* classer.

file (down) *vt* limer.

▶**file in** *vi* entrer à la queue leu leu.

▶**file out** *vi* sortir à la queue leu leu.

fil·ing cab·i·net classeur *m*.

fill **1** *vt* remplir (**with** de); *(tooth)* plomber. **2** *vi* se remplir.

fil·let filet *m*.

fill in *vt (form, hole)* remplir.

fill·ing **1** *adj (meal)* nourrissant. **2** *n (in tooth)* plombage *m*; *(in food)* garniture *f*.

▶**fill out** *vt (form)* remplir.

▶**fill up** **1** *vt (container, form)* remplir. **2** *vi* se remplir; *(with gas)* faire le plein.

film **1** *n* film *m*; *(for camera)* pellicule *f*. **2** *vt* filmer.

fil·ter filtre *m*; **f.-tipped cigarette** cigarette *f* (à bout) filtre.

filth saleté *f*.

filth·y *adj* sale.

fin *(of fish)* nageoire *f*.

fi·nal **1** *adj (last)* dernier. **2** *n (match)* finale *f*.

fi·nal·ize *vt* mettre au point; *(date)* fixer.

fi·nal·ly *adv* enfin.

fi·nance 1 *n* finance *f*. 2 *vt* financer.

fi·nan·cial *adj* financier.

find 1 *n* trouvaille *f*. 2 *vt** trouver; *(sth or sb lost)* retrouver;

▸ **find out** 1 *vt (secret etc)* découvrir; *(person)* démasquer. 2 *vi (inquire)* se renseigner (**about** sur); **to f. out about sth** *(discover)* découvrir qch.

fine¹ 1 *n* amende *f*, *(for driving offense)* contravention *f*. 2 *vt* **to f. sb ($100/etc)** infliger une amende (de cent dollars/etc) à qn.

fine² 1 *adj (thin, not coarse)* fin; *(very good)* excellent; **he's f.** *(healthy)* il va bien. 2 *adv (well)* très bien.

fin·ger doigt *m*; **little f.** petit doigt *m*.

fin·ger·nail ongle *m*.

fin·ger·print empreinte *f* (digitale); *(smudge)* trace *f* de doigt.

fin·ger·tip bout *m* du doigt.

fin·ish 1 *n* fin *f*, *(of race)* arrivée *f*. 2 *vt* finir; **to f. doing** finir de faire. 3 *vi* finir; **to have finished with** ne plus avoir besoin de; *(situation, person)* en avoir fini avec.

fin·ished *adj* fini.

fin·ish line ligne *f* d'arrivée.

▸ **finish off** *vti* finir.

▸ **finish up** 1 *vt* finir. 2 *vi* **to f. up in** se retrouver à; **to f. up doing** finir par faire.

Finn Finlandais, -aise *mf*.

Finn·ish 1 *adj* finlandais. 2 *(language)* finnois *m*.

fir sapin *m*.

fire¹ feu *m*; *(accidental)* incendie *m*; **to set f. to** mettre le feu à; **on f.** en feu; **(there's a) f.!** au feu!

fire² 1 *vt* **to f. a gun** tirer un coup de fusil or de revolver; **to f. sb** *(dismiss)* renvoyer qn. 2 *vi* tirer (**at** sur).

fire a·larm alarme *f* d'incendie.

fire·crack·er pétard *m*.

fire de·part·ment pompiers *mpl*.

fire en·gine voiture *f* de pompiers.

fire es·cape escalier *m* de secours.

fire·man, *pl* **-men** pompier *m*.

fire·place cheminée *f*.

fire sta·tion caserne *f* de pompiers.

fire·wood bois *m* de chauffage.

fire·works **f.** *(display)* feu *m* d'artifice.

firm 1 *n* entreprise *f*. 2 *adj* ferme.

firmly *adv* fermement.

first 1 *adj* premier. 2 *adv (firstly)* premièrement; *(for the first time)* pour la première fois; **(at) f.** d'abord. 3 *n* premier, -ière *mf*; **f. (gear)** *(of vehicle)* première *f*.

first aid premiers secours *mpl*.

first-class 1 *adj* excellent; *(ticket, seat)* de première; *(mail)* ordinaire. 2 *adv (to travel)* en première.

first floor rez-de-chaussée *m inv*.

first grade cours *m* préparatoire.

first·ly *adv* premièrement.

first name prénom *m*.

fish 1 *n inv* poisson *m*. 2 *vi* pêcher.

fish·er·man, *pl* **-men** pêcheur *m*.

fish·ing pêche *f*; **to go f.** aller à la pêche.

fish·ing rod canne *f* à pêche.

fish·mar·ket poissonnerie *f*.

fish sticks bâtonnets *mpl* de poisson.

fist poing *m*.

fit¹ *adj* en bonne santé; *(in good shape)* en forme; *(suitable)* propre (**for** à; **to do** à faire); *(worthy)* digne (**for** de; **to do** de faire); *(able)* apte (**for** à; **to do** à faire); **f. to eat** bon à manger.

fit² 1 *vt (of clothes)* aller (bien) à *(qn)*. 2 *vi* **this shirt fits** *(fits me)* cette chemise me va (bien).

fit³ *(attack)* accès *m*.

fit (in) 1 *vt (object)* faire entrer; **to f. sb in** *(find time to see)* prendre qn. 2 *vti* **to f. (in) sth** *(go in)* aller dans qch; **he doesn't f. in** il ne peut pas s'intégrer.

fit (on) 1 *vt* to f. sth (on) to sth *(put)* poser qch sur qch; *(fix)* fixer qch à qch. **2** *vti* to f. (on) sth *(go on sth)* aller sur qch.

fit·ness *(health)* santé *f*.

▶ **fit (out) with** *vt (house etc)* équiper de.

fit·ting 1 *adj* approprié (**to** à). **2** *n (of dress)* essayage *m*; **fittings** *(in house)* installations *fpl*; **f. room** cabine *f* d'essayage.

five *adj & n* cinq (*m*).

fix *vt (make firm, decide)* fixer; *(mend)* réparer; *(deal with)* arranger; *(prepare, cook)* préparer.

fix·ture *Sports* rencontre *f*; **fixtures** *(in building)* installations *fpl*.

▶ **fix up** *vt (trip etc)* arranger; **to f. sb up with a job/etc** procurer un travail/*etc* à qn.

fiz·zy *adj* pétillant.

flag drapeau *m*; *(on ship)* pavillon *m*.

flake *(of snow)* flocon *m*.

flake (off) *vi (of paint)* s'écailler.

flame flamme *f*; **to burst into f., to go up in flames** prendre feu.

flam·ma·ble *adj* inflammable.

flan tarte *f*.

flan·nel flanelle *f*.

flap 1 *vi (of wings etc)* battre. **2** *vt* **to f. its wings** battre des ailes. **3** *n (of pocket, envelope)* rabat *m*.

▶ **flare up** *vi (of fire)* prendre; *(of violence)* éclater.

flash 1 *n (of light)* éclat *m*; *(for camera)* flash *m*. **2** *vi (shine)* briller; *(on and off)* clignoter. **3** *vt (a light)* projeter; *(aim)* diriger (**on, at** sur); **to f. one's headlights** faire un appel de phares.

flash·ers *(of vehicle)* feux *mpl* de détresse.

flash·light lampe *f* électrique, lampe *f* de poche.

flask *(bottle)* bouteille *f*; *(for pocket)* flasque *f*.

flat¹ 1 *adj* plat; *(punctured)* crevé; *(deflated)* à plat; *(beer)* éventé; *(rate, fare)* fixe; **to put sth (down) f.** mettre qch à plat; **f. (on one's face)** à plat ventre. **2** *adv* **f. out** *(to work)* d'arrache-pied; *(to run)* à toute vitesse. **3** *n* crevaison *f*.

flat² *(rooms)* appartement *m*.

flat·ly *adv (to deny, refuse)* catégoriquement.

flat·ten (out) *vt* aplatir.

flat·ter *vt* flatter.

fla·vor goût *m*; *(of ice cream etc)* parfum *m*.

fla·vor·ing *(in cake etc)* parfum *m*.

flaw défaut *m*.

flea puce *f*.

flea mar·ket marché *m* aux puces.

flee* 1 *vi* s'enfuir. **2** *vt (place)* s'enfuir de.

fleet *(of ships)* flotte *f*.

Flem·ish 1 *adj* flamand. **2** *n (language)* flamand *m*.

flesh chair *f*.

flex 1 *vt (limb)* fléchir. **2** *n (wire)* fil *m* (souple); *(for telephone)* cordon *m*.

flex·i·ble *adj* souple.

flick *(with finger)* chiquenaude *f*.

flick·er 1 *n (of eyes)* tremblement *m*; *(of flame, light)* vacillement *m*; **a f. of hope** l'ombre d'un espoir. **2** *vi (eyes)* trembler; *(flame, light)* vaciller.

▶ **flick off** *vt* enlever (d'une chiquenaude).

flight *(of bird, aircraft)* vol *m*; *(escape)* fuite *f*; **f. of stairs** escalier *m*.

flight at·ten·dant *(male)* steward *m*; *(female)* hôtesse *f* de l'air.

flim·sy *adj (light)* (trop) léger; *(thin)* (trop) mince.

fling* *vt* lancer.

flint *(for lighter)* pierre *f*.

flip 1 *n (flick)* petit coup *m*; **f. chart** tableau *m* à feuilles. **2** *vt (with finger)* donner un petit coup à; *(toss)* envoyer; **to f. a coin** jouer à pile ou face.

flip-flops npl tongs fpl.

flip·per (of swimmer) palme f.

▶ **flip through** vt (book) feuilleter.

float 1 n Fishing flotteur m; (at carnival) char m. **2** vi flotter (**on** sur).

flock 1 n (of sheep) troupeau m; (of birds) volée f. **2** vi venir en foule.

flood 1 n inondation f; (of letters, tears) flot m. **2** vt (field, house etc) inonder. **3** vi (of river) déborder.

▶ **flood in** vt (of tourists etc) affluer.

▶ **flood into** vt (of tourists etc) envahir (un pays etc).

flood·light projecteur m.

floor (ground) sol m; (wooden etc in building) plancher m; (story) étage m; **on the f.** par terre; **on the first f.** au rez-de-chaussée.

floor·board planche f.

floor lamp lampadaire m.

flop 1 vi (of play etc) faire un four. **2** n four m.

flop·py adj (soft) mou (f molle).

flop·py disk disquette f.

flo·rist fleuriste mf.

floss (dental) f. fil m dentaire.

flour farine f.

flour·ish 1 n (gesture) grand geste m; (decoration) fioriture f. **2** vt brandir. **3** vi (business, economy, plant) prospérer; (person) être en pleine santé.

flow 1 vi couler; (of electric current, information) circuler; (of traffic) s'écouler. **2** n (of river) courant m; (of current, information) circulation f.

flow chart tableau m.

flow·er 1 n fleur f; **in f.** en fleur(s). **2** vi fleurir.

flow·er bed parterre m de fleurs, plate-bande f.

flow·er shop (boutique f de) fleuriste mf.

flu grippe f.

flu·ent adj **he's f. in Russian, his Russian is f.** il parle couramment le russe.

flu·ent·ly (to speak a language) couramment.

fluff (of material) peluche(s) f(pl); (on floor) moutons mpl.

flu·id adj & n fluide (m).

flunk vt (exam) Fam être collé à.

flu·o·res·cent adj fluorescent.

flush vt **to f. the toilet** tirer la chasse d'eau.

flute flûte f.

flut·ter vi (of bird) voltiger; (of flag) flotter.

fly[1] (insect) mouche f.

fly[2] **1** vi voler; (of passenger) aller en avion; (of flag) flotter. **2** vt (aircraft) piloter; (airline) voyager par.

fly[3] (on pants) braguette f.

▶ **fly across** or **over** vt (country etc) survoler.

▶ **fly away** or **off** vi s'envoler.

fly·ing vol m; (air travel) l'avion m; **f. saucer** soucoupe f volante.

foam écume f; (on beer) mousse f; **f. rubber** caoutchouc m mousse; **f. mattress**/etc matelas m/etc mousse.

fo·cus 1 n (of attention) centre m; **in f.** au point. **2** vt (image) mettre au point. **3** vti **to f. (one's attention) on** se tourner vers.

fog brouillard m.

fog·gy adj **it's f.** il y a du brouillard; **f. weather** brouillard m.

foil (for cooking) papier m alu(minium).

fold 1 n (in paper etc) pli m. **2** vt plier; (wrap) envelopper (**in** dans); **to f. one's arms** (se) croiser les bras. **3** vi (of chair etc) se plier.

▶ **fold back** or **over 1** vt (blanket etc) replier. **2** vi se replier.

fold·er (file holder) chemise f.

fold·ing adj (chair etc) pliant.

▶ **fold up 1** vt (chair etc) plier. **2** vi se plier.

folk 1 adj (dance etc) folklorique; **f. music** (musique f) folk m. **2** npl **folks** gens mpl or fpl.

fol·low 1 vt suivre; (career) poursuivre; **followed by** suivi de. **2** *vi* suivre.

▸**follow around** *vt* suivre partout.

fol·low·er partisan *m*.

fol·low·ing 1 *n* suivant *m*. **2** *prep* à la suite de.

▸**follow through** *vt* (*plan etc*) poursuivre jusqu'au bout.

▸**follow up** *vt* (*idea, story*) creuser; (*clue*) suivre.

fond *adj* **to be (very) f. of** aimer (beaucoup).

food nourriture *f*; (*particular substance*) aliment *m*; (*for cats, dogs*) pâtée *f*.

fool 1 *n* imbécile *mf*; **to play the f.** faire l'imbécile. **2** *vt* (*trick*) rouler.

▸**fool around** *vi* faire l'imbécile; (*waste time*) perdre son temps.

fool·ish *adj* bête.

fool·ish·ly *adv* bêtement.

foot, *pl* **feet** pied *m*; (*of animal*) patte *f*; (*measure*) pied *m* (= 30,48cm); **at the f. of** (*page, stairs*) au bas de; **on f.** à pied.

foot·ball (*game*) football *m* américain; (*ball*) ballon *m* (de football américain).

foot·ball play·er joueur, -euse *mf* de football américain.

foot·bridge passerelle *f*.

foot·path sentier *m*.

foot·print empreinte *f* (de pied *or* de pas).

foot·step pas *m*.

foot·stool repose-pieds *m inv*; (*cushioned*) pouf *m*.

for *prep* pour; (*in exchange for*) contre; (*for a distance of*) pendant; **what's it f.?** ça sert à quoi?; **he was away f. a month** il a été absent pendant un mois; **he won't be back f. a month** il ne sera pas de retour avant un mois; **he's been here/I haven't seen him f. a month** il est ici/je ne l'ai pas vu depuis un mois; **I haven't seen him f. ten years** voilà dix ans que je ne l'ai pas vu; **it's f. you to say** c'est à toi de dire; **f.**

that to be done pour que ça soit fait.

for·bid* *vt* interdire (**sb to do** à qn de faire); **she is forbidden to leave** il lui est interdit de partir.

force 1 *n* force *f*; **the armed forces** les forces armées. **2** *vt* forcer (*qn*) (**to do** à faire); (*door*) forcer; **forced to do** obligé *or* forcé de faire; **to f. one's way into** entrer de force dans.

fore·cast 1 *vt** prévoir. **2** *n* prévision *f*; (*of weather*) météo *f*.

fore·head front *m*.

for·eign *adj* étranger; (*trade*) extérieur; (*travel*) à l'étranger.

for·eign·er étranger, -ère *mf*.

fore·man, *pl* **-men** (*worker*) contremaître *m*.

fore·most *adj* principal.

fore·run·ner précurseur *m*.

fore·see* *vt* prévoir.

for·est forêt *f*.

for·ev·er *adv* pour toujours; (*continually*) sans cesse.

forge *vt* (*signature, money*) contrefaire; (*document*) falsifier.

▸**forge ahead** *vi* (*progress*) aller de l'avant.

for·ger·y faux *m*.

for·get* *vti* oublier (**to do** de faire).

▸**forget about** *vt* oublier.

for·get·ful *adj* **he's f.** il n'a pas de mémoire.

for·give* *vt* pardonner (**sb sth** qch à qn).

fork 1 *n* (*for eating*) fourchette *f*; (*for gardening*) fourche *f*; (*in road*) bifurcation *f*. **2** *vi* (*of road*) bifurquer.

▸**fork out** *vt* (*money*) *Fam* allonger.

form 1 *n* forme *f*; (*document*) formulaire *m*. **2** *vt* (*group, basis etc*) former; (*habit*) contracter; (*an opinion*) se former; **to f. part of** faire partie de. **3** *vi* (*appear*) se former.

for·mal *adj* (*person, tone etc*) cérémonieux; (*stuffy*) compassé; (*of-*

ficial) officiel; **f. dress** tenue de cérémonie.

for·mal·i·ty formalité *f.*

for·mat 1 *n* format *m.* **2** *vt* Comput formater.

for·ma·tion formation *f.*

for·mer 1 *adj* (*previous*) ancien; (*of two*) premier. **2** *pron* **the f.** celui-là, celle-là.

for·mer·ly *adv* autrefois.

for·mu·la, *pl* -as or -ae formule *f*; (*pl* -as) (*baby food*) lait *m* maternisé.

fort fort *m.*

forth *adv* **and so f.** et ainsi de suite; **to walk back and f.** faire les cent pas.

forth·com·ing *adj* (*event*) à venir; (*communicative*) expansif (**about** sur); **no answer was f.** il n'y a eu aucune réponse.

for·ti·eth *adj & n* quarantième (*mf*).

for·tress forteresse *f.*

for·tu·nate *adj* (*choice etc*) heureux; **to be f.** (*of person*) avoir de la chance; **it's f. that** c'est heureux que (+ *subjunctive*).

for·tu·nate·ly *adv* heureusement.

for·tune *n* fortune *f*; **to make one's f.** faire fortune; **to have the good f. to do** avoir la chance de faire.

for·ty *adj & n* quarante (*m*).

fo·rum forum *m.*

for·ward 1 *adv* forward(s) en avant; **to go f.** avancer. **2** *vt* (*letter*) faire suivre; (*goods*) expédier.

fos·sil fossile *m.*

fos·ter 1 *vt* (*child*) accueillir; (*hope, idea*) nourrir, entretenir; (*relations*) favoriser. **2** *adj* **f. child** enfant *mf* placé(e) dans une famille d'accueil; **f. parents** parents *mpl* nourriciers.

foul 1 *adj* (*smell, taste*) infect; (*language*) grossier. **2** *n* Sports faute *f.*

found[1] *pt & pp de* **find**.

found[2] *vt* (*town etc*) fonder.

found·er[1] fondateur, -trice *mf.*

foun·der[2] *vi* (*ship*) sombrer; (*plan, hopes*) s'effondrer.

foun·tain fontaine *f.*

foun·tain pen stylo *m* à encre.

four *adj & n* quatre (*m*).

four·teen *adj & n* quatorze (*m*).

fourth *adj & n* quatrième (*mf*).

fowl volaille *f.*

fox renard *m.*

foy·er (*in theater*) foyer *m.*

frac·tion fraction *f.*

frac·ture 1 *n* fracture *f.* **2** *vt* **to f. one's leg/etc** se fracturer la jambe/etc.

frag·ile *adj* fragile.

frag·ment fragment *m.*

fra·grance parfum *m.*

frail *adj* fragile.

frame 1 *n* (*of picture, bicycle*) cadre *m*; (*of window*) châssis *m*; **f. of mind** humeur *f.* **2** *vt* (*picture*) encadrer.

frame·work structure *f*; **in the f. of** dans le cadre de.

franc franc *m.*

fran·chise (*right to vote*) droit *m* de vote; (*right to sell product*) franchise *f.*

frank *adj* franc (*f* franche).

frank·ly *adv* franchement.

frank·ness franchise *f.*

fran·tic *adj* (*activity*) frénétique; (*rush*) effréné; (*person*) hors de soi.

fran·ti·cal·ly *adv* comme un fou.

fraud (*crime*) fraude *f*, (*person*) imposteur *m.*

fray *vi* (*of garment*) s'effilocher.

freck·le tache *f* de rousseur.

freck·led *adj* couvert de taches de rousseur.

free 1 *adj* libre; (*lavish*) généreux (**with** de); **f. (of charge)** gratuit; **to get f.** se libérer; **f. to do** libre de faire; **f. of** (*pain etc*) débarrassé de. **2** *adv* **f. (of charge)** gratuitement. **3** *vt* (*pt & pp* freed) (*prisoner*) libérer; (*trapped person*) dégager.

free·dom liberté *f*; **f. from** (*worry*) absence *f* de.

free·ly adv librement; (to give) libéralement.

free-range adj (chicken) fermier; **f. eggs** œufs mpl de poules élevées en plein air.

free·way autoroute f.

freeze* 1 vi geler. **2** vt (food) congeler; (prices) bloquer.

freez·er congélateur m; (in fridge) freezer m.

▸**freeze up** or **over** vi geler; (of window) se givrer.

freez·ing adj (weather) glacial; (hands, person) gelé; **it's f.** on gèle.

freight (goods) fret m; **f. car** wagon m de marchandises; **f. train** train m de marchandises.

French 1 adj français; (teacher) de français; (embassy) de France. **2** n (language) français m; **the F.** les Français mpl.

French bread a loaf of F. une baguette.

French fries frites fpl.

French·man, pl -men Français m.

French-speak·ing adj francophone.

French·wom·an, pl -women Française f.

fre·quent adj fréquent; **f. visitor** habitué, -ée mf (**to** de).

fre·quent·ly adv fréquemment.

fresh adj frais (f fraîche); (new) nouveau (f nouvelle); **to get some f. air** prendre l'air.

fresh·en·er air f. désodorisant m.

▸**freshen up** vi faire un brin de toilette.

fret vi (worry) se faire du souci.

Fri·day vendredi m; **Good F.** Vendredi Saint.

fridge frigo m.

fried (pt & pp of fry) adj (fish) frit; **f. egg** œuf m sur le plat.

friend ami, -ie mf; (from school, work) camarade mf; **to be friends with sb** être ami avec qn.

friend·ly adj aimable (**to** avec); **to be f. with** être ami avec.

friend·ship amitié f.

fright peur f; **to get a f.** avoir peur; **to give sb a f.** faire peur à qn.

fright·en vt effrayer.

▸**frighten away** or **off** vt (animal, person) faire fuire.

fright·ened adj effrayé; **to be f.** avoir peur (**of** de).

fright·en·ing adj effrayant.

frill (on dress etc) volant m.

fringe frange f; **on the f. of society** en marge de la société; **f. benefits** avantages mpl en nature.

fro adv **to go to and f.** aller et venir.

frog grenouille f.

from prep de; **where are you f.?** d'où êtes-vous?; **a train f.** un train en provenance de. ■ (time onwards) à partir de, dès; **f. today (on), as f. today** à partir d'aujourd'hui, dès aujourd'hui. ■ (numbers, prices onwards) à partir de. ■ (away from) à; **to take/borrow f.** prendre/emprunter à. ■ (out of) dans; sur; **to take f.** (box) prendre dans; (table) prendre sur; **to drink f. a cup/the bottle** boire dans une tasse/à la bouteille. ■ (according to) d'après. ■ (cause) par. ■ (on behalf of) de la part de; **tell her f. me** dis-lui de ma part.

front 1 n (of garment, building) devant m; (of boat, car) avant m; (of book) début m; **in f. (of)** devant; **in f.** (ahead) en race; (in race) en tête; **in the f.** (in vehicle) à l'avant. **2** adj (tooth) de devant; (part, wheel, car seat) avant; (row, page) premier; **f. door** porte f d'entrée.

fron·tier frontière f.

frost gel m; (on window) givre m.

frost·bite gelure f.

▸**frost up** vi (of window etc) se givrer.

frost·y adj (window) givré; **it's f.** il gèle.

froth mousse f.

frown vi froncer les sourcils.

fro·zen adj (vegetables etc) surgelé; **f. food** surgelés mpl.

fruit fruit *m*; **(some) f.** *(one piece)* un fruit; *(more than one)* des fruits; **f. drink** boisson *f* aux fruits; **f. salad** salade *f* de fruits; **f. tree** arbre *m* fruitier.

fruit·cake cake *m*.

frus·trate *vt* frustrer.

frus·trat·ed *adj* frustré.

frus·trat·ing *adj* irritant.

frus·tra·tion frustration *f*.

fry 1 *vt* faire frire. **2** *vi* frire.

fry pan poêle *f* (à frire).

fudge caramel *m* mou.

fu·el combustible *m*; *(for vehicle)* carburant *m*.

fu·gi·tive fugitif, -ive *mf*.

ful·fill *vt* (ambition) réaliser; *(condition)* remplir; *(desire)* satisfaire.

ful·fill·ing *adj* satisfaisant.

full 1 *adj* plein (of de); *(bus, theater etc)* complet; *(life, day)* rempli; **the f. price** le prix fort; **to pay f. fare** payer plein tarif; **to be f.** *(of person)* n'avoir plus faim; *(of hotel)* être complet; **f. name** *(on form)* nom et prénom. **2** *n* **in f.** *(to read sth etc)* en entier.

full-scale, full-size *adj* (model) grandeur nature *inv*.

full-time *adj & adv* à plein temps.

ful·ly *adv* entièrement.

fumes *npl* vapeurs *fpl*; *(from car exhaust)* gaz *m inv*.

fun amusement *m*; **to be f.** être très amusant; **to have (some) f.** s'amuser; **to make f. of** se moquer de; **for f.** pour le plaisir.

func·tion fonction *f*; *(meeting)* réunion *f*.

func·tion·al *adj* fonctionnel.

fund 1 *n* (for pension etc) caisse *f*; **funds** *(money, resources)* fonds *mpl*. **2** *vt* fournir des fonds à.

fu·ner·al enterrement *m*; **f. home** entreprise *f* de pompes funèbres.

fun·nel *(of ship)* cheminée *f*; *(for pouring)* entonnoir *m*.

fun·ny *adj* drôle; *(strange)* bizarre;

a **f. idea** une drôle d'idée; **to feel f.** ne pas se sentir très bien.

fur fourrure *f*.

fu·ri·ous *adj* furieux (**with, at** contre).

fur·nace fourneau *m*.

fur·nish *vt* (room) meubler.

fur·nished room pièce *f* meublée.

fur·ni·ture meubles *mpl*; **a piece of f.** un meuble.

fur·ther 1 *adv* = **farther**; *(more)* davantage. **2** *adj* supplémentaire; **f. details** de plus amples détails; **a f. case/etc** un autre cas/*etc*.

fur·ther·more *adv* en outre.

fur·thest *adj & adv* = **farthest**.

fu·ry fureur *f*.

fuss *n* chichis *mpl*; **what a f.!** quelle histoire! **2** *vi* faire des chichis.

fuss (a·round) *vi* s'agiter.

▸ **fuss over** *vt* être aux petits soins pour.

fuss·y *adj* tatillon; *(difficult)* difficile (**about** sur).

fu·ture 1 *n* avenir *m*; *Grammar* futur *m*; **in the f.** *(one day)* un jour (futur). **2** *adj* futur; *(date)* prochain.

fuze *(wire)* plomb *m*, fusible *m*; *(of bomb)* amorce *f*; **to blow a f.** faire sauter un plomb; **we've blown a f.** un plomb a sauté.

fuzz·y *adj* (picture, idea) flou.

G

gadg·et gadget *m*.

Gael·ic *adj & n* gaélique (*m*).

gag 1 *n* *(over mouth)* bâillon *m*; *(joke)* gag *m*. **2** *vt* (victim) bâillonner. **3** *vi* (choke) s'étouffer (**on** avec).

gai·e·ty gaieté *f*.

gai·ly *adv* gaiement.

gain 1 vt (obtain) gagner; (experience) acquérir; **to g. speed/weight** prendre de la vitesse/du poids. **2** n (increase) augmentation f (**in** de); (profit) bénéfice m.

▸**gain on** vt (catch up with) rattraper.

ga·la gala m.

ga·lax·y galaxie f.

gale grand vent m.

gal·lant adj (chivalrous) galant.

gal·ler·y galerie f, (for public) tribune f, **art g.** (private) galerie f d'art; (public) musée m d'art.

gal·li·vant Fam vadrouiller.

gal·lon gallon m.

gal·lop 1 vi galoper. **2** n galop m.

gam·ble (a·way) vt (lose) perdre (au jeu).

gam·ble 1 vi jouer (**on** sur; **with** avec). **2** vt jouer. **3** n coup m risqué.

gam·bler joueur, -euse mf.

gam·bling jeu m.

game n jeu m; (of football, etc) match m; (of tennis, chess, cards) partie f, **to play a g. of** (football etc) jouer un match de; (tennis, chess, cards) faire une partie de.

game ar·cade f galerie de jeux.

gang (of children, criminals) bande f, gang m; (of workers) équipe f.

gang·ster gangster m.

▸**gang up on** vt se mettre à plusieurs contre.

gang·way (to ship, aircraft) passerelle f.

gap (empty space) trou m; (in time) intervalle m; (in knowledge) lacune f, **the g. between** (difference) l'écart m entre.

gape vi rester bouche bée.

▸**gape at** vt regarder bouche bée.

ga·rage garage m.

gar·bage ordures fpl, (nonsense) idioties fpl, **g. bag** sac m poubelle; **g. man** éboueur m; **g. truck** camion-benne m.

gar·ban·zo (bean) pois m chiche.

gar·den 1 n jardin m. **2** vi jardiner.

gar·den·er jardinier, -ière mf.

gar·den hose tuyau m.

gar·den·ing jardinage m.

gar·gle vi se gargariser.

gar·land guirlande f.

gar·lic ail m.

gar·ment vêtement m.

gas 1 n gaz m inv; (gasoline) essence f, **g. mask/meter/etc** masque m/compteur m/etc à gaz; **g. heat** chauffage m au gaz; **g. heater** appareil m de chauffage à gaz; **g. station** station-service f, **g. stove** cuisinière f à gaz; (portable) réchaud m à gaz. **2** vt (poison) asphyxier (qn).

gash 1 n entaille f. **2** vt entailler.

gas·o·line essence f.

gasp 1 vi to g. (for breath) haleter. **2** n halètement m.

gas·sy adj (drink) gazeux.

gas·works usine f à gaz.

gate (at grade crossing, field etc) barrière f, (metal) grille f, (of castle, in airport) porte f, (at stadium) entrée f, (for tickets) portillon m.

gate·crash vi s'inviter (de force).

gath·er 1 vt (people, objects) rassembler; (pick up) ramasser; (information) recueillir; **I g. that...** je crois comprendre que...; **to g. speed** prendre de la vitesse. **2** vi (of people) se rassembler.

gath·er·ing (group) réunion f.

▸**gather round** vi (come closer) s'approcher.

gaud·y adj voyant.

gauge 1 n (instrument) jauge f. **2** vt (estimate) évaluer.

gaunt adj décharné.

gauze gaze f.

gave pt de **give**.

gay 1 adj homo(sexuel). **2** n homo (sexuel) m.

gaze 1 n regard m (fixe). **2** vi regarder.

▸**gaze at** vt regarder (fixement).

gear 1 n équipement m; (belong-

ings) affaires *fpl; (clothes) Fam* vêtements *mpl; (speed in vehicle)* vitesse *f;* **in g.** en prise; **not in g.** au point mort. **2** *vt* adapter (**to** à).

▸ **gear up** *vt* to be geared up to do être prêt à faire; **to g. oneself up for** se préparer pour.

geese *see* **goose**.

gel gel *m.*

gem pierre *f* précieuse.

gen·der *Grammar* genre *m.*

gen·er·al 1 *adj* général; **in g.** en général; **the g. public** le (grand) public; **for g. use** à l'usage du public. **2** *n (in army)* général *m.*

gen·er·al·ly *adv* généralement.

gen·er·a·tion génération *f.*

gen·er·a·tor groupe *m* électrogène.

gen·er·os·i·ty générosité *f.*

gen·er·ous *adj* généreux (**with** de); *(helping)* copieux.

gen·er·ous·ly *adv* généreusement.

gen·ius *(ability, person)* génie *m.*

gen·tle *adj (person, slope etc)* doux *(f* douce); *(touch)* léger; *(exercise, speed)* modéré.

gen·tle·man, *pl* **-men** monsieur *m.*

gen·tle·ness douceur *f.*

gent·ly *adv* doucement.

gen·u·ine *adj* véritable, authentique; *(sincere)* sincère.

gen·u·ine·ly *adv* véritablement, sincèrement.

ge·o·graph·i·cal *adj* géographique.

ge·og·ra·phy géographie *f.*

ge·o·met·ric, ge·o·met·ri·cal *adj* géométrique.

ge·om·e·try géométrie *f.*

germ *(in body, food etc)* microbe *m.*

Ger·man 1 *adj* allemand. **2** *n (person)* Allemand, -ande *mf; (language)* allemand *m.*

Ger·man mea·sles rubéole *f.*

Ger·man shep·herd *(dog)* berger *m* allemand.

ges·ture geste *m.*

get* **1** *vt (obtain)* obtenir; *(find)* trouver; *(buy)* acheter; *(receive)* recevoir; *(catch)* attraper; *(bus, train)* prendre; *(seize)* saisir; *(fetch)* aller chercher; *(put)* mettre; *(derive)* tirer (**from** de); *(understand)* comprendre; *(prepare)* préparer; *(hit with fist, stick etc)* atteindre; *(reputation)* se faire; **I have got** j'ai; **to g. sb to do sth** faire faire qch à qn; **to g. sth built**/*etc* faire construire/*etc* qch. **2** *vi (go)* aller; *(arrive)* arriver (**to** à); *(become)* devenir; **to g. caught**/*etc* se faire prendre/*etc;* **to g. cleaned up** se laver; **where have you gotten to?** où en es-tu?; **you've got to stay** *(must)* tu dois rester; **to g. working** se mettre à travailler.

▸ **get across 1** *vt (road)* traverser; *(message)* communiquer. **2** *vi* traverser.

▸ **get along** *vi (manage)* se débrouiller; *(be on good terms)* s'entendre (**with** avec).

▸ **get around** *vi* se déplacer; **to g. around to doing** en venir à faire.

▸ **get at** *vt (reach)* parvenir à.

▸ **get away** *vi (leave)* partir; *(escape)* s'échapper.

▸ **get back 1** *vt (recover)* récupérer; *(replace)* remettre. **2** *vi (return)* revenir; *(move back)* reculer.

▸ **get by** *vi* passer; *(manage)* se débrouiller.

▸ **get down** *vti* descendre.

▸ **get in 1** *vt (laundry etc)* rentrer; *(call for)* faire venir (qn). **2** *vi (enter)* entrer; *(come home)* rentrer; *(enter vehicle or train)* monter; *(of plane, train)* arriver.

▸ **get in (to)** *vt* entrer dans; *(vehicle, train)* monter dans; **to g. in (to) bed** se mettre au lit.

▸ **get off 1** *vi (leave)* partir; *(from vehicle or train)* descendre (**from** de); *(in court)* être acquitté. **2** *vt (remove)* enlever; *(send)* expédier; **to g. off a bus** descendre d'un bus.

▶ **get on 1** vt (shoes, clothes) mettre; (bus, train) monter dans. **2** vi (progress) marcher; (manage) se débrouiller; (succeed) réussir; (enter bus or train) monter; **to g. on with** (task) continuer.

▶ **get out 1** vi sortir; (from vehicle or train) descendre (**of** de); **to g. out of** (danger) se tirer de; (habit) perdre. **2** vt (remove) enlever; (bring out) sortir (qch), faire sortir (qn).

▶ **get over 1** vt (road) traverser; (obstacle) surmonter; (fence) franchir; (illness) se remettre de. **2** vi (cross) traverser; (visit) passer.

▶ **get through 1** vi passer; (finish) finir; **to g. through to sb** (on phone) contacter qn. **2** vt passer par; (meal) venir à bout de.

▶ **get to to g. sth to sb** faire parvenir qch à qn; **to g. sb to the airport** amener qn à l'aéroport.

get-to-geth-er réunion f.

▶ **get up 1** vi (rise) se lever (**from** de); **to g. up to something** or **to mischief** faire des bêtises. **2** vt (bring up) monter (qch); (wake up) réveiller.

ghast-ly adj (horrible) affreux.

ghet-to, pl -os ghetto m.

ghost fantôme m.

gi-ant 1 n géant m. **2** adj (tree, packet) géant.

gid-dy adj **to be** or **feel g.** avoir le vertige; **to make g.** donner le vertige à.

gift cadeau m; (talent) don m.

gift-ed adj doué.

gift vouch-er bon-cadeau m.

gig Fam (pop or rock concert) concert m.

gi-gan-tic adj gigantesque.

gig-gle 1 vi pouffer (de rire). **2** n **to get/have the giggles** attraper/avoir le fou rire.

gills npl (of fish) ouïes fpl.

gim-mick truc m.

gin (drink) gin m.

gin-ger gingembre m.

gi-raffe girafe f.

girl (jeune) fille f, (daughter) fille f; **American g.** jeune Américaine f.

girl-friend amie f, (of boy) petite amie f.

girl scout éclaireuse f.

give* vt donner (**to** à); (support) apporter; (a smile) faire; (a sigh) pousser; (a look) jeter.

▶ **give away** vt (free of charge) donner; (prizes) distribuer; (betray) trahir (qn).

▶ **give back** vt (return) rendre.

▶ **give in 1** vi (surrender) céder (**to** à). **2** vt (hand in) remettre.

giv-en 1 adj (specified) donné; **at a g. moment** à un moment donné; **to be g. to sth** (prone to) avoir une tendance à qch. **2** conj (considering) étant donné.

▶ **give out** vt (hand out) distribuer.

▶ **give over** vt (devote) consacrer (**to** à).

▶ **give up 1** vi abandonner. **2** vt abandonner; (seat) céder (**to** à); (prisoner) livrer (**to** à); **to g. up smoking** cesser de fumer.

▶ **give way** vi (of branch, person etc) céder (**to** à); (in vehicle) céder la priorité (**to** à).

glad adj content (**of, about** de).

glad-ly adv volontiers.

glam-or (charm) enchantement m; (splendor) éclat m.

glam-or-ous adj séduisant.

glance 1 n coup m d'œil. **2** vi jeter un coup d'œil (**at** à, sur).

gland glande f.

glare 1 n (light) lumière f éblouissante; (look) regard m furieux. **2** vi (dazzle) briller d'un éclat éblouissant; **to g. at sb** regarder qn avec colère.

glar-ing adj (light) éblouissant; (injustice) flagrant.

glass verre m; (mirror) miroir m; **a pane of g.** une vitre.

glass-es npl (for eyes) lunettes fpl.

glee joie f.

glen vallon *m*.

glide *vi* glisser; *(of aircraft, bird)* planer.

glid·ing *(sport)* vol *m* à voile.

glim·mer *(of hope)* lueur *f*.

glimpse aperçu *m*; **to catch** *or* **get a g. of** entrevoir.

glit·ter·ing *adj* scintillant.

globe globe *m*.

gloom *(sadness)* tristesse *f*.

gloom·y *adj* triste; *(pessimistic)* pessimiste.

glo·ri·fied *adj* **it's a g. barn/***etc* ce n'est guère plus qu'une grange/*etc*.

glo·ri·ous *adj* glorieux; *(splendid)* magnifique.

glo·ry gloire *f*.

gloss *(shine)* brillant *m*.

gloss·y *adj (paint, finish)* brillant; *(magazine)* de luxe.

glove gant *m*.

glove box, glove com·part·ment *(in car)* boîte *f* à gants.

glow *vi (of sky, fire)* rougeoyer.

glue 1 *n* colle *f*. **2** *vt* coller **(to, on** à**); with eyes glued to** les yeux fixés sur.

glum *adj* triste.

glut *(of oil etc)* surplus *m*.

glut·ton glouton, -onne *mf*.

gnat *(insect)* cousin *m*.

gnaw *vti* ronger.

go[1]* *vi* aller **(to** à; **from** de); *(depart)* partir, s'en aller; *(disappear)* disparaître, partir; *(function)* marcher; *(become)* devenir; *(of material)* s'user; **to go well/badly** *(of event)* se passer bien/mal; **she's going to do** *(is about to, intends to)* elle va faire; **it's all gone** il n'y en a plus; **to go and get** aller chercher; **to go riding/on a trip/***etc* faire du cheval/un voyage/*etc*; **to let go of** lâcher; **to go to a doctor/***etc* aller voir un médecin/*etc*; **two hours/** *etc* **to go** encore deux heures/*etc*.

go[2], *pl* **goes** *(attempt)* coup *m*; **to have a go at (doing) sth** essayer (de faire) qch; **on the go** actif.

▸ **go about** *or* **(a)round 1** *vi* se déplacer; *(of news)* circuler. **2** *vt* **to know how to go about it** savoir s'y prendre.

▸ **go across** *vti (cross)* traverser.

▸ **go after** *vt (chase)* poursuivre; *(seek)* (re)chercher.

▸ **go ahead** *vi* avancer; *(continue)* continuer; *(start)* commencer; **go ahead!** allez-y!; **to go ahead with** *(plan etc)* poursuivre.

go-a·head to get the g. avoir le feu vert.

▸ **go along** *vi* aller; **to go along with** *(agree)* être d'accord avec.

▸ **go around 1** *vi (turn)* tourner; *(be sufficient)* suffire. **2** *vt (corner)* tourner; *(world)* faire le tour de.

goat chèvre *f*.

▸ **go away** *vi* partir, s'en aller.

▸ **go back** *vi* retourner; *(in time)* remonter; *(step back)* reculer; **to go back on** *(promise)* revenir sur.

go-be·tween intermédiaire *mf*.

god dieu *m*; **G.** Dieu *m*.

god·daugh·ter filleule *f*.

god·fa·ther parrain *m*.

god·moth·er marraine *f*.

▸ **go down 1** *vi* descendre; *(fall down)* tomber; *(of ship)* couler; *(of sun)* se coucher; *(of price etc)* baisser. **2** *vt* **to go down the stairs/ street** descendre l'escalier/la rue.

god·send to be a g. tomber à pic.

god·son filleul *m*.

goes *see* **go**[1].

gog·gles *npl* lunettes *fpl (de protection, de plongée)*.

▸ **go in 1** *vi* (r)entrer; *(of sun)* se cacher. **2** *vt* **to go in a room/***etc* entrer dans une pièce/*etc*.

▸ **go (in) for** *vt* s'intéresser à.

go·ing 1 *n (conditions)* conditions *fpl*; **it's slow** *or* **tough g.** c'est difficile. **2** *adj* **the g. price** le prix pratiqué **(for** pour).

go·ings-on *npl* activités *fpl*.

▸**go into** vt (room etc) entrer dans.
gold or m; **g. watch**/etc montre/etc en or.
gold·en adj (in color) doré; (rule) d'or.
gold·fish poisson m rouge.
gold mine mine f d'or.
gold·plat·ed adj plaqué or.
golf golf m.
golf·er golfeur, -euse mf.
gone pp de **go**¹.
good 1 adj bon (f bonne); (kind) gentil; (weather) beau (f belle); (well-behaved) sage; **very g.!** (all right) très bien!; **to feel g.** se sentir bien; **g. at French**/etc bon ou fort en français/etc; **to be g. with** (children) savoir s'y prendre avec; **it's a g. thing (that)...** heureusement que...; **a g. many, a g. deal (of)** beaucoup (de); **g. morning** bonjour; (on leaving) au revoir; **g. evening** bonsoir; **g. night** bonsoir; (going to bed) bonne nuit. **2** n (advantage, virtue) bien m; **for her own g.** pour son bien; **it's no g. crying**/etc ça ne sert à rien de pleurer/etc; **that's no g.** (worthless) ça ne vaut rien; (bad) ça ne va pas; **what's the g.?** à quoi bon?; **for g.** pour de bon.
good·bye int au revoir.
good·look·ing adj beau (f belle).
good·ness bonté f; **my g.!** mon Dieu!; **thank g.!** Dieu merci!; **for g.' sake!** bon sang!
goods npl marchandises fpl; (articles for sale) articles mpl.
good·will bonne volonté f.
▸**go off** vi (leave) partir; (of alarm) se déclencher.
▸**go on** vi continuer (**doing** à faire); (happen) se passer; (last) durer.
goose, pl **geese** oie f.
goose·ber·ry groseille f à maquereau.
goose bumps npl chair f de poule.
▸**go out** vi sortir; (of light, fire) s'éteindre.

▸**go over 1** vi aller (**to** à); (to enemy) passer (**to** à); **to go over to sb's** faire un saut chez qn. **2** vt examiner; (in one's mind) repasser.
gorge (ravine) gorge f.
gor·geous adj magnifique.
go·ril·la gorille m.
Gos·pel Évangile m.
gos·sip 1 n (talk) bavardage(s) m(pl); (person) commère f. **2** vi (to talk) bavarder; (ill-naturedly) se livrer à des commérages.
got pt & pp de **get**.
▸**go through 1** vi passer. **2** vt (suffer) subir; (examine) examiner; (search) fouiller; (spend) dépenser; (wear out) user.
got·ten pp de **get**.
▸**go under** vi (of ship, company) couler.
▸**go up 1** vi monter; (of prices) augmenter. **2** vt to go up the stairs/street monter l'escalier/la rue.
gour·met gourmet m.
gov·ern 1 vt (rule) gouverner; (city) administrer; (influence) déterminer. **2** vi gouverner.
gov·ern·ment gouvernement m; (local) administration f.
gov·er·nor gouverneur m.
▸**go with** vt (accompany) accompagner, aller avec; (colors) aller avec.
▸**go without** vt se passer de.
gown (of woman) robe f.
grab vt to g. (hold of) saisir; to g. sth from sb arracher qch à qn.
grace (charm) grâce f.
grace·ful adj gracieux.
grade 1 n catégorie f, (in exam etc) note f, (class in school) classe f. **2** vt (classify) classer; (school paper) noter, corriger.
grade cross·ing passage m à niveau.
grade school école f primaire.
grad·u·al adj progressif.
gradu·al·ly adv progressivement.
grad·u·ate 1 vi obtenir son diplôme. **2** n diplômé, -ée mf.

grad·u·a·tion remise f des diplômes.

graf·fi·ti npl graffiti mpl.

graft 1 n greffe f. **2** vt greffer.

grain (seed) grain m; (cereal) céréales fpl.

gram gramme m.

gram·mar grammaire f.

gram·mar school = **grade school**.

gram·mat·i·cal adj grammatical.

grand adj (splendid) magnifique.

grand·dad(·dy) Fam papi m.

grand·child, pl **-children** petit(e)-enfant mf.

grand·daugh·ter petite-fille f.

grand·fa·ther grand-père m.

grand·ma Fam mamie f.

grand·moth·er grand-mère f.

grand·par·ents npl grands-parents mpl.

grand·son petit-fils m.

gran·ny Fam mamie f.

gra·no·la muesli m.

grant 1 vt accorder (to à); (request) accéder à; **to take sth for granted** considérer qch comme acquis; **I take it for granted that** je présume que. **2** n subvention f; (for study) bourse f.

grape grain m de raisin; **grapes** le raisin, les raisins mpl; **to eat (some) grapes** manger du raisin or des raisins.

grape·fruit pamplemousse m.

graph courbe f; **g. paper** papier m millimétré.

graph·ic adj graphique; **g. designer** graphiste mf.

graph·ics 1 n (study) art m graphique. **2** npl graphiques mpl.

grasp 1 vt (seize, understand) saisir. **2** n (hold) prise f; (understanding) compréhension f.

grass herbe f; (lawn) gazon m.

grass·hop·per sauterelle f.

grate 1 n (for fireplace) grille f de foyer. **2** vt (cheese etc) râper.

grate·ful adj reconnaissant (to à;

for de); **I'm g. (to you) for your help** je vous suis reconnaissant de votre aide.

grat·er râpe f.

grat·i·fy·ing adj très satisfaisant or agréable.

grat·i·tude reconnaissance f, gratitude f (for de).

grave[1] tombe f.

grave[2] adj (serious) grave.

grav·el gravier m.

grave·yard cimetière m.

grav·i·ty (force) pesanteur f.

gra·vy jus m de viande.

gray adj gris m; **to be going g.** grisonner.

graze 1 vi (of cattle) paître. **2** vt (skin) écorcher. **3** n (wound) écorchure f.

grease 1 n graisse f. **2** vt graisser.

greas·y adj plein de graisse; (hair) gras.

great adj grand; (excellent) Fam magnifique; **a g. deal (of),** a **g. many beaucoup (of); the greatest team**/etc (best) la meilleure équipe/etc.

great-grand·fa·ther arrière-grand-père m.

great-grand·moth·er arrière-grand-mère f.

great·ly (much) beaucoup; (very) très.

greed avidité f; (for food) gourmandise f.

greed·y adj avide; (for food) gourmand.

Greek 1 adj grec (f grecque). **2** n Grec m, Grecque f; (language) grec m.

green 1 adj vert; **to turn** or **go g.** verdir. **2** (color) vert m; (lawn) pelouse f; **greens** légumes mpl verts.

green·house serre f; **g. effect** effet m de serre.

greet vt saluer.

greet·ing salutation f; **greetings** (for birthday, festival) vœux mpl.

gre·nade (bomb) grenade f.

grey·hound lévrier m.

grid (on map) quadrillage m; (bars) grille f.

grief chagrin m.

grieve vi to g. for sb pleurer qn.

grill 1 n (utensil) gril m; (dish) grillade f. **2** vti griller.

grim adj (face, future) sombre; (bad) Fam affreux.

grime crasse f.

grim·y adj crasseux.

grin 1 vi avoir un large sourire. **2** n large sourire m.

grind* vt moudre; **to g. one's teeth** grincer des dents.

grind·er coffee g. moulin m à café.

grip 1 vt saisir; (hold) tenir serré. **2** n (hold) prise f; (with hand) poigne f; **in the g. of** en proie à.

grip·ping adj (book etc) prenant.

groan 1 vi gémir. **2** n gémissement m.

gro·cer épicier, -ière mf.

gro·cer·y g. **store** magasin m d'alimentation; **groceries** (food) épicerie f.

groin aine f.

groom (bridegroom) marié m.

groove (slot) rainure f.

▶ **grope around** vi tâtonner.

▶ **grope for** vt chercher à tâtons.

gross adj (total) (income etc) brut.

gross·ly adv (very) extrêmement.

ground terre f, sol m; (for camping etc) terrain m; **grounds** (reasons) raisons fpl; (gardens) parc m; **on the g.** (lying, sitting) par terre.

ground meat hachis m (de viande).

ground·work préparation f.

group groupe m.

group (to·geth·er) vti (se) grouper.

grow* 1 vi (of person) grandir; (of plant, hair) pousser; (increase) augmenter, grandir; (of company, town) se développer. **2** vt (plant, crops) cultiver; (beard) laisser pousser.

▶ **grow into** vt devenir.

growl vi grogner (**at** contre).

grown adj (man, woman) adulte.

grown-up grande personne f.

▶ **grow out of** vt (clothes) devenir trop grand pour; (habit) perdre.

growth croissance f; (increase) augmentation f (**in** de); (lump) tumeur f (**on** à).

▶ **grow up** vi devenir adulte.

grub (food) Fam bouffe f.

grub·by adj sale.

grudge rancune f; **to have a g. against** garder rancune à.

gru·el·ing adj éprouvant.

grue·some adj horrible.

grum·ble vi râler, grogner (**about**, **at** contre).

grump·y adj grincheux.

grunt 1 vti grogner. **2** n grognement m.

guar·an·tee 1 n garantie f. **2** vt garantir (**against** contre; **sb that** à qn que).

guard 1 n (vigilance, soldiers) garde f; (individual person) garde m; **to keep a g. on** surveiller; **under g.** sous surveillance; **on one's g.** sur ses gardes; **on g. (duty)** de garde; **to stand g.** monter la garde. **2** vt protéger; (watch over) surveiller.

guard·i·an gardien, -enne mf; (of minor) tuteur, -trice mf; (of museum) conservateur, -trice mf; **g. angel** ange m gardien.

guess 1 n conjecture f; (intuition) intuition f; **to make a g.** (essayer de) deviner. **2** vt deviner (**that** que); (length, number) estimer; (suppose) supposer; (think) croire (**that** que).

guess·work hypothèse f; **by g.** au jugé.

guest invité, -ée mf; (in hotel) client, -ente mf; (at meal) convive mf.

guest room chambre f d'amis.

guid·ance conseils mpl.

guide 1 n guide m; **g. (book)** guide m. **2** vt guider; **guided tour** visite f guidée.

guide·lines npl indications fpl (à suivre).

guild association f.

guilt culpabilité f.

guilt·y adj coupable; **g. person** coupable mf.

gui·nea pig cobaye m.

gui·tar guitare f.

gui·tar·ist guitariste mf.

gulf (in sea) golfe m; **a g. between** un abîme entre.

gull (bird) mouette f.

gulp (of drink) gorgée f.

▸ **gulp down** vt avaler (vite).

gum¹ (around teeth) gencive f.

gum² 1 n (for chewing) chewing-gum m; (glue) colle f. 2 vt coller.

gun pistolet m; (rifle) fusil m; (firing shells) canon m.

▸ **gun down** vt abattre.

gun·fire coups mpl de feu.

gun·man, pl -men bandit m armé.

gun·point at g. sous la menace d'une arme.

gun·pow·der poudre f à canon.

gun·shot coup m de feu.

gush (out) vi jaillir (of de).

gust g. (of wind) rafale f (de vent).

gut 1 n intestin m; **guts** (insides) entrailles fpl; Fam (courage) cran m. 2 vt (poultry, fish) étriper; (house) ravager.

gut·ter (on roof) gouttière f; (in street) caniveau m.

guy Fam type m.

gym gym(nastique) f; (gymnasium) gymnase m.

gym·nas·tics gymnastique f.

gy·ne·col·o·gist gynécologue mf.

H

hab·it habitude f; **to be in/get into the h. of doing** avoir/prendre l'habitude de faire.

hab·i·tat habitat m.

hack vt (cut) tailler.

hack·er (computer) h. pirate m informatique.

had pt & pp de **have**.

had·dock aiglefin m; **smoked h.** haddock m.

hag (old) h. (vieille) sorcière f.

hag·gle vi marchander; **to h. over the price** discuter le prix.

hail 1 n grêle f. 2 vi grêler; **it's hailing** il grêle.

hail·stone grêlon m.

hair (on head) cheveux mpl; (on body, of animal) poils mpl; **a h.** (on head) un cheveu; (on body, of animal) un poil.

hair·brush brosse f à cheveux.

hair·cut coupe f de cheveux; **to get a h.** se faire couper les cheveux.

hair·do, pl -dos Fam coiffure f.

hair·dress·er coiffeur, -euse mf.

hair dry·er sèche-cheveux m inv.

-haired suffix long-/red-h. aux cheveux longs/roux.

hair·pin épingle f à cheveux.

hair·rais·ing adj effrayant.

hair spray (bombe f de) laque f.

hair·style coiffure f.

hair·y adj (person, animal, body) poilu.

half 1 n (pl halves) moitié f, demi, -ie mf; **h. (of) the apple/etc** la moitié de la pomme/etc; **ten and a h.** dix et demi; **ten and a h. weeks** dix semaines et demie; **to cut in h.** couper en deux. 2 adj demi; **h. a day, a h.-day** une demi-journée; **h. a dozen, a h.-dozen** une demi-douzaine; **at h. price** à moitié prix. 3 adv (full etc) à demi, à moitié; **h. past one** une heure et demie.

half-heart·ed adj peu enthousiaste.

half-hour demi-heure f.

half-time (in game) mi-temps f.

half·way adv à mi-chemin (between entre); **to fill**/*etc* h. remplir/*etc* à moitié.

hal·i·but *(fish)* flétan *m*.

hall salle *f*; **lecture** h. amphithéâtre *m*.

Hal·low·e·en Halloween *m (la veille de la Toussaint)*.

hall·way entrée *f*.

halt halte *f*; **to call a** h. **to** mettre fin à.

halve *vt (time, expense)* réduire de moitié.

ham jambon *m*; h. **and eggs** œufs *mpl* au jambon.

ham·burg·er hamburger *m*; *(raw meat)* bœuf *m* haché.

ham·mer 1 *n* marteau *m*. **2** *vt (nail)* enfoncer **(into** dans).

ham·mer·ing *(defeat)* Fam raclée *f*.

ham·mock hamac *m*.

ham·per 1 *vt* gêner. **2** *n* panier *m*; *(laundry basket)* panier *m* à linge.

ham·ster hamster *m*.

hand¹ main *f*; *(of clock)* aiguille *f*; *Cards* jeu *m*; **to hold in one's** h. **te**nir à la main; **to give sb a (helping)** h. donner un coup de main à qn; **by** h. *(to make, sew etc)* à la main; **at** *or* **to** h. sous la main; **on** h. disponible; **out of** h. *(situation)* incontrôlable.

hand² *vt (give)* donner, passer **(to** à).

▸ **hand around** *vt (cookies)* passer.

hand·bag sac *m* à main.

hand·book manuel *m*; *(guide)* guide *m*.

hand·brake frein *m* à main.

hand·cuff *vt* passer les menottes à.

hand·cuffs *npl* menottes *fpl*.

hand·ful *(group)* poignée *f*.

hand·i·cap 1 *n* handicap *m*. **2** *vt* handicaper; **to be handicapped** *(after an accident etc)* rester handicapé.

hand·i·capped *adj* handicapé.

▸ **hand in** *vt* remettre.

hand·ker·chief, *pl* **-fs** mouchoir *m*.

han·dle 1 *n (of door)* poignée *f*; *(of knife)* manche *m*; *(of bucket)* anse *f*; *(of saucepan)* queue *f*. **2** *vt (manipulate)* manier; *(touch)* toucher à; *(vehicle)* manœuvrer; *(deal with)* s'occuper de.

han·dle·bars *npl* guidon *m*.

hand lug·gage bagages *mpl* à main.

hand·made *adj* fait à la main.

▸ **hand out** *vt* distribuer.

hand·out *(leaflet)* prospectus *m*; *(money)* aumône *f*; *(papers for course, workshop)* photocopies *fpl*.

▸ **hand over** *vt* remettre.

hand·rail rampe *f*.

hand·shake poignée *f* de main.

hand·some *adj* beau *(f* belle*)*; *(profit)* considérable.

hand·writ·ing écriture *f*.

hand·y *adj* commode, pratique; *(skillful)* habile **(at doing** à faire); *(within reach)* sous la main; *(place)* accessible.

hand·y·man, *pl* **-men** bricoleur *m*.

hang¹* 1 *vt (pt & pp* hung) suspendre **(on, from** à); *(let dangle)* laisser pendre **(from, out of** de). **2** *vi* pendre; *(of fog)* flotter. **3** *n* **to get the** h. **of sth** *Fam* arriver à comprendre qch.

hang² *vt (pt & pp* hanged) *(criminal)* pendre **(for** pour).

han·gar hangar *m*.

▸ **hang around** *vi* traîner; *(wait)* attendre.

▸ **hang down** *vi* pendre.

hang·er *(coat)* h. cintre *m*.

hang·glid·er deltaplane® *m*.

hang·ing *adj* suspendu **(from** à).

▸ **hang on** *vi* résister; *(wait)* attendre; **to** h. **on to** ne pas lâcher; *(keep)* garder.

▸ **hang out 1** *vt (laundry)* étendre; *(flag)* arborer. **2** *vi (of tongue, shirt)* pendre.

hang·o·ver gueule f de bois.

▶**hang up 1** vt (picture) accrocher. **2** vi (on phone) raccrocher.

hang-up complexe m.

hap·pen vi arriver, se passer; **to h. to sb/sth** arriver à qn/qch; **I h. to know** il se trouve que je le sais; **do you h. to have…?** est-ce que par hasard vous avez…?

hap·pen·ing événement m.

hap·pi·ly adv joyeusement; (contentedly) tranquillement; (fortunately) heureusement.

hap·pi·ness bonheur m.

hap·py adj heureux (**to do de faire**; **about sth** de qch); **I'm not h. about it** ça ne me plaît pas beaucoup; **H. New Year!** bonne année!

ha·rass vt harceler.

ha·rass·ment harcèlement m.

har·bor port m.

hard 1 adj (not soft, severe, difficult) dur; **h. worker** gros travailleur m; **h. on sb** dur avec qn; **h. of hearing** malentendant. **2** adv (to work, hit) dur; (to pull) fort; (to rain) à verse; **to think h.** réfléchir bien.

hard·ball (game) base-ball m; (ball) balle f de base-ball.

hard-boiled adj (egg) dur.

hard cop·y (document) copie f (sur) papier.

hard-core (group) noyau m.

hard disk disque m dur.

hard·en vti durcir; **to become hardened** to s'endurcir à.

hard·ly adv à peine; **h. anyone** presque personne; **h. ever** presque jamais.

hard·ness dureté f.

hard·ship épreuve(s) f(pl).

hard up adj (broke) Fam fauché.

hard·ware n inv quincaillerie f; (of computer) matériel m.

hard·ware store quincaillerie f.

hard-work·ing adj travailleur.

hare lièvre m.

harm 1 n (hurt) mal m; (wrong) tort m. **2** vt (physically) faire du mal à; (health, interests etc) nuire à.

harm·ful adj nuisible.

harm·less adj inoffensif.

har·mon·i·ca harmonica m.

har·mo·ni·ous adj harmonieux.

har·mo·ny harmonie f.

har·ness (for horse) harnais m; (to carry baby) porte-bébé m ventral.

harp harpe f.

▶**harp on** vt Fam ne pas s'arrêter de parler de.

harsh adj dur, sévère; (sound, taste) âpre.

harsh·ly adv durement.

harsh·ness dureté f.

har·vest 1 n moisson f; (of fruit) récolte f. **2** vt moissonner; récolter.

has see **have**.

has·sle Fam (trouble) histoires fpl; (aggravation) **it's a h.** c'est casse-pieds inv.

haste hâte f; **to make h.** se hâter.

has·ten 1 vi se hâter (**to do de faire**). **2** vt hâter.

has·ti·ly adv à la hâte.

hast·y adj précipité; (visit) rapide.

hat chapeau m; (of child) bonnet m; (cap) casquette f.

hatch vi (of chick, egg) éclore.

hatch·back (three-door) trois-portes f inv; (five-door) cinq-portes f inv.

hate vt détester, haïr; **to h. doing** or **to do** détester faire.

hate·ful adj haïssable.

ha·tred haine f.

haul vt (pull) tirer.

haunt 1 n (place) lieu m de prédilection; (of criminal) repaire m. **2** vt hanter.

haunt·ed adj hanté.

▶**have* 1** vt avoir; (meal, drink etc) prendre; **to h. a party/dream** faire une fête/un rêve; **will you h…?** (some cake, tea etc) est-ce que tu veux…?; **to let sb h. sth** donner qch à qn; **you've had it!** *Fam* tu es fichu! **2** *v aux* avoir; (*with 'monter', 'sortir' etc and reflexive verbs*) être; **to h. decided/been** avoir décidé/été; **to h. gone** être allé; **to h. cut oneself** s'être coupé; **I've got to go, I h. to go** je dois partir; **to h. sth done** faire faire qch; **he's had his suitcase brought up** il a fait monter sa valise; **haven't I?, hasn't she?/etc** n'est-ce pas?; **no I haven't!** non!; **yes I h.!** oui!; (*after negative question*) si!

hav·oc ravages *mpl*.

hawk faucon *m*.

hay foin *m*.

hay fe·ver rhume *m* des foins.

hay·stack meule *f* de foin.

haz·ard 1 *n* risque *m*. **2** *vt* risquer; **to h. a guess** essayer de deviner.

haze brume *f*.

ha·zel·nut noisette *f*.

haz·y *adj* (*weather*) brumeux; (*photo, idea*) flou.

he *pron* il; (*stressed*) lui; **he's a happy man** c'est un homme heureux.

head 1 *n* (*of person, hammer etc*) tête *f*, (*leader*) chef *m*; **it didn't enter my h.** ça ne m'est pas venu à l'esprit; **heads or tails?** pile ou face?; **per h., a h.** (*each*) par personne. **2** *adj* (*salesperson etc*) principal. **3** *vt* (*group, company*) être à la tête de; (*list*) être en tête de.

head·ache mal *m* de tête; **to have a h.** avoir mal à la tête.

head·band bandeau *m*.

▶**head for, be head·ing** or **head·ed for** *vt* (*place*) se diriger vers; (*disaster*) aller à.

head·ing (*of chapter etc*) titre *m*; (*of subject*) rubrique *f*.

head·light (*of vehicle*) phare *m*.

head·line (*of newspaper*) manchette *f*; **the headlines** les titres *mpl*.

head·mas·ter (*of school*) directeur *m*.

head·mis·tress (*of school*) directrice *f*.

head·phones *npl* casque *m* (à écouteurs).

head·quar·ters *npl* siège *m* (central); (*military*) quartier *m* général.

head·wait·er maître *m* d'hôtel.

head·way progrès *m*.

heal *vi* (*of wound*) se cicatriser; (*of bruise*) disparaître; (*of bone*) se ressouder.

health santé *f*.

health care soins *mpl* médicaux.

health food aliment *m* naturel; **h. food store** magasin *m* diététique.

health in·sur·ance assurance *f* maladie.

health·y *adj* (*person*) en bonne santé; (*food, attitude etc*) sain.

heap 1 *n* tas *m*; **heaps of** (*money, people*) *Fam* des tas de. **2** *vt* entasser.

▶**heap on** *vt* **to h. sth on sb** (*praise*) couvrir qn de qch; (*insults*) accabler qn de qch.

hear* 1 *vt* entendre; (*listen to*) écouter; (*learn*) apprendre (**that** que). **2** *vi* entendre; (*get news*) recevoir des nouvelles (**from** de); **I've heard of** or **about him** j'ai entendu parler de lui.

hear·ing (*sense*) ouïe *f*.

hear·ing aid appareil *m* auditif.

hearse corbillard *m*.

heart cœur *m*; **heart(s)** *Cards* cœur *m*; **by h.** par cœur.

heart at·tack crise *f* cardiaque.

heart·beat battement *m* de cœur.

heart·break·ing *adj* navrant.

heart·en·ing *adj* encourageant.

heart·y *adj* (*appetite*) gros (*f* grosse).

heat chaleur *f*; (*heating*) chauffage *m*.

heat (up) *vti* chauffer.

heat·er radiateur *m*.

heath lande *f*.

heat·ing chauffage m.

heat wave vague f de chaleur.

heave 1 vt (lift) soulever; (pull) tirer; (a sigh) pousser. **2** (feel sick) avoir des haut-le-cœur.

heav·en ciel m; **h. knows when** Dieu sait quand.

heav·i·ly adv lourdement; (to smoke, drink) beaucoup; **to rain h.** pleuvoir à verse.

heav·y adj lourd; (rain) fort; (traffic) dense; (smoker, drinker) grand.

heav·y·weight Boxing poids m lourd; (important person) personnage m important.

He·brew (language) hébreu m.

hec·tic adj fiévreux; (period) très agité.

hedge haie f.

hedge·hog hérisson m.

heel talon m.

heft·y adj gros (f grosse).

height hauteur f, (of person) taille f, (of success etc) sommet m; **at the h. of** (summer) au cœur de.

heir héritier m.

heir·ess héritière f.

held pt & pp de **hold**.

hel·i·cop·ter hélicoptère m.

hell enfer m; **a h. of a lot (of)** (very many, very much) Fam énormément (de); **h.!** Fam zut!

hel·lo! int bonjour!; (answering phone) allô!; (surprise) tiens!

helm (of boat) barre f.

hel·met casque m.

help 1 n aide f, secours m; (cleaning woman) femme f de ménage; (workers in office, store) employés, -ées mfpl; **h.!** au secours! **2** vt aider (**do, to do** à faire); **to h. oneself (to)** se servir (de); **I can't h. laughing/etc** je ne peux pas m'empêcher de rire/etc.

help·er assistant, -ante mf.

help·ful adj utile; (person) serviable.

help·ing (serving) portion f.

help·less adj (powerless) impuissant; (disabled) impotent.

▸ **help out** vti aider.

hem ourlet m.

hem·i·sphere hémisphère m.

hemmed in adj enfermé; (surrounded) cerné.

hem·or·rhage hémorragie f.

hen poule f.

hep·a·ti·tis hépatite f.

her 1 pron la, l'; (after prep, 'than', 'it is') elle; (to) h. lui; **I see h.** je la vois; **I give it to h.** je le/la lui donne. **2** poss adj son, sa, pl ses.

herb herbe f; **herbs** (in cooking) fines herbes fpl.

herd troupeau m.

here adv ici; **h. is, h. are** voici; **h. she is** la voici; **summer is h.** l'été est là; **h.!** (answering roll call) présent!; **h. (you are)!** (take this) tenez!

he·red·i·tar·y adj héréditaire.

her·mit solitaire mf.

he·ro, pl -oes héros m.

he·ro·ic adj héroïque.

her·o·in (drug) héroïne f.

her·o·ine héroïne f.

her·ring hareng m.

hers poss pron le sien, la sienne, pl les sien(ne)s; **this hat is h.** ce chapeau est à elle or est le sien.

her·self pron elle-même; (reflexive) se, s'; (after prep) elle.

hes·i·tant adj hésitant.

hes·i·tate vi hésiter (**about** sur; **to do** à faire).

hes·i·ta·tion hésitation f.

hey! int hé!; (calling attention) holà!

hi! int Fam salut!

hic·cups npl **to have (the) h.** avoir le hoquet.

hide¹ * **1** vt cacher (**from** à). **2** vi se cacher (**from** de).

hide² (skin) peau f.

hide-and-seek cache-cache m inv.

hid·e·ous adj horrible.

hid·e·ous·ly adv horriblement.

hide-out cachette f.

hid·ing **a good h.** (beating) une bonne raclée.

hid·ing place cachette f.

hi·er·ar·chy hiérarchie f.

hi-fi hi-fi f inv.

high 1 adj haut; (speed) grand; (price, number) élevé; (on drugs) Fam défoncé; **h. fever** forte fièvre f; **to be 16 feet h.** avoir 5 mètres de haut. **2** adv **h. (up)** (to fly, throw etc) haut. **3** n **an all-time h.** un nouveau record.

high·chair chaise f haute.

high-class adj (service) de premier ordre; (building) de luxe.

high·er adj supérieur (**than** à).

high·er ed·u·ca·tion enseignement m supérieur.

high·lands npl régions fpl montagneuses.

high·light 1 n (of visit, day) point m culminant; (of show) clou m. **2** vt souligner.

high·ly adv (very) très; (to recommend) chaudement; **h. paid** très bien payé.

high-pitched adj (sound) aigu (f -uë)

high-rise adj **h. apartment building** tour f.

high school (ages 11–15) = collège m; (ages 15–18) = lycée m.

high school di·plo·ma = baccalauréat m.

high-speed adj ultra-rapide; **h. train** rapide m.

high·way autoroute f.

hi·jack vt (aircraft) détourner.

hi·jack·er pirate m de l'air.

hi·jack·ing piraterie f aérienne; (one incident) détournement m.

hike 1 n excursion f à pied. **2** vi marcher à pied.

hik·er excursionniste mf.

hi·lar·i·ous adj hilarant.

hill colline f.

hill·side **on the h.** à flanc de colline.

hill·y adj accidenté.

him pron le, l'; (after prep, 'than', 'it is') lui; (to) h. lui; **I see h.** je le vois; **I give it to h.** je le/la lui donne.

him·self pron lui-même; (reflexive) se, s'; (after prep) lui.

hin·der vt gêner.

Hin·du 1 n Hindou, -oue mf. **2** adj hindou, -oue.

hinge charnière f.

hint 1 n allusion f, (sign) indication f; **hints** (advice) conseils mpl. **2** vt laisser entendre (**that** que).

▶ **hint at** vt faire allusion à.

hip hanche f.

hip·po·pot·a·mus hippopotame m.

hire vt (worker) engager, embaucher.

his 1 poss adj son, sa, pl ses. **2** poss pron le sien, la sienne, pl les sien(ne)s; **this hat is h.** ce chapeau est à lui or est le sien.

His·pan·ic 1 n Hispano-Américain, -aine mf. **2** adj hispano-américain, -aine.

hiss 1 vti siffler. **2** n sifflement m.

his·tor·i·c, his·tor·i·cal adj historique.

his·to·ry histoire f.

hit* 1 vt (beat etc) frapper; (bump into) heurter; (reach) atteindre; (affect) toucher. **2** n (blow) coup m; (play, film) succès m; **h. (song)** chanson f à succès.

hit-and-run driv·er chauffard m.

hitch 1 n (snag) problème m. **2** vti **to h. (a ride)** Fam faire du stop (**to** jusqu'à).

hitch·hike vi faire de l'auto-stop (**to** jusqu'à).

hitch·hik·er auto-stoppeur, -euse mf.

hitch·hik·ing auto-stop m.

▶ **hit (up)on** vt (find) tomber sur.

HIV abbr (human immunodeficiency virus) VIH m, HIV m; **to be H. positive/negative** être séropositif/séronégatif.

hive ruche f.

hoard vt amasser.

hoarse adj enroué.

hoax canular m.

hob·by passe-temps *m inv.*

ho·bo, *pl* **-os** vagabond, -onde *mf.*

hock·ey hockey *m*; **ice h.** hockey *m* sur glace.

hold 1 *n (grip)* prise *f*; *(of ship)* cale *f*; *(of aircraft)* soute *f*; **to get h. of** *(seize)* saisir; *(contact)* joindre; *(find)* trouver. **2** *vt** tenir; *(breath, interest, attention)* retenir; *(a post)* occuper; *(a record)* détenir; *(possess)* posséder; *(contain)* contenir; **to h. hands** se tenir par la main; **please h.** *(on phone)* ne quittez pas; **to be held** *(of event)* avoir lieu. **3** *vi (of nail, rope)* tenir; **if the rain holds off** s'il ne pleut pas.

▸**hold back** *vt (crowd)* contenir; *(hide)* cacher.

▸**hold down** *vt (price)* maintenir bas; *(job)* garder.

hold·er *(of passport)* titulaire *mf*; *(of record)* détenteur, -trice *mf*; *(container)* support *m.*

▸**hold on** *vi* attendre; *(stand firm)* tenir bon; **h. on!** *(on phone)* ne quittez pas!; **h. on (tight)** tenez bon!

▸**hold onto** *vt (cling to)* tenir bien; *(keep)* garder.

▸**hold out 1** *vt* offrir; *(arm)* étendre. **2** *vi* résister; *(last)* durer.

▸**hold up** *vt* lever; *(support)* soutenir; *(delay)* retarder; *(bank)* attaquer.

hold·up *(attack)* hold-up *m inv*; *(traffic jam)* bouchon *m.*

hole trou *m.*

hol·i·day *(legal)* jour *m* férié; **holidays** *(from school, work etc)* vacances *fpl.*

hol·low *adj* creux.

hol·ly houx *m.*

ho·ly *adj* saint; *(water)* bénit.

home 1 *n* maison *f*; *(country)* pays *m (natal)*; **at h.** à la maison, chez soi; **to make oneself at h.** se mettre à l'aise; **a good h.** une bonne famille; **(retirement) h.** maison *f* de retraite; **h. life/cooking/etc** la vie/cuisine/*etc* familiale. **2** *adv* à la maison, chez soi; **to go** *or* **come (back) h.** rentrer; **to be h.** être rentré.

home·land patrie *f.*

home·less *adj* sans abri.

home·made *adj* (fait à la) maison *inv.*

home·sick *adj* **to be h.** *(when abroad)* avoir le mal du pays; *(in general)* être nostalgique.

home·town ville *f* natale.

home·work devoir(s) *m(pl).*

ho·mo·sex·u·al *adj & n* homosexuel, -elle *(mf).*

hon·est *adj* honnête; *(frank)* franc *(f* franche*)* **(with** avec*).*

hon·es·ty honnêteté *f*; *(frankness)* franchise *f.*

hon·ey miel *m*; *(person)* Fam chéri, -ie *mf.*

hon·ey·moon lune *f* de miel; *(trip)* voyage *m* de noces.

honk *vi (in vehicle)* klaxonner.

hon·or 1 *n* honneur *m*; **in h. of** en l'honneur de; **with honors** *(academic distinction)* avec mention. **2** *vt* honorer **(with** de*).*

hon·or·a·ble *adj* honorable.

hood capuchon *m*; *(mask of robber)* cagoule *f*; *(car or carriage roof)* capote *f*; *(of car engine)* capot *m.*

hoof, *pl* **-fs** *or* **-ves** sabot *m.*

hook crochet *m*; *(on clothes)* agrafe *f*, Fishing hameçon *m*; **off the h.** *(phone)* décroché.

hooked *adj (nose, object)* recourbé; **h. on** *(drugs, chess etc)* Fam accro de.

▸**hook on** *or* **up** *vt* accrocher **(to** à*).*

hook·y **to play h.** sécher (la classe).

hoo·li·gan vandale *m.*

hoop cerceau *m.*

hoot 1 *vi (of owl)* hululer. **2** *n* hululement *m.*

hop 1 vi sauter (à cloche-pied); (of bird) sautiller; **h. in!** (in car) montez! **2** n saut m.

hope 1 n espoir m. **2** vi espérer; **I h. so** j'espère que oui. **3** vt espérer (**to do** faire; **that** que).

▸ **hope for** vt espérer.

hope·ful adj optimiste; (promising) prometteur; **to be h. that** avoir bon espoir que.

hope·ful·ly (one hopes) on espère (que).

hope·less adj désespéré; (useless) nul.

hope·less·ly (extremely) complètement.

hops npl houblon m.

hop·scotch marelle f.

ho·ri·zon horizon m; **on the h.** à l'horizon.

hor·i·zon·tal adj horizontal.

horn (of animal) corne f, (on vehicle) klaxon® m.

hor·ri·ble adj horrible.

hor·ri·bly adv horriblement.

hor·rif·ic adj horrible.

hor·ri·fy vt horrifier.

hor·ror horreur f.

horse cheval m.

horse·back **on h.** à cheval.

horse·pow·er cheval(-vapeur) m; **10 h.** 10 chevaux.

horse·ra·cing courses fpl.

horse·shoe fer m à cheval.

hose tuyau m; (pantyhose) collant m.

hos·pi·ta·ble adj accueillant.

hos·pi·tal hôpital m; **in the h.** à l'hôpital.

hos·pi·tal·i·ty hospitalité f.

hos·pi·tal·ize vt hospitaliser.

host hôte m; (of TV show) présentateur, -trice mf.

hos·tage otage m; **to take sb h.** prendre qn en otage.

hos·tel foyer m; **youth h.** auberge f de jeunesse.

host·ess hôtesse f.

hos·tile adj hostile (**to, towards** à).

hos·til·i·ty hostilité f(**to, towards** envers).

hot adj chaud; (spice) fort; **to be** or **feel h.** avoir chaud; **it's h.** (of weather) il fait chaud.

hot·cake crêpe f.

hot dog hot-dog m.

ho·tel hôtel m.

hot-wa·ter bottle bouillotte f.

hound vt (pursue) traquer.

hour heure f; **half an h.** une demi-heure; **a quarter of an h.** un quart d'heure.

hour·ly 1 adj (pay) horaire; **an h. bus/etc** bus/etc toutes les heures. **2** adv toutes les heures.

house[1], pl **-ses** maison f, (audience in theatre) salle f.

house[2] vt loger; (of building) abriter.

house·hold famille f.

house·keep·er gouvernante.

house·keep·ing ménage m (entretien).

House of Rep·re·sen·ta·tives Chambre f des représentants.

house·warm·ing **to have a h.** (party) pendre la crémaillère.

house·wife, pl **-wives** ménagère f.

house·work (travaux mpl de) ménage m.

hous·ing logement m; (houses) logements mpl.

hov·el taudis m.

hov·er vi (of bird etc) planer.

hov·er·craft aéroglisseur m.

how adv comment; **h. kind!** comme c'est gentil!; **h. do you do?** enchanté; **h. long/high is?** quelle est la longueur/hauteur de?; **h. much?, h. many?** combien?; **h. much time/etc?** combien de temps/etc?; **h. many apples/etc?** combien de pommes/etc?; **h. about some coffee?** du café?

how·e·ver 1 adv **h. big he may be** quelque grand qu'il soit; **h. she may do it** de quelque manière qu'elle le fasse. **2** conj cependant.

howl 1 *vi* hurler. **2** *n* hurlement *m*.
HQ *abbr (headquarters)* QG *m*.
hub·cap enjoliveur *m*.
hud·dle *vi* se blottir.
hug 1 *vt* serrer (dans ses bras). **2** *n* **to give sb a h.** serrer qn (dans ses bras).
huge *adj* énorme.
huh? *int Fam* hein?
hull *(of ship)* coque *f*.
hum 1 *vi (of insect)* bourdonner; *(of person)* fredonner. **2** *vt (tune)* fredonner.
hu·man *adj* humain; **h. being** être *m* humain.
hu·man·i·ty humanité *f*.
hum·ble *adj* humble.
hu·mid *adj* humide.
hu·mid·i·ty humidité *f*.
hu·mil·i·ate *vt* humilier.
hu·mil·i·a·tion humiliation *f*.
hu·mor·ous *adj (book etc)* humoristique; *(person)* plein d'humour.
hu·mor *(fun)* humour *m*.
hump *(lump)* bosse *f*.
hunch *Fam* intuition *f*.
hun·dred *adj & n* cent *(m)*; **a h. pages** cent pages; **hundreds of** des centaines de.
hun·dredth *adj & n* centième *(mf)*.
hun·ger faim *f*.
hun·gry *adj* **to be** *or* **feel h.** avoir faim; **to make h.** donner faim à.
hunt 1 *n (search)* recherche *f* (**for** de). **2** *vt (animals)* chasser; *(pursue)* poursuivre; *(seek)* chercher. **3** *vi* chasser.
▸ **hunt down** *vt* traquer.
hunt·er chasseur *m*.
▸ **hunt for** *vt* (re)chercher.
hunt·ing chasse *f*.
hur·dle *(fence)* haie *f*; *(problem)* obstacle *m*.
hurl *vt* lancer.
hur·ray! *int* hourra!
hur·ri·cane ouragan *m*.
hur·ry 1 *n* hâte *f*; **in a h.** à la hâte; **to**

be in a h. être pressé. **2** *vi* se dépêcher (**to do** de faire); **to h. through a meal** manger à toute vitesse; **to h. towards** se précipiter vers. **3** *vt (person)* bousculer.
▸ **hurry up** *vi* se dépêcher.
hurt* 1 *vt* faire du mal à; *(emotionally)* faire de la peine à; *(reputation etc)* nuire à; **to h. sb's feelings** blesser qn. **2** *vi* faire mal. **3** *n* mal *m*.
hus·band mari *m*.
hush silence *m*.
hus·tle 1 *vt (shove)* bousculer (qn). **2** *n* **h. and bustle** tourbillon *m*.
hut cabane *f*.
hy·dro·gen hydrogène *m*.
hy·giene hygiène *f*.
hy·gi·en·ic *adj* hygiénique.
hymn cantique *m*.
hy·phen trait *m* d'union.
hy·phen·at·ed *adj (word)* à trait d'union.
hyp·no·tize *vt* hypnotiser.
hy·poc·ri·sy hypocrisie *f*.
hyp·o·crite hypocrite *mf*.
hy·poth·e·sis, *pl* **-ses** hypothèse *f*.
hys·ter·i·cal *adj (upset)* qui a une crise de nerfs; *(funny) Fam* désopilant.
hys·ter·i·cal·ly *adv (to cry)* sans pouvoir s'arrêter.

I

I *pron* je, j'; *(stressed)* moi.
ice glace *f*; *(on road)* verglas *m*.
ice·berg iceberg *m*.
ice-cold *adj* glacial; *(drink)* glacé.
ice cream glace *f*.
ice cream bar esquimau® *m*.
ice cube glaçon *m*.
ice-skat·ing patinage *m* (sur glace).

▶**ice up** *vi (of windshield)* givrer.

i·ci·cle *(on cake)* glaçon *m*.

ic·ing *(on cake)* glaçage *m*.

ic·y *adj* glacé; *(weather)* glacial; *(road)* verglacé.

ID pièce *f* d'identité.

i·de·a idée *f*, **I have an i.** that j'ai l'impression que.

i·de·al 1 *adj* idéal *(mpl* -aux *or* -als). **2** *n* idéal *m (pl* -aux *or* -als).

i·de·al·ly *adv* idéalement; **i. we should stay** l'idéal, ce serait que nous restions.

i·den·ti·cal *adj* identique (**to,** **with** à).

i·den·ti·fi·ca·tion *(document)* pièce *f* d'identité.

i·den·ti·fy *vt* identifier; **to i.** (oneself) with s'identifier avec.

i·den·ti·ty identité *f*.

id·i·om expression *f* idiomatique.

id·i·ot idiot, -ote *mf*.

id·i·ot·ic *adj* idiot.

i·dle *adj (unoccupied)* inactif; *(lazy)* paresseux.

i·dler paresseux, -euse *mf*.

i·dol idole *f*.

i·dol·ize *vt (adore)* traiter comme une idole.

i.e. *abbr* c'est-à-dire.

if *conj* si; **if he comes** s'il vient; **even if** même si; **if only I were rich** si seulement j'étais riche.

ig·loo igloo *m*.

ig·no·rance ignorance *f* (**of** de).

ig·no·rant *adj* ignorant (**of** de).

ig·nore *vt* ne prêter aucune attention à *(qch)*; *(pretend not to recognize)* faire semblant de ne pas reconnaître *(qn)*.

ill 1 *adj (sick)* malade; *(bad)* mauvais. **2** *n* **ills** maux *mpl*.

il·le·gal *adj* illégal.

il·leg·i·ble *adj* illisible.

il·lit·er·ate *adj* illettré.

ill·ness maladie *f*.

ill-treat *vt* maltraiter.

il·lu·sion illusion *f* (**about** sur).

il·lus·trate *vt* illustrer (**with** de).

il·lus·tra·tion illustration *f*.

im·age image *f*; **i. (public) i.** *(of firm)* image *f* de marque.

i·mag·i·nar·y *adj* imaginaire.

i·mag·i·na·tion imagination *f*.

i·mag·ine *vt* (s')imaginer (**that** que).

im·i·tate *vt* imiter.

im·i·ta·tion imitation *f*; **i. jewelry** bijoux *mpl* fantaisie.

im·mac·u·late *adj* impeccable.

im·ma·ture *adj (person)* qui manque de maturité.

im·me·di·ate *adj* immédiat.

im·me·di·ate·ly 1 *adv (at once)* tout de suite, immédiatement. **2** *conj (as soon as)* dès que.

im·mense *adj* immense.

im·mense·ly *adv* extraordinairement.

im·mi·grant *n & adj* immigré, -ée *(mf)*.

im·mi·gra·tion immigration *f*.

im·mi·nent *adj* imminent.

im·mor·tal *adj* immortel.

im·mune *adj (naturally)* immunisé (**to** contre); *(vaccinated)* vacciné.

im·mu·nize *vt* vacciner (**against** contre).

im·pact effet *m* (**on** sur).

im·pa·tience impatience *f*.

im·pa·tient *adj* impatient (**to do** de faire).

im·pa·tient·ly *adv* avec impatience.

im·per·a·tive *Grammar* impératif *m*.

im·per·son·ate *vt* se faire passer pour; *(on TV etc)* imiter.

im·per·son·a·tor *(on TV etc)* imitateur, -trice *mf*.

im·per·ti·nent *adj* impertinent (**to** envers).

im·pe·tus impulsion *f*.

im·ple·ment[1] *(tool)* instrument *m*; *(utensil)* ustensile *m*.

im·ple·ment[2] *vt* mettre en œuvre.

im·pli·ca·tion conséquence f, (impact) portée f.

im·plic·it adj (implied) implicite; (absolute) absolu.

im·ply vt laisser entendre (that que); (assume) impliquer.

im·po·lite adj impoli.

im·port 1 vt importer (from de). **2** n importation f.

im·por·tance importance f; of no i. sans importance.

im·por·tant adj important.

im·port·er importateur, -trice mf.

im·pose 1 vt imposer (on à); (fine) infliger (on à). **2** vi (cause trouble) déranger; to i. on sb déranger qn.

im·pos·ing adj (building) impressionnant.

im·po·si·tion (inconvenience) dérangement m.

im·pos·si·bil·i·ty impossibilité f.

im·pos·si·ble adj impossible (to do à faire); it is i. (for us) to do it il (nous) est impossible de le faire.

im·pos·tor imposteur m.

im·prac·ti·cal adj peu réaliste.

im·press vt impressionner (qn).

im·pres·sion impression f.

im·pres·sive adj impressionnant.

im·pris·on vt emprisonner.

im·prob·a·ble adj peu probable.

im·prop·er adj (obscene) indécent; (inappropriate) inopportun, peu approprié.

im·prove 1 vt améliorer. **2** vi s'améliorer; (of business) reprendre.

im·prove·ment amélioration f.

▶**improve on** vt faire mieux que.

im·pro·vise vti improviser.

im·pu·dent adj impudent.

im·pulse impulsion f; on i. sur un coup de tête.

im·pul·sive adj impulsif.

im·pul·sive·ly adv de manière impulsive.

im·pu·ri·ty impureté f.

in 1 prep dans; in the box/etc dans la boîte/etc; in an hour('s) time dans une heure. ▪ à; in school à l'école; in Paris à Paris; in Portugal au Portugal; in ink à l'encre. ▪ en; in summer/May/French en été/mai/français; in Spain en Espagne; in an hour (within that period) en une heure; in doing en faisant. ▪ de; in a soft voice d'une voix douce; the best in le meilleur de. ▪ in the morning le matin; one in ten un sur dix. **2** adv to be in (home) être là, être à la maison; (of train) être arrivé; (in fashion) être en vogue.

in- prefix in-.

in·a·bil·i·ty incapacité f (to do de faire).

in·ac·ces·si·ble adj inaccessible.

in·ac·cu·ra·cy (error) inexactitude f.

in·ac·cu·rate adj inexact.

in·ad·e·qua·cy insuffisance f.

in·ad·e·quate adj insuffisant; (person) pas à la hauteur.

in·ap·pro·pri·ate adj peu approprié.

in·au·gu·rate vt (building) inaugurer.

in·au·gu·ra·tion inauguration f.

Inc abbr (Incorporated) = SARL.

in·ca·pa·ble adj incapable (of doing de faire).

in·cense vt mettre en colère.

in·cen·tive encouragement m, motivation f.

inch pouce m (= 2,54cm).

in·ci·dent incident m; (in film etc) épisode m.

in·ci·dent·al·ly (by the way) à propos.

in·cite vt inciter (to do à faire).

in·cite·ment incitation f.

in·cli·na·tion (desire) envie f (to do de faire).

in·cline vt (bend) incliner; to be inclined to do (feel a wish to) avoir

in·clude *vt (contain)* comprendre; **to be included** être compris; *(on list)* être inclus.

in·clud·ing *prep* y compris; **i. ser·vice** service *m* compris; **up to and i. Monday** jusqu'à lundi inclus.

in·clu·sive *adj* inclus; **to be i. of** comprendre.

in·come revenu *m (from* de); **pri·vate i.** rentes *fpl.*

in·come tax impôt *m* sur le revenu.

in·com·pat·i·ble *adj* incompatible (**with** avec).

in·com·pe·tent *adj* incompétent.

in·com·plete *adj* incomplet.

in·con·ceiv·a·ble *adj* inconcevable.

in·con·sid·er·ate *adj (remark)* irréfléchi; *(person)* pas très gentil (**towards** avec).

in·con·sis·ten·cy incohérence *f.*

in·con·sis·tent *adj* en contradiction (**with** avec).

in·con·spic·u·ous *adj* peu en évidence.

in·con·ven·ience 1 *n (bother)* dérangement *m; (disadvantage)* inconvénient *m.* **2** *vt* déranger, gêner.

in·con·ven·ient *adj (moment, situation etc)* gênant; *(house)* mal situé; **it's i. (for me) to** ça me dérange de.

in·cor·po·rate *vt (contain)* contenir.

in·cor·rect *adj* inexact; **you're i.** vous avez tort.

in·crease 1 *vi* augmenter; *(of effort, noise)* s'intensifier. **2** *vt* augmenter; intensifier. **3** *n* augmentation *f* (**in, of** de); *(of effort, noise)* intensification *f,* **on the i.** en hausse.

in·creas·ing *adj (amount)* croissant.

in·creas·ing·ly *adv* de plus en plus.

in·cred·i·ble *adj* incroyable.

in·cred·i·bly *adv* incroyablement.

in·cu·ba·tor *(for baby, eggs)* couveuse *f.*

in·cur *vt (expenses)* faire; *(loss)* subir.

in·cur·a·ble *adj* incurable.

in·de·cent *adj (obscene)* indécent.

in·de·ci·sive *adj* indécis.

in·deed *adv* en effet; **very good/ etc i.** vraiment très bon/*etc;* **yes i.!** bien sûr!; **thank you very much i.!** merci infiniment!

in·def·i·nite *adj* indéfini.

in·def·i·nite·ly *adv* indéfiniment.

in·de·pend·ence indépendance *f.*

in·de·pend·ent *adj* indépendant (**of** de).

in·de·pend·ent·ly *adv* de façon indépendante; **i. of** indépendamment de.

in·dex 1 *n (in book)* index *m.* **2** *vt (classify)* classer.

in·dex card fiche *f.*

in·dex fin·ger index *m.*

in·dex-linked *adj* indexé (**to** sur).

In·di·an 1 *n* Indien, -ienne *mf.* **2** *adj* indien, -ienne.

in·di·cate *vt* indiquer (**that** que).

in·di·ca·tion *(sign)* indice *m,* indication *f.*

in·di·ca·tor *(instrument)* indicateur *m; (in vehicle)* clignotant *m.*

in·dif·fer·ence indifférence *f* (**to** à).

in·dif·fer·ent *adj* indifférent (**to** à).

in·di·ges·tion problèmes *mpl* de digestion; **(an attack of) i.** une indigestion.

in·dig·nant *adj* indigné (**at** de).

in·dig·na·tion indignation *f.*

in·di·rect *adj* indirect.

in·di·rect·ly *adv* indirectement.

in·dis·creet adj indiscret.
in·dis·crim·i·nate (random) fait/donné/etc au hasard.
in·dis·crim·i·nate·ly adv (at random) au hasard.
in·dis·tin·guish·a·ble adj indifférenciable (from de).
in·di·vid·u·al 1 adj individuel; (specific) particulier. **2** n (person) individu m.
indi·vidu·al·ly adv (separately) individuellement.
in·door adj (games, shoes etc) d'intérieur; (swimming pool) couvert.
in·doors adv à l'intérieur.
in·duce vt persuader (to do de faire); (cause) provoquer.
in·dulge 1 vt (person) gâter; (whim) satisfaire; **to i.** oneself se faire plaisir. **2** vi se faire plaisir.
▸ **indulge** in vt se permettre.
in·dul·gent adj indulgent (to envers).
in·dus·tri·al adj industriel; (conflict) du travail; **i. park** zone f industrielle.
in·dus·try industrie f.
in·ed·i·ble adj immangeable.
in·ef·fec·tive adj (measure) inefficace.
in·ef·fi·cien·cy inefficacité f.
in·ef·fi·cient adj (person, measure) inefficace.
in·ept adj (unskilled) peu habile (at à); (incompetent) incapable.
in·e·qual·i·ty inégalité f.
in·ev·i·ta·ble adj inévitable.
in·ev·i·ta·bly adv inévitablement.
in·ex·cus·a·ble adj inexcusable.
in·ex·pen·sive adj bon marché inv.
in·ex·pe·ri·ence inexpérience f.
in·ex·pe·ri·enced adj inexpérimenté.
in·ex·pli·ca·ble adj inexplicable.
in·fal·li·ble adj infaillible.
in·fa·mous adj (evil) infâme.
in·fan·cy petite enfance f.

in·fant petit(e) enfant mf; (baby) nourrisson m.
in·fan·try infanterie f.
in·fat·u·at·ed adj amoureux (with de).
in·fat·u·a·tion engouement m (for, with pour).
in·fect vt infecter; **to get infected** s'infecter.
in·fec·tion infection f.
in·fec·tious adj contagieux.
in·fer vt déduire (from de).
in·fe·ri·or adj inférieur (to à); (goods, work) de qualité inférieure.
in·fe·ri·or·i·ty infériorité f.
in·fer·nal adj infernal.
in·fest vt infester (with de).
in·fi·nite adj infini.
in·fi·nite·ly adv infiniment.
in·fin·i·tive Grammar infinitif m.
in·fin·i·ty infini m.
in·firm adj infirme.
in·flamed adj (throat etc) enflammé.
in·flam·ma·tion inflammation f.
in·flate vt gonfler.
in·fla·tion inflation f.
in·flex·i·ble adj inflexible.
in·flict vt (a wound) occasionner (on à); **to i. pain on sb** faire souffrir qn.
in·flu·ence 1 n influence f; **under the i. (of drink)** en état d'ébriété. **2** vt influencer.
in·flu·en·tial adj **to be i.** avoir une grande influence.
in·flu·en·za grippe f.
in·flux flot m.
in·fo Fam renseignements mpl (on sur).
in·form vt informer (of de; that que).
in·for·mal adj simple, décontracté; (expression) familier; (meeting) non-officiel.
in·for·mal·ly adv sans cérémonie; (to dress) simplement; (to discuss) à titre non-officiel.
in·for·ma·tion renseignements

mpl (**about, on** sur); **a piece of i.** un renseignement.

in·form·a·tive *adj* instructif.

▸ **inform on** *vt* dénoncer.

in·fu·ri·ate *vt* exaspérer.

in·gen·ious *adj* ingénieux.

in·grat·i·tude ingratitude *f*.

in·gre·di·ent ingrédient *m*.

in·hab·it *vt* habiter.

in·hab·i·tant habitant, -ante *mf*.

in·hale *vt* aspirer.

in·her·it *vt* hériter (de).

in·her·i·tance héritage *m*.

in·hib·it *vt* (*hinder*) gêner; **to be inhibited** avoir des inhibitions.

in·hi·bi·tion inhibition *f*.

in·hos·pi·ta·ble *adj* peu accueillant, inhospitalier.

in·hu·man *adj* inhumain.

in·i·tial 1 *adj* premier. **2** *n* **initials** initiales *fpl*; (*signature*) paraphe *m*. **3** *vt* parapher.

in·i·tial·ly *adv* au début.

in·i·ti·ate *vt* (*reform, negotiations*) amorcer; (*quarrel*) provoquer, déclencher; (*lawsuit*) entamer; (*into society*) initier (**into** à).

in·ject *vt* injecter (**into** dans).

in·jec·tion injection *f*, piqûre *f*.

in·jure *vt* (*physically*) blesser, faire du mal à.

in·jured 1 *adj* blessé. **2** *n* **the i.** les blessés *mpl*.

in·ju·ry blessure *f*; (*fracture*) fracture *f*; (*sprain*) foulure *f*.

in·jus·tice injustice *f*.

ink encre *f*.

in·kling (petite) idée *f*.

in·land 1 *adj* intérieur. **2** *adv* à l'intérieur.

in-laws *npl* belle-famille *f*.

in·mate (*of prison*) détenu, -ue *mf*.

inn auberge *f*.

in·ner *adj* intérieur; **the i. city** les quartiers défavorisés du centre-ville.

in·ner tube (*of tire*) chambre *f* à air.

inn·keep·er aubergiste *mf*.

in·no·cence innocence *f*.

in·no·cent *adj* innocent.

in·oc·u·late *vt* vacciner (**against** contre).

in·oc·u·la·tion vaccination *f*.

in·put (*computer operation*) entrée *f*; (*data*) données *fpl*.

in·quire 1 *vi* se renseigner (**about** sur). **2** *vt* demander; **to i. how to get to** demander le chemin de.

▸ **inquire into** *vt* faire une enquête sur.

in·quir·y demande *f* de renseignements; (*investigation*) enquête *f*.

in·quis·i·tive *adj* curieux.

in·sane *adj* fou (*f* folle).

in·san·i·ty folie *f*.

in·scrip·tion inscription *f*, (*in book*) dédicace *f*.

in·sect insecte *m*.

in·sec·ti·cide insecticide *m*.

in·se·cure *adj* (*not securely fixed*) mal fixé; (*uncertain*) incertain; (*person*) qui manque d'assurance.

in·sen·si·tive *adj* insensible (**to** à).

in·sen·si·tiv·i·ty insensibilité *f*.

in·sert *vt* introduire, insérer (**in, into** dans).

in·side 1 *adv* dedans, à l'intérieur. **2** *prep* à l'intérieur de. **3** *n* dedans *m*, intérieur *m*; **on the i.** à l'intérieur (**of** de); **i. out** (*socks etc*) à l'envers. **4** *adj* intérieur.

in·sid·er initié, -ée *mf*.

in·sight (*into question*) aperçu *m* (**into** de).

in·sig·nif·i·cant *adj* insignifiant.

in·sin·cere *adj* peu sincère.

in·sist 1 *vi* insister (**on doing** pour faire). **2** *vt* (*order*) insister (**that** pour que + *subjunctive*); (*declare*) affirmer (**that** que).

in·sis·tence insistance *f*; **her i. on seeing me** l'insistance qu'elle met à vouloir me voir.

in·sis·tent *adj* **to be i.** insister (**that** pour que + *subjunctive*).

▸ **insist on** *vt* (*demand*) exiger; (*assert*) affirmer.

in·so·lence insolence f.

in·so·lent adj insolent.

in·som·ni·a insomnie f.

in·spect vt contrôler.

in·spec·tion inspection f; (of tickets) contrôle m.

in·spec·tor inspecteur, -trice mf.

in·spi·ra·tion inspiration f.

in·spire vt inspirer (**sb with sth** qch à qn).

in·stall vt installer.

in·stall·ment (of money) acompte m; (of serial) épisode m.

in·stance (example) cas m; **for i.** par exemple.

in·stant 1 adj immédiat; **i. coffee** café m soluble. **2** (moment) instant m.

in·stant·ly adv immédiatement.

in·stead adv plutôt; **i. of (doing)** sth au lieu de (faire) qch; **i. of sb** à la place de qn; **i. (of him)** à sa place.

in·stinct instinct m.

in·stinc·tive adj instinctif.

in·stinc·tive·ly adv instinctivement.

in·sti·tu·tion institution f.

in·struct vt (teach) enseigner (**sb in sth** qch à qn); **to i. sb to do** (order) charger qn de faire.

in·struc·tions npl (for use) mode m d'emploi; (orders) instructions fpl.

in·struc·tive adj instructif.

in·struc·tor (for skiing etc) moniteur, -trice mf; **driving i.** moniteur, -trice mf d'auto-école.

in·stru·ment instrument m.

in·stru·men·tal adj Music instrumental; **to be i. in sth** contribuer à qch.

in·suf·fi·cient adj insuffisant.

in·su·late vt (against cold and electrically) isoler.

in·su·la·tion (material) isolant m.

in·sult 1 vt insulter. **2** n insulte f (**to** à).

in·sur·ance assurance f; **i. company** compagnie f d'assurances.

in·sure vt assurer (**against** contre).

in·tact adj intact.

in·take (of water) prise f, arrivée f; (of food, alcohol etc) consommation f, (of students, recruits) admission f.

in·te·grate 1 vt intégrer. **2** vi s'intégrer.

in·teg·ri·ty intégrité f.

in·tel·lect intelligence f.

in·tel·lec·tu·al adj & n intellectuel, -elle (mf).

in·tel·li·gence intelligence f.

in·tel·li·gent adj intelligent.

in·tel·li·gi·ble adj compréhensible.

in·tend vt (gift etc) destiner (**for** à); **to be intended to do/for sb** être destiné à faire/à qn; **to i. to do** avoir l'intention de faire.

in·tense adj intense; (interest) vif.

in·ten·si·fy 1 vt intensifier. **2** vi s'intensifier.

in·ten·si·ty intensité f.

in·ten·sive adj intensif; **i. care** réanimation f.

in·tent adj **i. on doing** résolu à faire.

in·ten·tion intention f (**of doing** de faire).

in·ten·tion·al adj **it wasn't i.** ce n'était pas fait exprès.

in·ten·tion·al·ly adv exprès.

in·ter·act vi (people) communiquer.

in·ter·ac·tive adj interactif, -ive.

in·ter·cept vt intercepter.

in·ter·change (on road) échangeur m.

in·ter·change·a·ble adj interchangeable.

in·ter·com interphone m.

in·ter·con·nect·ed adj (facts etc) liés.

in·ter·course (sexual) rapports mpl sexuels.

in·ter·est 1 n intérêt m; (money) intérêts mpl; **to take an i. in** s'intéresser à; **to be of i. to sb** intéresser qn. **2** vt intéresser.

in·ter·est·ed *adj* intéressé; **to be i. in sth/sb** s'intéresser à qch/qn; **I'm i. in doing** ça m'intéresse de faire.

in·ter·est·ing *adj* intéressant.

in·ter·fere *vi* se mêler des affaires d'autrui.

▸ **interfere in** *vt* s'ingérer dans.

in·ter·fer·ence ingérence *f*; *(on radio)* parasites *mpl*.

▸ **interfere with** *vt (upset)* déranger.

in·ter·im 1 *n* **in the i.** entretemps. 2 *adj* provisoire.

in·te·ri·or 1 *adj* intérieur. 2 *n* intérieur *m*.

in·ter·jec·tion *Grammar* interjection *f*.

in·ter·me·di·ar·y intermédiaire *mf*.

in·ter·me·di·ate *adj* intermédiaire; *(course)* de niveau moyen.

in·ter·mis·sion *(in theater)* entracte *m*.

in·tern interne *mf* (des hôpitaux).

in·ter·nal *adj* interne; *(flight)* intérieur.

In·ter·nal Rev·e·nue Ser·vice service *m* des impôts.

in·ter·na·tion·al *adj* international.

in·ter·pret *vt* interpréter.

in·ter·pret·er interprète *mf*.

in·ter·ro·gate *vt* interroger.

in·ter·ro·ga·tion *(by police)* interrogatoire *m*.

in·ter·rog·a·tive *adj & n Grammar* interrogatif *(m)*.

in·ter·rupt *vt* interrompre.

in·ter·rup·tion interruption *f*.

in·ter·sect 1 *vt* couper. 2 *vi* s'entrecouper.

in·ter·sec·tion *(of roads, lines)* intersection *f*.

in·ter·state autoroute *f*.

in·ter·val intervalle *m*.

in·ter·vene *vi (of person)* intervenir; *(of event)* survenir.

in·ter·ven·tion intervention *f*.

in·ter·view 1 *n* entrevue *f* (**with** avec); *(on TV etc)* interview *f*. 2 *vt* avoir une entrevue avec; *(on TV etc)* interviewer.

in·ter·view·er *(on TV etc)* interviewer *m*.

in·ti·mate *adj* intime.

in·tim·i·date *vt* intimider.

in·to *prep* dans; **to put i.** mettre dans. ▪ **en; to translate i.** traduire en; **i. pieces** en morceaux. ▪ **to be i. yoga/etc** *Fam* être à fond dans le yoga/etc.

in·tol·er·a·ble *adj* intolérable (**that** que + *subjunctive*).

in·tox·i·cate *vt* enivrer.

in·tox·i·cat·ed *adj* ivre.

in·tran·si·tive *adj Grammar* intransitif.

in·tri·cate *adj* complexe.

in·tro·duce *vt (bring in)* introduire (**into** dans); *(program)* présenter; **to i. sb to sb** présenter qn à qn.

in·tro·duc·tion introduction *f*; *(of person to person)* présentation *f*; **i. to** *(initiation)* premier contact avec.

in·trude *vi* déranger (**on sb** qn).

in·trud·er intrus, -use *mf*.

in·tru·sion *(disturbance)* dérangement *m*.

in·tu·i·tion intuition *f*.

in·un·dat·ed *adj* submergé (**with work/letters/etc** de travail/lettres/etc).

in·vade *vt* envahir.

in·vad·er envahisseur, -euse *mf*.

in·val·id[1] malade *mf*; *(through injury)* infirme *mf*.

in·val·id[2] *adj* non valable.

in·val·u·a·ble *adj* inestimable.

in·va·ri·a·bly *adv (always)* toujours.

in·va·sion invasion *f*.

in·vent *vt* inventer.

in·ven·tion invention *f*.

in·ven·tor inventeur, -trice *mf*.

in·ven·to·ry inventaire *m*.

in·vest vt (money) placer, investir (in dans).

in·ves·ti·gate vt examiner; (crime) enquêter sur.

in·ves·ti·ga·tion examen m; (inquiry by journalist, police etc) enquête f (of, into sur).

in·ves·ti·ga·tor enquêteur, -euse mf.

▶ **invest in** vt placer son argent dans; (firm) investir dans.

in·vest·ment investissement m, placement m.

in·ves·tor (in shares) actionnaire mf; (saver) épargnant, -ante mf.

in·vig·or·at·ing adj stimulant.

in·vis·i·ble adj invisible.

in·vi·ta·tion invitation f.

in·vite vt inviter (to do à faire); (ask for) demander; (give occasion for) provoquer.

in·vit·ing adj engageant.

in·voice 1 n facture f. 2 vt facturer.

in·voke vt invoquer.

in·volve vt (person) mêler (in à); (entail) entraîner; the job involves le poste nécessite

in·volved adj (concerned) concerné; (committed) engagé (in dans); (complicated) compliqué; (at stake) en jeu; the person i. la personne en question; to be i. with sb avoir des liens intimes avec qn.

in·volve·ment participation f (in à); (commitment) engagement m; (emotional) liaison f.

in·ward(s) adv vers l'intérieur.

IOU abbr (I owe you) reconnaissance f de dette.

IQ abbr (intelligence quotient) QI m inv.

IRA abbr (individual retirement account) plan m d'épargne retraite personnel.

i·ris (plant, of eye) iris m.

I·rish 1 npl the I. les Irlandais mpl. 2 adj irlandais.

I·rish·man, pl -men Irlandais m.

I·rish·wom·an, pl -women Irlandaise f.

i·ron 1 n fer m; (for clothes) fer m (à repasser). 2 vt (clothes) repasser.

i·ron·ic, **i·ron·i·cal** adj ironique.

i·ron·ing repassage m.

i·ron·ing board planche f à repasser.

i·ro·ny ironie f.

ir·ra·tion·al adj (person) peu rationnel.

ir·reg·u·lar adj irrégulier.

ir·rel·e·vance manque m de rapport.

ir·rel·e·vant adj sans rapport (to avec); that's i. ça n'a rien à voir.

ir·re·sist·i·ble adj irrésistible.

ir·re·spec·tive of prep sans tenir compte de.

ir·ri·gate vt irriguer.

ir·ri·ta·ble adj irritable.

ir·ri·tate vt (annoy, inflame) irriter.

ir·ri·tat·ing adj irritant.

ir·ri·ta·tion irritation f.

is see be.

Is·lam·ic adj islamique.

is·land île f.

i·so·late vt isoler (from de).

i·so·lat·ed adj isolé.

i·so·la·tion isolement m; in i. isolément.

is·sue 1 vt publier; (tickets) distribuer; (passport) délivrer; (an order) donner; (warning) lancer; (supply) fournir (with de; to à). 2 n (matter) question f, (newspaper) numéro m.

it pron (subject) il, elle; (object) le, la, l'; (to) it (indirect object) lui; it's ringing il sonne; I've done it je l'ai fait. ▪ (impersonal) il; it's snowing il neige. ▪ (non specific) ce, cela, ça; who is it? qui est-ce?; it was Paul who... c'est Paul qui... ▪ of it, from it, about it en; in it, to it, at it y; on it dessus; under it dessous.

I·tal·ian 1 n Italien, -ienne mf; (language) italien m. 2 adj italien, -ienne.

i·tal·ics *npl* italique *m*.

itch 1 *n* démangeaison(s) *f(pl)*. **2** *vi* démanger; **his arm itches** son bras le démange.

itch·ing démangeaison(s) *f(pl)*.

itch·y *adj* **I have an i. hand** j'ai une main qui me démange.

i·tem (*object*) article *m*; (*matter*) question *f*. (**news**) **i.** information *f*.

its *poss adj* son, sa, *pl* ses.

it·self *pron* lui-même, elle-même; (*reflexive*) se, s'.

i·vo·ry ivoire *m*.

i·vy lierre *m*.

J

jab 1 *vt* enfoncer (**into** dans); (*prick*) piquer (*qn*) (**with sth** du bout de qch). **2** *n* (*blow*) coup *m*.

jack (*for car*) cric *m*; *Cards* valet *m*. **j. of all trades** homme *m* à tout faire.

jack·et veste *f*, **j. potato** pomme *f* de terre en robe des champs.

jack·ham·mer marteau *m* piqueur.

Ja·cuz·zi® Jacuzzi® *m*.

jag·ged *adj* déchiqueté.

jag·uar jaguar *m*.

jail 1 *n* prison *f*. **2** *vt* emprisonner.

jam¹ confiture *f*.

jam² **1** *n* (*traffic* **j.**) embouteillage *m*. **2** *vt* (*squeeze, make stuck*) coincer; (*street etc*) encombrer. **3** *vi* (*get stuck*) se coincer.

▸ **jam into** *vt* **to j. sth into sth** (*cram*) (en)tasser qch dans qch.

jammed *adj* (*machine etc*) coincé, bloqué; (*street etc*) encombré.

jam-packed *adj* bourré de monde.

jan·i·tor concierge *m*.

Jan·u·ar·y janvier *m*.

Jap·a·nese 1 *n* Japonais, -aise *mf*; (*language*) japonais *m*. **2** *adj* japonais, -aise.

jar pot *m*; (*large, glass*) bocal *m*.

jaun·dice jaunisse *f*.

jave·lin javelot *m*.

jaw mâchoire *f*.

jay·walk·ing = délit *m* mineur qui consiste à traverser une rue en dehors des clous ou au feu vert.

jazz jazz *m*.

jea·lous *adj* jaloux (*f* -ouse) (**of** de).

jeal·ous·y jalousie *f*.

jeans *npl* (**pair of**) **j.** (blue-)jean *m*.

jeep® jeep® *f*.

jeer (at) *vti* railler; (*boo*) huer.

jeer·ing (*of crowd*) huées *fpl*.

jeers *npl* huées *fpl*.

Jell-O® *inv* gelée *f*.

jel·ly (*preserve, dessert*) gelée *f*.

jeop·ard·ize *vt* mettre en danger.

jeop·ard·y danger *m*.

jerk 1 *vt* donner une secousse à. **2** *n* secousse *f*; (*stupid*) **j.** *Fam* crétin, -ine *mf*.

jer·sey (*garment*) maillot *m*.

jet (*plane*) avion *m* à réaction.

jet lag fatigue *f* (due au décalage horaire).

jet-lagged *adj* qui souffre du décalage horaire.

jet·ty jetée *f*.

Jew (*man*) Juif *m*; (*woman*) Juive *f*.

jew·el bijou *m* (*pl* -oux); (*in watch*) rubis *m*.

jew·el·er bijoutier, -ière *mf*.

jew·el·ry bijoux *mpl*.

Jew·ish *adj* juif.

jig·saw **j.** (*puzzle*) puzzle *m*.

jin·gle *vi* (*of keys*) tinter.

jit·ter·y *adj* **to be j.** *Fam* avoir la frousse.

job (*task*) travail *m*; (*post*) poste *m*.

job·less *adj* au chômage.

jock·ey jockey *m*.

jog 1 *n* (*shake*) secousse *f*. **2** *vt* secouer; (*push*) pousser; (*memory*) rafraîchir. **3** *vi* faire du jogging.

john *Fam* cabinets *mpl*.

join[1] **1** *vt* (*put together*) joindre; (*wires, pipes*) raccorder; (*words, towns*) relier; **to j. sb** (*catch up with, meet*) rejoindre qn; (*go with*) se joindre à qn (**in doing** pour faire). **2** *vi* (*of roads etc*) se rejoindre; (*of objects*) se joindre. **3** *n* raccord *m*.

join[2] **1** *vt* (*become a member of*) s'inscrire à (*club, parti*); (*firm, army*) entrer dans. **2** *vi* devenir membre.

▸**join in 1** *vt* **to join in sth** prendre part à qch. **2** *vi* prendre part.

joint 1 *n* (*in body*) articulation *f*. **2** *adj* (*account*) joint; (*effort*) conjugué.

joint·ly *adv* conjointement.

joke 1 *n* plaisanterie *f*; (*trick*) tour *m*. **2** *vi* plaisanter (**about** sur).

jok·er plaisantin *m*; *Cards* joker *m*.

jol·ly *adj* gai.

jolt *vti* secouer.

jos·tle 1 *vti* (*push*) bousculer. **2** *vi* (*push each other*) se bousculer.

▸**jot down** *vt* noter.

jour·nal·ist journaliste *mf*.

jour·ney voyage *m*; (*distance*) trajet *m*.

joy joie *f*.

joy·ful *adj* joyeux.

joy·stick manche *m* à balai.

judge 1 *n* juge *m*. **2** *vti* juger.

judg·ment jugement *m*.

ju·di·cial *adj* judiciaire.

ju·do judo *m*.

jug cruche *f*; (*for milk*) pot *m*.

jug·ger·naut force *f* irrésistible.

jug·gle *vi* jongler (**with** avec).

jug·gler jongleur, -euse *mf*.

juice jus *m*.

juic·y *adj* (*fruit*) juteux.

Ju·ly juillet *m*.

jum·ble (up) *vt* mélanger.

jum·bo *adj* géant.

jum·bo jet gros-porteur *m*.

jump 1 *n* saut *m*; (*start*) sursaut *m*; (*increase*) hausse *f*. **2** *vi* sauter; (*start*) sursauter; **to j. off sth** sauter de qch. **3** *vt* **to j. rope** sauter à la corde.

jump·er (*garment*) robe-chasuble *f*.

▸**jump in** *or* **on 1** *vt* (*train, vehicle*) monter dans. **2** *vi* monter.

jump rope corde *f* à sauter.

jump·y *adj* nerveux.

junc·tion carrefour *m*.

June juin *m*.

jun·gle jungle *f*.

jun·ior 1 *adj* (*younger*) plus jeune; (*in rank*) subalterne; (*doctor*) jeune. **2** *n* cadet, -ette *mf*; (*in school*) petit(e) élève *mf*.

jun·ior high (school) = collège *m* d'enseignement secondaire.

junk bric-à-brac *m inv*; (*metal*) ferraille *f*; (*goods*) camelote *f*; (*garbage*) ordures *fpl*; **j. food** malbouffe *f*.

ju·ry jury *m*.

just *adv* (*exactly, only*) juste; **she has/had j. left** elle vient/venait de partir; **he'll (only) j. catch the bus** il aura son bus de justesse; **he j. missed it** il l'a manqué de peu; **j. as big/etc** tout aussi grand/*etc* (**as** que); **j. over ten** un peu plus de dix; **j. one** un(e) seul(e); **j. about** à peu près; (*almost*) presque; **j. about to do** sur le point de faire.

jus·tice justice *f*.

jus·ti·fi·ca·tion justification *f*.

jus·ti·fy *vt* justifier; **to be justified in doing** être fondé à faire.

▸**jut out** *vi* faire saillie.

K

kan·ga·roo, *pl* -oos kangourou *m*.

ka·ra·te karaté *m*.

ke·bab brochette *f*.

keen *adj* (*interest, emotion*) vif; **k. eyesight** vue *f* perçante; **he's a k. athlete** c'est un passionné de sport;

to be k. on doing *(want)* tenir (beaucoup) à faire.

keep* *1 vt* garder; *(shop, car)* avoir; *(diary, promise)* tenir; *(family)* entretenir; *(rule)* respecter; *(delay)* retenir; **to k. doing** continuer à faire; **to k. sb waiting/working** faire attendre/travailler qn; **to k. sb in/out** empêcher qn de sortir/d'entrer. *2 vi (remain)* rester; *(of food)* se garder; **to k. going** continuer; **to k. (to the) right** tenir sa droite. *3 n (food)* nourriture *f*, subsistance *f*.

▸**keep away 1** *vt (person)* éloigner (**from** de). *2 vi* ne pas s'approcher (**from** de).

▸**keep back 1** *vt (crowd)* contenir; *(delay)* retenir; *(hide)* cacher (**from** à). *2 vi* ne pas s'approcher (**from** de).

▸**keep down** *vt (restrict)* limiter; *(price)* maintenir bas.

keep·er *(in park, zoo)* gardien, -ienne *mf*.

▸**keep from** *vt (hide)* cacher à; **to k. sb from doing** *(prevent)* empêcher qn de faire.

▸**keep off** *vi (not go near)* ne pas s'approcher; **the rain kept off** il n'a pas plu.

▸**keep on** *vt (hat, employee)* garder; **to k. on doing** continuer à faire.

▸**keep up** *vti* continuer (**doing sth** à faire qch); **to k. up (with sb)** *(follow)* suivre (qn).

ken·nel niche *f*.

kept *pt & pp de* **keep**.

ker·o·sene pétrole *m* (lampant).

ketch·up ketchup *m*.

ket·tle bouilloire *f*; **the k. is boiling** l'eau bout.

key *1 n* clef *f*; *(of piano, typewriter, computer)* touche *f*. *2 adj (industry, post etc)* clef *(f inv)*.

key·board clavier *m*.

key ring porte-clefs *m inv.*

kick *1 n* coup *m* de pied. *2 vt* donner un coup de pied à. *3 vi* donner des coups de pied.

▸**kick down** *or* **in** *vt (door etc)* démolir à coups de pied.

▸**kick off** *vi Sports* donner le coup d'envoi.

kick-off *Fam* coup *m* d'envoi.

▸**kick out** *vt (throw out) Fam* flanquer dehors.

kid *1 n (child) Fam* gosse *mf*. *2 vti (tease) Fam* blaguer.

kid·nap *vt* kidnapper.

kid·nap·per ravisseur, -euse *mf*.

kid·ney rein *m*; *(as food)* rognon *m*.

kill *vti* tuer.

kill·er tueur, -euse *mf*.

kill·ing *(of person)* meurtre *m*; *Fam* **to make a k.** se remplir les poches.

ki·lo, *pl* **-os** kilo *m*.

kil·o·gram kilogramme *m*.

kil·o·me·ter kilomètre *m*.

kin **my next of k.** mon plus proche parent.

kind¹ *(sort)* sorte *f*, genre *m*, espèce *f* (**of** de); **all kinds of** toutes sortes de; **what k. of drink/etc is it?** qu'est-ce que c'est comme boisson/etc?; **k. of worried/etc** plutôt inquiet/etc.

kind² *adj (pleasant)* gentil (**to** avec).

kin·der·gar·ten jardin *m* d'enfants.

kind·ly 1 *adj* bienveillant. *2 adv* gentiment; **k. wait** ayez la bonté d'attendre.

kind·ness gentillesse *f*.

king roi *m*.

king·dom royaume *m*.

ki·osk kiosque *m*.

kiss *1 n* baiser *m*. *2 vt (person)* embrasser; **to k. sb's hand** baiser la main de qn. *3 vi* s'embrasser.

kit équipement *m*; *(set of articles)* trousse *f*; **(do-it-yourself) k.** kit *m*; **tool k.** trousse *f* à outils.

kitch·en cuisine *f*.

kite *(toy)* cerf-volant *m*.

kit·ten chaton *m*.

klutz *Fam* balourd, -ourde *mf*.

knack to have a or the k. of doing
avoir le don de faire.
knee genou m (pl genoux).
kneel* (down) vi s'agenouiller;
to be kneeling (down) être à genoux.
knew pt de **know**.
knick·ers knickers mpl.
knife, pl **knives** couteau m; (penknife) canif m.
knight chevalier m, Chess cavalier m.
knit vti tricoter.
knit·ting (activity, material) tricot
m; **k. needle** aiguille f à tricoter.
knob (on door etc) bouton m.
knock 1 vt (strike) frapper; (collide
with) heurter; **to k. one's head on
sth** se cogner la tête contre qch. **2**
vi frapper. **3** n coup m; **there's a k.
at the door** quelqu'un frappe; **I
heard a k.** j'ai entendu frapper.
▶ **knock against** or **into** vt (bump
into) heurter.
▶ **knock down** vt (vase, pedestrian
etc) renverser; (house, wall etc)
abattre.
knock·er (for door) marteau m.
▶ **knock in** vt (nail) enfoncer.
▶ **knock off** vt (person, object) faire
tomber (**from** de).
▶ **knock out** vt (make unconscious)
assommer; Boxing mettre k.-o.;
(beat in competition) éliminer.
▶ **knock over** vt (pedestrian, vase
etc) renverser.
knot 1 n nœud m. **2** vt nouer.
know* 1 vt (facts, language etc) savoir; (person, place etc) connaître;
(recognize) reconnaître (**by** à); **to
k. that** savoir que; **to k. how to do**
savoir faire; **I'll let you k.** je te le ferai savoir; **to k. (a lot) about** (person, event) en savoir long sur; (cars, sewing etc) s'y connaître en;
to get to k. sb apprendre à mieux
connaître qn. **2** vi savoir; **I wouldn't
k.** je n'en sais rien; **I k. about that** je
suis au courant; **do you k. how to a**

good dentist/etc? connais-tu un
bon dentiste/etc?
know-how savoir-faire m inv.
know-it-all Fam je-sais-tout mf.
knowl·edge connaissance f (**of**
de); (learning) connaissances fpl.
known adj connu; **well k.** (bien)
connu (**that** que); **she is k. to be**
on sait qu'elle est.
knuck·le articulation f (du doigt).
Ko·ran the K. le Coran m.

L

lab Fam labo m.
la·bel 1 n étiquette f. **2** vt (goods)
étiqueter.
la·bor 1 n (work) travail m; (workers) main-d'œuvre f; **in l.** en train
d'accoucher. **2** adj (market, situation) du travail.
lab·o·ra·to·ry laboratoire m.
La·bor Day fête f du travail.
la·bor·er manœuvre m; (on farm)
ouvrier m agricole.
la·bor pro·test mouvement m
revendicatif.
la·bor un·ion syndicat m.
lace (cloth) dentelle f; (of shoe) lacet
m.
lace (up) vt (shoe) lacer.
lack 1 n manque m. **2** vt manquer de.
3 vi **to be lacking** manquer (**in** de).
lad gamin m.
lad·der échelle f.
la·dle louche f.
la·dy dame f; **a young l.** une jeune
fille; (married) une jeune femme;
the ladies' room les toilettes fpl
pour dames.
la·dy·bug coccinelle f.
la·ger bière f blonde.
lake lac m.
lamb agneau m.

lame *adj* to be l. boiter.

lamp lampe *f*.

lamp·post l. réverbère *m*.

lamp·shade abat-jour *m inu*

land 1 *n* terre *f*; *(country)* pays *m*; *(plot of)* l. terrain *m*. **2** *vi (of aircraft)* atterrir; *(of passengers)* débarquer. **3** *vt (aircraft)* poser.

land·ing *(of aircraft)* atterrissage *m*; *(at top of stairs)* palier *m*.

land·la·dy propriétaire *f*; *(of pub)* patronne *f*.

land·lord propriétaire *m*; *(of pub)* patron *m*.

land·own·er propriétaire *m* foncier.

land·scape paysage *m*.

land·slide éboulement *m*.

lane *(in country)* chemin *m*; *(in town)* ruelle *f*, *(division of road)* voie *f*.

lan·guage 1 *n (English etc)* langue *f*; *(means of expression, style)* langage *m*. **2** *adj (laboratory)* de langues; *(teacher, studies)* de langue(s).

lan·tern lanterne *f*.

lap *(of person)* genoux *mpl*; *(in race)* tour *m* (de piste).

la·pel *(of coat etc)* revers *m*.

lap·top portable *m*.

lar·ce·ny vol *m* simple.

lar·der *(storeroom)* garde-manger *m inu*

large *adj* grand; *(in volume)* gros *(f* grosse).

large·ly *adv* en grande mesure.

large-scale *adj* de grande envergure.

lark *(bird)* alouette *f*; *(joke) Fam* rigolade *f*.

la·ser laser *m*.

last¹ 1 *adj* dernier; **next to l.** avant-dernier. **2** *adv (lastly)* en dernier lieu; *(on the last occasion)* (pour) la dernière fois; **to leave l.** sortir en dernier. **3** *n (person, object)* dernier, -ière *mf*; **the l. of the beer/etc** la reste de la bière/*etc*; **at (long) l.** enfin.

last² *vi* durer; *(endure)* tenir.

last·ly *adv* en dernier lieu, enfin.

latch loquet *m*.

late 1 *adj (not on time)* en retard (**for** à); *(meal, hour)* tardif; **he's an hour l.** il a une heure de retard; **it's l.** il est tard; **at a later date** à une date ultérieure; **at the latest** au plus tard; **of l.** dernièrement. **2** *adv (in the day, season etc)* tard; *(not on time)* en retard; **it's getting l.** il se fait tard; **later (on)** plus tard.

late·com·er retardataire *mf*.

late·ly *adv* dernièrement.

Lat·in 1 *adj* latin. **2** *n (language)* latin *m*.

La·tin A·mer·i·ca l'Amérique *f* latine.

lat·ter 1 *adj (last-named)* dernier; *(second)* deuxième. **2** *n (last)* dernier, -ière *mf*; *(second)* second, -onde *mf*.

laugh 1 *n* rire *m*. **2** *vi* rire (**at, about** de).

laugh·ter rire(s) *m(pl)*.

launch 1 *vt (rocket, fashion etc)* lancer. **2** *n* lancement *m*.

laun·dro·mat laverie *f* automatique.

laun·dry *(place)* blanchisserie *f*, *(clothes)* linge *m*.

laun·dry de·ter·gent lessive *f*.

lav·a·to·ry cabinets *mpl*.

law loi *f*; *(study, profession)* droit *m*; **court of l.**, **l. court** cour *f* de justice.

lawn pelouse *f*, gazon *m*; **l. mower** tondeuse *f* (à gazon).

law·suit procès *m*.

law·yer avocat *m*; *(for wills, sales)* notaire *m*.

lay* *vt (put down)* poser; *(table)* mettre; *(blanket)* étendre (**over** sur); *(trap)* tendre; *(egg)* pondre.

► **lay down** *vt (put down)* poser.

lay·er couche *f*.

► **lay in** *vt (supplies)* faire provision de.

► **lay off** *vt (worker)* licencier.

► **lay out** *vt (garden)* dessiner; *(dis-*

play) disposer; *(money) Fam* mettre (on dans).

lay·out disposition *f.*

lay·per·son profane *mf.*

la·zy *adj* paresseux.

la·zy·bones *Fam* fainéant, -ante *mf.*

lead¹ 1 *vt* (conduct)* mener, conduire (to à); *(team, government etc)* diriger; *(life)* mener; **to l. sb in/out/etc** faire entrer/sortir/etc qn; **to l. sb to do** amener qn à faire. **2** *vi (of street, door etc)* mener (to à); *(in race)* être en tête; *(in match)* mener; *(go ahead)* aller devant. **3** *n (distance or time ahead)* avance *f (on* sur); *(example)* exemple *m; (leash)* laisse *f, (electric wire)* fil *m;* **to be in the l.** *(in race)* être en tête; *(in match)* mener.

lead² *(metal)* plomb *m; (of pencil)* mine *f.*

▸ **lead away** *or off vt* emmener.

lead·er chef *m; (of country, party)* dirigeant, -ante *mf.*

lead·ing *adj (main)* principal.

▸ **lead on 1** *vi (go ahead)* aller devant. **2** *vt (deceive)* tromper.

▸ **lead to** *vt (result in)* aboutir à; *(cause)* causer.

▸ **lead up to** *vt (of street etc)* conduire à; *(precede)* précéder.

leaf, *pl* **leaves** feuille *f, (of book)* feuillet *m.*

leaf·let prospectus *m; (containing instructions)* notice *f.*

▸ **leaf through** *vt (book)* feuilleter.

leak 1 *n (of gas etc)* fuite *f.* **2** *vi (of liquid, pipe etc)* fuir.

lean* 1 *vi (of object)* pencher; *(of person)* se pencher; **to l. against/on sth** *(of person)* s'appuyer contre/sur qch. **2** *vt* appuyer (against contre); **to l. one's head on/out of sth** pencher la tête sur/par qch.

▸ **lean forward** *vi (of person)* se pencher (en avant).

▸ **lean over** *vi (of person)* se pencher; *(of object)* pencher.

leap 1 *n* bond *m.* **2** *vi** bondir.

leap year année *f* bisextile.

learn* *vt* apprendre (**that** que); **to l. (how) to do** apprendre à faire. **2** *vi* apprendre; **to l. about** *(study)* étudier; *(hear about)* apprendre.

learn·er débutant, -ante *mf.*

learn·ing *(of language)* apprentissage *m (of* de).

lease 1 *n* bail *m;* **to give sb a new l. on life** redonner du tonus à qn. **2** *vt* louer à bail.

leash laisse *f.*

least 1 *adj* **the l.** *(smallest amount of)* le moins de; *(slightest)* le or la moindre. **2** *n* **the l.** le moins; **at l.** du moins; *(with quantity)* au moins. **3** *adv (to work etc)* le moins; *(with adjective)* le or la moins.

leath·er cuir *m.*

leave 1 *n (vacation)* congé *m.* **2** *vt** laisser; *(go away from)* quitter; **to be left (over)** rester; **there's no bread/etc left** il ne reste plus de pain/etc; **to l. go of** *(release)* lâcher. **3** *vi (go away)* partir (**from** de; **for** pour).

▸ **leave behind** *vt (not take)* laisser; *(in race, at school)* distancer.

▸ **leave on** *vt (hat, gloves)* garder.

▸ **leave out** *vt (forget to add)* oublier (de mettre); *(word, line)* sauter; *(exclude)* exclure.

lec·ture 1 *n (public speech)* conférence *f,* **to give a l.** faire une conférence. **2** *vt* **to l. sb** sermonner qn.

lec·tur·er conférencier, -ière *mf.*

leek poireau *m.*

left¹ *pt & pp de* **leave.**

left² 1 *adj (side, hand etc)* gauche. **2** *adv* à gauche. **3** *n* gauche *f,* **on or to the l.** à gauche (of de).

left-hand *adj* à or de gauche; **on the l. side** à gauche (of de).

left-hand·ed *adj (person)* gaucher.

left·o·vers *npl* restes *mpl.*

leg jambe *f, (of dog etc)* patte *f, (of table)* pied *m;* **l. (of chicken)** cuisse *f* (de poulet); **l. of lamb** gigot *m* (d'agneau).

le·gal *adj* légal.

le·gal·ly *adv* légalement.

leg·end légende *f*.

leg·i·ble *adj* lisible.

leg·is·la·tion legislation *f*.

leg·is·la·tive *adj* legislatif.

leg·is·la·ture (corps *m*) legislatif *m*.

le·git·i·mate *adj* légitime.

lei·sure **l.** (time) loisirs *mpl*. **l. activities** loisirs *mpl*.

lem·on citron *m*; **tea with l.** thé *m* au citron.

lem·on·ade citronnade *f*.

lend* *vt* prêter (**to** à); (color, charm etc) donner (**to** à).

length longueur *f*, (section of rope etc) morceau *m*; (duration) durée *f*, **l. of time** temps *m*.

length·en *vt* allonger; (in time) prolonger.

length·y *adj* long (*f* longue).

le·nient *adj* indulgent (**to** envers).

lens lentille *f*, (in spectacles) verre *m*; (of camera) objectif *m*.

len·til lentille *f* (graine).

leop·ard léopard *m*.

le·o·tard collant *m* (de danse).

less 1 *adj & n* moins (de) (**than** que); **l. time/etc** moins de temps/*etc*; **l. than a quart/ten** (with quantity, number) moins d'un litre/de dix. **2** *adv* moins (**than** que); **l. (often)** moins souvent; **l. and l.** de moins en moins; **one l.** un(e) de moins. **3** *prep* moins.

les·son leçon *f*.

let* *vt* (allow) laisser (**sb do** qn faire); **to l. sb have sth** donner qch à qn; **l. us** *or* **l.'s eat/etc** mangeons/ *etc*; **l.'s go for a stroll** allons nous promener; **l. him come** qu'il vienne.

▶**let down** *vt* (lower) baisser; **to l. sb down** (disappoint) décevoir qn.

let·down déception *f*.

▶**let in** *vt* (person) faire entrer; (noise, light) laisser entrer.

▶**let off** *vt* (firework, gun) faire partir; **to l. sb off** (not punish) ne pas punir qn; **to l. sb off doing** dispenser qn de faire.

▶**let out** *vt* (person) laisser sortir; (cry, secret) laisser échapper.

let·ter lettre *f*.

let·ter·box boîte *f* aux *or* à lettres.

let·ter o·pen·er coupe-papier *m inv*.

let·tuce laitue *f*.

▶**let up** *vi* (of rain etc) s'arrêter.

lev·el 1 *n* niveau *m*; (rate) taux *m*. **2** *adj* (surface) plat; (object on surface) d'aplomb; (equal in score) à égalité (**with** avec); (in height) au même niveau (**with** que).

lev·er levier *m*.

li·a·ble *adj* **to be l. to do** être capable *or* susceptible de faire.

li·ar menteur, -euse *mf*.

li·bel 1 *n* diffamation *f*. **2** *vt* diffamer.

lib·er·ty liberté *f*, **at l. to do** libre de faire.

li·brar·i·an bibliothécaire *mf*.

li·brar·y bibliothèque *f*.

lice *npl* poux *mpl*.

li·cense (document) permis *m*; **l. plate/number** plaque *f*/numéro *m* d'immatriculation.

lick *vt* lécher.

lic·o·rice réglisse *f*.

lid (of box etc) couvercle *m*.

lie¹* *vi* (in flat position) s'allonger; (remain) rester; (be) être; **to be lying** (on the grass etc) être allongé.

lie² 1 *vi** (tell lies) mentir. **2** *n* mensonge *m*.

▶**lie around** *vi* (of objects, person) traîner.

▶**lie down** *vi* s'allonger; **lying down** allongé.

life, *pl* **lives** vie *f*, **to come to l.** s'animer.

life·belt ceinture *f* de sauvetage.

life·boat canot *m* de sauvetage.

life·guard maître nageur *m* (sauveteur).

life in·sur·ance assurance-vie *f*.
life jack·et gilet *m* de sauvetage.
life pre·ser·ver ceinture *f* de sauvetage.
life·time in my l. de mon vivant.
lift 1 *vt* lever. **2** *n* (*elevator*) ascenseur *m*; to give sb a l. emmener qn (en voiture) (to à).
▸**lift down** *or* **off** *vt* (*take down*) descendre (from de).
▸**lift out** *vt* (*take out*) sortir (of de).
▸**lift up** *vt* (*arm, object*) lever.
light¹ lumière *f*; (*on vehicle*) feu *m*; (*vehicle headlight*) phare *m*; do you have a l.? (*for cigarette*) est-ce que vous avez du feu?
light²*vt* (*match, fire, gas*) allumer.
light³ *adj* (*not dark*) clair; a l. green jacket une veste vert clair.
light⁴ *adj* (*in weight, quantity etc*) léger; to travel l. voyager avec peu de bagages.
light (up) *vt* (*room*) éclairer; (*cigarette*) allumer.
light bulb ampoule *f* (électrique).
light·er (*for cigarettes*) briquet *m*; (*for stove*) allume-gaz *m inv*.
light·house phare *m*.
light·ing (*lights*) éclairage *m*.
light·ning (*charge*) foudre *f*; (*flash of*) l. éclair *m*.
like¹ 1 *prep* comme; l. this comme ça; what's he l.? comment est-il?; to be *or* look l. ressembler à; what was the book l.? comment as-tu trouvé le livre? **2** *conj* (*as*) Fam comme; do l. I do fais comme moi.
**like² ** *vt* aimer (bien) (to do, doing faire); she likes it here elle se plaît ici; to l. sth best aimer mieux qch; I'd l. to come je voudrais (bien) *or* j'aimerais (bien) venir; I'd l. some cake je voudrais du gâteau; would you l. an apple? voulez-vous une pomme?; if you l. si vous voulez.
like·a·ble *adj* sympathique.
like·li·hood there's not much l. that il y a peu de chances que (+ subjunctive).

like·ly 1 *adj* probable; (*excuse*) vraisemblable; it's l. (that) she'll come, she's l. to come il est probable qu'elle viendra. **2** *adv* very l. très probablement.
like·wise *adv* de même.
lik·ing a l. for (*person*) de la sympathie pour; (*thing*) du goût pour.
lil·y lis *m*.
limb membre *m*.
lime (*fruit*) citron *m* vert.
lim·it 1 *n* limite *f* (to à). **2** *vt* limiter (to à).
lim·ou·sine (*airport shuttle*) voiture-navette *f*.
limp 1 *vi* (*of person*) boiter. **2** *n* to have a l. boiter.
line¹ 1 *n* ligne *f*; (*of poem*) vers *m*; (*wrinkle*) ride *f*; (*track*) voie *f*; (*rope*) corde *f*; (*row*) rangée *f*; (*of vehicles, people*) file *f*; on the l. (*phone*) au bout du fil; to stand in l. faire la queue; to drop a l. (*send a letter*) envoyer un mot (to à). **2** *vt* to l. the street (*of trees*) border la rue; (*of people*) faire la haie le long de la rue.
line² *vt* (*clothes*) doubler.
lin·en (*sheets etc*) linge *m*.
lin·er (*ocean*) l. paquebot *m*.
▸**line up 1** *vt* (*children, objects*) aligner; (*arrange*) organiser. **2** *vi* s'aligner; (*of people*) faire la queue.
lin·ger *vi* (*of person*) s'attarder; (*of smell, memory*) persister; (*of doubt*) subsister.
lin·guis·tics linguistique *f*.
lin·ing (*of clothes*) doublure *f*.
link 1 *vt* (*connect*) relier; (*relate*) lier (to à). **2** *n* lien *m*; (*of chain*) maillon *m*; (*by road, rail*) liaison *f*.
▸**link up** *vi* (*of people etc*) s'associer; (*of roads*) se rejoindre.
li·on lion *m*.
lip lèvre *f*.
lip·stick bâton *m* de rouge; (*substance*) rouge *m* (à lèvres).
li·queur liqueur *f*.
liq·uid *n & adj* liquide (*m*).

liq·ui·date *vt* liquider.

liq·uor alcool *m*.

list 1 *n* liste *f*. **2** *vt* faire la liste de; *(names)* mettre sur la liste, inscrire; *(name one by one)* énumérer.

lis·ten (to) *vt* écouter.

lis·ten·er *(to radio)* auditeur, -trice *mf*.

▸ **listen (out) for** *vt* guetter *(un bruit ou les cris etc de)*.

li·ter litre *m*.

lit·er·al·ly *adv* litéralement.

lit·er·ar·y *adj* littéraire.

lit·er·a·ture littérature *f*; *(pamphlets etc)* documentation *f*.

lit·i·ga·tion litige *m*.

lit·ter *(rubbish)* détritus *m*; *(papers)* papiers *mpl*; *(young animals)* portée *f*.

lit·tle 1 *adj (small)* petit. **2** *adj & n (not much)* peu (de); **l. time/***etc* peu de temps/*etc*; **she eats l.** elle mange peu; **as l. as possible** le moins possible; **a l. money/***etc (some)* un peu d'argent/*etc*. **3** *adv* **a l. heavy/***etc* un peu lourd/*etc*; **to work/***etc* **a l.** travailler/*etc* un peu; **l. by l.** peu à peu.

live¹ *vi* vivre; *(reside)* habiter, vivre. **2** *vt (life)* mener.

live² **1** *adj (electric wire)* sous tension; *(switch)* mal isolé. **2** *adj & adv (broadcast)* en direct.

live·ly *adj (person, style, interest, mind)* vif; *(discussion)* animé.

▸ **live off** *or* **on** *vt (eat)* vivre de.

liv·er foie *m*.

▸ **live through** *vt (experience)* vivre; *(survive)* survivre à.

liv·ing 1 *adj (alive)* vivant. **2** *n* vie *f*; **to make** *or* **earn** *a or* **one's l.** gagner sa vie; **the cost of l.** le coût de la vie.

living room salle *f* de séjour.

liz·ard lézard *m*.

load 1 *n* charge *f*; *(weight)* poids *m*; **a l. of, loads of** *(people, money etc) Fam* un tas de. **2** *vt (truck, gun etc)* charger *(with de)*.

▸ **load up 1** *vt (car, ship etc)* charger

(with de). **2** *vi* charger la voiture, le navire *etc*.

loaf, *pl* **loaves** pain *m*.

loan 1 *n (money lent)* prêt *m*; *(money borrowed)* emprunt *m*. **2** *vt (lend)* prêter *(to à)*.

lob·by *(of hotel)* hall *m*.

lob·ster homard *m*.

lo·cal *adj* local; *(regional)* régional; *(of the neighborhood)* du *or* de quartier; *(of the region)* de la région.

lo·cal·i·ty environs *mpl*.

lo·cal·ly *adv* dans le coin.

lo·cate *vt (find)* trouver, repérer; **to be located** être situé.

lo·ca·tion *(site)* emplacement *m*.

lock 1 *vt (door etc)* fermer à clef. **2** *n (on door etc)* serrure *f*; *(on canal)* écluse *f*; *(of hair)* mèche *f*.

▸ **lock away** *vt (prisoner, jewels etc)* enfermer.

lock·er *(for luggage)* casier *m* de consigne automatique; *(for clothes)* vestiaire *m* (métallique).

lock·et médaillon *m*.

▸ **lock in** *vt* enfermer; **to l. sb in sth** enfermer qn dans qch.

▸ **lock out** *vt (accidentally)* enfermer dehors.

▸ **lock up 1** *vt (house etc)* fermer à clef; *(prisoner, jewels etc)* enfermer. **2** *vi* fermer à clef.

lodge 1 *n (porter's)* loge *f*, *(hunter's)* pavillon *m*; *(in park, resort)* bâtiment *m* central. **2** *vt (accommodate)* héberger, loger; *(claim)* déposer; **to l. a complaint** porter plainte. **3** *vi (live)* loger, être logé; *(get stuck)* se loger.

lodg·er *(room and meals)* pensionnaire *mf*; *(room only)* locataire *mf*.

lodg·ing hébergement *m*; lodgings chambre(s) *f(pl)* meublée(s).

loft *(attic)* grenier *m*.

log *(tree trunk)* tronc *m* d'arbre; *(for fire)* bûche *f*.

log·ic logique *f*.

log·i·cal *adj* logique.

lol·li·pop sucette f.

lone adj solitaire.

lone·li·ness solitude f.

lone·ly adj solitaire.

long 1 adj long (f longue); **to be 33 feet l.** avoir dix mètres de long; **to be six weeks l.** durer six semaines; **a l. time** longtemps. **2** adv longtemps; **has he been here l.?** il y a longtemps qu'il est ici?; **how l. ago?** il y a combien de temps?; **before l.** sous peu; **she no longer swims** elle ne nage plus; **I won't be l.** je n'en ai pas pour longtemps; **all summer l.** tout l'été; **as l. as, so l. as** (provided that) pourvu que (+ subjunctive).

long-dis·tance (phone call) interurbain; (flight) long-courrier.

long johns caleçon m (long).

long-term adj à long terme.

look 1 n regard m; (appearance) air m; **to have a l. (at)** jeter un coup d'œil (à); **to have a l. (for)** chercher; **to have a l. around** regarder; (walk) faire un tour; **let me have a l.** fais voir. **2** vi regarder; **to l. tired/etc** sembler or avoir l'air fatigué/etc; **you l. like or as if you're tired** on dirait que tu es fatigué; **to l. well or good** (of person) avoir bonne mine; **you l. good in that hat/etc** ce chapeau/etc te va très bien.

▶**look around 1** vt visiter. **2** vi regarder; (walk around) faire un tour; (look back) se retourner.

▶**look at** vt regarder.

▶**look back** vi regarder derrière soi; (remember) regarder en arrière.

▶**look down** vi baisser les yeux; (from a height) regarder en bas.

▶**look for** vt chercher.

▶**look forward to** vt (event) attendre avec impatience; **to l. forward to doing** avoir hâte de faire.

▶**look into** vt examiner; (find out about) se renseigner sur.

▶**look (out) on to** vt (of window etc) donner sur.

▶**look out** vi (be careful) faire attention (**for** à).

look·out (high place) observatoire m; **to be on the l.** faire le guet; **to be on the l. for** guetter.

▶**look over** or **through** vt examiner; (briefly) parcourir; (region, town) parcourir.

▶**look up 1** vi lever les yeux; (into the air) regarder en l'air; (improve) s'améliorer. **2** vt (word) chercher.

loom¹ métier m à tisser.

loom² vi (of mountain) apparaître indistinctement; (of event) paraître imminent.

loop boucle f.

loose 1 adj (screw, belt, knot) desserré; (tooth) branlant; (page) détaché; (clothes) flottant; (tea etc) au poids; (having escaped) (animal) échappé; (prisoner) évadé; **l. change** petite monnaie f; **to set** or **turn l.** (dog etc) lâcher. **2** n **on the l.** (prisoner) évadé; (animal) échappé.

loos·en vt (knot, belt, screw) desserrer.

lord seigneur m.

lose* 1 vt perdre; **to get lost** (of person) se perdre; **the ticket/etc got lost** on a perdu le billet/etc. **2** vi perdre.

los·er (in contest etc) perdant, -ante mf.

▶**lose to** vt être battu par.

loss perte f.

lost adj perdu.

lost and found objets mpl trouvés.

lot **a l. of, lots of** beaucoup de; **a l.** beaucoup; **quite a l.** pas mal (**of** de); **such a l.** tellement (**of** de); **what a l. of flowers/water/etc!** regarde toutes ces fleurs/toute cette eau/etc!

lo·tion lotion f.

lot·ter·y loterie f.

loud 1 adj (voice, music) fort; (noise, cry) grand; **the radio/TV is**

too l. le son de la radio/télé est trop fort. **2** adv (to shout etc) fort; **out** l. tout haut.

loud·ly adv (to speak etc) fort.

loud·speak·er haut-parleur m; (for speaking to crowd) porte-voix m inv.

lounge salon m; **teachers'** l. salle f des professeurs.

lous·y adj (food, weather etc) Fam infect.

love 1 n amour m; **in** l. amoureux (with de); **they're in** l. ils s'aiment. **2** vt aimer (beaucoup) (**to do, do·ing** faire).

love·ly adj agréable; (excellent) excellent; (pretty) joli; (charming) charmant; (kind) gentil.

lov·er a l. of music/etc un amateur de musique/etc.

lov·ing adj affectueux.

low 1 adj bas (f basse); (speed, income, intelligence) faible; (opinion, quality) mauvais; **to feel** l. être déprimé; **in** a l. **voice** à voix basse; **lower** inférieur. **2** adv bas; **to turn down** l. baisser.

low beams (of vehicle) codes mpl.

low·er vt baisser; (by rope) descendre.

low-fat adj (milk) écrémé; (cheese) allégé.

loy·al adj fidèle (to à), loyal (to envers).

loy·al·ty loyauté f.

loz·enge (tablet) pastille f.

luck (chance) chance f; **bad** l. malchance f.

luck·i·ly adv heureusement.

luck·y adj (person) chanceux; (guess, event) heureux; **to be** l. avoir de la chance (**to do** de faire); **it's** l. **that** c'est une chance que; l. **charm** porte-bonheur m inv; l. **number/etc** chiffre m/etc porte-bonheur.

lu·di·crous adj ridicule.

lug·gage bagages mpl.

luke·warm adj tiède.

lull·a·by berceuse f.

lum·ber bois m de charpente.

lum·ber·yard dépôt m de bois.

lu·mi·nous adj lumineux.

lump morceau m; (bump) bosse f; (swelling) grosseur f.

lump sum somme f forfaitaire.

lu·na·tic n, m, folle f.

lunch déjeuner m; **to have** l. déjeuner; l. **break,** l. **hour,** l. **time** heure f du déjeuner.

lung poumon m.

lux·u·ri·ous adj luxueux.

lux·u·ry 1 n luxe m. **2** adj (goods etc) de luxe.

M

MA abbr = **Master of Arts.**

mac·a·ro·ni macaroni(s) m(pl).

ma·chine machine f.

ma·chine gun (heavy) mitrailleuse f, (portable) mitraillette f.

ma·chin·er·y machines fpl; (works) mécanisme m.

mack·er·el n inv maquereau m.

mad adj fou (f folle); **m.** (at) (angry) furieux (contre); **m. about** (person) fou de; (films etc) passionné de; **like m.** comme un fou or une folle.

Mad·am madame f; (unmarried) mademoiselle f.

made pt & pp de **make.**

mad·man, pl -men fou m.

mad·ness folie f.

mag·a·zine magazine m, revue f.

mag·got ver m.

mag·ic 1 n magie f. **2** adj (wand etc) magique.

mag·i·cal adj magique.

ma·gi·cian magicien, -ienne mf.

mag·is·trate magistrat m.

mag·net aimant m.

mag·nif·i·cent adj magnifique.

mag·ni·fy·ing glass loupe *f*.

ma·hog·a·ny acajou *m*.

maid *(servant)* bonne *f*.

mail 1 *n (system)* poste *f*, *(letters)* courrier *m*. **2** *adj (bag etc)* postal. **3** *vt (letter)* poster.

mail·box boîte *f* aux or à lettres.

mail·man, *pl* **-men** facteur *m*.

main¹ *adj* principal; *the* m. thing is to l'essentiel est de; **m. road** grand-route *f*.

main² water/gas **m.** conduite *f* d'eau/de gaz; **the mains** *(electricity)* le secteur.

main·land continent *m*.

main·ly *adv* surtout.

main street grand-rue *f*.

main·tain *vt (vehicle etc)* entretenir; *(law and order)* faire respecter; **to m. that** affirmer que.

main·te·nance *(of vehicle, road)* entretien *m*; *(alimony)* pension *f* alimentaire.

mai·son·ette duplex *m*.

maî·tre d' maître *m* d'hôtel.

maj·es·ty majesté *f*; **Your M.** Votre Majesté.

ma·jor 1 *adj* majeur; **a m. road** une grande route. **2** *n (officer)* commandant *m*.

ma·jor·ette majorette *f*.

ma·jor·i·ty majorité *f* (of de); **the m. of people** la plupart des gens.

make* 1 *vt* faire; *(tool, vehicle etc)* fabriquer; *(decision)* prendre; *(friends, salary)* se faire; *(destination)* arriver à; **to m. happy/etc** rendre heureux/etc; **to m. sb do sth** faire faire qch à qn; **to m. do** *(manage)* se débrouiller (**with** avec); **to m. do with** *(be satisfied with)* se contenter de; **to m. it** arriver; *(succeed)* réussir; **what do you m. of it?** qu'en penses-tu? **2** *n (brand)* marque *f*.

▸ **make for** *vt* aller vers.

▸ **make good** *vt (loss)* compenser; *(damage)* réparer.

▸ **make off** *vi (run away)* se sauver.

▸ **make out 1** *vt (see)* distinguer; *(understand)* comprendre; *(write)* faire *(chèque, liste)*; *(claim)* prétendre (**that** que). **2** *vi* se débrouiller.

mak·er *(of product)* fabricant, -ante *mf*.

▸ **make up 1** *vt (story)* inventer; *(put together)* faire *(collection, liste etc)*; *(form)* former; *(loss)* compenser; *(quantity)* compléter; *(quarrel)* régler; *(one's face)* maquiller. **2** *vti* **to m. (it) up** *(of friends)* se réconcilier.

make-up *(for face)* maquillage *m*.

▸ **make up for** *vt (loss, damage)* compenser; *(lost time, mistake)* rattraper.

ma·lar·i·a malaria *f*.

male 1 *adj* mâle; *(clothes, sex)* masculin. **2** *n* mâle *m*.

mal·ice méchanceté *f*.

ma·li·cious *adj* malveillant.

mall *(shopping)* **m.** galerie *f* marchande; *(large complex)* centre *m* commercial.

ma·ma, ma·mma *Fam* maman *f*.

mam·mal mammifère *m*.

man, *pl* **men** homme *m*.

man·age 1 *vt (run)* diriger; *(handle)* manier; **to m. to do** *(succeed)* réussir à faire; *(by being smart)* se débrouiller pour faire; **I'll m. it** j'y arriverai. **2** *vi (succeed)* y arriver; *(make do)* se débrouiller (**with** avec); **to m. without sth** se passer de qch.

man·age·ment *(running, managers)* direction *f*.

man·ag·er directeur, -trice *mf*; *(of shop, café)* gérant, -ante *mf*.

man·ag·ing di·rec·tor PDG *m*.

mane crinière *f*.

ma·neu·ver 1 *n* manœuvre *f*. **2** *vti* manœuvrer.

ma·ni·ac fou *m*, folle *f*.

man·kind l'humanité *f*.

man·made *adj* artificiel.

man·ner *(way)* manière *f*, *(behavior)* attitude *f*; **manners** *(social ha-*

bits) manières *fpl*; **to have no man-ners** être mal élevé.

man·pow·er *n* main *f* d'œuvre.

man·tel·piece *(shelf)* cheminée *f*.

man·u·al 1 *adj* manuel. **2** *n (book)* manuel *m*.

man·u·fac·ture 1 *vt* fabriquer. **2** *n* fabrication *f*.

man·u·fac·tur·er fabricant, -ante *mf*.

ma·nure fumier *m*.

man·y *adj & n* beaucoup (de); **m. things** beaucoup de choses; **I don't have m.** j'en ai pas beaucoup; **m. came** beaucoup sont venus; **(a good** *or* **great) m. of** un (très) grand nombre de; **m. times** bien des fois; **as m. books/etc as** autant de livres/etc que.

map *(of country, region)* carte *f*; *(of town etc)* plan *m*.

mar·a·thon marathon *m*.

mar·ble marbre *m*; *(toy)* bille *f*.

March mars *m*.

march 1 *n* marche *f (militaire)*. **2** *vi (of soldiers)* défiler.

mare jument *f*.

mar·ga·rine margarine *f*.

mar·gin *(of page)* marge *f*.

ma·rine 1 *adj* marin. **2** *n* marine *m*; **the M. Corps** les Marines *mpl*.

mark 1 *n (symbol)* marque *f*; *(stain, trace)* trace *f*; *(token, sign)* signe *m*; *(for school exercise etc)* note *f*; *(target)* but *m*. **2** *vt* marquer; *(exam etc)* corriger.

mark·er *(pen)* marqueur *m*.

mar·ket marché *m*.

mar·ket·ing marketing *m*.

▶ **mark off** *vt (area)* délimiter.

mar·ma·lade confiture *f* d'oranges.

mar·riage mariage *m*.

mar·ried *adj* marié; **to get m.** se marier.

mar·row *(of bone)* moelle *f*.

mar·ry *vt* épouser, se marier avec; *(of priest etc)* marier. **2** *vi* se marier.

marsh marais *m*.

mar·shal 1 *n (in army)* maréchal *m*; *(district police officer)* commis-saire *m*; *(police chief)* commissaire *m* de police; *(fire chief)* capitaine *m* des pompiers. **2** *vt (troops)* masser, rassembler; *(facts, arguments etc)* rassembler.

mar·vel·ous *adj* merveilleux.

mar·zi·pan pâte *f* d'amandes.

mas·ca·ra mascara *m*.

mas·cot mascotte *f*.

mas·cu·line *adj* masculin.

mash *vt* to m. (up) écraser, broyer; *(food)* faire une purée de; **mashed potatoes** purée *f* (de pommes de terre).

mask masque *m*.

mass¹ 1 *n (quantity)* masse *f*; **a m. of** *(many)* une multitude de; *(pile)* un tas de; **masses of** des masses de. **2** *adj (protests, departure)* en masse.

mass² *(church service)* messe *f*.

mas·sa·cre 1 *n* massacre *m*. **2** *vt* massacrer.

mas·sage 1 *n* massage *m*. **2** *vt* masser.

mas·seur masseur *m*.

mas·seuse masseuse *f*.

mas·sive *adj (huge)* énorme.

mast *(of ship)* mât *m*.

mas·ter 1 *n* maître *m*; **M. of Arts/Science** *(person)* Maître *m* ès let-tres/sciences; **M. of Ceremonies** animateur, -trice *mf*. **2** *vt (control)* maîtriser; *(subject, situation)* domi-ner; **she has mastered Latin** elle possède le latin.

mas·ter·piece chef-d'œuvre *m*.

mat tapis *m*; *(of straw)* natte *f*; *(at door)* paillasson *m*; **(place) m.** set *m* (de table).

match¹ *(stick)* allumette *f*.

match² 1 *n (game)* match *m*; *(equal)* égal, -ale *mf*; **to be a good m.** *(of colors, people etc)* être bien assortis. **2** *vt (clothes, color etc)* aller (bien) avec; **to be well-matched** être (bien) assortis. **3** *vi* être assortis.

match (up) vt (plates etc) assortir.
match (up to) vt égaler; (sb's hopes or expectations) répondre à.
match·box boîte f d'allumettes.
match·ing adj (dress etc) assorti.
match·stick allumette f.
mate (friend) camarade mf.
ma·te·ri·al matière f, (cloth) tissu m; **material(s)** (equipment) matériel m; **building materials** matériaux mpl de construction.
ma·ter·nal adj maternel.
math maths fpl.
math·e·mat·i·cal adj mathématique.
math·e·mat·ics mathématiques fpl.
mat·i·nee (in theater) matinée f.
matt adj (paint, paper) mat.
mat·ter 1 n matière f, (subject, affair) affaire f, **what's the m. with you?** qu'est-ce que tu as?; **there's sth the m.** il y a qch qui ne va pas; **there's something the m. with my leg** j'ai quelque chose à la jambe. **2** vi importer (**to** à); **it doesn't m. if/who/etc** peu importe si/qui/etc; **it doesn't m.!** ça ne fait rien!
mat·tress matelas m.
ma·ture adj mûr; (cheese) fait.
max·i·mum adj & n maximum (m).
May mai m.
may v aux (pt might) (possibility) pouvoir; **he m. come** il peut arriver; **he might come** il pourrait arriver; **I m.** or **might have forgotten it** je l'ai peut-être oublié; **we m.** or **might as well go** nous ferions aussi bien de partir. ▪ (permission) pouvoir; **m. I stay?** puis-je rester?; **m. I?** vous permettez?; **you m. go** tu peux partir. ▪ (wish) **m. you be happy** (que tu) sois heureux.
may·be adv peut-être.
may·on·naise mayonnaise f.
may·or maire m.
maze labyrinthe m.
MBA abbr (Master of Business Ad-

ministration) MBA m, maîtrise f de gestion.
me pron me, m'; (after prep, 'than', 'it is') moi; (**to**) **me** me, m'; **she knows me** elle me connaît; **he gives** (**to**) **me** il me donne.
mead·ow pré m.
meal repas m.
mean[1]* vt(signify) vouloir dire; (intend) destiner (**for** à); (result in) entraîner; **to m. to do** avoir l'intention de faire; **I m. it** je suis sérieux; **to m. sth to sb** avoir de l'importance pour qn; **I didn't m. to!** je ne l'ai pas fait exprès!
mean[2] adj méchant.
mean·ing sens m.
mean·ing·ful adj significatif.
mean·ing·less adj qui n'a pas de sens.
mean·ness méchanceté f.
means n(pl) (method) moyen(s) m(pl) (**to do, of doing** de faire); (wealth) moyens mpl; **by m. of** (stick etc) au moyen de; (work etc) à force de; **by all m.!** très certainement!; **by no m.** nullement.
mean·time adv & n (**in the**) **m.** entre-temps.
mean·while adv entre-temps.
mea·sles rougeole f.
meas·ure 1 n (action, amount) mesure f. **2** vt mesurer.
meas·ure·ment (of chest etc) tour m; **measurements** mesures fpl.
▸ **measure up** vt (plank etc) mesurer.
▸ **measure up to** vt (task) être à la hauteur de.
meat viande f.
me·chan·ic mécanicien, -ienne mf.
me·chan·i·cal adj mécanique.
mech·a·nism mécanisme m.
med·al médaille f.
med·al·ist **to be a gold m.** être médaillé d'or.
me·di·a npl **the** (**mass**) **m.** les médias mpl.

me·di·an (in road) refuge m.
med·i·cal adj médical; (school, studies) de médecine; (student) en médecine.
med·i·ca·tion médicaments mpl.
med·i·cine médicament m; (science) médecine f.
med·i·cine cab·i·net, med·i·cine chest (armoire f à) pharmacie f.
me·di·e·val adj médiéval.
Med·i·ter·ra·ne·an 1 adj méditerranéen. **2** n the M. la Méditerranée.
me·di·um adj moyen.
me·di·um-sized adj moyen.
meet* 1 vt (person, team) rencontrer; (person by arrangement) retrouver; (pass in street etc) croiser; (fetch) (aller or venir) chercher; (wait for) attendre; (be introduced to) faire la connaissance de. **2** vi (of people, teams) se rencontrer; (of people by arrangement) se retrouver; (be introduced) se connaître; (of club) se réunir.
meet·ing réunion f; (large) assemblée f; (between two people) rencontre f; (arranged) rendez-vous m inv.
▸ **meet up** vi (of people) se rencontrer; (by arrangement) se retrouver.
▸ **meet up with** vt rencontrer; (by arrangement) retrouver.
▸ **meet with** vt (accident) avoir; (difficulty) rencontrer; (person) rencontrer; (by arrangement) retrouver.
mel·o·dy mélodie f.
mel·on melon m.
melt 1 vi fondre. **2** vt (faire) fondre.
mem·ber membre m.
mem·o, pl -os note f.
mem·o·ra·ble adj mémorable.
me·mo·ri·al 1 adj (plaque etc) commémoratif. **2** n mémorial m.
mem·o·ry mémoire f; (recollection) souvenir m; in m. of à la mémoire de.

men see **man**.
mend vt réparer; (clothes) raccommoder.
men·tal adj mental.
men·tal·ly adv he's m. handicapped c'est un handicapé mental; she's m. ill c'est une malade mentale.
men·tion 1 vt mentionner; not to m… sans parler de…; don't m. it! il n'y a pas de quoi! **2** n mention f.
men·u menu m.
me·ow vi (of cat) miauler.
mer·cy pitié f; at the m. of à la merci de.
mere adj simple; (only) ne…que; she's a m. child ce n'est qu'une enfant.
mere·ly adv (tout) simplement.
merge vi (blend) se mêler (with à); (of roads) se (re)joindre; (of firms) fusionner.
merg·er fusion f.
mer·it 1 n mérite m. **2** vt mériter.
mer·ry adj gai.
mer·ry-go-round (at fair) manège m.
mesh (of net) maille f.
mess (confusion) désordre m; (dirt) saleté f; in a m. sens dessus dessous; (trouble) dans le pétrin.
mes·sage message m.
▸ **mess around** vi (have fun) s'amuser; (play the fool) faire l'idiot.
▸ **mess around with** vt (fiddle with) s'amuser avec.
mes·sen·ger messager m; (in office, hotel) coursier, -ière mf.
▸ **mess up** vt (ruin) gâcher; (dirty) salir; (room) mettre sens dessus dessous.
mess·y adj (untidy) en désordre; (dirty) sale.
met·al métal m; m. ladder/etc échelle f/etc métallique.
met·a·phor métaphore f.
me·ter¹ (device) compteur m; (parking) m. parcmètre m.
me·ter² mètre m.

meth·od méthode f.

me·thod·i·cal adj méthodique.

met·ric adj métrique.

mice see **mouse**.

mi·cro prefix micro-.

mi·cro·chip puce f.

mi·cro·phone micro m.

mi·cro·scope microscope m.

mi·cro·wave (ov·en) four m à micro-ondes.

mid adj **(in)** m.-June (à) la mi-juin; **in** m. **air** en plein ciel.

mid·day midi m.

mid·dle 1 n milieu m; (waist) taille f; (right) in the m. of au (beau) milieu de; in the m. of saying/etc en train de dire/etc. **2** adj du milieu; (class) moyen; (name) deuxième.

mid·dle-aged adj d'un certain âge.

mid·dle-class adj bourgeois.

mid·night minuit m.

mid·se·mes·ter break vacances fpl scolaires.

midst in the m. of au milieu de.

mid·way adv à mi-chemin.

mid·wife, pl **-wives** sage-femme f.

might see **may**.

might·y 1 adj (powerful) puissant; (great) énorme. **2** adv Fam rudement.

mild adj doux (f douce); (beer, punishment) léger; (medicine, illness) bénin (f bénigne).

mile mile m (= 1,6km).

mile·age = kilométrage m.

mil·i·tar·y adj militaire.

milk 1 n lait m. **2** adj (chocolate) au lait; (bottle) à lait. **3** vt (cow) traire.

milk·man, pl **-men** laitier m.

milk shake milk-shake m.

mill moulin m; (factory) usine f.

mil·li·me·ter millimètre m.

mil·lion million m; a m. men/etc un million d'hommes/etc.

mil·lion·aire millionnaire mf.

mime vti mimer.

mim·ic vt (-ck-) imiter.

mince vt hacher; **she doesn't m. words** elle ne mâche pas ses mots.

mind 1 n esprit m; (sanity) raison f; (memory) mémoire f; **to change one's m.** changer d'avis; **to make up one's m.** se décider; **to be on sb's m.** préoccuper qn; **to have in m.** (person, plan) avoir en vue. **2** vti faire attention à; (look after) garder; (noise etc) être gêné par; **do you m. if?** (I smoke) ça vous gêne si?; (I leave) ça ne vous fait rien si?; **I don't m.** ça m'est égal; **I wouldn't m. a cup of tea** j'aimerais bien une tasse de thé; **never m.!** ça ne fait rien!; (don't worry) ne vous en faites pas!

mine¹ poss pron le mien, la mienne, pl les mien(ne)s; **this hat is m.** ce chapeau est à moi or est le mien.

mine² (for coal etc, explosive) mine f.

min·er mineur m.

min·er·al adj & n minéral (m).

min·i- prefix mini-.

min·i·a·ture adj (train etc) miniature inv; **in m.** en miniature.

min·i·bus minibus m.

min·i·mum adj & n minimum (m).

min·ing 1 n exploitation f minière, extraction f. **2** adj minier.

min·is·ter (clergyman) pasteur m.

min·is·try **to enter the m.** devenir pasteur.

mi·nor adj (detail, operation) petit.

mi·nor·i·ty minorité f.

mint (herb) menthe f; (candy) bonbon m à la menthe; **m. tea**/etc thé m/etc à la menthe.

mi·nus prep moins; (without) sans.

min·ute¹ minute f.

min·ute² adj (tiny) minuscule.

mir·a·cle miracle m.

mi·rac·u·lous adj miraculeux.

mir·ror miroir m, glace f, (in vehicle) rétroviseur m.

mis·be·have vi se conduire mal.

mis·cel·la·ne·ous adj divers.

mis·chief espièglerie f; (malice) méchanceté f; **to get into m.** faire des bêtises.

mis·chie·vous adj espiègle; (harmful) méchant, nuisible.

misdemeanor délit m.

mi·ser avare mf.

mis·er·a·ble adj (wretched) misérable; (unhappy) malheureux.

mi·ser·ly adj avare.

mis·er·y souffrances fpl; (sadness) tristesse f.

mis·for·tune malheur m.

mis·hap contretemps m.

mis·lay* vt égarer.

mis·lead vt tromper.

mis·lead·ing adj trompeur.

miss¹ 1 vt (train, opportunity etc) manquer; (not see) ne pas voir; (not understand) ne pas comprendre; **he misses Paris/her** Paris/elle lui manque. **2** vi manquer.

miss² (woman) mademoiselle f; **Miss Brown** Mademoiselle or Mlle Brown.

mis·sile (rocket) missile m; (object thrown) projectile m.

miss·ing adj absent; (after disaster) disparu; (object) manquant; **there are two cups m.** il manque deux tasses.

mis·sion mission f.

▸ **miss out 1** vt (leave out) sauter. **2** vi rater l'occasion.

▸ **miss out on** vt (opportunity etc) rater.

mist (fog) brume f; (on glass) buée f.

mis·take 1 n erreur f, faute f; **to make a m.** se tromper; **by m.** par erreur. **2** vt* (meaning etc) se tromper sur; **to m. sb/sth for** prendre qn/qch pour; **you're mistaken** tu te trompes.

mis·ta·ken·ly adv par erreur.

mis·treat vt maltraiter.

mis·tress maîtresse f.

mis·trust 1 n méfiance f. **2** vt se méfier de.

mist·y adj brumeux.

mis·un·der·stand* vt mal comprendre.

mis·un·der·stand·ing malentendu m.

mit·ten (glove) moufle f.

mix 1 vt mélanger, mêler; (cake) préparer; (salad) remuer. **2** vi se mêler; **she doesn't m.** elle n'est pas sociable.

mixed adj (school) mixte; (chocolates etc) assortis.

mix·er (electric, for cooking) mixe(u)r m.

mix·ture mélange m.

mix-up confusion f.

▸ **mix up** vt (drink, papers etc) mélanger; (make confused) embrouiller (qn); (mistake) confondre (**with** avec).

▸ **mix with** vt fréquenter.

moan vi (groan) gémir; (complain) se plaindre (**to** à; **about** de; **that** que).

mob 1 n foule f. **2** vt assiéger.

mo·bile adj mobile.

mod·el 1 n (example etc) modèle m; (fashion) mannequin m; (scale) m. modèle m (réduit). **2** adj (car, plane etc) modèle réduit inv; **m. train** train m miniature.

mod·el·ing clay pâte f à modeler.

mo·dem modem m.

mod·er·ate adj modéré.

mod·er·a·tion modération f.

mod·ern adj moderne; **m. languages** langues fpl vivantes.

mod·ern·ize 1 vt moderniser. **2** vi se moderniser.

mod·est adj modeste.

mod·es·ty modestie f.

mod·i·fi·ca·tion modification f.

mod·i·fy vt modifier.

moist adj humide; (sticky) moite.

mois·ture humidité f; (on glass) buée f.

mold 1 n (shape) moule m; (growth) moisissure f. **2** vt (clay etc) mouler.

mold·y *adj* moisi; **to get m.** moisir.
mole *(on skin)* grain *m* de beauté; *(animal)* taupe *f.*
mom *Fam* maman *f.*
mo·ment moment *m*; **the m. she leaves** dès qu'elle partira.
mom·my *Fam* maman *f.*
Mon·day lundi *m.*
mon·ey argent *m.*
mon·ey or·der mandat *m.*
mon·i·tor *(computer screen)* moniteur *m* (d'ordinateur).
monk moine *m.*
mon·key singe *m.*
mo·nop·o·lize *vt* monopoliser.
mo·not·o·nous *adj* monotone.
mo·not·o·ny monotonie *f.*
mon·ster monstre *m.*
month mois *m.*
month·ly 1 *adj* mensuel. **2** *adv* mensuellement.
mon·u·ment monument *m.*
moo *vi* meugler.
mood *(of person)* humeur *f, Grammar* mode *m*; **in a good/bad m.** de bonne/mauvaise humeur; **to be in the m. to do** être d'humeur à faire.
mood·y *adj (bad-tempered)* de mauvaise humeur.
moon lune *f.*
moon·light clair *m* de lune.
moor lande *f.*
moose *inv* élan *m.*
mop **1** *n* balai *m* (à laver). **2** *vt (floor etc)* essuyer.
mo·ped mobylette® *f.*
▸ mop up *vt (liquid)* éponger.
mor·al *(of story)* morale *f.*
mo·rale moral *m.*
more 1 *adj & n* plus (de) (**than** que); *(other)* d'autres; **m. cars**/*etc* plus de voitures/*etc*; **he has m. (than you)** il en a plus (que toi); **a few m. months** encore quelques mois; **(some) m. tea**/*etc* encore du thé/ *etc*; **m. than a quart/ten** *(with quantity, number)* plus d'un litre/de dix; **many m., much m.** beaucoup plus (de). **2** *adv* plus (**than** que);

m. and m. de plus en plus; **m. or less** plus ou moins; **she doesn't have any m.** elle n'en a plus.
more·o·ver *adv* de plus.
morn·ing *(in) matin m; (duration of morning)* matinée *f*; **in the m.** le matin; *(tomorrow)* demain matin; **at seven in the m.** à sept heures du matin; **every Tuesday m.** tous les mardis matin.
mor·tal *adj & n* mortel, -elle *(mf).*
mort·gage prêt-logement *m.*
Mos·lem *adj & n* musulman, -ane *(mf).*
mosque mosquée *f.*
mos·qui·to, *pl* **-oes** moustique *m.*
moss mousse *f (plante).*
most 1 *adj & n* le plus (de); **I have the m. books** j'ai le plus de livres; **I have the m.** j'en ai le plus; **m. (of the) books**/*etc* la plupart des livres/*etc*; **m. of the cake**/*etc* la plus grande partie du gâteau/*etc*; **at (the very) m.** tout au plus. **2** *adv* **(the) m.** *(of)* le plus; *(very)* très; **the m. beautiful** le plus beau, la plus belle (**in, of** de); **to talk (the) m.** parler le plus; **m. of all** surtout.
most·ly *adv* surtout.
mo·tel motel *m.*
moth papillon *m* de nuit; *(in clothes)* mite *f.*
moth·er mère *f*; **M.'s Day** la fête des Mères.
moth·er-in-law, *pl* **mothers-in-law** belle-mère *f.*
mo·tion 1 *n (of arm etc)* mouvement *m.* **2** *vti* **to m. (to) sb to do** faire signe à qn de faire.
mo·ti·vat·ed *adj* motivé.
mo·tive motif *m* (**for** de).
mo·tor *(engine)* moteur *m.*
mo·tor·bike moto *f.*
mo·tor·boat canot *m* automobile.
mo·tor·cy·cle motocyclette *f.*
mo·tor·cy·clist motocycliste *mf.*
mo·tor·ist automobiliste *mf.*
mount 1 *n (frame for photo)* cadre

m. **2** *vt (horse, photo)* monter. **3** *vi (on horse)* se mettre en selle.

moun·tain montagne *f;* **m. bike** VTT *m inv.*

moun·tain·eer alpiniste *mf.*

moun·tain·eer·ing alpinisme *m.*

moun·tain·ous *adj* montagneux.

▸ **mount up** *vi (add up)* chiffrer **(to** à**);** *(accumulate)* s'accumuler.

mourn *vt* to m. **(for)** sb, to m. the loss of sb pleurer (la perte de) qn; **she's mourning** elle est en deuil.

mourn·ing deuil *m;* **in m.** en deuil.

mouse, *pl* **mice** souris *f.*

mousse mousse *f (dessert).*

mouth, *pl* **-s** bouche *f; (of dog, lion etc)* gueule *f; (of river)* embouchure *f.*

mouth·wash bain *m* de bouche.

move 1 *n* mouvement *m; (change of house)* déménagement *m; (in game)* coup *m; (one's turn)* tour *m; (act)* démarche *f;* **to make a m.** *(leave)* se préparer à partir; **to get a m. on** se remuer. **2** *vt* déplacer; *(arm, leg)* remuer; *(put)* mettre; *(transport)* transporter; *(piece in game)* jouer; **to m. sb** *(emotionally)* émouvoir qn; *(transfer in job)* muter qn. **3** *vi* bouger; *(go)* aller **(to** à**);** *(out of house)* déménager; *(change seats)* changer de place; *(play)* jouer; **to m. to a new house**/*etc* aller habiter une nouvelle maison/*etc;* **to m. into a house** emménager dans une maison.

▸ **move along** *vi* avancer.

▸ **move around** *vi* se déplacer; *(fidget)* remuer.

▸ **move away** *vi* s'éloigner; *(to new house)* déménager.

▸ **move back 1** *vt (chair etc)* reculer; *(to its position)* remettre. **2** *vi* reculer; *(return)* retourner.

▸ **move down** *vti* descendre.

▸ **move forward** *vti* avancer.

▸ **move in** *vi (into house)* emménager.

move·ment *(action, group etc)* mouvement *m.*

▸ **move off** *vi (go away)* s'éloigner; *(of vehicle)* démarrer.

▸ **move on** *vi* avancer.

▸ **move out** *vi (out of house)* déménager.

▸ **move over 1** *vt* pousser. **2** *vi* se pousser.

mov·er déménageur *m.*

▸ **move up 1** *vt (meeting)* avancer. **2** *vi (on seats etc)* se pousser.

mov·ie film *m;* **the movies** *(art, movie theater)* le cinéma.

mov·ie cam·er·a caméra *f.*

mov·ie star vedette *f* (de cinéma).

mov·ie the·a·ter cinéma *m.*

mov·ing *adj* en mouvement; *(touching)* émouvant.

mov·ing van camion *m* de déménagement.

mow *vt (pp* **mown** *or* **mowed)** to m. the lawn tondre le gazon.

mow·er (lawn) m. tondeuse *f* (à gazon).

Mr Mr Brown Monsieur *or* M. Brown.

Mrs Mrs Brown Madame *or* Mme Brown.

Ms Ms Brown Madame *or* Mme Brown.

MS *abbr* = **Master of Science**.

much 1 *adj & n* beaucoup (de); **not m. time**/*etc* pas beaucoup de temps/*etc;* **I don't have m.** je n'en ai pas beaucoup; **as m. as** autant que; **as m. wine**/*etc* **as** autant de vin/*etc* que; **twice as m.** deux fois plus (de). **2** *adv* **very m.** beaucoup; **not (very) m.** pas beaucoup.

mud boue *f.*

mud·dle *(mix-up)* confusion *f; (mess)* désordre *m;* **in a m.** *(person)* désorienté; *(mind, ideas)* embrouillé.

mud·dle (up) *vt (person, facts)* embrouiller; *(papers)* mélanger.

▸**muddle through** *vi* se tirer d'affaire.

mud·dy *adj (water, road)* boueux; *(hands etc)* couvert de boue.

mues·li muesli *m*.

muf·fin muffin *m*.

mug[1] *(cup)* grande tasse *f*; **(beer)** m. chope *f*.

mug[2] *vt (in street)* agresser, attaquer.

mug·ger agresseur *m*.

mule *(male)* mulet *m*; *(female)* mule *f*.

mul·ti·ple *adj & n* multiple *(m)*.

mul·ti·pli·ca·tion multiplication *f*.

mul·ti·ply *vt* multiplier.

mum·ble *vti* marmotter.

mumps oreillons *mpl*.

mu·nic·i·pal *adj* municipal.

mur·der 1 *n* meurtre *m*, assassinat *m*. **2** *vt* tuer, assassiner.

mur·der·er meurtrier, -ière *mf*, assassin *m*.

mur·mur *vti* murmurer.

mus·cle muscle *m*.

mus·cu·lar *adj (arm etc)* musclé.

mu·se·um musée *m*.

mush·room champignon *m*.

mu·sic musique *f*.

mu·si·cal 1 *adj* musical; *(instrument)* de musique; **to be m.** être musicien. **2** *n* comédie *f* musicale.

mu·si·cian musicien, -ienne *mf*.

Mus·lim *adj & n* musulman, -ane *(mf)*.

mus·sel moule *f*.

must *v aux (necessity)* devoir; **you m. obey** tu dois obéir, il faut que tu obéisses. ▪ *(certainty)* devoir; **she m. be smart** elle doit être intelligente; **I m. have seen it** j'ai dû le voir.

mus·tache moustache *f*.

mus·tard moutarde *f*.

must·y to smell m. sentir le moisi.

mute 1 *adj* muet. **2** *n (person)* muet, -ette *mf*; *(on musical instrument)* sourdine *f*.

mut·ter *vti* marmonner.

mut·ton *(meat)* mouton *m*.

mu·tu·al *adj (help etc)* mutuel; *(friend)* commun.

muz·zle *(for animal)* muselière *f*.

my *poss adj* mon, ma, *pl* mes.

my·self *pron* moi-même; *(reflexive)* me, m'; *(after prep)* moi.

mys·te·ri·ous *adj* mystérieux.

mys·ter·y mystère *m*; *(novel)* roman *m* policier; *(movie)* film *m* policier.

myth mythe *m*.

N

nail *(of finger, toe)* ongle *m*; *(metal)* clou *m*; **n. file/polish** lime *f*/vernis *m* à ongles.

nail (down) *vt* clouer.

na·ive *adj* naïf.

na·ked *adj* nu.

name 1 *n* nom *m*; *(reputation)* réputation *f*; **my n. is...** je m'appelle...; **first n.** prénom *m*; **last n.** nom *m* de famille. **2** *vt* nommer; *(date, price)* fixer; **he was named after** *or* **for** il a reçu le nom de.

name·ly *adv* à savoir.

nan·a *(grandmother) Fam* mamie *f*.

nan·ny nourrice *f*; *(grandmother) Fam* mamie *f*.

nap *(sleep)* petit somme *m*; **to have** *or* **take a n.** faire un petit somme.

nap·kin serviette *f*.

nar·ra·tive 1 *n* récit *m*. **2** *adj* narratif.

nar·row *adj* étroit.

nar·row (down) *vt (choice etc)* limiter.

nar·row·ly **he n. escaped being killed/etc** il a failli être tué/etc.

nast·i·ly *adv (to behave)* méchamment.

nas·ty adj mauvais; (spiteful) méchant (to(wards) avec).

na·tion f.

na·tion·al adj national.

na·tion·al·i·ty nationalité f.

na·tive 1 adj (country) natal (mpl -als); **to be an English n. speaker** avoir l'anglais comme langue maternelle. **2** n **to be a n. of** être originaire de.

nat·u·ral adj naturel; (actor etc) né.

nat·u·ral·ly adv (as normal, of course) naturellement; (to behave etc) avec naturel.

na·ture (natural world, character) nature f.

na·ture stud·y sciences fpl naturelles.

naught rien m.

naugh·ty adj (child) vilain.

nau·se·at·ing adj écœurant.

nau·seous adj **to feel n.** avoir envie de vomir.

na·val adj naval (mpl -als); (officer) de marine.

na·vel nombril m.

nav·i·gate 1 vi naviguer. **2** vt (boat) diriger.

nav·i·ga·tion navigation f.

na·vy 1 n marine f. **2** adj n. (blue) bleu marine inv.

near 1 adv près; **very n.** tout près; **n. to** près de; **to come n. to being killed/etc** faillir être tué/etc; **n. enough** (more or less) plus ou moins. **2** prep **n. (to)** près de; **n. (to) the end** vers la fin; **to come n. sb** s'approcher de qn. **3** adj proche; **in the n. future** dans un avenir proche.

near·by 1 adv tout près. **2** adj proche.

near·ly adv presque; **she (very) n. fell** elle a failli tomber; **not n. as smart/etc** loin d'être aussi intelligent/etc que.

neat adj (clothes, work) soigné; (room) bien rangé.

neat·ly adv avec soin.

nec·es·sar·i·ly adv **not n.** pas forcément.

nec·es·sar·y adj nécessaire (**to do** de faire); **to do what's n.** faire le nécessaire.

ne·ces·si·ty nécessité f.

neck cou m; (of dress, horse) encolure f.

neck·lace collier m.

nec·tar·ine nectarine f.

need 1 n besoin m; **to be in n. of** avoir besoin de; **there's no n. (for you) to do** tu n'as pas besoin de faire; **if n. be** si besoin est. **2** vt avoir besoin de; **her hair needs cutting** il faut qu'elle se fasse couper les cheveux; **I needn't have rushed** ce n'était pas la peine de me presser.

nee·dle aiguille f.

need·less·ly adv inutilement.

nee·dle·work couture f; (object) ouvrage m.

neg·a·tive 1 adj négatif. **2** n (of photo) négatif m; Grammar forme f négative.

ne·glect vt (person, work, duty etc) négliger; (garden, car) ne pas s'occuper de.

ne·glect·ed adj (appearance) négligé; (garden, house) mal tenu; **to feel n.** se sentir délaissé.

neg·li·gence négligence f.

neg·li·gent adj négligent.

ne·go·ti·ate vti (discuss) négocier.

ne·go·ti·a·tion négociation f.

neigh vi (of horse) hennir.

neigh·bor voisin, -ine mf.

neigh·bor·hood quartier m; (neighbors) voisinage m.

neigh·bor·ing adj voisin.

nei·ther 1 adv **n....nor** ni...ni; **he n. sings nor dances** il ne chante ni ne danse. **2** conj (not either) **if you won't go, n. will I** si tu n'y vas pas, je n'irai pas non plus. **3** adj **n. boy (came)** aucun des deux garçons (n'est venu). **4** *pron* n. *(of them)* ni l'un(e) ni l'autre.

ne·on *adj (lighting etc)* au néon.

neph·ew neveu *m*.

nerve nerf *m; (courage)* courage *m* (**to do** de faire); *(calm)* sang-froid *m; (cheek)* culot *m* (**to do** de faire); **you get on my nerves** tu me tapes sur les nerfs.

nerv·ous *adj (tense)* nerveux; *(worried)* inquiet (**about** de); *(uneasy)* mal à l'aise; **to be** *or* **feel n.** *(before exam etc)* avoir le trac.

nest nid *m*.

net *n* filet *m*. **2** *adj (profit, weight etc)* net (*f* nette).

net·ting (wire) n. grillage *m*.

net·tle ortie *f*.

net·work réseau *m*.

neu·tral **1** *adj* neutre. **2** *n* **in n.** (gear) au point mort.

nev·er *adv* (ne…) jamais; **she n. lies** elle ne ment jamais; **n. again** plus jamais.

nev·er-end·ing *adj* interminable.

nev·er·the·less *adv* néanmoins.

new *adj* nouveau (*f* nouvelle); *(brand-new)* neuf (*f* neuve); **a n. glass**/*etc (different)* un autre verre/ *etc*; **what's n.?** *Fam* quoi de neuf?

new·born *adj* **a n. baby** un nouveau-né, une nouveau-née.

new·ly *adv (recently)* nouvellement.

news nouvelle(s) *f(pl); (in the media)* informations *fpl*; **sports n.** *(newspaper column)* chronique *f* sportive; **a piece of n., some n.** une nouvelle; *(in the media)* une information.

news flash flash *m*.

news·let·ter bulletin *m*.

news·pa·per journal *m*.

news·stand kiosque *m* (à journaux).

next 1 *adj* prochain; *(room, house)* d'à-côté; *(following)* suivant; **n. month** *(in the future)* le mois pro-

chain; **the n. day** le lendemain; **the n. morning** le lendemain matin; **(by) this time n. week** d'ici (à) la semaine prochaine; **to live n. door** habiter à côté (**to** de); **n.-door neighbor** voisin *m* d'à côté. **2** *n* suivant, -ante *mf*. **3** *adv (afterwards)* ensuite; *(now)* maintenant; **when you come n.** la prochaine fois que tu viendras. **4** *prep* **n. to** *(beside)* à côté de.

nib *(of pen)* plume *f*.

nib·ble *vti (eat)* grignoter; *(bite)* mordiller.

nice *adj (pleasant)* agréable; *(pretty)* joli; *(kind)* gentil (**to** avec); **it's n. here** c'est bien ici; **n. and warm**/*etc (very)* bien chaud/*etc*.

nice·ly *adv* agréablement; *(kindly)* gentiment.

nick·el *(coin)* pièce *f* de cinq cents.

nick·el-and-dime-store = magasin *m* à prix unique.

nick·name surnom *m*.

niece nièce *f*.

night nuit *f, (evening)* soir *m*; **last n.** *(evening)* hier soir; *(night)* la nuit dernière; **to have an early/late n.** se coucher tôt/tard; **to have a good n.('s sleep)** bien dormir.

night·club boîte *f* de nuit.

night·gown, Fam **nightie** chemise *f* de nuit.

night·in·gale rossignol *m*.

night·mare cauchemar *m*.

night·stand table *f* de nuit.

night·time nuit *f.*

night watch·man veilleur *m* de nuit.

nil zéro *m*.

nine *adj & n* neuf *(m)*.

nine·teen *adj & n* dix-neuf *(m)*.

nine·ti·eth *adj & n* quatre-vingt-dixième *(mf)*.

nine·ty *adj & n* quatre-vingt-dix *(m)*.

ninth *adj & n* neuvième *(mf)*.

nip 1 *n (bite)* (petite) morsure *f; (drink)* petit verre; *(coldness)* there's a n. in the air le fond de l'air est frais. **2** *vt* pincer.

nip·ple bout *m* de sein; *(of bottle)* tétine *f.*

ni·tro·gen azote *m.*

no 1 *adv* & *n* non *(m inv)*; **no more than ten/etc** pas plus de dix/*etc*; **no more time/etc** plus de temps/*etc.* **2** *adj* aucun(e); pas de; **I have no idea** je n'ai aucune idée; **no child came** aucun enfant n'est venu; **I have no time/etc** je n'ai pas de temps/*etc*, **of no importance/etc** sans importance/*etc*; **'no smoking'** 'défense de fumer'; **no way!** *Fam* pas question!; **no one = nobody.**

no·ble *adj* noble.

no·bod·y *pron* (ne…) personne; **n. came** personne n'est venue; **n.!** personne!

nod 1 *vti* **to n. (one's head)** faire un signe de tête. **2** *n* signe *m* de tête.

▸ **nod off** *vi* s'assoupir.

noise bruit *m*; *(of bell, drum)* son *m*; **to make a n.** faire du bruit.

nois·i·ly *adv* bruyamment.

nois·y *adj* bruyant.

nom·i·nate *vt (appoint)* nommer.

nom·i·na·tion *(proposal)* proposition *f*, *(appointment)* nomination *f.*

non- *prefix* non-.

none *pron* aucun(e) *mf*; *(in filling out a form)* néant; **she has n. (at all)** elle n'en a pas (du tout); **n. (at all) came** pas un(e) seul(e) n'est venu(e); **n. of the cake/etc** pas une seule partie du gâteau/*etc*; **n. of the trees/etc** aucun des arbres/*etc.*

none·the·less *adv* néanmoins.

non·ex·ist·ent *adj* inexistant.

non-fic·tion *(in library)* ouvrages *mpl* généraux.

non-sense absurdités *fpl*; **that's n.** c'est absurde.

non-smok·er non-fumeur, -euse *mf.*

non-stick *adj (pan)* anti-adhésif.

non-stop 1 *adj* sans arrêt; *(train,*

flight) direct. **2** *adv* sans arrêt; *(to fly)* sans escale.

noo·dles *npl* nouilles *fpl*; *(in soup)* vermicelle(s) *m(pl).*

noon midi *m*; **at n.** à midi.

nor *conj* ni; **neither you n. me/I** ni toi ni moi; **she neither drinks n. smokes** elle ne fume ni ne boit; **I do not know, n. do I care** je ne sais pas et d'ailleurs je m'en moque.

norm norme *f.*

nor·mal 1 *adj* normal. **2** *n* **above/ below n.** au-dessus/au-dessous de la normale.

nor·mal·ly *adv* normalement.

north 1 *n* nord *m*; **(to the) n. of** au nord de. **2** *adj (coast)* nord *inv.* **3** *adv* au nord.

North A·mer·i·can 1 *n* Nord-Américain, -aine *mf.* **2** *adj* nord-américain, -aine.

north·bound *adj* en direction du nord.

north-east *n* & *adj* nord-est *(m & adj inv).*

north·ern *adj (coast)* nord *inv*; *(town)* du nord.

north·ern·er habitant, -ante *mf* du nord.

north·ward(s) *adj* & *adv* vers le nord.

north-west *n* & *adj* nord-ouest *(m & adj inv).*

Nor·we·gian 1 *n* Norvégien, -ienne *mf.* **2** *adj* norvégien, -ienne *mf.*

nose nez *m*; **her n. is bleeding** elle saigne du nez.

nose·bleed saignement *m* de nez.

nos·tril *(of person)* narine *f*, *(horse)* naseau *m.*

nos·(e)y *adj* indiscret.

not *adv* (ne…) pas; **he's n. there, he isn't there** il n'est pas là; **n. yet** pas encore; **why n.?** pourquoi pas?; **n. one reply/etc** pas une seule réponse/*etc*; **n. at all** pas du tout; *(after 'thank you')* je vous en prie. ■

non; **I think/hope** n. je pense/j'espère que non; **isn't she?, don't you?/**etc non?

no·ta·ble adj notable.

no·ta·bly adv (noticeably) notablement; (particularly) notamment.

note 1 n (comment, musical etc) note f; (money) billet m; (message) petit mot m; **to make a n. of** prendre note de. **2** vt noter.

note·book carnet m; (for school) cahier m.

▸**note down** vt (word etc) noter.

note·pad bloc-notes m.

note·pa·per papier m à lettres.

noth·ing pron (ne...) rien; **he knows** n. il ne sait rien; **to eat/** etc rien à manger/etc; **n. big/**etc rien de grand/etc; **n. much** pas grand-chose; **I've got** n. **to do with it** je n'y suis pour rien; **to come to** n. (of efforts etc) ne rien donner; **for** n. (in vain, free of charge) pour rien; **to have** n. **on** être tout nu.

no·tice 1 n avis m; (sign) pancarte f; (poster) affiche f; **to give** n. donner sa démission; **to give sb (advance)** n. avertir qn (**of** de); **to take** n. faire attention (**of** à); **until further** n. jusqu'à nouvel ordre. **2** vt remarquer (**that** que).

no·tice·a·ble adj visible.

no·ti·fi·ca·tion avis m.

no·ti·fy vt avertir (**sb of sth** qn de qch).

no·tion idée f.

no·to·ri·ous adj tristement célèbre; (criminal) notoire.

noun nom m.

nour·ish·ing adj nourrissant.

nov·el 1 n roman m. **2** adj nouveau (f nouvelle).

nov·el·ist romancier, -ière mf.

No·vem·ber novembre m.

now 1 adv maintenant; **just** n., **right** n. en ce moment; **I saw her**

just n. je l'ai vue à l'instant; **for** n. pour le moment; **from** n. **on** désormais; **before** n. avant; **n. and then** de temps à autre. **2** conj n. (**that**) maintenant que.

now·a·days adv aujourd'hui.

no·where adv nulle part; **n. near the house** loin de la maison; **n. near enough** loin d'être assez.

noz·zle (hose) jet m.

nu·clear adj nucléaire.

nude **in the** n. (tout) nu.

nudge 1 vt pousser du coude. **2** n coup m de coude.

nui·sance embêtement m; (person) peste f; **that's a** n. c'est embêtant.

numb adj (hand etc) engourdi.

num·ber 1 n nombre m; (of page, house, telephone etc) numéro m; **a** n. **of** un certain nombre de. **2** vt (page etc) numéroter.

nu·mer·al chiffre m.

nu·mer·ous adj nombreux.

nun religieuse f.

nurse 1 n infirmière f; (male) n. infirmier m. **2** vt (take care of) soigner; (baby) allaiter. **3** vi (of baby) téter.

nurs·er·y (in house) chambre f d'enfants; (for plants) pépinière f.

nurs·er·y rhyme chanson f enfantine.

nurs·er·y school école f maternelle.

nurs·ing home (for elderly people) maison f de retraite; (for convalescents) maison f de repos; (for mentally ill) maison f de santé.

nut[1] (walnut) noix f; (hazelnut) noisette f; (peanut) cacah(o)uète f.

nut[2] (for bolt) écrou m.

nut·crack·er casse-noix m inv.

nut·shell **in a** n. en un mot.

ny·lon 1 n nylon m; **nylons** bas mpl nylon. **2** adj (shirt etc) en nylon.

O

oak chêne m.

oar aviron m.

oat·meal flocons mpl d'avoine.

oats npl avoine f.

o·be·di·ence obéissance f (**to** à).

o·be·di·ent adj obéissant.

o·bey 1 vt obéir à (qn); **to be obeyed** être obéi. **2** vi obéir.

ob·ject[1] (thing, aim) objet m; Grammar complément m (d'objet).

ob·ject[2] vi to o. to sth/sb désapprouver qch/qn; **I o. to you(r) doing that** ça me gêne que tu fasses ça.

ob·jec·tion objection f.

ob·jec·tive (aim) objectif m.

ob·li·ga·tion obligation f.

o·blige vt (compel) contraindre (**sb to do** qn à faire); (help) rendre service à.

o·blig·ing adj serviable.

o·blique adj oblique.

ob·scene adj obscène.

ob·scure 1 adj obscur. **2** vt (hide) cacher; (confuse) obscurcir.

ob·ser·vant adj observateur.

ob·ser·va·tion observation f.

ob·serve vt observer; (say) remarquer (**that** que).

ob·ses·sion obsession f.

ob·sta·cle obstacle m.

ob·sti·nate adj (person, resistance) obstiné.

ob·struct vt (block) boucher; (hinder) gêner.

ob·tain vt obtenir.

ob·tain·a·ble adj disponible.

ob·vi·ous adj évident (**that** que).

ob·vi·ous·ly adv évidemment.

oc·ca·sion (time, opportunity) occasion f; (event, ceremony) événement m.

oc·ca·sion·al adj (odd) qu'on fait/ voit/etc de temps en temps; **she drinks the o. whisky** elle boit un whisky de temps en temps.

oc·ca·sion·al·ly adv de temps en temps.

oc·cu·pant occupant, -ante mf.

oc·cu·pa·tion (activity) occupation f; (job) emploi m; (trade) métier m; (profession) profession f.

oc·cu·py vt occuper; **to keep oneself occupied** s'occuper (**doing** à faire).

oc·cur vi (happen) avoir lieu; (be found) se rencontrer; **it occurs to me that…** il me vient à l'esprit que…

oc·cur·rence (event) événement m.

o·cean océan m.

o'clock adv (it's) three o'c./etc (il est) trois heures/etc.

Oc·to·ber octobre m.

oc·to·pus pieuvre f.

odd adj (strange) bizarre. ▪ (number) impair. ▪ (left over) **I have an o. penny** il me reste un penny; **a few o. stamps** quelques timbres (qui restent); **the o. man out** l'exception f; **sixty o.** soixante et quelques; **an o. glove/etc** un gant/etc dépareillé. ▪ qu'on fait/voit/etc de temps en temps; **I smoke the o. cigarette** je fume une cigarette de temps en temps; **o. jobs** menus travaux mpl.

oddly adv bizarrement.

odds npl (in betting) cote f; (chances) chances fpl; **at o.** en désaccord (**with** avec); **o. and ends** des petites choses.

o·dor odeur f.

of prep de, d' (de + le = du, de + les = des); **of the woman** de la femme; **of a book** d'un livre; **she has a lot of it** or **of them** elle en a beaucoup; **a friend of his** un ami à lui; **there are ten of us** nous sommes dix; **that's nice of you** c'est gentil de ta part.

off 1 adv (gone away) parti; (light, radio etc) éteint; (faucet) fermé; (detached) détaché; (removed) enlevé; (canceled) annulé; **6 miles o.** à 10km (d'ici or de là); **to be ou go o.** (leave) partir; **a day o.** un jour de congé; **time o.** du temps libre; **5% o.** une réduction de 5%; **hands o.!** pas touche!; **to be better o.** être mieux. **2** prep (from) de; (distant) éloigné de; **to get o. the bus**/etc descendre du bus/etc; **to take sth o. the table**/etc prendre qch sur la table/etc; **o. New York** au large de New York.

off•col•or adj risqué.

of•fend vt froisser (qn); **to be offended (at)** se froisser (de).

of•fend•er (criminal) délinquant, -ante mf.

of•fense (crime) délit m; **to take o.** s'offenser (**at** de).

of•fen•sive adj (words etc) insultant (**to sb** pour qn); (person) insultant (**to sb** avec qn).

of•fer 1 n offre f, special **o.** (in store) promotion f. **2** vt offrir (**to do** de faire).

of•fer•ing offre f, (in church) offrande f.

off•hand 1 adj (abrupt) brusque, impoli. **2** adv (to say, know etc) comme ça.

of•fice (room) bureau m; (of doctor, lawyer) cabinet m; (post) fonction f; **head o.** siège m central; **o. building** immeuble m de bureaux.

of•fi•cer (in the army etc) officier m; (police) **o.** agent m (de police).

of•fi•cial 1 adj officiel. **2** n (civil servant) fonctionnaire mf.

of•fi•cial•ly adv officiellement.

off-line adj Comput non connecté; (printer) déconnecté.

off•spring inv (children) progéniture f.

of•ten adv souvent; **how o.?**

combien de fois?; **how o. do they run?** (train etc) il y en a tous les combien?; **every so o.** de temps en temps.

oh! int oh!, ah!; **oh yes!** mais oui!; **oh yes?** ah oui?

oil 1 n huile f, (extracted from ground) pétrole m; (fuel) mazout m. **2** vt (machine) graisser.

oil•can burette f.

oil change (in vehicle) vidange f.

oint•ment pommade f.

OK, o•kay 1 adj (satisfactory) bien inv, (unharmed) sain et sauf; (undamaged) intact; (without worries) tranquille; **it's o.** ça va; **I'm o.** (healthy) je vais bien. **2** adv (well) bien; **o.!** (agreement) d'accord!

old adj vieux (f vieille); (former) ancien; **how o. is he?** quel âge a-t-il?; **he's ten years o.** il a dix ans; **he's older than me** il est plus âgé que moi; **an older son** un fils aîné; **the oldest son** le fils aîné; **o. man** vieillard m; **o. woman** vieille femme f, **to get o.** grow **old(er)** vieillir; **o. age** vieillesse f.

old-fash•ioned adj démodé; (person) rétro inv.

ol•ive olive f, **o. oil** huile f d'olive.

O•lym•pic adj (games etc) olympique.

om•e•let(te) omelette f, **cheese/** etc **o.** omelette au fromage/etc.

o•mis•sion omission f.

o•mit vt omettre.

on 1 prep (position) sur; **to put on (to)** mettre sur. ▪ (about) sur; **to speak on** parler sur. ▪ (manner, means) **on foot** à pied; **on the train**/etc dans le train/etc; **to be on (salary)** toucher; (team) être membre de; **to keep or stay on** (path etc) suivre. ▪ (time) **on Monday** lundi; **on Mondays** le lundi; **on May 3rd** le 3 mai. ▪ (+ present participle) en; **on seeing this** en voyant ceci. **2** adv (ahead) en avant; (in *progress)* en cours; *(lid, brake)* mis; *(light, radio)* allumé; *(gas, faucet)* ouvert; **on (and on)** sans cesse; **to play/***etc* **on** continuer à jouer/*etc*; **what's on?** *(television)* qu'y a-t-il à la télé?; **from then on** à partir de là.

once 1 *adv* une fois; *(formerly)* autrefois; **o. a month** une fois par mois; **o. again, o. more** encore une fois; **at o.** tout de suite; **all at o.** tout à coup; *(at the same time)* à la fois. **2** *conj* une fois que.

one 1 *adj* un, une; **o. man** un homme; **o. woman** une femme; **page o.** la page un; **twenty-o.** vingt-et-un. ▪ *(only)* seul; **my o. (and only) aim** mon seul (et unique) but. ▪ *(same)* même; **on the o. bus** dans le même bus. **2** *pron* un, une; **do you want o.?** en veux-tu (un)?; **o. of them** l'un d'eux, l'une d'elles; **a big/***etc* **o.** un grand/ *etc*; **that o.** celui-là, celle-là; **the o. who** *or* **which** celui *or* celle qui; **another o.** un(e) autre. ▪ *(impersonal)* on; **o. knows** on sait; **it helps o.** ça nous *or* vous aide; **one's family** sa famille.

one·self *pron* soi-même; *(reflexive)* se, s'.

one-way *adj (street)* à sens unique; *(ticket)* simple.

on·ion oignon *m*.

on-line *adj* Comput en ligne.

on·look·er spectateur, -trice *mf*.

on·ly 1 *adj* seul; **the o. one** le seul, la seule; **an o. son** un fils unique. **2** *adv* seulement, ne… que; **I o. have ten** je n'en ai que dix, j'en ai dix seulement; **not o.** non seulement; **I have o. just seen it** je viens tout juste de le voir; **o. he knows** lui seul le sait. **3** *conj (but)* Fam seulement.

on·to *prep* = **on to**.

on·ward(s) *adv* en avant; **from that time o.** à partir de là.

o·paque *adj* opaque.

o·pen 1 *adj* ouvert; *(ticket)* open

inv; **wide o.** grand ouvert. **2** *n* **(out)** in the **o.** en plein air. **3** *vt* ouvrir. **4** *vi (of flower, door, eyes etc)* s'ouvrir; *(of shop, office, person)* ouvrir.

o·pen-air *adj (pool, market etc)* en plein air.

o·pen·ing ouverture *f*; *(career prospect)* débouché *m*.

o·pen·ly *adv* ouvertement.

o·pen-mind·ed *adj* à l'esprit ouvert.

o·pen·ness franchise *f*.

▸**open out 1** *vt* ouvrir. **2** *vi* s'ouvrir; *(widen)* s'élargir.

▸**open up 1** *vt* ouvrir. **2** *vi* s'ouvrir; *(open the door)* ouvrir.

op·er·a opéra *m*.

op·er·ate 1 *vi (of surgeon)* opérer (**on sb** qn; **for** de); *(of machine etc)* fonctionner; *(proceed)* opérer. **2** *vt* faire fonctionner; *(business)* gérer.

op·er·a·tion opération *f*; *(working)* fonctionnement *m*.

op·er·a·tor *(on phone)* standardiste *mf*.

o·pin·ion opinion *f*, avis *m*; **in my o.** à mon avis.

op·po·nent adversaire *mf*.

op·por·tu·ni·ty occasion *f* (**to do** de faire).

op·pose *vt* s'opposer à.

op·posed *adj* opposé (**to** à).

op·pos·ing *adj (team)* opposé.

op·po·site 1 *adj (direction, opinion etc)* opposé; *(house)* d'en face. **2** *adv (to sit etc)* en face. **3** *prep* **o. (to)** en face de. **4** *n* **the o.** le contraire.

op·po·si·tion opposition *f* (**to** à).

opt *vi* **to o. for sth** décider pour qch.

op·ti·cal *adj* optique.

op·ti·cian opticien, -ienne *mf*.

op·ti·mist **to be an o.** être optimiste.

op·ti·mis·tic *adj* optimiste.

op·tion *(choice)* choix *m*.

op·tion·al *adj* facultatif.

or *conj* ou; **he doesn't drink or smoke** il ne boit ni ne fume.

o·ral 1 *adj* oral. **2** *n (exam)* oral *m.*

or·ange 1 *n (fruit)* orange *f*; **o. juice** jus *m* d'orange. **2** *adj & n (color)* orange (*m & adj inv*).

or·ange·ade orangeade *f.*

or·bit orbite *f.*

or·chard verger *m.*

or·ches·tra orchestre *m.*

or·deal épreuve *f.*

or·der 1 *n (command, arrangement)* ordre *m; (purchase)* commande *f;* **in o.** *(passport etc)* en règle; **in o. to do** pour faire; **in o. that** pour que (+ *subjunctive)*; **out of o.** *(machine)* en panne; *(telephone)* en dérangement. **2** *vt* ordonner (**sb to do** à qn de faire); *(meal, goods etc)* commander; *(taxi)* appeler. **3** *vi (in café etc)* commander.

▸ **order around** *vt* commander.

or·di·nance ordonnance *f.*

or·di·nar·y *adj (usual, commonplace)* ordinaire; *(average)* moyen; **it's out of the o.** ça sort de l'ordinaire.

ore minerai *m.*

or·gan *(in body)* organe *m; (instrument)* orgue *m,* orgues *fpl.*

or·gan·ic *adj (vegetables etc)* biologique.

or·gan·i·za·tion organisation *f.*

or·gan·ize *vt* organiser.

or·gan·iz·er organisateur, -trice *mf.*

o·ri·en·tal *adj* oriental.

or·i·gin origine *f.*

o·rig·i·nal 1 *adj (idea, artist etc)* original; *(first)* premier; *(copy, version)* original. **2** *n (document etc)* original *m.*

o·rig·i·nal·i·ty originalité *f.*

o·rig·i·nal·ly *adv (at first)* au départ.

o·rig·i·nate *vi (begin)* prendre naissance (**in** dans); **to o. from** émaner de.

or·na·ment *(on dress etc)* ornement *m; (vase etc)* bibelot *m.*

or·phan orphelin, -ine *mf.*

or·phan·age orphelinat *m.*

or·tho·dox *adj* orthodoxe.

os·trich autruche *f.*

oth·er 1 *adj* autre; **o. doctors** d'autres médecins; **the o. one** l'autre *mf.* **2** *pron* **the o.** l'autre *mf;* **(some)** **others** d'autres; **some do, others don't** les uns le font, les autres ne le font pas. **3** *adv* **o. than** autrement que.

oth·er·wise *adv* autrement.

ouch! *int* aïe!

ought *v aux (obligation, desirability)* devoir; **you o. to leave** tu devrais partir; **I o. to have done it** j'aurais dû le faire; **he said he o. to stay** il a dit qu'il devait rester. ■ *(probability)* devoir; **it o. to be ready** ça devrait être prêt.

ounce once *f (= 28,35g).*

our *poss adj* notre, *pl* nos.

ours *pron* le nôtre, la nôtre, *pl* les nôtres; **this book is o.** ce livre est à nous *or* est le nôtre.

our·selves *pron* nous-mêmes; *(reflexive, after prep)* nous.

out 1 *adv (outside)* dehors; *(not at home etc)* sorti; *(light, fire)* éteint; *(news, secret)* connu; *(book)* publié; *(eliminated from game)* éliminé; **to be** *or* **go o. a lot** sortir beaucoup; **to have a day o.** sortir pour la journée; **the tide's o.** la marée est basse; **o. there** là-bas. **2** *prep* **o. of** en dehors de; *(danger, water)* hors de; *(without)* sans; **o. of pity/etc** par pitié/*etc;* **o. of the window** par la fenêtre; **to drink/take/copy o. of sth** boire/prendre/copier dans qch; **made o. of** *(wood etc)* fait en; **to make sth o. of a box/etc** faire qch avec une boîte/*etc;* **she's o. of town** elle n'est pas en ville; **four o. of five** quatre sur cinq; **to feel o. of place** ne pas se sentir intégré.

out·bound adj o. journey or trip aller m.

out·break (of war) début m; (of violence) éruption f.

out·burst (of anger, joy) explosion f.

out·come résultat m.

out·dat·ed adj démodé.

out·do* vt surpasser (in en).

out·door adj (pool, market) en plein air; o. clothes tenue f pour sortir.

out·doors adv dehors.

out·er adj extérieur.

out·er space l'espace m (cosmique).

out·fit (clothes) costume m; (for woman) toilette f; (toy) panoplie f (de cow-boy etc); ski/etc o. tenue f de ski/etc.

out·grow vt (habit) passer l'âge de; (clothes) devenir trop grand pour.

out·ing sortie f, excursion f.

out·law 1 n hors-la-loi m inv. 2 vt proscrire.

out·let (market for goods) débouché m.

out·line (shape) contour m.

out·look inv (for future) perspective(s) f(pl); (point of view) perspective f (on sur).

out·num·ber vt être plus nombreux que.

out-of-date adj (expired) périmé; (old-fashioned) démodé.

out·put rendement m; (computer data) données fpl de sortie.

out·rage 1 n scandale m; (anger) indignation f. 2 vt outraged by sth indigné de qch.

out·ra·geous (shocking) scandaleux.

out·right adv (to say, tell) franchement.

out·set at the o. au début; from the o. dès le début.

out·side 1 adv (au) dehors; to go o. sortir. 2 prep en dehors de. 3 n extérieur m. 4 adj extérieur.

out·sid·er (stranger) étranger, -ère mf; (athlete, horse etc) outsider m.

out·skirts npl banlieue f.

out·stand·ing adj remarquable; (problem) non réglé; (debt) impayé.

out·ward adj (sign, appearance) extérieur.

out·ward(s) adv vers l'extérieur.

o·val adj & n ovale (m).

ov·en four m.

ov·en mitt gant m isolant.

o·ver 1 prep (on) sur; (above) au-dessus de; (on the other side of) de l'autre côté de; to jump/look/etc sth sauter/regarder/etc par-dessus qch; o. it (on) dessus; (above) au-dessus de; (to jump etc) par-dessus; to be upset/etc o. sth (about) avoir de la peine/etc à cause de qch; o. the phone au téléphone; o. the holidays pendant les vacances; o. ten days (more than) plus de dix jours; men o. sixty les hommes de plus de soixante ans; all o. Spain dans toute l'Espagne; all o. the carpet partout sur le tapis. 2 adv (above) (par-)dessus; o. here ici; o. there là-bas; to come or go o. (visit) passer; to ask o. inviter (à venir); all o. (everywhere) partout; it's (all) o. (finished) c'est fini; a pound or o. une livre ou plus; I have ten o. il m'en reste dix; o. and o. (again) à plusieurs reprises; o. pleased/etc trop content/etc.

o·ver·all adj (length etc) total.

o·ver·alls npl (of workman) bleu m de travail; (of child) salopette f.

o·ver·board adv à la mer.

o·ver·charge to o. sb for sth faire payer qch trop cher à qn.

o·ver·coat pardessus m.

o·ver·come vt (problem) surmonter.

o·ver·do* vt to o. it ne pas y aller doucement; don't o. it! vas-y doucement!

o·ver·draft découvert m.

o·ver·due *adj (train etc)* en retard.

o·ver·eat* *vi* manger trop.

o·ver·ex·cit·ed *adj* surexcité.

o·ver·flow *vi (of river, bath etc)* déborder.

o·ver·head *adv* au-dessus.

o·ver·hear *vt (pt & pp* overheard*)* surprendre.

o·ver·heat *vi (of engine)* chauffer.

o·ver·joyed *adj* fou (*f* folle) de joie.

o·ver·lap 1 *vi* se chevaucher. **2** *vt* chevaucher.

ov·er·leaf *adv* au verso.

o·ver·load *vt* surcharger.

o·ver·look *vt* ne pas remarquer; *(forget)* oublier; *(ignore)* passer sur; *(of window etc)* donner sur.

o·ver·night 1 *adv* (pendant) la nuit; **to stay o.** passer la nuit. **2** *adj (train)* de nuit.

o·ver·pass *(bridge)* toboggan *m*.

o·ver·rat·ed *adj* surfait.

o·ver·seas 1 *adv (abroad)* à l'étranger. **2** *adj (visitor etc)* étranger; *(trade)* extérieur.

o·ver·sight oubli *m*.

o·ver·sleep* *vi (pt & pp* overslept*)* dormir trop longtemps.

o·ver·spend* *vi* dépenser trop.

o·ver·take* *vti (in vehicle)* dépasser.

o·ver·time 1 *n* heures *fpl* supplémentaires. **2** *adv* **to work o.** faire des heures supplémentaires.

o·ver·turn *vi (of car, boat)* se retourner.

o·ver·weight *adj* **to be o.** *(of person)* avoir des kilos en trop.

o·ver·whelm *vt* accabler; **overwhelmed with** *(work, offers)* submergé de.

o·ver·work 1 *n* surmenage *m*. **2** *vi* se surmener.

owe *vt (money etc)* devoir (**to** à).

ow·ing *prep* **o.** to à cause de.

owl hibou *m (pl* hiboux*)*.

own 1 *adj* propre; **my o. house** ma propre maison. **2** *pron* **it's my** **(very) o.** c'est à moi (tout seul); **a house of his o.** sa propre maison; **(all) on one's o.** tout seul; **to get one's o. back** se venger. **3** *vt* posséder; **who owns this ball/etc?** à qui appartient cette balle/*etc*?

▸ **own up** *vi* avouer (**to sth** qch).

own·er propriétaire *mf*.

ox, *pl* **oxen** bœuf *m*.

ox·y·gen oxygène *m*.

oys·ter huître *f*.

o·zone ozone *m*; **o. layer** couche *f* d'ozone.

P

pa *Fam* papa *m*.

pace pas *m*.

Pa·cif·ic 1 *adj* pacifique. **2** *n* **the P.** le Pacifique.

pac·i·fi·er *(of baby)* sucette *f*.

pack 1 *n* paquet *m*; *(backpack)* sac *m* à dos; *(of wolves)* meute *f*; *(of cards)* jeu *m*; *(of lies)* tissu *m*. **2** *vt* *(fill)* remplir (**with** de); *(suitcase)* faire; *(object into box etc)* emballer; *(object into suitcase)* mettre dans sa valise.

pack (down) *vt (crush)* tasser.

pack·age paquet *m*; *Comput* progiciel *m*.

pack·age tour voyage *m* organisé.

pack·ag·ing emballage *m*.

▸ **pack away** *vt (put away)* ranger.

packed *adj (bus etc)* bourré.

packed lunch panier-repas *m*.

pack·et paquet *m*.

▸ **pack in** *vt (quit) Fam* laisser tomber.

pack·ing emballage *m*.

▸ **pack into 1** *vt (cram)* entasser dans. **2** *vi (crowd into)* s'entasser dans.

▶ **pack up 1** *vt (put into box)* emballer; *(give up) Fam* laisser tomber. **2** *vi Fam (stop)* s'arrêter; *(of machine)* tomber en panne.

pact pacte *m*.

pad *(of cloth etc)* tampon *m*; *(for writing etc)* bloc *m*.

pad·ded *adj (armchair etc)* rembourré.

pad·dle 1 *vi (dip one's feet)* se mouiller les pieds. **2** *n (for boat)* pagaie *f*; *(for ping-pong)* raquette *f*. **3** *vt* **to p. a canoe** pagayer.

pad·dle boat pédalo *m*.

pad·lock cadenas *m*; *(on bicycle)* antivol *m*.

page *(of book etc)* page *f*.

pain douleur *f*; *(grief)* peine *f*; **pains** *(efforts)* efforts *mpl*; **to be in p.** souffrir; **to take (great) pains to do** se donner du mal à faire.

pain·ful *adj* douloureux.

pain·kill·er calmant *m*; **on painkillers** sous calmants.

paint 1 *n* peinture *f*; **paints** *(in box, tube)* couleurs *fpl*. **2** *vti* peindre; **to p. sth blue/***etc* peindre qch en bleu/ *etc*.

paint·brush pinceau *m*.

paint·er peintre *m*.

paint·ing *(activity, picture)* peinture *f*.

paint strip·per décapant *m*.

pair *(two)* paire *f*; *(of people)* couple *m*.

pa·ja·mas *npl* pyjama *m*; **a pair of p.** un pyjama.

Pa·ki·sta·ni 1 *n* Pakistanais, -aise *mf*. **2** *adj* pakistanais, -aise.

pal *Fam* copain *m*, copine *f*.

pal·ace palais *m*.

pal·ate *(in mouth)* palais *m*.

pale *adj* pâle.

pal·ette *(of artist)* palette *f*.

palm *(of hand)* paume *f*; **p. (tree)** palmier *m*; **p. (leaf)** palme *f*.

pam·phlet brochure *f*.

pan casserole *f*; *(for frying)* poêle *f*.

pan·cake crêpe *f*.

pane vitre *f*.

pan·el *(of door etc)* panneau *m*; *(of judges)* jury *m*; *(of experts)* groupe *m*; **(control) p.** console *f*.

pan·ic 1 *n* panique *f*. **2** *vi* s'affoler.

pant *vi* haleter.

pant·ies *npl (female)* slip *m*.

pan·to·mime spectacle *m* de mime.

pan·try *(larder)* garde-manger *m inv*.

pants *npl (trousers)* pantalon *m*.

pant·y·hose collant *m*.

pa·per 1 *n* papier *m*; *(newspaper)* journal *m*; *(wallpaper)* papier *m* peint; *(in high school, college)* dissertation *f*; **brown p.** papier *m* d'emballage; **to put down on p.** mettre par écrit. **2** *adj (bag, towel etc)* en papier; *(cup, plate)* en carton.

pa·per·back livre *m* de poche.

pa·per clip trombone *m*.

pa·per tow·el essuie-tout *m inv*.

pa·per·work écritures *fpl*.

par *(parity)* égalité *f*; *(in golf)* par *m*; **on a p.** au même niveau (**with** de); **that's about p. for the course** c'est ce à quoi il faut s'attendre.

par·a·chute parachute *m*.

pa·rade *(procession)* défilé *m*; *(street)* avenue *f*.

par·a·dise paradis *m*.

par·a·graph paragraphe *m*; **'new p.'** 'à la ligne'.

par·a·keet perruche *f*.

par·a·le·gal assistant, -ante *mf (d'un avocat)*.

par·al·lel *adj* parallèle (**with, to** à).

par·a·lyze *vt* paralyser.

par·a·site parasite *m*.

par·a·sol *(over table, on beach)* parasol *m*.

par·cel colis *m*, paquet *m*.

par·don 1 *n* **I beg your p.** je vous prie de m'excuser; *(not hearing)* vous dites?; **p.?** *(not hearing)* comment?; **p. (me)!** *(sorry)* pardon!

2 *vt* pardonner (**sb for sth** qch à qn).

par·ent père *m*, mère *f*, **one's parents** ses parents *mpl*.

par·ish paroisse *f*.

Pa·ris·ian 1 *n* Parisien, -ienne *mf*. **2** *n* parisien, -ienne.

park 1 *n* parc *m*. **2** *vt* (*vehicle*) garer. **3** *vi* se garer; (*remain parked*) stationner.

par·ka anorak *m*.

park·ing stationnement *m*; 'no p.' 'défense de stationner'.

park·ing en·force·ment of-fi·cer contractuel, -elle *mf*.

park·ing light (*of vehicle*) veilleuse *f*.

park·ing lot parking *m*.

park·ing me·ter parcmètre *m*.

park·ing place, parking space place *f* de parking.

park·ing tick·et contravention *f*.

par·lia·ment parlement *m*.

par·rot perroquet *m*.

pars·ley persil *m*.

pars·nip panais *m*.

part 1 *n* partie *f*, (*of machine*) pièce *f*; (*of serial*) épisode *m*; (*role*) rôle *m*; (*in hair*) raie *f*, **to take p.** participer (**in** à); **in p.** en partie; **for the most p.** dans l'ensemble; **to be a p. of sth** faire partie de qch; **in these parts** dans ces parages. **2** *adv* (*partly*) en partie. **3** *vi* (*of friends etc*) se quitter; (*of married couple*) se séparer.

par·tial *adj* partiel; **to be p. to sth** (*fond of*) *Fam* avoir un faible pour qch.

par·tic·i·pant participant, -ante *mf*.

par·tic·i·pate *vi* participer (**in** à).

par·tic·i·pa·tion participation *f*.

par·tic·i·ple *Grammar* participe *m*.

par·tic·u·lar 1 *adj* particulier; (*fussy*) difficile (**about** sur); (*showing care*) méticuleux; **in p.** en particulier. **2** *npl* **particulars** détails *mpl*; **sb's particulars** les coordonnées *fpl* de qn.

par·tic·u·lar·ly *adv* particulièrement.

par·ti·tion (*in room*) cloison *f*.

part·ly *adv* en partie.

part·ner partenaire *mf*; (*in business*) associé, -ée *mf*; **(dancing) p.** cavalier, -ière *mf*.

part·ner·ship association *f*.

part·ridge perdrix *f*.

part-time *adj & adv* à temps partiel.

par·ty (*formal*) réception *f*, (*with friends*) soirée *f*, (*for birthday*) fête *f*, (*group*) groupe *m*; (*political*) parti *m*.

pass 1 *n* (*entry permit*) laissez-passer *m inv*; (*over mountains*) col *m*; *Sports* passe *f*, (*for transportation*) carte *f* d'abonnement. **2** *vi* passer (**to** à; **through** par); (*overtake*) dépasser; (*in exam*) être reçu (**in French**/*etc* en français/*etc*). **3** *vt* passer (**to** à); (*go past*) passer devant (*immeuble etc*); (*vehicle*) dépasser; (*exam*) être reçu à; **to p. sb** (*in street*) croiser qn.

pass·a·ble *adj* (*not bad*) passable; (*road*) praticable.

pas·sage (*of text etc*) passage *m*; (*corridor*) couloir *m*.

pas·sage·way (*corridor*) couloir *m*.

▸ **pass around** *vt* (*cake etc*) faire passer.

▸ **pass away** *vi* (*die*) mourir.

pass·book livret *m* de caisse d'épargne.

▸ **pass by 1** *vi* passer (à côté). **2** *vt* (*building etc*) passer devant; **to p. by sb** (*in street*) croiser qn.

pas·sen·ger passager, -ère *mf*; (*on train*) voyageur, -euse *mf*.

pas·ser-by, *pl* **passers-by** passant, -ante *mf*.

pass·ing 1 *n* (*of time*) écoulement *m*; (*of law*) vote *m*; **in p.** en passant. **2** *adj* qui passe.

pass·ing grade (*in school*) moyenne *f*.

pas·sion passion f.

pas·sion·ate adj passionné.

pas·sive 1 adj passif. **2** n Grammar passif m.

▸ **pass off** vt to p. oneself off as se faire passer pour.

▸ **pass on** vt (message etc) transmettre (**to** à).

▸ **pass out** vi (faint) s'évanouir.

▸ **pass over** vt (ignore) passer sur.

pass·port passeport m.

▸ **pass through** vi passer.

▸ **pass up** vt (chance) laisser passer.

pass·word mot m de passe.

past 1 n passé m; **in the p.** (formerly) dans le temps. **2** adj (gone by) passé; (former) ancien; **these p. months** ces derniers mois; **in the p. tense** au passé. **3** prep (in front of) devant; (after) après; (further than) plus loin que; **p. four o'clock** quatre heures passées. **4** adv devant; **to go p.** passer.

pas·ta pâtes fpl.

paste 1 n (of meat) pâté m; (of fish) beurre m; (glue) colle f. **2** vt coller.

pas·teur·ized adj (milk) pasteurisé.

pas·tille pastille f.

pas·time passe-temps m inv.

pas·try pâte f; (cake) pâtisserie f.

pas·ture pâturage m.

pat vt (cheek etc) tapoter; (animal) caresser.

patch (for clothes) pièce f; (over eye) bandeau m; (of color) tache f; **cabbage p.** carré m de choux; **bad p.** mauvaise période f.

patch (up) vt (clothing) rapiécer.

pat·ent¹ 1 n brevet m d'invention. **2** vt (faire) breveter.

pat·ent² p. (leather) cuir m verni.

path, pl -s sentier m; (in park) allée f.

pa·thet·ic adj (results etc) lamentable.

path·way sentier m.

pa·tience patience f; **to lose p.** perdre patience (**with sb** avec qn).

pa·tient 1 adj patient. **2** n malade mf; (on doctor's or dentist's list) patient, -ente mf.

pa·tient·ly adv patiemment.

pat·i·o, pl -os patio m.

pa·tri·ot·ic adj patriotique; (person) patriote.

pa·trol 1 n patrouille f. **2** vi patrouiller. **3** vt patrouiller dans.

pa·tron (of charity) patron, -onne mf; (of arts) mécène m; (customer) client, -e mf, **to p. saint** (saint, -e mf) patron, -onne mf.

pat·tern dessin m; (paper model for garment) patron m.

pause 1 n pause f, (in conversation) silence m. **2** vi faire une pause; (hesitate) hésiter.

pave vt paver; **to p. the way for sth** ouvrir la voie à qch.

paved adj pavé.

pave·ment (roadway) chaussée f.

pa·vil·ion pavillon m.

pav·ing stone pavé m.

paw patte f.

pawn Chess pion m.

pay* 1 n salaire m; (of workman, soldier) paie f; **p. slip** bulletin m de paie. **2** vt (person, sum) payer; (deposit) verser; (of investment) rapporter; (compliment, visit) faire (**to** à); **to p. sb to do** or **for doing** payer qn pour faire; **to p. sb for sth** payer qch à qn; **to p. money into one's account** verser de l'argent sur son compte. **3** vi payer; **to p. a lot** payer cher.

pay·a·ble adj payable; **a check p. to** un chèque à l'ordre de.

▸ **pay back** vt (person, loan) rembourser.

pay·check chèque m de règlement de salaire.

▸ **pay for** vt payer.

pay·ment paiement m; (of deposit) versement m.

▸ **pay off** vt (debt, person) rembourser.

▸ **pay out** vt (spend) dépenser.

pay phone téléphone *m* public.
▶ **pay up** *vti* payer.

PE *abbr (physical education)* éducation *f* physique, EPS *f*.

pea pois *m*; **(green) peas** petits pois *mpl*; **p. soup** soupe *f* aux pois.

peace paix *f*; **p. of mind** tranquillité *f* d'esprit; **in p.** en paix; **to have (some) p. and quiet** avoir la paix.

peace·ful *adj* paisible; *(demonstration)* pacifique.

peach pêche *f*.

pea·cock paon *m*.

peak 1 *n (mountain top)* sommet *m*; *(mountain)* pic *m*; **to be at its p.** être à son maximum. **2** *adj (hours, period)* de pointe.

peaked *adj Fam (ill)* patraque.

pea·nut cacah(o)uète *f*; **p. butter** beurre *m* de cacah(o)uètes.

pear poire *f*; **p. tree** poirier *m*.

pearl perle *f*.

peb·ble caillou *m* (*pl* cailloux); *(on beach)* galet *m*.

pe·can noix *f* de pécan.

peck *vti* **to p. (at)** *(of bird)* picorer *(du pain etc)*; donner un coup de bec à *(qn)*.

pe·cu·liar *adj* bizarre; *(special)* particulier (**to** à).

pe·cu·li·ar·i·ty *(feature)* particularité *f*.

ped·al 1 *n* pédale *f*. **2** *vi* pédaler. **3** *vt* **to p. a bicycle** faire marcher un vélo; *(ride)* rouler en vélo.

pe·des·tri·an piéton *m*; **p. crossing** passage *m* pour piétons; **p. street** rue *f* piétonne.

peek **to have a p.** jeter un petit coup d'œil (**at** à).

peel 1 *n* épluchure(s) *f(pl)*; **a piece of p.**, **some p.** une épluchure. **2** *vt (apple, potato etc)* éplucher. **3** *vi (of sunburnt skin)* peler; *(of paint)* s'écailler.

peel·er **(potato) p.** éplucheur *m*.
▶ **peel off** *vt (label etc)* décoller.

peep 1 *n* coup *m* d'œil *(furtif)*. **2** *vi* **to p. (at)** regarder furtivement.

peer *vi* **to p. (at)** regarder attentivement.

peg *(for tent)* piquet *m*; *(for clothes)* pince *f* (à linge); *(for coat, hat)* patère *f*.

pen *(fountain, ballpoint)* stylo *m*; *(enclosure)* parc *m*.

pen·al·ty *(prison sentence)* peine *f*; *(fine)* amende *f*; *Sports* penalty *m*.

pen·cil crayon *m*; **in p.** au crayon.

pen·cil case trousse *f*.
▶ **pencil in** *vt (note down)* noter provisoirement.

pen·cil sharp·en·er taille-crayon(s) *m inv*.

pen·e·trate *vt (substance)* pénétrer; *(forest)* pénétrer dans.

pen·guin manchot *m*.

pen·i·cil·lin pénicilline *f*.

pen·in·su·la presqu'île *f*.

pen·knife, *pl* **-knives** canif *m*.

pen·ni·less *adj* sans le sou.

pen·ny, *pl* **pennies** *(coin)* cent *m*; **not a p.!** pas un sou!

pen pal correspondant *m*, -ante *mf*.

pen·sion pension *f*; **(retirement) p.** retraite *f*.

pen·sion·er **(old age) p.** retraité *m*, -ée *mf*.

peo·ple 1 *npl* gens *mpl* or *fpl*; *(specific persons)* personnes *fpl*; **the p.** *(citizens)* le peuple; **old p.** les personnes *fpl* âgées; **old p.'s home** maison *f* de retraite; **English p.** les Anglais *mpl*. **2** *n (nation)* peuple *m*.

pep·per poivre *m*; *(vegetable)* poivron *m*.

pep·per·mint *(flavor)* menthe *f*; *(candy)* bonbon *m* à la menthe.

per *prep* par; **p. year** par an; **p. person** par personne; **p. cent** pour cent; **10 dollars p. pound** 10 dollars la livre.

per·ceive *vt* percevoir; *(notice)* remarquer.

per·cent·age pourcentage *m*.

perch 1 *n (for bird)* perchoir *m*. **2** *vi (of bird, person)* se percher.

per·co·la·tor cafetière f, (in café etc) percolateur m.

per·fect 1 adj parfait; Grammar p. tense parfait m. **2** n Grammar parfait m. **3** vt (technique) mettre au point; (one's French etc) parfaire ses connaissances en.

per·fec·tion perfection f.

per·fect·ly adv parfaitement.

per·form 1 vt (task, miracle) accomplir; (one's duty) remplir; (surgical operation) pratiquer (**on** sur); (a play, piece of music) jouer. **2** vi (act, play) jouer; (sing) chanter; (dance) danser; (of machine) fonctionner.

per·form·ance (in theater) représentation f, (in movie theater, concert hall) séance f, (of actor, musician) interprétation f, (of athlete, machine) performance f.

per·form·er (entertainer) artiste mf.

per·fume parfum m.

per·haps adv peut-être; **p. not** peut-être que non.

per·il péril m.

pe·ri·od période f, (historical) époque f, (lesson) leçon f, (punctuation mark) point m; (**monthly**) **period** (of woman) règles fpl.

pe·ri·od·i·cal périodique m.

perk (in job) avantage m en nature.

▸**perk up** vi (become livelier) reprendre du poil de la bête.

perm 1 n permanente f. **2** vt to have one's hair permed se faire faire une permanente.

per·ma·nent adj permanent; (address) fixe.

per·ma·nent·ly adv à titre permanent.

per·mis·sion permission f (**to do** de faire); **to ask p.** demander la permission.

per·mit 1 vt permettre (**sb to do** à qn de faire). **2** n permis m; (entrance pass) laissez-passer m inv.

per·pen·dic·u·lar adj perpendiculaire (**to** à).

per·se·cute vt persécuter.

per·se·cu·tion persécution f.

per·se·ver·ance persévérance f.

per·se·vere vi persévérer (**in** dans).

per·sist vi persister (**in doing** à faire; **in sth** dans qch).

per·sist·ent adj (person) obstiné; (noise etc) continuel.

per·son personne f, **in p.** en personne.

per·son·al adj personnel; (application) en personne; (friend) intime; (life) privé; (indiscreet) indiscret.

per·son·al·i·ty personnalité f.

per·son·al·ly adv personnellement; (in person) en personne.

per·son·nel personnel m.

per·suade vt persuader (**sb to do** qn de faire).

per·sua·sion persuasion f.

per·ti·nent adj pertinent.

pes·si·mist to be a p. être pessimiste.

pes·si·mis·tic adj pessimiste.

pest animal m or insecte m nuisible; (person) casse-pieds mf inv.

pes·ter vt harceler (**with** questions de questions); **to p. sb to do sth/for sth** harceler qn pour qu'il fasse qch/jusqu'à ce qu'il donne qch.

pet 1 n animal m (domestique); (favorite person) chouchou, -oute mf. **2** adj (dog, cat etc) domestique; (favorite) favori (f -ite).

pet·al pétale m.

pe·ti·tion (signatures) pétition f.

pet·ti·coat jupon m.

pet·ty adj (minor) petit; (mean) mesquin; **p. cash** petite caisse f.

phar·ma·cist pharmacien, -ienne mf.

phar·ma·cy pharmacie f.

phase phase f.

▸**phase in** vt introduire progressivement.

▸**phase out** vt supprimer progressivement.

PhD abbr (Doctor of Philosophy) doctorat m.

pheas·ant faisan m.

phe·nom·e·nal adj phénoménal.

phe·nom·e·non, pl -ena phénomène m.

phi·los·o·pher philosophe mf.

phil·o·soph·i·cal adj philosophique; (resigned) philosophe.

phi·los·o·phy philosophie f.

phlegm (in throat) glaires fpl.

phone 1 n téléphone m; on the p. au téléphone; (at other end) au bout du fil. **2** vt téléphoner à. **3** vi téléphoner.

▸**phone back** vti rappeler.

phone book annuaire m.

phone booth cabine f téléphonique.

phone call coup m de fil; to make a p. call téléphoner (to à).

phone num·ber numéro m de téléphone.

pho·net·ic adj phonétique.

pho·to, pl -os photo f; to take a p. of prendre une photo de; to have one's p. taken se faire prendre en photo.

pho·to·cop·i·er photocopieuse f.

pho·to·cop·y 1 n photocopie f. **2** vt photocopier.

pho·to·graph photographie f.

pho·tog·ra·pher photographe mf.

pho·to·graph·ic adj photographique.

pho·tog·ra·phy photographie f.

phrase expression f, (idiom) locution f.

phrase·book manuel m de conversation.

phys·i·cal adj physique; p. examination examen m médical; p. education éducation f physique.

phy·si·cian médecin m.

phys·ics physique f.

pi·an·ist pianiste mf.

pi·an·o, pl -os piano m.

pick 1 n to take one's p. faire son choix. **2** vt choisir; (flower, fruit) cueillir; (hole) faire (in dans); to p. one's nose se mettre les doigts dans le nez.

pick·ax pioche f.

pick·le cornichon m.

pick·led adj (onion etc) au vinaigre.

▸**pick off** vt enlever.

▸**pick on** vt s'en prendre à.

pick out vt choisir; (identify) reconnaître.

pick·pock·et pickpocket m.

▸**pick up 1** vt (sth dropped) ramasser; (fallen person or chair) relever; (person into air, weight) soulever; (a cold) attraper; (habit, accent, speed) prendre; (fetch) (passer) prendre; (find) trouver; (learn) apprendre. **2** vi (improve) s'améliorer; (of business) reprendre; (of patient) aller mieux.

pic·nic pique-nique m.

pic·ture 1 n image f, (painting) tableau m; (photo) photo f; (film) film m. **2** vt (imagine) s'imaginer (that que).

pic·ture frame cadre m.

pic·tur·esque adj pittoresque.

pie (open) tarte f; (with pastry on top) tourte f.

piece morceau m; (of fabric, machine, in game) pièce f; (coin) pièce f; in pieces en morceaux; to take to pieces (machine) démonter; a p. of news/etc une nouvelle/etc; in one p. intact; (person) indemne.

pier jetée f.

pierce vt percer (qch).

pierc·ing adj (cry, cold) perçant.

pig cochon m.

pi·geon pigeon m.

pi·geon·hole casier m.

pig·gy·back to give sb a p. porter qn sur le dos.

pig·gy·bank tirelire f.

pig·tail (hair) natte f.

pile 1 n tas m; (neatly arranged) pile f; **piles of** Fam beaucoup de. **2** vt entasser; (neatly) empiler.
▶ **pile into** vt (crowd into) s'entasser dans.
piles npl (illness) hémorroïdes fpl.
▶ **pile up 1** vt entasser; (neatly) empiler. **2** vi s'accumuler.
pile-up (on road) carambolage m.
pill pilule f; **to be on the p.** prendre la pilule.
pil·lar pilier m.
pil·low oreiller m.
pil·low·case taie f d'oreiller.
pi·lot pilote m.
pim·ple bouton m.
pin épingle f; (drawing pin) punaise f.
pin (on) vt épingler (to sur, à); (to wall) punaiser (to, on à).
pin·a·fore (apron) tablier m.
pin·ball flipper m; **p. machine** flipper m.
pin·cers npl (tool) tenailles fpl.
pinch 1 n (of salt) pincée f; **to give sb a p.** pincer qn. **2** vt pincer; (steal) Fam piquer (**from** à).
pin·cush·ion pelote f (à épingles).
pine pin m.
pine·ap·ple ananas m.
pink adj & n (color) rose (m).
pink·ie petit doigt m.
pint pinte f (= 0.47 litre).
▶ **pin up** vt (on wall) punaiser (**on** à); (notice) afficher.
pi·o·neer 1 n (settler) pionnier, -ère mf. **2** vt **to p. sth** être le premier/la première à mettre au point qch.
pipe tuyau m; (of smoker) pipe f; **to smoke a p.** fumer la pipe.
pi·rate pirate m.
pis·ta·chi·o pistache f.
pis·tol pistolet m.
pit (hole) trou m; (coalmine) mine f; (quarry) carrière f; (stone of fruit) noyau m; (smaller) pépin m.
pitch vt (tent) dresser; (ball) lancer.

pitch-black, pitch-dark adj noir comme dans un four.
pitch·er (container) cruche f.
pit·y 1 n pitié f; **(what) a p.!** (quel) dommage!; **it's a p.** c'est dommage (**that** que (+ subjunctive); **to do** de faire). **2** vt plaindre.
piz·za pizza f.
plac·ard (notice) affiche f.
place 1 n endroit m, lieu m; (house) maison f; (seat, position, rank) place f; **in the first p.** en premier lieu; **to take p.** avoir lieu; **p. of work** lieu m de travail; **market p.** place f du marché; **at my p., to my p.** (house) chez moi; **all over the p.** partout; **to take the p. of** remplacer; **in p. of** à la place de. **2** vt placer; (an order) passer (**with sb** à qn); **to p. sb** (identify) remettre qn.
place mat set m (de table).
place set·ting couvert m.
plague 1 n peste f; (nuisance) plaie f. **2** vt harceler (**with** de).
plain¹ adj (clear) clair; (simple) simple; (madness) pur; (without pattern) uni; (woman, man) sans beauté; **to make it p. to sb that** faire comprendre à qn que.
plain² plaine f.
plain·ly adv clairement; (frankly) franchement.
plait 1 n tresse f. **2** vt tresser.
plan 1 n projet m; (economic, of house etc) plan m; **according to p.** comme prévu. **2** vt (foresee) prévoir; (organize) organiser; (design) concevoir; **to p. to do** or **on doing** avoir l'intention de faire; **as planned** comme prévu.
plane (aircraft) avion m; (tool) rabot m.
plan·et planète f.
plane tree platane m.
▶ **plan for** vt (rain, disaster) prévoir.
plank planche f.
plant 1 n plante f; (factory) usine f; **house p.** plante f verte. **2** vt (flower etc) planter.

plas·ter plâtre *m*; **in p.** dans le plâtre.

plas·tic 1 *adj (object)* en plastique. **2** *n* plastique *m*.

plas·tic bag sac *m* en plastique.

plas·tic sur·ger·y chirurgie *f* esthétique.

plas·tic wrap film *m* alimentaire.

plate *(dish)* assiette *f*; *(metal sheet)* plaque *f*.

plat·form *(at train station)* quai *m*; *(on bus etc)* plate-forme *f*; *(for speaker etc)* estrade *f*.

plau·si·ble *adj* plausible.

play 1 *n (in theater)* pièce *f* (de théâtre). **2** *vt (part, tune etc)* jouer; *(game)* jouer à; *(instrument)* jouer de; *(team)* jouer contre; *(record, CD)* passer; **to p. a part in doing/ in sth** contribuer à faire/à qch. **3** *vi* jouer (**at** à); *(of tape recorder etc)* marcher; **what are you playing at?** qu'est-ce tu fais?; **what's playing?** *(at movies etc)* qu'est-ce qu'on joue?

▸ **play around** *vi* jouer.

▸ **play back** *vt (tape)* réécouter.

▸ **play down** *vt* minimiser.

play·er *(in game, of instrument)* joueur, -euse *mf*; **cassette/CD p.** lecteur *m* de cassettes/CD.

play·ground *(in school)* cour *f* de récréation; *(with swings etc)* terrain *m* de jeux.

play·ing card carte *f* à jouer.

play·ing field terrain *m* de jeux.

▸ **play on** *vt (feelings, fears etc)* jouer sur.

play·pen parc *m* (pour enfants).

play·school garderie *f* (d'enfants).

play·time récréation *f*.

plea *(request)* appel *m*; *Law (argument)* argument *m*; *(defense)* défense *f*.

plead 1 *vt (argue)* plaider; *(as excuse)* alléguer. **2** *vi (beg)* supplier; **to p. with sb to do sth** supplier qn de faire qch; *Law* **to p. guilty/not guilty** plaider coupable/non coupable.

pleas·ant *adj* agréable.

pleas·ant·ly *adv* agréablement.

please 1 *adv* s'il vous plaît, s'il te plaît. **2** *vt* **to p. sb** plaire à qn; *(satisfy)* contenter qn. **3** *vi* plaire; **do as you p.** fais comme tu veux.

pleased *adj* content (**with** de; **that** que (+ *subjunctive*); **to do** de faire); **p. to meet you!** enchanté!

pleas·ing *adj* agréable.

pleas·ure plaisir *m*.

pleat *(in skirt)* pli *m*.

pleat·ed *adj* plissé.

pledge 1 *n* promesse *f*. **2** *vt* promettre.

plen·ti·ful *adj* abondant.

plen·ty **p. of** beaucoup de; **that's p.** c'est assez.

pli·ers *npl* pince(s) *f(pl)*.

plot 1 *n* complot *m* (**against** contre); **p. (of land)** terrain *m*. **2** *vti* comploter (**to do** de faire).

plot (out) *vt (route)* déterminer.

plow 1 *n* charrue *f*. **2** *vt (field)* labourer.

pluck *vt (fowl)* plumer; *(flower)* cueillir.

plug *(of cotton wool)* tampon *m*; *(for sink, bath)* bonde *f*, *(electrical)* fiche *f*, prise *f (mâle)*; *(socket)* prise *f* de courant; **(wall) p.** *(for screw)* cheville *f*.

plug (up) *vt* boucher.

▸ **plug in** *vt (radio etc)* brancher.

plum prune *f*.

plumb·er plombier *m*.

plumb·ing plomberie *f*.

plump *adj* potelé.

plunge 1 *vt* plonger (**into** dans). **2** *vi (dive)* plonger (**into** dans); *(fall)* tomber (**from** de).

plu·ral 1 *adj (form)* pluriel; *(noun)* au pluriel. **2** *n* pluriel *m*; **in the p.** au pluriel.

plus 1 *prep* plus; **two p. two** deux plus deux. **2** *adj* **twenty p.** vingt et quelques.

p.m. *adv* de l'après-midi; *(evening)* du soir.

poach vt (egg) pocher.
PO Box boîte f postale.
pock·et poche f; **p. money**/etc argent m/etc de poche.
pock·et·book (handbag) sac m à main.
pock·et·ful a **p. of** une pleine poche de.
pock·et·knife, pl -knives canif m.
po·em poème m.
po·et poète m.
po·et·ic adj poétique.
po·et·ry poésie f.
point 1 n (position, score etc) point m; (decimal) virgule f; (meaning) sens m; (of knife etc) pointe f; **points** (for train) aiguillage m; **p. of view** point m de vue; **at this p.** (in time) en ce moment; **what's the p.?** à quoi bon? (of waiting/ etc attendre/etc); **there's no p. (in) staying**/etc ça ne sert à rien de rester/etc. **2** vt (aim) pointer (**at** sur); **to p. one's finger (at)** montrer du doigt.
▶ **point (at** or **to)** vt (with finger) montrer du doigt.
point·ed adj pointu.
point·less adj inutile.
▶ **point out** vt (show) indiquer; (mention) signaler (**that**).
▶ **point to** vt (indicate) indiquer.
poi·son 1 n poison m; (of snake) venin m. **2** vt empoisonner.
poi·son·ous adj toxique; (snake) venimeux; (plant) vénéneux.
poke vt pousser (du doigt etc); (fire) tisonner; **to p. sth into sth** fourrer qch dans qch; **to p. one's head out of the window** passer la tête par la fenêtre.
▶ **poke around in** vt (drawer etc) fouiner dans.
pok·er (for fire) tisonnier m.
po·lar bear ours m blanc.
Pole Polonais, -aise mf.
pole (rod) perche f; (fixed) poteau m; (for flag) mât m; **North/South P.** pôle m Nord/Sud.

po·lice police f.
po·lice car voiture f de police.
po·lice force police f.
po·lice·man, pl -men agent m de police.
po·lice·wom·an, pl -women femme-agent f.
pol·i·cy (plan etc) politique f; (insurance) **p.** police f (d'assurance).
po·li·o polio f.
Po·lish 1 adj polonais. **2** n (language) polonais m.
pol·ish 1 vt cirer; (metal) astiquer; (rough surface) polir. **2** n (for shoes) cirage m; (for floor etc) cire f; (shine) vernis m; **to give sth a p.** faire briller qch.
▶ **polish off** vt (food etc) Fam avaler.
▶ **polish up** vt (one's French etc) perfectionner.
po·lite adj poli (**to, with** avec).
po·lite·ly adv poliment.
po·lite·ness politesse f.
po·lit·i·cal adj politique.
pol·i·ti·cian homme m or femme f politique.
pol·i·tics politique f.
poll (voting) scrutin m; **to go to the polls** aller aux urnes; **(opinion) p.** sondage m (d'opinion).
pol·len pollen m.
poll·ing place bureau m de vote.
polls urnes fpl; **to go to the p.** aller aux urnes.
pol·lute vt polluer.
pol·lu·tion pollution f.
po·lo shirt polo m.
pol·y·es·ter 1 n polyester m. **2** adj (shirt etc) en polyester.
pome·gran·ate (fruit) grenade f.
pond étang m; (artificial) bassin m.
po·ny poney m.
po·ny·tail (hair) queue f de cheval.
poo·dle caniche m.
pool (puddle) flaque f; (for swimming) piscine f; (billiards) billard m américain.
pooped adj (tired) Fam vanné.

poor 1 *adj* pauvre; *(bad)* mauvais; *(weak)* faible. **2** *npl* **the p.** les pauvres *mpl*.

poor·ly *adv (badly)* mal.

pop¹ *vti (burst)* crever. **2** *vt (put) Fam* mettre.

pop² **1** *n (music)* pop *m*; *(drink)* soda *m*; *(father) Fam* papa *m*. **2** *adj (concert etc)* pop *inv*.

pop·corn pop-corn *m*.

pope pape *m*.

▸ **pop in** *vi* entrer un instant.

▸ **pop out** *vi* sortir un instant.

▸ **pop over** *vi* faire un saut (**to** chez).

pop·py coquelicot *m*.

pop·si·cle® glace *f* à eau.

pop·u·lar *adj* populaire; *(fashionable)* à la mode; **to be p. with** plaire beaucoup à.

pop·u·lar·i·ty popularité *f*.

pop·u·lat·ed *adj* highly/sparsely/*etc* p. très/peu/*etc* peuplé; **p. by** peuplé de.

pop·u·la·tion population *f*.

porch porche *m*; *(veranda)* véranda *f*.

pork *(meat)* porc *m*.

por·ridge porridge *m (bouillie de flocons d'avoine)*.

port *(harbor)* port *m*.

por·ta·ble *adj* portable, portatif.

por·ter *(for luggage)* porteur *m*.

port·fo·li·o *(for documents)* porte-documents *m inv*; *(of politician)* portefeuille *m*; *(of model, artist etc)* book *m*.

port·hole hublot *m*.

por·tion *(share)* portion *f*, *(of train, book etc)* partie *f*.

por·trait portrait *m*.

Por·tu·guese 1 *adj* portugais, -aise. **2** *n* Portugais, -aise *mf*, *(language)* portugais *m*.

pose 1 *n (of model)* pose *f*. **2** *vi* poser (**for** pour).

posh *adj Fam* chic *inv*.

po·si·tion position *f*, *(job, circumstances)* situation *f*; **in a p. to do** en mesure de faire.

pos·i·tive *adj* positif; *(progress, change)* réel; *(answer)* affirmatif; *(sure)* certain (**of** de; **that** que).

pos·sess *vt* posséder.

pos·ses·sions *npl* biens *mpl*.

pos·ses·sive *adj & n Grammar* possessif (*m*).

pos·si·bil·i·ty possibilité *f*.

pos·si·ble *adj* possible; **it is p. (for us) to do it** il (nous) est possible de le faire; **it is p. that** il est possible que (+ *subjunctive*); **if p.** si possible; **as much** *or* **as many as p.** le plus possible.

pos·si·bly *adv (perhaps)* peut-être; **if you p. can** si cela t'est possible; **to do all one p. can** faire tout son possible.

post¹ *(job, place)* poste *m*.

post² *(pole)* poteau *m*; *(of door)* montant *m*.

post (up) *vt (notice etc)* afficher.

post·age tarif *m* (postal) (**to** pour).

post·age stamp timbre-poste *m*.

post·al *adj (services etc)* postal.

post·card carte *f* postale.

post·er affiche *f*, *(for decoration)* poster *m*.

post·grad·u·ate étudiant, -ante *mf* de troisième cycle.

post·man, *pl* -**men** facteur *m*.

post·mark cachet *m* de la poste.

post of·fice *(bureau m* de) poste *f*.

post·pone *vt* remettre (**for** de; **until** à).

post·pone·ment remise *f*.

pot pot *m*; *(for cooking)* marmite *f*; *(drug) Fam* hasch *m*; **pots and pans** casseroles *fpl*.

po·ta·to, *pl* -**oes** pomme *f* de terre.

po·tent *adj* puissant.

po·ten·tial 1 *adj (client, sales)* éventuel. **2** *n* **to have p.** *(of firm etc)* avoir de l'avenir.

pot·ter potier *m*.

pot·ter·y *(art)* poterie *f*; *(objects)* poteries *fpl*; **a piece of p.** une poterie.

pot·ty pot *m* (de bébé).

pouch petit sac *m*; *(of kangaroo)* poche *f*.

poul·try volaille *f*.

pounce *vi* sauter (**on** sur).

pound *(weight)* livre *f* (= 453,6g); *(money)* livre *f* (sterling); *(for cars, dogs)* fourrière *f*.

pour *vt* *(liquid)* verser; **to p. money into sth** investir beaucoup d'argent dans qch.

pour (down) *vi* **it's pouring (down)** il pleut à verse.

▸ **pour in 1** *vt (liquid)* verser. **2** *vi (of water, rain)* entrer à flots; *(of people)* affluer.

▸ **pour off** *vt (liquid)* vider.

▸ **pour out 1** *vt (liquid)* verser; *(cup etc)* vider. **2** *vi (of liquid)* couler à flots; *(of people)* sortir en masse.

pov·er·ty pauvreté *f*.

pow·der 1 *n* poudre *f*. **2** *vt* **to p. one's face** se poudrer.

pow·dered *adj (milk, eggs)* en poudre; **p. sugar** sucre *m* glace.

pow·er *(ability, authority)* pouvoir *m*; *(strength, nation)* puissance *f*; *(energy)* énergie *f*; *(current)* courant *m*; **in p.** au pouvoir; **p. outage** coupure *f* de courant.

pow·er·ful *adj* puissant.

pow·er plant centrale *f* (électrique).

prac·ti·cal *adj* pratique.

prac·ti·cal joke farce *f*.

prac·ti·cal·ly *adv (almost)* pratiquement.

prac·tice 1 *n (exercise, way of proceeding)* pratique *f*; *(habit)* habitude *f*; *(sports training)* entraînement *m*; *(rehearsal)* répétition *f*; **to be out of p.** avoir perdu la pratique. **2** *vt (sports, art etc)* pratiquer; *(medicine, law)* exercer; *(flute, piano etc)* s'exercer à; *(language)* (s'exercer à) parler (**on** guage) (s'exercer à) parler (**on**

avec). **3** *vi* s'exercer; *(of doctor, lawyer)* exercer.

praise 1 *vt* louer (**for sth** de qch); **to p. sb for doing** louer qn d'avoir fait. **2** *n* louange(s) *f(pl)*.

prank *(trick)* farce *f*.

prawn crevette *f* (rose).

pray 1 *vi* prier; **to p. for good weather/a miracle** prier pour avoir du beau temps/pour un miracle. **2** *vt* **to p. that** prier pour que (+ *subjunctive*).

prayer prière *f*.

preach *vi* prêcher.

pre·cau·tion précaution *f* (**of doing** de faire); **as a p.** par précaution.

pre·cede *vti* précéder.

prec·e·dent précédent *m*.

pre·ced·ing *adj* précédent.

pre·cinct *(electoral district)* circonscription *f*; *(police district)* secteur *m*.

pre·cious *adj* précieux.

pre·cise *adj* précis; *(person)* minutieux.

pre·co·cious *adj (child)* précoce.

pred·a·tor prédateur *m*.

pred·e·ces·sor prédécesseur *m*.

pre·dic·a·ment situation *f* fâcheuse.

pre·dict *vt* prédire.

pre·dict·a·ble *adj* prévisible.

pre·dic·tion prédiction *f*.

pref·ace préface *f*.

pre·fer *vt* préférer (**to** à); **to p. to do** préférer faire.

pref·er·a·ble *adj* préférable (**to** à).

pref·er·a·bly *adv* de préférence.

pref·er·ence préférence *f* (**for** pour).

pre·fix préfixe *m*.

preg·nan·cy grossesse *f*.

preg·nant *adj (woman)* enceinte; **five months p.** enceinte de cinq mois.

pre·his·tor·ic *adj* préhistorique.

prej·u·dice préjugé *m*; **to be full of p.** être plein de préjugés.

pre·lim·i·nar·y *adj* préliminaire.

pre·ma·ture adj prématuré.

prem·is·es npl locaux mpl; **on the p.** sur les lieux.

pre·mi·um (insurance) **p.** prime f (d'assurance).

prep·a·ra·tion préparation f; **preparations** préparatifs mpl (**for** de).

pre·pare 1 vt préparer (**sth for** qch pour; **sb for** qn à); **to p. to do** se préparer à faire. 2 vi **to p. for** (journey, occasion) faire des préparatifs pour; (exam) préparer.

pre·pared adj (ready) prêt (**to do** à faire); **to be p. for sth** (expect) s'attendre à qch.

prep·o·si·tion Grammar préposition f.

prep school école f préparatoire.

pre·school adj préscolaire.

pre·scribe vt (of doctor) prescrire.

pre·scrip·tion (for medicine) ordonnance f.

pres·ence présence f; **in the p. of** en présence de.

pres·ent¹ 1 adj (not absent) présent (**at** à; **in** dans); (year, state, job, house etc) actuel; Grammar **p. tense** présent m. 2 n (gift) cadeau m; Grammar (tense) présent m; **at p.** à présent.

pre·sent² vt présenter (**to** à); **to p. sb with** (gift) offrir à qn; (prize) remettre à qn.

pres·en·ta·tion présentation f; (of prize) remise f.

pres·ent·ly adv (soon) tout à l'heure; (now) à présent.

pres·er·va·tion conservation f.

pre·ser·va·tive agent m de conservation.

pre·serve 1 vt (keep) conserver. 2 n (jam) confiture f.

pre·side vi présider; **to p. over** or **at** sth présider qch.

pres·i·den·cy présidence f.

pres·i·dent président, -ente mf.

pres·i·den·tial adj présidentiel.

press¹ 1 n (newspapers, machine)

presse f. 2 adj (conference etc) de presse.

press² 1 vt (button etc) appuyer sur; (clothes) repasser; **to p. sb to do** (urge) presser qn de faire. 2 vi (with finger) appuyer (**on** sur); (of weight) faire pression (**on** sur).

▸ **press down** vt (button etc) appuyer sur.

pressed adj **to be p. (for time)** être très bousculé.

▸ **press on** vi (carry on) continuer (**with sth** qch).

pres·sure pression f; **the p. of work** le surmenage; **under p.** (worker, to work) sous pression.

pres·sure cook·er cocotteminute f.

pre·sume vt présumer (**that** que).

pre·tend vti (make believe) faire semblant (**to do** de faire; **that** que).

pre·text prétexte m; **on the p. of/ that** sous prétexte de/que.

pret·ty 1 adj joli. 2 adv (rather, quite) assez; **p. well, p. much** (almost) pratiquement.

pre·vail vi prédominer; **to p. upon** or **on sb to do sth** (persuade) persuader qn de faire qch.

pre·vent vt empêcher (**from doing** de faire).

pre·ven·tion prévention f.

pre·vi·ous adj précédent; (experience) préalable; **p. to** avant.

pre·vi·ous·ly adv avant.

prey proie f; **bird of p.** rapace m.

price prix m.

price list tarif m.

prick vt piquer (**with** avec); (burst) crever.

prick·ly adj (plant, beard) piquant.

pride (satisfaction) fierté f; (exaggerated) orgueil m; (self-respect) amour-propre m; **to take p. in** être fier de; (take care of) prendre soin de.

▸ **pride on** vt **to p. oneself on sth/ on doing** s'enorgueillir de qch/de faire.

priest prêtre m.

pri·mar·i·ly adv essentiellement.

pri·mar·y 1 adj principal; **p. color** couleur f primaire. **2** n (election) (élection f) primaire f.

pri·mar·y school école f primaire.

prime min·is·ter premier ministre m.

prime num·ber nombre m premier.

prim·i·tive adj primitif.

prim·rose primevère f.

prince prince m.

prin·cess princesse f.

prin·ci·pal (of school) directeur, -trice mf.

print 1 n (of finger, foot etc) empreinte f, (letters) caractères mpl; (engraving) gravure f, (photo) épreuve f, **out of p.** épuisé; **p. shop** imprimerie f. **2** vt (book etc) imprimer; (photo) tirer; (write) écrire en caractères d'imprimerie.

print·er (of computer) imprimante f.

print·ing (industry, process) imprimerie f, (print run) tirage m; **p. plant** imprimerie f; **p. press** presse fd'imprimerie.

▶**print out** vti (of computer) imprimer.

print-out (of computer) sortie f sur imprimante.

pri·or adj précédent; (experience) préalable.

pri·or·i·ty priorité f (over sur).

pris·on prison f; **in p.** en prison.

pris·on·er prisonnier, -ière mf; **to take sb p.** faire qn prisonnier.

pri·va·cy intimité f.

pri·vate 1 adj privé; (lesson, car, secretary etc) particulier; (report) confidentiel; (dinner etc) intime. **2** n (soldier) (simple) soldat m; **in p.** en privé; (to have dinner etc) dans l'intimité.

pri·vate·ly adv en privé; (to have dinner etc) dans l'intimité.

prize prix m; (in lottery) lot m.

prize-win·ner lauréat, -ate mf; (in lottery) gagnant, -ante mf.

pro¹ pro m; **the pros and cons** le pour et le contre.

pro² abbr (professional) pro mf.

pro- prefix (in favour of) pro-.

prob·a·ble adj probable (**that** que); (convincing) vraisemblable.

prob·a·bly adv probablement.

probe 1 n (device) sonde f, (investigation) enquête f. **2** vt sonder; (investigate) enquêter sur.

▶**probe into** vt enquêter sur.

prob·lem problème m; **no p.!** Fam pas de problème!; **to have a p. doing** avoir du mal à faire.

prob·lem·at·ic, prob·lem·at·i·cal adj problématique.

pro·ceed vi (go) avancer; (act) procéder; (continue) continuer.

pro·ceeds npl recette f.

proc·ess (method) procédé m (**for doing** pour faire); (chemical, economic etc) processus m; **in the p. of doing** en train de faire.

proc·essed cheese fromage m en tranches.

pro·ces·sion cortège m.

pro·duce 1 vt (manufacture, cause etc) produire; (bring out) sortir (pistolet, mouchoir etc); (passport) présenter. **2** n produits mpl.

pro·duc·er (of goods, film) producteur, -trice mf.

prod·uct produit m.

pro·duc·tion production f, (of play) mise f en scène.

pro·duc·tive adj productif.

pro·duc·tiv·i·ty productivité f.

pro·fes·sion profession f.

pro·fes·sion·al 1 adj professionnel; (piece of work) de professionnel. **2** n professionnel, -elle mf.

pro·fes·sor professeur m (d'université).

prof·it 1 n profit m, bénéfice m; **to sell at a p.** vendre à profit. **2** vi **to p. by** or **from sth** tirer profit de qch.

prof·it·a·ble adj rentable.

pro·found adj profond.

pro·gram 1 n (schedule, of computer) programme m; (broadcast) emission f. **2** vt programmer.

prog·ress 1 n progrès m(pl); **to make p.** faire des progrès; (when driving etc) bien avancer; **in p.** en cours. **2** vi progresser; (of story, meeting) se dérouler.

pro·gres·sive adj progressif.

pro·hib·it vt interdire (**sb from doing** à qn de faire).

proj·ect projet m (**for sth** pour qch); (at school) étude f.

pro·jec·tor (for films etc) projecteur m.

pro·long vt prolonger.

prom·i·nent adj (person) important.

prom·ise 1 n promesse f; **to show p.** être prometteur. **2** vt promettre (**sb sth, sth to sb** qch à qn; **to do** de faire; **that** que). **3** vi **I p.!** je te le promets!; **p.?** promis?

prom·is·ing adj (situation) prometteur (f -euse).

pro·mote vt **to p. sb** (in job etc) donner de l'avancement à qn.

pro·mo·tion (of person) avancement m.

prompt adj (speedy) rapide.

prone adj **p. to** (illnesses, accidents) prédisposé à.

pro·noun pronom m.

pro·nounce vt prononcer.

pro·nun·ci·a·tion prononciation f.

proof (evidence) preuve(s) f(pl).

prop 1 n (physical support) support m; (psychological support) soutien m. **2** vt (lean) appuyer.

prop·a·gan·da propagande f.

pro·pel·ler hélice f.

prop·er adj (suitable, respectable) convenable; (downright) véritable; (noun, meaning) propre; **the p. address/method/**etc (correct) la bonne adresse/méthode/etc.

prop·er·ly adv comme il faut, convenablement.

prop·er·ty (building, possessions) propriété f.

pro·por·tion (ratio) proportion f; (portion) partie f; **proportions** (size) dimensions fpl.

pro·por·tion·al adj proportionnel (**to** à).

pro·pos·al proposition f; (of marriage) demande f (en mariage).

pro·pose 1 vt (suggest) proposer (**to** à; **that** que + subjunctive). **2** vi faire une demande (en mariage) (**to** à).

prop·o·si·tion proposition f.

props npl (in theater) accessoires mpl.

▶ **prop up** vt (ladder etc) appuyer (**against** contre); (one's head) caler; (wall) étayer.

prose prose f.

pros·e·cute vt poursuivre (en justice).

pros·e·cu·tion (action) poursuites fpl judiciaires; **the p.** = le ministère public.

pros·pect (outlook, possibility) perspective f (**of** de); (future) prospects perspectives fpl d'avenir.

pros·per·i·ty prospérité f.

pros·per·ous adj riche.

pro·tect vt protéger (**from** de; **against** contre).

pro·tec·tion protection f.

pro·tec·tive adj (clothes etc) de protection.

pro·test 1 n protestation f (**against** contre); (demonstration) manifestation f. **2** vi protester (**against** contre); (of students etc) contester.

Prot·es·tant adj & n protestant, -ante (mf).

pro·test·er (student etc) contestataire mf.

pro·trac·tor (for measuring) rapporteur m.

proud adj fier (**of** de; **to do** de faire); (conceited) orgueilleux.

proud·ly adv fièrement; (conceitedly) orgueilleusement.

prove 1 vt prouver (**that** que). **2** vi **to p. difficult**/etc s'avérer difficile/etc.

prov·erb proverbe m.

pro·vide vt (supply) fournir (**sb with sth** qch à qn); **to p. sb with sth** (equip) pourvoir qn de qch.

pro·vid·ed, **pro·vid·ing** conj p. (that) pourvu que (+ subjunctive).

▸ **provide for** vt pourvoir aux besoins de.

prov·ince province f; **the provinces** la province.

pro·vin·cial adj provincial.

pro·vi·sion·al adj provisoire.

pro·voke vt (annoy) agacer.

prowl (a·round) vi rôder.

prowl·er rôdeur, -euse mf.

prune 1 n pruneau m. **2** vt (tree, bush) tailler.

prun·ing shears sécateur m.

psy·chi·at·ric adj psychiatrique.

psy·chi·a·trist psychiatre mf.

psy·cho·log·i·cal adj psychologique.

psy·chol·o·gist psychologue mf.

psy·chol·o·gy psychologie f.

pub pub m.

pub·lic 1 adj public (f -ique); (library, swimming pool) municipal. **2** n public m; **in p.** en public.

pub·li·ca·tion publication f.

pub·lic·i·ty publicité f.

pub·lish vt publier; (book, author) éditer.

pub·lish·er éditeur, -trice mf.

pub·lish·ing (profession) édition f.

pud·ding pudding m; **rice p.** riz m au lait.

pud·dle flaque f (d'eau).

puff n (of smoke, wind) bouffée f. **2** vi souffler.

▸ **puff at** vt (cigar etc) tirer sur.

pull 1 n **to give sth a p.** tirer qch. **2** vt tirer; (trigger) appuyer sur;

(tooth) arracher; (muscle) se claquer; **to p. apart** or **to pieces** mettre en pièces. **3** vi tirer (**at**, **on** sur); (go, move) aller.

▸ **pull along** vt traîner (**to** jusqu'à).

▸ **pull away 1** vt (move) éloigner; (snatch) arracher (**from** à). **2** vi (in vehicle) démarrer; **to pull away from** s'éloigner de.

▸ **pull back 1** vi se retirer. **2** vt retirer; (curtains) ouvrir.

▸ **pull down** vt baisser; (knock down) faire tomber; (demolish) démolir.

▸ **pull in 1** vt (into room etc) faire entrer (de force); (crowd) attirer. **2** vi arriver; (stop in vehicle) se garer.

▸ **pull off** vt (remove) enlever.

▸ **pull on** vt (boots etc) mettre.

▸ **pull out 1** vt (tooth, hair) arracher; (cork, pin) enlever; (from pocket etc) tirer, sortir (**from** de). **2** vi (move out in vehicle) déboîter; (withdraw) se retirer (**from**, **of** de).

▸ **pull over 1** vt traîner (**to** jusqu'à); (knock down) faire tomber. **2** vi (in vehicle) se ranger (sur le côté).

pull·o·ver pull(-over) m.

▸ **pull through** vi s'en tirer.

▸ **pull up 1** vt (socks, sleeve, collar, shade) remonter, relever; (plant, tree) arracher; (chair) approcher. **2** vi (in vehicle) s'arrêter.

pulse pouls m.

pump 1 n pompe f; (air) p. (in service station) gonfleur m. **2** vt pomper.

pump·kin potiron m, citrouille f.

▸ **pump up** vt (mattress etc) gonfler.

punch¹ n (blow) coup m de poing. **2** vt donner un coup de poing à (qn).

punch² n (for paper) perforeuse f. **2** vt (ticket) poinçonner; (with date) composter; **to p. a hole in sth** faire un trou dans qch.

punc·tu·al adj (on time) à l'heure; (regularly) ponctuel.

punc·tu·a·tion ponctuation f.

punc·ture 1 *n* crevaison *f*. **2** *vti* (*burst*) crever.

pun·ish *vt* punir (**for sth** de qch; **for doing** pour avoir fait).

pun·ish·ment punition *f*.

pup (*dog*) chiot *m*.

pu·pil élève *mf*, (*of eye*) pupille *f*.

pup·pet marionnette *f*.

pup·py chiot *m*.

pur·chase 1 *n* achat *m*. **2** *vt* acheter (**from sb** à qn; **for sb** à or pour qn).

pur·chas·er acheteur, -euse *mf*.

pure *adj* pur.

pure·ly *adv* (*only*) strictement.

pur·ple 1 *adj* violet (*f* -ette). **2** *n* violet *m*.

pur·pose (*aim*) but *m*; **for this p.** dans ce but; **on p.** exprès.

pur·pose·ly *adv* exprès.

purse (*for coins*) porte-monnaie *m inv*; (*handbag*) sac *m* à main.

pur·sue *vt* (*inquiry, aim etc*) poursuivre.

pur·suit poursuite *f*, (*of pleasure, glory*) quête *f*, (*pastime*) occupation *f*.

push 1 *n* to give sb/sth a p. pousser qn/qch. **2** *vt* pousser (**to, as far as** jusqu'à); **to p. sth into/between** enfoncer qch dans/entre; **to p. sb into doing** pousser qn à faire. **3** *vi* pousser.

push (**down**) *vt* (*button*) appuyer sur; (*lever*) abaisser.

▸ **push around** *vt* (*bully*) marcher sur les pieds à.

▸ **push aside** *vt* écarter.

▸ **push away** or **back** *vt* repousser.

push-but·ton bouton *m*; (*of phone*) touche *f*; **p. phone** téléphone *m* à touches.

▸ **push on** *vi* continuer (**with sth** qch).

▸ **push over** *vt* renverser.

▸ **push through** *vt* to p. one's way through se frayer un chemin (**a crowd** à travers une foule).

▸ **push up** *vt* (*lever, sleeve, collar*) relever; (*increase*) augmenter.

push·y *adj Fam* batailleur, -euse.

puss (*cat*) minou *m*.

put* *vt* mettre; (*money*) placer (**into** dans); (*question*) poser (**to** à); (*say*) dire.

▸ **put across** *vt* (*message etc*) communiquer (**to** à).

▸ **put aside** *vt* (*money, object*) mettre de côté.

▸ **put away** *vt* (*book, car etc*) ranger; (*criminal*) mettre en prison.

▸ **put back** *vt* (*replace, postpone*) remettre; (*telephone receiver*) raccrocher.

▸ **put by** *vt* (*money*) mettre de côté.

▸ **put down** *vt* (*on floor etc*) poser; (*passenger*) déposer; (*a deposit*) verser; (*write down*) inscrire.

▸ **put forward** *vt* (*candidate*) proposer (**for** à).

▸ **put in** *vt* (*sth into box etc*) mettre dedans; (*insert*) introduire; (*add*) ajouter; (*install*) installer; (*application*) faire.

▸ **put off** *vt* renvoyer (à plus tard); (*gas, radio*) fermer; **to p. sb off** dissuader qn (**doing** de faire); (*disgust*) dégoûter qn.

▸ **put on** *vt* (*clothes etc*) mettre; (*weight*) prendre; (*gas, radio*) mettre; (*record, cassette*) passer; (*clock*) avancer; (*lid*) mettre en place.

▸ **put out** *vt* (*take outside*) sortir; (*arm, leg*) étendre; (*hand*) tendre; (*gas, light*) éteindre; (*bother*) déranger.

▸ **put through** *vt* (*on phone*) passer qn (**to** à).

▸ **put together** *vt* mettre ensemble; (*assemble*) assembler; (*compose*) composer.

put·ty mastic *m*.

▸ **put up 1** *vi* (*stay*) descendre (**at a hotel** à un hôtel). **2** *vt* (*lift*) lever; (*window*) remonter; (*tent, statue, ladder*) dresser; (*building*) construire; (*umbrella*) ouvrir; (*picture*) mettre; (*price*) augmenter; (*candidate*) proposer (**for** à); (*guest*) loger.

▸**put up with** *vt* supporter.

puz·zle 1 *n* mystère *m*; *(jigsaw)* puzzle *m*. **2** *vt* laisser perplexe.

puz·zled *adj* perplexe.

puz·zling *adj* curieux.

py·lon pylône *m*.

pyr·a·mid pyramide *f*.

Q

qual·i·fi·ca·tion diplôme *m*; **qualifications** *(skills)* qualités *fpl* nécessaires (**for** pour; **to do** pour faire).

qual·i·fied *adj (able)* qualifié (**to do** pour faire); *(teacher etc)* diplômé.

qual·i·fy *vt* obtenir son diplôme (**as a** doctor/*etc* de médecin/*etc*); *(in sports)* se qualifier (**for** pour).

qual·i·ty qualité *f*.

quan·ti·ty quantité *f*.

quar·rel 1 *n* dispute *f*; **to pick a q.** chercher des histoires (**with sb** à qn). **2** *vi* se disputer (**with sb** avec qn).

quar·rel·ing disputes *fpl*.

quar·ry *(to extract stone etc)* carrière *f*.

quart litre *m (mesure approximative = 0.95 litre)*.

quar·ter¹ quart *m*; *(money)* quart *m* de dollar; *(of fruit)* quartier *m*; *(of school/fiscal year)* trimestre *m*; **to divide sth into quarters** diviser qch en quatre; **q. (of a) pound** quart *m* de livre; **a q. past** or **after nine** neuf heures et quart or un quart; **a q. to nine** neuf heures moins le quart.

quar·ter² *(district)* quartier *m*.

quar·ter·back quarterback *m*.

quartz *adj (watch etc)* à quartz.

quay quai *m*, débarcadère *m*.

queen reine *f*; *Chess, Cards* dame *f*.

quench *vt* **to q. one's thirst** se désaltérer.

que·ry *(question)* question *f*.

ques·tion 1 *n* question *f*; **it's out of the q.** il n'en est pas question. **2** *vt* interroger *(qn)* (**about** sur); *(doubt)* mettre *(qch)* en question.

ques·tion·a·ble *adj* discutable.

ques·tion mark point *m* d'interrogation.

ques·tion·naire questionnaire *m*.

quib·ble *vi* ergoter (**over** sur).

quiche quiche *f*.

quick 1 *adj* rapide; **be q.!** fais vite!; **to have a q. meal**/*etc* manger/*etc* en vitesse. **2** *adv* vite.

quick·ly *adv* vite.

qui·et *adj (silent, peaceful)* tranquille; *(machine, vehicle)* silencieux; *(voice, sound)* doux (*f* douce); **to be** or **keep q.** *(shut up)* se taire; *(make no noise)* ne pas faire de bruit; **q.!** silence!; **to keep q. about sth** ne pas parler de qch.

qui·et·ly *adv* tranquillement; *(not loudly)* doucement; *(silently)* silencieusement.

quilt édredon *m*.

quit* **1** **to q. doing** arrêter de faire. **2** *vi* abandonner; *(resign)* démissionner.

quite *adv (entirely)* tout à fait; *(really)* vraiment; *(rather)* assez; **q. a lot** pas mal (**of** de).

quiz, *pl* **quizzes** *(in school)* contrôle *m*; **q. show** jeu(-concours) *m*.

quo·ta quota *m*.

quo·ta·tion citation *f*; *(estimate)* devis *m*.

quo·ta·tion marks guillemets *mpl*; **in q. marks** entre guillemets.

quote *vt* citer; *(reference)* rappeler; *(price)* indiquer. **2** *vi* **to q. from** citer. **3** *n* = **quotation**.

R

rab·bi rabbin m.

rab·bit lapin m.

ra·bies rage f.

race¹ 1 n (contest) course f. **2** vt (horse) faire courir; **to r. (against or with)** sb faire une course avec qn. **3** vi (run) courir.

race² (group) race f.

race·car voiture f de course.

race·car driv·er coureur m automobile.

race·horse cheval m de course.

race·track champ m de courses.

ra·cial adj racial.

ra·cial·ism, rac·ism racisme m.

rac·ing courses fpl.

ra·cist adj & n raciste (mf).

rack (for bottles, letters etc) casier m; (for drying dishes) égouttoir m; (luggage) r. (on bus, train) filet m à bagages.

rack·et (for tennis) raquette f; (din) vacarme m.

ra·dar radar m.

ra·di·a·tion radiation f.

ra·di·a·tor radiateur m.

rad·i·cal adj radical.

ra·di·o, pl -os radio f; (set) poste m de radio; **on** or **over the r.** à la radio.

ra·di·o·ac·tive adj radioactif.

rad·ish radis m.

ra·di·us, pl -dii (of circle) rayon m.

raf·fle tombola f.

raft (boat) radeau m.

rag (old clothing) haillon m; (for dusting etc) chiffon m; **in rags** (clothes) en loques; (person) en haillons.

rage rage f; **to fly into a r.** se mettre en rage.

rag·ged adj (clothes) en loques; (person) en haillons.

raid 1 n (military) raid m; (by police)

descente f; (by thieves) hold-up m inv; **air r.** raid m aérien. **2** vt faire un raid dans; (of police) faire une descente dans; (of thieves) faire un hold-up dans.

rail (for train) rail m; (rod on balcony) balustrade f; (on stairs) rampe f; **by r.** (to travel) par le train; (to send) par chemin de fer.

rail·ing (of balcony) balustrade f; **railings** (fence) grille f.

rail·road 1 n chemin m de fer; **r. (track)** voie f ferrée. **2** adj (ticket) de chemin de fer; **r. line** ligne f de chemin de fer.

rain 1 n pluie f; **in the r.** sous la pluie. **2** vi pleuvoir; **it's raining** il pleut.

rain·bow arc-en-ciel m.

rain·coat imper(méable) m.

rain·y adj pluvieux.

raise 1 vt (lift) lever; (child, family, voice) élever; (salary, price) augmenter; (question) soulever; **to r. money** réunir des fonds. **2** n augmentation f (de salaire).

rai·sin raisin m sec.

rake 1 n râteau m. **2** vt (garden) ratisser.

rake (up) vt (leaves) ratisser.

ral·ly (political) rassemblement m.

▶**rally around** or **round 1** vt venir en aide à. **2** vi venir en aide.

ram 1 n (animal) bélier m. **2** vt (vehicle) emboutir; **to r. sth into sth** enfoncer qch dans qch.

ram·ble randonnée f.

ramp (slope for wheelchair etc) rampe f (d'accès).

ran pt de **run**.

ranch ranch m.

ran·dom 1 n **at r.** au hasard. **2** adj (choice) (fait) au hasard; (sample) prélevé au hasard; **r. check** (by police) contrôle-surprise m.

range 1 n (of gun, voice etc) portée f; (of singer's voice) étendue f; (of colors, prices, products) gamme f; (of sizes) choix m; (of mountains) chaîne *f; (stove)* cuisinière *f.* **2** *vi (vary)* varier (**from** de; **to** à).

rank rang *m.*

ran·som *(money)* rançon *f.*

rape 1 *vt* violer. **2** *n* viol *m.*

rap·id *adj* rapide.

rap·id·ly *adv* rapidement.

rap·ist violeur *m.*

rare *adj* rare; *(meat)* saignant.

rare·ly *adv* rarement.

ras·cal coquin, -ine *mf.*

rash 1 *n* éruption *f.* **2** *adj* irréfléchi.

rash·ly *adv* sans réfléchir.

rasp·ber·ry framboise *f; * r. **jam** confiture *f* de framboises.

rat rat *m.*

rate 1 *n (level)* taux *m; (speed)* vitesse *f; (price)* tarif *m;* **at the r. of** à une vitesse de; *(amount)* à raison de; **at this r.** *(slow speed)* à ce train-là; **at any r.** en tout cas. **2** *vt* évaluer (**at** à); *(regard)* considérer (**as** comme); *(deserve)* mériter.

rath·er *adv (preferably, quite)* plutôt; **I'd r. stay** j'aimerais mieux rester (**than** que); **r. than leave/***etc* plutôt que de partir/*etc.*

rat·ing *(ranking)* classement *m; (appraisal)* évaluation *f;* **ratings** *(for TV, radio program)* indice *m* d'écoute.

ra·tio, *pl* **-os** proportion *f.*

ra·tion 1 *n* ration *f;* **rations** *(food)* vivres *mpl.* **2** *vt* rationner.

ra·tion·al *adj (person)* raisonnable.

ra·tion·ing rationnement *m.*

rat·tle 1 *n (baby's toy)* hochet *m.* **2** *vi* faire du bruit; *(of window)* trembler. **3** *vt (shake)* secouer.

rav·en·ous *adj* **I'm r.** j'ai une faim de loup.

raw *adj (vegetable etc)* cru; *(skin)* écorché; **r. material** matière *f* première.

ray *(of light, sun)* rayon *m.*

ra·zor rasoir *m.*

re- *prefix* ré-, re-, r-.

reach 1 *vt (place, distant object,*

aim) atteindre; *(gain access to)* accéder à; *(of letter)* parvenir à (**qn**); *(contact)* joindre (**qn**); *(conclusion)* arriver à; **to r. sb sth** passer qch à qn. **2** *vi* s'étendre (**to** à); *(with arm)* (é)tendre le bras (**for** pour prendre). **3** *n* portée *f; * **within r. of** à portée de; *(near)* à proximité de; **within (easy) r.** *(object)* à portée de main.

▸ **reach out** *vi* (é)tendre le bras (**for** pour prendre).

re·act *vi* réagir (**against** contre; **to** à).

re·ac·tion réaction *f.*

re·ac·tor réacteur *m (nucléaire).*

read¹ 1 *vt* lire; *(meter)* relever; *(of instrument)* indiquer. **2** *vi* lire; **to r. to sb** faire la lecture à qn.

▸ **read aloud** *or* **out loud** *vt* lire (à haute voix).

▸ **read back** *or* **over** *vt* relire.

read·er lecteur, -trice *mf; (book)* livre *m* de lecture.

read·i·ly *adv (willingly)* volontiers; *(easily)* facilement.

read·ing lecture *f; (of meter)* relevé *m; (by instrument)* indication *f.*

▸ **read through** *vt* parcourir.

▸ **read up (on)** *vt* étudier.

read·y *adj* prêt (**to do** à faire; **for sth** à *or* pour qch); **to get sth/sb r.** préparer qch/qn; **to get r.** se préparer (**for sth** à *or* pour qch; **to do** à faire); **r. cash** argent *m* liquide.

read·y-made *adj* tout fait.

read·y-to-wear *adj* **r. clothes** prêt-à-porter *m inv.*

re·al *adj* vrai; *(life, world)* réel.

re·al es·tate biens *mpl* immobiliers; **r. estate agent** agent *m* immobilier.

re·al·is·tic *adj* réaliste.

re·al·i·ty réalité *f.*

re·al·ize *vt (know)* se rendre compte de; *(understand)* comprendre (**that** que).

re·al·ly *adv* vraiment.

Real·tor® agent *m* immobilier.

rear 1 *n (back part)* arrière *m;* **in or**

at the r. à l'arrière. **2** adj arrière inv, de derrière. **3** vt (family, animals) élever.

rear (up) vi (of horse) se cabrer.

re·ar·range vt (hair, room) réarranger; (plans) changer.

rea·son 1 n raison f; **the r. for/why...** la raison de/pour laquelle...; **for no r.** sans raison. **2** vi raisonner.

rea·son·a·ble adj raisonnable.

rea·son·a·bly adv (fairly, rather) assez.

rea·son·ing raisonnement m.

▸**reason with** vt raisonner.

re·as·sure vt rassurer.

re·as·sur·ing adj rassurant.

re·bel 1 n rebelle mf; (against parents etc) révolté, -ée mf. **2** vi se révolter (**against** contre).

re·bel·lion révolte f.

re·bound 1 vi (of ball) rebondir; (of stone) ricocher. **2** n rebond m; ricochet m.

re·build vt reconstruire.

re·call vt (remember) se rappeler (**that** que; **doing** avoir fait); **to r. sth to sb** rappeler qch à qn.

re·ceipt (for payment, object left etc) reçu m (**for** de); **on r. of** dès réception de.

re·ceive vt recevoir.

re·ceiv·er (of phone) combiné m; **to pick up the r.** (of phone) décrocher.

re·cent adj récent; **in r. months** ces mois-ci.

re·cent·ly adv récemment.

re·cep·tion (party, of radio etc) réception f; **r. (desk)** réception f, accueil m.

re·cep·tion·ist secrétaire mf, réceptionniste mf.

re·charge vt (battery) recharger.

rec·i·pe recette f (**for** de).

re·cip·i·ent (of gift, letter) destinataire mf; (of award) lauréat, -ate mf.

re·cite vt (poem) réciter; (list) énumérer.

reck·less adj (rash) imprudent.

reck·on vt (calculate) calculer; (think) Fam penser (**that** que).

▸**reckon on** vt (rely on) compter sur; **to r. on doing** compter faire.

▸**reckon with** vt (take into account) compter avec.

re·claim vt (baggage at airport) récupérer.

rec·og·nize vt reconnaître (**by** à).

rec·ol·lect vt se souvenir de; **to r. that** se souvenir que.

rec·ol·lec·tion souvenir m.

rec·om·mend vt recommander (**to** à; **for** pour); **to r. sb to do** recommander à qn de faire.

rec·om·men·da·tion recommandation f.

re·cord 1 n (best performance) record m; (register) registre m; (mention) mention f; (background) antécédents mpl; (public) records archives fpl; **to keep a r. of** noter. **2** adj (time, number etc) record inv. **3** vt (on tape, in register) enregistrer; (in diary) noter. **4** vi enregistrer.

re·cord·ed adj (music, message, tape) enregistré; (TV broadcast) en différé.

re·cord·er flûte f à bec; (tape) r. magnétophone m; (video) r. magnétoscope m.

re·cord·ing enregistrement m.

re·cov·er 1 vt (get back) retrouver. **2** vi (from illness etc) se remettre (**from** de); (of economy) se redresser.

rec·re·a·tion récréation f.

re·cruit recrue f.

rec·tan·gle rectangle m.

rec·tan·gu·lar adj rectangulaire.

re·cy·cle vt recycler.

red 1 adj rouge; (hair) roux (f rousse); **to turn r.** rougir; **r. light** (traffic light) feu m rouge. **2** n (color) rouge m; **in the r.** (company, account) dans le rouge, en déficit.

red·hand·ed *adj* caught r. pris en flagrant délit.

red·head roux *m*, rousse *f*.

red-hot *adj* brûlant.

re·di·rect *vt (mail)* faire suivre.

re·do* *vt (exercise, house etc)* refaire.

re·duce *vt* réduire (**to** à; **by** de); **at a reduced price** *(ticket, goods)* à prix réduit.

re·duc·tion réduction *f* (**in** de).

re·dun·dan·cy superfluité *f*.

re·dun·dant *adj* superflu.

reed *(plant)* roseau *m*.

reef récif *m*.

reel *(of thread, film)* bobine *f; (film itself)* bande *f.*

re·fec·to·ry réfectoire *m*.

re·fer **1** *vi* **to r. to** *(mention)* faire allusion à; *(speak of)* parler de; *(apply to)* s'appliquer à. **2** *vt* **to r. sth to sb** soumettre qch à qn.

ref·e·ree 1 *n Sports* arbitre *m*. **2** *vt* arbitrer.

ref·er·ence *(in book, for job)* référence *f; (mention)* mention *f* (**to** de); **with r. to** concernant; **r. book** ouvrage *m* de référence.

ref·er·en·dum référendum *m*.

re·fill 1 *vt* remplir (à nouveau); *(lighter, pen)* recharger. **2** *n* recharge *f;* **a r.** *(drink)* un autre verre.

re·flect *vt (light etc)* refléter; **to be reflected** se refléter.

re·flec·tion *(image)* reflet *m*.

re·flex réflexe *m*.

re·form réforme *f*.

re·frain *vi* s'abstenir (**from doing** de faire).

re·fresh *vt (of bath, drink)* rafraîchir; *(of sleep, rest)* délasser.

re·fresh·er course cours *m* de recyclage.

re·fresh·ing *adj (drink)* rafraîchissant.

re·fresh·ments *npl (drinks)* rafraîchissements *mpl, (snacks)* petites choses *fpl* à grignoter.

re·frig·er·ate *vt (food)* conserver au frais.

re·frig·er·a·tor réfrigérateur *m*.

ref·uge refuge *m;* **to take r.** se réfugier.

ref·u·gee réfugié, -ée *mf*.

re·fund 1 *vt* rembourser. **2** *n* remboursement *m*.

re·fus·al refus *m*.

re·fuse *vt* refuser (**sb sth** qch à qn; **to do** faire). **2** *vi* refuser.

re·gain *vt (lost ground)* regagner; *(health, strength)* retrouver.

re·gard *vt* considérer; **as regards** en ce qui concerne. **2** *n* considération *f* (**for** pour); **to have (a) high r. for sb** estimer qn; **to give one's regards to sb** transmettre son meilleur souvenir à qn.

re·gard·ing *prep* en ce qui concerne.

re·gard·less 1 *adj* **r. of** sans tenir compte de. **2** *adv (all the same)* quand même.

reg·i·ment régiment *m*.

re·gion région *f;* **in the r. of $50/ etc (about)** dans les 50 dollars/ etc.

re·gion·al *adj* régional.

reg·is·ter 1 *n* registre *m*. **2** *vt (birth etc)* déclarer; **registered letter** lettre recommandée; **to send by registered mail** envoyer en recommandé. **3** *vi (enroll)* s'inscrire (**for a course** à un cours); *(in hotel)* signer le registre.

reg·is·tra·tion *(enrollment)* inscription *f;* **r. (number)** *(of vehicle)* numéro *m* d'immatriculation.

re·gret 1 *vt* regretter (**doing, to do** de faire; **that** que (+ *subjunctive*)). **2** *n* regret *m*.

reg·u·lar *adj (steady)* régulier; *(surface)* uni; *(usual)* habituel; *(price, size)* normal; *(listener)* fidèle.

reg·u·lar·ly *adv* régulièrement.

reg·u·late *vt (adjust)* régler; *(control)* réglementer.

reg·u·la·tions *npl (rules)* règlement *m*.

re·hears·al répétition *f*.

re·hearse vt (a play etc) répéter. **2** vi répéter.

reign 1 n règne m; **in the r. of** sous le règne de. **2** vi régner (**over** sur).

rein·deer inv renne m.

re·in·force vt renforcer (**with** de).

re·in·force·ments npl (troops) renforts mpl.

reins npl (for horse) rênes fpl; (for baby) bretelles fpl de sécurité (avec laisse).

re·ject vt rejeter.

re·jec·tion rejet m; (of candidate) refus m.

re·joice vi (celebrate) faire la fête; (be delighted) se réjouir (**over** or **at sth** de qch).

re·lat·ed adj (linked) lié (**to** à); **to be r. to sb** (by family) être parent de qn.

▸ **relate to** vt (apply to) se rapporter à.

re·la·tion (relative) parent, -ente mf; (relationship) rapport m; **international relations** relations fpl internationales.

re·la·tion·ship (in family) lien(s) m(pl) de parenté; (relations) relations fpl; (connection) rapport m.

rel·a·tive 1 n (person) parent, -ente mf. **2** adj relatif; **r. to** en rapport avec.

rel·a·tive·ly adv relativement.

re·lax 1 vt (person) détendre; (grip, pressure) relâcher. **2** vi se détendre; **r.!** (calm down) du calme!

re·lax·a·tion (rest) détente f.

re·laxed adj décontracté.

re·lease 1 vt (free) libérer (**from** de); (bomb) lâcher; (brake) desserrer; (film, record) sortir; (trapped person) dégager. **2** n (of prisoner) libération f; (of film etc) sortie f; **press r.** communiqué m de presse.

rel·e·vant adj pertinent (**to** à); (useful) utile; **that's not r.** ça n'a rien à voir.

re·li·a·bil·i·ty fiabilité f; (of person) sérieux m.

re·li·a·ble adj fiable; (person) sérieux.

re·lief (from pain etc) soulagement m (**from** à); (help) secours m; (in geography etc) relief m.

re·lieve vt (pain, person etc) soulager; (take over from) relayer (qn).

re·li·gion religion f.

re·li·gious adj religieux.

rel·ish 1 n condiment m. **2** vt (food, wine) savourer.

re·load vt (gun, camera) recharger.

re·luc·tance manque m d'enthousiasme (**to do** de faire).

re·luc·tant adj peu enthousiaste (**to do** pour faire).

re·luc·tant·ly adv sans enthousiasme.

▸ **re·ly on** vt (count on) compter sur; (be dependent on) dépendre de.

re·main vi rester.

re·main·ing adj qui reste(nt).

re·mark 1 n remarque f. **2** vt (faire) remarquer (**that** que). **3** vi **to r. on sth** faire des remarques sur qch.

re·mark·a·ble adj remarquable (**for** par).

re·mark·a·bly adv remarquablement.

re·match Sports revanche f.

re·me·di·al adj **r. class** cours m de rattrapage.

rem·e·dy 1 n remède m. **2** vt remédier à.

re·mem·ber 1 vt se souvenir de, se rappeler; **to r. that/doing** se rappeler que/d'avoir fait; **to r. to do** penser à faire. **2** vi se souvenir, se rappeler.

re·mind vt rappeler (**sb of sth** qch à qn; **sb that** qn que); **to r. sb to do** faire penser à qn à faire.

re·mind·er rappel m; **to give sb a r. to do** faire penser à qn à faire.

re·morse remords m(pl).

re·mote adj (far-off) lointain; (isolated) isolé; (slight) petit.

re·mote con·trol télécommande f.

re·mov·al (of clothes, stain etc) enlèvement m; (of obstacle, word) suppression f.

re·move vt (clothes, stain etc) enlever (**from sb** à qn; **from sth** de qch); (obstacle, word) supprimer.

re·new vt renouveler; (resume) reprendre; (library book) renouveler le prêt de.

rent 1 n (for house etc) loyer m. **2** vt louer.

rent·al (of house, car) location f.

▸ **rent out** vt louer.

re·or·gan·ize vt (firm etc) réorganiser.

re·pair 1 vt réparer. **2** n réparation f; **in bad r.** en mauvais état.

re·pair·man, pl **-men** réparateur m, dépanneur m.

re·pay vt (pt & pp **repaid**) (pay back) rembourser; (reward) récompenser (**for** de).

re·pay·ment (paying back) remboursement m; (rewarding) récompense f.

re·peat 1 vt répéter (**that** que); (promise, threat) réitérer; (class) redoubler; **to r. oneself** se répéter. **2** n (on TV, radio) rediffusion f.

re·peat·ed adj (attempts etc) répétés.

re·peat·ed·ly adv à maintes reprises, de nombreuses fois.

re·pel vt repousser.

rep·e·ti·tion répétition f.

re·pet·i·tive adj répétitif.

re·place vt (take the place of) remplacer (**by, with** par); (put back) remettre; (telephone receiver) raccrocher.

re·place·ment (person) remplaçant, -ante mf; (machine part) pièce f de rechange.

re·play 1 n match m rejoué; (instant or action) **r.** répétition f d'une séquence précédente. **2** vt (match) rejouer.

rep·li·ca copie f exacte.

re·ply 1 vti répondre (**to** à; **that** que). **2** n réponse f.

re·port 1 n (account) rapport m; (of meeting) compte rendu m; (in media) reportage m; (of pupil) bulletin m; (rumor) rumeur f. **2** vt rapporter; (announce) annoncer (**that** que); (notify) signaler (**to** à); (inform on) dénoncer (**to** à). **3** vi faire un rapport; (of journalist) faire un reportage (**on** sur); (go) se présenter (**to** à; **to sb** chez qn).

re·port card bulletin m (scolaire).

re·port·ed adj (speech) indirect.

re·port·er reporter m.

rep·re·sent vt représenter.

rep·re·sen·ta·tive représentant, -ante mf.

re·pro·duce 1 vt reproduire. **2** vi se reproduire.

re·pro·duc·tion reproduction f.

rep·tile reptile m.

re·pub·lic république f.

rep·u·ta·ble adj de bonne réputation.

rep·u·ta·tion réputation f; **to have a r. for being** avoir la réputation d'être.

re·quest 1 n demande f (**for** de). **2** vt demander (**sth from sb** qch à qn; **sb to do** à qn de faire).

re·quire vt (of thing) demander; (of person) avoir besoin de; **if required** s'il le faut.

re·quired adj **the r. qualities**/etc les qualités/etc qu'il faut.

re·run (on TV, radio) rediffusion f.

res·cue 1 vt (save) sauver; (set free) délivrer (**from** de). **2** n sauvetage m (**of** de); (help) secours m; **to go to sb's r.** aller au secours de qn.

re·search 1 n recherches fpl (**on, into** sur). **2** vi faire des recherches.

re·search·er chercheur, -euse mf.

re·sem·blance ressemblance f (**to** avec).

re·sem·ble vt ressembler à.

re·sent vt (person) en vouloir à; (remark, criticism) ne pas apprécier.

re·sent·ment ressentiment m.

res·er·va·tion (of hotel room etc) réservation f; (doubt) réserve f.

re·serve 1 vt réserver; (right) se réserver. **2** n nature r. réserve f naturelle; **in r.** en réserve.

re·served adj (person, place) réservé.

re·serve tank réservoir m de secours.

res·er·voir réservoir m.

re·side vi to r. in New York résider à New York.

res·i·dence (home) résidence f; (of students) foyer m.

res·i·dent habitant, -ante mf; (of hotel) pensionnaire mf.

res·i·den·tial adj (district) résidentiel.

re·sign 1 vt to r. oneself to sth/to doing se résigner à qch/à faire. **2** vi démissionner; **to r. from one's job** démissionner.

res·ig·na·tion (from job) démission f.

re·sist 1 vt (attack etc) résister à; **to r. doing sth** se retenir de faire qch; **she can't r. cakes** elle ne peut pas résister devant des gâteaux. **2** vi résister.

re·sis·tance résistance f (to à).

re·sort¹ vi to r. to doing en venir à faire; **to r. to sth** avoir recours à qch. **2** n as a last r. en dernier ressort.

re·sort² (vacation) r. station f de vacances; **beach r.** station f balnéaire; **ski r.** station f de ski.

re·sour·ces npl (wealth, means) ressources fpl.

re·spect 1 n respect m (for pour, de); **with r. to** en ce qui concerne. **2** vt respecter.

re·spect·a·ble adj (honorable, quite good) respectable; (clothes, behavior) convenable.

re·spec·tive adj respectif.

re·spond vi répondre (to à); **to r. to treatment** bien réagir au traitement.

re·sponse réponse f.

re·spon·si·bil·i·ty responsabilité f.

re·spon·si·ble adj responsable (for de; to sb devant qn); (job) à responsabilités.

rest¹ 1 n repos m; (support) support m; **to have** or **take a r.** se reposer. **2** vi (relax) se reposer; **to be resting on sth** (of hand etc) être posé sur qch. **3** vt (lean) appuyer (on sur; against contre).

rest² (remaining part) reste m (of de); **the r.** (others) les autres mfpl; **the r. of the men/etc** les autres hommes/etc.

res·tau·rant restaurant m.

rest·ful adj reposant.

rest·less adj agité.

re·store vt (give back) rendre (to à); (building etc) restaurer.

re·strain vt (person, dog) maîtriser; (crowd, anger) contenir; **to r. oneself from doing sth** s'empêcher de faire qch.

re·straint (restriction) restriction f; (moderation) mesure f.

re·strict vt restreindre (to à).

re·strict·ed adj restreint.

re·stric·tion restriction f.

rest·room toilettes fpl.

re·sult résultat m; **as a r. of** par suite de.

re·sume vti reprendre.

ré·su·mé CV m inv

re·tail 1 adj (price, shop) de détail. **2** adv (to sell) au détail.

re·tail·er détaillant, -ante mf.

re·tain vt (freshness etc) conserver.

re·take vt (exam) repasser.

re·tire vi (from work) prendre sa retraite; (withdraw) se retirer (from de; to à); (go to bed) aller se coucher.

re·tired adj (no longer working) retraité.

re·tir·ee retraité, -ée mf.

re·tire·ment retraite f.

re·treat 1 n (withdrawal) retraite f; (shelter) refuge m. 2 vi se retirer; (of army) battre en retraite.

re·trieve vt (recover) récupérer; (of dog) rapporter.

re·turn 1 vi (come back) revenir; (go back) retourner; (go back home) rentrer. 2 vt (give back) rendre; (put back) remettre; (send back) renvoyer. 3 n retour m; (on investment) rendement m; **tax r.** déclaration f de revenus; **in r.** en échange (**for** de). 4 adj (flight etc) (de) retour.

re·turn·a·ble adj (bottle) consigné.

re·veal vt (make known) révéler (**that** que).

rev·e·la·tion révélation f.

re·venge vengeance f; **to get one's r.** se venger (**on sb** de qn; **for sth** de qch); **in r.** pour se venger.

re·verse 1 adj (order) inverse. 2 n contraire m; **in r.** (gear) en marche arrière. 3 vti **to r.** (the car) faire marche arrière; **to r. in/out** rentrer/sortir en marche arrière.

re·vert vi **to r.** to revenir à.

re·view 1 vt (book) faire la critique de. 2 n critique f.

re·vise 1 vt (opinion, notes, text) réviser. 2 vi (for exam) réviser (**for** pour).

re·vi·sion révision f.

re·viv·al (of custom, business, play) reprise f; (of fashion) renouveau m.

re·vive vt (unconscious person) ranimer.

re·volt révolte f.

re·volt·ing adj dégoûtant.

rev·o·lu·tion révolution f.

rev·o·lu·tion·ar·y adj & n révolutionnaire (mf).

re·volve vi tourner (**around** autour de).

re·volv·er revolver m.

re·volv·ing door(s) (porte f à) tambour m.

re·ward 1 n récompense f (**for** de, pour). 2 vt récompenser (**sb for sth** qn de or pour qch).

re·wind* 1 vt (tape) rembobiner. 2 vi se rembobiner.

rhet·o·ric rhétorique f.

rheu·ma·tism rhumatisme m; **to have r.** avoir des rhumatismes.

rhi·noc·er·os rhinocéros m.

rhu·barb rhubarbe f.

rhyme 1 n rime f, (poem) vers mpl. 2 vi rimer (**with** avec).

rhythm rythme m.

rhyth·mi·cal adj rythmé.

rib (in body) côte f.

rib·bon ruban m.

rice riz m.

rich 1 adj riche. 2 npl **the r.** les riches mpl.

rich·es npl richesses fpl.

rid adj **to get r. of** se débarrasser de.

rid·dle (puzzle) énigme f.

ride 1 n (on bicycle, by car, on horse etc) promenade f; (distance) trajet m; **to go for a r.** (in car) faire une promenade (en voiture); **to give sb a r.** (in car) emmener qn en voiture. 2 vi* aller (à bicyclette/à moto/à cheval/etc (**to** à); **to r., to go riding** (on horse) monter (à cheval). 3 vt (a particular horse) monter; (distance) faire (à cheval etc); **to r. a horse** or **horses** monter à cheval; I was riding a bicycle j'étais à bicyclette; **to r. a bicycle to** aller à bicyclette à.

rid·er (on horse) cavalier, -ière mf.

ridge crête f, (of roof) faîte m.

ri·dic·u·lous adj ridicule.

rid·ing (horseback) **r.** équitation f.

ri·fle fusil m.

rig (oil) **r.** derrick m; (at sea) plateforme f pétrolière.

right¹ 1 adj (correct) bon (f bonne); (fair) juste; (angle) droit; **to be r.** (of *person*) avoir raison (**to do de** faire); **the r. choice/time** le bon choix/moment; **it's the r. time** (*accurate*) c'est l'heure exacte; **the clock's r.** la pendule est à l'heure; **it's not r. to steal** ce n'est pas bien de voler; **to put r.** (*error*) corriger; **r.!** bien!; **that's r.** c'est ça. **2** *adv* (*straight*) (tout) droit; (*completely*) tout à fait; (*correctly*) juste; (*well*) bien; **she did r.** elle a bien fait; **r. here** ici même; **r. away, r. now** tout de suite. **3** *n* **r. and wrong** le bien et le mal.

right² **1** *adj* (*hand, side etc*) droit. **2** *adv* à droite. **3** *n* droite *f*; **on** *or* **to the r.** à droite (**of** de).

right³ (*claim*) droit *m* (**to do de** faire); **to have a r. to sth** avoir droit à qch.

right-hand *adj* à *or* de droite; **on the r. side** à droite (**of** de).

right-hand·ed *adj* (*person*) droitier.

right·ly *adv* à juste titre.

rig·id *adj* rigide.

rim (*of cup etc*) bord *m*.

rind (*of cheese*) croûte *f*.

ring¹ (*on finger, curtain etc*) anneau *m*; (*with jewel*) bague *f*; (*of people, chairs*) cercle *m*; *Boxing* ring *m*; **diamond r.** bague *f* de diamants; **to make a r. around** entourer (**with** de).

ring² **1** *n* (*sound*) sonnerie *f*; **to give sb a r.** (*phone call*) passer un coup de fil à qn. **2** *vi** (*of bell, phone, person*) sonner. **3** *vt* sonner; **to r. the (door)bell** sonner (à la porte).

ring-lead·er meneur, -euse *mf*.

▸ **ring out** *vi* (*of bell*) sonner; (*of sound*) retentir.

rinse **1** *vt* rincer; **to r. one's hands** se rincer les mains. **2** *n* **to give sth a r.** rincer qch.

▸ **rinse out** *vt* rincer.

ri·ot **1** *n* (*uprising*) émeute *f*; (*fight*) bagarre *f*. **2** *vi* faire une émeute; (*fight*) se bagarrer.

rip **1** *vt* déchirer. **2** *vi* (*of fabric*) se déchirer. **3** *n* déchirure *f*.

ripe *adj* mûr; (*cheese*) fait.

rip·en *vti* mûrir.

▸ **rip off** *vt* (*button etc*) arracher (**from** de); **to r. sb off** *Fam* rouler qn.

rip-off *Fam* **it's a r.** c'est du vol organisé.

▸ **rip out** *vt* arracher (**from** de).

▸ **rip up** *vt* déchirer.

rise **1** *vi** (*of temperature, balloon, price*) monter; (*of sun, curtain, person*) se lever; **to r. in price** augmenter de prix. **2** *n* (*in price etc*) hausse *f* (**in** de); (*slope in ground*) montée *f*; **to give r. to sth** donner lieu à qch.

ris·ing **1** *adj* (*sun*) levant; (*prices*) en hausse. **2** *n* (*of sun*) lever *m*; (*of prices*) hausse *f*.

risk **1** *n* risque *m* (**of doing** de faire; **in doing** à faire); **at r.** (*person*) en danger; (*job*) menacé. **2** *vt* risquer; **she won't r. leaving** elle ne se risquera pas à partir.

risk·y *adj* risqué.

rit·u·al *adj & n* rituel (*m*).

ri·val **1** *adj* (*company etc*) rival. **2** *n* rival, -ale *mf*. **3** *vt* (*compete with*) rivaliser avec (**in** de); (*equal*) égaler (**in** en).

riv·er rivière *f*; (*flowing into sea*) fleuve *m*.

Riv·i·er·a **the (French) R.** la Côte d'Azur.

roach (*cockroach*) cafard *m*.

road **1** *n* route *f* (**to** qui va à); (*small*) chemin *m*; (*in town*) rue *f*; (*roadway*) chaussée *f*; **across the r.** (*building etc*) en face; **by r.** par la route. **2** *adj* (*map, safety*) routier; (*accident*) de la route; **r. sign** panneau *m* (routier).

road·side bord *m* de la route; **r. bar/hotel/**etc bar *m*/ hôtel *m*/etc situé au bord de la route.

road·way chaussée *f*.

road·work travaux *mpl*.

roam *vt* parcourir; **to r. the streets**

(of child, dog etc) traîner dans les rues.

roar 1 *vi (of lion)* rugir; *(of person)* hurler. **2** *n (of lion)* rugissement *m.*

roast 1 *vt* rôtir; *(coffee)* griller. **2** *vi (of meat)* rôtir. **3** *n (meat)* rôti *m.* **4** *adj (chicken etc)* rôti; **r. beef** rosbif *m.*

rob *vt (person)* voler; *(bank)* attaquer; *(by breaking in)* cambrioler; **to r. sb of sth** voler qch à qn.

rob·ber voleur, -euse *mf.*

rob·ber·y vol *m.*

robe *(bathrobe)* robe *f* de chambre.

rob·in rouge-gorge *m.*

ro·bot robot *m.*

rock¹ *vt (baby, boat)* bercer. **2** *vi (sway)* se balancer; *(of building)* trembler. **3** *n (music)* rock *m.*

rock² *(substance)* roche *f*, *(boulder, rock face)* rocher *m*; *(stone)* pierre *f*; **r. face** paroi *f* rocheuse.

rock·et fusée *f.*

rock·ing chair fauteuil *m* à bascule.

rod *(wooden)* baguette *f*; *(metal)* tige *f*, *(of curtain)* tringle *f*; *(for fishing)* canne *f* (à pêche).

rogue *(dishonest)* crapule *f*, *(mischievous)* coquin, -ine *mf.*

role rôle *m.*

roll 1 *n (of paper etc)* rouleau *m*; *(small bread loaf)* petit pain *m*; *(of drum)* roulement *m*; *(attendance list)* cahier *m* d'appel; **to call** *or* **take the r.** faire l'appel. **2** *vi (of ball etc)* rouler; *(of person, animal)* se rouler. **3** *vt* rouler.

▸**roll down** *vt (car window etc)* baisser; *(slope)* descendre (en roulant).

roll·er *(for hair, painting etc)* rouleau *m.*

roll·er-skate 1 *n* patin *m* à roulettes. **2** *vi* faire du patin à roulettes.

roll·ing pin rouleau *m* à pâtisserie.

▸**roll over 1** *vi (many times)* se rouler; *(once)* se retourner. **2** *vt* retourner.

▸**roll up** *vt (map, cloth)* rouler; *(sleeve, pants)* retrousser.

Ro·man 1 *n* Romain, -aine *mf.* **2** *adj* romain, -aine.

Ro·man Cath·o·lic *adj & n* catholique *(mf).*

ro·mance *(love)* amour *m*; *(affair)* aventure *f* amoureuse.

ro·man·tic *adj* romantique.

roof toit *m*; *(of tunnel, cave)* plafond *m.*

roof rack *(of car)* galerie *f.*

room *(in house etc)* pièce *f*, *(bedroom)* chambre *f*, *(large, public)* salle *f*, *(space)* place *f* (**for** pour); **men's r., ladies' r.** toilettes *fpl.*

room·mate colocataire *mf.*

room·y *adj* spacieux; *(clothes)* ample.

root racine *f*, *(origin)* origine *f*; **to take r.** *(of plant)* prendre racine.

▸**root for** *vt Fam* encourager.

rope corde *f.*

▸**rope off** *vt (of police etc)* interdire l'accès de.

rose *(flower)* rose *f*, **r. bush** rosier *m.*

ro·ta·tion rotation *f.*

rot (a·way) *vti* pourrir.

rot·ten *adj (fruit, weather etc)* pourri; *(bad) Fam* moche; **to feel r.** *(ill)* être mal fichu.

rough¹ *adj (surface, plank)* rugueux; *(ground)* inégal; *(brutal)* brutal; *(sea)* agité.

rough² *adj (calculation etc)* approximatif; **r. guess** approximation *f*, **r. draft** brouillon *m.*

rough·ly¹ *adv (not gently)* rudement; *(brutally)* brutalement.

rough·ly² *adv (more or less)* à peu (de choses) près.

round 1 *adj* rond. **2** *n Boxing* round *m*; *(of drinks, visits)* tournée *f*, *(of policeman)* ronde *f.*

round·a·bout *adj* indirect.

▸**round off** vt (meal etc) terminer (with par); (figure) arrondir.
round trip aller (et) retour m.
▸**round up** vt (people, animals) rassembler.
route itinéraire m; (of ship, aircraft) route f; bus r. ligne f d'autobus.
rou·tine routine f.
row[1] n (line) rang m, rangée f; (one behind another) file f; **two days in a r.** deux jours de suite. 2 vi (in boat) ramer. 3 vt (boat) faire aller à la rame.
row[2] 1 n Fam (noise) vacarme m; (quarrel) dispute f. 2 vi Fam se disputer (with avec).
row·boat bateau m à rames.
row house maison f attenante aux maisons voisines.
roy·al adj royal.
roy·al·ty personnages mpl royaux.
rub vti frotter; (person) frictionner.
rub·ber caoutchouc m; (eraser) gomme f.
rub·ber band élastique m.
rub·ber boots bottes fpl de caoutchouc.
rub·ber stamp tampon m.
rub·ble décombres mpl.
▸**rub down** vt (person) frictionner; (wall, door) poncer.
▸**rub in** vt (cream) faire pénétrer (en massant).
▸**rub off** or **out** vt (mark) effacer.
ru·by rubis m.
ruck·sack sac m à dos.
rud·der gouvernail m.
rude adj impoli (to envers); (coarse, insolent) grossier (to envers).
rude·ness impolitesse f; (coarseness, insolence) grossièreté f.
rug carpette f.
rug·by rugby m.
ru·in 1 n ruine f; **in ruins** (building) en ruine. 2 vt (health, person etc) ruiner; (clothes) abîmer.
rule 1 n règle f; **against the rules**

contraire au règlement; **as a r.** en règle générale; (of country) gouverner. 3 vi (of king etc) régner (over sur).
▸**rule out** vt exclure.
rul·er (for measuring) règle f; (king, queen etc) souverain, -aine mf.
rul·ing 1 adj (party) au pouvoir; (monarch) régnant; (class) dirigeant. 2 n décision f.
rum rhum m.
rum·mage sale vente f de charité.
ru·mor bruit m, rumeur f.
run 1 n (period) période f; (for skiing) piste f; **to go for a r.** (aller) faire une course à pied; **on the r.** (prisoner) en fuite; **in the long r.** à la longue. 2 vi* courir; (of river, nose, faucet) couler; (of color in laundry) déteindre; (of play, movie) se jouer; (function) marcher; (of car engine) tourner; **to r. down/in/etc** descendre/entrer/etc en courant; **to go running** faire du jogging. 3 vt (race, risk) courir; (temperature, errand) faire; (business, country etc) diriger; (bath) faire couler.
▸**run across** vt (meet) tomber sur.
▸**run along** vi filer.
▸**run away** vi s'enfuir (from de).
▸**run down** vt (pedestrian) renverser.
rung (of ladder) barreau m.
▸**run into** vt (meet) tomber sur; (crash into) percuter.
run·ner (athlete) coureur m.
run·ner-up second, -onde mf.
run·ning 1 n (on foot) course f. 2 adj r. **water** eau f courante; **six days/etc r.** six jours/etc de suite.
run·ny adj (nose) qui coule.
▸**run off** vi (flee) s'enfuir.
▸**run out** vi (of inventory) s'épuiser; (of lease) expirer; **to r. out of** (time, money) manquer de; **we've r. out of coffee** on n'a plus de café.
▸**run over** vt (kill pedestrian) écra-

ser; *(knock down pedestrian)* renverser.

run·way piste *f* (d'envol).

rush 1 *vi* se précipiter (**at** sur; **towards** vers); *(hurry)* se dépêcher (**to do** de faire). **2** *vt (hurry)* bousculer (*qn*); **to r. sb to the hospital** transporter qn d'urgence à l'hôpital; **to r. (through) sth** *(job, meal etc)* faire/manger/*etc* qch en vitesse. **3** *n* ruée *f* (**for** vers); *(confusion)* bousculade *f*; *(hurry)* hâte *f*, **in a r.** pressé (**to do** de faire).

rush hour heure *f* de pointe.

▸**rush out** *vi* partir en vitesse.

Russian 1 *adj* russe. **2** *n* Russe *mf*; *(language)* russe *m*.

rust 1 *n* rouille *f*. **2** *vi* (se) rouiller.

rust·y *adj (metal, memory etc)* rouillé.

RV *abbr (recreational vehicle)* camping-car *m*.

rye bread pain *m* de seigle.

S

sack 1 *n (bag)* sac *m*; **to get the s.** *(from one's job)* se faire virer; **to give sb the s.** virer qn. **2** *vt (dismiss)* virer.

sa·cred *adj* sacré.

sac·ri·fice 1 *n* sacrifice *m*. **2** *vt* sacrifier (**to** à; **for** pour).

sad *adj* triste.

sad·den *vt* attrister.

sad·dle selle *f*.

sad·ly *adv* tristement; *(unfortunately)* malheureusement.

sad·ness tristesse *f*.

safe¹ *adj (person)* en sécurité; *(equipment, toy, animal)* sans danger; *(place, investment, method)* sûr; *(bridge, ladder)* solide; **s. (and sound)** sain et sauf; **it's s. to go**

out on peut sortir sans danger; **s. from** à l'abri de.

safe² *(for money etc)* coffre-fort *m*.

safe·guard 1 *n* sauvegarde *f*. **2** *vt* sauvegarder.

safe·ly *adv (without accident)* sans accident; *(without risk)* sans risque; *(in a safe place)* en lieu sûr.

safe·ty sécurité *f*.

safe·ty pin épingle *f* de sûreté.

sag *vi (of roof, ground)* s'affaisser.

sail 1 *vi* naviguer; *(leave)* partir; *(as sport)* faire de la voile; **to s. around the world/an island** faire le tour du monde/d'une île en bateau. **2** *vt (boat)* piloter. **3** *n* voile *f*.

sail·board planche *f* (à voile).

sail·boat voilier *m*.

sail·ing navigation *f*; *(sport)* voile *f*; *(departure)* départ *m*.

sail·or marin *m*.

saint saint *m*, sainte *f*.

sake for my/your/his/*etc* **s.** pour moi/toi/lui/*etc*; **(just) for the s. of eating/***etc* simplement pour manger/*etc*.

sal·ad salade *f*.

sal·ad bowl saladier *m*.

sal·ad dress·ing sauce *f* pour salade.

sal·a·ry *(professional)* salaire *m*, traitement *m*; *(wage)* salaire *m*.

sale vente *f*, **sale(s)** *(at reduced prices)* soldes *mpl*; **on s.** *(cheaply)* en solde; *(available)* en vente; **(up) for s.** à vendre.

sales·clerk vendeur, -euse *mf*.

sales·man, *pl* -men *(in store)* vendeur *m*; **(traveling) s.** représentant *m* (de commerce).

sales tax = TVA *f*.

sales·wom·an, *pl* -women vendeuse *f*, *(who travels)* représentante *f* (de commerce).

sa·li·va salive *f*.

salm·on saumon *m*.

sa·lon salon *m*.

salt 1 *n* sel *m*; **bath salts** sels *mpl* de bain. **2** *vt* saler.

salt·cel·lar, salt·sha·ker salière f.

salt·y adj salé.

sal·va·tion salut m; **S. Army** Armée f du salut.

same 1 adj même; **the (very) s. house as** (exactement) la même maison que. **2** pron **the s.** le or la même, (pl) les mêmes; **it's all the s. to me** ça m'est égal; **all** or **just the s.** tout de même; **to do the s.** en faire autant.

sam·ple 1 n échantillon m; (of blood) prélèvement m. **2** vt (wine etc) goûter.

sand 1 n sable m. **2** vt (road) sabler.

san·dal sandale f.

sand·cas·tle château m de sable.

sand·pa·per papier m de verre.

sand·wich sandwich m; **cheese/** etc **s.** sandwich au fromage/etc; **s. shop** sandwicherie f.

sand·y adj (beach) de sable; (road) sablonneux.

san·i·tar·y nap·kin serviette f hygiénique.

San·ta Claus le père Noël.

sar·dine sardine f.

sat pt & pp de **sit**.

satch·el cartable m.

sat·el·lite satellite m.

sat·in satin m.

sat·is·fac·tion satisfaction f.

sat·is·fac·to·ry adj satisfaisant.

sat·is·fy vt satisfaire (qn); **to s. oneself that** s'assurer que; **satisfied (with)** satisfait (de).

sat·is·fy·ing adj satisfaisant.

sat·su·ma (fruit) mandarine f, satsuma f.

sat·u·rate vt (soak) tremper.

Sat·ur·day samedi m.

sauce sauce f; (stewed fruit) compote f; **tomato s.** sauce f tomate.

sauce·pan casserole f.

sau·cer soucoupe f.

sau·na sauna m.

sau·sage saucisse f; (dried, for slicing) saucisson m.

save 1 vt (rescue) sauver (**from** de); (keep) garder; (money, time) économiser; (stamps) collectionner; **to s. sb from doing** empêcher qn de faire; **that will s. him the trouble of going** ça lui évitera d'y aller. **2** n Sports arrêt m.

▶ **save up 1** vt (money) économiser. **2** vi faire des économies (**for sth, to buy sth** pour acheter qch).

sav·ings npl (money) économies fpl.

sav·ings and loan = société f de crédit immobilier.

sav·ings bank caisse f d'épargne.

saw¹ n scie f. **2** vt* scier.

saw² pt de **see**.

saw·dust sciure f.

▶ **saw off** vt scier.

sax·o·phone saxophone m.

say* vt dire (**to** à; **that** que); (of dial etc) marquer; **to s. again** répéter; **(let's) s. tomorrow** disons demain; **that is to s.** c'est-à-dire.

say·ing proverbe m.

scab (of wound) croûte f.

scaf·fold·ing échafaudage m.

scald vt ébouillanter.

scale (of map, wages etc) échelle f; (on fish) écaille f, (in music) gamme f.

scales npl (for weighing) balance f; (bathroom) **s.** pèse-personne m.

scal·lion oignon m vert.

scan 1 vt (text, graphics) passer au scanner; (scrutinize) scruter; (glance at) parcourir. **2** n échographie f; **to have a s.** passer une échographie.

scan·dal scandale m; (gossip) médisances fpl.

Scan·di·na·vi·an 1 n Scandinave mf. **2** adj scandinave.

scan·ner scanner m.

scar cicatrice f.

scarce adj rare.

scarce·ly adv à peine.

scare vt faire peur à.

scare·crow épouvantail m.

scared adj effrayé; **to be s. (stiff)** avoir (très) peur.

scarf, pl **scarves** (long) écharpe f; (square, for women) foulard m.

scar·let fe·ver scarlatine f.

scar·y adj it's s. ça fait peur.

scat·ter 1 vt (crowd, clouds etc) disperser; (throw around) éparpiller (papiers etc). **2** vi (of crowd) se disperser.

sce·nar·i·o scénario m.

scene (setting, fuss, part of play or movie) scène f; (of crime, accident) lieu m; (view) vue f.

scen·er·y paysage m; (for play or movie) décor(s) m(pl).

scent (fragrance, perfume) parfum m.

sched·ule 1 n (of work etc) programme m; (timetable) horaire m; **on s.** (on time) à l'heure; **according to s.** comme prévu. **2** vt (to plan) prévoir; (event) fixer le programme de.

sched·uled adj (planned) prévu; (service, flight) régulier.

scheme plan m (**to do** pour faire); (dishonest trick) combine f.

schmuck Fam andouille f.

schol·ar (learned person) érudit, -ite mf.

schol·ar·ship (grant) bourse f (d'études).

school 1 n école f; (teaching, lessons) classe f; **in** or **at s.** à l'école; **public s.** école f publique; **summer s.** cours mpl d'été. **2** adj (year etc) scolaire.

school·boy écolier m.

school·girl écolière f.

school·teach·er (primary) instituteur, -trice mf; (secondary) professeur m.

sci·ence science f; **to study s.** étudier les sciences.

sci·ence fic·tion science-fiction f.

sci·en·tif·ic adj scientifique.

sci·en·tist scientifique mf, savant m.

scis·sors npl ciseaux mpl.

scold vt gronder (**for doing** pour avoir fait).

scone petit pain m au lait.

scoot·er (child's) trottinette f; (motorcycle) scooter m.

scope (range) étendue f, (limits) limites fpl; **s. for sth/for doing** (opportunity) des possibilités fpl de qch/de faire.

scorch vt roussir.

score¹ 1 n (in sports) score m; (at cards) marque f; (music) partition f. **2** vt (point, goal) marquer. **3** vi (point) marquer un point; (goal) marquer un but; (count points) marquer les points.

score² a s. (of) une vingtaine (de).

scorn mépris m.

Scot Écossais, -aise mf.

Scotch (whisky) scotch m.

scotch (tape)® Scotch® m.

Scots·man, pl **-men** Écossais m.

Scots·wom·an, pl **-women** Écossaise f.

Scot·tish adj écossais.

scoun·drel vaurien m.

scout (boy) s. scout m; **girl s.** éclaireuse f.

scram·ble 1 vi **to s. up a hill** gravir une colline en s'aidant des mains. **2** vt (message) brouiller; **scrambled eggs** œufs mpl brouillés. **3** n (rush) bousculade f.

scrap 1 n petit morceau m (**of** de); (of information) fragment m; (metal) ferraille f, **scraps** (food) restes mpl. **2** vt se débarrasser de; (vehicle) mettre à la ferraille; (plan) abandonner.

scrap·book album m (pour collages etc).

scrape 1 vt racler; (skin, knee etc) érafler. **2** vi **to s. against sth** frotter contre qch. **3** n (on skin) éraflure f.

▶**scrape away** or **off** vt (mud etc) racler.

▶**scrape through** vi (in exam) réussir de justesse.

▶**scrape together** vt (money, people) réunir (difficilement).

scrap met·al ferraille f.

scrap pa·per (papier m) brouillon m.

scratch 1 n (mark, injury) éraflure f, **to start from s.** (re)partir de zéro; **it isn't up to s.** ce n'est pas au niveau. **2** vt (arm etc that itches) gratter; (skin, furniture etc) érafler; (one's name) (**on** sur). **3** vi (relieve an itch) se gratter.

scratch pa·per (for draft) (papier m) brouillon m.

scream 1 vti crier; **to s. at sb** crier après qn. **2** n cri m (perçant).

screen écran m; (folding) **s.** paravent m.

screw 1 n vis f. **2** vt visser (**to** à).

screw an·chor cheville f.

▶**screw down** vt visser.

screw·driv·er tournevis m.

▶**screw on** vt visser.

scrib·ble vti griffonner.

script (of movie) scénario m; (of play) texte m.

scrub vt nettoyer (à la brosse); (pan) récurer.

scrub brush brosse f dure.

scu·ba div·ing plongée f sous-marine.

sculp·tor sculpteur m.

sculp·ture (art, object) sculpture f.

scum (on liquid) écume f, Fam (people) racaille f.

sea mer f, (**out**) **at s.** en mer; **by s.** par mer; **by** or **beside the sea** au bord de la mer.

sea·food fruits mpl de mer.

sea·front bord m or front m de mer.

sea·gull mouette f.

seal 1 n (animal) phoque m; (mark, design) sceau m; (of wax) cachet m (de cire). **2** vt (document, container) sceller; (envelope) cacheter; (with putty) boucher.

sea li·on otarie f.

▶**seal off** vt (of police etc) interdire l'accès de.

seam (in cloth) couture f.

search 1 n recherche f (**for** de); (of person, place) fouille f, **in s. of** à la recherche de. **2** vt (person, place) fouiller (**for** pour trouver); **to s. (through) one's papers/etc** chercher qch dans ses papiers/etc. **3** vi chercher; **to s. for sth** chercher qch.

sea·shell coquillage m.

sea·shore bord m de la mer.

sea·sick adj **to be s.** avoir le mal de mer.

sea·sick·ness mal m de mer.

sea·side bord m de la mer.

sea·son 1 n saison f. **2** vt (food) assaisonner.

sea·son·al adj saisonnier.

sea·son·ing assaisonnement m.

sea·son tick·et abonnement m.

seat 1 n siège m; (on train, bus) banquette f, (in theater) fauteuil m; (place) place f, **to take** or **have a s.** s'asseoir. **2** vt (at table) placer (qn); **the room seats 50** la salle a 50 places (assises); **be seated!** asseyez-vous!

seat belt ceinture f de sécurité.

seat·ed adj (sitting) assis.

seat·ing (seats) places fpl assises.

sea·weed algue(s) f(pl).

sec·ond¹ adj deuxième, second; **every s. week** une semaine sur deux; **in s. (gear)** en second. **2** adv **to come s.** se classer deuxième. **3** n (person, object) deuxième mf, second, -onde mf.

sec·ond² (part of minute) seconde f.

sec·ond·ar·y adj secondaire.

sec·ond-class adj (ticket) de seconde (classe); (mail) non urgent.

sec·ond·hand adj & adv (not new) d'occasion.

sec·ond·ly adv deuxièmement.

se·cret adj & n secret (m); **in s.** en secret.

sec·re·tar·y secrétaire *mf; (cabinet official)* ministre *m*; **S. of State** Ministre des Affaires étrangères.

se·cret·ly *adv* en secret, secrètement.

sec·tion *(of town, book etc)* partie *f; (of machine, furniture)* élément *m; (in store)* rayon *m*; **the sports/etc s.** *(of newspaper)* la page des sports/etc.

sec·u·lar *adj (music, art)* profane; *(education, school)* laïque.

se·cure 1 *adj (person, valuables)* en sûreté; *(place)* sûr; *(solid)* solide; *(door, window)* bien fermé. **2** *vt (fasten)* attacher; *(window etc)* bien fermer.

se·cure·ly *adv (firmly)* solidement; *(safely)* en sûreté.

se·cu·ri·ty sécurité *f; (for loan)* caution *f.*

se·dan berline *f.*

se·da·tion under **s.** sous calmants.

sed·a·tive calmant *m.*

see* *vti* voir; **we'll s.** on verra (bien); **I saw him run(ning)** je l'ai vu courir; **s. you (later)!** à tout à l'heure!; **s. you (soon)!** à bientôt!; **to s. that** *(take care that)* veiller à ce que (+ *subjunctive*); *(check)* s'assurer que.

▸ **see about** *vt* s'occuper de; *(consider)* songer à.

seed graine *f; (in grape)* pépin *m.*

see·ing *conj* **s. (that)** vu que.

seek* *vt* chercher (**to do** à faire); *(ask for)* demander (**from** à).

seem *vi* sembler (**to do** faire); **it seems that** *(impression)* il semble que (+ *subjunctive or indicative*); *(rumor)* il paraît que (+ *indicative*); **it seems to me that** il me semble que (+ *indicative*).

seem·ing·ly *adv* apparemment.

▸ **see off** *vt* accompagner *(qn).*

▸ **see out** *vt* raccompagner *(qn).*

see·saw *(jeu m de)* bascule *f.*

▸ **see through** *vt* **to s. sth through** *(carry out)* mener qch à bien; **to s.**

through sb voir dans le jeu de qn; **$20 should s. me through** 20 dollars devraient me suffire.

▸ **see to** *vt (deal with)* s'occuper de; *(mend)* réparer; **to see to it that** veiller à ce que (+ *subjunctive*); *(check)* s'assurer que.

seg·ment segment *m; (of orange)* quartier *m.*

seize *vt* saisir; *(power, land)* s'emparer de.

sel·dom *adv* rarement.

se·lect *vt* choisir (**from** parmi); *(candidates, players etc)* sélectionner.

se·lec·tion sélection *f.*

se·lec·tive *adj* sélectif.

self-as·sur·ance assurance *f.*

self-as·sured *adj* sûr de soi.

self-con·fi·dence assurance *f.*

self-con·fi·dent *adj* sûr de soi.

self-con·scious *adj* gêné.

self-con·trol maîtrise *f* de soi.

self-de·fense légitime défense *f.*

self-em·ployed *adj* qui travaille à son compte.

self-ev·i·dent *adj* évident.

self·ish *adj* égoïste.

self-re·spect amour-propre *m.*

self-righ·teous *adj* suffisant.

self-serv·ice *n & adj* libre-service *(m inv).*

sell* 1 *vt* vendre; **to have or be sold out of sth** n'avoir plus de qch. **2** *vi (of product)* se vendre.

sell·er vendeur, -euse *mf.*

se·mes·ter semestre *m.*

sem·i- *prefix* demi-, semi-.

sem·i·cir·cle demi-cercle *m.*

sem·i·co·lon point-virgule *m.*

sem·i·de·tached house maison *f* jumelle.

sem·i·fi·nal demi-finale *f.*

sem·i·nar séminaire *m.*

sem·i·trail·er semi-remorque *m.*

sem·o·li·na semoule *f.*

sen·a·tor sénateur *m.*

send* *vt* envoyer (**to** à); **to s. sb for sth/sb** envoyer qn chercher qch/qn.

▶**send away** or **off 1** vt envoyer (**to**
à); (dismiss) renvoyer. **2** vi **to s.**
away or **off for sth** commander
qch (par courrier).
▶**send back** vt renvoyer.
send·er expéditeur, -trice mf.
▶**send for** vt (doctor etc) faire venir;
(by mail) commander (par cour-
rier).
▶**send in** vt (form etc) envoyer; (person) faire entrer.
▶**send on** vt (letter, luggage) faire
suivre.
▶**send out** vt (invitation etc) envoyer; (from room etc) faire sortir
(qn); **to s. out for** (meal) envoyer
chercher.
▶**send up** vt (luggage) faire monter.
sen·ior 1 adj (older) plus âgé; (position, rank) supérieur. **2** n aîné, -ée
mf; (in school) grand m, grande f,
étudiant, -ante mf de dernière
année.
sen·ior high (school) = lycée
m.
sen·sa·tion sensation f.
sen·sa·tion·al adj (terrific) Fam
sensationnel.
sense 1 n (meaning) sens m; **s. of**
smell odorat m; **a s. of** (shame etc)
un sentiment de; **to have a s. of hu-**
mor avoir de l'humour; **to have**
(good) s. avoir du bon sens; **to have**
the s. to do avoir l'intelligence de
faire; **to make s.** (of story) avoir un
sens, tenir debout. **2** vt sentir (intui-
tivement) (**that** que).
sense·less adj (stupid) insensé.
sen·si·ble adj (wise) raisonnable.
sen·si·tive adj sensible (**to** à);
(skin) délicat; (touchy) susceptible
(**about** à propos de).
sen·tence 1 n Grammar phrase f;
(punishment, in prison) peine f. **2**
vt **to s. sb to 3 years (in prison)**
condamner qn à 3 ans de prison.
sen·ti·ment sentiment m.
sen·ti·ment·al adj sentimental.
sep·a·rate 1 adj (distinct) séparé;

(independent) indépendant; (different) différent. **2** vt séparer (**from**
de). **3** vi se séparer (**from** de).
sep·a·rate·ly adv séparément.
sep·a·ra·tion séparation f.
Sep·tem·ber septembre m.
se·quence (order) ordre m; (series) succession f.
se·quin paillette f.
ser·geant sergent m; (in police
force) brigadier m.
se·ri·al (story, film) feuilleton m.
se·ries inv série f.
se·ri·ous adj sérieux; (illness, mistake) grave.
se·ri·ous·ly adv sérieusement;
(ill) gravement; **to take s.** prendre
au sérieux.
ser·vant (in house etc) domestique mf.
serve vt servir (**to sb** à qn; **sb with**
sth qch à qn); (of train, bus etc) desservir (un village etc); (it) **serves**
you right! ça t'apprendra!
▶**serve out** or **up** vt (meal etc) servir.
serv·ice 1 n service m; (machine or
vehicle repair) révision f; **s. charge**
(in restaurant) service m. **2** vt (machine, vehicle) réviser.
ser·vice ar·e·a (on highway) aire
f de service.
ser·vice sta·tion station-service
f.
ses·sion séance f.
set 1 n (of keys, tools etc) jeu m; (of
stamps, numbers) série f; (of people) groupe m; (in mathematics) ensemble m; (of books) collection f;
(scenery) décor m; (hairstyle) mise
f en plis; Tennis set m; chess **s.** jeu
m d'échecs. **2** adj (time, price etc)
fixe; **the s. menu** le plat du jour; **s.**
on doing résolu à faire; **to be s. on**
sth vouloir qch à tout prix; **all s.**
(ready) prêt (**to do** pour faire). **3**
vt* (put) mettre; (date, limit etc) fixer; (record) établir; (mechanism,
clock) régler; (alarm clock) mettre

(*for* pour); (*arm etc in plaster*) plâtrer; (*task*) donner (*for sb* à qn); (*trap*) tendre; **to have one's hair s.** se faire faire une mise en plis. **4** *vi* (*of sun*) se coucher; (*of jelly*) prendre.

▸ **set about** *vt* **to s. about sth/ about doing** (*begin*) se mettre à qch/à faire.

▸ **set back** *vt* (*clock*) retarder.
  set·back revers *m*.

▸ **set down** *vt* (*object*) déposer.

▸ **set forward** *vt* (*clock*) avancer.

▸ **set off 1** *vt* (*bomb*) faire exploser; (*mechanism*) déclencher. **2** *vi* (*leave*) partir.

▸ **set out 1** *vt* (*display, explain*) exposer (**to** à); (*arrange*) disposer. **2** *vi* (*leave*) partir; **to s. out to do** entreprendre de faire.
  set·tee canapé *m*.
  set·ting (*surroundings*) cadre *m*.

▸ **set·tle 1** *vt* (*decide, arrange, pay*) régler; (*date*) fixer; **that's (all) settled** c'est décidé. **2** *vi* (*live*) s'installer.

▸ **settle down** *vi* (*in chair or house*) s'installer; (*calm down*) se calmer; (*in one's lifestyle*) se ranger.
  set·tle·ment (*agreement*) accord *m*.
  set·tler colon *m*.

▸ **settle (up) with** *vt* (*pay*) régler.

▸ **set up 1** *vt* (*tent*) dresser; (*business*) créer. **2** *vi* **to s. up shop** monter une affaire.
  sev·en *adj & n* sept (*m*).
  sev·en·teen *adj & n* dix-sept (*m*).
  sev·enth *adj & n* septième (*mf*).
  sev·en·ti·eth *adj & n* soixante-dixième (*mf*).
  sev·en·ty *adj & n* soixante-dix (*m*); **s.-one** soixante et onze.
  sev·er·al *adj & pron* plusieurs (**of** d'entre).
  se·vere *adj* (*tone etc*) sévère; (*winter*) rigoureux; (*test*) dur.
  sew* *vti* coudre.
  sew·er égout *m*.

  sew·ing couture *f*.
  sew·ing ma·chine machine *f* à coudre.

▸ **sew on** *vt* (*button*) (re)coudre.

▸ **sew up** *vt* (*tear*) (re)coudre.
  sex 1 *n* sexe *m*; (*activity*) relations *fpl* sexuelles; **to have s. with sb** coucher avec qn. **2** *adj* (*education, life etc*) sexuel.
  sex·u·al *adj* sexuel.
  sex·y *adj* sexy *inv*.
  sh! *int* chut!
  shab·by *adj* (*room etc*) minable.
  shade ombre *f*; (*of colour*) ton *m*; (*of lamp*) abat-jour *m inv*; (*window*) store *m*; **in the s.** à l'ombre.
  shad·ow ombre *f*.
  shad·y *adj* (*place*) ombragé.
  shaft (*of tool*) manche *m*; (*in mine*) puits *m*; (*of elevator*) cage *f*; (*of light*) rayon *m*.
  shake 1 *vt* secouer; (*bottle*) agiter; (*upset*) bouleverser; **to s. one's head** (*say no*) secouer la tête; **to s. hands with sb** serrer la main à qn; **we shook hands** nous nous sommes serré la main. **2** *vi* trembler (**with** de).
  shall *v aux* (*future*) **I s. come, I'll come** je viendrai; **we s. not come, we shan't come** nous ne viendrons pas. ▪ (*question*) **s. I leave?** veux-tu que je parte?; **s. we leave?** on part?
  shal·low *adj* (*water, river etc*) peu profond.
  shame (*feeling, disgrace*) honte *f*; **it's a s.** c'est dommage (**to do** de faire); **it's a s. (that)** c'est dommage que (+ *subjunctive*); **what a s.!** (quel) dommage!
  shame·ful *adj* honteux.
  sham·poo 1 *n* shampooing *m*. **2** *vt* **to s. sb's hair** faire un shampooing à qn.
  shan't = shall not.
  shape forme *f*; **in (good) s.** (*fit*) en (pleine) forme; **to stay in s.** se maintenir en forme; **to be in good/bad s.** (*of vehicle etc*) être en

bon/mauvais état; *(of business)* marcher bien/mal; **to take s.** *(of plan, book etc)* prendre forme; *(progress well)* avancer.

-shaped *suffix* pear-s./etc en forme de poire/etc.

share 1 *n* part *f* (**of**, in de); *(of stock)* action *f*. **2** *vt (meal, opinion etc)* partager (**with** avec); *(characteristic)* avoir en commun.

share·hold·er actionnaire *mf*.

▸ **share in** *vt* avoir sa part de.

▸ **share out** *vt* partager, répartir (**among** entre).

shark requin *m*.

sharp 1 *adj (knife etc)* tranchant; *(pointed)* pointu; *(point, pain)* aigu (*f* -uë); *(bend)* brusque. **2** *adv* **five o'clock/etc** à cinq heures/etc pile.

sharp·en *vt (knife)* aiguiser; *(pencil)* tailler.

sharp·ly *adv (suddenly)* brusquement.

shat·ter 1 *vt (door, arm etc)* fracasser; *(glass)* faire voler en éclats. **2** *vi* fracasser; *(of glass)* voler en éclats.

shave 1 *vt (person, head)* raser; **to s. off one's beard** se raser la barbe. **2** *vi* se raser. **3** *n* **to have a s.** se raser.

shav·er rasoir *m* électrique.

shav·ing cream crème *f* à raser.

shav·ing kit trousse *f* de toilette (d'homme).

shawl châle *m*.

she *pron* elle; **she's a happy woman** c'est une femme heureuse.

shed¹ *(in garden)* abri *m* (de jardin); *(for goods or machines)* hangar *m*.

shed² *vt (lose)* perdre; *(tears)* répandre.

sheep *inv* mouton *m*.

sheep·skin peau *f* de mouton.

sheer *adj (utter)* pur; *(cliff)* à pic; *(stockings, fabric)* extra fin.

sheet *(on bed)* drap *m*; *(of paper)* feuille *f*; *(of glass, ice)* plaque *f*.

shelf, *pl* **shelves** étagère *f*; *(in shop)* rayon *m*.

shell 1 *n (of egg etc)* coquille *f*; *(of tortoise)* carapace *f*; *(seashell)* coquillage *m*; *(explosive)* obus *m*. **2** *vt (peas)* écosser.

shell·fish *(oysters etc)* fruits *mpl* de mer.

shel·ter 1 *n* abri *m*; **to take s.** se mettre à l'abri (**from** de). **2** *vt* abriter (**from** de). **3** *vi* s'abriter.

shelv·ing rayonnage(s) *m(pl)*.

shep·herd berger *m*.

sher·iff shérif *m*.

sher·ry sherry *m*.

shield 1 *n* bouclier *m*; *(screen)* écran *m*. **2** *vt* protéger (**from** de).

shift 1 *n (change)* changement *m* (**of**, in de); *(period of work)* poste *m*; *(workers)* équipe *f*; **gear s.** levier *m* de vitesse. **2** *vt (move)* bouger; **to s. gear(s)** changer de vitesse. **3** *vi* bouger.

shin tibia *m*.

shine 1 *vi** briller. **2** *vt (polish)* faire briller; **to s. a light on sth** éclairer qch. **3** *n (on shoes, cloth)* brillant *m*.

shin·y *adj* brillant.

ship navire *m*, bateau *m*; **by s.** en bateau.

ship·ping *(traffic)* navigation *f*.

ship·wreck naufrage *m*.

ship·wrecked *adj* naufragé; **to be s.** faire naufrage.

ship·yard chantier *m* naval.

shirt chemise *f*; *(of woman)* chemisier *m*; *(of sportsman)* maillot *m*.

shiv·er 1 *vi* frissonner (**with** de). **2** *n* frisson *m*.

shock 1 *n (emotional, physical)* choc *m*; **(electric) s.** décharge *f* (électrique); **suffering from s.,** in s. en état de choc. **2** *vt (offend)* choquer; *(surprise)* stupéfier.

shock ab·sorb·er amortisseur *m*.

shock·ing *adj* affreux; *(outrageous)* scandaleux.

shoe chaussure *f*, soulier *m*.

shoe·lace lacet *m*.

shoe pol·ish cirage *m*.

shoe re·pair shop cordonnerie f.

shoe store magasin m de chaussures.

shoot* 1 vt (kill) tuer (d'un coup de feu); (wound) blesser (d'un coup de feu); (execute) fusiller; (gun) tirer un coup de; (film) tourner. **2** vi (with gun) tirer (at sur).

▶ **shoot ahead** vi (rush) avancer à toute vitesse.

shoot·ing (shots) coups mpl de feu; (murder) meurtre m.

▶ **shoot off** vi (rush) partir à toute vitesse.

▶ **shoot up** vi (of price) monter en flèche.

shop 1 n magasin m; (small) boutique f; **at the flower s.** chez le fleuriste. **2** vi faire ses courses (**at** chez).

shop·keep·er commerçant, -ante mf.

shop·ping to go s. faire des courses.

shop·ping bag sac m à provisions.

shop·ping cen·ter centre m commercial.

shop·ping dis·trict quartier m commerçant.

shore (of sea, lake) rivage m; (coast) côte f.

short 1 adj court; (person, distance) petit; **a s. time** or **while (ago)** (il y a) peu de temps; **to be s. of money/time** être à court d'argent/de temps; **we're s. ten men** il nous manque dix hommes; **to be s. for sth** (of name) être l'abréviation de qch. **2** adv **to cut s.** (hair) couper court; (visit etc) raccourcir; (person) couper la parole à; **to get** or **run s.** manquer (**of** de).

short·age manque m.

short·cut raccourci m.

short·en vt (dress, text etc) raccourcir.

short·ly adv (soon) bientôt; **s. af·ter** peu après.

shorts npl (a pair of) s. un short.

short·sight·ed adj myope.

short-term adj à court terme.

shot (from gun) coup m; (with camera) prise f de vues.

shot·gun fusil m (de chasse).

should v aux (ought to) **you s. do it** vous devriez le faire; **I s. have stayed** j'aurais dû rester; **that s. be Paul** ça doit être Paul. ▪ (would) **it's strange she s. say no** il est étrange qu'elle dise non. ▪ (possibility) **if he s. come** s'il vient.

shoul·der épaule f; (hard) s. (of highway) bas-côté m.

shoul·der bag sac m à bandoulière.

shout 1 n cri m. **2** vti crier; **to s. to sb to do** crier à qn de faire.

▶ **shout at** vt (scold) crier après.

shout·ing (shouts) cris mpl.

▶ **shout out** vti crier.

shove 1 n poussée f; **to give a s. (to)** pousser. **2** vt pousser; (put) Fam fourrer. **3** vi pousser.

shov·el 1 n pelle f. **2** vt (snow etc) enlever à la pelle.

show 1 n (in theater) spectacle m; (at movies) séance f; **the Auto S.** le Salon de l'Automobile; **on s.** (painting etc) exposé. **2** vt* montrer (**to** à; **that** que); (in exhibition) exposer; (movie) passer; (indicate) indiquer; **to s. sb to the door** reconduire qn. **3** vi (be visible) se voir; (of movie) passer.

▶ **show around** vt faire visiter; **to s. sb around the house** faire visiter la maison à qn.

show·er (bath) douche f; (of rain) averse f.

▶ **show in** vt (visitor) faire entrer.

show·ing (of movie) séance f.

▶ **show off** vi crâner.

show-off crâneur, -euse mf.

▶ **show out** vt (visitor) reconduire.

▶ **show up** vi (of person) arriver. **2** vt (embarrass) mettre (qn) dans l'embarras.

shrimp crevette *f* (grise).

shrink* *vi* (of clothes) rétrécir.

shrub arbuste *m*.

shrug *vt* to s. one's shoulders hausser les épaules.

shud·der *vi* frémir (**with** de).

shuf·fle *vt* (cards) battre.

shush! *int* chut!

shut* 1 *vt* fermer. **2** *vi* (of door etc) se fermer; (of shop etc) fermer.

▸ **shut down** *vti* fermer.

▸ **shut in** *vt* enfermer.

▸ **shut off** *vt* (gas etc) fermer; (engine) arrêter; (isolate) isoler.

▸ **shut out** *vt* (light) empêcher d'entrer; **to s. sb out** (accidentally) enfermer qn dehors.

shut·ter (on window) volet *m*; (of store) rideau *m* (métallique).

shut·tle s. (service) navette *f*, **space s.** navette spatiale.

▸ **shut up 1** *vt* (house etc) fermer; (lock up) enfermer (personne, objet précieux). **2** *vi* (be quiet) se taire.

shy *adj* timide.

shy·ness timidité *f*.

sick 1 *adj* malade; **to be s.** (vomit) vomir; **off s.** en congé de maladie; **to feel s.** avoir mal au cœur; **to be s. (and tired) of sth/sb** *Fam* en avoir marre de qch/qn. **2** *npl* **the s.** les malades *mpl*.

sick·ness maladie *f*.

side côté *m*; (of hill, animal) flanc *m*; (of road, river) bord *m*; (team) équipe *f*; **at** or **by the s. of** à côté de; **at** or **by my s.** à côté de moi, à mes côtés; **s. by s.** l'un à côté de l'autre; **to move to one's s.** s'écarter; **on this s.** de ce côté; **on the other s.** de l'autre côté; **to take sides with sb** se ranger du côté de qn; **on our s.** de notre côté.

side·board buffet *m*.

side·burns *npl* pattes *fpl*.

side·walk trottoir *m*.

side·ways *adv & adj* de côté.

sid·ing (for train) voie *f* d'évite-

ment; (of wall) parement *m* (extérieur).

siege siège *m*; **under s.** assiégé.

sieve tamis *m*; (for liquids) passoire *f*.

sift *vt* (flour etc) tamiser.

sigh 1 *n* soupir *m*. **2** *vi* soupirer.

sight vue *f*; (thing seen) spectacle *m*; **to lose s. of** perdre de vue; **to catch s. of** apercevoir; **by s.** de vue; **in s.** (target etc) en vue; **out of s.** caché; **the (tourist) sights** les attractions *fpl* touristiques.

sight·see·ing to go s. faire du tourisme.

sign 1 *n* signe *m*; (notice) panneau *m*; (over shop, inn) enseigne *f*; **no s. of** aucune trace de. **2** *vti* (with signature) signer.

sig·nal 1 *n* signal *m*; (of vehicle) clignotant *m*; **traffic signals** feux *mpl* de signalisation. **2** *vi* faire signe (**to** à); **to s. (left/right)** (in car) mettre son clignotant (à gauche/à droite).

sig·na·ture signature *f*.

sig·nif·i·cant *adj* (important, large) important.

sig·nif·i·cant·ly *adv* sensiblement.

sig·ni·fy *vt* signifier.

▸ **sign in** *vi* (in hotel etc) signer le registre.

▸ **sign on** *or up vi* (of soldier, worker) s'engager; (for course) s'inscrire (**for** à).

sign·post poteau *m* indicateur.

si·lence 1 *n* silence *m*; **in s.** en silence. **2** *vt* faire taire.

si·lent *adj* silencieux; (movie) muet (*f* muette); **to keep s.** garder le silence (**about** sur).

si·lent·ly *adv* silencieusement.

silk soie *f*.

sill (of window) rebord *m*.

sil·ly *adj* bête; **to do something s.** faire une bêtise.

sil·ver 1 *n* argent *m*; (plates etc) argenterie *f*. **2** *adj* (spoon etc) en argent; **s. paper** papier *m* d'argent.

sil·ver-plat·ed *adj* plaqué argent.

sil·ver·ware *inv* argenterie *f*.

sim·i·lar *adj* semblable (**to** à).

sim·i·lar·i·ty ressemblance *f* (**to** avec).

sim·ple *adj* simple.

sim·pli·fy *vt* simplifier.

sim·ply *adv* (*plainly, merely*) simplement; (*absolutely*) absolument.

si·mul·ta·ne·ous *adj* simultané.

si·mul·ta·ne·ous·ly *adv* simultanément.

sin péché *m*.

since 1 *prep* depuis. **2** *conj* depuis que; (*because*) puisque; **s. she's been here** depuis qu'elle est ici; **it's a year s. I saw him** ça fait un an que je ne l'ai pas vu. **3** *adv* (*ever*) **s.** depuis.

sin·cere *adj* sincère.

sin·cere·ly *adv* sincèrement; **yours s.** (*in letter*) veuillez croire à mes sentiments dévoués.

sin·cer·i·ty sincérité *f*.

sing* *vti* chanter.

sing·er chanteur, -euse *mf*.

sin·gle *adj* seul; (*room, bed*) pour une personne; (*unmarried*) célibataire; **not a s. book/etc** pas un seul livre/*etc*; **every s. day** tous les jours sans exception.

Sin·gle Mar·ket Marché *m* unique.

sin·gle-mind·ed *adj* résolu.

▸ **single out** *vt* choisir.

sin·gu·lar 1 *adj* (*form*) singulier; (*noun*) au singulier. **2** *n* singulier *m*; **in the s.** au singulier.

sin·is·ter *adj* sinistre.

sink¹ (*in kitchen*) évier *m*; (*washbasin*) lavabo *m*.

sink*² *vi* (*of ship, person etc*) couler.

▸ **sink (down) into** *vt* (*mud*) s'enfoncer dans; (*armchair*) s'affaler dans.

sip *vi* boire à petites gorgées.

sir monsieur *m*; **S.** (*title*) sir.

si·ren (*of factory etc*) sirène *f*.

sis·ter sœur *f*.

sit* 1 *vi* s'asseoir; **to be sitting** être assis; **she was sitting reading** elle était assise à lire. **2** *vt* (*child on chair etc*) asseoir.

sit (for) *vt* (*exam*) se présenter à.

▸ **sit around** *vi* traîner; (*do nothing*) ne rien faire.

▸ **sit down 1** *vi* s'asseoir; **to be sitting down** être assis. **2** *vt* asseoir (*qn*).

site (*position*) emplacement *m*; (*building*) **s.** chantier *m*.

sit·ting room salon *m*.

sit·u·ate *vt* situer; **to be situated** être situé, se situer.

sit·u·a·tion situation *f*.

▸ **sit up (straight)** *vi* s'asseoir (bien droit).

six *adj & n* six (*m*).

six·teen *adj & n* seize (*m*).

sixth *adj & n* sixième (*mf*).

six·ti·eth *adj & n* soixantième (*mf*).

six·ty *adj & n* soixante (*m*).

size (*of person, clothes, packet etc*) taille *f*; (*measurements*) dimensions *fpl*; (*of town, sum*) importance *f*; (*of shoes, gloves*) pointure *f*; (*of shirt*) encolure *f*; **hip/chest s.** tour *m* de hanches/de poitrine.

skate 1 *n* patin *m*. **2** *vi* patiner.

skate·board planche *f* (à roulettes).

skat·er patineur, -euse *mf*.

skat·ing patinage *m*; **to go s.** faire du patinage.

skat·ing rink (*ice-skating*) patinoire *f*.

skel·e·ton squelette *m*.

sketch 1 *n* (*drawing*) croquis *m*; (*comic play*) sketch *m*. **2** *vi* faire un ou des croquis.

skew·er (*for meat etc*) broche *f*; (*for kebab*) brochette *f*.

ski 1 *n* ski *m*. **2** *vi* faire du ski.

skid 1 *vi* déraper; **to s. into sth** déraper et heurter qch. **2** *n* dérapage *m*.

ski·er skieur, -euse *mf*.

ski·ing 1 *n* ski *m*. **2** *adj* (school, clothes, etc) de ski.

ski lift remonte-pente *m*.

skill habileté *f* (at à); (technique) technique *f*.

skilled *adj* habile.

skilled work·er ouvrier, -ière qualifié(e).

skill·ful *adj* habile (at doing à faire; at sth à qch).

skim milk lait *m* écrémé.

skin peau *f*.

skin div·ing plongée *f* sousmarine.

skin·ny *adj* maigre.

skip 1 *vi* (hop) sautiller; (with rope) sauter à la corde. **2** *vt* (miss) sauter (repas, classe etc).

skirt jupe *f*.

skull crâne *m*.

sky ciel *m*.

sky·scrap·er gratte-ciel *m inv*.

slack *adj* (knot, spring) lâche; to be s. (of rope) avoir du mou; (in office etc) être calme.

slack·en *vt* (rope) relâcher.

slacks *npl* pantalon *m*.

slam 1 *vt* (door, lid) claquer. **2** *vi* (of door) claquer. **3** *n* claquement *m*.

slang argot *m*.

slant 1 *n* inclinaison *f*. **2** *vi* (of roof) être en pente.

slap 1 *n* tape *f*, (on face) gifle *f*. **2** *vt* (person) donner une tape à; to s. sb's face gifler qn; to s. sb's bottom donner une fessée à qn.

slate ardoise *f*.

slaugh·ter 1 *vt* massacrer; (animal) abattre. **2** *n* massacre *m*; (of animal) abattage *m*.

slave esclave *mf*.

▸**slave away** *vi* se crever (au travail).

slav·er·y esclavage *m*.

sled luge *f*, (horse-drawn) traîneau *m*.

sleep 1 *n* sommeil *m*; to get some s. dormir. **2** *vi** dormir; (spend the night) coucher; to go or get to s. s'endormir.

sleep·er (bed in train) couchette *f*; (train) train *m* couchettes.

sleep·ing *adj* (asleep) endormi.

sleep·ing bag sac *m* de couchage.

sleep·ing car wagon-lit *m*.

sleep·ing pill somnifère *m*.

sleep·y *adj* to be s. (of person) avoir sommeil.

sleet 1 *n* neige *f* fondue. **2** *vi* it's sleeting il tombe de la neige fondue.

sleeve (of shirt etc) manche *f*, (of record) pochette *f*, long-/short-sleeved à manches longues/courtes.

sleigh traîneau *m*.

slen·der *adj* (person) svelte; (wrist, neck etc) fin; (hope, chance) maigre, faible.

slept *pt & pp de* sleep.

slice tranche *f*.

slice (up) *vt* couper (en tranches).

slide 1 *n* (in playground) toboggan *m*; (film) diapositive *f*. **2** *vi** glisser. **3** *vt* (letter etc) glisser (into dans); (table, chair etc) faire glisser.

slid·ing door porte *f* à glissière or coulissante.

slight *adj* (noise, mistake etc) léger, petit; (chance) faible; the slightest thing la moindre chose; not in the slightest pas le moins du monde.

slight·ly *adv* légèrement.

slim 1 *adj* mince. **2** *vi* maigrir.

sling (for arm) écharpe *f*, in a s. en écharpe.

slip 1 *n* (mistake) erreur *f*, (woman's undergarment) combinaison *f*, a s. of paper un bout de papier. **2** *vi* glisser. **3** *vt* (slide) glisser (qch) (to à; into dans).

▸**slip away** *vi* s'esquiver.

▸**slip·cov·er** (on furniture) housse *f*.

▸**slip in** *vi* entrer furtivement.

▸**slip into** *vt* (room etc) se glisser dans; (bathrobe etc) mettre, passer.

▸ **slip off** vt (garment) enlever.

▸ **slip on** vt (garment) mettre.

▸ **slip out** vi sortir furtivement; (for a moment) sortir (un instant).

slip·per pantoufle f.

slip·per·y adj glissant.

▸ **slip up** vi (make a mistake) gaffer.

slit (opening) fente f, (cut) coupure f.

slo·gan slogan m.

slope 1 n pente f, (of mountain) versant m, (of skiing) piste f. **2** vi (of ground, roof etc) être en pente.

slop·ing adj en pente.

slot (slit) fente f, (groove) rainure f.

slot ma·chine distributeur m automatique; (for gambling) machine f à sous.

slow 1 adj lent; **to be s.** (of clock, watch) retarder; **to be five minutes s.** retarder de cinq minutes; **in s. motion** au ralenti. **2** adv lentement.

▸ **slow down** or **up** vti ralentir.

slow·ly adv lentement; (bit by bit) peu à peu.

slow·poke Fam tortue f.

slug limace f.

slum (house) taudis m; **the slums** les quartiers mpl pauvres.

slump 1 n (in sales, prices etc) baisse f soudaine; (economic depression) crise f. **2** vi (sales, prices, person) s'effondrer; (morale) baisser soudainement.

sly adj (cunning) rusé.

smack 1 n claque f, gifle f, (on bottom) fessée f. **2** vt (person) donner une claque à; **to s. sb's face** gifler qn; **to s. sb's bottom** donner une fessée à qn.

small 1 adj petit. **2** adv (to cut, chop) menu.

small·pox petite vérole f.

smart adj (fashionable, elegant) élégant; (clever) intelligent.

smash 1 vt (break) briser; (shatter) fracasser. **2** vi se briser.

smash·ing adj Fam formidable.

▸ **smash into** vt (of vehicle) (r)entrer dans.

smash-up collision f.

smell 1 n odeur f, (sense of) s. odorat m. **2** vt* sentir. **3** vi (stink) sentir (mauvais); (have a smell) avoir une odeur; **to s. of smoke/etc** sentir la fumée/etc.

smell·y adj qui sent mauvais, qui pue; **to be s.** sentir mauvais, puer.

smile 1 n sourire m. **2** vi sourire (**at sb** à qn).

smock blouse f.

smoke 1 n fumée f, **to have a s.** fumer une cigarette/etc. **2** vti fumer; **'no smoking'** 'défense de fumer'; **smoking compartment** compartiment m fumeurs.

smok·er fumeur, -euse mf, (train compartment) compartiment m fumeurs.

smooth adj (surface, skin etc) lisse; (flight) agréable.

▸ **smooth down** or **out** vt (dress, hair etc) lisser.

smug·gle vt passer (en fraude).

smug·gler contrebandier, -ière mf.

smug·gling contrebande f.

snack (meal) casse-croûte m inv; **snacks** (things to eat) petites choses fpl à grignoter; (candies) friandises fpl; **to eat a s.** or **snacks** grignoter.

snack bar snack(-bar) m.

snail escargot m.

snake serpent m.

snap 1 vt (break) casser (avec un bruit sec). **2** vi se casser net. **3** n (fastener) bouton-pression m.

snap(-shot) photo f.

snatch vt saisir (d'un geste vif); **to s. sth from sb** arracher qch à qn.

sneak·er (chaussure f de) tennis m.

sneer vi ricaner.

sneeze 1 vi éternuer. **2** n éternuement m.

sniff vti **to s. (at)** renifler.

snip (off) vt couper.

snook·er snooker m (sorte de jeu de billard).

snore vi ronfler.

snor·ing ronflements mpl.

snout museau m.

snow 1 n neige f. **2** vi neiger; **it's snowing** il neige.

snow·ball boule f de neige.

snow·drift congère f.

snow·flake flocon m de neige.

snow·man bonhomme m de neige.

snow·plow chasse-neige m inv.

snow·storm tempête f de neige.

so 1 adv (to such a degree) si, tellement (**that** que); (thus) ainsi; **so that** (purpose) pour que (+ subjunctive); (result) si bien que (+ indicative); **so as to do** pour faire; **I think so** je le pense; **if so** si oui; **is that so?** c'est vrai?; **so am I, so do I**/etc moi aussi; **so much** (to work etc) tant (**that** que); **so much courage**/etc tant de courage/etc; **so many** tant; **so many books**/etc tant de livres/etc; **ten or so** environ dix; **and so on** et ainsi de suite. **2** conj (therefore) donc; **so what?** et alors?

soak 1 vt (drench) tremper (qn); (laundry, food) faire tremper. **2** vi (of laundry etc) tremper.

soaked through adj (person) trempé jusqu'aux os.

soak·ing adj & adv **s.** (**wet**) trempé.

▶ **soak up** vt absorber.

soap savon m.

soap pow·der lessive f.

soap·y adj savonneux.

sob 1 n sanglot m. **2** vi sangloter.

so·ber adj **he's s.** (not drunk) il n'est pas ivre.

soc·cer football m.

so·cial adj social; **s. club** club m; **s. evening** soirée f; **to have a good s. life** sortir beaucoup; **s. security** (pension) pension f de retraite; **s. services, S. Security** = Sécurité f sociale; **s. worker** assistant, -ante mf social(e).

so·cial·ist adj & n socialiste (mf).

so·ci·e·ty société f.

sock chaussette f.

sock·et (for electric plug) prise f de courant.

so·da (pop) soda m.

so·da (wa·ter) eau f gazeuse.

so·fa canapé m; **s. bed** canapé-lit m.

soft adj (gentle, not stiff) doux (f douce); (butter, ground) mou (f molle); **s. drink** boisson f non alcoolisée.

soft·ball = sorte de base-ball.

soft·en 1 vt (object) ramollir; (skin) adoucir. **2** vi (object) ramollir; (skin) s'adoucir.

soft·ly adv doucement.

soft·ware inv logiciel m.

soil sol m, terre f.

so·lar adj solaire.

sol·dier soldat m.

sole (of shoe) semelle f; (of foot) plante f; (fish) sole f; **lemon s.** limande f.

sol·emn adj (formal) solennel; (serious) grave.

sol·id 1 adj (car, meal etc) solide; (wall, time) plein; (gold) massif; **s. line** ligne f continue. **2** n solide m.

sol·i·dar·i·ty solidarité f.

so·lo adj & n solo (m).

so·lu·tion solution f (**to** de).

solve vt (problem) résoudre.

sol·vent 1 n solvant m. **2** adj (financially) solvable.

some 1 adj (amount, number) du, de la, des; **s. wine** du vin; **s. water** de l'eau; **s. dogs** des chiens; **s. pretty flowers** de jolies fleurs. ▪ (unspecified) un, une; **s. man (or other)** un homme (quelconque). ▪ (a few) quelques; (a little) un peu de. **2** pron (number) quelques-un(e)s (**of** des); ▪ (a certain quantity) en; **I want s.** j'en veux.

some·bod·y pron = **someone**.

some·day *adv* un jour.

some·how *adv* d'une manière ou d'une autre; *(for some reason)* on ne sait pourquoi.

some·one *pron* quelqu'un; **s. small**/*etc* quelqu'un de petit/*etc*.

some·place *adv* quelque part.

som·er·sault culbute *f*.

some·thing *pron* quelque chose; **s. awful**/*etc* quelque chose d'affreux/*etc*, **s. of a liar**/*etc* un peu menteur/*etc*.

some·time *adv* un jour.

some·times *adv* quelquefois.

some·what *adv* quelque peu.

some·where *adv* quelque part.

son fils *m*.

song chanson *f*.

son-in-law, *pl* **sons-in-law** gendre *m*.

soon *adv* bientôt; *(quickly)* vite; *(early)* tôt; **s. after** peu après; **as s. as she leaves** aussitôt qu'elle partira; **no sooner had he spoken than** à peine avait-il parlé que; **I'd sooner leave** je préférerais partir; **I'd just as s. leave** j'aimerais autant partir; **sooner or later** tôt ou tard.

soot suie *f*.

soothe *vt (pain, nerves)* calmer.

sore 1 *adj (painful)* douloureux; *(angry) Fam* fâché (**at** contre); **she has a s. throat** elle a mal à la gorge. 2 *n* plaie *f*.

sor·row chagrin *m*.

sor·ry *adj* **to be s.** *(regret)* être désolé (**to do** de faire); **I'm s. she can't come** je regrette qu'elle ne puisse pas venir; **I'm s. about the delay** je m'excuse pour ce retard; **s.!** pardon!; **to feel** *or* **be s. for sb** plaindre qn.

sort¹ sorte *f*, espèce *f* (**of** de); **all sorts of** toutes sortes de; **what s. of drink**/*etc* **is it?** qu'est-ce que c'est comme boisson/*etc*?

sort² *vt (papers etc)* trier.

▸ **sort out** *vt (classify, select)* trier; *(separate)* séparer (**from** de); *(tidy)* ranger; *(problem)* régler.

soul âme *f*.

sound¹ 1 *n* son *m*; *(noise)* bruit *m*; **I don't like the s. of it** ça ne me plaît pas du tout. 2 *vt (bell, alarm etc)* sonner; **to s. one's horn** klaxonner. 3 *vi (of bell etc)* sonner; *(seem)* sembler; **to s. like** sembler être; *(resemble)* ressembler à.

sound² 1 *adj (healthy)* sain; *(good, reliable)* solide. 2 *adv* **s. asleep** profondément endormi.

sound·proof *vt* insonoriser.

soup soupe *f*, potage *m*.

sour *adj* aigre.

source source *f*.

south 1 *n* sud *m*; *(to the)* **s. of** au sud de. 2 *adj (coast)* sud *inv* 3 *adv* au sud.

south·bound *adj* en direction du sud.

south·east *n & adj* sud-est (*m & adj inv*).

south·ern *adj (town)* du sud; *(coast)* sud *inv*

south·ern·er habitant, -ante *mf* du sud.

south·ward(s) *adj & adv* vers le sud.

south·west *n & adj* sud-ouest (*m & adj inv*).

sou·ve·nir *(object)* souvenir *m*.

sow* *vt (seeds)* semer.

space *(gap, emptiness, atmosphere)* espace *m*; *(period)* période *f*; *(for parking)* place *f*; **to take up s.** *(room)* prendre de la place.

space heat·er radiateur *m* d'appoint.

▸ **space out** *vt* espacer.

space·ship engin *m* spatial.

space·suit combinaison *f* spatiale.

spa·cious *adj* spacieux.

spade bêche *f*; *(of child)* pelle *f*; **spade(s)** *Cards* pique *m*.

spa·ghet·ti spaghetti(s) *mpl*.

span 1 *n (of hand, wing)* envergure *f*; *(of arch)* portée *f*; *(of bridge)* travée *f*; *(duration)* durée *m*. 2 *vt (river* *etc)* enjamber; *(period of time etc)* couvrir.

Span·iard Espagnol, -ole *mf.*

Span·ish 1 *adj* espagnol. **2** *n (language)* espagnol *m.*

spank *vt* donner une fessée à.

spank·ing fessée *f.*

spare 1 *adj (extra)* de trop; *(clothes)* de rechange; *(wheel)* de secours; *(bed, room)* d'ami; **s. time** loisirs *mpl.* **2** *n* **s. (part)** pièce *f* détachée. **3** *vt (do without)* se passer de *(qn, qch)*; **to s. sb** *(details etc)* épargner à qn; *(time)* accorder à qn; *(money)* donner à qn.

spark étincelle *f.*

spar·kle *vi (of diamond, star)* étinceler.

spar·kling *adj (wine, water)* pétillant.

spark·plug bougie *f.*

spar·row moineau *m.*

speak* 1 *vi* parler (**about, of** de); **English-/French-speaking** qui parle anglais/français. **2** *vt (language)* parler; *(say)* dire.

speak·er *(public)* orateur *m; (loudspeaker)* haut-parleur *m; (of stereo system)* enceinte *f.*

▸ **speak up** *vi* parler plus fort.

spear lance *f.*

spe·cial 1 *adj* spécial; *(care, attention)* (tout) particulier. **2** *n* **today's s.** *(in restaurant)* le plat du jour.

spe·cial·ist spécialiste *mf* (**in** de).

spe·cial·ize *vi* se spécialiser (**in** dans).

spe·cial·ly *adv* spécialement.

spe·cial·ty spécialité *f.*

spe·cies *inv* espèce *f.*

spe·cif·ic *adj* précis.

spec·i·fi·ca·tion spécification *f.*

spec·i·men *(example, person)* spécimen *m.*

spec·ta·cle spectacle *m;* **spectacles** *(glasses)* lunettes *fpl.*

spec·tac·u·lar *adj* spectaculaire.

spec·ta·tor spectateur, -trice *mf.*

spec·trum spectre *m; (range)* gamme *f.*

spec·u·late *vi* s'interroger; *(financially)* spéculer; **to s. that** conjecturer que.

speech *(talk, lecture)* discours *m* (**on, about** sur); *(power of language)* parole *f, (spoken language)* langage *m.*

speed 1 *n (rate)* vitesse *f, (quickness)* rapidité *f;* **s. limit** limitation *f* de vitesse. **2** *vi* (drive too fast)* aller trop vite.

speed·boat vedette *f.*

speed·om·e·ter compteur *m* (de vitesse).

▸ **speed* up 1** *vt* accélérer. **2** *vi (of person)* aller plus vite.

spell¹ *(period)* (courte) période *f; (magic)* charme *m;* **cold s.** vague *f* de froid.

spell*² ** *vt (write)* écrire; *(say aloud)* épeler; *(of letters)* former *(mot);* **how is it spelled? comment cela s'écrit-il?

spell·ing orthographe *f.*

spend* 1 *vt (money)* dépenser (**on** pour); *(time etc)* passer (**on sth** sur qch; **doing** à faire). **2** *vi* dépenser.

sphere sphère *f.*

spice 1 *n* épice *f.* **2** *vt* épicer.

spic·y *adj (food)* épicé.

spi·der araignée *f;* **s.'s web** toile *f* d'araignée.

spike pointe *f.*

spill* 1 *vt* répandre, renverser. **2** *vi* se répandre, se renverser (**on, over** sur).

▸ **spill out 1** *vt (empty)* vider *(café, verre etc).* **2** *vi (of coffee etc)* se renverser.

▸ **spill over** *vi* déborder.

spin* *vt (wheel etc)* faire tourner; *(washing)* essorer.

spin·ach *(food)* épinards *mpl.*

spin (a·round) *vi (of dancer, wheel etc)* tourner.

spine *(of back)* colonne *f* vertébrale.

spi·ral spirale f.

spire flèche f.

spir·its npl (drinks) alcool m.

spir·i·tu·al adj spirituel.

spit 1 vti* cracher. **2** n (for meat) broche f.

spite in s. of malgré.

spite·ful adj malveillant.

splash 1 vt éclabousser (**with** de; **over** sur). **2** n (mark) éclaboussure f.

splash (a·round) vi (in river, mud) patauger; (in bath) barboter.

splen·did adj splendide.

splin·ter (in finger) écharde f.

split 1 n fente f, (tear) déchirure f. **2** vt* (break apart) fendre; (tear) déchirer.

split (up) 1 vt (group) diviser; (money, work) partager (**between** entre). **2** vi (of group) se diviser (**in·to** en); (because of disagreement) se séparer.

spoil* vt gâter; (damage, ruin) abîmer; (child, dog) gâter.

spoke (of wheel) rayon m.

spoke, spo·ken pt & pp de **speak**.

spokes·man, pl **-men** porte-parole m inv (**for, of** de).

sponge éponge f.

sponge cake gâteau m de Savoie.

▶**sponge down** vt **to s. oneself down** se laver à l'éponge.

spon·sor 1 vt sponsoriser. **2** n sponsor mf.

spon·ta·ne·ous adj spontané.

spool bobine f.

spoon cuillère f.

spoon·ful cuillerée f.

sport sport m; **sports** (in general) sport m; **my favorite s.** mon sport préféré; **to play sports** faire du sport; **sports club** club m sportif; **sports car/jacket/ground** voiture f/veste f/terrain m de sport.

sports·man, pl **-men** sportif m.

sports·wom·an, pl **-women** sportive f.

spot¹ (stain, mark) tache f; (dot) point m; (place) endroit m; **on the s.** sur place.

spot² vt (notice) apercevoir.

spot·less adj (clean) impeccable.

spot·light (in theater etc) projecteur m; (for photography) spot m.

spot·ted adj (animal) tacheté.

spouse époux, -ouse mf.

spout (of teapot etc) bec m.

sprain 1 n foulure f. **2** vt **to s. one's ankle/wrist** se fouler la cheville/le poignet.

spray 1 n (can) bombe f; **hair s.** laque f à cheveux. **2** vt (liquid, surface) vaporiser; (plant) arroser; (car) peindre à la bombe.

spread 1 vt* (stretch, open out) étendre; (legs, fingers) écarter; (distribute) répandre (**over** sur); (paint, payment, visits) étaler; (news, germs) propager. **2** vi (of fire) s'étendre; (of news, epidemic) se propager. **3** n (paste) pâte f (à tartiner); **cheese s.** fromage m à tartiner.

▶**spread out 1** vt (stretch, open out) étendre; (legs, fingers) écarter; (distribute) répandre; (paint, payment, visits) étaler. **2** vi (of people) se disperser.

spring¹ 1 n (metal device) ressort m. **2** vi* (leap) bondir.

spring² (season) printemps m; **in (the) s.** au printemps.

spring³ (of water) source f.

spring·board tremplin m.

spring on·ion oignon m vert.

spring·time printemps m.

sprin·kle vt (sand etc) répandre (**on, over** sur); **to s. with water, to s. water on** asperger d'eau; **to s. with** (sugar, salt, flour) saupoudrer de.

sprin·kler (in garden) arroseur m.

sprout (Brussels) s. chou m (pl choux) de Bruxelles.

spur (of horse rider) éperon m.

spurt (out) vi (of liquid) jaillir.

spy espion, -onne mf.

spy·ing espionnage *m*.

▸ **spy on** *vt* espionner.

square 1 *n* carré *m*; *(in town)* place *f*; *(for drawing right angles)* équerre *f*. **2** *adj* carré; *(meal)* solide.

squash 1 *vt (crush)* écraser; *(squeeze)* serrer. **2** *n (game)* squash *m*; *(vegetable)* courge *f*.

squat (down) *vi* s'accroupir.

squeak *vi (of door)* grincer; *(of shoe)* craquer.

squeal 1 *vi* pousser des cris aigus. **2** *n* cri *m* aigu.

squeeze 1 *vt* presser; **to s. sb's hand** serrer la main à qn. **2** *vi (force oneself)* se glisser **(through/into/** *etc* par/dans/*etc*). **3** *n (pressure)* pression *f*, *(hug)* étreinte; **to give sth a s.** presser qch; **a s. of lemon** quelques gouttes de citron.

▸ **squeeze in** *vi (of person)* trouver un peu de place.

▸ **squeeze into** *vt* **to s. sth into sth** faire rentrer qch dans qch.

▸ **squeeze out** *vt (juice etc)* faire sortir **(from de)**.

▸ **squeeze up** *vi* se serrer **(against** contre).

squint 1 *n* to have a s. loucher. **2** *vi* loucher; *(in the sunlight etc)* plisser les yeux.

squir·rel écureuil *m*.

squirt 1 *vt (liquid)* faire gicler. **2** *vi* gicler.

stab *vt (with knife)* poignarder.

sta·bil·i·ty stabilité *f*.

sta·ble¹ *adj* stable.

sta·ble² écurie *f*.

stack *(heap)* tas *m*; **stacks of** *Fam* un *or* des tas de.

stack (up) *vt* entasser.

sta·di·um stade *m*.

staff personnel *m*; *(of school)* professeurs *mpl*; *(of army)* état-major *m*.

stag cerf *m*.

stage¹ 1 *n (platform)* scène *f*. **2** *vt (play)* monter.

stage² *(phase, of journey)* étape *f*.

stage·coach diligence *f*.

stag·ger *vi* chanceler.

stain 1 *vt (to mark)* tacher **(with** de). **2** *n* tache *f*.

stained glass win·dow vitrail *m (pl* vitraux).

stain·less steel *adj (knife etc)* en inox.

stain re·mov·er détachant *m*.

stair·case escalier *m*.

stairs *npl* escalier *m*.

stake *(post)* pieu *m*.

stale *adj (bread etc)* rassis *(f* rassie).

stalk *(of plant)* tige *f*.

stall 1 *n (in market)* étal *m (pl* étals); *(for newspapers, flowers)* kiosque *m*. **2** *vti (of car engine)* caler.

stam·mer *vti* bégayer.

stamp 1 *n (for postage, instrument)* timbre *m*; *(mark)* cachet *m*. **2** *vt (document)* tamponner; *(letter)* timbrer; **self-addressed stamped en·velope** enveloppe *f* timbrée à votre adresse. **3** *vti* **to s. (one's feet)** taper des pieds.

stance position *f*.

stand 1 *n (support)* support *m*; *(at exhibition)* stand *m*; *(for spectators)* tribune *f*; **news/flower s.** kiosque *m* à journaux/à fleurs. **2** *vt* (pain, person etc)* supporter; *(put)* mettre (debout); **to s. a chance** avoir une chance. **3** *vi* être *or* se tenir (debout); *(get up)* se lever; *(remain)* rester (debout); *(be situated)* se trouver.

stan·dard 1 *n* norme *f*; *(level)* niveau *m*; **standards (of behavior)** principes *mpl*; **s. of living** niveau *m* de vie; **up to s.** *(of work etc)* au niveau. **2** *adj (model, size)* standard *inv*.

▸ **stand around** *vi* traîner.

▸ **stand aside** *vi* s'écarter.

▸ **stand back** *vi* reculer.

▸ **stand by 1** *vi* rester là (sans rien faire); *(be ready)* être prêt. **2** *vt (friend)* rester fidèle à.

stand·by *adj (ticket)* sans garantie.

▸ **stand for** *vt (mean)* signifier, représenter; *(put up with)* supporter.

▸ **stand in for** *vt* remplacer.

stand·ing *adj* debout *inv.*

▸ **stand out** *vi* ressortir (**against** sur).

stand·point point *m* de vue.

stand·still to bring to a s. immobiliser; **to come to a s.** s'immobiliser.

▸ **stand up 1** *vt* mettre debout. **2** *vi* se lever.

▸ **stand up for** *vt* défendre.

▸ **stand up to** *vt* résister à *(qch)*; *(defend oneself)* tenir tête à *(qn)*.

sta·ple 1 *n (for paper etc)* agrafe *f.* **2** *vt* agrafer.

sta·pler agrafeuse *f.*

star 1 *n* étoile *f*, *(person)* vedette *f.* **2** *vi (of actor)* être la vedette (**in** de). **3** *vt (of movie)* avoir pour vedette.

stare 1 *n* regard *m* (fixe). **2** *vi* **to s. at** fixer (du regard).

Star-Span·gled Ban·ner *(flag)* drapeau *m* américain; *(hymn)* hymne *m* national américain.

start¹ 1 *n* commencement *m*, début *m*; *(of race)* départ *m*; *(lead)* avance *f* (**on** sur); **to make a s.** commencer. **2** *vt* commencer; **to s. doing** *or* **to do** commencer à faire. **3** *vi* commencer (**with sth** par qch; **by doing** par faire); **starting from** *(price etc)* à partir de.

start² *vi (jump)* sursauter.

start (off *or* **out)** *vi* partir (**for** pour).

start (up) 1 *vt (engine, vehicle)* mettre en marche; *(business)* fonder. **2** *vi (of engine, vehicle)* démarrer.

start·er *(in vehicle)* démarreur *m.*

star·tle *vt (make jump)* faire sursauter.

▸ **start on** *vt* commencer.

star·va·tion faim *f.*

starve *vi* souffrir de la faim; *(die)* mourir de faim; **I'm starving!** *(hungry)* je meurs de faim!

state¹ *(condition)* état *m*; **S.** *(nation etc)* État *m*; **the States** *Fam* les États-Unis *mpl.*

state² *vt* déclarer (**that** que); *(time, date)* fixer.

state·ment déclaration *f*, **(bank) s.** relevé *m* de compte.

states·man, *pl* **-men** homme *m* d'État.

stat·ic 1 *adj* statique. **2** *n (on radio)* parasites *mpl*; *(electricity)* électricité *f* statique.

sta·tion *(for trains)* gare *f*, *(underground)* station *f*; **(police) s.** commissariat *m* (de police); **bus s.** gare *f* routière; **radio s.** station *f* de radio; **service** *or* **gas s.** station-service *f.*

sta·tion·ar·y *adj (vehicle)* à l'arrêt.

sta·tion·er·y articles *mpl* de bureau.

sta·tion·er·y store papeterie *f.*

sta·tion·mas·ter chef *m* de gare.

sta·tion wag·on break *m*, commerciale *f.*

sta·tis·tic *(fact)* statistique *f.*

stat·ue statue *f.*

stay 1 *n (visit)* séjour *m.* **2** *vi* rester; *(reside)* loger; *(visit)* séjourner; **to s. put** ne pas bouger.

▸ **stay away** *vi* ne pas s'approcher (**from** de); **to s. away from** *(school etc)* ne pas aller à.

▸ **stay in** *vi* rester à la maison; *(of nail, screw)* tenir.

▸ **stay out** *vi* rester dehors; *(not come home)* ne pas rentrer.

▸ **stay out of** *vt (not interfere in)* ne pas se mêler de.

▸ **stay up** *vi* ne pas se coucher; *(of fence etc)* tenir; **to s. up late** se coucher tard.

stead·i·ly *adv (gradually)* progressivement; *(regularly)* régulièrement; *(without stopping)* sans arrêt.

stead·y *adj* stable; *(hand)* sûr; *(progress, speed)* régulier; **s. (on one's feet)** solide sur ses jambes.

steak steak *m*, bifteck *m*.

steal* *vti* voler (**from sb** à qn).

steam 1 *n* vapeur *f*; *(on glass)* buée *f*. **2** *vt (food)* cuire à la vapeur.

steam·roll·er rouleau *m* compresseur.

steel acier *m*.

steep *adj (stairs, slope etc)* raide; *(hill, path)* escarpé; *(price)* excessif.

stee·ple clocher *m*.

steer *vt (vehicle, ship, person)* diriger (**towards** vers).

steer·ing wheel volant *m*.

stem *(of plant)* tige *f*.

step 1 *n* pas *m*; *(of stairs)* marche *f*; *(on train, bus)* marchepied *m*; *(doorstep)* pas *m* de la porte; *(action)* mesure *f*; **(flight of) steps** escalier *m*; *(outdoors)* perron *m*; **(pair of) steps** *(ladder)* escabeau *m*. **2** *vi (walk)* marcher (**on** sur).

▸ **step aside** *vi* s'écarter.

▸ **step back** *vi* reculer.

step·broth·er demi-frère *m*.

step·daugh·ter belle-fille *f*.

step·fa·ther beau-père *m*.

▸ **step forward** *vi* faire un pas en avant.

▸ **step into** *vt (car etc)* monter dans.

▸ **step out of** *vt (car etc)* descendre de.

step·lad·der escabeau *m*.

step·mo·ther belle-mère *f*.

▸ **step over** *vt (obstacle)* enjamber.

step·sis·ter demi-sœur *f*.

step·son beau-fils *m*.

▸ **step up** *vt (increase)* augmenter; *(quicken)* accélérer.

ster·e·o 1 *n (pl* -os*) (equipment)* chaîne (stéréo *inv*). **2** *adj* stéréo *inv*.

ster·il·ize *vt* stériliser.

ster·ling *(currency)* sterling *m inv*; **s. silver** argent *m* fin; **the pound s.** la livre sterling.

stew ragoût *m*.

stew·ard *(on plane, ship)* steward *m*.

stew·ard·ess hôtesse *f*.

stewed fruit compote *f*.

stick¹ *n* bâton *m*; *(for walking)* canne *f*.

stick*² 1 *vt (glue)* coller; *(put) Fam* mettre, fourrer; **to s. sth into sth** fourrer qch dans qch. **2** *vi* coller (**to** à); *(of food in pan)* attacher (**to** dans); *(of drawer etc)* se coincer, être coincé.

stick·er autocollant *m*.

▸ **stick on** *vt (stamp)* coller.

▸ **stick out 1** *vt (tongue)* tirer. **2** *vi (of petticoat etc)* dépasser.

▸ **stick up** *vt (notice)* afficher.

▸ **stick up for** *vt* défendre.

stick·y *adj* collant; *(label)* adhésif.

stiff *adj* raide; *(leg etc)* ankylosé; *(brush)* dur; **to have a s. neck** avoir le torticolis; **to feel s.** être courbaturé.

sti·fle *vi* **it's stifling** on étouffe.

still¹ *adv* encore, toujours; *(even)* encore; *(nevertheless)* tout de même.

still² *adj (not moving)* immobile; *(calm)* calme; **to keep** *or* **stand s.** rester tranquille.

stim·u·late *vt* stimuler.

sting 1 *vti* (of insect, ointment etc)* piquer. **2** *n* piqûre *f*.

stin·gy *adj* avare.

stink* *vi* puer; **to s. of smoke/etc** empester la fumée/etc.

▸ **stink up** *vt (room)* empester.

stir *vt (coffee, leaves etc)* remuer.

stitch point *m*; *(in knitting)* maille *f*; *(in wound)* point *m* de suture.

stitch (up) *vt (sew)* coudre; *(repair)* recoudre.

stock 1 *n (supply)* provision *f*; *(soup)* bouillon *m*; **stock(s)** *(securities)* valeurs *fpl* (boursières); **in s.** en magasin, en stock; **out of s.** épuisé; **the S. Market** la Bourse. **2** *vt (sell)* vendre.

stock·ing bas m.
stock·pile 1 n réserve f. **2** vt faire des réserves de.
▸ **stock up** vi s'approvisionner (**with** de, en).
stock·y adj trapu.
sto·len pp of **steal**.
stom·ach (for digestion) estomac m; (front of body) ventre m.
stom·ach·ache mal m de ventre; **to have a s.** avoir mal au ventre.
stone pierre f; (pebble) caillou m (pl cailloux); (in fruit) noyau m.
stood pt & pp de **stand**.
stool tabouret m.
stop 1 n (place, halt) arrêt m; (for plane, ship) escale f; **bus s.** arrêt m d'autobus; **to put a s. to sth** mettre fin à qch; **s. sign** (on road) stop m. **2** vt arrêter; (end) mettre fin à; (prevent) empêcher (**from doing** de faire). **3** vi s'arrêter; (of pain, conversation etc) cesser; (stay) rester; **to s. eating/etc** s'arrêter de manger/etc; **to s. snowing/etc** cesser de neiger/etc; **'no stopping (no standing)'** (street sign) 'arrêt interdit'.
▸ **stop by** vi passer (**sb's** chez qn).
stop·light (on vehicle) stop m.
▸ **stop off** or **over** vi (on journey) s'arrêter.
stop·off, stop·o·ver halte f.
stop·per bouchon m.
▸ **stop up** vt (sink, pipe etc) boucher.
stop·watch chronomètre m.
store (supply) provision f; (warehouse) entrepôt m; (shop) magasin m.
store (a·way) vt (furniture) entreposer.
store (up) vt (in warehouse etc) stocker; (for future use) mettre en réserve.
store·keep·er commerçant, -ante mf.
store·room (in house) débarras m; (in office, store) réserve f.
stork cigogne f.

storm tempête f; (thunderstorm) orage m.
storm·y adj orageux.
sto·ry¹ histoire f; (newspaper article) article m; (plot) intrigue f; **short s.** nouvelle f.
sto·ry² (of building) étage m.
stove (for cooking) cuisinière f; (portable) réchaud m; (for heating) poêle m.
straight 1 adj droit; (hair) raide; (route) direct; (tidy) en ordre; (frank) franc (f franche). **2** adv (to walk etc) droit; (directly) tout droit; (to drink whisky etc) sec; **s. away** tout de suite; **s. ahead** or **on** tout droit.
straight·en vt (wire, tie, picture) redresser; (hair) défriser; (room, papers) ranger.
▸ **straighten out** vt (problem) résoudre.
straight·for·ward adj (easy, clear) simple.
strain 1 n (tiredness) fatigue f; (mental) tension f nerveuse. **2** vt (eyes) fatiguer; (voice) forcer; **to s. one's back** se faire mal au dos.
strain·er passoire f.
strand (of wool) brin m; (of hair) mèche f.
strand·ed adj (of) en rade.
strange adj (odd) étrange; (unknown) inconnu.
stran·ger (unknown) inconnu, -ue mf; (person from outside) étranger, -ère mf.
stran·gle vt étrangler.
strap sangle f, courroie f; (on dress) bretelle f; (on watch) bracelet m; (on sandal) lanière f.
▸ **strap (down** or **in)** vt attacher (avec une courroie).
straw paille f; **a (drinking) s.** une paille.
straw·ber·ry 1 n fraise f. **2** adj (ice cream) à la fraise; (jam) de fraises; (tart) aux fraises.
streak (line) raie f; (of color) strie f; (of paint) traînée f.

stream (*brook*) ruisseau m; (*flow*) flot m.

street rue f; **s. door** porte f d'entrée.

street·car (*tram*) tramway m.

street lamp, street light réverbère m.

street map plan m des rues.

strength force f; (*health, energy*) forces fpl; (*of wood etc*) solidité f.

strength·en vt renforcer.

stress 1 n (*mental*) stress m; (*emphasis*) & Grammar accent m; **under s.** stressé. **2** vt insister sur; (*word*) accentuer; **to s. that** souligner que.

stretch 1 vt (*rope, neck*) tendre; (*shoe, rubber*) étirer; **to s. one's legs** se dégourdir les jambes. **2** vi (*of person, elastic*) s'étirer. **3** n (*area*) étendue f.

stretch (out) 1 vt (*arm, leg*) étendre; **to s. (out) one's arm** (*reach out*) tendre le bras (**to take** pour prendre). **2** vi (*of plain etc*) s'étendre.

stretch·er brancard m.

strict adj strict.

strict·ly adv strictement; **s. forbidden** formellement interdit.

strict·ness sévérité f.

stride (*gen*) pas m, enjambée f.

▸ **stride* along/out**/etc vi avancer/sortir/etc à grands pas.

strike*¹ vt (*hit, impress*) frapper; (*collide with*) heurter; (*a match*) frotter; (*of clock*) sonner (*l'heure*); **it strikes me that** il me semble que (+ indicative).

strike² (*of workers*) grève f; **to go (out) on s.** se mettre en grève (**for** pour obtenir).

▸ **strike out 1** vt (*cross out*) rayer, barrer. **2** vi **to s. out at sb** essayer de frapper qn.

strik·er (*worker*) gréviste mf.

strik·ing adj (*impressive*) frappant.

string ficelle f; (*of parka, apron*) cordon m; (*of violin, racket etc*) corde f; (*of pearls*) collier m.

strip (*piece*) bande f; (*thin*) **s.** (*of metal etc*) lamelle f.

strip (off) vi se déshabiller.

stripe rayure f.

striped adj rayé.

strip mall = centre m commercial qui longe une route.

strive vi **to s. to do sth** s'efforcer de faire qch.

stroke 1 n (*movement*) coup m; (*illness*) hémorragie f cérébrale; (*swimming*) **s.** nage f; **a s. of luck** un coup de chance. **2** vt (*beard, cat etc*) caresser.

stroll 1 n promenade f. **2** vi se promener.

stroll·er (*for baby*) poussette f.

strong adj fort; (*shoes, chair etc*) solide.

struc·ture structure f; (*building*) construction f.

strug·gle 1 n (*fight*) lutte f (**to do** pour faire). **2** vi (*fight*) lutter, se battre (**with** avec); (*thrash around*) se débattre; **to s. to do** (*try hard*) s'efforcer de faire; (*have difficulty*) avoir du mal à faire.

stub (*of cigarette etc*) bout m; (*of ticket, check*) talon m, souche f.

stub·born adj (*person*) entêté.

stub·born·ness entêtement m.

▸ **stub out** vt (*cigarette*) écraser.

stuck (*pt & pp de* stick) adj (*caught, jammed*) coincé.

stud (*for collar*) bouton m de col.

stu·dent 1 n étudiant, -ante mf; (*at school*) élève mf; **music**/etc **s.** étudiant, -ante en musique/etc. **2** adj (*life, protest*) étudiant; (*restaurant, housing*) universitaire.

stu·di·o, pl -os (*of artist etc*) studio m; **s. apartment** studio m.

stud·y 1 n étude f; (*office*) bureau m. **2** vt (*learn, observe*) étudier. **3** vi étudier; **to s. to be a doctor**/etc faire des études de médecine/etc; **to s. for an exam** préparer un examen.

stuff 1 n (*thing*) truc m; (*things*)

trucs *mpl*; (*possessions*) affaires *fpl*;
it's good s. c'est bon. **2** *vt* (*fill*) bourrer (**with** de); (*cushion etc*) rem-
bourrer (**with** avec); (*put*) fourrer
(**into** dans); (*chicken etc*) farcir.
stuffed (up) *adj* (*nose*) bouché.
stuff·ing (*for chicken etc*) farce *f*.
stuff·y *adj* (*room etc*) mal aéré; **it
smells s.** ça sent le renfermé.
stum·ble *vi* trébucher (**over** sur).
stump (*of tree*) souche *f*.
stun *vt* (*with punch etc*) étourdir.
stunned *adj* (*amazed*) stupéfait
(**by** par).
stun·ning *adj* (*astounding*) stupéfiant; (*beautiful*) superbe.
stu·pid *adj* stupide; **a s. thing** une
stupidité; **s. fool** idiot, -ote *mf*.
stu·pid·i·ty stupidité *f*.
stur·dy *adj* robuste.
stut·ter 1 *vi* bégayer. **2** *n* to have a
s. être bègue.
sty (*for pigs*) porcherie *f*.
style style *m*; (*fashion*) mode *f*; (*design of dress etc*) modèle *m*; (*of hair*)
coiffure *f*.
styl·ish *adj* chic *inv*.
sub·ject (*matter*) & *Grammar* sujet *m*; (*at school, university*) matière *f*; (*citizen*) ressortissant, -ante
mf.
sub·junc·tive *Grammar* subjonctif *m*.
sub·ma·rine sous-marin *m*.
sub·scrib·er abonné, -ée *mf*.
▸**sub·scribe to** *vt* (*take out subscription*) s'abonner à (*journal etc*);
(*be a subscriber*) être abonné à
(*journal etc*).
sub·scrip·tion (*to newspaper
etc*) abonnement *m*.
sub·side *vi* (*of ground*) s'affaisser.
sub·si·dy subvention *f*.
sub·stance substance *f*.
sub·stan·tial *adj* important;
(*meal*) copieux.
sub·sti·tute produit *m* de remplacement; (*person*) remplaçant,
-ante *mf* (**for** de).

sub·ti·tle sous-titre *m*.
sub·tle *adj* subtil.
sub·tract *vt* soustraire (**from** de).
sub·trac·tion soustraction *f*.
sub·urb banlieue *f*; **the suburbs** la
banlieue.
sub·ur·ban *adj* (*train etc*) de banlieue.
sub·way métro *m*.
suc·ceed *vi* réussir (**in doing** à
faire; **in sth** dans qch).
suc·cess succès *m*, réussite *f*; **he
was a s.** il a eu du succès; **it was a
s.** c'était réussi.
suc·cess·ful *adj* (*effort etc*) cou-
ronné de succès; (*firm*) prospère;
(*candidate in exam*) admis; (*writer,
film etc*) à succès; **to be s.** réussir
(**in** dans; **in an exam** à un examen;
in doing à faire).
suc·cess·ful·ly *adv* avec succès.
suc·ces·sion succession *f*, série *f*;
ten days in s. dix jours consécutifs.
suc·ces·sive *adj* successif.
suc·ces·sor successeur *m* (**to** de).
such 1 *adj* tel, telle; **s. a car/etc** une
telle voiture/etc; **s. happiness/etc**
tant de bonheur/etc; **s. as** comme,
tel que. **2** *adv* (*so very*) si; (*in com-
parisons*) aussi; **s. a large helping**
une si grosse portion; **s. a kind woman as you** une femme aussi gen-
tille que vous.
suck *vt* sucer.
suck (up) *vi* (*with straw*) aspirer.
sud·den *adj* soudain; **all of a s.**
tout à coup.
sud·den·ly *adv* subitement.
suds *npl* (*soap*) **s.** mousse *f* de
savon.
sue 1 *vt* poursuivre (**en justice**).
2 *vi* engager des poursuites judiciaires.
suede 1 *n* daim *m*. **2** *adj* de daim.
suf·fer 1 *vi* souffrir (**from** de). **2** *vt*
(*loss*) subir; (*pain*) ressentir.
suf·fer·er victime *f*; **AIDS s.** malade *mf* du SIDA.
suf·fer·ing souffrance(s) *f(pl)*.

suf·fi·cient adj (quantity) suffisant; **s. money**/etc suffisamment d'argent/etc.

suf·fi·cient·ly adv suffisamment.

suf·fix suffixe m.

suf·fo·cate vti étouffer.

sug·ar 1 n sucre m; **granulated/ lump s.** sucre cristallisé/en morceaux. **2** vt sucrer.

sug·ar bowl sucrier m.

sug·gest vt (propose) suggérer, proposer (**to** à; **doing** de faire; **that** que (+ subjunctive)); (imply) suggérer.

sug·ges·tion suggestion f.

su·i·cide suicide m; **to commit s.** se suicider.

suit[1] (man's) costume m; (woman's) tailleur m; Cards couleur f; **flying/ diving/ski s.** combinaison f de vol/plongée/ski.

suit[2] vt (please, be acceptable to) convenir à; (of dress, color etc) aller (bien) à; **it suits me to stay** ça m'arrange de rester; **suited to** (job, activity) fait pour.

suit·a·ble adj qui convient (**for** à), convenable (**for** pour); (dress, color) qui va (bien).

suit·case valise f.

suite (rooms) suite f; (furniture) mobilier m.

sulk vi bouder.

sul·len adj maussade.

sum (amount of money, total) somme f; (calculation) calcul m.

sum·ma·rize vt résumer.

sum·ma·ry résumé m.

sum·mer 1 n été m; **in (the) s.** en été. **2** adj d'été; **s. vacation** grandes vacances fpl.

sum·mer·time été m.

sum·mon vt (meeting, person) convoquer; (aid) appeler à; (to court etc) citer.

sum·mons 1 n (to court etc) assignation f à comparaître. **2** vt (to court etc) assigner à comparaître.

summon up vt to **s. up one's cou-**

rage/strength rassembler son courage/ses forces.

▸ **sum up** vti (facts etc) résumer.

sun soleil m; **in the s.** au soleil; **the sun is shining** il fait (du) soleil.

sun·bathe vi prendre un bain de soleil, se faire bronzer.

sun·burn coup m de soleil.

sun·burned, sun·burnt adj brûlé par le soleil.

sun·dae glace f aux fruits.

Sun·day dimanche m.

sun·glass·es npl lunettes fpl de soleil.

sun·lamp lampe f à bronzer.

sun·light (lumière f du) soleil m.

sun·ny adj (day etc) ensoleillé; **it's s.** il fait (du) soleil; **s. periods** or **intervals** éclaircies fpl.

sun·rise lever m du soleil.

sun·roof toit m ouvrant.

sun·set coucher m du soleil.

sun·shine soleil m.

sun·stroke insolation f.

sun·tan bronzage m; **s. lotion/oil** crème f/huile f solaire.

sun·tanned adj bronzé.

su·per adj Fam sensationnel.

su·perb adj superbe.

su·per·fi·cial adj superficiel.

su·per·glue colle f extra-forte.

su·per·in·ten·dent (of apartment building) gardien, -enne mf; (police) **s.** = commissaire mf (de police).

su·pe·ri·or adj supérieur (**to** à).

su·pe·ri·or·i·ty supériorité f.

su·per·mar·ket supermarché m.

su·per·sti·tion superstition f.

su·per·sti·tious adj superstitieux.

su·per·vise vt (person, work) surveiller; (office, research) diriger.

su·per·vi·sor surveillant, -ante mf; (in office) chef m de service; (in store) chef m de rayon.

sup·per dîner m; (late-night) souper m; **to have s.** dîner; (late at night) souper.

sup·ple adj souple.
sup·ple·ment 1 n supplément m. **2** vt compléter.
sup·ply 1 vt fournir; (with electricity, gas, water) alimenter (**with** en); (equip) équiper (**with** de); **to s. sb with sth, to s. sth to sb** fournir qch à qn. **2** n (stock) provision f, (food) supplies vivres mpl.
sup·port 1 vt (bear weight of, help, encourage) soutenir; (be in favor of) être en faveur de; (family etc) subvenir aux besoins de. **2** n (help) soutien m; (object) support m.
sup·port·er partisan m; (in sport) supporter m.
sup·pose vti supposer (**that** que); I'm supposed to work or be working je suis censé travailler; he's supposed to be rich on le dit riche; **I s. (so)** je pense; you're tired, **I s.** vous êtes fatigué, je suppose; **s. we go** (suggestion) si nous partions; **s. or supposing you're right** supposons que tu aies raison.
sup·press vt (feelings, smile, revolt) supprimer; (news, truth, evidence) faire disparaître.
sure adj sûr (**of** de; **that** que); she's **s. to accept** il est sûr qu'elle acceptera; **to make s. of sth** s'assurer de qch; **be s. to do it!** ne manquez pas de le faire!
sure·ly adv sûrement; **s. he didn't refuse?** (I hope) il n'a tout de même pas refusé?
sur·face surface f; **s. area** superficie f; **s. mail** courrier m par voie normale.
surf·board planche f (de surf).
surf·ing surf m; **to go s.** faire du surf.
surge 1 n (increase) augmentation f, (of anger, pity) accès m. **2** vi **to s. forward** (people) se ruer en avant.
sur·geon chirurgien, -enne mf.
sur·ger·y to have s. avoir une opération (**for** pour).

sur·gi·cal adj chirurgical.
sur·name nom m de famille.
sur·plus 1 n surplus m. **2** adj en surplus.
sur·prise 1 n surprise f; **to take sb by s.** prendre qn au dépourvu. **2** adj (visit etc) inattendu. **3** vt (astonish) étonner, surprendre.
sur·prised adj surpris (**that** que (+ subjunctive); **at sth** de qch); **I'm s. to see you** je suis surpris de te voir.
sur·pris·ing adj surprenant.
sur·ren·der vi se rendre (**to** à).
sur·round vt entourer (**with** de); (of army, police) encercler; **surrounded by** entouré de.
sur·round·ing adj environnant.
sur·round·ings npl environs mpl, (setting) cadre m.
sur·veil·lance surveillance f.
sur·vey enquête f, (of opinion) sondage m.
sur·vey·or (of land) géomètre m.
sur·vive 1 vi survivre. **2** vt survivre à.
sur·vi·vor survivant, -ante mf.
sus·pect 1 n suspect, -ecte mf. **2** vt soupçonner (**that** que; **of sth** de qch; **of doing** d'avoir fait).
sus·pend vt (postpone, dismiss) suspendre; (student) renvoyer; (driver's license) retirer.
sus·pend·ers npl bretelles fpl.
sus·pense (in book etc) suspense m.
sus·pen·sion (of vehicle) suspension f.
sus·pi·cion soupçon m.
sus·pi·cious adj (person) méfiant; (behavior) suspect; **s.(-looking)** suspect; **to be s. of** se méfier de.
swal·low 1 vti avaler. **2** n (bird) hirondelle f.
▸ **swallow down** vt avaler.
swamp marécage m.
swan cygne m.
swap 1 n échange m. **2** vt échanger

(**for** contre); **to s. seats** changer de place. **3** vi échanger.

swarm (of bees etc) essaim m.

sway vi se balancer.

swear* 1 vt (promise) jurer (**to do** de faire; **that** que). **2** vi (curse) jurer (**at** contre).

swear·word gros mot m.

sweat 1 n sueur f. **2** vi transpirer, suer; **I'm sweating** je suis en sueur.

sweat·er pull m.

sweat shirt sweat-shirt m.

Swede Suédois, -oise mf.

Swed·ish 1 adj suédois. **2** n (language) suédois m.

sweep* 1 vt (with broom) balayer; (chimney) ramoner. **2** vi balayer.

▸**sweep aside** vt écarter.

▸**sweep away** vt (leaves etc) balayer; (carry off) emporter.

▸**sweep out** vt (room etc) balayer.

▸**sweep up** vt balayer.

sweet adj (not sour) doux (f douce); (tea, coffee etc) sucré; (child, house, cat) mignon (f mignonne); (kind) aimable.

sweet·corn maïs m.

sweet·en vt (tea etc) sucrer.

sweet·ly adv (kindly) aimablement; (agreeably) agréablement.

swell* (up) vi (of hand, leg etc) enfler; (of wood, dough) gonfler.

swell·ing enflure f.

swerve vi (of vehicle) faire une embardée.

swift 1 adj rapide. **2** n (bird) martinet m.

swim 1 n to go for a s. se baigner. **2** vi* nager; (as sport) faire de la natation; **to go swimming** aller nager. **3** vt (crawl etc) nager.

swim meet (competition) concours m de natation.

swim·mer nageur, -euse mf.

swim·ming natation f.

swim·ming pool piscine f.

swim·ming trunks slip m de bain.

swim·suit maillot m de bain.

swing 1 n (in playground etc) balançoire f. **2** vi* (sway) se balancer. **3** vt (arms etc) balancer.

▸**swing around** vi (turn) virer; (of person) se retourner (vivement).

Swiss 1 adj suisse. **2** n inv Suisse m, Suissesse f; **the S.** les Suisses mpl.

switch 1 n (electric) bouton m (électrique). **2** vt (money, employee) transférer (**to** à); (exchange) échanger (**for** contre); **to s. places** or **seats** changer de place.

▸**switch off** vt (lamp, gas etc) éteindre; (engine) arrêter.

▸**switch on** vt (lamp, gas etc) mettre, allumer; (engine) mettre en marche.

swol·len (pp de swell) adj (leg etc) enflé; (stomach) gonflé.

sword épée f.

syl·la·ble syllabe f.

syl·la·bus programme m (scolaire).

sym·bol symbole m.

sym·bol·ic adj symbolique.

sym·pa·thet·ic adj (showing pity) compatissant; (understanding) compréhensif.

sym·pa·thize vi **I s. (with you)** (pity) je suis désolé (pour vous); (understanding) je vous comprends.

sym·pa·thy (pity) compassion f; (understanding) compréhension f; (when sb dies) condoléances fpl.

sym·pho·ny symphonie f.

symp·tom symptôme f.

syn·a·gogue synagogue f.

syn·o·nym synonyme m.

sy·ringe seringue f.

syr·up sirop m.

sys·tem système m; (human body) organisme m; (order) méthode f.

tab 188 **talk**

T

tab (cloth etc flap) patte f.
ta·ble (furniture, list) table f; **bed·side t.** table f de chevet; **to lay** or **set/clear the t.** mettre/débarrasser la table.
ta·ble·cloth nappe f.
ta·ble·mat (of cloth) napperon m; (hard) dessous-de-plat m inv.
ta·ble·spoon = cuillère f à soupe.
ta·ble·spoon·ful = cuillerée f à soupe.
tab·let (pill) comprimé m.
tack (nail) petit clou m; (thumbtack) punaise f.
tack·le vt (problem etc) s'attaquer à; Rugby, Football plaquer; Soccer tacler.
tack·y adj (remark etc) de mauvais goût.
tact tact m.
tact·ful adj to be t. (of person) avoir du tact.
tac·tic a t. une tactique; **tactics** la tactique.
taf·fy caramel n (dur).
tag (label) étiquette f.
tail (of animal etc) queue f.
tai·lor tailleur m.
take* vt prendre; (prize) remporter; (exam) passer; (subtract) soustraire (**from** de); (tolerate) supporter; (bring) amener (qn) (**to** à); (by car) conduire (qn) (**to** à); **to t. sth to sb** (ap)porter qch à qn; **to t. sb (out) to the theater/** etc emmener qn au théâtre/etc; **to t. sth with one** emporter qch; **to t. sb home** ramener qn; **it takes courage/** etc il faut du courage/etc (**to do** pour faire); **it took me an hour to do it** j'ai mis une heure à le faire.

▸**take after** vt ressembler à.
▸**take along** vt (object) emporter; (person) emmener.
▸**take apart** vt (machine) démonter.
▸**take away** vt (thing) emporter; (person) emmener; (remove) enlever; (subtract) soustraire (**from** de).
▸**take back** vt reprendre; (return) rapporter; (accompany) ramener (qn) (**to** à).
▸**take down** vt (object) descendre; (notes) prendre.
▸**take in** vt (chair, car etc) rentrer; (include) inclure; (understand) comprendre; (deceive) Fam rouler.
tak·en adj (seat) pris.
▸**take off 1** vt (remove) enlever; (lead away) emmener; (subtract) déduire (**from** de). **2** vi (of aircraft) décoller.
take-off (of aircraft) décollage m.
▸**take on** vt (work, staff, passenger) prendre.
▸**take out** vt (from pocket etc) sortir; (stain) enlever; (tooth) arracher; (insurance) prendre.
take-out 1 adj (meal) à emporter; (restaurant) qui fait des plats à emporter. **2** n (food) plat m à emporter.
▸**take over 1** vt (company etc) racheter; **to t. over sb's job** remplacer qn. **2** vi prendre la relève (**from** de); (permanently) prendre la succession (**from** de).
take·o·ver (of company etc) rachat m; **t. bid** OPA f.
▸**take up** vt (carry up) monter; (space, time) prendre; (hobby) se mettre à.
tak·ings npl recette f.
tale (story) conte m.
tal·ent talent m; **to have a t. for** avoir du talent pour.
tal·ent·ed adj doué.
talk 1 n propos mpl; (gossip) bavar-

dage(s) *m(pl)*; *(conversation)* conversation f; *(lecture)* exposé m (on sur); **talks** pourparlers *mpl*; **to have a t. with sb** parler avec qn; **there's t. of** on parle de. **2** *vi* parler (**to** à; **with** avec; **about, of** de). **3** *vt* *(nonsense)* dire; **to t. sb into doing/out of doing** persuader qn de faire/de ne pas faire.

talk·a·tive *adj* bavard.

▶ **talk over** *vt* discuter (de).

tall *adj (person)* grand; *(tree, house)* haut; **how t. are you?** combien mesures-tu?

tam·bou·rine tambourin m.

tame 1 *adj (animal)* apprivoisé. **2** *vt* apprivoiser.

tam·pon tampon m hygiénique.

tan 1 *n (suntan)* bronzage m. **2** *vti* bronzer.

tan·ger·ine mandarine f.

tan·gled *adj* enchevêtré.

tank *(storing liquid or gas)* réservoir m; *(vehicle)* char m; *(fish)* **t.** aquarium m.

tank·er (oil) **t.** *(ship)* pétrolier m.

tap 1 *n (for water)* robinet m; *(blow)* petit coup m. **2** *vti (hit)* frapper légèrement.

tape¹ 1 *n (of cloth, paper)* ruban m; **(adhesive) t.** ruban m adhésif. **2** *vt (stick)* coller *(avec du ruban adhésif)*.

tape² 1 *n (for sound or video recording)* bande f *(magnétique/vidéo)*. **2** *vt (a movie etc)* enregistrer, magnétoscoper; *(music, voice)* enregistrer; *(event)* faire une cassette de. **3** *vi* enregistrer.

tape meas·ure mètre m (à) ruban.

tape re·cord·er magnétophone m.

tar goudron m.

tar·get cible f; *(objective)* objectif m.

tar·iff *(list of prices)* tarif m; *(at customs)* tarif m douanier.

tar·pau·lin bâche f.

tart *(pie) (open)* tarte f; *(with pastry on top)* tourte f.

tar·tan *adj (skirt etc)* écossais.

task travail m.

taste 1 *n* goût m. **2** *vt (eat, drink)* goûter à; *(make out the taste of)* sentir (le goût de). **3** *vi* **to t. of** *or* **like sth** avoir un goût de qch; **to t. delicious/etc** avoir un goût délicieux/etc.

tast·y *adj* savoureux.

tat·tered *adj (clothes)* en lambeaux.

tat·tle *vi* rapporter (on sur).

tat·tle·tale *Fam* rapporteur, -euse mf.

tat·too 1 *n (pl -oos) (on body)* tatouage m. **2** *vt* tatouer.

tax 1 *n (on goods)* taxe f; *(on income)* impôt m, contributions fpl; **t. free** *(goods)* non taxé; **t. collector** percepteur m d'impôt. **2** *vt (goods)* taxer; *(person, company)* imposer.

tax·a·ble *adj* imposable.

tax·i taxi m; **t. stand** station f de taxis.

tax·pay·er contribuable mf.

TB tuberculose f.

tea thé m; **to have t.** prendre le thé; **t. party** thé m; **t. set** service m à thé

tea·bag sachet m de thé.

teach* 1 *vt* apprendre (sb sth qch à qn; that que); *(in school etc)* enseigner (sb sth qch à qn); **to t. sb (how) to do** apprendre à qn à faire. **2** *vi* enseigner.

teach·er professeur m; *(in primary school)* instituteur, -trice mf.

teach·ing enseignement m; **t. staff** personnel m enseignant.

tea·cup tasse f à thé.

team équipe f.

▶ **team up** *vi* faire équipe (with avec).

tea·pot théière f.

tear¹ 1 *n (rip)* déchirure. **2** *vt** déchirer.

tear² *(in eye)* larme f; **in tears** en larmes.

▶ **tear off** *or* **out** *vt (with force)* arracher; *(receipt, stamp etc)* détacher.

▸**tear up** *vt (letter etc)* déchirer.

tease *vt* taquiner.

tea·spoon petite cuillère *f*, cuillère *f* à café.

tea·spoon·ful cuillerée *f* à café.

tech·ni·cal *adj* technique.

tech·ni·cian technicien, -ienne *mf*.

tech·nique technique *f*.

tech·no·log·i·cal *adj* technologique.

tech·nol·o·gy technologie *f*.

ted·dy bear ours *m* (en peluche).

teen·age *adj (boy, girl, behavior)* adolescent; *(magazine, fashion)* pour adolescents.

teen·ag·er adolescent, -ente *mf*.

tee-shirt tee-shirt *m*.

teeth *see* tooth.

tee·to·tal·er = personne *f* qui ne boit jamais d'alcool.

tele- *prefix* télé-.

tel·e·com·mu·ni·ca·tions *npl* télécommunications *fpl*.

tel·e·gram télégramme *m*.

tel·e·graph pole poteau *m* télégraphique.

tel·e·phone 1 *n* téléphone *m*; **on the t.** *(speaking)* au téléphone. **2** *adj (call, line etc)* téléphonique; *(number)* de téléphone; **t. booth** cabine *f* téléphonique; **t. directory** annuaire *m* du téléphone. **3** *vi* téléphoner. **4** *vt* **to t. sb** téléphoner à qn.

tel·e·scope télescope *m*.

tel·e·vise *vt* retransmettre à la télévision.

tel·e·vi·sion télévision *f*; **on t.** à la télévision; **t. set** téléviseur *m*.

tell* 1 *vt* dire *(sb sth* qch à qn; *that* que); *(story)* raconter; *(distinguish)* distinguer *(from* de); *(know)* savoir; **to t. sb to do** dire à qn de faire; **to t. the difference** voir la différence. **2** *vi* **to t. of** *or* **about sth/sb** parler de qch/qn; **to t. on sb** rapporter sur qn.

tell·er (bank) **t.** guichetier, -ière *mf (de banque)*.

▸**tell off** *vt* disputer.

tem·per **to lose one's t.** se mettre en colère; **in a bad t.** de mauvaise humeur.

tem·per·a·ture température *f*; **to have a t.** avoir de la température.

tem·ple *(building)* temple *m*.

tem·po·rar·i·ly *adj* temporairement.

tem·po·rar·y *adj* provisoire; *(job)* temporaire; *(secretary)* intérimaire.

tempt *vt* tenter; **tempted to do** tenté de faire.

temp·ta·tion tentation *f*.

tempt·ing *adj* tentant.

ten *adj & n* dix *(m)*.

ten·an·cy location *f*; *(period)* occupation *f*.

ten·ant locataire *mf*.

tend *vi* **to t. to do** avoir tendance à faire.

ten·den·cy tendance *f* (**to do** à faire).

ten·der *adj (soft, loving)* tendre; *(painful)* sensible.

ten·nis tennis *m*; **table t.** tennis *m* de table; **t. court** court *m* (de tennis); **t. shoes** chaussures *fpl* de tennis, tennis *fpl*.

tense 1 *adj (person, muscle, situation)* tendu. **2** *n (of verb)* temps *m*.

ten·sion tension *f*.

tent tente *f*.

tenth *adj & n* dixième *(mf)*.

term *(word)* terme *m*; *(period)* période *f*, *(semester)* semestre *m*; **terms** *(conditions)* conditions *fpl*; *(prices)* prix *mpl*; **on good/bad terms** en bons/mauvais termes *(with* avec).

ter·mi·nal (air) **t.** aérogare *f*; **(computer) t.** terminal *m* (d'ordinateur).

ter·mi·nate 1 *vt (work, project)* terminer; *(contract)* résilier; *(pregnancy)* interrompre. **2** *vi* se terminer.

ter·race *(next to house etc)* terrasse *f*.

ter·ri·ble *adj* affreux.

ter·ri·bly *adv (badly, very)* affreusement.

ter·ri·fic *adj Fam (excellent, very great)* formidable.

ter·ri·fy *vt* terrifier; **to be terrified of** avoir très peur de.

ter·ri·fy·ing *adj* terrifiant.

ter·ri·to·ry territoire *m*.

ter·ror terreur *f*.

ter·ror·ist *n & adj* terroriste *(mf)*.

test 1 *vt (try)* essayer; *(product, machine)* tester; *(pupil)* interroger; *(of doctor)* examiner *(les yeux etc)*; *(analyze)* analyser *(le sang etc)*. 2 *n* essai *m*; *(of product)* test *m*; *(in school)* interrogation *f*, test *m*; *(by doctor)* examen *m*; *(of blood etc)* analyse *f*; **eye t.** examen *m* de la vue.

tes·ta·ment testament *m*; *(tribute)* preuve *f*; **Old/New T.** Ancien/Nouveau Testament *m*.

tes·ti·mo·ny témoignage *m*.

test tube éprouvette *f*.

test-tube ba·by bébé-éprouvette *m*.

text 1 *n* texte *m*; **t. (message)** message *m* texte, mini-message *m*. 2 *vt (send text message to)* envoyer un message texte *or* un mini-message à.

text·book manuel *m* (scolaire).

tex·tile *adj & n* textile *(m)*.

tex·ture texture *f*.

than *conj* que; **happier t.** plus heureux que. ▪ *(with numbers)* de; **more t. six** plus de six.

thank 1 *vt* remercier *(for sth* pour qch; *for doing* d'avoir fait); **t. you!** merci!; **no t. you!** (non) merci! 2 **n thanks** remerciements *mpl*; *(many) thanks!* merci (beaucoup)!; **thanks to** *(because of)* grâce à.

thank·ful *adj* reconnaissant *(for* de).

Thanks·giv·ing (day) = 4ème

jeudi de novembre, fête commémorant la première action de grâce des colons anglais.

that 1 *conj* que; **to say t.** dire que. 2 *rel pron (subject)* qui; *(object)* que; *(after prep)* lequel, laquelle, *pl* lesquel(le)s; **the boy t. left** le garçon qui est parti; **the book t.** I read le livre que j'ai lu; **the carpet t.** I put it on le tapis sur lequel je l'ai mis; **the house t.** she told me about la maison dont elle m'a parlé; **the day/moment t.** le jour/moment où. 3 *dem adj (pl see* those*)* ce, cet *(before vowel or mute h)*, cette; *(opposed to 'this')* ce… + -là; **t. day** ce jour; ce jour-là; **t. girl** cette fille; cette fille-là. 4 *dem pron (pl see* those*)* ça, cela; **t. (one)** celui-là *m*, celle-là *f*; **give me t.** donne-moi ça *or* cela; **t.'s right** c'est juste; **who's t.?** qui est-ce?; **t.'s the house** c'est la maison; *(pointing)* voilà la maison; **t. is (to say)** c'est-à-dire. 5 *adv (so)* si; **not t. good** pas si bon; **t. much** *(to cost etc)* (au)tant que ça.

thaw 1 *n* dégel *m*. 2 *vi* dégeler; *(of snow)* fondre; *(of food)* décongeler; **it's thawing** ça dégèle. 3 *vt (food)* (faire) décongeler.

the le, l', la, *pl* les; **t. roof** le toit; **t. man** l'homme; **t. moon** la lune; **t. boxes** les boîtes; **of t., from t.** du, de l', de la, *pl* des; **to t., at t.** au, à l', à la, *pl* aux.

the·a·ter théâtre *m*.

theft vol *m*.

their *poss adj* leur, *pl* leurs.

theirs *poss pron* le leur, la leur, *pl* les leurs; **this book is t.** ce livre est à eux *or* est le leur.

them *pron* les; *(after prep, 'than', 'it is')* eux *mpl*, elles *fpl*; **(to) t.** leur; **I see t.** je les vois; **I give (to) t.** je leur donne; **ten of t.** dix d'entre eux *or* elles; **all of t. came** tous sont venus, toutes sont venues; **I like all of t.** je les aime tous *or* toutes.

them·selves *pron* eux-mêmes

mpl, elles-mêmes *fpl*; *(reflexive)* se, s'; *(after prep)* eux *mpl*, elles *fpl*.

then 1 *adv (at that time)* à cette époque-là; *(just a moment ago)* à ce moment-là; *(next)* ensuite; **from t. on** dès lors; **before t.** avant cela; **until t.** jusque-là. 2 *conj (therefore)* donc.

the·o·ry théorie *f*.

there *adv* là; *(down or over)* t. là-bas; **on t.** là-dessus; **t. is, t. are** il y a; *(pointing)* voilà; **t. he is** le voilà; **that man t.** cet homme-là.

there·fore *adv* donc.

ther·mom·e·ter thermomètre *m*.

Ther·mos® thermos® *m or f*.

ther·mo·stat thermostat *m*.

these 1 *dem adj (sing see this)* ces; *(opposed to 'those')* ces... + ci; **t. men** ces hommes; ces hommes-ci. 2 *dem pron (sing see this)* t. (ones) ceux-ci *mpl*, celles-ci *fpl*; **t. are my friends** ce sont mes amis.

the·sis, *pl* **-ses** thèse *f*.

they *pron* ils *mpl*, elles *fpl*; *(stressed)* eux *mpl*, elles *fpl*; **t. are doctors** ce sont des médecins. ▪ *(people in general)* on; **t. say** on dit.

thick 1 *adj* épais *(f* épaisse*)*. 2 *adv (to spread)* en couche épaisse.

thick·en *vt* épaissir. 2 *vi (of fog etc)* s'épaissir; *(of cream etc)* épaissir.

thick·ly *adv (to spread)* en couche épaisse.

thick·ness épaisseur *f*.

thief, *pl* **thieves** voleur, -euse *mf*.

thigh cuisse *f*.

thim·ble dé *m* (à coudre).

thin 1 *adj (slice, paper etc)* mince; *(person, leg)* maigre; *(soup)* peu épais *(f* épaisse*)*. 2 *adv (to spread)* en couche mince.

thin (down) *vt (paint etc)* diluer.

thing chose *f*; **one's things** *(belongings)* ses affaires *fpl*; **it's a good t.** (that) heureusement que.

think* 1 *vi* penser *(about, of* à*)*; **to t. (carefully)** réfléchir *(about, of*

à*)*; **to t. of doing** penser à faire; **she doesn't t. much of it** ça ne lui dit pas grand-chose. 2 *vt* penser *(that* que*)*; **I t. so** je pense que oui; **what do you t. of him?** que penses-tu de lui?

▸ **think over** *vt* réfléchir à.

▸ **think up** *vt* inventer.

thin·ly *adv (to spread)* en couche mince.

third 1 *adj* troisième. 2 *n* troisième *mf*; **a t.** *(fraction)* un tiers. 3 *adv* **to come t.** se classer troisième.

third·ly *adv* troisièmement.

thirst soif *f*.

thirst·y *adj* **to be** *or* **feel t.** avoir soif; **to make sb t.** donner soif à qn.

thir·teen *adj & n* treize *(m)*.

thir·teenth *adj & n* treizième *(mf)*.

thir·ti·eth *adj & n* trentième *(mf)*.

thir·ty *adj & n* trente *(m)*.

this 1 *dem adj (pl see these)* ce, cet *(before vowel or mute h)*, cette; *(opposed to 'that')* ce... + ci; **t. book** ce livre; ce livre-ci; **t. photo** cette photo; cette photo-ci. 2 *dem pron (pl see these)* ceci; **t. (one)** celui-ci *m*, celle-ci *f*; **give me t.** donne-moi ceci; **t. is Paul** c'est Paul; *(pointing)* voici Paul. 3 *adv* **t. high** *(pointing)* haut comme ceci; **t. far** jusqu'ici.

thorn épine *f*.

thor·ough *adj (careful)* minutieux; *(knowledge, examination)* approfondi; **to give sth a t. cleaning**/etc nettoyer/etc qch à fond.

thor·ough·ly *adv (completely)* tout à fait; *(carefully)* avec minutie; *(to know, clean etc)* à fond.

those 1 *dem adj (sing see that)* ces; *(opposed to 'these')* ces... + -là; **t. men** ces hommes; ces hommes-là. 2 *dem pron (sing see that)* t. (ones) ceux-là *mpl*, celles-là *fpl*; **t. are my friends** ce sont mes amis.

though 1 *conj (even)* bien que *(+ subjunctive)*; **as t.** comme si. 2 *adv (however)* cependant.

thought (pt & pp de **think**) pensée f, **(careful)** t. réflexion f.

thought·ful adj (considerate) gentil, attentionné.

thought·less adj (towards others) pas très gentil; (absent-minded) étourdi.

thou·sand adj & n mille (m & adj inv); **a t. pages** mille pages; **two t. pages** deux mille pages; **thousands of** des milliers de.

thread 1 n (yarn) fil m. 2 vt (needle, beads) enfiler.

threat menace f.

threat·en vt menacer (**to do** de faire; **with sth** de qch).

threat·en·ing adj menaçant.

three adj & n trois (m).

thresh·old seuil m.

threw pt de **throw**.

thrill frisson m.

thrilled adj ravi (**with sth** de qch; **to do** de faire).

thrill·er film m or roman m à suspense.

thrill·ing adj passionnant.

thrive vi (person, business, plant) prospérer; **to t. on sth** avoir besoin de qch pour s'épanouir.

thriv·ing adj prospère.

throat gorge f.

throne trône m.

through 1 prep (place) à travers; (window, door) par; (time) pendant; (means) par; **to go** or **get t.** (forest etc) traverser; (hole etc) passer par; (wall etc) passer à travers. 2 adv à travers; **to let t.** laisser passer; **to be t.** (finished) avoir fini; **t. to** or **till** jusqu'à; **I'll put you t. (to him)** (on phone) je vous le passe.

through·out 1 prep **t. the neighborhood**/etc dans tout le quartier/etc; **t. the day**/etc pendant toute la journée/etc. 2 adv (everywhere) partout; (all the time) tout le temps.

throw* vt jeter (**to, at** à); (party) donner.

▸ **throw away** vt (unwanted object) jeter.

▸ **throw out** vt (unwanted object) jeter; (expel) mettre à la porte.

▸ **throw up** vti (vomit) Fam rendre.

thrust 1 vt* **to t. sth into sth** enfoncer qch dans qch. 2 n (movement) mouvement m en avant; (of argument etc) idée f principale.

thud bruit m sourd.

thug voyou m.

thumb pouce m.

thumb·tack punaise f.

thun·der 1 n tonnerre m. 2 vi tonner; **it's thundering** il tonne.

thun·der·storm orage m.

Thurs·day jeudi m.

thus adv ainsi.

tick (off) vt (on list etc) cocher.

tick·et billet m; (for bus, subway, cloakroom) ticket m; (price) t. étiquette f.

tick·et col·lec·tor contrôleur, -euse mf.

tick·et of·fice guichet m.

tick·le vt chatouiller.

tick·lish adj chatouilleux.

tic-tac-toe morpion m (jeu).

tide marée f.

ti·di·ly adv (to put away) soigneusement.

ti·dy adj (place, toys etc) bien rangé; (clothes, hair) soigné; (person) ordonné; (in appearance) soigné.

tidy (up or **away)** vt ranger.

tie 1 n (around neck) cravate f; (game) match m nul. 2 vt (fasten) attacher (**to** à); (a knot) faire (**in** à); (shoe) lacer.

▸ **tie down** vt attacher.

▸ **tie up** vt attacher (**to** à); (person) ligoter.

ti·ger tigre m.

tight 1 adj (clothes fitting too closely) (trop) étroit; (drawer, lid) dur; (knot, screw) serré; (rope, wire) raide. 2 adv (to hold, shut) bien; (to squeeze) fort.

tight·en (up) *vt (bolt, screw)* (res)serrer; *(security)* renforcer.

tight·ly *adv (to hold)* bien; *(to squeeze)* fort.

tights *npl* collant(s) *m(pl).*

tile 1 *n (on roof)* tuile *f; (on wall or floor)* carreau *m.* **2** *vt (wall, floor)* carreler.

till 1 *prep & conj* = **until. 2** *n (for money)* caisse *f* (enregistreuse).

tilt *vti* pencher.

tim·ber bois *m* (de construction).

time 1 *n* temps *m; (point in time)* moment *m; (period in history)* époque *f; (on clock)* heure *f; (occasion)* fois *f;* **some/most of the t.** une partie/la plupart du temps; **all of the t.** tout le temps; **in a year's t.** dans un an; **it's t. (to do)** il est temps (de faire); **to have a good t.** s'amuser; **to have a hard t. doing** avoir du mal à faire; **in t.** *(to arrive)* à temps; **from t. to t.** de temps en temps; **what t. is it?** quelle heure est-il?; **on t.** à l'heure; **at the same t.** en même temps (**as** que); *(simultaneously)* à la fois; **for t. being** pour le moment; **one at a t.** un à un. **2** *vt (athlete etc)* chronométrer; *(activity)* minuter; *(choose the time of)* choisir le moment de.

tim·er *(device)* minuteur *m; (built into appliance)* programmateur *m; (plugged into socket)* prise *f* programmable.

time·ta·ble horaire *m; (of activities)* emploi *m* du temps.

tim·id *adj (afraid)* craintif; *(shy)* timide.

tim·ing **what good t.!** ça tombe bien!

tin *(metal)* étain *m; (coated steel or iron)* fer-blanc *m; (can)* boîte *f.*

tin·foil papier *m* (d')alu.

ti·ny *adj* tout petit.

tip 1 *n (end)* bout *m; (pointed)* pointe *f; (money)* pourboire *m; (advice)* conseil *m.* **2** *vt (waiter etc)* donner un pourboire à.

tip (out) *vt (liquid, load)* déverser (**into** dans).

▸ **tip (up** *or* **over) 1** *vt (tilt)* pencher; *(overturn)* faire basculer. **2** *vi (tilt)* pencher; *(overturn)* basculer.

tip·toe **on t.** sur la pointe des pieds.

tire¹ 1 *vt* fatiguer. **2** *vi* se fatiguer.

tire² pneu *m (pl* pneus).

tired *vt* fatigué; **to be t. of sth/sb/ doing** en avoir assez de qch/de qn/ de faire.

tired·ness fatigue *f.*

▸ **tire out** *vt* épuiser.

tir·ing *adj* fatigant.

tis·sue *(handkerchief etc)* mouchoir *m* en papier.

ti·tle titre *m.*

to *prep* à; *(towards)* vers; *(of attitude)* envers; *(right up to)* jusqu'à; **give it to him** donne-le-lui; **to France** en France; **to Portugal** au Portugal; **to the butcher(s)/etc** chez le boucher/*etc;* **the road to Paris** la route de Paris; **the train to Paris** le train pour Paris; **kind/cruel to sb** gentil/cruel envers qn; **it's ten (minutes) to one** il est une heure moins dix. ▪ *(with infinitive)* **to say/do/etc** dire/faire/*etc,* (in order) **to** pour. ▪ *(with adjective)* à; **happy/etc to do** heureux/*etc* de faire; **it's easy/difficult to do** c'est facile/difficile à faire.

toad crapaud *m.*

toad·stool champignon *m* (vénéneux).

toast 1 *n* pain *m* grillé; **piece** *or* **slice of t.** tranche *f* de pain grillé, toast *m.* **2** *vt (bread)* griller.

toast·er grille-pain *m inu.*

to·bac·co tabac *m.*

to·bac·co store (bureau *m* de) tabac *m.*

to·bog·gan luge *f.*

to·day *adv* aujourd'hui.

tod·dler enfant *mf* (en bas âge).

toe orteil *m.*

toe·nail ongle *m* du pied.

tof·fee caramel m (dur).

to·geth·er adv ensemble; (at the same time) en même temps; **t. with** avec.

took pt de **take**.

toi·let (room) toilettes fpl; (bowl, seat) cuvette f or siège m des cabinets; **to go to the t.** aller aux toilettes.

toi·let pa·per papier m hygiénique.

toi·let·ries npl articles mpl de toilette.

toi·let wa·ter (perfume) eau f de toilette.

to·ken (for subway etc) jeton m.

told pt & pp de **tell**.

tol·er·ance tolérance f.

tol·er·ant adj tolérant (**of** à l'égard de).

tol·er·ate vt tolérer.

toll (fee) péage m; **t. road/bridge** route f/pont m à péage.

toll-free num·ber = numéro m vert.

to·ma·to, pl -oes tomate f.

tomb tombeau m.

to·mor·row adv demain; **t. morning** demain matin; **the day after t.** après-demain.

ton tonne f (= 907kg); **tons of** (lots of) Fam des tonnes de.

tone ton m; (dial) **t.** tonalité f.

tongs npl pince f.

tongue langue f.

ton·ic (water) Schweppes® m; **gin and t.** gin-tonic m.

to·night adv (this evening) ce soir; (during the night) cette nuit.

tonne = **ton**.

ton·sil amygdale f.

ton·sil·li·tis **to have t.** avoir une angine.

too adv trop; (also) aussi; (moreover) en plus; **to be tired to play** trop fatigué pour jouer; **t. hard to solve** trop difficile à résoudre; **t. much, t. many** trop; **t. much salt/t. many people/etc** trop de sel/gens/etc; **one t. many** un de trop.

took pt de **take**.

tool outil m.

tooth, pl teeth dent f.

tooth·ache mal m de dents; **to have a t.** avoir mal aux dents.

tooth·brush brosse f à dents.

tooth·paste dentifrice m.

tooth·pick cure-dent m.

top¹ 1 n (of mountain, tower, tree) sommet m; (of wall, ladder, page, garment) haut m; (of table) dessus m; (of list) tête f; (of bottle, tube) bouchon m; (bottle cap) capsule f; (of saucepan) couvercle m; (of pen) capuchon m; **at the t. of the class** le premier de la classe; **on t. of** sur. 2 adj (drawer, shelf) du haut; (step, layer) dernier; (in competition) premier; (maximum) maximum; **on the t. floor** au dernier étage; **at t. speed** à toute vitesse.

top² (spinning) **t.** toupie f.

top·ic sujet m.

▸**top up** vt (glass) remplir; (coffee, tea) remettre.

torch torche f.

tor·ment vt (annoy) agacer.

tor·na·do, pl -oes tornade f.

tor·toise tortue f.

tor·toise·shell écaille f.

tor·ture 1 n torture f. 2 vt torturer.

toss 1 vt (throw) jeter (**to** à); **to t. a coin** jouer à pile ou face. 2 vi **let's t.** jouons à pile ou face.

to·tal adj & n total (m).

to·tal·ly adv totalement.

touch 1 n (contact) contact m; (sense) toucher m; **in t. with sb** en contact avec qn; **to get in t.** se mettre en contact. 2 vt toucher. 3 vi (of lines, hands etc) se toucher; **don't t.!** n'y or ne touche pas!

▸**touch down** vi (of aircraft) atterrir.

touch·down (of plane) atterrissage m; (in football) essai m.

touch·y adj susceptible.

tough adj (meat) dur; (sturdy) solide; (strong) fort; (difficult, harsh) dur.

tour 1 n (journey) voyage m; (visit) visite f; (by artist etc) tournée f. 2 vt visiter.

tour·ism tourisme m.

tour·ist 1 n touriste mf. 2 adj touristique.

tour·ist (in·for·ma·tion) of·fice syndicat m d'initiative.

tour·na·ment tournoi m.

tow vt (car, boat) remorquer; (trailer) tracter.

to·ward(s) prep vers; (of feelings) envers; **cruel/etc t. sb** cruel/etc envers qn.

tow·el serviette f (de toilette); (for dishes) torchon m.

tow·er tour f.

town ville f, **in t., (in)to t.** en ville.

town coun·cil conseil m municipal.

town hall mairie f.

town·house maison f mitoyenne (en ville).

town·ship canton m.

tow truck dépanneuse f.

tox·ic adj toxique.

toy 1 n jouet m. 2 adj (gun) d'enfant; (house, car) miniature.

toy·shop magasin m de jouets.

trace 1 n trace f (of de). 2 vt (with tracing paper) (dé)calquer; (find) retrouver.

trac·ing pa·per papier-calque m inv.

track (of animal, sports stadium etc) piste f; (of record) plage f; (for train) voie f; (path) chemin m; (racetrack) champ m de courses; **tracks** (of wheels) traces fpl; **on the right t.** sur la bonne voie.

track shoe (running shoe) jogging m.

track·suit survêtement m.

trac·tor tracteur m.

trac·tor-trail·er semi-remorque m.

trade 1 n commerce m; (job) métier m. 2 vi faire du commerce (with avec); (swap) échanger; **to t. places** changer de place. **3** vt échanger (**for** contre).

trade-in (car etc) reprise f.

trade·mark marque f de fabrique; **(registered) t.** marque déposée.

trad·er commerçant, -ante mf, marchand, -ande mf.

trade un·ion syndicat m.

trad·ing commerce m.

tra·di·tion tradition f.

tra·di·tion·al adj traditionnel.

traf·fic circulation f; (air, sea, rail) trafic m.

traf·fic jam embouteillage m.

traf·fic laws Code m de la route.

traf·fic lights npl feux mpl (de signalisation); (when red) feu m rouge.

traf·fic sign panneau m de signalisation.

trag·e·dy tragédie f.

trag·ic adj tragique.

trail 1 n (of smoke, blood etc) traînée f. 2 vti (on the ground etc) traîner.

trail·er (for car) remorque f; (caravan) camping-car m.

train¹ train m; (underground) rame f; **to go** or **come by t.** prendre le train; **t. set** petit train m; **t. ticket** billet m de train; **t. station** gare f; **t. tracks** voie f ferrée.

train² 1 vt (teach) former (**to do** à faire); (in sport) entraîner; (animal, child) dresser (**to do** à faire). 2 vi recevoir une formation (**as a doctor/etc** de médecin/etc); (of athlete) s'entraîner.

trained adj (skilled) qualifié; (nurse, engineer) diplômé.

train·ee stagiaire mf.

train·er (of athlete, sportsperson, racehorse) entraîneur, -euse mf; (of animal) dresseur, -euse mf.

train·ing formation f; (in sports) entraînement m.

trai·tor traître m.

tramp clochard, -arde mf.

tran·quil·iz·er tranquillisant m.

trans·fer 1 *vt* (*person, goods etc*) transférer (**to** à). **2** *n* transfert *m* (**to** à); (*image*) décalcomanie *f*.

trans·fu·sion (blood) t. transfusion *f* (sanguine).

tran·sis·tor t. (radio) transistor *m*.

tran·sit transit *m*; **in t.** en transit.

tran·si·tive *adj Grammar* transitif.

trans·late *vt* traduire (**from** de; **in to** en).

trans·la·tion traduction *f*.

trans·la·tor traducteur, -trice *mf*.

trans·mis·sion transmission *f*.

trans·mit *vt* transmettre.

trans·par·ent *adj* transparent.

trans·plant greffe *f*.

trans·port 1 *vt* transporter. **2** *n* transport *m* (**of** de); **means of t.** moyen *m* de transport; **public t.** les transports en commun.

trap 1 *n* piège *m*. **2** *vt* (*animal*) prendre (au piège); (*jam*) coincer; (*cut off by snow etc*) bloquer (**by** par).

trap door trappe *f*.

trash (*nonsense*) sottises *fpl*; (*junk*) bric-à-brac *m inv*; (*waste*) ordures *fpl*.

trash·can poubelle *f*.

trash·y *adj* (*book, movie*) nul; (*goods*) de mauvaise qualité.

trav·el 1 *vi* voyager. **2** *vt* (*country, distance*) parcourir. **3** *n* travel(s) voyages *mpl*; **t. agent** agent *m* de voyages; **t. guide** guide *m*.

trav·el·er voyageur, -euse *mf*.

trav·el·er's check chèque *m* de voyage.

trav·el·ing voyages *mpl*.

trav·el sick·ness (*in car*) mal *m* de la route; (*in aircraft*) mal *m* de l'air.

tray plateau *m*.

treach·er·ous *adj* (*road, conditions*) très dangereux.

tread* *vi* marcher (**on** sur).

treas·ure trésor *m*.

treas·ur·er trésorier, -ère *mf*.

treat 1 *vt* traiter; (*consider*) considérer (**as** comme); **to t. sb to sth** offrir qch à qn. **2** *n* (*special*) t. petit extra *m*; **to give sb a (special) t.** donner une surprise à qn.

treat·ment traitement *m*.

treb·le *vti* tripler.

tree arbre *m*.

trem·ble *vi* trembler (**with** de).

tre·men·dous *adj* (*huge*) énorme; (*dreadful*) affreux; *Fam* (*marvellous*) formidable.

trench tranchée *f*.

trend·y *adj Fam* branché.

tri·al (*in court*) procès *m*; **to go or be on t.** être jugé, passer en jugement.

tri·an·gle triangle *m*.

tri·an·gu·lar *adj* triangulaire.

tribe tribu *f*.

trib·ute (*mark of respect*) hommage *m*; **to pay t.** to rendre hommage à.

trick 1 *n* (*joke, of magician etc*) tour *m*; (*clever method*) astuce *f*; **to play a t. on sb** jouer un tour à qn. **2** *vt* tromper.

trick·le 1 *n* (*of liquid*) filet *m*. **2** *vi* dégouliner.

trick·y *adj* (*problem etc*) difficile.

tri·cy·cle tricycle *m*.

trig·ger (*of gun*) gâchette *f*.

trim *vt* couper (un peu).

trip (*journey*) voyage *m*; (*outing*) excursion *f*.

trip (over or **up)** *vi* trébucher; **to t. over sth** trébucher contre qch.

tri·ple *vti* tripler.

▸**trip up** *vt* faire trébucher.

tri·umph 1 *n* triomphe *m* (**over** sur). **2** *vi* triompher (**over** de).

triv·i·al *adj* (*unimportant*) insignifiant.

trol·ley (*streetcar*) tramway *m*.

trom·bone trombone *m*.

troop·er (*soldier*) soldat *m* de cavalerie; (*policeman*) gendarme *m*.

troops *npl* troupes *fpl*.

tro·phy coupe *f*, trophée *m*.

trop·i·cal adj tropical.

trot 1 n trot m. **2** vi trotter.

trou·ble 1 n (difficulty) ennui(s) m(pl); (effort) peine f; (disorder, illness) troubles mpl; **to be in t.** avoir des ennuis; **to get into t.** s'attirer des ennuis (**with** avec); **to go to the t. of doing, take the t. to do** se donner la peine de faire. **2** vt (inconvenience) déranger; (worry, annoy) ennuyer.

trou·sers npl pantalon m; **a pair of t., some t.** un pantalon.

trout truite f.

tru·ant to play t. sécher (la classe).

truck camion m.

truck driv·er, truck·er camionneur m; (over long distances) routier m.

true adj vrai; (accurate) exact; **t. to** (one's promise etc) fidèle à; **to come t.** se réaliser.

trump (card) atout m.

trum·pet trompette f.

trunk (of tree, body) tronc m; (of elephant) trompe f; (case) malle f; (of vehicle) coffre m; **trunks** (for swimming) slip m de bain.

trust 1 n (faith) confiance f (**in** en). **2** vt (person, judgment) avoir confiance en; **to t. sb with sth, to t. sth to sb** confier qch à qn.

truth vérité f.

try 1 vt essayer (**to do, doing** de faire); **to t. one's luck** tenter sa chance. **2** vi essayer; **to t. hard** faire un gros effort. **3** n (attempt) essai m; **to give sth/a t.** essayer qch.

try (out) vt (car, method etc) essayer; (person) mettre à l'essai.

try·ing adj (person) difficile.

T-shirt tee-shirt m.

tub (basin) baquet m; (bath) baignoire f.

tube tube m.

▸ **tuck in** vt (shirt, blanket) rentrer; (person in bed) border.

Tues·day mardi m.

tuft touffe f.

tug vti tirer (**at** sur).

tug(·boat) remorqueur m.

tu·i·tion enseignement m; (lessons) leçons fpl.

tu·lip tulipe f.

tum·ble dégringolade f.

tum·ble (down) vi dégringoler.

tum·ble dry·er sèche-linge m inv.

tum·bler (glass) gobelet m.

tum·my Fam ventre m.

tu·mor tumeur f.

tu·na (fish) thon m.

tune 1 n air m; **in t./out of t.** (instrument) accordé/désaccordé; **to sing in t./out of t.** chanter juste/ faux. **2** vt (instrument) accorder; (engine) régler.

tun·ing (of engine) réglage m.

tun·nel tunnel m.

tur·ban turban m.

tur·key dindon m, dinde f; (as food) dinde f.

turn 1 n (movement, in game) tour m; (in road) tournant m; **to take turns** se relayer; **it's your t.** (to play) c'est à toi or (à) ton tour (de jouer). **2** vt tourner; (mattress, pancake) retourner; **to t. sth red/etc** rendre qch rouge/etc; **she's turned twenty** elle a vingt ans passés. **3** vi (of wheel etc) tourner; (turn head or body) se (re)tourner; (become) devenir; **to t. red/etc** devenir rouge/ etc.

▸ **turn around 1** vt (head, object) tourner; (vehicle) faire faire demi-tour à. **2** vi (of person) se retourner.

▸ **turn away 1** vt (eyes) détourner; (person) renvoyer. **2** vi se détourner.

▸ **turn back** vi retourner.

▸ **turn down** vt (gas, radio etc) baisser; (offer, person) refuser.

▸ **turn into** vt (change) changer qn en qch; **to t. into sb/sth** se changer en qn/qch.

tur·nip navet m (plante).

▶**turn off** vt (light, radio etc) éteindre; (faucet) fermer; (machine) arrêter.

▶**turn on** vt (light, radio etc) mettre; (faucet) ouvrir; (machine) mettre en marche.

▶**turn out 1** vt (light) éteindre. **2** vi (happen) se passer.

▶**turn over 1** vt (page) tourner. **2** vi (of vehicle, person) se retourner.

turn·pike autoroute f à péage.

▶**turn up 1** vt (radio, light etc) mettre plus fort; (collar) remonter. **2** vi (arrive) arriver.

tur·tle tortue f, **sea t.** tortue f de mer.

tur·tle·neck (sweater) col m roulé.

tusk défense f.

tu·tor 1 n précepteur, -trice mf. **2** vt donner des cours particuliers à.

TV télé f.

tweez·ers npl pince f à épiler.

twelfth adj & n douzième (mf).

twelve adj & n douze (m).

twen·ti·eth adj & n vingtième (mf).

twen·ty adj & n vingt (m).

twice adv deux fois; **t. as heavy/etc** deux fois plus lourd/etc.

twig brindille f.

twi·light crépuscule m.

twin jumeau m, jumelle f; **t. brother** frère m jumeau; **t. sister** sœur f jumelle; **t. beds** lits mpl jumeaux.

twine (grosse) ficelle f.

twin·kle vi (of star) scintiller.

twirl 1 vt faire tournoyer. **2** vi tournoyer.

twist 1 vt (wire, arm etc) tordre; (roll) enrouler (**around** autour de); (knob) tourner; **to t. one's ankle** se tordre la cheville. **2** n (turn) tour m; (in road) zigzag m.

▶**twist off** vt (lid) dévisser.

two adj & n deux (m); **t.-way traffic** circulation f dans les deux sens.

type¹ (sort) genre m, type m; (print) caractères mpl.

type² vti (write) taper (à la machine).

typed adj tapé à la machine.

type·writ·er machine f à écrire.

typ·i·cal adj typique (of de); **that's t. (of him)!** c'est bien lui!

typ·ist dactylo f.

U

UFO abbr (unidentified flying object) OVNI m.

ug·li·ness laideur f.

ug·ly adj laid.

ul·cer ulcère m.

ul·ti·mate adj (last) final; (supreme, best) absolu.

um·brel·la parapluie m; (over table, on beach) parasol m.

um·pire arbitre m.

ump·teen adj Fam je ne sais combien de, des tas de.

un- prefix in-, peu, non, sans.

un·a·ble adj to be u. to do être incapable de faire; **he's u. to swim** il ne sait pas nager.

un·ac·cept·a·ble adj inacceptable.

un·ac·cus·tomed to be u. to sth/to doing ne pas être habitué à qch/à faire.

u·nan·i·mous adj unanime.

u·nan·i·mous·ly adv à l'unanimité.

un·at·trac·tive adj (idea, appearance) peu attrayant; (ugly) laid.

un·a·vail·a·ble adj (person) qui n'est pas disponible; (product) épuisé.

un·a·void·a·ble adj inévitable.

un·a·void·a·bly adv inévitablement; (delayed) pour une raison indépendante de sa volonté.

un·a·ware adj to be u. of sth

ignorer qch; **to be u. that** ignorer que.

un·a·wares *adv* to catch sb u. prendre qn au dépourvu.

un·bear·a·ble *adj* insupportable.

un·be·liev·a·ble *adj* incroyable.

un·break·a·ble *adj* incassable.

un·but·ton *vt* déboutonner.

un·cer·tain *adj* incertain (**about, of** de); **it's u. whether** il n'est pas certain que (+ *subjunctive*); **I'm u. whether to stay** je ne sais pas très bien si je dois rester.

un·cer·tain·ty incertitude *f*.

un·changed *adj* inchangé.

un·cle oncle *m*.

un·clear *adj* (*meaning*) qui n'est pas clair; (*result*) incertain; **it's u. whether** on ne sait pas très bien si.

un·com·fort·a·ble *adj* (*chair etc*) inconfortable; (*uneasy*) mal à l'aise.

un·com·mon *adj* rare.

un·con·nect·ed *adj* (*facts etc*) sans rapport (**with** avec).

un·con·scious *adj* (*person*) sans connaissance.

un·con·sti·tu·tion·al *adj* inconstitutionnel.

un·con·vinc·ing *adj* peu convaincant.

un·co·op·er·a·tive *adj* peu coopératif.

un·cork *vt* (*bottle*) déboucher.

un·cov·er *vt* découvrir.

un·dam·aged *adj* (*goods*) en bon état.

un·de·cid·ed *adj* (*person*) indécis (**about** sur).

un·de·ni·a·ble *adj* incontestable.

un·der 1 *prep* sous; (*less than*) moins de; (*according to*) selon; **children u. nine** les enfants de moins de neuf ans; **u. the circumstances** dans les circonstances; **u. there** là-dessous; **u. it** dessous. **2** *adv* au-dessous.

un·der- *prefix* sous-.

un·der·charge *vt* **I under-charged him (for it)** je ne (le) lui ai pas fait payer assez.

un·der·clothes *npl* sous-vêtements *mpl.*

un·der·done *adj* pas assez cuit.

un·der·es·ti·mate *vt* sous-estimer.

un·der·go* *vt* subir.

un·der·grad·u·ate étudiant, -ante *mf* (qui prépare la licence).

un·der·ground *adj* souterrain; **u. passage** passage souterrain.

un·der·line *vt* (*word etc*) souligner.

un·der·mine *vt* saper.

un·der·neath 1 *prep* sous. **2** *adv* (en) dessous; **the book u.** le livre d'en dessous. **3** *n* dessous *m.*

un·der·pants *npl* slip *m.*

un·der·pass (*on highway*) passage *m* inférieur.

un·der·shirt tricot *m* de corps; (*woman's*) chemise *f* (américaine).

un·der·stand* *vti* comprendre.

un·der·stand·a·ble *adj* compréhensible.

un·der·stand·ing 1 *n* compréhension *f*; (*agreement*) accord *m*; (*sympathy*) entente *f.* **2** *adj* (*person*) compréhensif.

un·der·stood *adj* (*agreed*) entendu.

un·der·take* *vt* entreprendre (**to do** de faire).

un·der·tak·er entrepreneur *m* de pompes funèbres.

un·der·tak·ing (*task*) entreprise *f.*

un·der·wa·ter 1 *adj* sous-marin. **2** *adv* sous l'eau.

un·der·wear sous-vêtements *mpl*; (*underpants*) slip *m.*

un·do* *vt* défaire.

un·done *adj* **to come u.** (*of knot etc*) se défaire.

un·doubt·ed·ly *adv* sans aucun doute.

un·dress 1 *vi* se déshabiller. **2** *vt*

déshabiller; **to get undressed** se déshabiller.

un·eas·y adj (ill at ease) mal à l'aise.

un·em·ployed 1 adj au chômage. **2** n **the u.** les chômeurs mpl.

un·em·ploy·ment chômage m; (payment) allocation f de chômage; **to go on u.** s'inscrire au chômage.

un·em·ploy·ment of·fice = agence f nationale pour l'emploi, ANPE f.

un·e·ven adj inégal.

un·e·vent·ful adj (trip etc) sans histoires.

un·ex·pect·ed adj inattendu.

un·ex·pect·ed·ly adv à l'improviste; (suddenly) subitement.

un·fair adj injuste (**to sb** envers qn).

un·fair·ly adv injustement.

un·fair·ness injustice f.

un·faith·ful adj infidèle (**to** à).

un·fa·mil·iar adj inconnu; **to be u. with sth** ne pas connaître qch.

un·fash·ion·a·ble adj (subject etc) démodé; (restaurant etc) peu chic inv.

un·fas·ten vt défaire.

un·fa·vor·a·ble adj défavorable.

un·fin·ished adj inachevé.

un·fit adj en mauvaise santé; (in bad shape) pas en forme; (unsuitable) impropre (**for** à; **to do** à faire); (unworthy) indigne (**for** de; **to do de** faire); (unable) inapte (**for** à; **to do** à faire).

un·fold vt déplier.

un·for·get·ta·ble adj inoubliable.

un·for·giv·a·ble adj impardonnable.

un·for·tu·nate adj malheureux; **you were u.** tu n'as pas eu de chance.

un·for·tu·nate·ly adv malheureusement.

un·friend·ly adj froid, peu aimable (**to** avec).

un·fur·nished adj non meublé.

un·grate·ful adj ingrat.

un·hap·pi·ness tristesse f.

un·hap·py adj (sad) malheureux; **u. with** or **about sth** mécontent de qch.

un·harmed adj (person) indemne.

un·health·y adj (climate etc) malsain; (person) en mauvaise santé.

un·help·ful adj (person) peu serviable.

un·hook vt (picture, curtain) décrocher; (dress) dégrafer.

un·hurt adj indemne.

un·hy·gi·en·ic adj pas très hygiénique.

u·ni·form uniforme m.

un·im·por·tant adj peu important.

un·in·hab·it·ed adj inhabité.

un·in·jured adj indemne.

un·in·ten·tion·al adj involontaire.

un·in·ter·est·ing adj (book etc) peu intéressant.

un·ion 1 n union f; (labor union) syndicat m. **2** adj syndical; **u. member** syndiqué, -ée mf.

u·nique adj unique.

u·nit unité f; (of furniture etc) élément m; (team) groupe m.

u·nite 1 vt unir; (country, party) unifier. **2** vi (of students etc) s'unir.

u·ni·ver·sal adj universel.

u·ni·verse univers m.

u·ni·ver·si·ty 1 n université f; **at u.** à l'université. **2** adj universitaire; (student) d'université.

un·just adj injuste.

un·kind adj peu gentil (**to sb** avec qn).

un·know·ing·ly adv inconsciemment.

un·known adj inconnu.

un·lead·ed adj (gasoline) sans plomb.

un·less conj à moins que (+ subjunctive); **u. she comes** à moins qu'elle ne vienne.

un·like *prep* u. me, she… à la différence de moi, elle…; **that's u. him** ça ne lui ressemble pas.

un·like·ly *adj* peu probable; *(unbelievable)* incroyable; **she's u. to win** il est peu probable qu'elle gagne.

un·lim·it·ed *adj* illimité.

un·list·ed *adj (phone number)* sur la liste rouge.

un·load *vt* décharger.

un·lock *vt* ouvrir *(avec une clef).*

un·luck·i·ly *adv* malheureusement.

un·luck·y *adj (person)* malchanceux; *(number etc)* qui porte malheur; **you're u.** tu n'as pas de chance.

un·made *adj (bed)* défait.

un·mar·ried *adj* célibataire.

un·nec·es·sar·y *adj* inutile.

un·no·ticed *adj* **to go u.** passer inaperçu.

un·oc·cu·pied *adj (house)* inoccupé; *(seat)* libre.

un·pack 1 *vt (suitcase)* défaire; *(goods, belongings)* déballer. **2** *vi* défaire sa valise.

un·paid *adj (bill, sum)* impayé; *(work, worker)* bénévole.

un·pleas·ant *adj* désagréable (**to sb** avec qn).

un·plug *vt (appliance)* débrancher.

un·pop·u·lar *adj* peu populaire; **to be u. with sb** ne pas plaire à qn.

un·pre·dict·a·ble *adj* imprévisible; *(weather)* indécis.

un·pre·pared *adj* **to be u. for sth** *(not expect)* ne pas s'attendre à qch.

un·rea·son·a·ble *adj* qui n'est pas raisonnable.

un·rec·og·niz·a·ble *adj* méconnaissable.

un·re·lat·ed *adj (facts etc)* sans rapport (**to** avec).

un·re·li·a·ble *adj (person)* peu sûr; *(machine)* peu fiable.

un·rest agitation *f.*

un·roll 1 *vt* dérouler. **2** *vi* se dérouler.

un·safe *adj (place, machine etc)* dangereux; *(person)* en danger.

un·sat·is·fac·to·ry *adj* peu satisfaisant.

un·screw *vt* dévisser.

un·skilled work·er ouvrier, -ière *mf* non qualifié(e).

un·sta·ble *adj* instable.

un·stead·i·ly *adv (to walk)* d'un pas mal assuré.

un·stead·y *adj (hand, step)* mal assuré; *(table, ladder etc)* instable.

un·suc·cess·ful *adj (attempt etc)* vain; *(candidate)* malheureux; **to be u.** ne pas réussir (**in doing** à faire).

un·suc·cess·ful·ly *adv* en vain.

un·suit·a·ble *adj* qui ne convient pas (**for** à).

un·suit·ed *adj* **u. to** *(job, activity)* peu fait pour.

un·sure *adj* incertain (**of, about** de).

un·tan·gle *vt* démêler.

un·ti·dy *adj (clothes, hair)* peu soigné; *(room)* en désordre; *(person)* désordonné; *(in appearance)* peu soigné.

un·tie *vt (person, hands)* détacher; *(knot, parcel)* défaire.

un·til 1 *prep* jusqu'à; **u. then** jusque-là; **I didn't come u. yesterday** je ne suis venu qu'hier; **not u. tomorrow** pas avant demain. **2** *conj* jusqu'à ce que (**+ subjunctive**); **do nothing u. I come** ne fais rien avant que j'arrive.

un·true *adj* faux *(f* fausse*).*

un·used *adj (new)* neuf *(f* neuve*).*

un·u·su·al *adj* exceptionnel; *(strange)* étrange.

un·u·su·al·ly *adv* exceptionnellement.

un·veil *vt* dévoiler.

un·want·ed *adj* non désiré.

un·well *adj* indisposé.

un·will·ing *adj* **he's u. to do** il ne veut pas faire.

un·will·ing·ly *adv* à contrecœur.

un·wor·thy adj indigne (**of** de).

un·wrap vt ouvrir.

un·zip vt ouvrir (la fermeture éclair® de).

up 1 adv en haut; (in the air) en l'air; (out of bed) levé, debout; **to come** or **go up** monter; **prices are up** les prix ont augmenté; **up there** là-haut; **further** or **higher up** plus haut; **up to** (as far as) jusqu'à; **it's up to you to do it** c'est à toi de le faire; **that's up to you** ça dépend de toi; **what are you up to?** que fais-tu?; **to walk up and down** marcher de long en large. **2** prep (a hill) en haut de; (a tree) dans; (a ladder) sur; **to go up** (hill, stairs) monter.

up·date vt mettre à jour.

up·grade 1 vt (improve) améliorer; (promote) promouvoir; (software) mettre à jour. **2** n (of software) mise f à jour.

up·hill adv **to go u.** monter.

up·hold vt maintenir.

up·on prep sur.

up·per adj supérieur.

up·right adj & adv (straight) droit.

up·roar vacarme m, tapage m.

up·scale adj haut de gamme.

up·set 1 vt* (stomach, routine etc) déranger; **to u. sb** (make sad) peiner qn; (offend) vexer qn. **2** adj (sad) peiné; (offended) vexé; (stomach) dérangé; **to have an u. stomach** avoir l'estomac dérangé.

up·side down adv à l'envers.

up·stairs 1 adv en haut; **to go u.** monter (l'escalier). **2** adj (people, room) du dessus.

up-to-date adj moderne; (information) à jour; (well-informed) au courant (**on** de).

up·town les quartiers mpl résidentiels.

up·ward(s) adv vers le haut; **upwards of five euros** cinq euros et plus.

urge vt **to u. sb to do** conseiller vivement à qn de faire.

ur·gen·cy urgence f.

ur·gent adj urgent.

ur·gent·ly adv d'urgence.

u·rine urine f.

us pron nous; **(to) us** nous; **she sees us** elle nous voit; **he gives (to) us** il nous donne; **all of us** nous tous; **let's** or **let us eat!** mangeons!

us·age usage m.

use 1 n usage m, emploi m; **to make u. of sth** se servir de qch; **not in u.** hors d'usage; **to be of u.** être utile; **it's no u. crying/etc** ça ne sert à rien de pleurer/etc; **what's the u. of worrying/etc?** à quoi bon s'inquiéter/etc? **2** vt se servir de, utiliser (**as** comme; **to do, for doing** pour faire); **it's used to do** or **for doing** ça sert à faire; **it's used as** ça sert de.

use (up) vt (fuel) consommer; (supplies) épuiser; (money) dépenser.

used 1 adj (secondhand) d'occasion. **2** v aux **I u. to sing/etc** avant, je chantais/etc. **3** adj **u. to sth/to doing** habitué à qch/à faire; **to get u. to** s'habituer à.

use·ful adj utile (**to** à); **to come in u.** être utile.

use·ful·ness utilité f.

use·less adj inutile; (person) nul.

us·er (of road) usager m; (of machine, dictionary) utilisateur, -trice mf.

us·er-friend·ly adj convivial.

u·su·al adj habituel; **as u.** comme d'habitude.

u·su·al·ly adv d'habitude.

u·ten·sil ustensile m.

u·til·i·ty (public) **u.** service m public.

ut·ter 1 adj complet; (idiot) parfait. **2** vt (a cry) pousser; (a word) dire.

ut·ter·ly adv complètement.

U-turn (in vehicle) demi-tour m.

V

va·can·cy *(post)* poste *m* vacant; *(room)* chambre *f* libre.

va·cant *adj (room, seat)* libre; **v. lot** terrain *m* vague.

va·ca·tion vacances *fpl*; **on v.** en vacances.

va·ca·tion·er vacancier, -ière *mf*.

vac·ci·nate *vt* vacciner.

vac·ci·na·tion vaccination *f*.

vac·cine vaccin *m*.

vac·u·um *vt (carpet etc)* passer à l'aspirateur.

vac·u·um clean·er aspirateur *m*.

vague *adj* vague; *(outline)* flou.

vague·ly *adv* vaguement.

vain *adj* **in v.** en vain.

val·id *adj (ticket etc)* valable.

val·ley vallée *f*.

val·u·a·ble **1** *adj (object)* de (grande) valeur. **2** *npl* **valuables** objets *mpl* de valeur.

val·ue valeur *f*; **it's good v. (for money)** ça a un bon rapport qualité/prix.

valve *(of machine)* soupape *f*; *(in pipe, tube, heart)* valve *f*.

van camionnette *f*, fourgonnette *f*; *(large)* camion *m*.

van·dal vandale *mf*.

van·dal·ize *vt* saccager.

va·nil·la **1** *n* vanille *f*. **2** *adj (ice cream)* à la vanille.

van·ish *vi* disparaître.

var·i·a·ble *adj & n* variable *(f)*.

var·i·ant variante *f*.

var·ied *adj* varié.

va·ri·e·ty variété *f*; **a v. of reasons/etc** diverses raisons/*etc*; **v. show** spectacle *m* de variétés.

var·i·ous *adj* divers.

var·nish **1** *vt* vernir. **2** *n* vernis *m*.

var·y *vti* varier.

vase vase *m*.

Vas·e·line® vaseline *f*.

vast *adj* vaste.

VCR *abbr (video cassette recorder)* magnétoscope *m*.

veal *(meat)* veau *m*.

veg·e·ta·ble légume *m*.

veg·e·tar·i·an *adj & n* végétarien, -ienne *(mf)*.

veg·e·ta·tion végétation *f*.

ve·hi·cle véhicule *m*.

veil voile *m*.

vein *(in body)* veine *f*.

vel·vet **1** *n* velours *m*. **2** *adj* de velours.

vend·ing ma·chine distributeur *m* automatique.

ven·dor vendeur, -euse *mf*.

ve·ne·tian blind store *m* vénitien.

ven·ti·la·tion *(in room)* aération *f*.

ven·ture **1** *vt* hasarder; **to v. to do sth** se hasarder à faire qch. **2** *vi* **to v. out of doors** se risquer à sortir. **3** *n* entreprise *f* (hasardeuse).

ven·ue *(meeting place)* lieu *m* (de rendez-vous); *(for concert etc)* salle *f*.

verb verbe *m*.

ver·bal *adj* verbal.

ver·dict verdict *m*.

verse *(part of song)* couplet *m*; *(poetry)* poésie *f*, **in v.** en vers.

ver·sion version *f*.

ver·sus *prep* contre.

ver·ti·cal *adj* vertical.

ver·y **1** *adv* très; **v. much** beaucoup; **at the v. latest** au plus tard. **2** *adj (actual)* même; **his** or **her v. brother** son frère même.

vest *(waistcoat)* gilet *m*.

vet vétérinaire *m*.

vet·er·an *(of war)* ancien combattant *m*; *(experienced person)* vétéran *m*.

vet·er·i·nar·i·an vétérinaire *mf*.

vi·a *prep* par.

vi·brate *vi* vibrer.

vi·bra·tion vibration *f*.

vic·ar pasteur *m*.

vice vice *m*; *(tool)* étau *m*.
vi·cious *adj (spiteful)* méchant; *(violent)* brutal.
vic·tim victime *f*; **to be the v. of** être victime de.
vic·to·ry victoire *f*.
vid·e·o 1 *n (cassette)* cassette *f*; **on v.** sur cassette. **2** *adj (game, camera etc)* vidéo *inv*. **3** *vt (event)* faire une (vidéo)cassette de.
vid·e·o·cas·sette vidéocassette *f*; **v. recorder** magnétoscope *m*.
vid·e·o game jeu *m* vidéo.
vid·e·o·tape cassette *f* vidéo.
view vue *f*; **to come into v.** apparaître; **in my v.** à mon avis; **in v. of** compte tenu de.
view·er *(person)* téléspectateur, -trice *mf*.
view·find·er viseur *m*.
view·point point *m* de vue.
vil·la villa *f*.
vil·lage village *m*.
vil·lag·er villageois, -oise *mf*.
vil·lain scélérat *m*; *(in movie, play)* méchant, -ante *mf*.
vin·e·gar vinaigre *m*.
vine·yard vignoble *m*.
vi·o·lence violence *f*.
vi·o·lent *adj* violent.
vi·o·lent·ly *adv* violemment.
vi·o·lin violon *m*.
VIP *abbr (very important person)* VIP *mf*.
vir·gin vierge *f*.
vir·tu·al *adj* quasi; **v. reality** réalité *f* virtuelle.
vir·tue *(goodness)* vertu *f*; *(advantage)* mérite *m*; **by v. of** en vertu de.
vi·rus virus *m*.
vi·sa visa *m*.
vise étau *m*.
vis·i·ble *adj* visible.
vis·it 1 *n* visite *f*; *(stay)* séjour *m*. **2** *vt (place)* visiter; **to v. sb** rendre visite à qn; *(stay with)* faire un séjour chez qn. **3** *vi* être en visite.
vis·it·ing hours heures *fpl* de visite.

vis·i·tor visiteur, -euse *mf*; *(guest)* invité, -ée *mf*.
vi·tal *adj* essentiel; **it's v. that** il est essentiel que (+ *subjunctive*).
vi·ta·min vitamine *f*.
viv·id *adj* vif; *(description)* vivant.
vo·cab·u·lar·y vocabulaire *m*.
vo·ca·tion·al *adj* profesionnel, -elle.
vod·ka vodka *f*.
voice voix *f*; **at the top of one's v.** à tue-tête.
vol·ca·no, *pl* -oes volcan *m*.
volt·age voltage *m*.
vol·ume *(book, capacity, loudness)* volume *m*.
vol·un·tar·y *adj* volontaire; *(unpaid)* bénévole.
vol·un·teer 1 *n* volontaire *mf*. **2** *vi* se proposer (**for sth** pour qch; **to do** pour faire).
vom·it *vti* vomir.
vote 1 *n* vote *m*. **2** *vi* voter; **to v. Republican** voter républicain.
vot·er électeur, -trice *mf*.
vouch·er *(for meal, gift etc)* chèque *m*.
vow·el voyelle *f*.
voy·age voyage *m* (par mer).
vul·gar *adj* vulgaire.

W

wad *(of money etc)* liasse *f*; *(of cotton wool)* tampon *m*.
wad·dle *vi* se dandiner.
▶**wade through** *vt (mud, water etc)* patauger dans.
wad·ing pool *(small, inflatable)* piscine *f* gonflable.
▶**wad up** *vt (paper)* chiffonner.
wa·fer gaufrette *f*.
waf·fle gaufre *f*.
wag *vti (tail)* remuer.

wage(·s) n(pl) salaire m.

wage earn·er salarié, -ée mf.

wag·on (horse-drawn) charrette f, chariot m.

waist taille f; stripped to the w. torse nu.

waist·coat gilet m.

wait 1 n attente f. **2** vi attendre; **to w. for sb/sth** attendre qn/qch; **w. until I've gone, w. for me to go** attends que je sois parti; **to keep sb waiting** faire attendre qn.

▶ **wait behind** vi rester.

wait·er garçon m (de café).

wait·ing attente f.

wait·ing room salle f d'attente.

wait·ress serveuse f.

wait·staff serveurs mpl.

▶ **wait up** vi veiller; **to w. up for sb** attendre le retour de qn avant de se coucher.

wake* (up) 1 vi se réveiller. **2** vt réveiller.

walk 1 n promenade f; (shorter) (petit) tour m; (path) allée f; **to go for a w.** faire une promenade; (shorter) faire un (petit) tour; **to take for a w.** (child) emmener se promener; (baby, dog) promener; **five minutes' w. (away)** à cinq minutes à pied. **2** vi marcher; (stroll) se promener; (go on foot) aller à pied. **3** vt (distance) faire à pied; (take for a walk) promener (chien).

▶ **walk away** vi s'éloigner (**from** de).

walk·er (for pleasure) promeneur, -euse mf.

▶ **walk in** vi entrer.

walk·ing stick canne f.

Walk·man®, pl Walkmans baladeur m.

▶ **walk off** vi s'en aller; **to walk off with sth** (steal) partir avec qch.

▶ **walk out** vi (leave) partir.

wall mur m; (of cabin, tunnel) paroi f.

wal·let portefeuille m.

wall·pa·per 1 n papier m peint. **2** vt tapisser.

wall-to-wall car·pet(·ing) moquette f.

wal·nut (nut) noix f.

wal·rus (animal) morse m.

wan·der (a·round) vi errer; (stroll) flâner.

want vt vouloir (**to do** faire); (ask for) demander (qn); (need) avoir besoin de; **I w. him to go** je veux qu'il parte; **you're wanted** on vous demande.

war guerre f; **at w.** en guerre (**with** avec).

ward (in hospital) salle f.

war·den directeur, -trice mf.

ward·robe (built-in) penderie f; (free-standing) armoire f.

ware·house, pl -ses entrepôt m.

warm 1 adj chaud; **to be** or **feel w.** avoir chaud; **it's (nice and) w.** (of weather) il fait (agréablement) chaud. **2** vt (person, food etc) réchauffer.

warmth chaleur f.

▶ **warm up 1** vt (person, food etc) réchauffer. **2** vi (of person, room, engine) se réchauffer; (of food, water) chauffer.

warn vt avertir (**that** que); **to w. sb against sth** mettre qn en garde contre qch; **to w. sb against doing** conseiller à qn de ne pas faire.

warn·ing avertissement m; (advance notice) (pré)avis m; **(hazard) w. flashers** (of vehicle) feux mpl de détresse.

war·rant 1 n (legal order) mandat m. **2** vt (justify) justifier.

war·ran·ty (for goods) garantie f.

war·ri·or guerrier, -ère mf.

war·ship navire m de guerre.

wart verrue f.

war·time in w. en temps de guerre.

was pt de **be**.

wash 1 n to give sth a w. laver qch; **in the w.** (of dirty clothes) au sale. **2** vt laver; **to w. one's hands** se laver les mains.

wash·a·ble adj lavable.
▸ **wash away** or **off** or **out 1** vt (stain) faire partir (en lavant). **2** vi partir au lavage).
wash·ba·sin lavabo m.
wash·cloth gant m de toilette.
wash·ing (act) lavage m.
wash·ing ma·chine machine f à laver.
▸ **wash out** (bowl etc) laver.
wash·room toilettes fpl.
▸ **wash up** vi (wash hands and face) se laver.
wasp guêpe f.
waste 1 n gaspillage m; (of time) perte f. **2** vt (money, food etc) gaspiller; (time, opportunity) perdre.
waste·pa·per vieux papiers mpl.
waste·pa·per bas·ket corbeille f (à papier).
watch 1 n (small clock) montre f. **2** vt regarder; (be careful of) faire attention à. **3** vi regarder.
watch·band bracelet m de montre.
▸ **watch (out) for** vt (wait for) guetter.
watch (o·ver) vt (suspect, baby etc) surveiller.
▸ **watch out** vi (take care) faire attention (for à); **w. out!** attention!
wa·ter 1 n eau f; **w. pistol** pistolet m à eau. **2** vt (plant etc) arroser.
wa·ter·col·or (picture) aquarelle f; (paint) couleur f pour aquarelle.
wa·ter·cress cresson m (de fontaine).
▸ **water down** vt (wine etc) couper (d'eau).
wa·ter·fall chute f d'eau.
wa·ter·front bord m or front m de mer.
wa·ter·ing can arrosoir m.
wa·ter·mel·on pastèque f.
wa·ter·proof adj (material) imperméable.
wa·ter ski·ing ski m nautique.
wa·ter·tight adj étanche.
wave 1 n (of sea) vague f; (in hair) ondulation f; **medium/short w.** (on radio) ondes fpl moyennes/courtes; **long w.** grandes ondes fpl, ondes fpl longues. **2** vi (with hand) faire signe (de la main); **to w. to sb** (greet) saluer qn de la main. **3** vt (arm, flag etc) agiter.
wave·length longueur f d'ondes.
wav·y adj (hair) ondulé.
wax 1 n cire f. **2** vt cirer.
wax pa·per papier m sulfurisé.
way¹ 1 n (path) chemin m (to de); (direction) sens m; (distance) distance f; **all the w., the whole w.** (to talk etc) pendant tout le chemin; **this w.** par ici; **that w.** par là; **which w.?** par où?; **to lose one's w.** se perdre; **the w. there** l'aller m; **the w. back** le retour; **the w. in** l'entrée f; **the w. out** la sortie; **on the w.** en route (to pour); **to be** or **stand in sb's w.** être sur le chemin de qn; **to get out of the w.** s'écarter; **a long w. (away** or **off)** très loin. **2** adv (behind etc) très loin; **w. ahead** très en avance (of sur).
way² 1 n (manner) façon f; (means) moyen m; **(in) this w.** de cette façon; **no w.!** Fam pas question!
we pron nous; **we teachers** nous autres professeurs.
weak adj faible; (tea, coffee) léger.
weak·en 1 vt affaiblir. **2** vi faiblir.
weak·ness faiblesse f; (fault) point m faible.
wealth richesse(s) f(pl).
wealth·y adj riche.
weap·on arme f.
wear* 1 vt (have on body) porter; (put on) mettre. **2** n **w. (and tear)** usure f.
▸ **wear off** vi (of color, effect etc) disparaître.
▸ **wear out 1** vt (clothes etc) user; (person) épuiser. **2** vi s'user.
wea·ry adj fatigué.
wea·sel belette f.
weath·er temps m; **what's the w. like?** quel temps fait-il?; **it's nice w.**

il fait beau; **under the w.** *(ill)* patraque.

weath·er fore·cast, weather report météo *f.*

weave* *vt (cloth)* tisser.

web *(of spider)* toile *f.*

wed·ding mariage *m.*

wed·ding ring alliance *f.*

wedge 1 *n (under wheel etc)* cale *f.* **2** *vt (table etc)* caler.

Wednes·day mercredi *m.*

weed mauvaise herbe *f.*

week semaine *f*; **a w. from tomorrow** demain en huit.

week·day jour *m* de semaine.

week·end week-end *m*; **over the w.** ce week-end.

week·ly 1 *adj* hebdomadaire. **2** *adv* toutes les semaines. **3** *n (magazine)* hebdomadaire *m.*

weep* *vi* pleurer.

weigh *vti* peser.

weight poids *m*; **by w.** au poids; **to put on w.** grossir; **to lose w.** maigrir.

weird *adj (odd)* bizarre.

wel·come 1 *adj* **to be w.** *(warmly received, of person)* être bien reçu; **w.!** bienvenue!; **to make sb (feel) w.** faire bon accueil à qn; **you're w.!** *(after 'thank you')* il n'y a pas de quoi!; **some coffee/a break would be w.** un café/une pause ne ferait pas de mal. **2** *n* accueil *m.* **3** *vt* accueillir; *(warmly)* faire bon accueil à.

weld *vt* souder.

wel·fare **to be on w.** vivre d'allocations.

well¹ *(for water)* puits *m*; *(oil)* puits *m* de pétrole.

well² **1** *adv* bien; **w. done!** bravo!; **as w.** *(also)* aussi; **as w. as** aussi bien que; **as w. as two cats, he has a dog** en plus de deux chats, il a un chien. **2** *adj* bien *inv*; **she's w.** *(healthy)* elle va bien; **to get w.** se remettre. **3** *int* eh bien!; **huge, w., very big** énorme, enfin, très grand.

well-be·haved *adj* sage.

well-be·ing bien-être *m.*

well-in·formed *adj* bien informé.

well-known *adj* (bien) connu.

well-man·nered *adj* bien élevé.

well-off *adj* riche.

well-to-do *adj* aisé.

Welsh 1 *adj* gallois. **2** *n (language)* gallois *m*; **the W.** les Gallois *mpl.*

Welsh·man, *pl* -men Gallois *m.*

Welsh·wom·an, *pl* -women Galloise *f.*

went *pt de* **go¹**.

were *pt de* **be**.

west 1 *n* ouest *m*; **(to the) w. of** à l'ouest de. **2** *adj (coast)* ouest *inv.* **3** *adv* à l'ouest.

west·bound *adj* en direction de l'ouest.

west·ern 1 *adj (coast)* ouest *inv*; *(culture etc)* occidental. **2** *n (film)* western *m.*

west·ward(s) *adj & adv* vers l'ouest.

wet 1 *adj* mouillé; *(damp, rainy)* humide; *(day, month)* de pluie; **'w. paint'** 'peinture fraîche'; **to get w.** se mouiller; **to make w.** mouiller; **it's w.** *(raining)* il pleut. **2** *vt* mouiller.

whale baleine *f.*

wharf quai *m*, débarcadère *m.*

what 1 *adj* quel, quelle, *pl* quel(le)s; **w. book?** quel livre?; **w. a fool!** quel idiot! **2** *pron (in questions)* qu'est-ce qui; *(object)* qu'est-ce que; *(after prep)* quoi; **w.'s happening?** qu'est-ce qui se passe?; **w. does he do?** qu'est-ce qu'il fait?, que fait-il?; **w. is it?** qu'est-ce que c'est?; **w.'s that book?** c'est quoi, ce livre?; **w.!** *(surprise)* quoi!; **w.'s it called?** comment ça s'appelle?; **w. for?** pourquoi?; **w. about me?** et moi?; **w. about leaving?** si on partait? **3** *pron (indirect, relative)* ce qui; *(object)* ce que; **I know w. will happen/w. she'll do** je sais ce qui arrivera/ce qu'elle fera; **w. I need** ce dont j'ai besoin.

what·ev·er 1 *adj* w. (the) mistake/*etc* quelle que soit l'erreur/*etc*; no chance w. pas la moindre chance; nothing w. rien du tout. **2** *pron (no matter what)* quoi que (+ *subjunctive*); w. you do quoi que tu fasses; w. is important tout ce qui est important; do w. you want fais tout ce que tu veux.

wheat blé *m*.

wheel 1 *n* roue *f*; at the w. *(driving)* au volant. **2** *vt* pousser.

wheel·bar·row brouette *f*.

wheel·chair fauteuil *m* roulant.

when 1 *adv* quand. **2** *conj* quand; w. I finish, w. I've finished quand j'aurai fini; w. I saw him *or* w. I'd seen him, I left après l'avoir vu, je suis parti; the day/moment w. le jour/moment où.

when·ev·er *conj* quand; *(each time that)* chaque fois que.

where 1 *adv* où; w. are you from? d'où êtes-vous? **2** *conj* (là) où; I found it w. she'd left it je l'ai trouvé là où elle l'avait laissé; the place/house w. l'endroit/la maison où.

where·a·bouts 1 *adv* où (donc). **2** *n* his w. l'endroit *m* où il est.

where·as *conj* alors que.

where·by *adv* par quoi.

wher·ev·er *conj* w. you go partout où tu iras; I'll go w. you like j'irai (là) où vous voudrez.

wheth·er *conj* si; I don't know w. to leave je ne sais pas si je dois partir; w. she does it or not qu'elle le fasse ou non.

which 1 *adj (in questions etc)* quel, quelle, *pl* quel(le)s; w. hat? quel chapeau?; in w. case auquel cas. **2** *rel pron (subject)* qui; *(object)* que; *(after prep)* lequel, laquelle, *pl* lesquel(le)s; *(after clause)* ce qui; ce que; the house w. is old la maison qui est vieille; the book w. I like le livre que j'aime; the table w. I put it

on la table sur laquelle je l'ai mis; the film of w. le film dont; she's sick, w. is sad elle est malade, ce qui est triste; he lies, w. I don't like il ment, ce que je n'aime pas. **3** *pron* w. (one) *(in questions)* lequel, laquelle, *pl* lesquel(le)s; w. (one) of us? lequel *or* laquelle d'entre nous *or* de nous? ▪ w. (one) *(the one that)* celui que, celle qui, *pl* ceux qui, celles qui; *(object)* celui *etc* que; show me w. (one) is red montrez-moi celui *or* celle qui est rouge; I know w. (ones) you want je sais ceux *or* celles que vous désirez.

which·ev·er *adj & pron* w. book/ *etc or* w. of the books/*etc* you buy quel que soit le livre/*etc* que tu achètes; take w. books interest you prenez les livres qui vous intéressent; take w. (one) you like prends celui *or* celle que tu veux; w. (ones) remain ceux *or* celles qui restent.

while 1 *conj (when)* pendant que; *(although)* bien que (+ *subjunctive)*; *(as long as)* tant que; *(whereas)* tandis que; while eating/*etc* en mangeant/*etc*. **2** *n* a w. un moment; all the w. tout le temps.

whim caprice *m*.

whine *vi* gémir.

whip 1 *n* fouet *m*. **2** *vt* fouetter.

▸ **whip out** *vt* sortir brusquement.

whirl (a·round) *vi* tourbillonner.

whisk 1 *n (for eggs etc)* fouet *m*. **2** *vt* fouetter.

whisk·ers *npl (of cat)* moustaches *fpl*.

whis·key whisky *m*.

whis·per 1 *vti* chuchoter. **2** *n* chuchotement *m*.

whis·tle 1 *n* sifflement *m*; *(object)* sifflet *m*; to blow the *or* one's w. siffler. **2** *vti* siffler.

white 1 *adj* blanc (*f* blanche); to turn w. blanchir; w. man blanc *m*; w. woman blanche *f*. **2** *n (color, of egg)* blanc *m*.

white·wash vt (wall) badigeonner.

▸ **whiz past** vi passer à toute vitesse.

who pron qui; **w. did it?** qui (est-ce qui) a fait ça?

who·ev·er pron qui que ce soit qui; (object) qui que ce soit que; **this man, w. he is** cet homme, quel qu'il soit.

whole 1 adj entier; (intact) intact; **the w. time/village/etc** tout le temps/village/etc; **the w. thing** le tout. **2** n on the w. dans l'ensemble.

whole·sale 1 adj (price) de gros. **2** adv (to sell) au prix de gros; (in bulk) en gros.

whole·sal·er grossiste mf.

whole-wheat adj (bread) complet.

whol·ly adv entièrement.

whom pron (object) que; (in questions and after prep) qui; **of w.** dont.

whoop·ing cough coqueluche f.

whose poss pron & adj à qui, de qui; **w. book is this?** à qui est ce livre?; **w. daughter are you?** de qui es-tu la fille?; **the woman w. book I have** la femme de qui j'ai le livre.

why 1 adv pourquoi; **w. not?** pourquoi pas? **2** conj **the reason w. they…** la raison pour laquelle ils …

wick mèche f (de bougie).

wick·ed adj (evil) méchant; (mischievous) malicieux.

wick·er 1 n osier m. **2** adj (basket etc) en osier.

wide 1 adj large; (choice, variety) grand; **to be three yards w.** avoir trois mètres de large. **2** adv (to open) tout grand.

wide-a·wake adj éveillé.

wide·ly adv (to travel) beaucoup.

wid·en 1 vt élargir. **2** vi s'élargir.

wide·spread adj (très) répandu.

wid·ow veuve f.

wid·ow·er veuf m.

width largeur f.

wife, pl **wives** femme f.

wig perruque f.

wild adj (animal, flower etc) sauvage.

wil·der·ness désert m.

wild·life nature f.

wild·ly adv (cheer) frénétiquement; (guess) au hasard.

will¹ v aux **he will come, he'll come** (future tense) il viendra; **you will not come, you won't come** tu ne viendras pas; **you'll come, w. you?** tu viendras, n'est-ce pas?; **w. you have a cup of tea?** veux-tu prendre un thé?; **w. you be quiet!** veux-tu te taire!; **I w.!** (yes) oui!

will² volonté f; (legal document) testament m; **ill w.** mauvaise volonté f; **against one's w.** à contrecœur.

will·ing adj (helper, worker) de bonne volonté; **to be w. to do** vouloir bien faire.

will·ing·ly adv (with pleasure) volontiers; (voluntarily) volontairement.

will·ing·ness bonne volonté f; **his or her w. to do** son empressement m à faire.

wil·low saule m.

win 1 n victoire f. **2** vi* gagner. **3** vt (money, prize, race) gagner.

wind¹ vent m.

wind²*1 vt (roll) enrouler (around autour de); (clock) remonter. **2** vi (of river, road) serpenter.

wind·break·er blouson m.

wind·mill moulin m à vent.

win·dow fenêtre f; (pane, in vehicle or train) vitre f; (in store) vitrine f; (counter) guichet m; **to go w. shopping** faire du lèche-vitrines.

win·dow box jardinière f.

win·dow-pane vitre f.

win·dow screen grillage m.

win·dow·sill (inside) appui m de (la) fenêtre; (outside) rebord m de (la) fenêtre.

wind·shield pare-brise *m inv*; **w. wiper** essuie-glace *m*.

wind·surf·ing **to go w.** faire de la planche (à voile).

wind·y *adj* **it's w.** *(of weather)* il y a du vent.

wine vin *m*; **w. bottle** bouteille *f* à vin; **w. list** carte *f* des vins.

wine-glass verre *m* à vin.

wing aile *f*.

wink 1 *vi* faire un clin d'œil (**at, to** à). **2** *n* clin *m* d'œil.

win·ner gagnant, -ante *mf*; *(of argument, fight)* vainqueur *m*.

win·ning 1 *adj* *(number, horse etc)* gagnant; *(team)* victorieux. **2** *n* **winnings** gains *mpl*.

win·ter 1 *n* hiver *m*; **in (the) w.** en hiver. **2** *adj* d'hiver.

win·ter·time hiver *m*.

wipe *vt* essuyer; **to w. one's feet/hands** s'essuyer les pieds/les mains.

▸ **wipe off** *or* **up** *vt (liquid)* essuyer.

wip·er *(in vehicle)* essuie-glace *m*.

wire fil *m*.

wir·ing *(electrical)* installation *f* électrique.

wis·dom sagesse *f*.

wise *adj (in knowledge)* sage; *(advisable)* prudent.

wish 1 *vt* souhaiter, vouloir (**to do** faire); **I w. (that) you could help me/could have helped me** je voudrais que/j'aurais voulu que vous m'aidiez; **I w. I hadn't done that** je regrette d'avoir fait ça; **if you w.** si tu veux; **I w. you a happy birthday** je vous souhaite un bon anniversaire; **I w. I could** si seulement je pouvais. **2** *vi* **to w. for sth** souhaiter qch. **3** *n (specific)* souhait *m*; *(general)* désir *m*; **best wishes** *(on greeting card)* meilleurs vœux *mpl*; *(in letter)* amitiés *fpl*; **send him or her my best wishes** fais-lui mes amitiés.

wit *(humor)* esprit *m*; *(person)* homme *m*/femme *f* d'esprit; **wits** *(intelligence)* intelligence *f*; **to be at one's wits' end** ne plus savoir que faire.

witch sorcière *f*.

with *prep* avec; **come w. me** viens avec moi; **w. no hat/etc** sans chapeau/*etc*. ▪ *(at the house etc of)* chez; **she's staying w. me** elle loge chez moi. ▪ *(cause)* de; **to jump w. joy** sauter de joie. ▪ *(instrument, means)* avec, de; **to write w. a pen** écrire avec un stylo; **to fill w.** remplir de. ▪ *(description)* à; **w. blue eyes** aux yeux bleus.

with·draw* **1** *vt* retirer. **2** *vi* se retirer (**from** de).

with·draw·al retrait *m*.

with·er *vi (of plant etc)* se flétrir.

with·hold* *vt (permission, help)* refuser (**from** à); *(decision)* différer; *(money)* retenir (**from** de); *(information)* cacher (**from** à).

with·in *prep (place, box etc)* à l'intérieur de; **w. 6 miles (of)** *(less than)* à moins de 10 km (de); *(inside an area of)* dans un rayon de 10 km (de); **w. a month** *(to return etc)* avant un mois; *(to finish sth)* en moins d'un mois.

with·out *prep* sans; **w. a tie/etc** sans cravate/*etc*; **w. doing** sans faire.

wit·ness 1 *n (person)* témoin *m*. **2** *vt (accident etc)* être (le) témoin de.

wob·bly *adj (table, tooth)* branlant.

wolf, *pl* **wolves** loup *m*.

wom·an, *pl* **women** femme *f*; **women's** *(clothes etc)* féminin.

won·der 1 *n* **(it's) no w.** ce n'est pas étonnant (**that** que (+ *subjunctive*)). **2** *vt* se demander (**if** si; **why** pourquoi). **3** *vi (think)* réfléchir; **I was just wondering** je réfléchissais.

won·der·ful *adj* merveilleux.

won't = will not.

wood *(material, forest)* bois *m*.

wood·en *adj* de *or* en bois.

wood·work (school subject) menuiserie f.

wool laine f.

wool·en 1 adj en laine. **2** n woollens lainages mpl.

word mot m; (spoken, promise) parole f; **words** (of song etc) paroles fpl; **to have a w. with sb** parler à qn; (advise, criticize) avoir un mot avec qn; **in other words** autrement dit.

word·ing termes mpl.

word proc·ess·ing traitement m de texte.

wore pt de wear.

work 1 n travail m; (product, book etc) œuvre f; (building or repair work) travaux mpl; **out of w.** au chômage; **a day off w.** un jour de congé; **he's off w.** il n'est pas allé travailler; **the works** (of clock etc) le mécanisme. **2** vi travailler; (of machine etc) marcher; (of drug) agir. **3** vt (machine) faire marcher; **to get worked up** s'exciter.

▸ **work at** or **on** vt (improve) travailler.

work·bench établi m.

work·er travailleur, -euse mf; (manual) ouvrier, -ière mf; (office) w. employé, -ée mf (de bureau).

work·force main-d'œuvre f.

work·ing adj w. class classe f ouvrière; **in w. order** en état de marche.

work·man, pl -men ouvrier m.

▸ **work on** vt (book, problem etc) travailler à.

▸ **work out 1** vi (succeed) marcher; (do exercises) s'entraîner; **it works out at 50 euros** ça fait 50 euros. **2** vt calculer; (problem) résoudre; (scheme) préparer; (understand) comprendre.

work·out séance f d'entraînement.

work·shop atelier m.

world 1 n monde m; **all over the w.** dans le monde entier. **2** adj (war

etc) mondial; (champion, cup, record) du monde.

world·wide adj mondial.

worm ver m.

worn (pp de wear) adj (clothes etc) usé.

worn-out adj (object) complètement usé; (person) épuisé.

wor·ri·some adj inquiétant.

wor·ry 1 n souci m. **2** vi s'inquiéter (about sth de qch; about sb pour qn). **3** vt inquiéter; **to be worried** être inquiet.

worse 1 adj pire, plus mauvais (than que); **to get w.** se détériorer; **he's getting w.** (in health) il va de plus en plus mal. **2** adv plus mal (than que); **to be w. off** aller moins bien financièrement.

wors·en vti empirer.

wor·ship vt (person, god) adorer.

worst 1 adj pire, plus mauvais. **2** adv (the) w. le plus mal. **3** n the w. (one) le or la pire, le or la plus mauvais(e); **at w.** au pire.

worth 1 n valeur f; **to buy 50 dollars w. of gas** acheter pour 50 dollars d'essence. **2** adj **to be w. sth** valoir qch; **how much** or **what is it w.?** ça vaut combien?; **the movie's w. seeing** le film vaut la peine d'être vu; **it's w. (one's) while** ça (en) vaut la peine; **it's w. (while) waiting** ça vaut la peine d'attendre.

worth·while adj (activity) qui vaut la peine; (book, movie) qui vaut la peine d'être lu/vu; (plan, contribution) valable; (cause) louable.

wor·thy adj w. of sth/sb digne de qch/qn.

would v aux **I w. stay, I'd stay** (conditional tense) je resterais; **he w. have done it** il l'aurait fait; **w. you help me, please?** voulez-vous m'aider, s'il vous plaît?; **w. you like some tea?** voudriez-vous (prendre) du thé?; **I w. see her every day** (in the past) je la voyais chaque jour.

wound 1 *vt* blesser; **the wounded** les blessés *mpl.* **2** *n* blessure *f*.

wrap (up) 1 *vt* envelopper; *(parcel)* emballer. **2** *vti* **to w. (oneself) up** *(dress warmly)* se couvrir. **3** *n* **plastic w.** film *m* plastique.

wrap·per *(of candy)* papier *m*.

wrap·ping *(action, material)* emballage *m*; **w. paper** papier *m* d'emballage.

wreath, *pl* **-s** couronne *f*.

wreck 1 *n (ship)* épave *f*; *(sinking)* naufrage *m*; *(train etc)* train *m* etc accidenté; *(accident)* accident *m*. **2** *vt* détruire.

wrench *(tool)* clef *f* (à écrous), clef *f* à molette.

wres·tle *vi* lutter (**with sb** avec qn).

wres·tler lutteur, -euse *mf*; *(no holds barred)* catcheur, -euse *mf*.

wres·tling *(sport)* lutte *f*; *(no holds barred)* catch *m*.

wring* (out) *vt (clothes by hand)* tordre.

wrin·kle *(on skin)* ride *f*.

wrist poignet *m*.

wrist·watch montre *f*.

write* *vti* écrire.

▸ **write away** *or* **off for** *vt (details etc)* écrire pour.

▸ **write back** *vi* répondre.

▸ **write down** *vt* noter.

▸ **write off** *vt (debt)* annuler.

▸ **write out** *vt* écrire; *(copy)* recopier.

writ·er auteur *m* (**of** de); *(literary)* écrivain *m*.

writ·ing *(handwriting)* écriture *f*; **to put sth (down) in w.** mettre qch par écrit; **some w.** *(on page)* quelque chose d'écrit.

writ·ing desk secrétaire *m*.

writ·ing pad bloc *m* de papier à lettres; *(for notes)* bloc-notes *m*.

writ·ing pa·per papier *m* à lettres.

wrong 1 *adj (sum, idea etc)* faux (*f* fausse); *(direction, time etc)* mauvais; *(unfair)* injuste; **to be w.** *(of person)* avoir tort (**to do** de faire); *(mistaken)* se tromper; **it's w. to swear/etc** c'est mal de jurer/etc; **the clock's w.** la pendule n'est pas à l'heure; **something's w.** quelque chose ne va pas; **something's w. with the phone** le téléphone ne marche pas bien; **something's w. with her arm** elle a quelque chose au bras; **what's w. with you?** qu'est-ce que tu as?; **the w. way around** *or* **up** à l'envers. **2** *adv* mal; **to go w.** *(of plan)* mal tourner. **3** *n* **to be in the w.** être dans son tort.

wrong·ly *adv (incorrectly)* mal.

X

X·mas *Fam* Noël *m*.

X-ray 1 *n (photo)* radio(graphie) *f*; *(beam)* rayon *m* X; **to have an X-ray** passer une radio. **2** *vt* radiographier.

Y

yacht yacht *m*.

yard *(of farm, school etc)* cour *f*; *(for storage)* dépôt *m*; *(measure)* yard *m* (= 91,44cm).

yarn *(thread)* fil *m*.

yawn 1 *vi* bâiller. **2** *n* bâillement *m*.

year an *m*, année *f*; **school/tax y.** année *f* scolaire/fiscale; **this y.** cette année; **in the y.** 1992 en (l'an) 1992; **he's ten years old** il a dix ans; **New Y.** Nouvel An; **New Year's Day**

le jour de l'An; **New Year's Eve** la Saint-Sylvestre.

year·ly adj annuel.

yeast levure f.

yell hurlement m.

yell (out) vti hurler.

▸ **yell at** vt (scold) crier après.

yel·low adj & n (color) jaune (m).

yes adv oui; (contradicting negative question) si.

yes·ter·day adv hier; **y. morning** hier matin; **the day before y.** avant-hier.

yet 1 adv encore; (already) déjà; **she hasn't come (as) y.** elle n'est pas encore venue; **has he come y.?** est-il déjà arrivé? **2** conj (nevertheless) pourtant.

yield vi 'y.' (road sign) 'cédez la priorité'.

yo·gurt yaourt m.

yolk jaune m (d'œuf).

you pron (polite form singular) vous; (familiar form singular) tu; (polite and familiar form plural) vous; (object) vous; te, t'; pl vous; (after prep, 'than', 'it is') vous; toi; pl vous; **(to) y.** vous; te, t'; pl vous; **y. are** vous êtes; tu es; **I see y.** je vous vois; je te vois; **y. teachers** vous autres professeurs; **y. idiot!** espèce d'imbécile! ▪ (indefinite) on; (object) vous; te, t'; pl vous; **y. never know** on ne sait jamais.

young 1 adj jeune; **my young(er) brother** mon (frère) cadet; **his or her youngest brother** le cadet de ses frères; **the youngest son** le cadet. **2** n (of animals) petits mpl; **the y. (people)** les jeunes mpl.

young·ster jeune mf.

your poss adj (polite form singular,

polite and familiar form plural) votre, pl vos; (familiar form singular) ton, ta, pl tes; (one's) son, sa, pl ses.

yours poss pron le vôtre, la vôtre, pl les vôtres; (familiar form singular) le tien, la tienne, pl les tien(ne)s; **this book is y.** ce livre est à vous or est le vôtre; ce livre est à toi or est le tien.

your·self pron (polite form) vous-même; (familiar form) toi-même; (reflexive) vous; te, t'; (after prep) vous; toi.

your·selves pron pl vous-mêmes; (reflexive, after prep) vous.

youth jeunesse f; (young man) jeune m; **y. center** maison f des jeunes.

Z

ze·bra zèbre m.

ze·ro, pl -os zéro m.

zig·zag 1 n zigzag m. **2** adj en zig-zag. **3** vi zigzaguer.

zip (up) vt fermer (avec une fermeture éclair®).

zip code code m postal; (geographic area) division f postale.

Zip® drive Comput lecteur m Zip®.

zip·per fermeture f éclair®.

zit (pimple) Fam bouton m.

zone zone f.

zoo, pl zoos zoo m.

zuc·chi·ni, pl -ni or -nis courgette f.

French verb conjugations

Regular verbs

	-ER Verbs	-IR Verbs	-RE Verbs
Infinitive	donn / er	fin / ir	vend / re
1 Present	je donne	je finis	je vends
	tu donnes	tu finis	tu vends
	il donne	il finit	il vend
	nous donnons	nous finissons	nous vendons
	vous donnez	vous finissez	vous vendez
	ils donnent	ils finissent	ils vendent
2 Imperfect	je donnais	je finissais	je vendais
	tu donnais	tu finissais	tu vendais
	il donnait	il finissait	il vendait
	nous donnions	nous finissions	nous vendions
	vous donniez	vous finissiez	vous vendiez
	ils donnaient	ils finissaient	ils vendaient
3 Past historic	je donnai	je finis	je vendis
	tu donnas	tu finis	tu vendis
	il donna	il finit	il vendit
	nous donnâmes	nous finîmes	nous vendîmes
	vous donnâtes	vous finîtes	vous vendîtes
	ils donnèrent	ils finirent	ils vendirent
4 Future	je donnerai	je finirai	je vendrai
	tu donneras	tu finiras	tu vendras
	il donnera	il finira	il vendra
	nous donnerons	nous finirons	nous vendrons
	vous donnerez	vous finirez	vous vendrez
	ils donneront	ils finiront	ils vendront
5 Subjunctive	je donne	je finisse	je vende
	tu donnes	tu finisses	tu vendes
	il donne	il finisse	il vende
	nous donnions	nous finissions	nous vendions
	vous donniez	vous finissiez	vous vendiez
	ils donnent	ils finissent	ils vendent
7 Present participle	donnant	finissant	vendant
8 Past participle	donné	fini	vendu

Note The conditional is formed by adding the following endings to the infinitive: -ais, -ais, -ait, -ions, -iez, -aient. Final 'e' is dropped in infinitives ending '-re'.

Spelling anomalies of -er verbs

Verbs in **-ger** (eg **manger**) take an extra **e** before endings beginning with **o** or **a**: *Present* je mange, nous mangeons; *Imperfect* je mangeais, nous mangions; *Past historic* je mangeai, nous mangeâmes; *Present participle* mangeant. Verbs in **-cer** (eg **commencer**) change **c** to **ç** before endings beginning with **o** or **a**: *Present* je commence, nous commençons; *Imperfect* je commençais, nous commencions; *Past historic* je commençai, nous commençâmes; *Present participle* commençant. Verbs containing mute **e** in their penultimate syllable fall into two groups. In the first (eg **mener, peser, lever**), **e** becomes **è** before an unpronounced syllable in the present and subjunctive, and in the future and conditional tenses (eg je mène, ils mèneront). The second group contains most verbs ending in **-eler** and **-eter** (eg **appeler, jeter**). These verbs change **l** to **ll** and **t** to **tt** before an unpronounced syllable (eg j'appelle, ils appelleront; je jette, ils jetteront). However, the following four verbs in **-eler** and **-eter** fall into the first group in which **e** changes to **è** before mute **e** (eg je pèle, ils pèleront; j'achète, ils achèteront): **geler, peler; acheter, haleter**. Derived verbs (eg **dégeler, racheter**) are conjugated in the same way. Verbs containing **é** in their penultimate syllable change **é** to **è** before the unpronounced endings of the present and subjunctive only (eg je cède but je céderai). Verbs in **-yer** (eg **essuyer**) change **y** to **i** before an unpronounced syllable in the present and subjunctive, and in the future and conditional tenses (eg j'essuie, ils essuieront). In verbs in **-ayer** (eg **balayer**), **y** may be retained before mute **e** (eg je balaie or balaye, ils balaieront or balayeront).

Irregular verbs

Listed below are those verbs considered to be the most useful. Forms and tenses not given are fully derivable, such as the third person singular of the present tense which is normally formed by substituting 't' for the final 's' of the first person singular, eg 'crois' becomes 'croit', 'dis' becomes 'dit'. Note that the endings of the past historic fall into three categories, the 'a' and 'i' categories shown at *donner*, and at *finir* and *vendre*, and the 'u' category which has the following endings: -us, -ut, -ûmes, -ûtes, -urent. Most of the verbs listed below form their past historic with 'u'. The imperfect may usually be formed by adding -ais, -ait, -ions, -iez, -aient to the stem of the first person plural of the present tense, eg 'je buvais' etc may be derived from 'nous buvons' (stem 'buv-' and ending '-ons'); similarly, the present participle may generally be formed by substituting -ant for -ons (eg buvant). The future may usually be formed by adding -ai, -as, -a, -ons, -ez, -ont to the infinitive or to an infinitive without final 'e' where the ending is -re (eg conduire). The imperative usually has the same forms as the second persons singular and plural and first person plural of the present tense.

1 = Present   2 = Imperfect   3 = Past historic   4 = Future
5 = Subjunctive   6 = Imperative   7 = Present participle
8 = Past participle   n = nous   v = vous   † verbs conjugated with **être** only.

Irregular French verbs

abattre	*like* **battre**
† **s'abstenir**	like **tenir**
accourir	*like* **courir**
accueillir	*like* **cueillir**
acquérir	1 j'acquiers, n acquérons 2 j'acquérais 3 j'acquis 4 j'acquerrai 5 j'acquière 7 acquérant 8 acquis
admettre	*like* **mettre**
† **aller**	1 je vais, tu vas, il va, n allons, v allez, ils vont 4 j'irai 5 j'aille, nous allions, ils aillent 6 va, allons, allez (*but note* vas-y)
apercevoir	*like* **recevoir**
apparaître	*like* **connaître**
appartenir	*like* **tenir**
apprendre	*like* **prendre**
asseoir	1 j'assieds, il assied, n asseyons, ils asseyent 2 j'asseyais 3 j'assis 4 j'assiérai 5 j'asseye 7 asseyant 8 assis
atteindre	1 j'atteins, n atteignons, ils atteignent 2 j'atteignais 3 j'atteignis 4 j'atteindrai 5 j'atteigne 7 atteignant 8 atteint
avoir	1 j'ai, tu as, il a, n avons, v avez, ils ont 2 j'avais 3 j'eus 4 j'aurai 5 j'aie, il ait, n ayons, ils aient 6 aie, ayons, ayez 7 ayant 8 eu
battre	1 je bats, il bat, n battons 5 je batte
boire	1 je bois, n buvons, ils boivent 2 je buvais 3 je bus 5 je boive, n buvions 7 buvant 8 bu
bouillir	1 je bous, n bouillons, ils bouillent 2 je bouillais 3 *not used* 5 je bouille 7 bouillant
combattre	*like* **battre**
commettre	*like* **mettre**
comprendre	*like* **prendre**
conclure	1 je conclus, n concluons, ils concluent 5 je conclue
conduire	1 je conduis, n conduisons 3 je conduisis 5 je conduise 8 conduit
connaître	1 je connais, il connaît, n connaissons 3 je connus 5 je connaisse 7 connaissant 8 connu
conquérir	*like* **acquérir**
consentir	*like* **conduire**
contenir	*like* **tenir**
contraindre	*like* **atteindre**
contredire	*like* **dire** *except* 1 v contredisez
convaincre	*like* **vaincre**
convenir	*like* **tenir**
coudre	1 je couds, il coud, n cousons, ils cousent 3 je cousis 5 je couse 7 cousant 8 cousu

French verb conjugations

courir	1 je cours, n courons 3 je courus 4 je courrai 5 je coure 8 couru
couvrir	1 je couvre, n couvrons 2 je couvrais 5 je couvre 8 couvert
craindre	*like* **atteindre**
croire	1 je crois, n croyons, ils croient 2 je croyais 3 je crus 5 je croie, n croyions 7 croyant 8 cru
cueillir	1 je cueille, n cueillons 2 je cueillais 4 je cueillerai 5 je cueille 7 cueillant
cuire	1 je cuis, n cuisons 2 je cuisais 3 je cuisis 5 je cuise 7 cuisant 8 cuit
débattre	*like* **battre**
décevoir	*like* **recevoir**
découvrir	*like* **couvrir**
décrire	*like* **écrire**
déduire	*like* **conduire**
défaire	*like* **faire**
déplaire	*like* **plaire**
déteindre	*like* **atteindre**
détruire	*like* **conduire**
† **devenir**	*like* **tenir**
devoir	1 je dois, n devons, ils doivent 2 je devais 3 je dus 4 je devrai 5 je doive, n devions 6 *not used* 7 devant 8 dû, due, *pl* dus, dues
dire	1 je dis, n disons, v dites 2 je disais 3 je dis 5 je dise 7 disant 8 dit
disparaître	*like* **connaître**
dissoudre	1 je dissous, n dissolvons 2 je dissolvais 5 je dissolve 7 dissolvant 8 dissous, dissoute
distraire	1 je distrais, n distrayons 2 je distrayais 3 *none* 5 je distraie 7 distrayant 8 distrait
dormir	*like* **mentir**
éclore	1 il éclôt, ils éclosent 8 éclos
écrire	1 j'écris, n écrivons 2 j'écrivais 3 j'écrivis 5 j'écrive 7 écrivant 8 écrit
élire	*like* **lire**
émettre	*like* **mettre**
émouvoir	1 j'émeus, n émouvons, ils émeuvent 2 j'émouvais 3 j'émus (*rare*) 4 j'émouvrai 5 j'émeuve, n émouvions 8 ému
endormir	*like* **mentir**
enfreindre	*like* **atteindre**
† **s'enfuir**	*like* **fuir**
entretenir	*like* **tenir**
envoyer	4 j'enverrai
éteindre	*like* **atteindre**
être	1 je suis, tu es, il est, n sommes, v êtes, ils sont 2 j'étais 3 je fus 4 je serai 5 je sois, n soyons, ils soient 6 sois, soyons, soyez 7 étant 8 été

French verb conjugations

exclure	*like* **conclure**
extraire	*like* **distraire**
faillir	*(defective)* 3 je faillis 4 je faillirai 8 failli
faire	1 je fais, n faisons, v faites, ils font 2 je faisais 3 je fis 4 je ferai 5 je fasse 7 faisant 8 fait
falloir	*(impersonal)* 1 il faut 2 il fallait 3 il fallut 4 il faudra 5 il faille 6 *none* 7 *none* 8 fallu
frire	*(defective)* 1 je fris, tu fris, il frit 4 je frirai *(rare)* 6 fris *(rare)* 8 frit *(for other persons and tenses use* faire frire*)*
fuir	1 je fuis, n fuyons, ils fuient 2 je fuyais 3 je fuis 5 je fuie 7 fuyant 8 fui
haïr	1 je hais, il hait, n haïssons
inscrire	*like* **écrire**
instruire	*like* **conduire**
interdire	*like* **dire** *except* 1 v interdisez
interrompre	*like* **rompre**
intervenir	*like* **tenir**
introduire	*like* **conduire**
joindre	*like* **atteindre**
lire	1 je lis, n lisons 2 je lisais 3 je lus 5 je lise 7 lisant 8 lu
maintenir	*like* **tenir**
mentir	1 je mens, n mentons 2 je mentais 5 je mente 7 mentant
mettre	1 je mets, n mettons 2 je mettais 3 je mis 5 je mette 7 mettant 8 mis
moudre	je mouds, il moud, n moulons 2 je moulais 3 je moulus 5 je moule 7 moulant 8 moulu
† mourir	1 je meurs, n mourons, ils meurent 2 je mourais 3 je mourus 4 je mourrai 5 je meure, n mourions
† naître	1 je nais, il naît, n naissons 2 je naissais 3 je naquis 4 je naîtrai 5 je naisse 7 naissant 8 né
nuire	1 je nuis, n nuisons 2 je nuisais 3 je nuisis 5 je nuise 7 nuisant 8 nui
obtenir	*like* **tenir**
offrir	*like* **couvrir**
ouvrir	*like* **couvrir**
paître	*(defective)* 1 il paît 2 il paissait 3 *none* 4 il paîtra 5 il paisse 7 paissant 8 *none*
paraître	*like* **connaître**
parcourir	*like* **courir**
† partir	*like* **mentir**
† parvenir	*like* **tenir**
peindre	*like* **atteindre**
permettre	*like* **mettre**
plaindre	*like* **atteindre**
plaire	1 je plais, il plaît, n plaisons 2 je plaisais 3 je plus 5 je plaise 7 plaisant 8 plu
pleuvoir	*(impersonal)* 1 il pleut 2 il pleuvait 3 il plut 4 il pleuvra 5 il pleuve 6 *none* 7 pleuvant 8 plu
poursuivre	*like* **suivre**

French verb conjugations

pouvoir	1 je peux *or* je puis, tu peux, il peut, n pouvons, ils peuvent 2 je pouvais 3 je pus 4 je pourrai 5 je puisse 6 *not used* 7 pouvant 8 pu
prédire	*like* dire *except* 1 v prédisez
prendre	1 je prends, il prend, n prenons, ils prennent 2 je prenais 3 je pris 5 je prenne 7 prenant 8 pris
prescrire	*like* écrire
pressentir	*like* mentir
prévenir	*like* tenir
prévoir	*like* voire *except* 4 je prévoirai
produire	*like* conduire
promettre	*like* mettre
† **provenir**	*like* tenir
rabattre	*like* battre
recevoir	1 je reçois, n recevons, ils reçoivent 2 je recevais 3 je reçus 4 je recevrai 5 je reçoive, n recevions, ils reçoivent 7 recevant 8 reçu
reconduire	*like* conduire
reconnaître	*like* connaître
reconstruire	*like* conduire
recoudre	*like* coudre
recouvrir	*like* couvrir
recueillir	*like* cueillir
redire	*like* dire
réduire	*like* conduire
refaire	*like* faire
rejoindre	*like* atteindre
relire	*like* lire
reluire	*like* nuire
rendormir	*like* mentir
renvoyer	*like* envoyer
† **repartir**	*like* mentir
repentir	*like* mentir
reprendre	*like* prendre
reproduire	*like* conduire
résoudre	1 je résous, n résolvons 2 je résolvais 3 je résolus 5 je résolve 7 résolvant 8 résolu
ressentir	*like* mentir
resservir	*like* mentir
ressortir	*like* mentir
restreindre	*like* atteindre
retenir	*like* tenir
† **revenir**	*like* tenir
revivre	*like* vivre
revoir	*like* voir
rire	1 je ris, n rions 2 je riais 3 je ris 5 je rie, n riions 7 riant 8 ri
rompre	*regular except* 1 il rompt
satisfaire	*like* faire

French verb conjugations

savoir	1 je sais, n savons, il savent 2 je savais 3 je sus 4 je saurai 5 je saurai 6 sache, sachons, sachez 7 sachant 8 su
sentir	*like* **mentir**
servir	*like* **mentir**
sortir	*like* **mentir**
souffrir	*like* **couvrir**
sourire	*like* **rire**
soustraire	*like* **distraire**
soutenir	*like* **tenir**
† **se souvenir**	*like* **tenir**
suffire	1 je suffis, n suffisons 2 je suffisais 3 je suffis 5 je suffise 7 suffisant 8 suffi
suivre	1 je suis, n suivons 2 je suivais 3 je suivis 5 je suive 7 suivant 8 suivi
surprendre	*like* **prendre**
survivre	*like* **vivre**
taire	1 je tais, n taisons 2 je taisais 3 je tus 5 je taise 7 taisant 8 tu
teindre	*like* **atteindre**
tenir	1 je tiens, n tenons, ils tiennent 2 je tenais 3 je tins, tu tins, il tint, n tînmes, v tîntes, ils tinrent 4 je tiendrai 5 je tienne 7 tenant 8 tenu
traduire	*like* **conduire**
traire	*like* **distraire**
transmettre	*like* **mettre**
vaincre	1 je vaincs, il vainc, n vainquons 2 je vainquais 3 je vainquis 5 je vainque 7 vainquant 8 vaincu
valoir	1 je vaux, il vaut, n valons 2 je valais 3 je valus 4 je vaudrai 5 je vaille 6 *not* used 7 valant 8 valu
† **venir**	*like* **tenir**
vivre	1 je vis, n vivons 2 je vivais 3 je vécus 5 je vive 7 vivant 8 vécu
voir	1 je vois, n voyons 2 je voyais 3 je vis 4 je verrai 5 je voie, n voyions 7 voyant 8 vu
vouloir	1 je veux, il veut, n voulons, ils veulent 2 je voulais 3 je voulus 4 je voudrai 5 je veuille 6 veuille, veuillons, veuillez 7 voulant 8 voulu

Countries and regions

Africa *(African)*	Afrique *f (africain)*
South/North Africa *(South/North African)*	A. du Sud/Nord *(sud-/nord-africain)*
Algeria *(Algerian)*	Algérie *f (algérien)*
America *(American)*	Amérique *f (américain)*
South/North America *(South/North American)*	A. du Sud/Nord *(sud-/nord-américain)*
Argentina *(Argentinian)*	Argentine *f (argentin)*
Asia *(Asian)*	Asie *f (asiatique)*
Australia *(Australian)*	Australie *f (australien)*
Austria *(Austrian)*	Autriche *f (autrichien)*
Belgium *(Belgian)*	Belgique *f (belge)*
Brazil *(Brazilian)*	Brésil *m (brésilien)*
Canada *(Canadian)*	Canada *m (canadien)*
Caribbean (the) *(Caribbean)*	Antilles *fpl (antillais)*
China *(Chinese)*	Chine *f (chinois)*
CIS *(abbr* Commonwealth of Independent States)	CEI *f (abrév* Communauté des États Indépendants)
Cuba *(Cuban)*	Cuba *m (cubain)*
Cyprus *(Cypriot)*	Chypre *f (c(h)ypriote)*
Czech Republic *(Czech)*	République *f* tchèque *(tchèque)*
Denmark *(Danish)*	Danemark *m (danois)*
Egypt *(Egyptian)*	Égypte *f (égyptien)*
England *(English)*	Angleterre *f (anglais)*
Europe *(European)*	Europe *f (européen)*
Finland *(Finnish)*	Finlande *f (finlandais)*
France *(French)*	France *f (français)*
Germany *(German)*	Allemagne *f (allemand)*
Great Britain *(British)*	Grande-Bretagne *f (britannique)*
Greece *(Greek)*	Grèce *f (grec)*
Holland *(Dutch)*	Pays-Bas *mpl (hollandais)*
Hungary *(Hungarian)*	Hongrie *f (hongrois)*
India *(Indian)*	Inde *f (indien)*
Indonesia *(Indonesian)*	Indonésie *f (indonésien)*
Iran *(Iranian)*	Iran *m (iranien)*
Iraq *(Iraqi)*	Irak *m (irakien)*
Ireland *(Irish)*	Irlande *f (irlandais)*
Israel *(Israeli)*	Israël *m (israélien)*

Countries and regions

Italy *(Italian)*	Italie f *(italien)*
Jamaica *(Jamaican)*	Jamaïque f *(jamaïcain)*
Japan *(Japanese)*	Japon m *(japonais)*
Kenya *(Kenyan)*	Kenya m *(kényan)*
Korea *(Korean)*	Corée f *(coréen)*
North/South Korea	C. du Sud/Nord
Lebanon *(Lebanese)*	Liban m *(libanais)*
Libya *(Libyan)*	Libye f *(libyen)*
Luxembourg *(Luxembourgish)*	Luxembourg m *(luxembourgeois)*
Malaysia *(Malaysian)*	Malaisie *(malais)*
Mexico *(Mexican)*	Mexique m *(mexicain)*
Morocco *(Moroccan)*	Maroc m *(marocain)*
New Zealand	Nouvelle-Zélande f *(néo-zélandais)*
Nigeria *(Nigerian)*	Nigéria m *(nigérian)*
Norway *(Norwegian)*	Norvège f *(norvégien)*
Pakistan *(Pakistani)*	Pakistan m *(pakistanais)*
Philippines *(Filipino)*	Philippines fpl *(philippin)*
Poland *(Polish)*	Pologne f *(polonais)*
Portugal *(Portuguese)*	Portugal m *(portugais)*
Romania *(Romanian)*	Roumanie f *(roumain)*
Russia *(Russian)*	Russie f *(russe)*
Saudi Arabia *(Saudi)*	Arabie f Saoudite *(saoudien)*
Scotland *(Scottish)*	Écosse f *(écossais)*
Slovakia *(Slovak)*	Slovaquie *(slovaque)*
Spain *(Spanish)*	Espagne f *(espagnol)*
Sweden *(Swedish)*	Suède f *(suédois)*
Switzerland *(Swiss)*	Suisse f *(suisse)*
Syria *(Syrian)*	Syrie f *(syrien)*
Thailand *(Thai)*	Thaïlande f *(thaïlandais)*
Tunisia *(Tunisian)*	Tunisie f *(tunisien)*
Turkey *(Turkish)*	Turquie f *(turc)*
United Kingdom *(British)*	Royaume-Uni m *(britannique)*
United States *(American)*	États-Unis mpl *(américain)*
Vietnam *(Vietnamese)*	Viêt-nam m *(vietnamien)*
Wales *(Welsh)*	Pays m de Galles *(gallois)*
West Indies *(West Indian)*	Antilles fpl *(antillais)*

A

a *voir* **avoir**.

à *prép* (à + le = au [o], à + les = aux [o]) (*direction: lieu*) to; (*temps*) till, to; **aller à Paris** to go to Paris; **de 3 à 4 h** from 3 till *ou* to 4 (o'clock). ▪ (*position: lieu*) at, in; (*surface*) on; (*temps*) at; **être au bureau/à la ferme/au jardin/à Paris** to be at *ou* in the office/on *ou* at the farm/in the garden/in Paris; **à 8 h** at 8 (o'clock); **à mon arrivée** on (my) arrival; **à lundi!** see you (on) Monday! ▪ (*description*) **l'homme à la barbe** the man with the beard; **verre à liqueur** liqueur glass. ▪ (*attribution*) **donner qch à qn** to give sth to sb, to give sb sth. ▪ (*devant infinitif*) **apprendre à lire** to learn to read; **travail à faire** work to do; **maison à vendre** house for sale. ▪ (*appartenance*) **c'est (son livre) à lui** it's his (book); **c'est à vous de** (*décider, protester etc*) it's up to you to; (*lire, jouer etc*) it's your turn to. ▪ (*prix*) for; **pain à un euro** loaf for one euro. ▪ (*poids*) by; **vendre au poids** to sell by weight. ▪ (*moyen, manière*) **à bicyclette** by bicycle; **à la main** by hand; **à pied** on foot; **au crayon** in pencil; **au galop** at a gallop; **deux à deux** two by two. ▪ (*appel*) **au voleur!** (stop) thief!

abaisser *vt* to lower.

abaisser (s') *vpr* (*barrière*) to lower; (*température*) to drop.

abandon *m* (*de sportif*) withdrawal; **à l'a.** in a neglected state.

abandonner 1 *vt* (*travail*) to give up; (*endroit*) to desert. **2** *vi* to give up; (*sportif*) to withdraw.

abasourdi, -ie *adj* stunned.

abat-jour *m inv* lampshade.

abattoir *m* slaughterhouse.

abattre* *vt* (*mur*) to knock down; (*arbre*) to cut down; (*animal*) to slaughter; (*avion*) to shoot down; (*personne*) to shoot.

abattre (s') *vpr* **s'a. sur** (*pluie*) to come down on; (*tempête*) to hit.

abattu, -ue *adj* (*mentalement*) dejected; (*physiquement*) exhausted.

abbaye *f* abbey.

abbé *m* (*prêtre*) priest.

abcès *m* abscess.

abdomen *m* stomach, abdomen.

abeille *f* bee.

aberrant, -ante *adj* absurd.

abîmer *vt* to ruin.

abîmer (s') *vpr* to get ruined.

aboiement *m* bark; **aboiements** barking.

abolir *vt* to abolish.

abominable *adj* terrible.

abondance *f* une a. de plenty of.

abondant, -ante *adj* plentiful.

abonné, -ée *mf* (à un journal, au téléphone) subscriber.

abonnement *m* subscription; (carte d')a. (de train) season pass.

abonner (s') *vpr* to subscribe, to take out a subscription (à to).

abord (d') *adv* first.

abordable *adj* (prix, marchandises) affordable.

abordage *m* (assaut) boarding.

aborder 1 *vi* to land. **2** *vt* (personne) to approach; (problème) to tackle; (navire) to board.

aboutir *vi* to succeed; **a. à** to lead to; **n'a. à rien** to come to nothing.

aboyer *vi* to bark.

abréger *vt* (récit) to shorten.

abreuvoir *m* (récipient) drinking trough.

abréviation *f* abbreviation.

abri *m* shelter; **a. (de jardin)** (garden) shed; **à l'a. de** (vent) sheltered from; (besoin) safe from; **sans a.** homeless.

abricot *m* apricot.

abricotier *m* apricot tree.

abriter *vt* to shelter.

abriter (s') vpr to (take) shelter.

abrupt, -e adj (pente etc) steep.

abrutir vt (télévision) to stupefy, to numb; (travail) to exhaust.

absence f absence.

absent, -ente 1 adj absent, away. **2** mf absentee.

absenter (s') vpr to go away (de from).

absolu, -ue adj absolute.

absolument adv absolutely.

absorbant, -ante adj (papier) absorbent; (travail, lecture) absorbing.

absorber vt to absorb.

abstenir* (s') vpr to refrain (de faire from doing).

absurde adj absurd.

absurdité f absurdity; **dire des absurdités** to talk nonsense.

abus m abuse; (de nourriture) overindulgence (de in).

abuser vi to go too far; **a. de** (situation, personne) to take unfair advantage of; (friandises) to overindulge in.

acajou m mahogany.

accabler vt to overwhelm (de with).

accalmie f lull.

accéder vi **a. à** (lieu) to reach.

accélérateur m accelerator.

accélérer vi to accelerate.

accélérer (s') vpr to speed up.

accent m accent; (sur une syllabe) stress.

accepter vt to accept; **a. de faire** to agree to do.

accès m access (à to); (de folie, colère, toux) fit; (de fièvre) bout; **'a. interdit'** 'no entry'.

accessoires mpl (de voiture etc) accessories; (de théâtre) props.

accident m accident; **a. d'avion/ de train** plane/train crash.

accidentel, -elle adj accidental.

acclamations fpl cheers.

acclamer vt to cheer.

accolade f (embrassade) embrace; (signe) curly bracket.

accommoder vt (assaisonner) to prepare.

accompagnateur, -trice mf (musical) accompanist; (d'un groupe) guide.

accompagnement m (musical) accompaniment.

accompagner vt (personne) to go ou come with; (chose, musique) to accompany.

accomplir vt to carry out.

accord m agreement; (musical) chord; **tomber d'a.** to reach an agreement; **être d'a.** to agree (avec with); **d'a.!** all right!

accordéon m accordion.

accorder vt (donner) to grant; (instrument) to tune; (verbe) to make agree.

accorder (s') vpr (s'entendre) to get along.

accotement m (of road) shoulder.

accouchement m delivery.

accoucher vi to give birth (de to).

accouder (s') vpr **s'a. à** ou **sur** to lean on (with one's elbows).

accoudoir m armrest.

accourir* vi to come running.

accoutumer (s') vpr to get accustomed (à to).

accroc m tear (à in).

accrochage m (de voitures) minor collision.

accrocher vt (déchirer) to catch; (fixer) to hook; (suspendre) to hang up (on a hook); (heurter) to hit.

accrocher (s') vpr (se cramponner) to cling (à to); (ne pas céder) to persevere.

accroissement m increase (de in).

accroître vt, **s'accroître** vpr to increase.

accroupi, -ie adj squatting.

accroupir (s') vpr to squat (down).

accueil m welcome.

accueillant, -ante adj welcoming.

accueillir* *vt* to welcome.
accumuler *vt*, **s'accumuler** *vpr* to pile up.
accusation *f* accusation; *(au tribunal)* charge.
accusé, -ée *mf* accused; *(à la cour d'assises)* defendant.
accuser *vt* to accuse (**de** of); *(rendre responsable)* to blame (**de** for).
acharnement *m* (stubborn) determination.
acharner (s') *vpr* **s'a. sur** *(attaquer)* to lay into; **s'a. à faire** to struggle to do.
achat *m* purchase; **faire des achats** to go shopping.
acheter *vti* to buy; **a. à qn** to buy from sb; *(pour qn)* to buy for sb.
acheteur, -euse *mf* buyer; *(dans un magasin)* shopper.
achever *vt* to finish (off); **a. de faire qch** *(personne)* to finish doing sth; **a. qn** *(tuer)* to finish sb off.
acide 1 *adj* sour. **2** *m* acid.
acier *m* steel.
acné *f* acne.
acompte *m* deposit.
acquéreur *m* purchaser.
acquérir* *vt* *(acheter)* to purchase; *(obtenir)* to acquire.
acquisition *f* *(achat)* purchase.
acquittement *m* *(d'un accusé)* acquittal.
acquitter *vt* *(dette)* to pay; *(accusé)* to acquit.
acquitter (s') *vpr* **s'a. envers qn** to repay sb.
acrobate *mf* acrobat.
acrobatie(s) *f(pl)* acrobatics.
acrobatique *adj* acrobatic.
acte *m* *(action, de pièce de théâtre)* act.
acteur, -trice *mf* actor, actress.
actif, -ive 1 *adj* active. **2** *m* Grammaire active.
action *f* action; *(en Bourse)* share, stock.
actionnaire *mf* shareholder.
activer *vt* *(feu)* to boost.

activer (s') *vpr* *(se dépêcher)* Fam to get a move on.
activité *f* activity.
actualité *f* *(événements)* current events; **actualités** *(à la télévision etc)* news.
actuel, -elle *adj* *(présent)* present; *(contemporain)* topical.
actuellement *adv* at the present time.
adaptateur *m* adapter.
adaptation *f* adjustment; *(de roman)* adaptation.
adapter *vt* to adapt; *(ajuster)* to fit (**à** to).
adapter (s') *vpr* **s'a. à** *(s'habituer)* to adapt to, to adjust to; *(tuyau etc)* to fit.
additif *m* additive.
addition *f* addition; *(au restaurant)* check.
additionner *vt* to add (**à** to); *(nombres)* to add up.
adepte *mf* follower.
adéquat, -ate *adj* appropriate; *(quantité)* adequate.
adhérent, -ente *mf* member.
adhérer *vi* **a. à** *(coller)* to stick to; *(s'inscrire)* to join.
adhésif, -ive *adj & m* adhesive.
adieu, -x *int & m* farewell.
adjectif *m* adjective.
adjoint, -ointe *mf* assistant; **a. au maire** deputy mayor.
adjuger *vt* **a. qch à qn** *(prix, contrat)* to award sth to sb; *(aux enchères)* to knock sth down to sb.
admettre* *vt* *(laisser entrer, accueillir, reconnaître)* to admit; *(autoriser, tolérer)* to allow; *(candidat)* to pass; **être admis à** *(examen)* to have passed.
administratif, -ive *adj* administrative.
administration *f* administration; **l'A.** *(service public)* the Civil Service.
administrer *vt* *(gérer, donner)* to administer.

admirable *adj* admirable.

admirateur, -trice *mf* admirer.

admiratif, -ive *adj* admiring.

admiration *f* admiration.

admirer *vt* to admire.

admissible *adj (tolérable)* acceptable, admissible; **candidat a.** = candidate who has qualified for the oral examination.

admission *f* admission (**à, dans** to).

adolescent, -ente *mf* adolescent, teenager.

adopter *vt* to adopt.

adoptif, -ive *adj (fils, patrie)* adopted.

adoption *f* adoption.

adorable *adj* adorable.

adoration *f* worship.

adorer *vt* to love, to adore (**faire** doing); *(dieu)* to worship.

adosser (s') *vpr* to lean back (**à** against).

adoucir *vt (voix, traits)* to tone down.

adoucir (s') *vpr (temps)* to turn milder.

adresse *f (domicile)* address; *(habileté)* skill.

adresser *vt (lettre)* to send; *(compliment, remarque)* to address; **a. la parole à** to speak to.

adresser (s') *vpr* **s'a. à** to speak to; *(aller trouver)* to go and see; *(bureau)* to (go and) ask at; *(être destiné à)* to be aimed at.

adroit, -oite *adj* skillful.

adulte *mf* adult, grown-up.

adverbe *m* adverb.

adversaire *mf* opponent.

aération *f* ventilation.

aérer *vt* to air (out).

aérien, -ienne *adj (photo)* aerial; **attaque/transport aérien(ne)** air attack/transport.

aérobic *m* aerobics.

aérogare *f* air terminal.

aéroglisseur *m* hovercraft.

aéroport *m* airport.

aérosol *m* aerosol.

affaiblir *vt*, **s'affaiblir** *vpr* to weaken.

affaire *f (question)* matter; **affaires** business; *(effets)* things; **avoir a. à** to have to deal with; **c'est mon a.** that's my business; **faire une bonne a.** to get a bargain.

affamé, -ée *adj* starving.

affection *f (attachement)* affection.

affectueux, -euse *adj* affectionate, loving.

affichage *m* **panneau d'a.** billboard.

affiche *f* poster.

afficher *vt (affiche)* to stick up.

affirmatif, -ive *adj (ton, réponse)* positive, affirmative.

affirmation *f* assertion.

affirmer *vt* to assert.

affliger *vt* to distress.

affluence *f* crowd; **heure(s) d'a.** rush hour(s).

affluent *m* tributary.

affolant, -ante *adj* terrifying.

affolement *m* panic.

affoler *vt* to drive crazy.

affoler (s') *vpr* to panic.

affranchir *vt (lettre)* to stamp.

affranchissement *m (tarif)* postage.

affreux, -euse *adj* horrible.

affront *m* insult; **faire un a. à** to insult.

affrontement *m* confrontation.

affronter *vt* to confront; *(mauvais temps, difficultés etc)* to brave.

affûter *vt* to sharpen.

afin 1 *prép* **a. de** (+ *infinitif*) in order to. **2** *conj* **a. que** (+ *subjonctif*) so that.

africain, -aine 1 *adj* African. **2** *mf* **A.** African.

agaçant, -ante *adj* irritating.

agacer *vt* to irritate.

âge *m* age; **quel â. as-tu?** how old are you?; **d'un certain â.** middle-aged; **le moyen â.** the Middle Ages.

âgé, -ée *adj* elderly; **â. de six ans** six years old; **enfant â. de six ans** six-year-old child.

agence *f* agency; *(succursale)* branch office; **a. immobilière** real estate office.

agenda *m* appointment book.

agenouiller (s') *vpr* to kneel (down); **être agenouillé** to be kneeling (down).

agent *m* agent; **a. (de police)** policeman; **a. immobilier** real estate agent.

agglomération *f* built-up area; *(ville)* town.

aggloméré *n* fiberboard.

aggravation *f* *(de maladie)* aggravation; *(de situation)* worsening.

aggraver *vt*, **s'aggraver** *vpr* *(situation, maladie)* to get worse; *(état de santé)* to deteriorate; *(difficultés)* to increase.

agile *adj* agile.

agilité *f* agility.

agir *vpr* to act.

agir (s') *vpr* **il s'agit d'argent/etc** it's a question *ou* matter of money/ *etc*; **de quoi s'agit-il?** what is it?, what's it about?

agitation *f* *(de la mer)* roughness; *(d'une personne)* restlessness.

agité, -ée *adj* *(mer)* rough; *(personne)* restless.

agiter *vt* *(remuer)* to stir; *(secouer)* to shake; *(brandir)* to wave.

agiter (s') *vpr* *(enfant)* to fidget.

agneau, -x *m* lamb.

agrafe *f* hook; *(pour papiers)* staple.

agrafer *vt* *(robe)* to do up; *(papiers)* to staple.

agrafeuse *f* stapler.

agrandir *vt* to enlarge.

agrandir (s') *vpr* to expand.

agrandissement *m* *(de ville)* expansion; *(de maison)* extension; *(de photo)* enlargement.

agréable *adj* pleasant.

agréer *vt* **veuillez a. (l'expression**

de) mes salutations distinguées *(dans une lettre)* sincerely yours.

agresser *vt* to attack.

agresseur *m* attacker; *(dans la rue)* mugger.

agressif, -ive *adj* aggressive.

agression *f* *(dans la rue)* mugging.

agressivité *f* aggressiveness.

agricole *adj* **ouvrier/machine a.** farm worker/machine; **travaux agricoles** farm work.

agriculteur *m* farmer.

agriculture *f* farming.

aguets (aux) *adv* on the look-out.

ah! *int* ah!, oh!

ai *voir* **avoir**.

aide 1 *f* help; **à l'a. de** with the aid of. **2** *mf* *(personne)* assistant.

aider *vt* to help *(à faire* to do).

aider (s') *vpr* **s'a. de** to make use of.

aïe! *int* ouch!

aie(s), aient *voir* **avoir**.

aigle *m* eagle.

aigre *adj* sour.

aigu, -uë *adj* *(douleur)* acute; *(dents)* sharp; *(voix)* shrill.

aiguillage *m* *(pour train)* switches.

aiguille *f* *(à coudre, de pin)* needle; *(de montre)* hand.

aiguiller *vt* *(train)* to switch.

aiguilleur *m* signalman; **a. du ciel** air-traffic controller.

aiguiser *vt* to sharpen.

ail *m* garlic.

aile *f* wing; *(de moulin à vent)* sail; *(d'automobile)* fender.

ailier *m* Sport wing.

aille(s), aillent *voir* **aller**[1].

ailleurs *adv* somewhere else; **d'a.** *(du reste)* anyway.

aimable *adj* *(gentil)* kind; *(sympathique)* likeable.

aimant *m* magnet.

aimanter *vt* to magnetize.

aimer *vt* to love; **a. (bien)** *(apprécier)* to like, to be fond of; **a. faire** to like doing *ou* to do; **a. mieux** to prefer.

aimer (s') *vpr* **ils s'aiment** they're in love.

aîné, -ée 1 *adj (de deux frères etc)* elder, older; *(de plus de deux)* eldest, oldest. **2** *mf (de deux)* elder *ou* older (child); *(de plus de deux)* eldest *ou* oldest (child).

ainsi *adv (comme ça)* (in) this *ou* that way; **a. que** as well as; **et a. de suite** and so on.

air¹ *m* air; *(mélodie)* tune; **en plein a.** in the open (air), outdoors; **ficher en l'a.** *Fam (jeter)* to chuck, to pitch; *(gâcher)* to mess up; **en l'a.** *(jeter)* (up) in the air; *(paroles)* empty.

air² *m (expression)* look; **avoir l'a.** to look, to seem; **avoir l'a. de** to look like.

aire *f* area; **a. de stationnement** parking area.

aisance *f (facilité)* ease; *(prospérité)* affluence.

aise *f* **à l'a.** *(dans un vêtement etc)* comfortable; *(dans une situation)* at ease; **mal à l'a.** uncomfortable.

aisé, -ée *adj (facile)* easy; *(riche)* comfortably off.

aisselle *f* armpit.

ait *voir* **avoir**.

ajourner *vt* to postpone; *(après le début de la séance)* to adjourn.

ajout *m* addition (à to).

ajouter *vti* to add (à to).

ajuster *vt (pièce, salaires)* to adjust; **a. à** *(adapter)* to fit to.

alaise *f* (waterproof) undersheet.

alarme *f (signal)* alarm; **a. antivol/d'incendie** burglar/fire alarm.

alarmer *vt* to alarm.

album *m (de timbres etc)* album.

alcool *m* alcohol; *(spiritueux)* spirits; **a. à 90°** rubbing alcohol.

alcoolique *adj & mf* alcoholic.

alcoolisé, -ée *adj* alcoholic.

alcootest® *m* breath test; *(appareil)* Breathalyzer®.

alentours *mpl* surroundings.

alerte *f* alarm; **en état d'a.** on the alert.

alerter *vt* to warn.

algèbre *f* algebra.

algérien, -ienne 1 *adj* Algerian. **2** *mf* A. Algerian.

algue(s) *f(pl)* seaweed.

alibi *m* alibi.

aliéné, -ée *mf* insane person.

alignement *m* alignment.

aligner *vt*, **s'aligner** *vpr* to line up.

aliment *m* food.

alimentaire *adj* ration/*etc* **a.** food rations/*etc*; **produits alimentaires** foods.

alimentation *f (action)* feeding; *(régime)* diet; *(nourriture)* food; **magasin d'a.** grocery store.

alimenter *vt (nourrir)* to feed.

allaiter *vti* to breastfeed.

allécher *vt* to tempt.

allée *f (de parc etc)* path; *(de cinéma, supermarché etc)* aisle.

allégé, -ée *adj (fromage etc)* low-fat.

alléger *vt* to make lighter.

allemand, -ande 1 *adj* German. **2** *mf* A. German. **3** *m (langue)* German.

aller¹* *vi (aux* être) to go; **a. à** *(convenir à)* to suit; **a. avec** *(vêtement)* to go with; **a. bien/mieux** *(personne)* to be well/better; **il va savoir/***etc* he'll know/*etc*, he's going to know/*etc*; **il va partir** he's about to leave, he's going to leave; **vas-y!** go and see!; **comment vas-tu?**, **(comment) ça va?** how are you?; **ça va!** all right!, fine!; **allez-y!** go on!, go ahead!; **allez! au lit!** come on *ou* go on to bed!

aller² *m* outward journey; **a. (simple)** one-way (ticket); **a. (et) retour** round-trip (ticket).

aller (s'en) *vpr* to go away; *(tache)* to come out.

allergie *f* allergy.

allergique *adj* allergic (à to).

alliance *f (anneau)* wedding ring; *(de pays)* alliance.

allié, -ée *mf* ally.

allier *vt* to combine (**à** with); *(pays)* to ally (**à** with).

allier (s') *vpr (pays)* to become allied (**à** with, to).

allô! *int* hello!

allocation *f* allowance, benefit; **a. (de) chômage** unemployment benefit; **allocations familiales** child benefit.

allongé, -ée *adj (étiré)* elongated.

allonger 1 *vt (bras)* to stretch out; *(jupe)* to lengthen. **2** *vi (jours)* to get longer.

allonger (s') *vpr* to stretch out.

allouer *vt* **a. qch à qn** *(ration)* to allocate sb sth; *(indemnité)* to grant sb sth.

allumage *m (de voiture)* ignition.

allumer *vt (feu, cigarette, gaz)* to light; *(électricité)* to turn *ou* switch on.

allumer (s') *vpr (lumière)* to come on.

allumette *f* match.

allure *f (vitesse)* pace; *(de véhicule)* speed; *(air)* look.

allusion *f* allusion; **faire a. à** to refer to.

alors *adv (en ce cas-là)* so; **a. que** *(tandis que)* whereas.

alouette *f* (sky)lark.

alourdir *vt* to weigh down.

alourdir (s') *vpr* to become heavy *ou* heavier.

Alpes (les) *fpl* the Alps.

alphabet *m* alphabet.

alphabétique *adj* alphabetical.

alpinisme *m* mountain climbing.

alpiniste *mf* mountain climber.

alterner *vti* to alternate.

altitude *f* height.

alu *m* papier (d')a. tinfoil.

aluminium *m* aluminum; **papier a.** tinfoil.

amabilité *f* kindness.

amaigri, -ie *adj* thin(ner).

amaigrissant *adj* **régime a.** (weight-loss) diet.

amande *f* almond.

amant *m* lover.

amarrer *vt* to moor.

amarres *fpl* moorings.

amas *m* heap, pile.

amasser *vt*, **s'amasser** *vpr* to pile up.

amateur *m (d'art etc)* lover; *(sportif)* amateur; **une équipe a.** an amateur team.

ambassade *f* embassy.

ambassadeur, -drice *mf* ambassador.

ambiance *f* atmosphere.

ambigu, -uë *adj* ambiguous.

ambitieux, -euse *adj* ambitious.

ambition *f* ambition.

ambulance *f* ambulance.

ambulant, -ante *adj* traveling.

âme *f* soul.

amélioration *f* improvement.

améliorer *vt*, **s'améliorer** *vpr* to improve.

aménagement *m (disposition)* fitting out; *(transformation)* conversion.

aménager *vt (arranger)* to fit out (**en** as); *(transformer)* to convert (**en** into).

amende *f* fine.

amener *vt* to bring.

amer, -ère *adj* bitter.

américain, -aine 1 *adj* American. **2** *mf* **A.** American.

amertume *f* bitterness.

ameublement *m* furniture.

ami, -ie *mf* friend; *(de la nature etc)* lover (**de** of); **petit a.** boyfriend; **petite amie** girlfriend.

amical, -e, -aux *adj* friendly.

amincir *vt* to make thin *or* thinner; **cette robe t'amincit** that dress makes you look thinner.

amiral, -aux *m* admiral.

amitié *f* friendship.

amonceler (s') *vpr* to pile up.

amont (en) *adv* upstream.

amorce *f (de pêcheur)* bait; *(de pistolet d'enfant)* cap.

amortir *vt (coup)* to cushion; *(bruit)* to deaden.

amortisseur *m* shock absorber.

amour *m* love; **pour l'a. de** for the sake of.

amoureux, -euse 1 *mf* lover. **2** *adj* **a. de qn** in love with sb.

amour-propre *m* self-respect.

amovible *adj* removable.

amphithéâtre *m* (*romain*) amphitheater; (*à l'université*) lecture hall.

ample *adj* (*vêtement*) full, ample.

amplement *adv* fully, amply; **c'est a. suffisant** it's more than enough.

ampleur *f* (*de robe*) fullness.

amplificateur *m* amplifier.

amplifier *vt* (*son, courant*) to amplify.

ampoule *f* (*électrique*) (light) bulb; (*aux pieds etc*) blister; (*de médicament*) phial.

amputer *vt* to amputate.

amusant, -ante *adj* amusing.

amusement *m* amusement.

amuser *vt* to entertain.

amuser (s') *vpr* to enjoy oneself, to have fun; **s'a. avec** to play with; **s'a. à faire** to amuse oneself doing.

amygdales *fpl* tonsils.

an *m* year; **il a dix ans** he's ten (years old); **Nouvel A.** New Year.

analogue *adj* similar.

analphabète *adj & mf* illiterate.

analyse *f* analysis.

analyser *vt* to analyze.

ananas *m* pineapple.

anarchie *f* anarchy.

anatomie *f* anatomy.

ancêtre *m* ancestor.

anchois *m* anchovy.

ancien, -ienne *adj* old; (*meuble*) antique; (*qui n'est plus*) former; (*antique*) ancient; (*dans une fonction*) senior.

anciennement *adv* formerly.

ancienneté *f* (*âge*) age; (*expérience*) seniority.

ancre *f* anchor.

ancrer *vt* to anchor.

andouille *f* *Fam* fool; **espèce d'a.!** (you) fool!

âne *m* (*animal*) donkey; (*personne*) ass.

anéantir *vt* to wipe out.

anecdote *f* anecdote.

ânesse *f* female donkey.

anesthésie *f* anesthesia; **a. générale** general anesthetic.

anesthésier *vt* to anesthetize.

ange *m* angel.

angine *f* throat infection.

anglais, -aise 1 *adj* English. **2** *mf* **A.** Englishman, Englishwoman; **les A.** the English. **3** *m* (*langue*) English.

angle *m* angle; (*de rue*) corner.

anglophone 1 *adj* English-speaking. **2** *mf* English speaker.

angoissant, -ante *adj* distressing.

angoisse *f* (great) anxiety, anguish.

angoisser (s') *vpr* to get anxious.

anguille *f* eel.

animal, -e, -aux *m & adj* animal.

animateur, -trice *mf* (*de télévision*) emcee; (*de club*) leader, organizer.

animation *f* (*des rues*) activity; (*de réunion*) liveliness.

animé, -ée *adj* lively.

animer *vt* (*débat*) to lead; (*soirée*) to liven up; (*mécanisme*) to drive.

animer (s') *vpr* (*rue etc*) to come to life.

anis *m* aniseed.

ankylosé, -ée *adj* stiff.

anneau, -x *m* ring.

année *f* year; **bonne a.!** Happy New Year!

annexe *f* (*bâtiment*) annex(e).

anniversaire *m* (*d'événement*) anniversary; (*de naissance*) birthday.

annonce *f* (*publicitaire*) advertisement; **petites annonces** classified advertisements.

annoncer *vt* to announce; (*vente*) to advertise.

annoncer (s') *vpr* **s'a. pluvieux/difficile/etc** to look rainy/difficult/etc.

annuaire m (téléphonique) directory, phone book.
annuel, -elle adj yearly.
annulaire m ring finger.
annulation f cancellation.
annuler vt to cancel.
ânonner vt to stumble through.
anonymat m anonymity; **garder l'a.** to remain anonymous.
anonyme adj & mf anonymous (person).
anorak m parka.
anorexie f anorexia.
anormal, -e, -aux adj abnormal.
anse f (de tasse etc) handle.
Antarctique (l') m the Antarctic.
antécédent m Grammaire antecedent; **antécédents (de personne)** past record; **antécédents médicaux** medical history.
antenne f (de radio, d'insecte) antenna.
antérieur, -eure adj (précédent) former; (placé devant) front.
antibiotique m antibiotic.
antibrouillard adj & m (phare) a. fog light.
antichoc adj inv shockproof.
anticipé, -ée adj (retraite, retour) early; (paiement) advance.
anticorps m antibody.
antilope f antelope.
antipathique adj disagreeable.
antiquaire mf antique dealer.
antique adj ancient.
antiquité f (temps, ancienneté) antiquity; (objet ancien) antique.
antivol m anti-theft device.
anxiété f anxiety.
anxieux, -euse adj anxious.
août m August.
apaisant, -ante adj soothing.
apaiser vt (personne) to calm; (douleur) to soothe.
apercevoir* vt to see; (brièvement) to catch a glimpse of.
apercevoir (s') vpr s'a. de to realize.
aperçu m (idée) general idea.

apéritif m aperitif.
aphte m mouth ulcer.
apitoyer (s') vpr s'a. sur son sort to feel sorry for oneself.
aplanir vt (terrain) to level; (difficulté) to iron out, to smooth out.
aplati, -ie adj flat.
aplatir vt to flatten (out).
aplomb (d') adv (meuble etc) level, straight.
apostrophe f (signe) apostrophe.
apparaître* vi to appear.
appareil m (électrique) appliance; (téléphonique) telephone; (avion) aircraft; (dentaire) braces; (digestif) system; **a. (photo)** camera.
apparemment adv apparently.
apparence f appearance.
apparent, -ente adj apparent; (visible) conspicuous, noticeable.
apparition f appearance; (spectre) apparition.
appartement m apartment.
appartenance f (de groupe) belonging (à to); (de parti) membership (à of).
appartenir* vi to belong (à to).
appât m bait.
appâter vt to lure.
appauvrir (s') vpr to become impoverished.
appauvrissement m impoverishment.
appel m (cri) call; (en justice) appeal; **faire l'a.** to call the roll; **faire a. à** to call upon.
appeler vt (personne, nom etc) to call; (en criant) to call out to (sb); **a. à l'aide** to call for help.
appeler (s') vpr to be called; **il s'appelle Paul** his name is Paul.
appellation f (nom) term; **a. contrôlée** (de vin) guaranteed vintage.
appendicite f appendicitis.
appétissant, -ante adj appetizing.
appétit m appetite (de for); **bon a.!** enjoy your meal!

applaudir *vti* to applaud.
applaudissements *mpl* applause.
application *f* application.
applique *f* wall lamp.
appliqué, -ée *adj* painstaking.
appliquer (s') *vpr* s'a. à (*un travail*) to apply oneself to; (*concerner*) to apply to; **s'a. à faire** to take pains to do.
appoint *m* faire l'a. to give the exact money.
apporter *vt* to bring.
appréciation *f* (*de professeur*) comment (**sur** on).
apprécier *vt* (*aimer, percevoir*) to appreciate.
appréhender *vt* (*craindre*) to dread (**a. faire** doing).
apprendre* *vt* (*étudier*) to learn; (*événement, fait*) to hear of; (*nouvelle*) to hear; **a. à faire** to learn to do; **a qch à qn** to teach sb sth; (*informer*) to tell sb sth; **a. à qn à faire** to teach sb to do; **a. que** to learn that; (*être informé*) to hear that.
apprenti, -ie *mf* apprentice.
apprentissage *m* apprenticeship; (*d'une langue*) learning (**de** of).
apprêter (s') *vpr* to get ready (**à faire** to do).
apprivoisé, -ée *adj* tame.
apprivoiser *vt* to tame.
approcher 1 *vt* (*chaise etc*) to draw up (**de** to); (*personne*) to come ou get close to, to approach. **2** *vi* to draw near(er), to get close(r) (**de** to).
approcher (s') *vpr* to come ou get near(er) (**de** to); **il s'est approché de moi** he came up to me.
approfondir *vt* (*trou*) to dig deeper; (*question*) to go into thoroughly.
approprier (s') *vpr* to take, to help oneself to.
approuver *vt* to approve.
approvisionner (s') *vpr* to get one's supplies (**de** of).

approximatif, -ive *adj* approximate.
appui *m* support; (*pour coude etc*) rest.
appuyer 1 *vt* (*soutenir*) to support; **a. qch sur** (*poser*) to rest sth on. **2** *vi* **a. sur** to rest on; (*bouton*) to press.
appuyer (s') *vpr* s'a. sur to lean on, to rest on.
après 1 *prép* (*temps*) after; (*espace*) beyond; **a. un an** after a year; **a. le pont** beyond the bridge; **a. avoir mangé** after eating. **2** *adv* after(-wards); **l'année d'a.** the following year.
après (d') *prép* according to.
après-demain *adv* the day after tomorrow.
après-midi *m ou f inv* afternoon.
après-rasage, *pl* **après-rasages** *m* aftershave.
après-shampooing *m inv* conditioner.
après-ski, *pl* **après-skis** *m* snowboot.
apte *adj* capable (**à** of).
aptitudes *fpl* aptitude (**pour** for).
aquarelle *f* watercolor.
aquarium *m* aquarium.
aquatique *adj* aquatic.
arabe 1 *adj* Arab. **2** *mf* A. Arab. **3** *adj & m* (*langue*) Arabic; **chiffres arabes** Arabic numerals.
arachide *f* peanut.
araignée *f* spider.
arbitre *m* Football, Boxe referee; *Tennis* umpire.
arbitrer *vt* Football, Boxe to referee; *Tennis* to umpire.
arbre *m* tree.
arbuste *m* (small) shrub.
arc *m* (*arme*) bow; (*voûte*) arch; (*de cercle*) arc.
arcades *fpl* arcade, arches.
arc-en-ciel, *pl* **arcs-en-ciel** *m* rainbow.
arche *f* (*voûte*) arch.
archer *m* archer.

archiplein, -pleine *adj* jam-packed.

architecte *m* architect.

architecture *f* architecture.

archives *fpl* records.

Arctique (l') *m* the Arctic.

ardent, -ente *adj (passionné)* ardent.

ardeur *f (énergie)* enthusiasm.

ardoise *f* slate.

are *m* = 100 square meters.

arène *f (pour taureaux)* bullring; **arènes** *(romaines)* amphitheater.

arête *f (de poisson)* bone; *(de cube)* edge, ridge.

argent *m (métal)* silver; *(monnaie)* money; **a. comptant** cash.

argenterie *f* silverware.

argile *f* clay.

argot *m* slang.

argument *m* argument.

argumenter *vi* to argue.

arithmétique *f* arithmetic.

armature *f (de lunettes, tente)* frame.

arme *f* arm, weapon; **a. à feu** firearm.

armée *f* army; **a. de l'air** air force.

armement(s) *m(pl)* arms.

armer *vt (personne)* to arm (**de** with); *(fusil)* to cock.

armer (s') *vpr* to arm oneself (**de** with).

armoire *f (penderie)* wardrobe, closet; **a. à pharmacie** medicine chest *ou* cabinet.

armure *f* armor.

aromate *m (herbe)* herb; *(épice)* spice.

arôme *m (goût)* flavor; *(odeur)* (pleasant) smell.

arracher *vt (clou, dent, cheveux, page)* to pull out; *(plante)* to pull up; **a. qch à qn** to snatch sth from sb.

arranger *vt (chambre, visite etc)* to fix up; *(voiture, texte)* to put right; **ça m'arrange** that suits me.

arranger (s') *vpr* to come to an

agreement; *(finir bien)* to turn out fine; **s'a. pour faire** to manage to do.

arrestation *f* arrest.

arrêt *m (halte, endroit)* stop; *(action)* stopping; **temps d'a.** pause; **sans a.** constantly; **'a. interdit'** *(panneau de signalisation)* 'no stopping (no standing)'.

arrêté *m* order.

arrêter 1 *vt* to stop; *(voleur etc)* to arrest. **2** *vi* to stop; **il n'arrête pas de critiquer/etc** he's always criticizing/etc.

arrêter (s') *vpr* to stop (**de faire** doing).

arrière 1 *adv* en **a.** *(marcher)* backwards; *(rester)* behind. **2** *m & adj inv* rear, back; **faire marche a.** to reverse, to back. **3** *m Sport* (full)back.

arrière-boutique, *pl* **arrièreboutiques** *f* back (room) *(of a shop)*.

arrière-goût, *pl* **arrière-goûts** *m* aftertaste.

arrière-grand-mère, *pl* **arrière-grands-mères** *f* great-grandmother.

arrière-grand-père, *pl* **arrièregrands-pères** *m* great-grandfather.

arrière-pays *m inv* hinterland.

arrière-pensée, *pl* **arrière-pensées** *f* ulterior motive.

arrière-plan, *pl* **arrière-plans** *m* background; **à l'a.** in the background.

arrivage *m* shipment.

arrivée *f* arrival; **ligne d'a.** finish line.

arriver *vi (aux être)* to arrive; *(survenir)* to happen; **a. à** to reach; **a. à qn** to happen to sb; **a. à faire** to manage to do; **il m'arrive d'oublier/etc** I (sometimes) forget/etc.

arrogant, -ante *adj* arrogant.

arrondir *vt (chiffre, angle)* to round off.

arrondissement *m (d'une ville)* district.

arrosage m watering.

arroser vt (terre) to water.

arrosoir m watering can.

art m art.

artère f artery; (rue) main road.

artichaut m artichoke.

article m (de presse, de commerce, en grammaire) article; **articles de toilette** toiletries.

articulation f (de membre) joint; **a. (du doigt)** knuckle.

articuler vt (mot etc) to articulate.

artifice m **feu d'a.** firework display.

artificiel, -elle adj artificial.

artisan m craftsman.

artisanal, -e, -aux adj **objet a.** object made by craftsmen.

artisanat m craft industry.

artiste mf artist.

artistique adj artistic.

as¹ voir avoir.

as² m (carte, champion) ace.

ascenseur m elevator.

ascension f ascent; **l'A.** Ascension Day.

asiatique 1 adj Asian. **2** mf **A.** Asian.

asile m (abri) shelter.

aspect m (air) appearance.

asperge f asparagus.

asperger vt to spray (**de** with).

asphyxie f suffocation.

asphyxier vt to suffocate.

aspirateur m vacuum cleaner; **passer (à) l'a.** to vacuum.

aspirer vt (liquide) to suck up.

aspirine f aspirin.

assaisonnement m seasoning.

assaisonner vt to season.

assassin m murderer.

assassinat m murder.

assassiner vt to murder.

assaut m onslaught; **prendre d'a.** to (take by) storm.

assemblée f (personnes réunies) gathering; (parlement) assembly.

assembler vt to put together.

assembler (s') vpr to gather.

asseoir* (s') vpr to sit (down).

assez adv enough; **a. de pain/gens** enough bread/people; **j'en ai a.** I've had enough; **a. grand/etc (suffisamment)** big/etc enough (**pour faire** to do); **a. fatigué/etc (plutôt)** fairly ou quite tired/etc.

assiéger vt (magasin, vedette) to mob.

assiette f plate; **a. anglaise** (assorted) cold cuts.

assis, -ise (pp of asseoir) adj sitting (down).

assises fpl (cour d')a. court of assizes.

assistance f (assemblée) audience; (aide) assistance.

assistant, -ante mf assistant; **assistant(e) social(e)** social worker; **assistante maternelle** (dans une garderie) daycare worker; (à domicile) babysitter.

assister 1 vt (aider) to help. **2** vi **a. à** (réunion, cours etc) to attend; (accident) to witness.

association f association.

associé, -ée mf partner.

associer (s') vpr to associate (**à** with).

assoiffé, -ée adj thirsty.

assombrir (s') vpr (ciel) to cloud over.

assommer vt (personne) to knock unconscious.

assorti, -ie adj (objet semblable) matching; (bonbons) assorted; **a. de** accompanied by.

assortiment m assortment.

assortir vt, **s'assortir** vpr to match.

assoupir (s') vpr to doze off.

assouplir vt (corps) to limber up, to stretch.

assouplissement m **exercices d'a.** stretching exercises.

assourdir vt to deafen.

assourdissant, -ante adj deafening.

assumer vt (tâche, rôle) to assume, to take on; (risque) to take.

assurance f (aplomb) self-assurance; (contrat) insurance.

assuré, -ée 1 adj (succès) guaranteed; (air, personne) confident. **2** mf policyholder.

assurer vt (par un contrat) to insure; (travail) to carry out; **a. à qn que** to assure sb that; **a. qn de qch** to assure sb of sth.

assurer (s') vpr s'a. to insure oneself (contre against); s'a. que/de to make sure that/of.

astérisque m asterisk.

asthmatique adj & mf asthmatic.

asthme m asthma.

asticot m maggot.

astiquer vt to polish.

astre m star.

astrologie f astrology.

astronaute mf astronaut.

astronomie f astronomy.

astuce f (pour faire qch) knack, trick.

astucieux, -euse adj clever.

atelier m (d'ouvrier etc) workshop; (de peintre) studio.

athée 1 adj atheistic. **2** mf atheist.

athlète mf athlete.

athlétique adj athletic.

athlétisme m athletics.

atlantique 1 adj Atlantic. **2** m l'A. the Atlantic.

atlas m atlas.

atmosphère f atmosphere.

atome m atom.

atomique adj (bombe etc) atomic.

atout m trump (card).

atroce adj atrocious.

atrocités fpl atrocities.

attabler (s') vpr to sit down at the table.

attachant, -ante adj (enfant etc) likeable.

attaché-case, pl **attachés-cases** m attaché case, briefcase.

attacher vt (lier) to tie (up) (à to); (boucler, fixer) to fasten.

attacher (s') vpr s'a. à qn to become attached to sb.

attaquant, -ante mf attacker.

attaque f attack.

attaquer vti to attack.

attaquer (s') vpr s'a. à to attack.

attarder (s') vpr (en chemin) to dawdle.

atteindre* vt to reach; être atteint de (maladie) to be suffering from.

attelage m (crochet) hook (for towing).

atteler vt (bêtes) to harness; (remorque) to hook up.

attendre 1 vt to wait for; elle attend un bébé she's expecting a baby. **2** vi to wait; **a. que qn vienne** to wait for sb to come; **faire a. qn** to keep sb waiting; **en attendant** meanwhile; **en attendant que (+ subjonctif)** until.

attendre (s') vpr s'a. à to expect.

attendrir (s') vpr to be moved (sur by).

attendrissant, -ante adj moving.

attentat m attempt on sb's life; **a. (à la bombe)** (bomb) attack.

attente f wait(ing); **salle d'a.** waiting room.

attentif, -ive adj (personne) attentive; (travail, examen) careful.

attention f attention; faire a. to pay attention to; **a.!** watch out!, be careful!; **a. à la voiture!** watch out for the car!

attentionné, -ée adj considerate.

attentivement adv attentively.

atténuer vt (effet) to reduce; (douleur) to ease.

atténuer (s') vpr (douleur) to ease.

atterrir vi to land.

atterrissage m landing.

attestation f (document) certificate.

attester vt to testify to; **a. que...** to testify that...

attirant, -ante adj attractive.

attirer vt to attract; (attention) to draw (sur to).

attitude *f* attitude.

attraction *f* attraction.

attraper *vt* (*ballon, maladie, voleur, train etc*) to catch; (*accent, contravention etc*) to pick up; **se laisser a.** (*duper*) to get taken in.

attrayant, -ante *adj* attractive.

attribuer *vt* (*donner*) to assign (**à** to); (*décerner*) to award (**à** to).

attribut *m* attribute.

attrister *vt* to sadden.

attroupement *m* (disorderly) crowd.

attrouper *vt*, **s'attrouper** *vpr* to gather.

au *voir* **à**, **le**.

aube *f* dawn.

auberge *f* inn; **a. de jeunesse** youth hostel.

aubergine *f* eggplant.

aucun, -une 1 *adj* no, not any; **il n'a a. talent** he has no talent; **il n'a pas de talent** he doesn't have any talent; **a. professeur n'est venu** no teacher has come. **2** *pron* none, not any; **il n'en a a.** he has none (at all); **il n'en a pas** he doesn't have any (at all).

audace *f* (*courage*) daring.

audacieux, -euse *adj* daring.

au-delà 1 *adv* beyond; **100 euros mais pas a.** 100 euros but no more. **2** *prép* **a. de** beyond.

au-dessous 1 *adv* below, under; (*à l'étage inférieur*) downstairs. **2** *prép* **a. de** under, below.

au-dessus 1 *adv* above, over; (*à l'étage supérieur*) upstairs. **2** *prép* **a. de** above; (*âge, température, prix*) over.

audience *f* (*entretien*) audience; (*de tribunal*) hearing; **l'a. est suspendue** the case is adjourned.

audio *adj inv* audio.

auditeur, -trice *mf* listener; **les auditeurs** the audience.

auditoire *m* audience.

auge *f* (feeding) trough.

augmentation *f* increase (**de** in, of); **a. de salaire** (pay) raise.

augmenter *vti* to increase (**de** by).

aujourd'hui *adv* today.

auparavant *adv* (*avant*) before(-hand); (*d'abord*) first.

auprès de *prép* by, close to.

auquel *voir* **lequel**.

aura, aurai(t) *etc voir* **avoir**.

auriculaire *m* pinky, little finger.

aurore *f* dawn.

ausculter *vt* to examine (*with a stethoscope*).

aussi *adv* (*comparaison*) as; **a. sage que** as wise as. ▪ (*également*) too, also, as well; **moi a.** so do/can/am/ etc I. ▪ (*tellement*) so; **un repas a. délicieux** so delicious a meal, such a delicious meal.

aussitôt *adv* immediately; **a. que** as soon as; **a. levé, il partit** as soon as he was up, he left.

australien, -ienne 1 *adj* Australian. **2** *mf* **A.** Australian.

autant *adv* **a. de…que** (*quantité*) as much…as; (*nombre*) as many…as. ▪ **a. de** (*tant de*) so much; (*nombre*) so many. ▪ **a. (que)** (*souffrir, lire etc*) as much (as); **en faire a.** to do the same; **j'aimerais a. aller au cinéma** I'd just as soon go to the movies.

autel *m* altar.

auteur *m* (*de livre*) author; (*de chanson*) composer.

authentique *adj* genuine.

auto *f* car; **autos tamponneuses** bumper cars.

autobus *m* bus.

autocar *m* bus, coach.

autocollant *m* sticker.

auto-école *f* driving school.

autographe *m* autograph.

automatique *adj* automatic.

automatiquement *adv* automatically.

automne *m* autumn, fall.

automobile *f & adj* car, automobile.

automobiliste *mf* motorist, driver.

autonome *adj (région)* autono-
mous, self-governing; *(personne)*
self-sufficient.

autoradio *m* car radio.

autorisation *f* permission.

autoriser *vt* to permit (**à faire** to
do).

autoritaire *adj* authoritarian.

autorité *f* authority.

autoroute *f* highway.

auto-stop *m* hitchhiking; **faire de
l'a.** to hitchhike.

auto-stoppeur, -euse *mf* hitch-
hiker.

autour 1 *adv* around. **2** *prép* **a. de**
around.

autre *adj & pron* other; **un a. livre**
another book; **un a.** another (one);
d'autres others; **d'autres médecins**
other doctors; **d'autres questions?**
any other questions?; **quelqu'un/
personne/rien d'a.** someone/no
one/nothing else; **a. chose/part**
something/somewhere else; **qui/
quoi d'a.?** who/what else?; **l'un l'a.,
les uns les autres** each other; **l'un
et l'a.** both (of them); **l'un ou l'a.** either (of them); **ni l'un ni l'a.** neither
(of them); **les uns...les autres** some...others; **d'un moment à l'a.**
any moment.

autrefois *adv* in the past.

autrement *adv* differently; *(sinon)* otherwise.

autrichien, -ienne 1 *adj* Austrian. **2** *mf* A. Austrian.

autruche *f* ostrich.

aux *voir* **à, le**.

auxiliaire *adj & m* (verbe) **a.** auxiliary (verb).

auxquel(le)s *voir* **lequel**.

aval (en) *adv* downstream.

avalanche *f* avalanche.

avaler *vti* to swallow.

avance *f* **à l'a., d'a.** in advance; **en
a.** *(arriver, partir)* early; *(avant
l'horaire prévu)* ahead (of time); **en
a. sur** ahead of; **avoir une heure
d'a.** *(train etc)* to be an hour early.

avancement *m (de personne)*
promotion.

avancer 1 *vt (date)* to move up;
(main, chaise) to move forward;
(travail) to speed up. **2** *vi* to advance, to move forward; *(montre)*
to be fast.

avancer (s') *vpr* to move forward.

avant 1 *prép* before; **a. de voir** before seeing; **a. qu'il (ne) parte** before he leaves; **a. tout** above all. **2**
adv before; **en a.** *(mouvement)* forward; *(en tête)* ahead; **la nuit d'a.**
the night before. **3** *m & adj inv* front.
4 *m (joueur)* forward.

avantage *m* advantage.

avantager *vt* to favor.

avantageux, -euse *adj (offre)*
attractive; *(prix)* reasonable.

avant-bras *m inv* forearm.

avant-dernier, -ière *adj & mf*
last but one.

avant-hier *adv* the day before
yesterday.

avant-première, *pl* **avant-pre-
mières** *f* preview.

avant-veille *f* **l'a. (de)** two days
before.

avare 1 *adj* miserly, stingy. **2** *mf*
miser.

avarice *f* miserliness, avarice.

avarie *f* damage; **subir une a.** to be
damaged.

avarié, -ée *adj (aliment)* rotting,
rotten.

avec *prép* with; *(envers)* to(wards);
et a. ça? *(dans un magasin)* anything else?

avenir *m* future; **à l'a.** in future.

aventure *f* adventure.

aventurer (s') *vpr* to venture.

aventurier, -ière *mf* adventurer.

avenue *f* avenue.

avérer (s') *vpr (se révéler)* to prove
to be; **il s'avère que...** it turns out
that...

averse *f* shower.

avertir *vt (mettre en garde)* to
warn; *(informer)* to notify.

avertissement *m* warning; notification.

avertisseur *m (klaxon®)* horn; **a. d'incendie** fire alarm.

aveu, -x *m* confession.

aveugle 1 *adj* blind. **2** *mf* blind man, blind woman; **les aveugles** the blind.

aveugler *vt* to blind.

aveuglette (à l') *adv* **chercher qch à l'a.** to grope for sth.

aviateur, -trice *mf* airman, air-woman.

aviation *f (armée de l'air)* air force; *(avions)* aircraft *inv*; **l'a. (activité)** flying; **base d'a.** air base.

avide *adj (cupide)* greedy; *(passionné)* eager **(de** for).

avion *m* aircraft *inv*, (air)plane; **a. à réaction** jet; **a. de ligne** airliner; **par a. (lettre)** airmail; **en a., par a. (voyager)** by plane, by air.

aviron *m* oar; **l'a. (sport)** rowing.

avis *m* opinion; *(communiqué)* notice; **à mon a.** in my opinion; **changer d'a.** to change one's mind.

avocat, -ate 1 *mf* attorney. **2** *m (fruit)* avocado.

avoine *f* oats.

avoir* 1 *v aux* to have; **je l'ai vu** I've seen him. **2** *vt (posséder)* to have; *(obtenir)* to get; **qu'est-ce que tu as?** what's the matter with you?; **il n'a qu'à essayer** all he has to do is try; **a. faim/chaud/etc** to be *ou* feel hungry/hot/etc; **a. cinq ans** to be five (years old); **j'en ai pour dix minutes** this will take me ten minutes. **3** *(locution)* **il y a** there is, *pl* there are; **il y a six ans** six years ago; *(voir* **il)**.

avortement *m* abortion.

avouer *vti* to confess **(que** that).

avril *m* April.

axe *m (ligne)* axis; *(essieu)* axle; **grands axes** *(routes)* main roads.

ayant, ayez, ayons *voir* **avoir.**

azote *m* nitrogen.

azure *m (sky)* blue; **la Côte d'A.** the (French) Riviera.

B

baby-foot *m inv* foosball.

bac **1** *m (bateau)* ferry(boat); *(cuve)* tank. **2** *abrév* = **baccalauréat.**

baccalauréat *m* = high school diploma.

bâche *f* tarpaulin.

bachelier, -ière *mf* holder of the *baccalauréat.*

bâcher *vt* to cover over (with a tarpaulin).

bâcler *vt Fam* to botch (up).

badaud, -aude *m* onlooker.

badigeonner *vt (mur)* to white-wash; *(écorchure)* to coat, to paint.

bafouiller *vti* to stammer.

bagage *m* piece of luggage *ou* baggage; **bagages** luggage, baggage.

bagarre *f* fight(ing).

bagarrer (se) *vpr* to fight.

bagnole *f Fam* car.

bague *f (anneau)* ring.

baguette *f* stick; *(de chef d'orchestre)* baton; *(pain)* (long thin) loaf; **baguettes** *(de tambour)* drumsticks; *(pour manger)* chopsticks; **b. (magique)** (magic) wand.

baie *f (de côte)* bay.

baignade *f (bain)* bath, swim; *(endroit)* swimming place.

baigner 1 *vt* to bathe. **2** *vi* **b. dans** *(aliment)* to be steeped in.

baigner (se) *vpr* to go swimming.

baigneur, -euse 1 *mf* bather, swimmer. **2** *m (poupée)* baby doll.

baignoire *f* bath (tub).

bail, *pl* **baux** *m* lease; **ça fait un b. que je ne l'ai pas vu** *Fam* I haven't seen him for ages.

bâillement *m* yawn.

bâiller *vi* to yawn.

bâillon *m* gag.

bâillonner *vt* to gag.

bain *m* bath; **prendre un b. de so-**

leil to sunbathe; **salle de bain(s)** bathroom; **être dans le b.** *Fam* to have gotten into the swing of things; **b. de bouche** mouthwash.
baiser *m* kiss.
baisse *f* fall, drop (**de** in); **en b.** falling.
baisser 1 *vt* to lower, to drop; *(tête)* to bend; *(radio, chauffage)* to turn down. **2** *vi* to go down, to drop.
baisser (se) *upr* to bend down.
bal, *pl* **bals** *m* ball; *(populaire)* dance.
balade *f Fam* walk; *(en auto)* drive.
balader (se) *upr Fam (à pied)* to (go for a) walk; **se b. (en voiture)** to go for a drive.
baladeur *m* Walkman®.
balai *m* broom; **manche à b.** broomstick.
balance *f* (pair of) scales.
balancer *vt* to sway; *(lancer) Fam* to pitch; *(se débarrasser de) Fam* to chuck, to pitch.
balancer (se) *upr* to swing (from side to side).
balançoire *f (suspendue)* swing.
balayer *vt* to sweep (up); *(enlever)* to sweep away.
balayette *f* (hand)brush.
balayeur, -euse 1 *mf (personne)* roadsweeper. **2** *f (véhicule)* road-sweeper.
balbutier *vti* to stammer.
balcon *m* balcony.
baleine *f* whale.
balisage *m* beacons.
balise *f (pour naviguer)* beacon.
baliser *vt* to mark with beacons.
ballast *m* ballast.
balle *f (de tennis, golf etc)* ball; *(projectile)* bullet.
ballerine *f* ballerina.
ballet *m* ballet.
ballon *m (jouet d'enfant, appareil)* balloon; *(sports)* ball; **b. de football** soccer ball.
ballot *m* bundle.
ballottage *m (scrutin)* second ballot.

balnéaire *adj* **station b.** beach resort.
balustrade *f* (hand)rail.
bambin *m* tiny tot.
bambou *m* bamboo.
ban *m (applaudissements)* round of applause; **un (triple) b. pour...** three cheers for...
banal, -e, -als *adj (objet, gens)* ordinary; *(idée)* trite, banal; **pas b.** unusual.
banane *f* banana.
banc *m (siège)* bench; **b. de sable** sandbank.
bancaire *adj* **compte b.** bank account.
bancal, -e, -als *adj (meuble)* wobbly.
bandage *m* bandage.
bande¹ *f (de terrain, papier etc)* strip; *(de film)* reel; *(rayure)* stripe; *(pansement)* bandage; *(sur la chaussée)* line; **b. d'arrêt d'urgence** shoulder; **b. (magnétique)** tape; **b. vidéo** videotape; **b. dessinée** comic strip.
bande² *f (groupe)* gang.
bande-annonce, *pl* **bandes-annonces** *f* preview.
bandeau, -x *m (sur les yeux)* blindfold; *(pour la tête)* headband.
bander *vt (blessure)* to bandage; *(yeux)* to blindfold.
banderole *f (sur montants)* banner.
bandit *m* robber.
bandoulière *f (de sac)* shoulder strap; **en b.** slung across the shoulder.
banlieue *f* **la b.** the outskirts (of town).
banque *f* bank; *(activité)* banking.
banquette *f (de véhicule, train)* seat.
banquier *m* banker.
banquise *f* ice floe.
baptême *m* christening, baptism.
baptiser *vt (enfant)* to christen, to baptize.

baquet m tub, basin.

bar m (lieu, comptoir) bar.

baraque f hut, shack.

baraquement m (makeshift) huts.

baratin m Fam (verbiage) waffle; (de séducteur) sweet talk; (de vendeur) sales talk.

barbare adj (cruel) barbaric.

barbe f beard; **se faire la b.** to shave; **quelle b.!** Fam what a bore!

barbecue m barbecue.

barbelé adj **fil de fer b.** barbed wire.

barboter vi to splash around.

barbouillage m smear(ing); (gribouillage) scribble, scribbling.

barbouiller vt (salir) to smear; (gribouiller) to scribble.

barbu, -ue adj bearded.

barème m (de notes, de salaires, de prix) scale; (pour calculer) ready reckoner.

baril m barrel; **b. de poudre** powder keg.

barman, pl -men ou -mans m bartender.

baromètre m barometer.

baron m baron.

baronne f baroness.

barque f (small) boat.

barquette f (de fruit) punnet; (de plat cuisiné) container.

barrage m (sur une route) roadblock; (sur un fleuve) dam.

barre f bar; (de bateau) helm; (trait) stroke.

barreau, -x m (de fenêtre) bar; (d'échelle) rung.

barrer vt (route etc) to block; (mot, phrase) to cross out.

barrette f barrette.

barricade f barricade.

barricader vt to barricade.

barricader (se) vpr to barricade oneself (in).

barrière f (porte) gate; (clôture) fence; (obstacle) barrier.

barrique f (large) barrel.

bas, basse 1 adj low. **2** adv low; (parler) in a whisper; **plus b.** further ou lower down. **3** m (de côté, page, mur etc) bottom; **tiroir/etc du b.** bottom drawer/etc; **en b.** down (below); (par l'escalier) downstairs; **en ou au b. de** at the bottom of.

bas m (chaussette) stocking.

bas-côté m roadside, verge, shoulder.

bascule f weighing machine; (jeu d'enfant) seesaw.

basculer vti to topple over.

base f base; **bases** (d'un argument, accord etc) basis; **salaire de b.** base pay; **à b. de lait/citron** milk-/lemon-based.

baser vt to base (**sur** on).

basket(-ball) m basketball.

baskets fpl (chaussures) sneakers.

basque 1 adj Basque. **2** mf B. Basque.

basse voir **bas**.

basse-cour, pl **basses-cours** f farmyard.

bassin m pond; (rade) dock; (du corps) pelvis; **b. houiller** coalfield.

bassine f bowl.

bataille f battle.

batailleur, -euse 1 mf fighter. **2** adj fond of fighting, belligerent.

bateau, -x m boat; (grand) ship.

bateau-mouche, pl **bateaux-mouches** m river boat (on the Seine).

bâtiment m building; (navire) vessel; **le b.** (industrie) the construction industry.

bâtir vt to build; **bien bâti** well-built.

bâton m stick; (d'agent) baton; **b. de rouge** lipstick; **donner des coups de b. à qn** to beat sb (with a stick).

battante adj f **pluie b.** driving rain.

battement m beat(ing); (de paupières) blink(ing); (délai) interval; **b. de cœur** heartbeat.

batterie f battery; **la b.** (d'un orchestre) the drums.

batteur m (d'orchestre) drummer.

battre* 1 vt to beat. 2 vi to beat; **b. des mains** to clap (one's hands); **b. des paupières** to blink; **b. des ailes** (oiseau) to flap its wings.

battre (se) vpr to fight.

baume m balm.

bavard, -arde adj talkative.

bavardage m chatting.

bavarder vi to chat.

bave f drool.

baver vi to drool; **en b.** Fam to have a rough time of it.

bavoir m bib.

bavure f (tache) smudge.

bazar m (magasin) bazaar; (désordre) mess.

BD f abrév (bande dessinée) comic strip.

beau (or **bel** before vowel or mute h), **belle**, pl **beaux, belles** adj beautiful, attractive; (voyage, temps etc) fine, lovely; **au b. milieu** right in the middle; **j'ai b. crier/etc** it's no use (my) shouting/etc.

beaucoup adv (lire etc) a lot; **aimer b.** to like very much ou a lot; **b. de** (livres etc) many, a lot of; (courage etc) a lot of; **pas b. d'argent/etc** not much money/etc; **j'en ai b.** (quantité) I have a lot; (nombre) I have lots; **b. plus** much more; many more (**que** than).

beau-fils, pl **beaux-fils** m (gendre) son-in-law; (après remariage) stepson.

beau-frère, pl **beaux-frères** m brother-in-law.

beau-père, pl **beaux-pères** m (père du conjoint) father-in-law; (après remariage) stepfather.

beauté f beauty.

beaux-arts mpl fine arts; **école des b., les B.** art school.

beaux-parents mpl parents-in-law.

bébé m baby.

bec m (d'oiseau) beak; (de cruche) spout; **coup de b.** peck.

bécane f Fam bike.

bêche f spade.

bêcher vt (cultiver) to dig.

becquée f **donner la b. à** (oiseau) to feed.

bedonnant, -ante adj potbellied.

bégayer vi to stutter.

bègue 1 mf stutterer. 2 adj **être b.** to stutter.

beige adj & m beige.

beignet m (pâtisserie) fritter; (rond) doughnut.

bel voir **beau**.

bêler vi to bleat.

belette f weasel.

belge 1 adj Belgian. 2 mf **B.** Belgian.

bélier m ram.

belle voir **beau**.

belle-famille, pl **belles-familles** f in-laws.

belle-fille, pl **belles-filles** f (épouse du fils) daughter-in-law; (après remariage) stepdaughter.

belle-mère, pl **belles-mères** f (mère du conjoint) mother-in-law; (après remariage) stepmother.

belle-sœur, pl **belles-sœurs** f sister-in-law.

belliqueux, -euse adj (agressif) aggressive.

bénédiction f blessing.

bénéfice m (gain) profit; (avantage) benefit.

bénéficiaire 1 mf (de chèque) payee. 2 adj (entreprise) profit-making; (compte) in credit.

bénéficier vi to benefit (**de** from).

bénéfique adj beneficial.

bénévolat m voluntary work.

bénévole adj & mf voluntary (worker).

bénin, -igne adj (accident, opération) minor; (tumeur) benign.

bénir vt to bless; (remercier) to give thanks to.

bénit, -ite adj (pain) consecrated; **eau bénite** holy water.

benjamin, -ine mf youngest child.

benne f (de camion) (movable) container; **camion à b. basculante** dump truck.

BEP m abrév (brevet d'études professionnelles) = vocational diploma taken at 18.

béquille f (canne) crutch; (de moto) stand.

berceau, -x m cradle.

bercer vt (balancer) to rock; (apaiser) to soothe, to lull.

berceuse f lullaby.

béret m beret.

berge f (rive) (raised) bank.

berger m shepherd; **b. allemand** German shepherd.

bergère f shepherdess.

bergerie f sheepfold.

berline f (voiture) sedan.

berner vt to fool.

besogne f job, task.

besoin m need; **avoir b. de** to need.

bestiole f (insecte) bug.

bétail m livestock.

bête[1] f animal; (insecte) bug; **b. noire** pet peeve.

bête[2] adj stupid.

bêtement adv stupidly; **tout b.** quite simply.

bêtise f stupidity; (action, parole) stupid thing.

béton m concrete; **mur/etc en b.** concrete wall/etc.

betterave f beet.

beurre m butter.

beurrer vt to butter.

beurrier m butter dish.

biais m **regarder qn de b.** to look sideways at sb; **par le b. de** through.

bibelot m (small) ornament, trinket.

biberon m (feeding) bottle.

bible f bible; **la B.** the Bible.

bibliothécaire mf librarian.

bibliothèque f library; (meuble) bookcase.

bic® m ballpoint.

biceps m (muscle) biceps.

biche f doe.

bicyclette f bicycle.

bidon 1 m (jerry) can. **2** adj inv Fam phoney.

bidonville m shantytown.

bidule m (chose) Fam whatchamacallit.

bien 1 adv well; **b. fatigué/souvent/etc (très)** very tired/often/etc, **merci b.!** thanks very much!; **b.!** fine!, right!; **b. des fois/des gens/** etc lots of ou many times/people/ etc, **je l'ai b. dit (intensif)** I did say so; **tu as b. fait** you did right; **c'est b. fait (pour lui)** it serves him right. **2** adj inv (convenable, compétent etc) fine. **3** m (avantage) good; (chose) possession; **ça te fera du b.** it will do you good; **pour ton b.** for your own good; **le b. et le mal** good and evil.

bien-être m wellbeing.

bienfaisant, -ante adj beneficial.

bien que conj (+ subjonctif) although.

bientôt adv soon; **à b.!** see you soon!; **il est b. midi/etc** it's nearly twelve/etc.

bienveillant, -ante adj kind.

bienvenu, -ue 1 adj welcome. **2** f welcome; **souhaiter la bienvenue à** to welcome.

bière f beer; **b. pression** draft beer.

bifteck m steak.

bifurcation f (route etc) fork.

bifurquer vi to fork.

bigoudi m (hair) roller.

bijou, -x m jewel.

bijouterie f (commerce) jewelry store, jeweler's.

bijoutier, -ière mf jeweler.

bilan m (financier) balance sheet; (résultat) outcome; (d'un accident) (casualty) toll; **b. de santé** check-

up; **déposer le b.** to file for
bankruptcy.

bile *f* bile; **se faire de la b.** *Fam* to
worry.

bilingue *adj* bilingual.

billard *m (jeu)* billiards; *(table)* billiard table.

bille *f (d'enfant)* marble; **stylo à b.**
ballpoint (pen).

billet *m* ticket; **b. (de banque)** bill;
b. aller, b. simple one-way ticket; **b.
aller-retour** round trip ticket.

billeterie *f (lieu)* ticket office; **b.
automatique** *(de billet de transport)* ticket machine.

biologie *f* biology.

biologique *adj* biological; *(légumes etc)* organic.

bip *m* beeper.

biscotte *f* Melba toast.

biscuit *m* cookie.

bise¹ *f (vent)* north wind.

bise² *f (baiser) Fam* kiss; **faire la b. à
qn** to kiss sb on both cheeks.

bison *m (American)* buffalo.

bisou *m Fam* kiss.

bissextile *adj f* année b. leap year.

bistouri *m* scalpel.

bistro(t) *m Fam* bar.

bitume *m (revêtement)* asphalt.

bizarre *adj* peculiar, odd.

blague *f (plaisanterie, farce)* joke;
b. à part seriously.

blaguer *vi* to be joking.

blaireau, -x *m (animal)* badger;
(brosse) shaving brush.

blâmer *vt* to criticize, to blame.

blanc, blanche 1 *adj (robe etc)* white;
(page) blank. **2** *mf (personne)*
white man *ou* woman. **3** *m (couleur)*
white; *(de poulet)* breast; *(espace)*
blank; **b. (d'œuf)** (egg) white; **laisser en b.** to leave blank; **chèque en
b.** blank check; **donner carte blanche à qn** to give sb free rein.

blancheur *f* whiteness.

blanchir *vi* to turn white.

blanchisserie *f (lieu)* laundry.

blatte *f (cock)* roach.

blé *m* wheat.

blême *adj* sickly pale; **b. de colère**
livid.

blêmir *vi* to turn pale.

blessant, -ante *adj* hurtful.

blessé, -ée *mf* casualty.

blesser *vt* to injure, to hurt; *(avec
un couteau, une balle etc)* to wound;
(offenser) to hurt.

blesser (se) *vpr* se b. le *ou* au
bras/etc to hurt one's arm/etc.

blessure *f* injury; wound.

bleu, -e 1 *adj (mpl* bleus) blue. **2** *m
(pl* bleus) *(couleur)* blue; *(contusion)* bruise; *(vêtement)* overalls.

blindé, -ée *adj (voiture etc)* armored; **porte blindée** reinforced
steel door; **une vitre blindée** bulletproof glass.

bloc *m* block; *(de papier)* pad; **à b.**
(visser etc) tight.

bloc-notes, *pl* blocs-notes *m*
writing pad.

blond, -onde 1 *adj* fair(-haired),
blond. **2** *mf* fair-haired *ou* blond
man *ou* woman; **(bière) blonde**
beer.

bloquer *vt (obstruer)* to block;
(coincer) to jam; *(roue)* to lock;
(prix) to freeze.

bloquer (se) *vpr* to jam; *(roue)* to
lock.

blottir (se) *vpr* to crouch; *(dans
son lit)* to snuggle in; **se b. contre**
to snuggle up to.

blouse *f (tablier)* smock.

blouson *m* windbreaker.

bobine *f* reel, spool.

bocal, -aux *m* glass jar; *(à poisons)* bowl.

bœuf, *pl* **-fs** *m* ox *(pl* oxen);
(viande) beef.

boire* *vti* to drink; **offrir à b. à qn**
to offer sb a drink.

bois *m* wood; *(de construction)* timber; **en** *ou* **de b.** wooden; **b. de
chauffage** firewood.

boisé, -ée *adj* wooded.

boisson *f* drink.

boîte f box; (de conserve) can; **b. aux ou à lettres** mailbox. ▪ (entreprise) Fam firm; **b. de nuit** nightclub.

boiter vi to limp.

boîtier m (de montre) case.

bol m bowl; **un b. d'air** a breath of fresh air.

bombardement m bombing; shelling.

bombarder vt to bomb; (avec des obus) to shell.

bombe f bomb; (de laque etc) spray.

bon¹, bonne adj good; (qui convient) right; (apte) fit; **b. anniversaire!** happy birthday!; **le b. choix/ moment** the right choice/time; **b. à manger** fit to eat; **c'est b. à savoir** it's worth knowing; **croire b. de** to think it wise to; **b. en français/etc** good at French/etc; **un b. moment** (intensif) a good while; **pour de b.** really (and truly); **ah b.?** is that so?

bon² m (billet) coupon, voucher.

bonbon m candy.

bond m leap.

bondé, -ée adj packed.

bondir vi to leap.

bonheur m happiness; (chance) good luck; **par b.** luckily.

bonhomme, pl **bonshommes** m fellow; **b. de neige** snowman.

bonjour m & int good morning; (après-midi) good afternoon; **donner le b. à, dire b. à** to say hello to.

bonne¹ voir **bon.**

bonne² f maid.

bonnet m (de ski etc) cap; (de femme, d'enfant) bonnet, hat.

bonsoir m & int (en rencontrant qn) good evening; (en quittant qn) goodbye; (au coucher) good night.

bonté f kindness.

bord m (rebord) edge; (rive) bank; **au b. de la mer** at the beach; **au b. de la route** by the roadside; **b. du trottoir** curb; **à bord (de)** (avion, bateau) on board.

border vt (vêtement) to edge; (lit, personne) to tuck in; **b. la rue/etc** (maisons, arbres) to line the street/etc.

bordereau, -x m (de livraison etc) note.

bordure f border.

borne f boundary mark; **b. kilométrique** = milestone.

borné, -ée adj (personne) narrow-minded; (esprit) narrow.

bosse f (dans le dos) hump; (enflure, de terrain) bump.

bosser vi Fam to work (hard).

bossu, -ue 1 adj hunchbacked. **2** mf hunchback.

botte f (chaussure) boot; (de fleurs etc) bunch.

bottine f (ankle) boot.

bouc m billy goat; (barbe) goatee.

boucan m Fam din, row; **faire du b.** to kick up a row.

bouche f mouth; **b. de métro** métro entrance; **b. d'égout** drain opening.

bouché, -ée adj j'ai le nez b. my nose is stuffed up.

bouchée f mouthful.

boucher¹ vt (évier etc) to stop up; (bouteille) to cork; (vue, rue etc) to block.

boucher², -ère m butcher.

boucher (se) vpr se b. le nez to hold one's nose.

boucherie f butcher's (shop).

bouchon m stopper; (de liège) cork; (de tube, bidon) cap; (embouteillage) traffic jam.

boucle f (de ceinture) buckle; **b. d'oreille** earring; **b. (de cheveux)** curl.

bouclé, -ée adj (cheveux) curly.

boucler 1 vt (attacher) to fasten; (cheveux) to curl. **2** vi to be curly.

bouclier m shield.

bouder vi to sulk.

boudin m blood sausage.

boue f mud.

bouée f buoy; **b. de sauvetage** lifebuoy.

boueux, -euse *adj* muddy.

bouffe *f (nourriture) Fam* grub.

bouffée *f (de fumée)* puff.

bouffer *vti (manger) Fam* to eat.

bougeoir *m* candlestick.

bouger *vti* to move.

bougie *f* candle; *(d'automobile)* spark plug.

bouillie *f* porridge.

bouillir* *vi* to boil.

bouilloire *f* kettle.

bouillon *m (aliment)* broth; *(bulles)* bubbles.

bouillonner *vi* to bubble.

boulanger, -ère *mf* baker.

boulangerie *f* baker's (shop).

boule *f* ball; **boules** (French) bowling game; **b. de neige** snowball.

bouleau, -x *m* (silver) birch.

bouledogue *m* bulldog.

boulet *m* **b. de canon** cannonball.

boulette *f (de papier)* ball; *(de viande)* meatball.

boulevard *m* boulevard.

bouleversant, -ante *adj (perturbant)* distressing; *(émouvant)* deeply moving.

bouleversement *m* upheaval.

bouleverser *vt (déranger)* to turn upside down; *(perturber)* to distress; *(émouvoir)* to move deeply.

boulimie *f* bulimia.

boulon *m* bolt.

boulot *m Fam (emploi)* job; *(travail)* work.

bouquet *m (de fleurs)* bunch.

bouquin *m Fam* book.

bourdon *m (insecte)* bumblebee.

bourdonnement *m* buzzing.

bourdonner *vi* to buzz.

bourg *m* (small) market town.

bourgeois, -oise *adj & mf* middle-class (person).

bourgeon *m* bud.

bourgeonner *vi* to bud.

bourrasque *f* squall, gust of wind.

bourré, -ée *adj (ivre) Fam* wasted.

bourrer *vt* to stuff, to cram (**de** with); *(pipe)* to fill.

bourse *f (sac)* purse; *(d'études)* grant, scholarship; **la B.** the Stock Exchange.

bousculade *f* jostling.

bousculer *vt (heurter, pousser)* to jostle.

boussole *f* compass.

bout *m* end; *(de langue, canne, doigt)* tip; *(de papier, pain, ficelle)* piece; **un b. de temps** a little while; **au b. d'un moment** after a moment; **à b.** exhausted; **à b. de souffle** out of breath.

bouteille *f* bottle; *(de gaz)* cylinder.

boutique *f* shop.

bouton *m (bourgeon)* bud; *(au visage etc)* pimple; *(de vêtement)* button; *(poussoir)* (push-)button; *(de porte, télévision)* knob.

bouton-d'or, *pl* boutons-d'or *m* buttercup.

boutonner *vt*, **se boutonner** *vpr* to button (up).

boutonnière *f* buttonhole.

bouton-pression, *pl* boutons-pression *m* snap (fastener).

box, *pl* boxes *m (garage)* garage facility; *(de cheval)* stall; *(au bureau)* cubicle.

boxe *f* boxing.

boxer *vi* to box.

boxeur *m* boxer.

boycotter *vt* to boycott.

BP *f abrév (boîte postale)* PO Box.

bracelet *m* bracelet; *(de montre)* strap, band.

braconner *vi* to poach.

braconnier *m* poacher.

braguette *f (de pantalon)* fly.

brailler *vti* to bawl.

braise(s) *f(pl)* embers.

brancard *m (civière)* stretcher.

branchages *mpl (cut)* branches.

branche *f (d'arbre)* branch; *(de compas)* arm, leg.

branchement *m* connection.

brancher *vt* to plug in.

brandir *vt* to flourish.

branlant, -ante *adj (table etc)* wobbly, shaky.

braquer 1 *vt (arme etc)* to point (**sur** at). **2** *vi* to turn the steering wheel, to steer.

bras *m* arm; **b. dessus b. dessous** arm in arm; **à b. ouverts** with open arms.

brasier *m* blaze.

brassard *m* armband.

brasse *f (nage)* breaststroke.

brasserie *f (usine)* brewery; *(café)* brasserie.

brassière *f (de bébé)* undershirt.

brave *adj & m* brave (man).

bravement *adv* bravely.

bravo 1 *int* bravo. **2** *m* cheer.

bravoure *f* bravery.

break *m (voiture)* station wagon.

brebis *f* ewe.

brèche *f* gap.

bredouille *adj* **rentrer b.** to come back empty-handed.

bredouiller *vti* to mumble.

bref, brève 1 *adj* brief, short. **2** *adv* **(enfin) b.** in a word.

bretelle *f* strap; *(d'accès)* access road; **bretelles** *(pour pantalon)* suspenders.

breton, -onne 1 *adj* Breton. **2** *mf* **B.** Breton.

brevet *m* diploma; **b. (des collèges)** = exam at end of junior high school; **b. (d'invention)** patent.

bricolage *m (passe-temps)* do-it-yourself.

bricoler 1 *vi* to do odd jobs. **2** *vt (fabriquer)* to put together.

bricoleur, -euse *mf* handyman, handywoman.

bride *f* bridle.

brider *vt* to hold *ou* back.

bridés *adj* **avoir les yeux bridés** to have slit eyes.

brièvement *adv* briefly.

brièveté *f* shortness, brevity.

brigand *m* robber; *(enfant)* rascal.

brillamment *adv* brilliantly.

brillant, -ante 1 *adj (luisant)* shining; *(astiqué)* shiny; *(couleur)* bright; *(doué)* brilliant. **2** *m* shine; *(couleur)* brightness.

briller *vi* to shine; **faire b.** *(meuble)* to polish (up).

brin *m (d'herbe)* blade; *(de corde, fil)* strand; *(de muguet)* spray.

brindille *f* twig.

brioche *f* brioche *(light sweet bun)*.

brique *f* brick; *(de lait, jus de fruit)* carton.

briquet *m (cigarette)* lighter.

brise *f* breeze.

briser *vt*, **se briser** *vpr* to break.

britannique 1 *adj* British. **2** *mf* **B.** Briton; **les Britanniques** the British.

broc *m* pitcher, jug.

brocante *f (commerce)* second-hand trade *(in furniture etc)*.

brocanteur, -euse *mf* second-hand dealer *(in furniture etc)*.

broche *f (pour rôtir)* spit; *(bijou)* brooch.

brochet *m* pike.

brochette *f (tige)* skewer; *(plat)* kebab.

brochure *f* brochure, booklet.

brocolis *mpl* broccoli.

broder *vt* to embroider (**de** with).

broderie *f* embroidery.

bronches *fpl* bronchial tubes.

bronchite *f* bronchitis.

bronzage *m* (sun)tan.

bronze *m* bronze.

bronzer 1 *vt* to tan. **2** *vi* to get (sun)tanned.

bronzer (se) *vpr* **se (faire) b.** to sunbathe, to get a (sun)tan.

brosse *f* brush; **b. à dents** toothbrush.

brosser *vt* to brush.

brosser (se) *vpr* **se b. les dents/cheveux** to brush one's teeth/hair.

brouette *f* wheelbarrow.

brouhaha *m* hubbub.

brouillard *m* fog; **il y a du b.** it's foggy.

brouiller *vt (œufs)* to scramble; **b. la vue à qn** to blur sb's vision.

brouiller (se) *vpr (temps)* to cloud over; *(vue)* to get blurred; *(amis)* to fall out (**avec** with).

brouillon *m* rough draft.

broussailles *fpl* bushes.

brousse *f* **la b.** the bush.

brouter *vti* to graze.

broyer *vt* to grind.

brugnon *m* nectarine.

bruine *f* drizzle.

bruit *m* noise, sound; *(nouvelle)* rumor; **faire du b.** to make noise.

brûlant, -ante *adj (objet, soleil)* burning (hot).

brûlé *m* **odeur de b.** smell of burning.

brûler *vti* to burn; **b. un feu (rouge)** to go through the lights.

brûler (se) *vpr* to burn oneself.

brûlure *f* burn.

brume *f* mist, haze.

brumeux, -euse *adj* misty, hazy.

brun, brune 1 *adj* brown; *(cheveux)* dark, brown; *(personne)* dark-haired. **2** *m (couleur)* brown. **3** *mf* dark-haired person.

brunir *vi* to turn brown; *(cheveux)* to get darker.

brushing *m* blow-dry.

brusque *adj (manière, personne)* abrupt; *(subit)* sudden.

brusquement *adv* suddenly.

brusquerie *f* abruptness.

brut *adj (pétrole)* crude; *(poids, salaire)* gross.

brutal, -e, -aux *adj (violent)* brutal; *(franc)* rough.

brutaliser *vt* to ill-treat.

brutalité *f* brutality.

brute *f* brute.

bruyamment *adv* noisily.

bruyant, -ante *adj* noisy.

BTS *m abrév (brevet de technicien supérieur)* = advanced vocational training certificate.

bu, bue *pp of* **boire**.

bûche *f* log.

bûcheron *m* lumberjack.

bûcheur, -euse *mf Fam* grind.

budget *m* budget.

buée *f* mist.

buffet *m (armoire)* sideboard; *(table, repas)* buffet.

buisson *m* bush.

bulldozer *m* bulldozer.

bulle *f* bubble; *(de BD)* balloon.

bulletin *m (météo)* report; *(scolaire)* report card; **b. de paie** pay slip; **b. de vote** ballot paper.

bureau, -x *m (table)* desk; *(lieu)* office; **b. de change** foreign exchange office, bureau de change; **b. de tabac** tobacco store.

burette *f* oilcan.

bus *m* bus.

buste *m (torse)* chest; *(sculpture)* bust.

but *m (objectif)* aim, goal; *Sport* goal.

buté, -ée *adj* obstinate.

buter *vi* **b. contre** to stumble over.

butoir *m (de porte)* stop(per).

butte *f* mound.

buvard *m* blotting paper.

buvette *f* refreshment bar.

buveur, -euse *mf* drinker.

C

ça *pron dém (abrév de cela) (pour désigner)* that; *(plus près)* this; *(sujet indéfini)* it, that; **ça m'amuse que...** it amuses me that...; **où/ quand/comment/etc ça?** where?/ when?/how?/etc; **ça va (bien)?** how's it going?; **ça va!** fine!, OK!; **ça alors!** *(surprise, indignation)* I'll be!, how about that!; **c'est ça** that's right.

cabane *f* hut, cabin; *(à outils)* shed; *(à lapins)* hutch.

cabine *f (de bateau)* cabin; *(téléphonique)* phone booth *ou* box; *(à* *la piscine)* cubicle; **c. (de pilotage)** cockpit; *(d'un grand avion)* flight deck; **c. d'essayage** fitting room.

cabinet *m (de médecin)* office; *(de ministre)* department; **cabinets** *(toilettes)* toilet, lavatory; **c. de toilette** (small) bathroom; **c. de travail** study.

câble *m* cable; *(cordage)* rope; **la télévision par c.** cable television.

cabosser *vt* to dent.

cabrer (se) *vpr (cheval)* to rear (up).

cacah(o)uète *f* peanut.

cacao *m* cocoa.

cachalot *m* sperm whale.

cache-cache *m inv* hide-and-seek.

cache-nez *m inv* scarf, muffler.

cacher *vt* to hide (à from); **je ne cache pas que...** I don't hide the fact that...

cacher (se) *vpr* to hide.

cachet *m (de la poste)* postmark; *(comprimé)* tablet.

cacheter *vt* to seal.

cachette *f* hiding place; **en c.** in secret.

cachot *m* dungeon.

cactus *m* cactus.

cadavre *m* corpse.

caddie® *m (supermarket)* cart.

cadeau, -x *m* present, gift.

cadenas *m* padlock.

cadence *f (vitesse)* rate; **en c.** in time.

cadet, -ette 1 *adj (de deux frères etc)* younger; *(de plus de deux)* youngest. **2** *mf (de deux)* younger (child); *(de plus de deux)* youngest (child); *(sportif)* junior.

cadran *m (de téléphone)* dial; *(de montre)* face.

cadre *m (de photo, vélo etc)* frame; *(décor)* setting; *(sur un imprimé)* box; *(chef)* executive, manager.

cadrer 1 *vt (photo)* to center. **2** *vi (correspondre)* to tally (**avec** with).

cafard *m (insecte)* (cock)roach;

avoir le c. to be in the dumps; **ça me donne le c.** it depresses me.

café *m* coffee; *(bar)* café; **c. au lait, c. crème** coffee with milk; **c. noir, c. nature** black coffee; **c. soluble** *ou* **instantané** instant coffee; **tasse de c.** cup of black coffee.

cafétéria *f* cafeteria.

cafetière *f* coffeepot; *(électrique)* percolator.

cage *f* cage; *(d'escalier)* well; *Sport* goal (area).

cageot *m* crate, box.

cagnotte *f (caisse commune)* kitty; *(de jeu)* pool.

cagoule *f* ski mask; *(de bandit, moine)* hood.

cahier *m* exercise book; **c. de brouillon** scratch pad; **c. d'appel** roll *(in school)*.

cahot *m* jolt, bump.

cailler *vti (sang)* to clot; *(lait)* to curdle; **faire c.** *(lait)* to curdle.

caillot *m (blood)* clot.

caillou, -x *m* stone.

caisse *f* case, box; *(guichet)* cash desk; *(de supermarché)* checkout; *(tambour)* drum; **c. (enregistreuse)** till, cash register; **c. d'épargne** savings bank.

caissier, -ière *mf* cashier; *(de supermarché)* checkout assistant.

cake *m* fruit cake.

calcaire *adj (eau)* hard.

calciné, -ée *adj* charred.

calcul *m* calculation; *(discipline)* arithmetic.

calculatrice *f* calculator.

calculer *vt* to calculate.

cale *f (pour maintenir)* wedge; *(de bateau)* hold.

caleçon *m* underpants; **c. de bain** bathing trunks.

calendrier *m* calendar.

calepin *m* notebook.

caler 1 *vt (meuble etc)* to wedge; *(appuyer)* to prop (up). **2** *vti (moteur)* to stall.

calfeutrer *vt* to draftproof.

calfeutrer (se) *vpr* **se c. (chez soi)** to shut oneself away.

calibre *m* *(diamètre)* caliber; *(d'œuf)* grade.

califourchon (à) *adv* astride; **se mettre à c. sur** to straddle.

câlin, -ine 1 *adj* affectionate. **2** *m* cuddle.

calmant *m* *(pour la nervosité)* sedative; *(pour la douleur)* painkiller; **sous calmants** *(pour la nervosité)* under sedation; *(pour la douleur)* on painkillers.

calme 1 *adj* calm. **2** *m* calm(ness); **du c.!** keep quiet!; *(pas de panique)* keep calm!; **dans le c.** *(travailler, étudier)* in peace and quiet.

calmer *vt* *(douleur)* to soothe; *(inquiétude)* to calm; **c. qn** to calm sb (down).

calmer (se) *vpr* to calm down.

calomnie *f* *(en paroles)* slander; *(par écrit)* libel.

calorie *f* calorie.

calque *m* *(dessin)* tracing; **(papier-)c.** tracing paper.

camarade *mf* friend; **c. de jeu** playmate.

camaraderie *f* friendship.

cambouis *m* (dirty) oil.

cambrer (se) *vpr* to arch one's back.

cambriolage *m* burglary.

cambrioler *vt* to burglarize.

cambrioleur, -euse *mf* burglar.

camelote *f* junk.

camembert *m* Camembert (cheese).

caméra *f* (TV *ou* film) camera.

caméscope® *m* camcorder.

camion *m* truck.

camion-benne, *pl* **camions-bennes** *m* garbage truck.

camionnette *f* van.

camp *m* camp; **feu de c.** campfire; **lit de d.** camp bed; **dans mon c.** *(jeu)* on my side.

campagnard, -arde *mf* countryman, countrywoman.

campagne *f* country(side); *(électorale, militaire etc)* campaign; **à la c.** in the country.

camper *vi* to camp.

campeur, -euse *mf* camper.

camping *m* camping; *(terrain)* camp(ing) site.

camping-car *m* camper.

canadien, -ienne 1 *adj* Canadian. **2 C.** Canadian.

canal, -aux *m* *(pour bateaux)* canal.

canalisation *f* *(de gaz etc)* mains.

canaliser *vt* *(foule)* to channel.

canapé *m* *(siège)* sofa, couch, settee.

canapé-lit, *pl* **canapés-lits** *m* sofa bed.

canard *m* duck.

canari *m* canary.

cancer *m* cancer.

cancéreux, -euse *mf* cancer patient.

candidat, -ate *mf* candidate; **être** *ou* **se porter c.** to apply for.

candidature *f* application; *(aux élections)* candidacy; **poser sa c.** to apply (**à** for).

cane *f* (female) duck.

caneton *m* duckling.

canette *f* *(de bière)* (small) bottle.

caniche *m* poodle.

canicule *f* heatwave.

canif *m* penknife.

canine *f* canine (tooth).

caniveau, -x *m* gutter *(in street)*.

canne *f* (walking) stick; **c. à pêche** fishing rod.

cannelle *f* cinnamon.

cannibale *mf* cannibal.

canoë *m* canoe; *(sport)* canoeing.

canon *m* (big) gun; *(de fusil etc)* barrel.

canot *m* boat; **c. de sauvetage** lifeboat; **c. pneumatique** rubber dinghy.

canoter *vi* to go boating.

cantine *f* canteen; *(à l'école)* cafeteria.

cantique *m* hymn.

cantonnier *m* road mender.

caoutchouc *m* rubber; **balle/etc en c.** rubber ball/*etc*.

CAP *m abrév (certificat d'aptitude professionnelle)* technical and vocational diploma.

cap *m (pointe de terre)* cape; *(direction)* course; **mettre le c. sur** to steer a course for.

capable *adj* capable, able; **c. de faire** able to do, capable of doing.

capacité *f* ability; *(contenance)* capacity.

cape *f* cape; *(grande)* cloak.

capitaine *m* captain.

capitale *f (lettre, ville)* capital.

capitulation *f* surrender.

capituler *vi* to surrender.

capot *m (de véhicule)* hood.

capote *f (de véhicule)* (convertible) top.

caprice *m (passing)* whim.

capricieux, -euse *adj* temperamental.

capsule *f (spatiale)* capsule; *(de bouteille)* cap.

capter *vt (signal, radio)* to pick up.

captiver *vt* to fascinate.

capture *f* capture.

capturer *vt* to capture.

capuche *f* hood.

capuchon *m* hood; *(de stylo)* cap.

car 1 *conj* because, for. **2** *m* bus, coach; **c. de police** police van.

carabine *f* rifle; **c. à air comprimé** airgun.

caractère¹ *m (lettre)* character; **petits caractères** small letters; **caractères d'imprimerie** capitals.

caractère² *m (tempérament, nature)* character; **avoir bon c.** to be good-natured.

caractéristique *adj & f* characteristic.

carafe *f* decanter.

carambolage *m* pileup *(of vehicles)*.

caramel *m* caramel; *(bonbon dur)* taffy.

carapace *f* shell.

caravane *f (pour camper)* trailer.

carbone *m* **(papier) c.** carbon (paper).

carbonisé, -ée *adj (nourriture)* burnt to a cinder.

carburant *m* fuel.

carburateur *m* carburetor.

carcasse *f* carcass; *(d'immeuble etc)* frame, shell.

cardiaque *adj* **être c.** to have a weak heart; **crise/problème c.** heart attack/trouble.

cardinal, -aux 1 *adj (nombre, point)* cardinal. **2** *m* cardinal.

caressant, -ante *adj* loving.

caresse *f* caress.

caresser *vt* to stroke.

cargaison *f* cargo.

cargo *m* cargo boat.

carie *f* **la c. (dentaire)** tooth decay; **une c.** a cavity.

cariée *adj* **dent c.** decayed *ou* bad tooth.

carillon *m (cloches)* chimes; *(horloge)* chiming clock.

caritatif, -ive *adj* charitable.

carlingue *f (d'avion)* cabin.

carnaval, pl -als *m* carnival.

carnet *m* notebook; *(de timbres, chèques, adresses)* book; **c. de notes** report card.

carotte *f* carrot.

carpe *f* carp.

carpette *f* rug.

carré, -ée *adj & m* square.

carreau, -x *m (vitre)* (window) pane; *(pavé)* tile; **Cartes (couleur)** diamonds; **à carreaux** *(nappe etc)* check.

carrefour *m* crossroads.

carrelage *m (sol)* tiled floor.

carrément *adv (dire etc)* bluntly; *(complètement)* downright.

carrière *f (terrain)* quarry; *(métier)* career.

carrosse *m* (horse-drawn) carriage.

carrosserie *f* body(work).

carrure f build.

cartable m satchel.

carte f card; (routière) map; (menu) menu; **c. (postale)** (post)card; **c. à jouer** playing card; **jouer aux cartes** to play cards; **c. de visite** business card; **c. de crédit** credit card; **c. des vins** wine list; **c. grise** vehicle registration document.

carton m cardboard; (boîte) cardboard box.

cartonné adj livre c. hardback.

cartouche f cartridge; (de cigarettes) carton.

cas m case; **en tout c.** in any case; **en aucun c.** on no account; **en c. de besoin** if need be; **en c. d'accident** in the event of an accident; **en c. d'urgence** in an emergency; **au c. où elle tomberait** if she should fall; **pour le c. où il pleuvrait** in case it rains.

casanier, -ière adj stay-at-home.

cascade f waterfall; (de cinéma) stunt.

cascadeur, -euse mf stunt man, stunt woman.

case f pigeonhole; (de tiroir) compartment; (d'échiquier etc) square; (de fomulaire) box; (hutte) hut, cabin.

caserne f barracks; **c. de pompiers** fire station.

casier m pigeonhole; (fermant à clef) locker; **c. à bouteilles/à disques** bottle/record rack; **c. judiciaire** criminal record.

casino m casino.

casque m helmet; (de coiffeur) (hair)dryer; **c. (à écouteurs)** headphones.

casqué, -ée adj helmeted.

casquette f (coiffure) cap.

casse-cou mf inv (personne) daredevil.

casse-croûte m inv snack.

casse-noisettes m inv; **casse-noix** m inv nutcracker(s).

casse-pieds mf inv (personne) Fam pain.

casser 1 vt to break; (noix) to crack; **elle me casse les pieds** Fam she's getting on my nerves. **2** vi, **se casser** vpr to break; **se c. la figure** (tomber) Fam to take a spill.

casserole f (sauce)pan.

casse-tête m inv (problème) headache; (jeu) puzzle.

cassette f (audio) cassette; (vidéo) video (cassette); **sur c.** (film) on video.

cassis m (fruit) blackcurrant; (obstacle) dip (across road).

castor m beaver.

catalogue m catalog.

catastrophe f disaster; **atterrir en c.** to make an emergency landing.

catastrophique adj disastrous.

catch m (all-in) wrestling.

catcheur, -euse mf wrestler.

catéchisme m catechism.

catégorie f category.

cathédrale f cathedral.

catholique adj & mf Catholic.

cauchemar m nightmare.

cause f cause; **à c. de** because of, on account of.

causer 1 vt (provoquer) to cause. **2** vi (bavarder) to chat (**de** about).

caution f (d'appartement) deposit; (d'un détenu) bail; (personne) guarantor; (appui) backing.

cavalier, -ière mf rider; (pour danser) partner.

cave f cellar.

caveau, -x m (burial) vault.

caverne f cave.

cavité f hollow.

CCP m abrév (compte chèque postal) Post Office checking account.

ce¹ (c' before e and é) pron dém it, that; **c'est toi/bon/etc** it's ou that's you/good/etc; **c'est mon médecin** he's my doctor; **ce sont eux qui...** they are the ones who...; **c'est à elle de jouer** it's her turn to play; **est-ce que tu viens?** are you coming? ▪ **ce que, ce qui** what; **je sais ce qui**

est bon/ce que tu veux I know what is good/what you want; **ce que c'est beau!** it's so beautiful!

ce[2], **cette**, *pl* **ces** (*ce becomes cet before a vowel or mute h*) *adj dém* this, that, *pl* these; **(+ ci)** this, *pl* these; **(+ là)** that, *pl* those; **cet homme** this *ou* that man; **cet homme-ci** this man; **cet homme-là** that man.

ceci *pron dém* this.

céder 1 *vt* to give up (**à** to). **2** *vi* (*personne*) to give in (**à** to); (*branche, chaise etc*) to give way.

cédille *f Grammaire* cedilla.

CEI *f abrév* (*Communauté d'États Indépendants*) CIS.

ceinture *f* belt; (*taille*) waist; **c. de sécurité** seatbelt; **c. de sauvetage** life preserver.

cela *pron dém* (*pour désigner*) that; (*sujet indéfini*) it, that; **c. m'attriste que...** it saddens me that...; **quand/comment/etc c.?** when?/how?/etc.

célèbre *adj* famous.

célébrer *vt* to celebrate.

célébrité *f* fame.

céleri *m* (*en branches*) celery.

célibataire 1 *adj* single, unmarried. **2** *m* bachelor. **3** *f* unmarried woman.

cellophane® *f* cellophane®.

cellule *f* cell.

celui, **celle**, *pl* **ceux**, **celles** *pron dém* the one, *pl* those, the ones; **c. de Jean** Jean's (one); **ceux de Jean** Jean's (ones). ■ **(+ ci)** this one, *pl* these (ones) (*dont on vient de parler*) the latter; **(+ là)** that one, *pl* those (ones); the former; **ceux-ci sont gros** these (ones) are big.

cendre *f* ash.

cendrier *m* ashtray.

censé, **-ée** *adj* **être c. faire qch** to be supposed to do sth.

censure *f* (*activité*) censorship; (*comité*) board of censors.

censurer *vt* (*film*) to censor.

cent *adj & m* hundred; **c. pages** a *ou* one hundred pages; **cinq pour c.** five percent.

centaine *f* **une c.** a hundred (or so); **des centaines de** hundreds of.

centenaire 1 *adj* hundred-year-old; **être c.** to be a hundred. **2** *mf* centenarian. **3** *m* (*anniversaire*) centenary.

centième *adj & mf* hundredth.

centigrade *adj* centigrade.

centime *m* centime.

centimètre *m* centimeter; (*ruban*) tape measure.

central, **-e**, **-aux 1** *adj* central. **2** *m* **c. (téléphonique)** (telephone) exchange.

centrale *f* (*usine*) power plant.

centre *m* center; **c. commercial** shopping mall.

centre-ville *m inv* downtown area.

cependant *conj* however, yet.

céramique *f* (*matière*) ceramic; **de c.** ceramic.

cerceau, **-x** *m* hoop.

cercle *m* circle.

cercueil *m* coffin.

céréale *f* cereal.

cérémonie *f* ceremony.

cerf *m* deer.

cerf-volant, *pl* **cerfs-volants** *m* kite.

cerise *f* cherry.

cerisier *m* cherry tree.

cerne *m* ring.

cerner *vt* to surround; **avoir les yeux cernés** to have rings under one's eyes.

certain[1], **-aine** *adj* (*sûr*) certain, sure; **c'est c. que tu réussiras** you're certain *ou* sure to succeed; **je suis c. de réussir** I'm certain *ou* sure I'll succeed; **être c. de qch** to be certain *ou* sure of sth.

certain[2], **-aine** *adj* (*difficile à fixer*) certain; **un c. temps** a certain (amount of) time.

certainement *adv* certainly.

certains *pron pl* some (people).

certificat *m* certificate.

certifier *vt* to certify.

certitude *f* certainty; **avoir la c. que** to be certain that.

cerveau, -x *m* brain; **rhume de c.** head cold.

cervelle *f* brain; *(plat)* brains.

ces *voir* **ce²**.

CES *m abrév (collège d'enseignement secondaire)* = (junior) high school.

cesse *f* **sans c.** constantly.

cesser *vti* to stop; **faire c.** to put a stop to; **il ne cesse (pas) de parler** he doesn't stop talking.

cessez-le-feu *m inv* ceasefire.

c'est-à-dire *conj* that is (to say).

cet, cette *voir* **ce²**.

ceux *voir* **celui**.

chacun, -une *pron* each (one), every one; *(tout le monde)* everyone.

chagrin *m* grief; **avoir du c.** to be very upset.

chahut *m* racket.

chahuter *vi* to create a racket.

chahuteur, -euse *mf* rowdy.

chaîne *f* chain; *(de télévision)* channel; *(de montagnes)* chain, range; **travail à la c.** assembly-line work; **c. hi-fi** hi-fi system.

chaînette *f* (small) chain.

chair *f* flesh; *(couleur)* **c.** flesh-colored; **en c. et on os** in the flesh; **la c. de poule** goose pimples *ou* bumps; **c. à saucisses** sausage meat.

chaise *f* chair; **c. longue** deckchair; **c. haute** high-chair.

châle *m* shawl.

chalet *m* chalet.

chaleur *f* heat; *(douce)* warmth.

chaleureux, -euse *adj* warm.

chaloupe *f (bateau)* launch.

chalumeau, -x *m* blowtorch.

chalutier *m* trawler.

chamailler (se) *vpr* to squabble.

chambouler *vt Fam* to make topsy-turvy.

chambre *f* (bed)room; **c. à coucher** bedroom; *(mobilier)* bedroom suite *ou* set; **c. à air** *(de pneu)* inner tube; **c. de commerce** chamber of commerce; **c. d'amis** guest room; **garder la c.** to stay indoors.

chameau, -x *m* camel.

chamois *m* **peau de c.** chamois.

champ *m* field; **c. de bataille** battlefield; **c. de courses** racetrack.

champagne *m* champagne.

champignon *m* mushroom.

champion, -onne *mf* champion.

championnat *m* championship.

chance *f* luck; *(probabilité, occasion)* chance; **avoir de la c.** to be lucky; **c'est une c. que** it's lucky that.

chanceler *vi* to stagger.

chanceux, -euse *adj* lucky.

chandail *m* (thick) sweater.

chandelier *m* candlestick.

chandelle *f* candle; **en c.** *(tir)* straight into the air.

change *m (de devises)* exchange.

changement *m* change.

changer *vti* to change; **c. qn en** to change sb into; **ça la changera de ne pas travailler** it'll be a change for her not to be working; **c. de train/voiture/etc** to change trains/one's car/etc; **c. de vitesse/sujet** to change gear/the subject.

changer (se) *vpr* to change (one's clothes).

chanson *f* song.

chant *m* singing; *(chanson)* song; **c. de Noël** Christmas carol.

chantage *m* blackmail.

chanter 1 *vi* to sing; *(coq)* to crow; **si ça te chante** *Fam* if you feel like it. **2** *vt* to sing.

chanteur, -euse *mf* singer.

chantier *m* (building) site; **c. naval** shipyard, dockyard.

chantilly *f* whipped cream.

chantonner *vti* to hum.

chaos *m* chaos.

chapeau, -x *m* hat.

chapelet *m* rosary; **un c. de** (*saucisses etc*) a string of.

chapelle *f* chapel.

chapelure *f* breadcrumbs.

chapiteau, -x *m* (*de cirque*) big top; (*pour expositions etc*) marquee, tent.

chapitre *m* chapter.

chaque *adj* each, every.

char *m* (*romain*) chariot; (*de carnaval*) float; **c. (d'assaut)** tank.

charade *f* (*énigme*) riddle.

charbon *m* coal; **c. de bois** charcoal.

charcuterie *f* pork butcher's shop; (*aliments*) cooked pork meats.

charcutier, -ière *mf* pork butcher.

chardon *m* thistle.

charge *f* (*poids*) load; (*fardeau*) burden; **à la c. de qn** (*personne*) dependent on sb; (*frais*) payable by sb; **prendre en c.** to take charge of.

chargé, -ée *adj* (*véhicule, arme etc*) loaded; (*journée*) busy.

chargement *m* loading; (*objet*) load.

charger *vt* to load; (*soldats, batterie*) to charge; **c. qn de** (*travail etc*) to entrust sb with; **c. qn de faire** to instruct sb to do.

charger (se) *vpr* **se c. de** (*enfant, travail etc*) to take charge of.

chariot *m* (*à bagages etc*) cart.

charité *f* (*secours*) charity.

charmant, -ante *adj* charming.

charme *m* charm; (*magie*) spell.

charmer *vt* to charm.

charnière *f* hinge.

charpente *f* frame(work).

charpentier *m* carpenter.

charrette *f* cart.

charrier *vt* (*transporter*) to cart; (*rivière*) to carry along (*sand etc*).

charrue *f* plow.

charter *m* charter (flight).

chasse¹ *f* hunting, hunt; **c. à courre** hunting; **avion de c.** fighter plane; **faire la c. à** to hunt for.

chasse² *f* **c. d'eau** toilet flush; **tirer la c.** to flush the toilet.

chasse-neige *m inv* snowplow.

chasser **1** *vt* (*animal*) to hunt; (*personne, odeur*) to chase away; (*mouche*) to brush away. **2** *vi* to hunt.

chasseur, -euse *mf* hunter.

châssis *m* frame; (*d'automobile*) chassis.

chat *m* cat; **pas un c.** not a soul; **perché** (*jeu*) tag.

châtaigne *f* chestnut.

châtaignier *m* chestnut tree.

châtain *adj inv* (chestnut) brown.

château, -x *m* castle; (*palais*) palace; **c. fort** fortified castle; **c. d'eau** water tower.

châtiment *m* punishment.

chaton *m* kitten.

chatouiller *vt* to tickle.

chatouilleux, -euse *adj* ticklish.

chatte *f* (she-)cat.

chatterton *m* electrician's tape.

chaud, chaude **1** *adj* hot; (*doux*) warm. **2** *m* **avoir c.** to be hot; (*doux*) to be warm; **il fait c.** it's hot; **être au c.** to be in the warm.

chaudement *adv* warmly.

chaudière *f* boiler.

chauffage *m* heating.

chauffant, -ante *adj* (*couverture*) electric; **plaque chauffante** hot plate.

chauffard *m* reckless driver.

chauffé, -ée *adj* (*piscine etc*) heated.

chauffe-eau *m inv* water heater.

chauffer **1** *vt* to heat (up). **2** *vi* to heat (up); (*moteur*) to overheat.

chauffeur *m* driver; (*employé*) chauffeur.

chaume *m* (*pour toiture*) thatch; **toit de c.** thatched roof.

chaumière *f* thatched cottage.

chaussée *f* road(way).

chausse-pied, *pl* chausse-pieds *m* shoehorn.

chausser *vt* **c. qn** to put shoes on

(to) sb; **c. du 40** to take a size 40 shoe.

chausser (se) *vpr* to put on one's shoes.

chaussette *f* sock.

chausson *m* slipper; *(de danse)* shoe.

chaussure *f* shoe.

chauve *adj & mf* bald (person).

chauve-souris, *pl* **chauves-souris** *f* *(animal)* bat.

chauvin, -ine 1 *adj* chauvinistic. **2** *mf* chauvinist.

chaux *f* lime.

chavirer *vti* to capsize.

chef *m* leader, head; **c. d'entreprise** head of (a) company; **c. de gare** stationmaster; **c. d'orchestre** conductor; **en c.** *(commandant, rédacteur)* in chief.

chef-d'œuvre, *pl* **chefs-d'œuvre** *m* masterpiece.

chef-lieu, *pl* **chefs-lieux** *m* chief town *(of a département)*.

chemin *m* road, path; *(trajet, direction)* way; **beaucoup de c. à faire** a long way to go; **se mettre en c.** to set out.

chemin de fer *m* railroad.

cheminée *f* fireplace; *(encadrement)* mantelpiece; *(sur le toit)* chimney; *(de navire)* funnel.

cheminot *m* railroad employee.

chemise *f* shirt; *(cartonnée)* folder; **c. de nuit** *(de femme)* nightgown; *(d'homme)* nightshirt.

chemisette *f* short-sleeved shirt.

chemisier *m* blouse.

chêne *m* oak.

chenil *m* kennel.

chenille *f* caterpillar.

chèque *m* check; **c. de voyage** traveler's check.

chèque-repas, *pl* **chèques-repas** *m* meal voucher.

chéquier *m* checkbook.

cher, chère *adj (aimé)* dear (**à** to); *(coûteux)* expensive; **payer c.** *(objet)* to pay a lot for; *(erreur etc)* to pay dearly for.

chercher *vt* to look for; *(dans un dictionnaire)* to look up; **aller c.** to (go and) fetch *ou* get; **c. à faire** to attempt to do.

chercheur, -euse *mf* research worker.

chéri, -ie 1 *adj* dearly loved. **2** *mf* darling.

cherté *f* high cost.

chétif, -ive *adj* puny.

cheval, -aux *m* horse; **à c.** on horseback; **faire du c.** to go horseback riding; **chevaux de bois** merry-go-round.

chevalier *m* knight.

chevaline *adj f* **boucherie c.** horse butcher's (shop).

chevelure *f* (head of) hair.

chevet *m* **table/livre de c.** bedside table/book; **au c. de** at the bedside of.

cheveu, -x *m* **un c.** a hair; **cheveux** hair; **tiré par les cheveux** farfetched.

cheville *f* ankle; *(pour vis)* (wall) plug.

chèvre *f* goat.

chevreau, -x *m (petit de la chèvre)* kid.

chez *prép* **c. qn** at sb's house/apartment/*etc*; **il est c. Jean/c. le médecin** he's at Jean's (place)/at the doctor's; **il va c. Jean/c. le médecin** he's going to Jean's (place)/to the doctor's; **c. moi, c. nous** at home; **je vais c. moi** I'm going home; **une habitude c. elle** a habit with her; **c. Mme Dupont** *(adresse)* care of Mme Dupont.

chic 1 *adj inv* smart; *(gentil)* *Fam* nice. **2** *int* **c. (alors)!** great! **3** *m* style.

chicorée *f* *(à café)* chicory; *(pour salade)* endive.

chien *m* dog; **un mal de c.** an awful lot of trouble; **temps de c.** rotten weather.

chien-loup, *pl* **chiens-loups** *m* wolfhound.

chienne f dog, bitch.

chiffon m rag; **c. (à poussière)** dust cloth.

chiffonner vt to crumple.

chiffre m figure, number; (romain, arabe) numeral; **c. d'affaires** sales.

chimie f chemistry.

chimique adj chemical.

chimpanzé m chimpanzee.

chinois, -oise 1 adj Chinese. **2** mf **C.** Chinese man, Chinese woman, Chinese inv; **les C.** the Chinese. **3** m (langue) Chinese.

chiot m puppy.

chipoter vi (contester) to quibble (**sur** about).

chips mpl (potato) chips.

chirurgical, -e, -aux adj surgical.

chirurgie f surgery.

chirurgien m surgeon.

choc m (d'objets, émotion) shock.

chocolat m chocolate; **c. à croquer** bittersweet chocolate; **c. au lait** milk chocolate.

chocolaté, -ée adj chocolate-flavored.

chœur m (chanteurs, nef) choir; **en c.** (all) together.

choisir vt to choose, to pick.

choix m choice; (assortiment) selection.

cholestérol m cholesterol.

chômage m unemployment; **au c.** unemployed.

chômer vi to be unemployed.

chômeur, -euse mf unemployed person; **les chômeurs** the unemployed.

choquant, -ante adj shocking.

choquer vt to shock.

chorale f choral society.

chose f thing; **monsieur C.** Mr What's-his-name.

chou, -x m cabbage; **choux de Bruxelles** Brussels sprouts.

choucroute f sauerkraut.

chouette 1 f owl. **2** adj Fam super, great.

chou-fleur, pl **choux-fleurs** m cauliflower.

choyer vt to pamper.

chrétien, -ienne adj & mf Christian.

chrome m chrome.

chromé, -ée adj chrome-plated.

chronique f (à la radio) report; (dans le journal) column.

chronomètre m stopwatch.

chronométrer vt to time.

chrysanthème m chrysanthemum.

chuchotement m whisper(ing).

chuchoter vti to whisper.

chut! int sh!, shush!

chute f fall; **c. d'eau** waterfall; **c. de neige** snowfall; **c. de pluie** rainfall.

chuter vi (diminuer) to fall, to drop; (tomber) Fam to fall.

ci 1 adv par-ci par-là here and there. **2** pron dém comme ci comme ça so so.

cible f target.

cicatrice f scar.

cicatrisation f healing (up).

cicatriser vt, **se cicatriser** vpr to heal up (leaving a scar).

cidre m cider.

Cie abrév (compagnie) Co.

ciel m (pl ciels) sky; (pl cieux) (paradis) heaven.

cierge m candle.

cigale f (insecte) cicada.

cigare m cigar.

cigarette f cigarette.

cigogne f stork.

ci-joint, -jointe 1 adj le document c. the enclosed document. **2** adv vous trouverez c. copie de... please find enclosed a copy of...

cil m (eye)lash.

cime f (d'un arbre) top; (d'une montagne) peak.

ciment m cement.

cimenter vt to cement.

cimetière m cemetery.

ciné m Fam movies.

cinéaste m movie maker.

ciné-club m film club.

cinéma m (art, industrie) movies; (bâtiment) movie theater; **faire du c.** to make movies.

cinéphile mf movie enthusiast.

cinglé, -ée adj Fam crazy.

cinq adj & m five.

cinquantaine f about fifty.

cinquante adj & m fifty.

cinquantième adj & mf fiftieth.

cinquième adj & mf fifth.

cintre m coathanger.

cirage m (shoe) polish.

circonférence f circumference.

circonflexe adj Grammaire circumflex.

circonstance f circumstance; **pour la c.** for this occasion.

circonstanciel, -ielle adj Grammaire adverbial.

circuit m (électrique, sportif etc) circuit; (voyage) tour.

circulaire 1 adj circular. 2 f (lettre) circular.

circulation f circulation; (automobile) traffic.

circuler vi to circulate; (véhicule, train) to travel; (passant) to walk around; (rumeur) to go around; **faire c.** (piétons etc) to move on.

cire f wax.

ciré m (vêtement) oilskins.

cirer vt to polish.

cirque m circus.

ciseau, -x m chisel; **(une paire de) ciseaux** (a pair of) scissors.

citadin, -ine mf city dweller.

citation f quotation.

cité f city; **c. universitaire** (university) dormitory complex.

citer vt to quote.

citerne f (réservoir) tank.

citoyen, -enne mf citizen.

citoyenneté f citizenship.

citron m lemon; **c. pressé** (fresh) lemon juice.

citronnade f lemonade.

citrouille f pumpkin.

civière f stretcher.

civil, -e 1 adj civil; (non militaire) civilian; **année civile** calendar year. **2** m civilian; **en c.** (policier) in plain clothes.

civilisation f civilization.

civilisé, -ée adj civilized.

civique adj civic; **instruction c.** civics.

clair, -e 1 adj (distinct, limpide, évident) clear; (éclairé) light; (pâle) light(-colored); **bleu/vert c.** light blue/green. **2** adv (voir) clearly. **3** m **c. de lune** moonlight.

clairement adv clearly.

clairière f clearing.

clairon m bugle.

clairsemé, -ée adj sparse.

clairvoyant, -ante adj perceptive.

clandestin, -ine adj (journal, mouvement) underground; **passager c.** stowaway.

claque f smack, slap.

claquement m (de porte) slamming.

claquer 1 vt (porte) to slam, to bang. 2 vi (porte) to slam, to bang; (coup de feu) to ring out; **c. des mains** to clap one's hands; **elle claque des dents** her teeth are chattering.

claquer (se) vpr se c. un muscle to tear a muscle.

claquettes fpl tap dancing; **faire des c.** to do tap dancing.

clarinette f clarinet.

clarté f light; (précision) clarity.

classe f class; **aller en c.** to go to school.

classement m classification; filing; grading; (rang) place; (en sport) placing.

classer vt to classify; (papiers) to file; (candidats) to grade.

classer (se) vpr se c. premier to come first.

classeur m (meuble) filing cabinet; (portefeuille) (loose leaf) binder.

classique adj classical.

clavicule f collarbone.

clavier m keyboard.

clé, clef f key; (outil) wrench; **fermer à c.** to lock; **sous c.** under lock and key; **c. de contact** ignition key.

clémentine f tangerine.

clergé m clergy.

cliché m (de photo) negative.

client, -ente mf customer; (d'un avocat) client; (d'un médecin) patient; (d'hôtel) guest.

clientèle f customers; (d'un avocat, d'un médecin) practice.

cligner vi **c. des yeux** to blink; (fermer à demi) to squint; **c. de l'œil** to wink.

clignotant m (de voiture) turn signal.

clignoter vi to blink; (lumière) to flicker.

climat m climate.

climatisation f air conditioning.

climatisé, -ée adj air-conditioned.

clin d'œil m wink; **en un c.** in no time (at all).

clinique f (private) clinic.

cliquer vi to click (**sur** on); **c. deux fois** to double-click.

clochard, -arde mf down-and-out, tramp.

cloche f bell.

cloche-pied (à) adv **sauter à c.** to hop on one foot.

clocher m bell tower; (en pointe) steeple.

clochette f (small) bell.

cloison f partition.

clope m ou f Fam smoke, cigarette.

clopin-clopant adv **aller c.** to hobble.

cloque f blister.

clos, close adj closed.

clôture f (barrière) fence.

clôturer vt to enclose.

clou m nail; **les clous** (passage) crosswalk.

clouer vt to nail; **cloué au lit** confined to bed.

clouté, -ée adj (pneus) studded; **passage c.** crosswalk.

clown m clown.

club m (association) club.

cm abrév (centimètre) cm.

coaguler vti, **se coaguler** vpr to clot.

coalition f coalition.

cobaye m guinea pig.

coca mf (Coca-Cola®) coke.

cocaïne f cocaine.

coccinelle f ladybug.

cocher¹ vt to tick (off), to check (off).

cocher² m coachman.

cochon, -onne 1 m pig; **c. d'Inde** guinea pig. **2** mf (personne sale) (dirty) pig.

cochonnerie f (chose sans valeur) trash; (obscénité) smutty remark; **manger des cochonneries** to eat junk food.

cocorico int & m cock-a-doodle-doo.

cocotier m coconut palm.

cocotte f casserole; **c. minute®** pressure cooker.

code m code; **codes, phares c.** low beams; **C. de la route** traffic laws.

cœur m heart; (couleur), Cartes hearts; **au c. de** (ville, hiver etc) in the middle ou heart of; **par c.** by heart; **avoir mal au c.** to feel sick; **avoir le c. gros** to have a heavy heart; **avoir bon c.** to be kind-hearted; **de bon c.** (offrir) willingly; (rire) heartily.

coffre m chest; (de banque) safe; (de voiture) trunk.

coffre-fort, pl **coffres-forts** m safe.

coffret m (à bijoux etc) box.

cogner vti to knock, to bang.

cogner (se) vpr **se c. la tête/etc** to knock ou bang one's head/etc; **se c. à qch** to knock ou bang into sth.

cohabiter vi to live together; **c. avec qn** to live with sb.

cohérent, -ente adj (discours) coherent; (attitude) consistent.

cohue f crowd.

coiffer vt **c. qn** to do sb's hair.

coiffer (se) vpr to do one's hair.

coiffeur, -euse mf hairdresser.

coiffure f hat; (arrangement) hairstyle.

coin m (angle) corner; (endroit) spot; **du c.** (magasin etc) local; **dans le c.** in the (local) area.

coincé, -ée adj stuck.

coincer vt (mécanisme etc) to jam.

coincer (se) vpr to get stuck ou jammed; **se c. le doigt** to get one's finger stuck.

coïncidence f coincidence.

coing m quince.

col m collar; (de montagne) pass; **c. roulé** turtleneck.

colère f anger; **une c.** a fit of anger; **en c.** angry (**contre** with); **se mettre en c.** to lose one's temper.

coléreux, -euse adj quick-tempered.

colique f diarrhea.

colis m parcel.

collaboration f collaboration.

collaborer vi collaborate (**à** on).

collant, -ante 1 adj (papier) sticky; (vêtement) skin-tight. **2** m pantyhose; (opaque) tights; (de danse) leotard.

colle f glue; (blanche) paste.

collecte f (quête) collection.

collectif, -ive adj collective; **billet c.** group ticket.

collection f collection.

collectionner vt to collect.

collectionneur, -euse mf collector.

collectivité f (groupe) community.

collège m = (junior) high school.

collégien, -enne mf = (junior) high school student.

collègue mf colleague.

coller vt to stick; (à la colle transparente) to glue; (à la colle blanche) to paste; (affiche) to stick up; (papier peint) to hang; (mettre) Fam to stick; **c. contre** (nez, oreille etc) to press against.

collier m (bijou) necklace; (de chien) collar.

colline f hill.

collision f collision; **entrer en c. avec** to collide with.

colocataire mf roommate.

colombe f dove.

colonel m colonel.

colonie f colony; **c. de vacances** summer camp.

colonne f column; **c. vertébrale** spine.

coloré, -ée adj colorful; (verre, liquide) colored.

colorer vt to color.

coloriage m **album de coloriages** coloring book.

colorier vt (dessin) to color (in).

coloris m (nuance) shade.

colosse m giant.

colza m (plante) rape.

coma m coma; **dans le c.** in a coma.

combat m fight.

combatif, -ive adj eager to fight; (instinct, esprit) fighting.

combattant m fighter, brawler.

combattre* vti to fight.

combien 1 adv (quantité) how much; (nombre) how many; **c. de** (temps, argent etc) how much; (gens, livres etc) how many. ■ (à quel point) how; **c. y a-t-il d'ici à...?** how far is it to...? **2** m inv **le c. sommes-nous?** Fam what is the date?; **tous les c.?** Fam how often?

combinaison f combination; (vêtement de femme) slip; (de mécanicien) overalls; **c. de vol/plongée/ski** flying/diving/ski suit; **c. spatiale** spacesuit.

combiné m (de téléphone) receiver.

combiner vt (assembler) to combine.

comble 1 m **le c. de** (la joie etc) the height of; **c'est un ou le c.!** that's the limit! **2** adj (bondé) packed.

combler *vt (trou etc)* to fill; **c. son retard** to make up lost time.

combustible *m* fuel.

comédie *f* comedy; **c. musicale** musical; **jouer la c.** to put on an act, to pretend.

comédien *m* actor.

comédienne *f* actress.

comestible *adj* edible.

comique *adj (amusant)* funny; *(acteur etc)* comic.

comité *m* committee.

commandant *m (d'un navire)* captain; **c. de bord** *(d'un avion)* captain.

commande *f (achat)* order; **sur c.** to order; **les commandes** *(d'un avion etc)* the controls.

commandement *m (autorité)* command.

commander 1 *vt* to command; *(acheter)* to order. **2** *vi* **c. à qn de faire** to command sb to do.

comme 1 *adv & conj* like; **c. moi** like me; **c. cela** like that; **qu'as-tu c. vins?** what kind of wines do you have? ▪ as; **blanc c. neige** (as) white as snow; **c. si** as if; **c. pour faire** as if to do; **c. par hasard** as if by chance. **2** *adv (exclamatif)* regarde c. il pleut! look how (hard) it's raining!; **c. c'est petit!** how small it is! **3** *conj (temps, cause)* as; **c. elle entrait** as she was coming in.

commencement *m* beginning, start.

commencer *vti* to begin, to start (**à faire** to do, doing; **par** with; **par faire** by doing); **pour c.** to begin with.

comment *adv* how; **c. le sais-tu?** how do you know?; **c.?** *(répétition, surprise)* what?; **c. est-il?** what is he like?; **c. faire?** what's to be done?; **c. t'appelles-tu?** what's your name?; **c. allez-vous?** how are you?

commentaire *m (remarque)* comment; *(de radio, de télévision)* commentary.

commerçant, -ante *mf* merchant; **rue commerçante** shopping street.

commerce *m* trade, commerce; *(magasin)* store, business; **dans le c.** *(objet)* (on sale) in stores.

commercial, -e, -aux *adj* commercial.

commère *f* gossip.

commettre* *vt (délit etc)* to commit; *(erreur)* to make.

commissaire *m* **c. (de police)** police chief.

commissariat *m* **c. (de police)** (central) police station.

commission *f (course)* errand; *(pourcentage)* commission (**sur** on); **faire les commissions** to go shopping, to run (the) errands.

commode 1 *adj (pratique)* handy. **2** *f* chest of drawers, dresser.

commun, -une *adj (collectif, habituel etc)* common; *(frais, cuisine)* shared; **ami c.** mutual friend; **en c.** in common; **avoir** *ou* **mettre en c.** to share.

communautaire *adj (de la CE)* Community; **vie c.** community life.

communauté *f (collectivité)* community; **la C. (économique) européenne** the European (Economic) Community; **la C. des États indépendants** the Commonwealth of Independent States.

commune *f* commune.

communication *f* communication; **c. (téléphonique)** (telephone) call.

communier *vi* to receive (Holy) Communion.

communion *f* (Holy) Communion.

communiqué *m* (official) statement; *(publicitaire)* message; **c. de presse** press release.

communiquer *vti* to communicate.

communiste *adj & mf* communist.

compact, -e adj dense.

compagne f friend; (épouse) companion.

compagnie f (présence, société) company; **tenir c. à qn** to keep sb company.

compagnon m companion; **c. de jeu** playmate; **c. de travail** co-worker.

comparable adj comparable.

comparaison f comparison (**avec** with).

comparaître* vi (devant tribunal) to appear (**devant** before).

comparer vt to compare (**à** to, with).

compartiment m compartment.

compas m compass.

compatir vi to sympathize.

compatriote mf compatriot.

compenser 1 vt to compensate for. **2** vi to compensate.

compétence f competence.

compétent, -ente adj competent.

compétition f competition; (épreuve sportive) event; **de c.** (esprit, sport) competitive.

complaisance f kindness.

complaisant, -ante adj kind.

complément m Grammaire complement.

complet, -ète 1 adj complete; (train, hôtel etc) full; (aliment) whole. **2** m suit.

complètement adv completely.

compléter vt to complete; (somme) to make up.

complexe 1 adj complex. **2** m (sentiment, construction) complex.

complication f complication.

complice m accomplice.

compliment m compliment; **mes compliments!** congratulations!

complimenter vt to compliment (**sur, pour** on).

compliqué, -ée adj complicated.

compliquer vt to complicate.

compliquer (se) vpr to get complicated.

complot m plot.

comploter vti to plot (**de faire** to do).

comportement m behavior.

comporter (se) vpr to behave; (joueur, voiture) to perform.

composé, -ée adj & m (mot, en chimie etc) compound; **temps c.** compound tense; Grammaire **passé c.** perfect (tense).

composer vt to make up, to compose; (numéro) to dial; **être composé de** to be made up ou composed of.

composer (se) vpr **se c. de** to be made up ou composed of.

compositeur, -trice mf composer.

composter vt (billet) to cancel.

compote f sauce; **c. de pommes** applesauce.

compréhensible adj understandable.

compréhensif, -ive adj (personne) understanding.

comprendre* vt to understand; (comporter) to include; **je n'y comprends rien** I don't understand anything about it.

comprendre (se) vpr **ça se comprend** that's understandable.

comprimé m tablet.

comprimer vt to compress.

compris, -ise adj (inclus) included (**dans** in); **tout c.** (all) inclusive; **y c.** including.

compromettre* vt (personne) to compromise; (sécurité) to jeopardize.

comptabilité f (comptes) accounts; (science) bookkeeping, accounting; (service) accounts department.

comptable mf bookkeeper; (expert) accountant.

comptant 1 adj **argent c.** (hard) cash. **2** adv **payer c.** to pay (in) cash.

compte m account; (calcul) count;

(nombre) (right) number; **avoir un c. en banque** to have a bank(ing) account; **c. chèque** checking account; **c. à rebours** countdown; **tenir c. de** to take into account; **c. tenu de** considering; **se rendre c. de** to realize; **à son c.** *(travailler)* for oneself; *(s'installer)* on one's own; **en fin de c.** all things considered.

compte-gouttes *m inv* dropper.

compter 1 *vt (calculer)* to count; **c. faire** to expect to do; *(avoir l'intention de)* to intend to do; **c. qch à qn** *(facturer)* to charge sb for sth. **2** *vi (calculer, avoir de l'importance)* to count; **c. sur** to rely on.

compte rendu *m* report; *(de livre, film)* review.

compteur *m* meter; **c. (de vitesse)** speedometer; **c. (kilométrique)** odometer.

comptoir *m (de magasin)* counter; *(de café)* bar; *(de bureau)* (reception) desk.

comte *m* count; *Br* earl.

comtesse *f* countess.

concentré, -ée 1 *adj (lait)* condensed; *(attentif)* concentrating (hard). **2** *m* **c. de tomates** tomato purée.

concentrer *vt,* **se concentrer** *vpr* to concentrate.

concerner *vt* to concern.

concert *m* concert.

concerter (se) *vpr* to consult each other.

concessionnaire *mf* (authorized) dealer.

concevoir *vt* to conceive.

concierge *mf* caretaker, janitor.

concitoyen, -enne *mf* fellow citizen.

conclure* *vti* to conclude (**que** that).

conclusion *f* conclusion.

concombre *m* cucumber.

concordant, -ante *adj* in agreement.

concorder *vi* to agree; **c. avec** to match.

concours *m (examen)* competitive examination; *(jeu)* competition; **c. hippique** horse show.

concret, -ète *adj* concrete.

concrétiser *vt (rêve)* to realize; *(projet)* to carry out.

conçu, -ue *adj* **c. pour faire/pour qn** designed to do/for sb; **bien c.** *(maison etc)* well designed.

concubinage *m* cohabitation; **vivre en c.** to cohabit.

concurrence *f* competition; **faire c. à** to compete with.

concurrencer *vt* to compete with.

concurrent, -ente *mf* competitor.

condamnation *f* sentence; *(censure)* condemnation.

condamné, -ée *mf* condemned man *ou* woman.

condamner *vt* to condemn; *(accusé)* to sentence (**à** to); *(porte)* to block up; **c. à une amende** to fine.

condition *f* condition; **conditions** *(clauses, tarifs)* terms; **à c. de faire,** **à c. que l'on fasse** providing *ou* provided (that) one does.

conditionné *adj* **à air c.** *(pièce etc)* air-conditioned.

conditionnel *m Grammaire* conditional.

condoléances *fpl* sympathy.

conducteur, -trice *mf* driver.

conduire* *vt* to lead; *(voiture)* to drive; *(eau)* to carry; **c. qn à** *(accompagner)* to take sb to.

conduire (se) *vpr* to behave.

conduite *f* behavior; *(de voiture)* driving (**de** of); *(d'eau, de gaz)* main.

cône *m* cone.

confection *f* making (**de** of); **vêtements de c.** ready-to-wear clothes.

confectionner *vt* to make.

conférence *f* conference.

confesser *vt*, **se confesser** *vpr* to confess.

confession *f* confession.

confettis *mpl* confetti.

confiance *f* trust; **faire c. à qn, avoir c. en qn** to trust sb; **c. en soi** (self-)confidence.

confiant, -ante *adj* trusting; (*sûr de soi*) confident.

confidence *f* (*secret*) confidence; **faire une c. à qn** to confide in sb.

confidentiel, -ielle *adj* confidential.

confier *vt* **c. qch à qn** (*enfant, objet*) to give sb sth to take care of; **c. un secret**/*etc* **à qn** to confide a secret/*etc* to sb.

confier (se) *vpr* **se c. à qn** to confide in sb.

confirmation *f* confirmation.

confirmer *vt* to confirm (**que** that).

confiserie *f* candy store; **confiseries** (*produits*) candy.

confiseur, -euse *mf* confectioner.

confisquer *vt* to confiscate (**à qn** from sb).

confit *adj* **fruits confits** candied fruit.

confiture *f* jelly.

conflit *m* conflict.

confondre *vt* (*choses, personnes*) to mix up, to confuse; **c. avec** to mistake for.

conformément *adv* **c. à** in accordance with.

confort *m* comfort.

confortable *adj* comfortable.

confrère *m* colleague.

confus, -use *adj* confused; (*gêné*) embarrassed; **je suis c.!** (*désolé*) I'm terribly sorry!

confusion *f* confusion; (*gêne, honte*) embarrassment.

congé *m* (*vacances*) vacation; **c. de maladie** sick leave; **congés payés** paid vacation.

congélateur *m* freezer, deep-freeze.

congeler *vt* to freeze.

congère *f* snowdrift.

congrès *m* congress.

conjoint *m* spouse.

conjonction *f* Grammaire conjunction.

conjoncture *f* circumstances.

conjugaison *f* conjugation.

conjugal, -e, -aux *adj* (*bonheur*) marital; (*vie*) married; (*devoir*) conjugal.

conjuguer *vt* (*verbe*) to conjugate.

connaissance *f* knowledge; (*personne*) acquaintance; **connaissances** knowledge (**en** of); **faire la c. de qn, faire c. avec qn** to meet sb; **perdre c.** to lose consciousness; **sans c.** unconscious.

connaître *vt* to know; (*rencontrer*) to meet; **nous nous connaissons déjà** we've met before; **s'y c. à** *ou* **en qch** to know (all) about sth.

connu, -ue (*pp of* **connaître**) *adj* (*célèbre*) well-known.

conquérant, -ante *mf* conqueror.

conquérir* *vt* to conquer.

conquête *f* conquest; **faire la c. de** to conquer.

consacrer *vt* (*temps, vie etc*) to devote (**à** to).

consacrer (se) *vpr* **se c. à** to devote oneself to.

conscience *f* (*psychologique*) consciousness; (*morale*) conscience; **avoir/prendre c. de** to be/become conscious *ou* aware of; **c. professionnelle** conscientiousness.

consciencieux, -euse *adj* conscientious.

conscient, -ente *adj* **c. de** aware of.

conseil[1] *m* **un c.** a piece of advice; **des conseils** advice.

conseil[2] *m* (*assemblée*) council; **c. d'administration** board of directors; **c. des ministres** (*réunion*) cabinet meeting.

conseiller *vt* to advise; **c. qch à qn** to recommend sth to sb; **c. à qn de faire** to advise sb to do.

conseiller, -ère *mf* (expert) consultant, adviser; (d'un conseil) councilor; **c. municipal** city councilman *ou* -woman.

consentement *m* consent.

consentir* *vi* **c. à** to consent to.

conséquence *f* consequence.

conservation *f* preservation.

conservatoire *m* school (of music, drama).

conserve *f* **conserves** canned food; **de** *ou* **en c.** canned; **mettre en c.** to can.

conserver *vt* to keep; (fruits, vie, tradition etc) to preserve.

conserver (se) *vpr* (aliment) to keep.

considérable *adj* considerable.

considération *f* (respect) regard, esteem; **prendre qch en c.** to take sth into consideration.

considérer *vt* to consider (**que** that; **comme** to be).

consigne *f* (instruction) orders; (de gare) baggage check; (somme) deposit; **c. automatique** luggage *ou* baggage lockers.

consigner *vt* (bouteille etc) to charge a deposit on.

consistant, -ante *adj* (sauce etc) thick; (repas) solid.

consister *vi* **c. en/dans** to consist of/in; **c. à faire** to consist in doing.

consolation *f* comfort.

console *f* console.

consoler *vt* to comfort, to console (**de** for).

consoler (se) *vpr* **se c. de** (la mort de qn etc) to get over.

consolider *vt* to strengthen.

consommateur, -trice *mf* consumer; (au café) customer.

consommation *f* consumption; (boisson) drink.

consommer 1 *vt* (aliment etc) to consume. **2** *vi* (au café) to drink; **c.**

beaucoup/peu (véhicule) to get good/bad mileage.

consonne *f* consonant.

conspirateur, -trice *mf* conspirator.

conspiration *f* plot.

conspirer *vi* to plot (**contre** against).

constamment *adv* constantly.

constat *m* (official) report.

constatation *f* observation.

constater *vt* to note, to observe (**que** that); (enregistrer) to record.

consternation *f* distress.

consterner *vt* to distress.

constipé, -ée *adj* constipated.

constituer *vt* (composer) to make up; (représenter) to represent; **constitué de** made up of.

constituer (se) *vpr* **se c. prisonnier** to give oneself up.

constitution *f* constitution; (composition) composition.

constructeur *m* (bâtisseur) builder; (fabricant) maker (**de** of); **c. automobile** car manufacturer.

construction *f* construction; **matériaux/jeu de c.** construction materials/set.

construire* *vt* to build.

consul *m* consul.

consulat *m* consulate.

consultation *f* consultation; **cabinet de c.** (doctor's) office.

consulter *vt*, **se consulter** *vpr* to consult.

contact *m* contact; (toucher) touch; (de voiture) ignition; **être en c. avec** to be in touch *ou* contact with; **entrer en c. avec** to come into contact with; **mettre/couper le c.** (dans une voiture) to turn on/off the ignition; **lentilles** *ou* **verres de c.** contact lenses.

contacter *vt* to contact.

contagieux, -euse *adj* contagious, infectious.

contagion *f* infection.

conte *m* tale; **c. de fée** fairy tale.

contempler vt to gaze at.
contemporain, -aine adj & mf contemporary.
contenance f (d'un récipient) capacity.
contenir* vt to contain; (avoir comme capacité) to hold.
content, -ente adj pleased, happy (de faire to do; de qn/qch with sb/sth); **c. de soi** self-satisfied.
contenter vt to satisfy, to please.
contenter (se) vpr **se c. de** to be content ou happy with.
contenu m (de récipient) contents.
conter vt (histoire etc) to tell.
contestable adj debatable.
contestataire mf protester.
contestation f protest.
contesté, -ée adj (théorie, dirigeant) controversial.
contester 1 vi (étudiants etc) to protest. **2** vt to protest against.
conteur, -euse mf storyteller.
contexte m context.
continent m continent; (opposé à une île) mainland.
continu, -ue adj continuous.
continuel, -elle adj continual.
continuellement adv continually.
continuer 1 vt to continue, to carry on (à ou de faire doing). **2** vi to continue, to go on.
contour m outline.
contourner vt (colline etc) to go around.
contraceptif, -ive adj & m contraceptive.
contracter vt, **se contracter** vpr to contract.
contractuel, -elle mf parking enforcement officer.
contradiction f contradiction.
contradictoire adj contradictory; (théories) conflicting.
contraindre* vt to compel (à faire to do).
contrainte f compulsion.
contraire 1 adj opposite; **c. à** contrary to. **2** m opposite; **au c.** on the contrary.
contrairement adv **c. à** contrary to.
contrariant, -ante adj (action etc) annoying; (personne) difficult.
contrarier vt (projet etc) to spoil; (personne) to annoy.
contrariété f annoyance.
contraste m contrast.
contrat m contract.
contravention f (pour stationnement interdit) (parking) ticket.
contre prép & adv against; (en échange de) (in exchange) for; **échanger c.** to exchange for; **fâché c.** angry with; **six voix c. deux** six votes to two; **Nîmes c. Arras** (match) Nîmes versus Arras; **un médicament c.** (toux etc) medicine for; **par c.** on the other hand; **tout c.** qch/qn close to sth/sb.
contre- préfixe counter-.
contre-attaque f counterattack.
contrebande f (fraude) smuggling; **de c.** (tabac etc) smuggled; **passer qch en c.** to smuggle sth.
contrebandier, -ière mf smuggler.
contrebas (en) adv & prép (down) below; **en c. de** below.
contrebasse f (instrument) double bass.
contrecarrer vt to thwart.
contrecœur (à) adv reluctantly.
contrecoup m repercussions.
contredire* vt to contradict.
contredire (se) vpr **se c.** to contradict oneself.
contrefaçon f (pratique) counterfeiting; (produit) fake.
contre-jour (à) adv against the (sun)light.
contremaître m foreman.
contre-plaqué m plywood.
contretemps m hitch.
contribuable mf taxpayer.
contribuer vi to contribute (à to).
contribution f contribution; (impôt) tax.

contrôle *m* inspection, check(ing) (**de** of); *(des prix, de la qualité)* control; *(maîtrise)* control.

contrôleur, -euse *mf (de train)* conductor; *(au quai)* ticket collector; *(de bus)* conductor.

contrordre *m* change of orders.

contusion *f* bruise.

convaincant, -ante *adj* convincing.

convaincre* *vt* to convince (**de** of); **c. qn de faire** to persuade sb to do.

convaincu, -ue *adj (certain)* convinced (**de** of).

convalescence *f* convalescence; **être en c.** to convalesce.

convalescent, -ente 1 *mf* convalescent. **2** *adj* **être c.** to convalesce.

convenable *adj* suitable; *(correct)* decent.

convenablement *adv* suitably; decently.

convenir* *vi* **c. à** *(être fait pour)* to be suitable for; *(plaire à, aller à)* to suit; **ça convient** *(date etc)* that's suitable.

convention *f (accord)* agreement; *(règle)* convention.

convenu, -ue *adj (prix etc)* agreed.

conversation *f* conversation.

convertir *vt* to convert (**à** to; **en** into).

conviction *f (certitude)* conviction.

convive *mf* guest *(at table)*.

convivial, -e, -aux *adj* convivial; *(système informatique)* user-friendly.

convocation *f (lettre)* (written) notice to attend.

convoi *m (véhicules)* convoy.

convoquer *vt* to summon (**à** to).

coopération *f* cooperation.

coopérer *vi* to cooperate (**à** in; **avec** with).

coordonnées *fpl (adresse, télé-phone)* contact address and telephone number.

copain *m Fam (camarade)* pal; *(petit ami)* boyfriend; **être c. avec** to be pals with.

copeau, -x *m (de bois)* shaving.

copie *f* copy; *(devoir, examen)* paper.

copier *vti* to copy (**sur** from).

copieux, -euse *adj* plentiful.

copine *f Fam (camarade)* pal; *(petite amie)* girlfriend; **être c. avec** to be pals with.

copropriété *f* **(immeuble en) c.** condominium.

coq *m* rooster.

coque *f (de navire)* hull; *(de noix)* shell; *(fruit de mer)* cockle; **œuf à la c.** soft-boiled egg.

coquelicot *m* poppy.

coqueluche *f* whooping cough.

coquet, -ette *adj (chic)* stylish, chic.

coquetier *m* egg cup.

coquetterie *f (élégance)* style, elegance.

coquillage *m (mollusque)* shellfish; *(coquille)* shell.

coquille *f* shell; **c. Saint-Jacques** scallop.

coquin, -ine *adj* mischievous.

cor *m (instrument)* horn; *(au pied)* corn.

corail, -aux *m* coral.

Coran *m* **le C.** the Koran.

corbeau, -x *m* crow.

corbeille *f* basket; **c. à papier** waste paper basket.

corbillard *m* hearse.

corde *f* rope; *(plus mince)* cord; *(de raquette, violon etc)* string; **c. à linge** clothesline; **c. à sauter** jump rope.

cordial, -e, -aux *adj* warm.

cordon *m (de tablier, sac etc)* string; *(de rideau)* cord.

cordon-bleu, *pl* **cordons-bleus** *m* cordon-bleu cook.

cordonnerie *f* shoe repair shop.

cordonnier *m* shoe repairman.

coriace *adj* tough.

corne *f (de chèvre etc)* horn; *(de cerf)* antler; *(matière, instrument)* horn.

corneille *f* crow.

cornet *m (de glace)* cornet, cone; **c. (de papier)** (paper) cone.

cornichon *m (concombre)* pickle.

corps *m* body; **lutter c. à c.** to fight hand-to-hand; **prendre c.** *(projet)* to take shape.

correct, -e *adj (exact, décent)* correct.

correctement *adv* correctly.

correcteur, -trice 1 *adj* **verres correcteurs** corrective lenses. **2** *mf (d'examen)* examiner; *(en typographie)* proofreader. **3** *m* **c. d'orthographe** spellchecker.

correction *f* correction; *(punition)* whipping; *(exactitude, décence)* correctness; **la c. de** *(devoirs, examen)* the marking of.

correspondance *f* correspondence; *(de train, d'autocar)* connection, transfer.

correspondant, -ante 1 *adj* corresponding. **2** *mf (d'un adolescent etc)* pen pal; *(au téléphone)* caller.

correspondre *vi* to correspond (**à** to, with); *(écrire)* to correspond (**avec** with).

corrida *f* bullfight.

corriger *vt* to correct; *(devoir)* to mark; **c. qn de** *(défaut)* to cure sb of.

corrompu, -ue *adj* corrupt.

corsage *m (chemisier)* blouse.

cortège *m* procession; **c. officiel** *(automobiles)* motorcade.

corvée *f* chore.

cosmonaute *mf* cosmonaut.

cosmos *m (univers)* cosmos; *(espace)* outer space.

cosse *f (de pois etc)* pod.

costaud, -aude *adj Fam* brawny.

costume *m (déguisement)* costume; *(complet)* suit.

costumé *adj* **bal c.** costume ball.

côte *f* rib; *(de mouton)* chop; *(de veau)* cutlet; *(montée)* hill; *(littoral)* coast; **c. à c.** side by side.

côté *m* side; *(direction)* way; **de l'autre c.** on the other side (**de** of); *(direction)* the other way; **du c. de** *(vers, près de)* towards; **de c.** *(mettre de l'argent etc)* to one side; *(regarder)* sideways; **à c.** nearby; *(pièce)* in the other room; *(maison)* next door; **à c. de** next to, beside; *(comparaison)* compared to; **à mes côtés** by my side.

coteau, -x *m* (small) hill.

côtelette *f (d'agneau, de porc)* chop; *(de veau)* cutlet.

côtier, -ière *adj* coastal.

cotisation *f (de club)* dues.

cotiser *vi (à un cadeau, pour la retraite)* to contribute (**à** to; **pour** towards).

cotiser (se) *vpr* to club together (**pour acheter** to buy).

coton *m* cotton; **c. (hydrophile)** absorbent cotton.

cou *m* neck.

couchage *m* **sac de c.** sleeping bag.

couchant *adj (soleil)* setting.

couche *f (épaisseur)* layer; *(de peinture)* coat; *(linge de bébé)* diaper.

couché, -ée *adj* **être c.** to be in bed; *(étendu)* to be lying (down).

couche-culotte, *pl* **couches-culottes** *f* disposable diaper.

coucher 1 *vt* to put to bed; *(héberger)* to put up; *(allonger)* to lay (down *ou* out). **2** *vi* to sleep (**avec** with).

coucher (se) *vpr* to go to bed; *(s'allonger)* to lie flat *ou* down; *(soleil)* to set.

couchette *f (de train)* sleeper, sleeping berth; *(de bateau)* bunk.

coucou *m (oiseau)* cuckoo; *(fleur)* cowslip.

coude *m* elbow; **se serrer les cou-**

des to help one another; **c. à c.** side by side; **coup de c.** nudge; **pousser du c.** to nudge.

coudre* *vti* to sew.

couette *f* duvet, down comforter.

couler¹ *vi* (*eau etc*) to flow; (*robinet, nez, sueur*) to run; (*fuir*) to leak.

couler² *vti* (*bateau, nageur*) to sink.

couleur *f* color; *Cartes* suit; **couleurs** (*teint*) color; **de c.** colored; **photo/etc en couleurs** color photo/etc; **téléviseur c.** *ou* **en couleurs** color TV set.

couleuvre *f* (grass) snake.

coulisses *fpl* **dans les c.** in the wings, backstage.

couloir *m* corridor; (*de circulation, d'une piste*) lane.

coup *m* blow, knock; (*léger*) tap; (*choc moral*) blow; (*de fusil etc*) shot; (*de crayon, d'horloge*) stroke; (*aux échecs etc*) move; (*fois*) *Fam* time; **donner des coups à** to hit; **c. de brosse** brush(-up); **c. de chiffon** wipe (with a rag); **c. de sonnette** ring (on a bell); **c. de dents** bite; **c. de chance** stroke of luck; **tenter le c.** *Fam* to give it a try; **tenir le c.** to hold out; **sous le c. de** (*émotion*) under the influence of; **après c.** afterwards; **tué sur le c.** killed outright; **à c. sûr** for sure; **tout à c., tout d'un c.** suddenly; **d'un seul c.** all at once; **du c.** (*de ce fait*) as a result.

coupable 1 *adj* guilty (**de** of). **2** *mf* guilty person, culprit.

coupant, -ante *adj* sharp.

coupe *f* (*trophée*) cup; (*à boire*) goblet; (*de vêtement etc*) cut; **c. de cheveux** haircut.

coupe-ongles *m inv* (finger nail) clippers.

coupe-papier *m inv* letter opener.

couper 1 *vt* to cut; (*arbre*) to cut down; (*téléphone*) to cut off; (*courant etc*) to switch off; (*morceler*) to cut up; (*croiser*) to cut across; **c. la parole à qn** to cut sb short. **2** *vi* to

cut; **ne coupez pas!** (*au téléphone*) hold on!

couper (se) *vpr* (*routes*) to intersect; **se c. au doigt** to cut one's finger.

couple *m* pair, couple.

couplet *m* verse.

coupure *f* cut; (*de journal*) clipping; **c. d'électricité** blackout, power outage.

cour *f* court(yard); (*de roi*) court; **c. (de récréation)** playground.

courage *m* courage; **bon c.!** good luck!

courageux, -euse *adj* courageous.

couramment *adv* (*parler*) fluently; (*souvent*) frequently.

courant, -ante 1 *adj* (*fréquent*) common; (*eau*) running; (*modèle, taille*) standard. **2** *m* (*de l'eau, électrique*) current; (*d'air*) draft; **coupure de c.** blackout, power outage; **être/mettre au c.** to know/tell (**de** about).

courbature *f* ache; **avoir des courbatures** to be aching (all over).

courbaturé, -ée *adj* aching (all over).

courbe 1 *adj* curved. **2** *f* curve.

courber *vti* to bend.

coureur *m* runner; (*cycliste*) cyclist; (*automobile*) racecar driver.

courgette *f* zucchini.

courir* 1 *vi* to run; (*se hâter*) to rush; (*à bicyclette, en auto*) to race; **le bruit court que…** there's a rumor going around that… **2** *vt* (*risque*) to run; (*épreuve sportive*) to run (in); (*danger*) to face.

couronne *f* crown; (*de fleurs*) wreath.

couronnement *m* (*de roi etc*) coronation.

couronner *vt* to crown.

courrier *m* mail; **c. électronique** e-mail.

courroie *f* strap; (*de transmission*) belt.

cours m course; (d'une monnaie etc) rate; (leçon) class; (série de leçons) course; **c. d'eau** river, stream; **en c.** (travail) in progress; (année) current; **en c. de route** on the way; **au c. de** during.

course[1] f (action) run(ning); (épreuve de vitesse) race; **courses** (de chevaux) races; **cheval de c.** racehorse; **voiture de c.** racecar.

course[2] f (commission) errand; **courses** (achats) shopping; **faire une c.** to run an errand; **faire les courses** to go shopping.

coursier, -ière mf messenger.

court, courte 1 adj short. **2** adv (couper, s'arrêter) short; **à c. de** (argent etc) short of. **3** m Tennis court.

court-circuit, pl **courts-circuits** m short-circuit.

couscous m couscous.

cousin, -ine mf cousin.

coussin m cushion.

coût m cost; **le c. de la vie** the cost of living.

couteau, -x m knife.

coûter vti to cost; **ça coûte combien?** how much does it cost?; **coûte que coûte** at all costs.

coûteux, -euse adj costly, expensive.

coutume f custom; **avoir c. de faire** to be accustomed to doing.

couture f sewing; (métier) dressmaking; (raccord) seam.

couturier m fashion designer.

couturière f dressmaker.

couvée f (oiseaux) brood.

couvent m convent.

couver 1 vt (œufs) to sit on. **2** vi (poule) to brood.

couvercle m lid, cover.

couvert m (set of) cutlery; **mettre le c.** to set ou lay the table.

couvert, -erte adj covered (**de** with, in); (de ciel) overcast.

couverture f (de lit) blanket; (de livre etc) cover.

couveuse f incubator.

couvrir* vt to cover (**de** with).

couvrir (se) vpr (s'habiller) to wrap up; (ciel) to cloud over.

cow-boy m cowboy.

crabe m crab.

crachat m spit, spittle.

cracher 1 vi to spit. **2** vt to spit (out).

crachin m (fine) drizzle.

craie f chalk.

craindre* vt to be afraid of, to fear; (chaleur, froid) to be sensitive to; **c. de faire** to be afraid of doing; **ne craignez rien** don't be afraid.

crainte f fear.

craintif, -ive adj timid.

crampe f cramp.

cramponner (se) vpr se **c. à** to hold on to, to cling to.

crampons mpl (de chaussures) cleats.

cran m (entaille) notch; (de ceinture) hole; **couteau à c. d'arrêt** switchblade; **c. de sûreté** safety catch.

crâne m skull.

crapaud m toad.

craquement m snapping ou cracking (sound).

craquer vi (branche) to snap; (bois sec) to crack; (sous la dent) to crunch; (se déchirer) to split, to rip; (personne) to break down.

crasse f filth.

crasseux, -euse adj filthy.

cratère m crater.

cravate f tie.

crawl m (nage) crawl.

crayon m pencil; **c. de couleur** colored pencil; (en cire) crayon; **c. à bille** ballpoint (pen).

crayonner vt to pencil.

créancier, -ière mf debtor.

création f creation; **1000 créations d'emplois** 1000 new jobs.

créature f creature.

crèche f (de Noël) crib; (pour bébé) daycare (center).

crédit m credit; **à c.** on credit; **faire c.** *(prêter)* to give credit (à to).

créditeur adj **compte c.** account in credit.

créer vt to create.

crémaillère f **pendre la c.** to have a house-warming (party).

crématorium m crematorium.

crème f cream; *(dessert)* cream dessert; **c. Chantilly** whipped cream; **c. glacée** ice cream; **c. à raser** shaving cream; **c. anglaise** custard sauce.

créneau, -x m **faire un c.** to parallel park.

crêpe f pancake, crepe.

crépiter vi to crackle.

crépu, -ue adj frizzy.

crépuscule m twilight, dusk.

cresson m (water)cress.

crête f *(de montagne etc)* crest.

creuser vt to dig.

creuser (se) vpr **se c. la tête** to rack one's brains.

creux, -euse 1 adj hollow; *(estomac)* empty; **assiette creuse** soup plate. **2** m hollow; *(de l'estomac)* pit.

crevaison f *(de pneu)* flat.

crevasse f *(trou)* crevice.

crevé, -ée adj *(fatigué)* Fam worn out; *(mort)* Fam dead.

crever 1 vi *(bulle etc)* to burst; *(pneu)* to go flat; *(mourir)* Fam to die. **2** vt to burst; *(œil)* to put out.

crevette f *(grise)* shrimp; *(rose)* prawn.

cri m *(de joie, surprise)* cry, shout; *(de peur)* scream; *(de douleur)* cry; *(appel)* call, cry.

cric m *(de voiture)* jack.

crier 1 vi to shout (out), to cry (out); *(de peur)* to scream; **c. après qn** Fam to shout at sb. **2** vt *(injure, ordre)* to shout (out).

crime m crime; *(assassinat)* murder.

criminel, -elle 1 adj criminal. **2** mf criminal; *(assassin)* murderer.

crinière f mane.

crise f crisis; *(accès)* attack; *(de colère etc)* fit; **c. cardiaque** heart attack.

crisper vt *(visage)* to make tense; *(poing)* to clench.

cristal, -aux m crystal.

critique 1 adj critical. **2** f *(reproche)* criticism.

critiquer vt to criticize.

croc m *(dent)* fang.

croche-pied m **faire un c. à qn** to trip sb up.

crochet m hook; *(aiguille)* crochet hook; *(travail)* crochet; **faire qch au c.** to crochet sth; **faire un c.** *(personne)* to make a detour.

crochu, -ue adj *(nez)* hooked.

crocodile m crocodile.

croire* 1 vt to believe; *(estimer)* to think, to believe **(que** that); **j'ai cru la voir** I thought I saw her. **2** vi to believe (à, en in).

croisement m *(de routes)* crossroads.

croiser vt *(jambes, ligne etc)* to cross; **c. qn** to pass *ou* meet sb.

croiser (se) vpr *(voitures etc)* to pass (each other); *(routes)* to cross.

croisière f cruise.

croissance f growth.

croissant, -ante 1 adj *(nombre)* growing. **2** m crescent; *(pâtisserie)* croissant.

croix f cross.

croque-monsieur m inv = toasted cheese and ham sandwich.

croquer vti to crunch.

croquis m sketch.

crosse f *(de fusil)* butt.

crotte f *(de lapin etc)* droppings, dung.

crottin m *(horse)* dung.

crouler vi *(édifice)* to crumble; **c. sous le travail** to be snowed under with work.

croustillant, -ante adj *(pain)* crusty.

croustiller vi to be crusty.

croûte f *(de pain etc)* crust; *(de fromage)* rind; *(de plaie)* scab.

croûton m crust (at end of loaf).
croyant, -ante 1 adj être c. to be a believer. **2** mf believer.
CRS abrév mpl (Compagnies républicaines de sécurité) riot police.
cru¹, crue pp of **croire**.
cru², crue adj (aliment etc) raw.
cruauté f cruelty (**envers** to).
cruche f pitcher, jug.
crudités fpl assorted raw vegetables.
cruel, -elle adj cruel (**envers, avec** to).
crustacés mpl shellfish.
cube 1 m cube; **cubes** (jeu) building blocks. **2** adj (mètre etc) cubic.
cueillette f picking; (fruits cueillis) harvest.
cueillir* vt to pick.
cuiller, cuillère f spoon; petite c., c. à café teaspoon; **c. à soupe** soup spoon, tablespoon.
cuillerée f spoonful; **c. à café** teaspoonful; **c. à soupe** tablespoonful.
cuir m leather.
cuire* **1** vt to cook; (à l'eau) to boil; **c. (au four)** to bake; (viande) to roast. **2** vi to cook; (à l'eau) to boil; (au four) to bake; (viande) to roast; **faire c.** to cook.
cuisine f (pièce) kitchen; (art, aliments) cooking; **faire la c.** to cook, to do the cooking; **livre de c.** cook book.
cuisiner vti to cook.
cuisinier, -ière 1 mf cook. **2** f (appareil) stove, range.
cuisse f thigh; (de poulet) leg.
cuisson m cooking.
cuit, cuite (pp of cuire) adj cooked; **bien c.** well done.
cuivre m (rouge) copper; (jaune) brass.
culbute f (saut) somersault; (chute) (backward) tumble.
culbuter vi to tumble over (backwards).
cul-de-sac, pl culs-de-sac m dead end.

culot m (d'ampoule, de lampe) base; (audace) Fam nerve.
culotte f (de femme) (pair of) panties; **culottes (courtes)** knickers.
culpabiliser vt c. qn to make sb feel guilty.
culte m (de dieu) worship; (religion) form of worship.
cultivateur, -trice mf farmer.
cultivé, -ée adj (personne) cultivated.
cultiver vt (terre) to farm; (plantes) to grow.
cultiver (se) vpr to improve one's mind.
culture f culture; (agriculture) farming; (de légumes) growing.
culturel, -elle adj cultural.
cupide adj avaricious.
cure f (course of) treatment, cure.
curé m (parish) priest.
cure-dent m toothpick.
curer vt (fossé etc) to clean out.
curieux, -euse 1 adj (bizarre) curious; (indiscret) inquisitive, curious (**de** about). **2** mf inquisitive person; (badaud) onlooker.
curiosité f curiosity.
curriculum (vitae) m inv résumé.
curseur m (d'ordinateur) cursor.
cuve f (réservoir) tank.
cuvette f (récipient) basin, bowl; (des toilettes) bowl.
CV m abrév (curriculum vitae) résumé.
cycle m (série) cycle.
cyclisme m cycling.
cycliste mf cyclist; **course c.** cycling ou bicycle race; **champion c.** cycling champion.
cyclomoteur m moped.
cyclone m cyclone.
cygne m swan.
cylindre m cylinder.
cylindrée f (engine) capacity.
cylindrique adj cylindrical.
cymbale f cymbal.
cyprès m (arbre) cypress.

D

dactylo f (personne) typist; (action) typing.

daim m fallow deer; (cuir) suede.

dallage m paving.

dalle f paving stone.

dallé, -ée adj paved.

dame f lady; (mariée) married lady; Échecs, Cartes queen; (au jeu de dames) king; **(jeu de) dames** checkers.

damier m checkerboard.

dandiner (se) vpr to waddle.

danger m danger; **en d.** in danger; **mettre en d.** to endanger; **en cas de d.** in an emergency; **en d. de mort** in peril of death; **'d. de mort'** (panneau) 'danger'; **être sans d.** to be safe.

dangereusement adv dangerously.

dangereux, -euse adj dangerous (pour to).

danois, -oise 1 adj Danish. **2** mf D. Dane. **3** m (langue) Danish.

dans prép in; (changement de lieu) into; (à l'intérieur de) inside; **entrer d.** to go in(to); **boire/prendre/etc d.** to drink/take/etc from ou out of; **d. deux jours/etc** (temps futur) in two days/etc; **d. les dix euros/etc** about ten euros/etc.

danse f dance; (art) dancing.

danser vti to dance.

danseur, -euse mf dancer.

date f date; **en d. du...** dated the...; **d. d'expiration** expiry date; **d. limite** deadline.

dater 1 vt (lettre etc) to date. **2** vi d. **de** to date from; **à d. de** as from.

datte f (fruit) date.

dauphin m dolphin.

davantage adv (quantité) more; (temps) longer; **d. de temps/etc** more time/etc; **d. que** more than; longer than.

de¹ (**d'** before a vowel or mute h; de + le = du, de + les = des) prép (complément d'un nom) of; **les rayons du soleil** the rays of the sun; **le livre de Paul** Paul's book; **un pont de fer** an iron bridge; **une augmentation d'impôts/etc** an increase in taxes/etc. ■ (complément d'un adjectif) digne de worthy of; **heureux de** happy to; **content de qch/qn** pleased with sth/sb. ■ (complément d'un verbe) parler de to speak of ou about; **décider de faire** to decide to do. ■ (provenance: lieu & temps) from; **mes amis du village** my friends from the village. ■ (agent) accompagné de accompanied by. ■ (moyen) armé de armed with; **se nourrir de** to live on. ■ (manière) d'une voix douce in ou with a gentle voice. ■ (cause) mourir de faim to die of hunger. ■ (temps) travailler de nuit to work by night; **six heures du matin** six o'clock in the morning. ■ (mesure) avoir ou faire six mètres de haut to be 20 feet high; **homme de trente ans** thirty-year-old man; **gagner quinze euros de l'heure** to earn fifteen euros an hour.

de² art partitif some; **elle boit du vin** she drinks (some) wine; **il ne boit pas de vin** (négation) he doesn't drink (any) wine; **des fleurs** (some) flowers; **de jolies fleurs** (some) pretty flowers; **il y en a six de tués** (avec un nombre) six killed.

dé m (à jouer) dice; (à coudre) thimble; **jouer aux dés** to play dice.

déballer vt to unpack.

débarbouiller (se) vpr to wash one's face.

débarquement m (de passagers) landing; (de marchandises) unloading.

débarquer 1 vt (passagers) to

land; (*marchandises*) to unload. **2** *vi* (*passagers*) to land.

débarras *m* storeroom; **bon d.!** *Fam* good riddance!

débarrasser *vt* (*table etc*) to clear (**de** of); **d. qn de** (*ennemi, soucis etc*) to rid sb of; (*manteau etc*) to relieve sb of.

débarrasser (se) *upr* **se d. de** to get rid of.

débat *m* discussion, debate.

débattre* *vt* to discuss, to debate.

débattre (se) *upr* to struggle (to get free).

débile 1 *adj* (*esprit, enfant etc*) weak; *Fam* idiotic. **2** *mf Fam* idiot.

débit *m* (*vente*) sales; (*compte*) debit; (*de fleuve*) flow; **d. de boissons** bar, café.

débiter *vt* (*découper*) to cut up (**en** into); (*vendre*) to sell; (*compte*) to debit.

débiteur, -trice 1 *mf* debtor. **2** *adj* **compte d.** debit account.

déblayer *vt* (*terrain, décombres*) to clear.

débloquer *vt* (*mécanisme*) to unjam; (*crédits*) to release.

déboîter 1 *vt* (*tuyau*) to disconnect; (*os*) to dislocate. **2** *vi* (*véhicule*) to pull out, to change lanes.

déborder 1 *vi* (*fleuve, liquide*) to overflow; **l'eau déborde du vase** the water is overflowing the vase. **2** *vt* (*dépasser*) to go beyond; **débordé de travail** snowed under with work.

débouché *m* (*carrière*) opening; (*marché pour produit*) outlet.

déboucher *vt* (*bouteille*) to open, to uncork; (*lavabo, tuyau*) to unclog.

débourser *vti* to pay out.

debout *adv* standing (up); **mettre d.** (*planche etc*) to stand up, to put upright; **se mettre d.** to stand *ou* get up; **rester d.** to remain standing; **être d.** (*levé*) to be up; **d.!** get up!

déboutonner *vt* to unbutton, to undo.

débraillé, -ée *adj* (*tenue etc*) slovenly, sloppy.

débrancher *vt* to unplug, to disconnect.

débrayer *vi* (*conducteur*) to depress the clutch.

débris *mpl* fragments; (*restes*) remains; (*détritus*) garbage.

débrouillard, -arde *adj* smart, resourceful.

débrouiller (se) *upr* to manage (**pour faire** to do).

début *m* start, beginning; **au d.** at the beginning.

débutant, -ante *mf* beginner.

débuter *vi* to start, to begin.

décaféiné, -ée *adj* decaffeinated.

décalage *m* (*écart*) gap; **d. horaire** time difference.

décalcomanie *f* (*image*) decal.

décaler *vt* to shift.

décalquer *vt* (*dessin*) to trace.

décapant *m* cleaning agent; (*pour enlever la peinture*) paint stripper.

décaper *vt* (*métal*) to clean; (*surface peinte*) to strip.

décapiter *vt* to behead.

décapotable *adj* (*voiture*) convertible.

décapsuler *vt* **d. une bouteille** to take the top off a bottle.

décapsuleur *m* bottle-opener.

décéder *vi* to die.

déceler *vt* (*trouver*) to detect.

décembre *m* December.

décemment *adv* decently.

décennie *f* decade.

décent, -ente *adj* (*convenable*) decent.

déception *f* disappointment.

décerner *vt* (*prix*) to award.

décès *m* death.

décevant, -ante *adj* disappointing.

décevoir* *vt* to disappoint.

déchaîné, -ée *adj* (*foule*) wild.

déchaîner *vt* **d. les rires** to cause

an outburst of laughter; **d. la colère** to arouse anger.

déchaîner (se) *vpr (tempête, rires)* to break out; *(foule)* to run riot; *(personne)* to fly into a rage.

décharge *f* **d. (publique)** *(garbage)* dump; **d. (électrique)** *(electric)* shock.

déchargement *m* unloading.

décharger *vt* to unload; *(batterie)* to discharge.

décharger (se) *vpr (batterie)* to go dead.

déchausser (se) *vpr* to take one's shoes off.

déchet *m* **déchets** *(restes)* waste; **il y a du d.** there's some waste.

déchiffrer *vt* to decipher.

déchiqueter *vt* to tear to shreds.

déchirer *vt (page etc)* to tear (up); *(vêtement)* to tear; *(ouvrir)* to tear open.

déchirer (se) *vpr (robe etc)* to tear.

déchirure *f* tear.

décidé, -ée *adj (air, ton)* determined; **d. à faire** determined to do.

décidément *adv* undoubtedly.

décider 1 *vt (opération)* to decide on; **d. que** to decide that. 2 *vi* **d. de faire** to decide to do.

décider (se) *vpr* **se d. à faire** to make up one's mind to do.

décimal, -e, -aux *adj* decimal.

décimètre *m* decimeter; **double d.** ruler.

décisif, -ive *adj* decisive.

décision *f* decision; *(fermeté)* determination.

déclaration *f* declaration; *(de vol etc)* notification; *(commentaire)* statement; **d. de revenus** tax return.

déclarer *vt* to declare (**que** that); *(vol etc)* to notify.

déclarer (se) *vpr (incendie)* to break out.

déclencher *vt (mécanisme, réaction)* to trigger, to start (off); *(attaque)* to launch.

déclencher (se) *vpr (alarme etc)* to go off.

déclic *m (bruit)* click.

déclin *m* decline; **être en d.** to be in decline.

décoiffer *vt* **d. qn** to mess up sb's hair.

décollage *m (d'avion)* takeoff.

décoller 1 *vi (avion)* to take off. 2 *vt (timbre)* to unstick.

décoller (se) *vpr* to come unstuck.

décolleté, -ée 1 *adj (robe)* low-cut. 2 *m (de robe)* low neckline.

décolorer (se) *vpr* to fade.

décombres *mpl* rubble.

décongeler 1 *vt (faire)* **d.** *(aliment)* to thaw. 2 *vi* to thaw.

déconseiller *vt* **d. qch à qn** to advise sb against sth; **d. à qn de faire** to advise sb against doing.

décontracté, -ée *adj (ambiance, personne)* relaxed; *(vêtement)* casual.

décontracter (se) *vpr* to relax.

décor *m (théâtre, paysage)* scenery; *(d'intérieur)* decoration.

décorateur, -trice *mf (interior)* decorator.

décoratif, -ive *adj* decorative.

décoration *f* decoration.

décorer *vt (maison, soldat)* to decorate (**de** with).

découdre *vt* to unstitch.

découdre (se) *vpr* to come unstitched.

découpage *m (image)* cutout.

découper *vt (viande)* to carve; *(article)* to cut out.

découragement *m* discouragement.

décourager *vt* to discourage.

décourager (se) *vpr* to get discouraged.

découvert *m (d'un compte)* overdraft.

découverte *f* discovery.

découvrir (se) *vpr (dans son lit)* to push the bedcovers off; *(ciel)* to clear (up); (enlever son chapeau) to remove one's hat.

décrasser vt (nettoyer) to clean.

décrire* vt to describe.

décroché adj (téléphone) off the hook.

décrocher vt (détacher) to unhook; (tableau) to take down; **d. (le téléphone)** to pick up the phone.

décrocher (se) vpr (tableau) to fall down.

décrotter vt to clean (the mud off).

déçu, -ue (pp of décevoir) adj disappointed.

déculotter (se) vpr to take off one's pants.

dédaigner vt to scorn, to despise.

dédaigneux, -euse adj scornful.

dédain m scorn.

dedans 1 adv inside; **en d.** on the inside; **tomber d.** (trou) to fall in (it); **je me suis fait rentrer d.** (accident de voiture) someone crashed into me. **2** m **le d.** the inside.

dédommagement m compensation.

dédommager vt to compensate (de for).

déduction f deduction.

déduire* vt (soustraire) to deduct (de from).

déesse f goddess.

défaillance f (évanouissement) fainting fit; (faiblesse) weakness; (panne) failure; **avoir une d.** (s'évanouir) to faint; (faiblir) to feel weak.

défaire* vt (nœud etc) to undo.

défaire (se) vpr to come undone.

défait adj (lit) unmade.

défaite f defeat.

défaut m (faiblesse) fault; (de fabrication) defect.

défavorable adj unfavorable (à to).

défavorisé, -ée adj (milieu) underprivileged.

défavoriser vt to put at a disadvantage.

défectueux, -euse adj faulty, defective.

défendre¹ vt (protéger) to defend.

défendre² vt (interdire) **d. à qn de faire** to forbid sb to do; **d. qch à qn** to forbid sb sth.

défendre (se) vpr to defend oneself.

défense¹ f (protection) defense; (d'éléphant) tusk.

défense² f (interdiction) **'d. de fumer'** 'no smoking'; **'d. (absolue) d'entrer'** '(strictly) no entry'.

défenseur m defender.

défi m challenge; **lancer un d. à qn** to challenge sb.

déficitaire adj (budget) in deficit; (entreprise) loss-making; (compte) in debit.

défier vt to challenge (à to); **d. qn de faire** to challenge sb to do.

défiguré, -ée adj disfigured.

défilé m (militaire) parade; (gorge) pass.

défiler vi (soldats) to march.

définir vt to define; **article défini** Grammaire definite article.

définitif, -ive adj final, definitive.

définition f definition; (de mots croisés) clue.

définitivement adv (partir, exclure) for good.

défoncé, -ée adj (route) bumpy; (drogué) Fam high.

défoncer vt (porte, mur) to smash in, to knock down; (trottoir, route) to dig up.

déformé, -ée adj misshapen; **chaussée déformée** uneven road surface, bumpy road.

déformer vt to put out of shape.

déformer (se) vpr to lose its shape.

défouler (se) vpr to let off steam.

défricher vt (terrain) to clear.

défroisser vt to smooth out.

défunt, -unte 1 adj (mort) departed; **mon d. mari** my late husband. **2** mf **le d., la défunte** the deceased.

dégagé, -ée *adj (ciel)* clear.

dégagement *m (action)* clearing; *Football* kick (down the field); **itinéraire de d.** alternative route *(to ease traffic congestion)*.

dégager 1 *vt (table etc)* to clear (**de** of); *(odeur)* to give off; **d. qn de** *(décombres etc)* to pull sb out of. **2** *vi Football* to clear the ball (down the field); **dégagez!** get lost!

dégager (se) *vpr (ciel)* to clear; **se d. de** *(personne)* to pull oneself free from *(rubble)*; *(odeur)* to come out of *(room)*.

dégainer *vti (arme)* to draw.

dégarni, -ie *adj* bare; **front d.** receding hairline.

dégarnir *vt (arbre de Noël)* to take down the decorations from.

dégarnir (se) *vpr (crâne)* to go bald.

dégâts *mpl* damage.

dégel *m* thaw.

dégeler *vti* to thaw (out).

dégivrer *vt (réfrigérateur)* to defrost.

déglingué, -ée *adj* falling to pieces.

dégonfler *vt (pneu)* to deflate.

dégonfler (se) *vpr (pneu)* to deflate; *(se montrer lâche) Fam* to chicken out.

dégouliner *vt* to trickle.

dégourdi, -ie 1 *adj (malin)* smart. **2** *mf* smart boy *ou* girl.

dégourdir (se) *vpr* **se d. les jambes** to stretch one's legs.

dégoût *m* disgust; **avoir du d. pour qch** to have a (strong) dislike for sth.

dégoûtant, -ante *adj* disgusting.

dégoûté, -ée *adj* disgusted (**de** with, by); **il n'est pas d.** *(difficile)* he's not fussy.

dégoûter *vt* to disgust; **d. qn de qch** to (be enough to) make sb sick of sth.

dégrader (se) *vpr (situation)* to deteriorate.

degré *m (angle, température)* degree.

dégringolade *f* tumble.

dégringoler *vi* to tumble (down).

déguerpir *vi* to clear out, to make tracks.

dégueulasse *adj Fam* disgusting.

déguisement *m* disguise; *(de bal costumé)* costume.

déguiser *vt* to disguise; **d. qn (en)** *(costumer)* to dress sb up (as).

déguiser (se) *vpr* to dress oneself up (**en** as).

déguster *vt (goûter)* to taste.

dehors 1 *adv* out(side); **en d. on** the outside; **en d. de la maison** outside the house; **en d. de la ville** out of town; **au-d. (de), au d. (de)** outside. **2** *m (extérieur)* outside.

déjà *adv* already; **elle l'a d. vu** she's seen it before, she's already seen it; **quand partez-vous, d.?** when did you say you're leaving?

déjeuner 1 *vi (à midi)* to have lunch; *(le matin)* to have breakfast. **2** *m* lunch; **petit d.** breakfast.

delà *adv* **au-d. (de), au d. (de)** beyond.

délabré, -ée *adj* dilapidated.

délacer *vt (chaussures)* to undo, to untie.

délai *m* time limit; **sans d.** without delay; **dernier d.** final date.

délasser (se) *vpr* to relax.

délayer *vt (mélanger)* to mix (with liquid).

délégation *f* delegation.

délégué, -ée *mf* delegate.

délibérer *vi (se consulter)* to deliberate (**de** about).

délicat, -ate *adj (santé, travail)* delicate; *(geste)* tactful; *(exigeant)* particular.

délicatement *adv (doucement)* delicately.

délicatesse *f (tact)* tact.

délice *m* delight.

délicieux, -euse *adj (plat)* delicious.

délier vt to undo.

délier (se) vpr (paquet) to come undone.

délimiter vt (terrain) to mark off.

délinquant, -ante mf delinquent.

délirer vi (dire n'importe quoi) to rave.

délit m offense.

délivrer vt (prisonnier) to release, to (set) free; (billet) to issue.

déloger vt to drive out.

deltaplane® m hang glider.

déluge m flood; (de pluie) downpour.

demain adv tomorrow; **à d.!** see you tomorrow!

demande f request (**de qch** for sth); **demandes d'emploi** positions wanted.

demander vt to ask for; (nécessiter) to require; **d. le chemin/l'heure** to ask the way/the time; **d. qch à qn** to ask sb for sth; **d. à qn de faire** to ask sb to do; **ça demande du temps** it takes time; **être très demandé** to be in great demand.

demander (se) vpr to wonder (**pourquoi** why; **si** if).

demandeur, -euse mf **d. d'emploi** job seeker.

démangeaison f itch; **avoir des démangeaisons** to be itching.

démanger vti to itch; **son bras le démange** his arm itches.

démaquillant m cleanser.

démaquiller (se) vpr to take off one's make-up.

démarche f walk; **faire des démarches** to go through the process (**pour faire** of doing).

démarrage m start.

démarrer vi (moteur) to start (up); (voiture) to move off.

démarreur m starter.

démasquer vt to expose.

démêler vt (cheveux) to untangle.

déménagement m move, moving; **camion de d.** moving van.

déménager vi to move.

déménageur m mover.

démesuré, -ée adj excessive.

démettre (se) vpr **se d. le pied/etc** to dislocate one's foot/etc.

demeure f (belle maison) mansion.

demeurer vi (aux être) (rester) to remain; (aux avoir) (habiter) to live.

demi, -ie 1 adj half; **une heure et demie** an hour and a half; (horloge) half past one. **2** adv (**à) d. plein**/etc half-full/etc. **3** m (verre) (half-pint) glass of beer.

demi-cercle m semicircle.

demi-douzaine f **une d. (de)** half a dozen.

demi-finale f semifinal.

demi-frère m stepbrother.

demi-heure f **une d.** a half-hour, half an hour.

demi-journée f half-day.

demi-pension f breakfast and one meal.

demi-pensionnaire mf day student.

démission f resignation.

démissionner vt to resign.

demi-sœur f stepsister.

demi-tarif adj inv (billet) half-price.

demi-tour m (en voiture) U-turn; **faire d.** (à pied) to turn back; (en voiture) to make a U-turn.

démocratie f democracy.

démocratique adj democratic.

démodé, -ée adj old-fashioned.

demoiselle f (célibataire) single woman; **d. d'honneur** (à un mariage) bridesmaid.

démolir vt (maison) to demolish, to knock down.

démolition f demolition.

démonstratif, -ive adj & m Grammaire demonstrative.

démonstration f demonstration, proof.

démonter vt (mécanisme) to take apart; (tente) to take down.

démonter (se) *vpr* to come apart, to come down.

démontrer *vt* to show.

démoraliser *vt* to demoralize.

démoraliser (se) *vpr* to become demoralized.

déneiger *vt* to clear of snow.

dénicher *vt (trouver)* to dig up.

dénombrer *vt* to count.

dénoncer *vt* d. qn *(au professeur)* to tell on sb (**à** to).

dénoncer (se) *vpr* to own up (**à** to).

dénouement *m (de livre)* ending; *(de pièce de théâtre)* dénouement; *(d'affaire)* outcome.

dénouer *vt (corde)* to undo, to untie.

dénouer (se) *vpr (nœud)* to come undone *ou* untied.

denrées *fpl* d. alimentaires foods.

dense *adj* dense.

dent *f* tooth *(pl* teeth); *(de fourchette)* prong; **faire ses dents** *(enfant)* to be teething; **coup de d.** bite.

dentaire *adj* dental.

dentelle *f* lace.

dentier *m* (set of) false teeth.

dentifrice *m* toothpaste.

dentiste *mf* dentist.

déodorant *m* deodorant.

dépannage *m* (emergency) repair.

dépanner *vt (voiture)* to repair.

dépanneur *m (de télévision)* repairman; *(de voiture)* roadside mechanic.

dépanneuse *f (voiture)* tow truck.

départ *m* departure; *(d'une course)* start; **ligne de d.** starting post; **au d.** at the start.

départager *vt* to decide between.

département *m* department.

départementale *adj f* route d. secondary road.

dépassé, -ée *adj (démodé)* outdated; *(incapable)* unable to cope.

dépasser 1 *vt (véhicule)* to overtake; **d. qn** *(en hauteur)* to be taller

than sb; *(surclasser)* to be ahead of sb. **2** *vi (clou etc)* to stick out.

dépêcher (se) *vpr* to hurry (up).

dépeigné, -ée *adj* être d. to have untidy hair.

dépendre *vi* to depend (**de** on, upon).

dépense *f (frais)* expense.

dépenser *vt (argent)* to spend.

dépenser (se) *vpr* to exert oneself.

dépensier, -ière *adj* wasteful.

dépilatoire *adj* crème d. hair-removing cream.

dépister *vt (criminel)* to track down; *(maladie)* to detect.

dépit *m* en d. de in spite of; **en d. du bon sens** *(mal)* atrociously.

déplacé, -ée *adj (mal à propos)* out of place.

déplacement *m (voyage)* (business) trip.

déplacer *vt* to shift, to move.

déplacer (se) *vpr (voyager)* to travel (about).

déplaire* *vi* ça me déplaît I don't like it.

dépliant *m (prospectus)* leaflet.

déplier *vt*, **se déplier** *vpr* to unfold.

déplorable *adj* regrettable, deplorable.

déplorer *vt (regretter)* to deplore; **d. que** (+ subjonctif) to regret that.

déployer *vt (ailes)* to spread.

déporter *vt (dévier)* to carry (off course).

déposer *vt (poser)* to put down; *(laisser)* to leave; *(plainte)* to lodge; *(ordures)* to dump; **d. qn** *(en voiture)* to drop sb (off).

déposer (se) *vpr (poussière)* to settle.

dépôt *m (d'ordures)* dump; *(dans une bouteille)* deposit.

dépotoir *m* garbage dump.

dépouillé, -ée *adj (arbre)* bare.

dépression *f* depression; **d. nerveuse** nervous breakdown.

déprimé, -ée *adj* depressed.

déprimer *vt* to depress.

depuis **1** *prép* since; **d. lundi** since Monday; **d. qu'elle est partie** since she left; **j'habite ici d. un mois** I've been living here for a month; **d. quand êtes-vous là?** how long have you been here?; **d. Paris** from Paris. **2** *adv* since (then).

député *m* (*à l'Assemblée Nationale*) = Congressman, Congresswoman.

déraciner *vt* (*arbre*) to uproot.

déraillement *m* derailment.

dérailler *vi* (*train*) to jump the rails.

dérangement *m* **en d.** (*téléphone*) out of order.

déranger *vt* (*affaires*) to disturb, to upset; **d. qn** to disturb *ou* bother sb; **ça vous dérange si je fume?** do you mind if I smoke?

déranger (se) *vpr* (*se déplacer*) to bother to come *ou* go; **ne te dérange pas!** don't bother!

dérapage *m* skid.

déraper *vi* to skid.

déréglé, -ée *adj* out of order.

dérégler *vt* (*télévision etc*) to put out of order.

dérégler (se) *vpr* (*montre etc*) to go wrong.

dériver *vi* (*bateau*) to drift.

dernier, -ière **1** *adj* last; (*mode*) latest; (*étage*) top; **en d.** last. **2** *mf* last (*person ou one*); **ce d.** the latter; **être le d. de la classe** to be (at the) bottom of the class.

dernièrement *adv* recently.

dérober *vt* (*voler*) to steal (**à** from).

dérouiller (se) *vpr* **se d. les jambes** to stretch one's legs.

dérouler *vt* (*tapis*) to unroll; (*fil*) to unwind.

dérouler (se) *vpr* (*événement*) to take place.

derrick *m* oil rig.

derrière **1** *prép & adv* behind; **assis d.** (*dans une voiture*) sitting in the back; **par d.** (*attaquer*) from behind. **2** *m* back; (*fesses*) behind; **pattes de d.** hind legs.

des *voir* **de**[1,2], **le**.

dès *prép* from; **d. le début** (right) from the start; **d. qu'elle viendra** as soon as she comes.

désabusé, -ée *adj* disillusioned.

désaccord *m* disagreement.

désaccordé, -ée *adj* (*violon etc*) out of tune.

désaffecté, -ée *adj* (*gare etc*) disused.

désagréable *adj* unpleasant.

désaltérer *vt* **d. qn** to quench sb's thirst.

désaltérer (se) *vpr* to quench one's thirst.

désapprobation *f* disapproval.

désapprouver *vt* to disapprove of.

désarmement *m* (*de nation*) disarmament.

désarmer *vt* to disarm.

désastre *m* disaster.

désastreux, -euse *adj* disastrous.

désavantage *m* disadvantage.

désavantager *vt* to handicap.

desceller (se) *vpr* to come loose.

descendre **1** *vi* (*aux être*) to come *ou* go down; (*d'un train*) to get off; (*d'un arbre*) to climb down (**de** from); (*thermomètre*) to fall; (*marée*) to go out; **d. de cheval** to dismount; **d. en courant** to run down. **2** *vt* (*aux avoir*) (*escalier*) to come *ou* go down; (*objet*) to bring *ou* take down.

descente *f* (*d'avion etc*) descent; (*pente*) slope; **d. de lit** (*tapis*) bedside rug.

description *f* description.

désemparé, -ée *adj* (*personne*) at a loss.

désenchanté, -ée *adj* disillusioned.

désenfler *vi* to go down.

déséquilibre (en) *adv* (*meuble*) unsteady.

déséquilibrer *vt* to throw off balance.

désert, -erte *adj* deserted; **île déserte** desert island.

désert *m* desert.

désespérant, -ante *adj (enfant)* hopeless.

désespéré, -ée *adj (personne)* in despair; *(situation)* hopeless; *(efforts)* desperate.

désespérer *vt* to drive to despair.

désespoir *m* despair.

déshabiller *vt*, **se déshabiller** *vpr* to undress.

désherbant *m* weed killer.

désherber *vti* to weed.

désigner *vt (montrer)* to point to; *(élire)* to appoint; *(signifier)* to indicate.

désinfectant *m* disinfectant.

désinfecter *vt* to disinfect.

désintéresser (se) *vpr* **se d. de qch** to lose interest in sth.

désinvolte *adj (dégagé)* casual; *(insolent)* offhand.

désir *m* desire.

désirer *vt* to want; **je désire que tu viennes** I want you to come.

désister (se) *vpr* to withdraw.

désobéir *vi* to disobey; **d. à qn** to disobey sb.

désobéissant, -ante *adj* disobedient.

désobligeant, -ante *adj* disagreeable.

désodorisant *m* air freshener.

désolé, -ée *adj* **être d.** *(navré)* to be sorry (**que** (+ *subjonctif*) that; **de faire** to do).

désoler *vt* to upset (very much).

désordonné, -ée *adj (personne)* messy, untidy.

désordre *m (dans une chambre)* mess; *(dans une classe)* disturbance; **en d.** messy, untidy.

désorganisé, -ée *adj* disorganized.

désormais *adv* from now on.

desquel(le)s *voir* **lequel**.

dessécher (se) *vpr (plante)* to wither; *(peau)* to get dry.

desserrer *vt (ceinture)* to loosen; *(poing)* to open; *(frein)* to release.

desserrer (se) *vpr* to come loose.

dessert *m* dessert.

desservir *vt (table)* to clear; **le car dessert ce village** the bus stops at this village.

dessin *m* drawing; **d. (humoristique)** cartoon; **d. animé** *(film)* cartoon; **école de d.** art school.

dessinateur, -trice *mf* drawer; **d. humoristique** cartoonist.

dessiner *vt* to draw.

dessous 1 *adv* under(neath), below; **en d.** under(neath); **par-d.** *(passer)* under(neath). **2** *m* underside, underneath; **drap de d.** bottom sheet; **les gens du d.** the people downstairs.

dessous-de-plat *m inv* tablemat.

dessus 1 *adv (marcher, monter)* on it; *(passer)* over it; **par-d.** *(sauter)* over (it). **2** *m* top; **drap de d.** top sheet; **les gens du d.** the people upstairs.

dessus-de-lit *m inv* bedspread.

destin *m* fate.

destinataire *mf* addressee.

destination *f (lieu)* destination; **à d. de** *(train)* to, for.

destiner *vt* **d. qch à qn** to intend sth for sb.

destruction *f* destruction.

désuet, -ète *adj* obsolete.

détachant *m* stain remover.

détacher[1] *vt (ceinture)* to undo; *(personne)* to untie; *(ôter)* to take off.

détacher[2] *vt (linge)* to remove the stains from.

détacher (se) *vpr (chien)* to break loose; *(se dénouer)* to come undone; **se d. (de qch)** *(fragment)* to come off (sth).

détail[1] *m* detail; **en d.** in detail.

détail[2] *m* **de d.** *(magasin, prix)* retail; **vendre au d.** to sell retail.

détaillant, -ante mf retailer.

détaillé, -ée adj (récit etc) detailed.

détaler vi to run off.

détecteur m detector.

détective m d. (privé) (private) detective.

déteindre* vi (couleur) to run; **ton tablier bleu a déteint sur ma chemise** the blue of your apron has come off on my shirt.

détendre vt d. qn to relax sb.

détendre (se) vpr (se reposer) to relax; (corde etc) to slacken.

détendu, -ue adj relaxed; (ressort etc) slack.

détenir* vt (record, pouvoir, titre, prisonnier) to hold; (secret, objet volé) to be in possession of.

détente f (repos) relaxation.

détenu, -ue mf prisoner.

détergent m detergent.

détérioration f deterioration (de in).

détériorer (se) vpr to deteriorate.

déterminant, -ante adj decisive.

déterminer vt (préciser) to determine.

déterrer vt to dig up.

détester vt to hate (**faire** doing, to do).

détonation f explosion.

détour m (crochet) detour.

détourné, -ée adj (chemin) roundabout, indirect.

détournement m (d'avion) hijacking.

détourner vt (dévier) to divert; (tête) to turn (away); (avion) to hijack; **d. les yeux** to look away.

détourner (se) vpr to turn away; **se d. de** (chemin) to stray from.

détraqué, -ée adj out of order.

détraquer vt (mécanisme) to put out of order.

détraquer (se) vpr (machine) to break down.

détresse f distress; **en d.** (navire) in distress.

détritus mpl garbage.

détroit m strait(s).

détruire* vt to destroy.

dette f debt; **avoir des dettes** to be in debt.

deuil m (vêtements) mourning; **en d.** in mourning.

deux adj & m two; **d. fois** twice; **tous (les) d.** both.

deuxième adj & mf second.

deuxièmement adv secondly.

deux-pièces m inv (maillot de bain) bikini.

deux-points m inv Grammaire colon.

deux-roues m inv two-wheeled vehicle.

dévaler **1** vt (escalier) to race down. **2** vi (tomber) to tumble down.

dévaliser vt to rob.

devancer vt to get ou be ahead of.

devant **1** prép & adv in front (of); **d. (l'hôtel/etc)** in front (of the hotel/etc); **passer d. (l'église/etc)** to go past (the church/etc); **assis d.** (dans une voiture) sitting in the front. **2** m front; **roue de d.** front wheel; **patte de d.** foreleg.

devanture f (vitrine) shop ou store window.

dévaster vt to ruin, to devastate.

développement m development; (de photos) developing; **en plein d.** (entreprise, pays) growing fast.

développer vt, **se développer** to develop.

devenir* vi (aux être) to become; **qu'est-il devenu?** what's become of him?

déverser vt, **se déverser** vpr (liquide) to pour out (**dans** into).

déviation f (itinéraire provisoire) detour.

dévier **1** vt (circulation) to divert. **2** vi (de sa route) to veer (off course).

deviner vt to guess.

devinette f riddle.

devis m estimate (of cost of work to be done).

devise f (légende) motto; **devises** (argent) (foreign) currency.

dévisser vt to unscrew.

dévisser (se) vpr (bouchon) to unscrew; (se desserrer) to come loose.

dévoiler vt (secret) to disclose.

devoir*¹ v aux (nécessité) **je dois refuser** I must refuse, I have (got) to refuse; **j'ai dû refuser** I had to refuse. ▪ (probabilité) **il doit être tard** it must be late; **elle a dû oublier** she must have forgotten; **il ne doit pas être bête** he can't be stupid. ▪ (obligation) **tu dois apprendre tes leçons** you must study your lessons; **il aurait dû venir** he should have come; **vous devriez rester** you should stay. ▪ (événement prévu) **elle doit venir** she's supposed to be coming, she's due to come.

devoir*² **1** vt (argent etc) to owe (**à** to). **2** m (obligation) duty; (exercice) exercise; **devoirs** (à faire à la maison) homework; **d. sur table** exam(ination) in class.

dévorer vt (manger) to eat up.

dévoué, -ée adj (soldat etc) dedicated.

dévouement m dedication.

dévouer (se) vpr **se d. (pour qn)** to sacrifice oneself (for sb).

diabète m diabetes.

diabétique mf diabetic.

diable m devil; **habiter au d.** to live miles from anywhere.

diagnostic m diagnosis.

diagonale f diagonal (line); **en d.** diagonally.

dialecte m dialect.

dialogue m conversation; (de film) dialogue.

diamant m diamond.

diamètre m diameter.

diapositive, Fam **diapo** f (color) slide.

diarrhée f diarrhea.

dictature f dictatorship.

dictée f dictation.

dicter vt to dictate (**à** to).

dictionnaire m dictionary.

dicton m saying.

diesel adj & m (moteur) **d.** diesel (engine).

diète f (jeûne) **à la d.** on a diet.

diététique adj **produit d.** health food.

dieu, -x m god; **D.** God.

différence f difference (**de** in).

différent, -ente adj different (**de** than, from, to).

difficile adj difficult; (exigeant) fussy; **d. à faire** difficult to do; **il nous est d. de** it's difficult for us to.

difficulté f difficulty; **en d.** in a difficult situation.

diffuser vt (émission) to broadcast.

digérer vti to digest.

digestif, -ive 1 adj digestive. **2** m after-dinner liqueur.

digestion f digestion.

digne adj **d. de** worthy of.

digue f dike; (en bord de mer) sea wall.

dilater vt, **se dilater** vpr to expand.

diligence f (véhicule) stagecoach.

dimanche m Sunday.

dimension f dimension.

diminuer 1 vt to reduce. **2** vi (réserves) to decrease; (jours) to get shorter; (prix) to drop.

diminutif m (prénom) nickname.

diminution f reduction, decrease (**de** in).

dinde f turkey.

dindon m turkey (cock).

dîner 1 vi to have dinner; (au Canada, en Belgique) to have lunch. **2** m dinner.

dînette f (jouet) doll's dinner service ou set.

dinosaure m dinosaur.

diphtongue f diphthong.

diplôme m certificate, diploma.

diplômé, -ée 1 adj qualified; (de l'université) **être d. (de)** to be a graduate (of). **2** mf holder of a diploma; (de l'université) graduate.

dire* vt (mot) to say; (vérité, secret, heure) to tell; **d. des bêtises** to talk nonsense; **d. qch à qn** to tell sb sth, to say sth to sb; **d. à qn que** to tell sb that, to say to sb that; **d. à qn de faire** to tell sb to do; **on dirait un château/du Mozart** it looks like a castle/sounds like Mozart; **ça ne me dit rien** (envie) I don't feel like it; (souvenir) it doesn't ring a bell.

dire (se) vpr ça ne se dit pas you don't say that.

direct, -e 1 adj direct; **train d.** fast train. **2** m (émission) live.

directement adv directly.

directeur, -trice mf director; (d'école) principal.

direction f (sens) direction; **en d. de** (train) to, for; **sous la d. de** (orchestre) conducted by; **la d.** (équipe dirigeante) the management.

dirigeable adj & m (ballon) **d.** airship, dirigible.

dirigeant m (de parti etc) leader; (d'entreprise, club) manager.

diriger vt (société) to run; (parti, groupe) to lead; (véhicule) to steer; (orchestre) to conduct; (arme etc) to point (**vers** towards).

diriger (se) vpr se **d. vers** (lieu) to make one's way towards.

dis, disant voir dire.

discipline f (règle) discipline.

discipliné, -ée adj well-disciplined.

discipliner (se) vpr to discipline oneself.

disco f disco.

discontinu, -ue adj (ligne) broken; (bruit) intermittent.

discothèque f (club) discotheque.

discours m speech.

discret, -ète adj (personne) discreet.

discrètement adv discreetly.

discrétion f discretion.

discrimination f discrimination.

discussion f discussion; (conversation) talk; **pas de d.!** no argument!

discuter vi (parler) to talk (**de** about); (répliquer) to argue; **d. sur qch** to discuss sth.

dise(nt) etc voir dire.

disjoncter vi (circuit électrique) to fuze.

disloquer (se) vpr (meuble) to fall apart.

disparaître* vi to disappear; (être porté manquant) to be reported missing.

disparition f disappearance.

disparu, -ue adj (soldat) missing.

dispense f exemption.

dispenser vt **d. qn de** (obligation) to exempt sb from.

disperser vt (objets) to scatter.

disperser (se) vpr (foule) to disperse.

disponible adj (article, place etc) available.

disposé, -ée adj bien **d.** in a good mood; **d. à faire** prepared to do.

disposer 1 vt (objets) to arrange. **2** vi **d. de qch** to make use of sth.

disposer (se) vpr se **d. à faire** to prepare to do.

dispositif m (mécanisme) device.

disposition f arrangement; **à la d. de qn** at sb's disposal; **prendre ses dispositions** to make arrangements.

disproportionné, -ée adj disproportionate.

dispute f quarrel.

disputer vt (match) to play; (rallye) to compete in; **d. qn** (gronder) Fam to tell sb off.

disputer (se) vpr to quarrel (**avec** with).

disqualifier vt (équipe) to disqualify.

disque m disk; **d. compact** compact disk.

disquette f (d'ordinateur) floppy (disk), diskette.

dissertation f (au lycée etc) essay.

dissimuler vt, **se dissimuler** (cacher) to hide (à from).

dissipé, -ée adj (élève) unruly.

dissiper vt (brouillard) to dispel; **d. qn** to distract sb.

dissiper (se) vpr (brume) to lift; (élève) to misbehave.

dissolvant m solvent; (pour vernis à ongles) nail polish remover.

dissoudre* vt, **se dissoudre** vpr to dissolve.

dissuader vt to dissuade (de qch from sth; de faire from doing).

distance f distance; **à deux mètres de d.** seven feet apart.

distancer vt to leave behind.

distinct, -incte adj distinct.

distinctement adv clearly.

distinguer vt to distinguish; (voir) to make out; **d. le blé de l'orge** to tell wheat from barley.

distinguer (se) vpr **se d. de** to be distinguishable from.

distraction f amusement; (étourderie) absent-mindedness.

distraire* vt (divertir) to entertain.

distraire (se) vpr to amuse oneself.

distrait, -aite adj absent-minded.

distribuer vt (donner) to hand out; (courrier) to deliver; (cartes) to deal.

distributeur m **d. (automatique)** vending machine; **d. de billets** ticket machine; (de banque) automatic teller machine, ATM.

distribution f distribution; (du courrier) delivery.

dit, dite, dites voir **dire**.

divan m couch.

divergent, -ente adj (lignes) divergent; (opinions) differing.

divers, -erses adj pl (distincts) varied; (plusieurs) various.

diversifier vt, **se diversifier** vpr to diversify.

divertir vt to entertain.

divertir (se) vpr to enjoy oneself.

divertissement m entertainment.

diviser vt, **se diviser** vpr to divide (en into).

division f division.

divorce m divorce.

divorcé, -ée adj divorced.

divorcer vi to get divorced.

dix adj & m ten.

dix-huit adj & m eighteen.

dixième adj & mf tenth.

dix-neuf adj & m nineteen.

dix-sept adj & m seventeen.

dizaine f une d. (de) about ten.

docile adj docile.

docker m docker.

docteur m doctor.

doctorat m doctorate, = PhD.

document m document.

documentaire m (film) documentary.

documentaliste mf (à l'école) (school) librarian.

documentation f (documents) documentation.

documenter (se) vpr to collect information.

dodo m (langage enfantin) **faire d.** to sleep.

doigt m finger; **d. de pied** toe; **petit d.** little finger, pinkie.

dois, doit, doive(nt) voir **devoir**[1,2].

dollar m dollar.

domaine m (terres) estate.

dôme m dome.

domestique 1 adj (animal) domestic; **travaux domestiques** housework. **2** mf servant.

domicile m home; **livrer à d.** to deliver (to the house).

domination f domination.

dominer 1 vt to dominate. **2** vi (être le plus fort) to dominate.

domino m domino; **dominos** (jeu) dominoes.

dommage *m* **c'est d.!** it's a pity *ou* a shame! (**que** + *subjonctif* that); **dommages** (*dégâts*) damage.

dompter *vt* (*animal*) to tame.

dompteur, -euse *mf* (*de lions*) lion tamer.

DOM-TOM *mpl abrév* (*départements et territoires d'outre-mer*) = French overseas departments and territories.

don *m* (*cadeau, aptitude*) gift; (*charité*) donation.

donc *conj* (*par conséquent*) so; **asseyez-vous d.!** won't you sit down!

donjon *m* keep.

données *fpl* (*information*) data.

donner 1 *vt* to give; (*récolte*) to produce; (*sa place*) to give up; (*cartes*) to deal; **d. un coup à** to hit; **d. à réparer** to take (in) to be repaired; **ça donne soif/faim** it makes you thirsty/hungry. **2** *vi* **d. sur** (*fenêtre*) to overlook; (*porte*) to open onto.

donner (se) *vpr* **se d. du mal** to go to a lot of trouble (**pour faire** to do).

dont *pron rel* (= *de qui, duquel, de quoi etc*) (*personne*) of whom; (*chose*) of which; (*appartenance: personne, chose*) whose; **une mère d. le fils est malade** a mother whose son is ill; **la fille d. il est fier** the daughter he is proud of *ou* of whom he is proud; **la façon d.** the way in which.

doper (se) *vpr* to take drugs.

doré, -ée *adj* (*objet*) gilt, gold; (*couleur*) golden.

dorénavant *adv* from now on.

dorer *vt* (*objet*) to gild.

dorer (se) *vpr* **se d. au soleil** to sunbathe.

dormir* *vi* to sleep.

dortoir *m* dormitory.

dos *m* (*de personne, d'animal*) back; **à d. d'âne** (riding) on a donkey; **'voir au d.'** (*verso*) 'see over'.

dose *f* dose.

dossier *m* (*de siège*) back; (*papiers*) file.

doter *vt* (*équiper*) to equip (**de** with); **doté d'une grande intelligence** endowed with great intelligence.

douane *f* customs.

douanier *m* customs officer.

doublage *m* (*de film*) dubbing.

double 1 *adj* & *adv* double. **2** *m* **le d. (de)** (*quantité*) twice as much (as), double; **je l'ai en d.** I have two of them.

doubler 1 *vt* (*vêtement*) to line; (*film*) to dub. **2** *vti* (*augmenter*) to double; (*en voiture*) to overtake.

doublure *f* (*étoffe*) lining.

douce *voir* **doux.**

doucement *adv* (*délicatement*) gently; (*à voix basse*) softly; (*lentement*) slowly.

douceur *f* (*de miel*) sweetness; (*de peau*) softness; (*de temps*) mildness.

douche *f* shower.

doucher *vt* **d. qn** to give sb a shower.

doucher (se) *vpr* to take a shower.

doué, -ée *adj* gifted (**en** at); (*intelligent*) clever.

douillet, -ette *adj* (*lit*) soft, cozy; **tu es d.** (*délicat*) you're such a baby.

douleur *f* (*mal*) pain; (*chagrin*) sorrow.

douloureux, -euse *adj* painful.

doute *m* doubt; **sans d.** probably, no doubt.

douter *vi* to doubt.

douter (se) *vpr* **se d. de qch** to suspect sth; **je m'en doute** I would think so.

douteux, -euse *adj* (*peu certain*) doubtful; (*louche, médiocre*) dubious.

doux, douce *adj* (*miel etc*) sweet; (*peau*) soft; (*temps*) mild.

douzaine *f* dozen; (*environ*) about twelve; **une d. d'œufs/etc** a dozen eggs/etc.

douze *adj* & *m* twelve.

douzième *adj & mf* twelfth.

dragée *f* sugared almond.

dragon *m (animal)* dragon.

draguer *vt (rivière)* to dredge; *(personne) Fam* to come on to.

dramatique *adj* dramatic; **film d.** drama.

drame *m* drama; *(catastrophe)* tragedy.

drap *m (de lit)* sheet; **d. housse** fitted sheet; **d. de bain** bath towel.

drapeau, -x *m* flag.

dressage *m* training.

dresser *vt (échelle)* to put up; *(animal)* to train.

dresser (se) *vpr (personne)* to stand up; *(montagne)* to stand.

dribbler *vti Sport* to dribble.

drogue *f* une d. *(stupéfiant)* a drug; **la d.** drugs.

drogué, -ée *mf* drug addict.

droguer (se) *vpr* to take drugs.

droguerie *f* hardware store.

droit *m (privilège)* right (**de faire** to do); *(d'inscription etc)* fee(s); **le d.** *(science)* law; **avoir d. à** to be entitled to.

droit², droite 1 *adj (route etc)* straight; *(vertical)* upright; *(angle)* right. **2** *adv* straight; **tout d.** straight ahead.

droit³, droite *adj (côté etc)* right.

droite *f* la d. *(côté)* the right (side); **à d.** *(tourner)* (to the) right; *(rouler etc)* on the right; **de d.** *(fenêtre etc)* right-hand; **à d. de** on *ou* to the right of.

droitier, -ière *adj & mf* right-handed (person).

drôle *adj* odd, strange; **d. d'air/de type** strange look/guy.

drôlement *adv (extrêmement)* terribly.

du *voir* de¹,², le.

dû, due *(pp of* devoir¹,²) *adj* d. à due to.

duc *m* duke.

duchesse *f* duchess.

duel *m* duel.

dune *f* (sand) dune.

duplex *m* duplex.

duquel *voir* lequel.

dur, -e 1 *adj (substance)* hard; *(difficile)* hard, tough; *(hiver, personne, ton)* harsh; *(œuf)* hard-boiled. **2** *adv (travailler)* hard.

durable *adj* lasting.

durant *prép* during.

durcir *vti,* **se durcir** *vpr* to harden.

durée *f (de film etc)* length.

durer *vi* to last; **ça dure depuis** it's been going on for.

dureté *f* hardness; *(de ton etc)* harshness.

duvet *m (d'oiseau)* down; *(sac)* sleeping bag.

dynamique *adj* dynamic.

dynamite *f* dynamite.

dynamo *f* dynamo.

dyslexique *adj & mf* dyslexic.

E

eau, -x *f* water; **e. douce/salée** fresh/salt water; **e. de Cologne** cologne; **tomber à l'e.** *(projet)* to fall through.

eau-de-vie, *pl* eaux-de-vie *f* brandy.

ébahi, -ie *adj* astounded.

ébaucher *vt (tableau, roman)* to rough out.

ébéniste *m* cabinet-maker.

éblouir *vt* to dazzle.

éboueur *m* garbage collector.

ébouillanter (s') *vpr* to scald oneself.

éboulement *m* landslide.

ébouler (s') *vpr (falaise)* to crumble; *(roches)* to fall.

ébouriffé, -ée *adj (cheveux)* disheveled.

ébranler *vt* to shake; *(santé)* to weaken.

ébranler (s') *vpr (train etc)* to move off.

ébrécher *vt (assiette)* to chip.

ébruiter *vt, s'ébruiter vpr (nouvelle)* to spread.

ébullition *f* être en é. *(eau)* to be boiling.

écaille *f (de poisson)* scale; *(de tortue)* shell; *(pour lunettes)* tortoiseshell; *(de peinture)* flake.

écailler *vt (poisson)* to scale; *(huitre)* to shell.

écailler (s') *vpr (peinture)* to flake (off), to peel.

écarlate *adj* scarlet.

écarquiller *vt* é. les yeux to open one's eyes wide.

écart *m (intervalle)* gap; *(embardée)* swerve; *(différence)* difference (**de** in; **entre** between); à l'é. out of the way; à l'é. de away from.

écarté, -ée *adj (endroit)* remote; les jambes écartées with legs apart.

écarter *vt (objets)* to move apart; *(jambes, rideaux)* to open; é. qch de qch to move sth away from sth; é. qn de *(exclure)* to keep sb out of.

écarter (s') *vpr (s'éloigner)* to move away (**de** from).

échafaud *m* scaffold.

échafaudage *m (de peintre etc)* scaffold(ing).

échalote *f* shallot.

échancré, -ée *adj* low-cut.

échange *m* exchange; en é. in exchange (**de** for).

échanger *vt* to exchange (**contre** for).

échangeur *m (autoroute)* interchange.

échantillon *m* sample.

échapper *vi* é. à qn to escape from sb; é. à la mort to escape death; son nom m'échappe her name escapes me.

échapper (s') *vpr (s'enfuir)* to escape (**de** from); *(gaz, eau)* to escape.

écharde *f* splinter.

écharpe *f* scarf; *(de maire)* sash; en é. *(bras)* in a sling.

échauffer (s') *vpr (sportif)* to warm up.

échec *m* failure; les échecs *(jeu)* chess; é.! check!; é. et mat! checkmate!

échelle *f (marches)* ladder; *(dimension)* scale; faire la courte é. à qn to give sb a leg up *ou* a boost.

échelon *m (d'échelle)* rung; *(de fonctionnaire)* grade.

échiquier *m* chessboard.

écho *m (d'un son)* echo.

échographie *f (ultrasound)* scan; passer une é. to have a scan.

échouer *vi* to fail; é. à *(examen)* to fail.

échouer (s') *vpr (navire)* to run aground.

éclabousser *vt* to splash (**de** with).

éclaboussure *f* splash.

éclair *m (lumière)* flash; *(d'orage)* flash of lightning.

éclairage *m (de pièce etc)* lighting.

éclaircie *f (durée)* sunny interval.

éclaircir *vt (couleur etc)* to make lighter; *(mystère)* to clear up.

éclaircir (s') *vpr (ciel)* to clear (up); *(situation)* to become clear.

éclaircissement *m* explanation.

éclairé, -ée *adj* bien/mal é. well/badly lit.

éclairer *vt (pièce etc)* to light (up); é. qn *(avec une lampe)* to give sb some light.

éclairer (s') *vpr (visage)* to brighten up; *(situation)* to become clear; s'é. à la bougie to use candlelight.

éclaireur, -euse *mf* boy *ou* girl scout.

éclat[1] *m (de la lumière)* brightness; *(de phare)* glare.

éclat[2] *m (de verre ou de bois)* splinter; *(de rire)* (out)burst.

éclatant, -ante *adj (lumière, succès)* brilliant.

éclatement m (de ballon etc) bursting; (de bombe) explosion.

éclater vi (ballon etc) to burst; (bombe) to go off; (verre) to shatter; (guerre, incendie) to break out; (orage) to break; **é. de rire** to burst out laughing; **é. en sanglots** to burst into tears.

éclore* vi (œuf) to hatch.

éclosion f hatching.

écluse f (de canal) lock.

écœurant, -ante adj disgusting, sickening.

écœurer vt **é. qn** to make sb feel sick.

école f school; **à l'é.** in ou at school; **aller à l'é.** to go to school.

écolier, -ière mf schoolboy, schoolgirl.

écologiste mf environmentalist.

économe adj thrifty.

économie f economy; **économies** (argent) savings; **une é. de temps** time saved; **faire des économies** to save (up).

économique adj (bon marché) economical.

économiser vti to economize (**sur** on).

écorce f (d'arbre) bark; (de fruit) peel, skin.

écorcher vt (érafler) to scrape; **é. les oreilles** to grate on one's ears.

écorcher (s') vpr to scrape oneself.

écorchure f scrape.

écossais, -aise 1 adj Scottish; (tissu) tartan; (whisky) Scotch. **2** mf E. Scot.

écosser vt (pois) to shell.

écoulement m (de liquide) flow; (de temps) passage.

écouler (s') vpr (eau) to flow out; (temps) to pass.

écourter vt (séjour) to cut short; (texte, tige) to shorten.

écouter 1 vt to listen to. **2** vi to listen.

écouteur m (de téléphone) earpiece; **écouteurs** (casque) earphones.

écran m screen; **le petit é.** television.

écrasant, -ante adj overwhelming.

écraser vt to crush; (cigarette) to put ou stub out; (piéton) to run over; **se faire é.** to get run over.

écraser (s') vpr to crash (**contre** into).

écrémé adj (lait) skim.

écrevisse f crayfish.

écrier (s') vpr to exclaim (**que** that).

écrire* 1 vt to write; (en toutes lettres) to spell; **é. à la machine** to type. **2** vi to write.

écrire (s') vpr (mot) to be spelled ou spelt.

écrit m **par é.** in writing.

écriteau, -x m notice, sign.

écriture f writing.

écrivain m author, writer.

écrou m (de boulon) nut.

écrouler (s') vpr to collapse.

écueil m reef; (obstacle) pitfall.

écuelle f bowl.

écume f (de mer etc) foam.

écureuil m squirrel.

écurie f stable.

écusson m (en étoffe) badge.

édifice m building.

édifier vt to erect.

éditer vt to publish.

éditeur, -trice mf publisher.

édition f (livre, journal) edition; (métier) publishing.

édredon m eiderdown.

éducateur, -trice mf educator.

éducatif, -ive adj educational.

éducation f education; **avoir de l'é.** to have good manners.

éduquer vt to educate.

effacer vt to rub out, to erase; (en lavant) to wash out; (avec un chiffon) to wipe away.

effarant, -ante adj astounding.

effaroucher vt to scare away.

effectif m (de classe etc) total number.

effectivement adv actually.

effectuer vt (expérience etc) to carry out; (trajet etc) to make.

effet m effect (sur on); **faire de l'e.** (remède) to be effective; **en e.** indeed, in fact; **sous l'e. de la colère** in anger.

efficace adj (mesure etc) effective; (personne) efficient.

efficacité f (de mesure etc) effectiveness; (de personne) efficiency.

effilocher (s') vpr to fray.

effleurer vt to skim, to touch (lightly).

effondrer (s') vpr to collapse.

efforcer (s') vpr s'e. de faire to try (hard) to do.

effort m effort; **sans e.** (réussir etc) effortlessly.

effrayant, -ante adj frightening.

effrayer vt to frighten, to scare.

effronté, -ée adj (personne) impudent.

effroyable adj dreadful.

égal, -e, aux 1 adj equal (à to); (uniforme, régulier) even; **ça m'est é.** I don't care. **2** mf (personne) equal.

également adv (aussi) also, as well.

égaler vt to equal.

égaliser vi to equalize.

égalité f equality; (régularité) evenness; **à é. (de score)** even, equal (in points).

égard m **à l'é. de** (envers) towards.

égarer vt (objet) to mislay.

égarer (s') vpr to lose one's way.

égayer vt (pièce) to brighten up; **é. qn** to cheer sb up.

église f church.

égoïste adj & mf selfish (person).

égorger vt to cut the throat of.

égout m sewer; **eaux d'é.** sewage.

égoutter 1 vt to drain. **2** vi, s'égoutter vpr to drain; (linge) to drip.

égouttoir m (dish) drainer.

égratigner vt to scratch.

égratignure f scratch.

eh! int hey!; **eh bien!** well!

élaborer vt (plan, idée) to develop.

élan m (vitesse) momentum; (impulsion) impulse; **prendre son é.** to get a running start.

élancer (s') vpr (bondir) to leap ou rush (forward).

élargir (s') vpr (route etc) to widen.

élastique 1 adj (objet) elastic. **2** m (lien) elastic ou rubber band.

électeur, -trice mf voter.

élection f election.

électoral, -e, -aux adj campagne électorale election campaign.

électricien m electrician.

électricité f electricity.

électrique adj electric.

électrocuter vt to electrocute.

électroménager 1 adj m appareil é. household electrical appliance. **2** m household appliances.

électronique adj electronic.

électrophone m record player.

élégance f elegance; **avec é.** elegantly.

élégant, -ante adj elegant.

élément m element; (de meuble) unit; **éléments** (notions) rudiments.

élémentaire adj basic; (cours, école etc) elementary.

éléphant m elephant.

élevage m breeding, raising.

élève mf pupil.

élevé, -ée adj (haut) high; **bien/mal é.** well-/bad-mannered.

élever vt (prix, voix etc) to raise; (enfant) to bring up, to raise; (animal) to breed, to raise.

élever (s') vpr (prix, ton etc) to rise; **s'é. à** (prix) to amount to.

éleveur, -euse mf breeder.

éliminatoire adj & f (épreuve) é. heat.

éliminer vt to eliminate.

élire* vt to elect (**à** to).

elle pron (sujet) she; (chose, animal) it; **elles** they. ■ (complément) her; (chose, animal) it; **elles** them.

elle-même pron herself; (chose, animal) itself; **elles-mêmes** themselves.

éloigné, -ée adj (lieu) far away; (date) distant; **é. de** (village etc) far (away) from.

éloigner vt (chose, personne) to move ou go away (**de** from).

e-mail m e-mail; **envoyer un e.** to send an e-mail (**à** to).

émail, -aux m enamel.

emballage m (action) packing; wrapping; (caisse) packaging; (papier) wrapping (paper).

emballer vt (dans une caisse etc) to pack; (dans du papier) to wrap (up); **e. qn** (passionner) Fam to thrill sb.

emballer (s') vpr (personne) Fam to get carried away; (cheval) to bolt.

embarcadère m quay, wharf.

embarcation f (small) boat.

embardée f (sudden) swerve.

embarquement m (de passagers) boarding.

embarquer 1 vt (passagers) to take on board; (marchandises) to load (up). 2 vi, **s'embarquer** vpr to (go on) board.

embarras m (gêne) embarrassment.

embarrassant, -ante adj (paquet) cumbersome; (question) embarrassing.

embarrasser vt **e. qn** to be in sb's way; (question etc) to embarrass sb.

embarrasser (s') vpr **s'e. de** to burden oneself with.

embaucher vt (ouvrier) to hire.

embellir 1 vt (pièce, personne) to make more attractive. 2 vi (personne) to grow more attractive.

embêtant, -ante adj annoying, boring.

embêtement m trouble.

embêter vt (agacer) to bother; (ennuyer) to bore.

embêter (s') vpr Fam to get bored.

emboîter vt, **s'emboîter** vpr (tuyau(x)) to fit together.

embouchure f (de fleuve) mouth.

embourber (s') vpr to get bogged down.

embouteillage m traffic jam.

embouteillé, -ée adj (rue) congested.

emboutir vt (voiture) to crash into.

embranchement m (de voie) junction.

embrasser vt (donner un baiser à) to kiss.

embrasser (s') vpr to kiss (each other).

embrayage m (de véhicule) clutch.

embrocher vt to skewer.

embrouiller vt (fils) to tangle (up); (papiers etc) to mix up; **e. qn** to confuse sb.

embrouiller (s') vpr to get confused (**dans** in, with).

embuscade f ambush.

émerger vi to emerge (**de** from).

émerveiller vt to amaze, to fill with wonder.

émetteur m (poste) é. transmitter.

émettre* vt (lumière, son etc) to give out; (message radio) to broadcast; (timbre, monnaie) to issue.

émeute f riot.

émietter vt, **émietter (s')** vpr to crumble.

émigrer vi to emigrate.

émission f (de radio etc) broadcast; (diffusion) transmission; (de timbre, monnaie) issue.

emmanchure f arm hole.

emmêler vt to tangle (up).

emménager vi (dans un logement) to move in; **e. dans** to move into.

emmener vt to take (à to); **e. qn en promenade** to take sb for a walk.

emmitoufler (s') vpr to wrap (oneself) up.

émotif, -ive adj emotional.

émotion f emotion; (trouble) excitement; **une é.** (peur) a scare.

émouvant, -ante adj moving.

émouvoir* vt to move, to touch.

empailler vt to stuff.

empaqueter vt to pack.

emparer (s') vpr **s'e. de** to take, to grab.

empêchement m **j'ai eu un e.** something's come up at the last minute.

empêcher vt to prevent, to stop (**de faire** (from) doing).

empêcher (s') vpr **s'e. de faire qch** to stop oneself from doing sth; **elle ne peut pas s'e. de rire** she can't help laughing.

empereur m emperor.

empester 1 vt (tabac etc) to stink of; **e. qn** to stink sb out. **2** vi to stink.

empiler vt, **empiler (s')** vpr to pile up (**sur** on).

empire m empire.

empirer vi to worsen, to get worse.

emplacement m site; (de stationnement) place.

emplir vt, **emplir (s')** vpr to fill (**de** with).

emploi m (usage) use; (travail) job, employment; **e. du temps** schedule; **sans e.** (au chômage) unemployed.

employé, -ée mf employee; (de bureau, banque) clerk, employee.

employer vt (utiliser) to use; **e. qn** to employ sb.

employer (s') vpr (expression) to be used.

employeur, -euse mf employer.

empoigner vt to grab.

empoisonner vt to poison.

empoisonner (s') vpr to poison oneself; (par accident) to be poisoned.

emporter vt (prendre) to take (away) (**avec soi** with one); (entraîner) to carry away; (par le vent) to blow off ou away.

emporter (s') vpr to lose one's temper (**contre** with).

empreinte f mark; **e. (digitale)** fingerprint; **e. (de pas)** footprint.

empresser (s') vpr **s'e. de faire** to hasten to do.

emprisonner vt to jail.

emprunt m (argent etc) loan.

emprunter vt (argent) to borrow (**à** from); (route) to use.

ému, -ue adj moved; (attristé) upset.

en¹ prép (lieu) in; (direction) to; **être/aller en France** to be in/go to France. ▪ (temps) in; **en février** in February; **d'heure en heure** from hour to hour. ▪ (moyen, état etc) by; in; on; **en avion** by plane; **en groupe** in a group; **en congé** on leave ou vacation. ▪ (matière) in; **en bois** in wood; **chemise en nylon** nylon shirt; **c'est en or** it's (made of) gold. ▪ (comme) **en cadeau** as a present. ▪ (+ participe présent) **en mangeant**/etc while eating/etc; **en apprenant que** on hearing that; **en souriant** smiling, with a smile. ▪ (transformation) into; **traduire en** to translate into.

en² pron & adv (= de là) from there; **j'en viens** I've just come from there. ▪ (= de ça, lui etc) **il en est content** he's pleased with it ou him ou them; **en parler** to talk about it; **en mourir** to die of ou from it. ▪ (partitif) some; **j'en ai** I have some.

encadrer vt (tableau) to frame; (entourer d'un trait) to circle (word).

encaisser vt (argent, loyer etc) to collect.

enceinte adj (femme) pregnant; **e. de six mois** six months pregnant.

encens m incense.

encercler vt to surround.

enchaîner vt to chain (up); (idées etc) to link (up).

enchaîner (s') *vpr (idées etc)* to be linked (up).

enchanté, -ée *adj (ravi)* delighted (**de** with; **que** (+ *subjonctif*) that); **e. de faire votre connaissance!** pleased to meet you!

enchantement *m* delight; **comme par e.** as if by magic.

enchanter *vt (ravir)* to delight.

enchanteur *m* magician.

enchère *f (offre)* bid; **vente aux enchères** auction; **mettre qch aux enchères** to put sth up for auction, to auction sth.

enclos *m* enclosure.

encoche *f* nick (**à** in).

encolure *f* neck; *(tour du cou)* collar (size).

encombrant, -ante *adj (paquet)* bulky.

encombrement *m (d'objets)* clutter; *(de rue)* traffic jam.

encombrer *vt (pièce etc)* to clutter up (**de** with); *(rue)* to congest (**de** with); **e. qn** to hamper sb.

encore *adv (toujours)* still; **e. là** still here. ■ *(avec négation)* yet; **pas e.** not yet. ■ *(de nouveau)* again; **essaie e.** try again. ■ *(de plus)* **e. un café** another coffee, one more coffee; **e. une fois** (once) again, once more; **e. un** another (one), one more; **e. du pain** (some) more bread; **e. quelque chose** something else; **qui/quoi e.?** who/what else? ■ *(avec comparatif)* even, still; **e. mieux** even better, better still.

encourageant, -ante *adj* encouraging.

encouragement *m* encouragement.

encourager *vt* to encourage (**à faire** to do).

encrasser *vt* to clog up (with dirt).

encre *f* ink; **e. de Chine** India ink.

encrier *m* inkpot.

encyclopédie *f* encyclopedia.

endettement *m* debts.

endetter (s') *vpr* to get into debt.

endive *f* chicory, endive.

endommager *vt* to damage.

endormi, -ie *adj* asleep, sleeping.

endormir* *vt* to put to sleep.

endormir (s') *vpr* to fall asleep, to go to sleep.

endroit *m (lieu)* place; **à l'e.** *(vêtement)* right side out.

endurant, -ante *adj* tough.

endurcir *vt* **e. qn** to harden sb.

endurcir (s') *vpr* **s'e. à** to become hardened to *(pain etc)*.

endurer *vt* to endure.

énergie *f* energy.

énergique *adj* energetic; *(remède)* powerful; *(mesure, ton)* forceful.

énergiquement *adv* energetically.

énervé, -ée *adj* on edge.

énerver *vt* **é. qn** *(irriter)* to get on sb's nerves; *(rendre énervé)* to make sb nervous.

énerver (s') *vpr* to get worked up.

enfance *f* childhood.

enfant *m* child *(pl* children); **e. en bas âge** infant; **e. de chœur** altar boy.

enfantin, -ine *adj (voix, joie)* child-like; *(simple)* easy.

enfer *m* hell; **d'e.** *(bruit etc)* infernal; **à un train d'e.** at breakneck speed.

enfermer *vt* to lock up; **s'e. dans** *(chambre etc)* to lock oneself (up) in.

enfiler *vt (aiguille)* to thread; *(perles etc)* to string; *(vêtement)* to pull on.

enfin *adv (à la fin)* finally, at last; *(en dernier lieu)* lastly; **e. bref** in a word; **(mais) e.!** for heaven's sake!

enflammer *vt* to set fire to; *(allumette)* to light; *(irriter)* to inflame *(throat etc)*.

enflammer (s') *vpr* to catch on fire.

enfler *vti* to swell.

enflure *f* swelling.

enfoncer 1 *vt (clou)* to knock in, to hammer in; *(porte, voiture)* to smash in; **e. dans qch** *(couteau, mains etc)* to plunge into sth. **2** *vi,* **s'enfoncer** *vpr (s'enliser)* to sink (**dans** into).

enfouir *vt* to bury.

enfreindre* *vt* to infringe.

enfuir* (s') *vpr* to run away ou off (**de** from).

enfumer *vt (pièce)* to fill with smoke.

engagé, -ée *adj (écrivain)* committed.

engagement *m (promesse)* commitment; *(dans une compétition)* entry; **prendre l'e. de** to undertake to.

engager *vt (discussion, combat)* to start; **e. qn** *(embaucher)* to hire sb.

engager (s') *vpr (dans l'armée)* to enlist; *(sportif)* to enter (**pour** for); *(action, jeu)* to start; **s'e. à faire** to undertake to.

engelure *f* chilblain.

engin *m* machine; **e. spatial** spaceship.

englober *vt* to include.

engloutir *vt (nourriture)* to wolf down; *(faire disparaître)* to swallow up.

engouffrer (s') *vpr* s'e. dans to sweep *ou* rush into.

engourdir (s') *vpr* to go numb.

engrais *m* fertilizer; *(naturel)* manure.

engraisser 1 *vt (animal)* to fatten (up). **2** *vi* to get fat.

engrenage *m* gears.

engueuler *vt* **e. qn** *Fam* to give sb hell.

énigme *f* riddle.

enivrer (s') *vpr* to get drunk (**de** on).

enjambée *f* stride.

enjamber *vt* to step over; *(pont etc)* to span *(river etc).*

enjeu, -x *m (mise)* stake; *(de pari, de guerre)* stakes.

enjoliveur *m* hubcap.

enjoué, -ée *adj* playful.

enlaidir 1 *vt* to make ugly. **2** *vi* to grow ugly.

enlèvement *m (d'enfant)* kidnapping.

enlever *vt* to take away (**à qn** from sb); *(vêtement)* to take off; *(tache)* to take out; *(enfant etc)* to kidnap.

enlever (s') *vpr (tache)* to come out.

enliser (s') *vpr* to get bogged down (**dans** in).

enneigé, -ée *adj (montagne, route)* snow-covered; *(bloqué par la neige)* snowed in.

enneigement *m* **bulletin d'e.** snow report.

ennemi, -ie 1 *mf* enemy. **2** *adj* **pays/soldat e.** enemy country/soldier.

ennui *m* boredom; **un e.** *(tracas)* trouble; **l'e., c'est que** the annoying thing is that.

ennuyé, -ée *adj (air)* bored; **je suis e.** that bothers me.

ennuyer *vt (agacer, préoccuper)* to bother; *(fatiguer)* to bore.

ennuyer (s') *vpr* to get bored.

ennuyeux, -euse *adj* boring; *(contrariant)* annoying.

énoncer *vt* to state.

énorme *adj* enormous, huge.

énormément *adv* enormously; **e. de** an enormous amount of.

énormité *f (d'une demande, d'un crime, d'une somme)* enormity; *(faute)* glaring mistake.

enquête *f (de police)* investigation; *(judiciaire)* inquiry; *(sondage)* survey.

enquêter *vi* to investigate; **e. sur** to investigate.

enquêteur, -euse *mf* investigator.

enragé, -ée *adj (chien)* rabid; *(furieux)* furious.

enregistrement *m (des bagages)* check-in; *(sur bande etc)* recording.

enregistrer 1 vt (par écrit, sur bande etc) to record; **(faire) e.** (bagages) to check. **2** vi to record; **ça enregistre** it's recording.

enrhumer (s') vpr to catch a cold.

enrichir (s') vpr to get rich.

enrobé, -ée adj **e. de chocolat** chocolate-covered.

enroué, -ée adj hoarse.

enrouler vt to wind; (tapis) to roll up.

enrouler (s') vpr **s'e. dans** (couvertures) to wrap oneself up in.

ensanglanté, -ée adj blood-stained.

enseignant, -ante mf teacher.

enseigne f sign; **e. lumineuse** neon sign.

enseignement m education; (action, métier) teaching.

enseigner 1 vt to teach; **e. qch à qn** to teach sb sth. **2** vi to teach.

ensemble 1 adv together. **2** m (d'objets) set; (vêtement féminin) outfit; **l'e. du personnel** the whole staff; **l'e. des enseignants** all of the teachers; **dans l'e.** on the whole; **d'e.** (vue etc) general.

ensevelir vt to bury.

ensoleillé, -ée adj sunny.

ensuite adv (puis) next; (plus tard) afterwards.

entaille f (fente) notch; (blessure) gash.

entailler vt (bois) to notch; (peau) to gash.

entamer vt (pain, peau etc) to cut (into); (bouteille etc) to start (on).

entasser vt, **s'entasser** vpr (objets) to pile up; **(s')e. dans** (passagers etc) to crowd ou pile into.

entendre vt to hear; **e. parler de** to hear of; **e. dire que** to hear (it said) that.

entendre (s') vpr (être d'accord) to agree (sur on); **s'e. (avec qn)** to get on (with sb).

entendu, -ue adj (convenu) agreed; **e.!** all right!; **bien e.** of course.

entente f (accord) agreement; **(bonne) e.** (amitié) good relationship.

enterrement m burial; (funérailles) funeral.

enterrer vt to bury.

entêté, -ée adj stubborn.

entêtement m stubbornness; (à faire qch) persistence.

entêter (s') vpr to persist (à faire in doing).

enthousiasme m enthusiasm.

enthousiasmer vt to fill with enthusiasm.

enthousiasmer (s') vpr **s'e. pour** to be ou get enthusiastic about.

enthousiaste adj enthusiastic.

entier, -ière 1 adj (total) whole; (intact) intact; **le pays tout e.** the whole country. **2** m **en e.** completely.

entièrement adv entirely.

entonnoir m (ustensile) funnel.

entorse f sprain.

entortiller vt **e. qch autour de qch** to wrap sth around sth.

entourage m circle of family and friends.

entourer vt to surround (de with); **entouré de** surrounded by.

entracte m (au théâtre) intermission.

entraide f mutual aid.

entraider (s') vpr to help each other.

entrain m **plein d'e.** lively.

entraînant, -ante adj (musique) lively.

entraînement m (sportif) training.

entraîner vt to carry away; (causer) to bring about; (emmener de force) to drag (sb) (away); (athlète etc) to train (à for).

entraîner (s') vpr (sportif) to train.

entraîneur m (d'athlète) coach.

entre prép between; **l'un d'e. vous** one of you.

entrebâillé, -ée *adj* slightly open.

entrebâiller *vt* to open slightly.

entrechoquer (s') *vpr* to chink.

entrecôte *f* (filleted) rib steak.

entrée *f* (*action*) entry; (*porte*) entrance; (*accès*) admission (**de** to); (*vestibule*) entrance hall; (*billet*) ticket (for admission); (*plat*) first course; (*en informatique*) input; **à son e.** as he *ou* she came in; **'e. interdite'** 'no entry'; **'e. libre'** 'admission free'.

entreposer *vt* to store.

entrepôt *m* warehouse.

entreprendre* *vt* to undertake (**de faire** to do).

entrepreneur *m* (*en bâtiment*) contractor.

entreprise *f* company, firm.

entrer *vi* (*aux être*) to go in; (*venir*) to come in; **e. dans** (*pièce*) to come *ou* go into; (*arbre etc*) to crash into; **faire/laisser e. qn** to show/let sb in.

entre-temps *adv* meanwhile.

entretenir* *vt* to maintain; **e. sa forme** to stay in shape.

entretenir (s') *vpr* **s'e. de** to talk about (**avec** with).

entretien *m* maintenance; (*dialogue*) conversation; (*entrevue*) interview.

entrevoir* *vt* (*rapidement*) to catch a glimpse of; (*pressentir*) to foresee.

entrevue *f* interview.

entrouvert, -erte *adj* half-open.

énumération *f* list(ing).

énumérer *vt* to list.

envahir *vt* to invade; (*herbe etc*) to overrun (*garden*).

envahisseur *m* invader.

enveloppe *f* (*pour lettre*) envelope; **e. timbrée à votre adresse** self-addressed stamped envelope.

envelopper *vt* to wrap (up) (**dans** in).

envers 1 *prép* toward(s), to. **2** *m* **à l'e.** (*chaussette*) inside out; (*pantalon*) back to front; (*la tête en bas*) upside down.

envie *f* (*jalousie*) envy; (*désir*) desire; **avoir e. de qch** to want sth; **j'ai e. de faire** I feel like doing.

envier *vt* to envy (**qch à qn** sb sth).

environ *adv* (*à peu près*) about.

environnant, -ante *adj* surrounding.

environnement *m* environment.

environner *vt* to surround.

environs *mpl* surroundings; **aux environs de** around.

envisager *vt* to consider (**de faire** doing).

envoi *m* sending; (*paquet*) package; **coup d'e.** *Sport* kick-off.

envoler (s') *vpr* (*oiseau*) to fly away; (*avion*) to take off; (*chapeau etc*) to blow away.

envoyé, -ée *mf* (*reporter*) correspondent.

envoyer* *vt* to send; (*lancer*) to throw.

épais, -aisse *adj* thick.

épaisseur *f* thickness.

épaissir *vti*, **s'épaissir** *vpr* to thicken.

épanoui, -ie *adj* in full bloom; (*visage*) beaming.

épanouir (s') *vpr* to blossom; (*visage*) to beam.

épargne *f* (*action, vertu*) saving; (*sommes*) savings.

épargner *vt* (*argent*) to save; (*ennemi etc*) to spare; **e. qch à qn** (*ennuis etc*) to spare sb sth.

éparpiller *vt*, **s'éparpiller** *vpr* to scatter.

épatant, -ante *adj* marvelous.

épaule *f* shoulder.

épauler *vt* (*fusil*) to raise (to one's shoulder); **é. qn** (*aider*) to back sb up.

épave *f* wreck.

épée *f* sword.

épeler *vt* (*mot*) to spell.

éperon *m* spur.

épi *m* (*de blé etc*) ear.

épice f spice.
épicé, -ée adj spicy.
épicer vt to spice.
épicerie f grocery store; (produits) groceries.
épicier, -ière mf grocer.
épidémie f epidemic.
épiler (s') vpr to remove unwanted hair; s'é. les jambes à la cire to wax one's legs.
épinards mpl spinach.
épine f (de plante) thorn.
épineux, -euse adj thorny.
épingle f pin; é. de nourrice safety pin; é. à linge clothes pin; é. à cheveux hairpin.
épisode m episode.
épithète f (adjectif) attribute.
éplucher vt (carotte, pomme etc) to peel.
épluchure f peeling.
éponge f sponge.
éponger vt to sponge up.
époque f (date) time; (historique) age.
épouse f wife.
épouser vt é. qn to marry sb.
épousseter vt to dust.
épouvantable adj terrifying; (mauvais) appalling.
épouvantail m scarecrow.
épouvante f terror; film d'é. horror movie.
épouvanter vt to terrify.
époux m husband.
épreuve f (examen) test; (sportive) event; (malheur) ordeal.
éprouvant, -ante adj (pénible) trying.
éprouver vt to test; (sentiment etc) to feel.
éprouvette f test tube; bébé-é. test-tube baby.
épuisant, -ante adj exhausting.
épuisé, -ée adj exhausted; (marchandise) out of stock.
épuiser vt to exhaust.
épuiser (s') vpr (réserves) to run

out; s'é. à faire to exhaust oneself doing.
équateur m equator.
équation f equation.
équerre f (pour tracer) square.
équilibre m balance; tenir ou mettre en é. to balance (sur on); perdre l'é. to lose one's balance.
équilibrer vt (budget) to balance.
équipage m crew.
équipe f team; (d'ouvriers) crew; é. de secours search party.
équipement m equipment; (de camping, ski) gear.
équiper vt to equip (de with).
équipier, -ière mf team member.
équitable adj fair.
équitation f (horseback) riding.
équivalent, -ente adj & m equivalent.
équivaloir* vi é. à qch to be equivalent to sth.
érafler vt to scrape, to scratch.
éraflure f scrape, scratch.
errer vi to wander.
erreur f mistake.
éruption f (de boutons) rash.
es voir être.
escabeau, -x m stepladder.
escadrille f (groupe d'avions) flight.
escalade f climbing.
escalader vt to climb.
escale f faire e. à (avion) to stop (over) at; (navire) to put in at.
escalier m stairs; e. roulant escalator.
escalope f escalope (thin slice of meat).
escargot m snail.
escarpé, -ée adj steep.
esclavage m slavery.
esclave mf slave.
escorte f escort.
escorter vt to escort.
escrime f fencing.
escrimeur, -euse mf fencer.
escroc m crook.
espace m space; e. vert garden, park.

espacer *vt* to space out.

espagnol, -ole 1 *adj* Spanish. **2** *mf* E. Spaniard. **3** *m* (*langue*) Spanish.

espèce *f* (*race*) species; (*genre*) kind, sort; **e. d'idiot!** you fool!

espèces *fpl* (*argent*) cash; **en e.** in cash.

espérance *f* hope.

espérer 1 *vt* to hope for; **e. que** to hope that; **e. faire** to hope to do. **2** *vi* to hope.

espiègle *adj* mischievous.

espion, -onne *mf* spy.

espionnage *m* spying.

espionner *vt* to spy on.

espoir *m* hope; **sans e.** (*cas etc*) hopeless.

esprit *m* spirit; (*intellect*) mind; (*humour*) wit; **venir à l'e. de qn** to cross sb's mind.

Esquimau, -de, -aux *mf* Eskimo.

esquiver *vt* to dodge.

essai *m* (*épreuve*) test; (*tentative*) try, attempt.

essaim *m* swarm (*of bees etc*).

essayage *m* (*de costume*) fitting.

essayer *vt* to try (**de faire** to do); (*vêtement*) to try on.

essence *f* gas.

essentiel, -ielle 1 *adj* essential. **2** *m* **l'e.** the main thing.

essentiellement *adv* essentially.

essieu, -x *m* axle.

essor *m* (*d'oiseau*) flight; (*de pays, d'entreprise*) rapid growth; **en plein e.** booming; **prendre son e.** to take off.

essorer *vt* (*dans une essoreuse*) to spin-dry; (*dans une machine à laver*) to spin.

essoufflé, -ée *adj* out of breath.

essuie-glace, *pl* **essuie-glaces** *m* windshield wiper.

essuie-mains *m inv* (hand) towel.

essuyer *vt* to wipe.

est¹ *voir* **être**.

est² *m & adj inv* east; **d'e.** (*vent*) east(erly); **de l'e.** eastern.

estime *f* regard.

estimer *vt* (*objet*) to value; (*juger*) to consider (**que** that); **e. qn** to have a high regard for sb.

estimer (s') *vpr* **s'e. heureux/etc** to consider oneself happy/etc.

estivant, -ante *mf* vacationer.

estomac *m* stomach.

estrade *f* platform.

estropier *vt* to cripple.

estuaire *m* estuary.

et *conj* and; **vingt et un** twenty-one.

étable *f* cowshed.

établi *m* (work)bench.

établir *vt* (*installer*) to set up; (*plan, liste*) to draw up.

établir (s') *vpr* (*habiter*) to settle.

établissement *m* establishment; **é. scolaire** school.

étage *m* (*d'immeuble*) floor; **à l'é.** upstairs; **au premier é.** on the second floor.

étagère *f* shelf.

étais, était *etc voir* **être**.

étalage *m* (*vitrine*) display window.

étaler *vt* to lay out; (*en vitrine*) to display; (*beurre etc*) to spread.

étanche *adj* watertight; (*montre*) waterproof.

étang *m* pond.

étant *voir* **être**.

étape *f* stage; (*lieu*) stop(over).

État *m* (*nation*) State; **homme d'É.** statesman.

état *m* (*condition*) state; **en bon é.** in good condition; **être en é. de faire** to be up to doing.

étau, -x *m* vise.

été¹ *pp of* **être**.

été² *m* summer; **en é.** in (the) summer.

éteindre* 1 *vt* (*feu etc*) to put out; (*lampe etc*) to turn *ou* switch off. **2** *vi* to switch off.

éteindre (s') *vpr* (*feu*) to go out.

éteint, -einte *adj* (*feu, bougie*) out; (*lampe*) off.

étendre vt (nappe) to spread (out); (linge) to hang out; **é. le bras**/etc to stretch out one's arm/etc.

étendre (s') vpr (personne) to stretch out; (plaine) to stretch; (feu) to spread.

étendu, -ue adj (forêt etc) extensive; (personne) stretched out.

étendue f (importance) extent; (surface) area.

éterniser (s') vpr (débat) to drag on endlessly; (visiteur) Fam to stay for ever.

éternité f eternity.

éternuement m sneeze.

éternuer vi to sneeze.

êtes voir **être**.

étinceler vi to sparkle.

étincelle f spark.

étiqueter vt to label.

étiquette f label.

étirer (s') vpr to stretch (oneself).

étoffe f material.

étoile f star; **à la belle é.** in the open.

étoilé, -ée adj (ciel) starry.

étonnant, -ante adj surprising.

étonnement m surprise.

étonner vt to surprise.

étonner (s') vpr to be surprised (de qch at sth; que (+ subjonctif) that).

étouffant, -ante adj (air) stifling.

étouffer 1 vt (tuer) to suffocate, to smother; (bruit) to muffle; (feu) to smother; **é. qn** (chaleur) to stifle sb. **2** vi on étouffe! it's stifling!

étouffer (s') vpr (en mangeant) to choke (sur, avec on).

étourderie f thoughtlessness; **une é.** a thoughtless blunder.

étourdi, -ie adj thoughtless.

étourdir vt to stun; (vertige) to make dizzy.

étourdissant, -ante adj (bruit) deafening.

étourdissement m (malaise) dizzy spell.

étrange adj strange, odd.

étranger, -ère 1 adj (d'un autre pays) foreign; (non familier) strange (à to). **2** mf foreigner; (inconnu) stranger; **à l'é.** abroad; **de l'é.** from abroad.

étrangler vt (tuer) to strangle.

étrangler (s') vpr to choke.

être* 1 vi to be; **il est tailleur** he's a tailor; **est-ce qu'elle vient?** is she coming?; **il vient, n'est-ce pas?** he's coming, isn't he?; **est-ce qu'il aime le thé?** does he like tea?; **nous sommes dix** there are ten of us; **nous sommes le dix** today is the tenth (of the month); **il a été à Paris** he has been to Paris. **2** v aux (avec venir, partir etc) to have; **elle est arrivée** she has arrived. **3** m ê. **humain** human being.

étrennes fpl New Year's gift.

étrier m stirrup.

étroit, -oite adj narrow; (vêtement) tight; **être à l'é.** to be cramped.

étroitement adv (surveiller etc) closely.

étude f study; (salle) study hall; **à l'é.** (projet) under consideration; **faire des études de** (médecine etc) to study.

étudiant, -ante mf & adj student.

étudier vti to study.

étui m (à lunettes etc) case.

eu, eue pp of **avoir**.

euh! int hem!, er!

euro m (monnaie) euro.

euro- préfixe Euro-.

européen, -enne 1 adj European. **2** mf E. European.

eux pron (sujet) they; (complément) them; (réfléchi, emphase) themselves.

eux-mêmes pron themselves.

évacuer vt to evacuate.

évadé, -ée mf escaped prisoner.

évader (s') vpr to escape (de from).

évaluer vt to estimate; (bien) to value.

Évangile m Gospel.

évanouir (s') vpr to faint, to pass out.

évanouissement m blackout.

évasion f escape (**de** from).

éveiller vt (susciter) to arouse.

événement m event.

éventail m fan; (choix) range.

éventrer vt (sac, oreiller) to rip open; (animal) to open up.

éventuel, -elle adj possible.

éventuellement adv possibly.

évêque m bishop.

évidemment adv obviously.

évident adj obvious (**que** that); (facile) Fam easy.

évier m (kitchen) sink.

éviter vt to avoid (**de faire** doing); **é. qch à qn** to spare sb sth.

évoluer vi (changer) to develop; (société, situation) to evolve; (se déplacer) to move around.

ex- préfixe ex-; **ex-mari** ex-husband.

exact, -e adj (précis) exact, accurate; (juste, vrai) correct.

exactement adv exactly.

exactitude f (expression précise) accuracy; (justesse) correctness.

ex æquo adv être classés **e.** to tie.

exagération f exaggeration.

exagéré, -ée adj excessive.

exagérer vti to exaggerate.

examen m examination; (bac etc) exam(ination).

examinateur, -trice mf examiner.

examiner vt to examine.

exaspérer vt (personne) to exasperate.

excédent m **e. de bagages** excess baggage.

excellent, -ente adj excellent.

excepté prép except.

exception f exception; **à l'e. de** except (for).

exceptionnel, -elle adj exceptional.

exceptionnellement adv exceptionally.

excès m excess; **e. de vitesse** speeding.

excessif, -ive adj excessive.

excitant, -ante adj Fam exciting.

excitation f excitement.

excité, -ée adj excited.

exciter vt to excite.

exclamation f exclamation.

exclamer (s') vpr to exclaim.

exclure* vt to exclude (**de** from).

excursion f trip, outing; (à pied) hike.

excuse f (prétexte) excuse; **excuses** (regrets) apology; **faire des excuses** to apologize (**à** to).

excuser vt to excuse (**qn d'avoir fait, qn de faire** sb for doing).

excuser (s') vpr to apologize (**de** for; **auprès de** to).

exécuter vt (travail etc) to carry out; (jouer) to perform; **e. qn** (tuer) to execute sb.

exécution f (mise à mort) execution.

exemplaire m copy.

exemple m example; **par e.** for example; **donner l'e.** to set an example (**à** to).

exercer vt (muscles, droits) to exercise.

exercer (s') vpr to practice (**à qch** sth; **à faire** doing).

exercice m exercise; **faire de l'e.** to (take) exercise.

exigeant, -eante adj demanding.

exigence f demand.

exiger vt to demand (**de** from; **que** (+ subjonctif) that).

exiler (s') vpr to go into exile.

existence f existence.

exister vi to exist; **il existe** there is, pl there are.

exorbitant, -ante adj exorbitant.

expédier vt (envoyer) to send off.

expéditeur, -trice mf sender.

expédition f (envoi) dispatch; (voyage) expedition.

expérience *f (connaissance)* experience; *(scientifique)* experiment; **faire l'e. de qch** to experience sth.

expérimenté, -ée *adj* experienced.

expérimenter *vt (remède, vaccin)* to try out (**sur** on).

expert *m* expert (**en** on, in).

expirer *vi* to breathe out; *(mourir)* to pass away.

explicatif, -ive *adj* explanatory.

explication *f* explanation; *(mise au point)* discussion.

expliquer *vt* to explain (**à** to; **que** that).

expliquer (s') *vpr (discuter)* to talk things over (**avec** with).

exploit *m* feat, exploit.

exploitation *f (agricole)* farm.

exploiter *vt (champs)* to farm; *(profiter de)* to exploit.

explorateur, -trice *mf* explorer.

exploration *f* exploration.

explorer *vt* to explore.

exploser *vi* to explode.

explosif *m* explosive.

explosion *f* explosion.

exportateur, -trice 1 *mf* exporter. **2** *adj* exporting.

exportation *f* export.

exporter *vt* to export (**vers** to; **de** from).

exposé, -ée *adj* **e. au sud/etc** facing south/etc.

exposer *vt* to expose (**à** to); *(tableau etc)* to exhibit; *(vie)* to risk.

exposer (s') *vpr* **s'e. à** to expose oneself.

exposition *f (salon)* exhibition.

exprès *adv* on purpose; *(spécialement)* specially.

express *m inv (train)* express; *(café)* espresso.

expression *f (phrase, mine)* expression.

exprimer *vt* to express.

exprimer (s') *vpr* to express oneself.

expulser *vt* to expel (**de** from); *(joueur)* to send off.

exquis, -ise *adj (nourriture)* delicious.

exténué, -ée *adj* exhausted.

extérieur, -e 1 *adj* outside; *(surface)* outer, external; *(signe)* outward. **2** *m* outside; **à l'e. (de)** outside.

extérioriser *vt* to express.

externe *mf (élève)* day student.

extincteur *m* fire extinguisher.

extra- *préfixe* extra-.

extraire* *vt* to extract (**de** from).

extrait *m* extract.

extraordinaire *adj* extraordinary.

extrême *adj & m* extreme.

extrêmement *adv* extremely.

extrémité *f* end.

F

fable *f* fable.

fabricant, -ante *mf* manufacturer.

fabrication *f* manufacture.

fabriquer *vt* to make; *(en usine)* to manufacture; **qu'est-ce qu'il fabrique?** *Fam* what's he up to?

fabuleux, -euse *adj* fabulous.

fac *f* university.

façade *f (de bâtiment)* front.

face *f* face; *(de cube etc)* side; **en f.** opposite; **en f. de** opposite, facing; *(en présence de)* in front of, face to face with; **f. à un problème** faced with a problem; **regarder qn en f.** to look sb in the face; **f. à f.** face to face.

fâché, -ée *adj (air)* angry; *(amis)* on bad terms.

fâcher *vt* to anger.

fâcher (se) *vpr* to get angry

(contre with); **se f. avec qn** to fall
out with sb.
facile *adj* easy; **c'est f. à faire** it's
easy to do; **il nous est f. de** it's easy
for us to.
facilement *adv* easily.
facilité *f* easiness; *(à faire qch)*
ease.
faciliter *vt* to make easier.
façon *f* way; **la f. dont elle parle** the
way (in which) she talks; **f. (d'agir)**
behavior; **façons** *(manières)* manners; **de toute f.** anyway; **à ma f.**
my way.
facteur *m* mailman, postal carrier.
factrice *f* postal carrier.
facture *f* bill, invoice.
facturer *vt* to bill, to invoice.
facultatif, -ive *adj* optional.
faculté *f* university; **à la f.** at the
university, at school.
fade *adj (nourriture)* bland.
faible 1 *adj* weak; *(bruit)* faint;
(vent) slight; **f. en anglais/etc** poor
at English/etc. **2** *m* **avoir un f. pour**
to have a soft spot for.
faiblement *adv* weakly; *(légèrement)* slightly; *(éclairer)* faintly.
faiblesse *f* weakness; faintness;
slightness.
faiblir *vi (forces)* to weaken.
faïence *f (matière)* earthenware;
faïences *(objets)* earthenware.
faillir* *vi* **il a failli tomber** he almost fell.
faillite *f* **faire f.** to go bankrupt.
faim *f* hunger; **avoir f.** to be hungry;
donner f. à qn to make sb hungry.
fainéant, -ante *mf* lazy bones.
faire* 1 *vt (bruit, faute, gâteau etc)*
to make; *(devoir, ménage etc)* to do;
(rêve) to have; *(sourire)* to give;
(promenade, chute) to take; **ça fait
dix mètres/euros** *(mesure, prix)* it's
ou that's ten metres/euros; **qu'a-t-il
fait (de)?** what's he done (with)?;
que f.? what should I/you/we/etc.
do?; **f. du tennis/etc** to play tennis/
etc; **f. l'idiot** to play the fool; **ça ne**

fait rien that doesn't matter. **2** *vi
(agir)* to do; *(paraître)* to look; **il fait
vieux** he looks old; **elle ferait bien
de partir** she'd do well to leave; **il
fait beau/froid/etc** it's sunny/
cold/etc, **ça fait deux ans que je
ne l'ai pas vu** I haven't seen him for
two years; **ça fait un an que je suis
là** I've been here for a year. **3** *v aux
(+ infinitif)* **f. construire une maison** to have *ou* get a house built; **f.
crier/etc qn** to make sb shout/etc, **se
f. obéir/etc** to be obeyed/etc, **se
f. tuer/etc** to get *ou* be killed/etc.
faire (se) *vpr* **se f. des amis** to
make friends; **se f. vieux/etc** to get
old/etc; **il se fait tard** it's getting
late; **se f. à** to get used to; **ne t'en
fais pas!** don't worry!
faire-part *m inv* announcement.
fais, fait, faites *voir* **faire**.
faisable *adj* feasible.
faisan *m* pheasant.
faisceau, -x *m (rayons)* beam.
fait, faite *(pp of* **faire)** **1** *adj (fromage)* ripe; *(yeux)* made up; **tout f.**
ready made; **c'est bien f.!** it serves
you right! **2** *m* event; *(réalité)* fact;
prendre sur le f. to catch red-
handed; **f. divers** news item; **au f.**
by the way; **en f.** in fact.
falaise *f* cliff.
falloir* *vi* **il faut qch/qn** I/you/we/
etc need sth/sb; **il lui faut un stylo**
he *ou* she needs a pen; **il faut partir**
I/you/we/etc have to go; **il faut que
je parte** I have to go; **il faudrait
qu'elle reste** she ought to stay; **il
faut un jour** it takes a day (**pour
faire** to do).
fameux, -euse *adj* famous; *(excellent)* first-class.
familial, -e, -aux *adj (atmosphère, ennuis)* family; *(entreprise)*
family-run.
familiariser (se) *vpr* to familia-
rize oneself (**avec** with).
familiarité *f* familiarity (**avec**
with).

familier, -ière adj familiar (à to);
f. avec qn (over)familiar with sb;
animal f. pet.

familièrement adv (parler) in-
formally.

famille f family; **en f.** with one's
family.

fan m fan.

fana mf être **f. de** to be crazy about.

fané, -ée adj faded.

faner (se) vpr to fade.

fanfare f (orchestre) brass band.

fantaisie f (caprice) whim; **(de) f.**
(bouton etc) novelty.

fantastique adj fantastic.

fantôme m ghost.

faon m fawn.

farce¹ f practical joke.

farce² f (viande) stuffing.

farceur, -euse mf practical joker.

farcir vt to stuff.

fardeau, -x m burden.

farine f flour.

farouche adj (animal) easily
scared; (violent) fierce.

fascination f fascination.

fasciner vt to fascinate.

fasse(s), fassent etc voir **faire**.

fatal, -e, -als adj fatal; (inévitable)
inevitable.

fatalement adv inevitably.

fatigant, -ante adj tiring; (ennuyeux) tiresome.

fatigue f tiredness.

fatigué, -ée adj tired (**de** of).

fatiguer vt to tire.

fatiguer (se) vpr to get tired (**de**
of).

fauché, -ée adj Fam (flat) broke.

faucher vt (herbe) to mow; (blé) to
reap.

faucon m hawk.

faufiler (se) vpr to edge one's way
(**dans** through, into).

fausse voir **faux**.

fausser vt (réalité, résultat) to
distort.

faut voir **falloir**.

faute f mistake; (responsabilité)

fault; (péché) sin; **c'est ta f.** it's your
fault.

fauteuil m armchair; **f. roulant**
wheelchair.

fautif, -ive adj (personne) at fault;
(erroné) faulty.

fauve m wild animal, big cat.

faux, fausse 1 adj false; (pas exact) wrong; (monnaie) forged. **2**
adv (chanter) out of tune.

faux f scythe.

faux-filet m sirloin.

faveur f **en f. de** in aid ou favor
of.

favorable adj favorable (**à** to).

favori, -ite adj & mf favorite.

favoriser vt to favor.

fax m (appareil, message) fax.

faxer vt (message) to fax.

fée f fairy.

féerique adj fairy(-like).

feinte f (ruse) ruse.

fêler vt, **se fêler** vpr to crack.

félicitations fpl congratulations
(**pour** on).

féliciter vt to congratulate (**qn de**
ou **sur** sb on).

fêlure f crack.

femelle adj & f (animal) female.

féminin, -ine adj (prénom etc) female; (trait, pronom etc) feminine;
(mode, revue etc) women's.

femme f woman (pl women);
(épouse) wife; **f. médecin** woman
doctor; **f. de ménage** cleaning
woman.

fendre vt (bois etc) to split.

fendre (se) vpr to crack.

fenêtre f window.

fente f slit.

fer m iron; **barre de f.** iron bar; **f.
forgé** wrought iron; **f. à cheval** hor-
seshoe; **f. à repasser** iron (for
clothes); **santé de f.** cast-iron
constitution.

fera, ferai(t) etc voir **faire**.

fer-blanc, pl **fers-blancs** m tin.

férié adj jour **f.** holiday.

ferme¹ f farm.

ferme² 1 adj firm; (pas, voix) steady. **2** adv (travailler, boire) hard.

fermé, -ée adj (porte etc) closed, shut; (route etc) closed; (gaz etc) off.

fermement adv firmly.

fermer 1 vt to close, to shut; (gaz etc) to turn ou switch off; (vêtement) to do up; **f. (à clef)** to lock. **2** vi, **se fermer** vpr to close, to shut.

fermeté f firmness.

fermeture f closing; (heure) closing time; **f. éclair®** zipper.

fermier, -ière mf farmer.

féroce adj fierce, savage.

feront voir faire.

ferraille f scrap metal, old iron; **mettre à la f.** to scrap.

ferrée adj f **voie f.** railroad; (rails) track.

ferroviaire adj **compagnie f.** railroad company.

fertile adj fertile.

fesse f buttock; **les fesses** one's behind.

fessée f spanking.

festin m (banquet) feast.

festival, pl **-als** m festival.

fête f (civile) holiday; (religieuse) feast (day); (entre amis) party; **f. foraine** fair, carnival; **f. de famille** family celebration; **c'est sa f.** it's his ou her saint's ou feast day; **f. des Mères** Mother's Day; **jour de f.** holiday; **faire la f.** to have a good time.

fêter vt to celebrate.

feu, -x m fire; (de réchaud) burner; **feux de détresse** (hazard) warning flashers; **f. rouge** red light; (objet) traffic lights; **mettre le f. à** to set fire to; **en f.** on fire; **faire du f.** to light ou make a fire; **avez-vous du f.?** have you got a light?; **à f. doux** on low heat; **au f.!** fire!; **coup de f.** (bruit) gunshot.

feuillage m leaves.

feuille f leaf; (de papier etc) sheet; **f. d'impôt** tax form; **f. de paye** pay slip.

feuilleter vt to flip through; **pâte feuilletée** puff pastry ou paste.

feuilleton m serial.

feutre m crayon **f.** felt-tip (pen).

février m February.

fiabilité f reliability.

fiable adj reliable.

fiançailles fpl engagement.

fiancé m fiancé.

fiancée f fiancée.

fiancer (se) vpr to become engaged (**avec** to).

ficeler vt to tie up.

ficelle f string.

fiche f (carte) index card; (papier) form.

fiche(r) vt (pp fichu) Fam **f. le camp** to shove off; **fiche-moi la paix!** leave me alone!

fiche(r) (se) vpr se **f. de qn** to make fun of sb; **je m'en fiche!** I don't give a damn!

fichier m card index.

fichu, -ue adj c'est **f.** (abîmé) Fam it's had it.

fidèle adj faithful (**à** to); (client) regular.

fidélité f fidelity, faithfulness.

fier (se) vpr se **f. à** to trust.

fier, fière adj proud (**de** of).

fièrement adv proudly.

fierté f pride.

fièvre f fever; **avoir de la f.** to have a temperature ou a fever.

fiévreux, -euse adj feverish.

figer vti, **se figer** vpr to congeal.

figue f fig.

figurant, -ante mf (de film) extra.

figure f (géométrique) figure.

figurer vi to appear.

figurer (se) vpr to imagine.

fil¹ m thread; **f. dentaire** dental floss.

fil² m (métallique) wire; **f. de fer** wire; **passer un coup de f. à qn** to call sb (up).

file f line; (couloir) lane; **f. d'attente** line; **en f. (indienne)** in single file.

filer 1 vt f. qn (suivre) to shadow sb. **2** vi (partir) to rush off; (aller vite) to speed along.

filet m (à bagages) rack; (d'eau) trickle; (de poisson) fillet; **f. (à provisions)** string bag.

filiale f subsidiary (company).

filière f (voie obligée) channels; (domaine d'études) field of study; (organisation clandestine) network; **suivre la f. normale** to go through the official channels.

fille f girl; (parenté) daughter; **petite f.** (little ou young) girl; **jeune f.** girl, young lady.

fillette f little girl.

filleul m godson.

filleule f goddaughter.

film m movie, film; (pellicule) film; **f. plastique** plastic wrap.

filmer vt to film.

fils m son.

filtre m filter; (à bout) f. (cigarette) (filter-)tipped; **(bout) f.** filter tip.

filtrer vt to filter.

fin f end; **mettre f. à** to put an end to; **prendre f.** to come to an end; **sans f.** endless; **à la f.** in the end; **f. mai** at the end of May.

fin, fine 1 adj (pointe etc) fine; (peu épais) thin; (esprit, oreille) sharp. **2** adv (couper etc) finely.

final, -e, -aux ou **-als** adj final.

finale f final.

finalement adv finally.

finance f finance.

financement m financing.

financer vt to finance.

financier, -ière adj financial.

finir vt to finish; **f. de faire** to finish doing; (cesser) to stop doing; **f. par faire** to end up doing; **c'est fini** it's over.

finlandais, -aise 1 adj Finnish. **2** mf **F.** Finn. **finnois** m (langue) finnish.

fisc m = Internal Revenue.

fissure f crack.

fissurer (se) vpr to crack.

fixe adj fixed; **idée f.** obsession; **regard f.** stare.

fixement adv **regarder f.** to stare at.

fixer vt (attacher) to fix (à to); (date etc) to fix; **f. (du regard)** to stare at; **être fixé** (décidé) to be decided.

flacon m (small) bottle.

flair m (d'un chien etc) (sense of) smell; (intuition) insight.

flairer vt to smell.

flamand, -ande 1 adj Flemish. **2** m (langue) Flemish.

flamber vi to burn.

flamme f flame; **en flammes** on fire.

flan m (dessert) custard tart, baked custard.

flanc m side.

flâner vi to stroll.

flaque f puddle.

flash, pl **flashes** m (de photographie) flash(light); (dispositif) flash(gun); (d'informations) (news)-flash.

flatter vt to flatter.

flatterie f flattery.

fléau, -x m (catastrophe) scourge.

flèche f arrow; (d'église) spire; **monter en f.** (prix) to shoot up.

flécher vt to mark (with arrows).

fléchette f dart; **fléchettes** (jeu) darts.

fléchir 1 vt (membre) to flex. **2** vi (poutre) to sag.

flétrir vt, **se flétrir** vpr to wither.

fleur f flower; (d'arbre) blossom; **en fleur(s)** (arbre) flowered, flowery; **à fleurs** (tissu) flowered, flowery.

fleuri, -ie adj in bloom; (tissu) flowered, flowery.

fleurir vi to flower; (arbre) to blossom.

fleuriste mf florist.

fleuve m river.

flexible adj pliable.

flic m Fam cop.

flipper m (jeu) pinball; (appareil) pinball machine.

flocon *m (de neige)* flake.

flot *m (de souvenirs etc)* flood; **à f.** afloat; **les flots** the waves.

flotte *f (de bateaux)* fleet; *(pluie)* Fam rain; *(eau)* Fam water.

flotter *vi* to float; *(drapeau)* to fly.

flotteur *m Pêche* float.

flou, -e *adj* fuzzy, blurred.

fluide *adj & m* fluid.

fluo *adj inv (couleur etc)* luminous, fluorescent.

fluorescent, -ente *adj* fluorescent.

flûte 1 *f* flute; *(verre)* champagne glass. **2** *int* heck!

foi *f* faith; **être de bonne/mauvaise f.** to be/not to be (completely) sincere.

foie *m* liver.

foin *m* hay.

foire *f* fair.

fois *f* time; **une f.** once; **deux f.** twice; **chaque f. que** whenever; **une f. qu'il sera arrivé** once he has arrived; **à la f.** at the same time; **des f.** sometimes; **une f. pour toutes** once and for all.

fol *voir* **fou.**

folie *f* madness.

folklore *m* folklore.

folklorique *adj* **musique f.** folk music.

folle *voir* **fou.**

foncé, -ée *adj (couleur)* dark.

foncer *vi (aller vite)* to tear along; **f. sur qn** to charge at sb.

fonction *f* function; **la f. publique** public *ou* civil service.

fonctionnaire *mf* civil servant.

fonctionnement *m* working.

fonctionner *vi (machine etc)* to work; **faire f.** to operate.

fond *m (de boîte, jardin etc)* bottom; *(de salle etc)* back; *(arrière-plan)* background; **au f. de** at the bottom of; at the back of; **f. de teint** foundation (makeup); **à f. (connaître etc)** thoroughly.

fonder *vt (ville etc)* to found.

fondre 1 *vt* to melt; *(métal)* to melt down; **faire f.** *(sucre etc)* to dissolve. **2** *vi* to melt; *(sucre etc)* to dissolve; **f. en larmes** to burst into tears.

fonds *mpl (argent)* funds.

font *voir* **faire.**

fontaine *f* fountain.

fonte *f (des neiges)* melting; *(fer)* cast iron.

football *m* soccer; **f. américain** football.

footballer, -euse *mf* soccer player.

footing *m* jogging.

force *f* force; *(physique, morale)* strength; **ses forces** one's strength; **de f.** by force; **à f. de lire/etc** through reading/etc, after much reading/etc.

forcément *adv* obviously; **pas f.** not necessarily.

forcer *vt (porte etc)* to force; **f. qn à faire** to force sb to do.

forcer (se) *vpr* to force oneself (**à faire** to do).

forêt *f* forest.

forfait *m* **déclarer f.** to withdraw from the game.

formalité *f* formality.

format *m* size.

formation *f* education, training.

forme *f (contour)* shape, form; **en f. de poire/etc** pear/etc-shaped; **en (pleine) f.** in good shape *ou* form.

formel, -elle *adj (absolu)* formal.

former *vt* to form; *(apprenti etc)* to train.

former (se) *vpr (apparaître)* to form.

formidable *adj* terrific, tremendous.

formulaire *m (feuille)* form.

formule *f* formula; *(phrase)* (set) expression; **f. de politesse** polite form of address.

fort, forte 1 *adj* strong; *(pluie, mer)* heavy; *(voix, radio)* loud; *(fièvre)* high; *(élève)* bright; **f. en**

(maths etc) good at; **c'est plus f. qu'elle** she can't help it. **2** *adv (frapper, pleuvoir)* hard; *(parler)* loud(ly); *(serrer)* tight; **sentir f.** to have a strong smell.

fort *m* fort.

forteresse *f* fortress.

fortifiant *m* tonic.

fortune *f* fortune; **faire f.** to make one's fortune.

fosse *f (trou)* pit; *(tombe)* grave.

fossé *m* ditch.

fou *(or* **fol** *before vowel or mute h)*, **folle 1** *adj* crazy; *(succès, temps)* tremendous; **f. de** *(musique etc)* crazy about; **f. de joie** wildly happy. **2** *mf* madman, madwoman. **3** *m Echecs* bishop; **faire le f.** to play the fool.

foudre *f* la f. lightning.

foudroyant, -ante *adj (succès etc)* staggering.

foudroyer *vt (tuer)* to electrocute.

fouet *m* whip; *(de cuisine)* whisk.

fouetter *vt* to whip; *(œufs)* to whisk.

fougère *f* fern.

fouiller 1 *vt (personne, maison etc)* to search. **2** *vi* **f. dans** *(tiroir etc)* to search through.

fouillis *m* jumble, mess.

foulard *m* (head)scarf.

foule *f* crowd; **une f. de** *(objets etc)* a mass of.

fouler (se) *upr* **se f. la cheville/**etc to sprain one's ankle/*etc*.

foulure *f* sprain.

four *m* oven.

fourche *f (embranchement)* fork.

fourchette *f (pour manger)* fork.

fourgon *m* van; *(mortuaire)* hearse.

fourgonnette *f (small)* van.

fourmi *f* ant; **avoir des fourmis** to have pins and needles *(dans* in).

fourneau, -x *m (poêle)* stove.

fournée *f* batch.

fournir *vt* to supply; *(effort)* to make; **f. qch à qn** to supply sb with sth.

fournisseur *m (commerçant)* supplier; **f. d'accès** access provider.

fournitures *fpl* **f. de bureau** office supplies; **f. scolaires** school stationery.

fourré, -ée *adj (gant etc)* furlined.

fourrer *vt Fam (mettre)* to stick.

fourre-tout *m inv (sac)* carryall.

fourrière *f (lieu)* pound.

fourrure *f* fur.

foyer *m (maison, famille)* home; *(résidence de jeunes etc)* hostel.

fracas *m* din.

fracasser *vt,* **se fracasser** *upr* to smash.

fraction *f* fraction.

fracture *f* fracture; **se faire une f. au bras/**etc to fracture one's arm/*etc*.

fracturer *vt (porte etc)* to break (open).

fracturer (se) *upr* **se f. la jambe/** etc to fracture one's leg/*etc*.

fragile *adj* fragile.

fragment *m* fragment.

fraîcheur *f* freshness; *(du temps)* coolness.

frais, fraîche 1 *adj* fresh; *(temps)* cool; *(boisson)* cold; **servir f.** *(vin etc)* to serve chilled. **2** *m* **il fait f.** it's cool; **mettre au f.** to put in a cool place; *(au frigo)* to refrigerate.

frais *mpl* expenses; **à mes f.** at my (own) expense.

fraise *f* strawberry.

framboise *f* raspberry.

franc, franche *adj (personne etc)* frank; **coup f.** *Football* free kick; *Basket-ball* foul shot.

franc *m (monnaie)* franc.

français, -aise 1 *adj* French. **2** *mf* **F.** Frenchman, Frenchwoman; **les F.** the French. **3** *m (langue)* French.

franchement *adv* frankly; *(vraiment)* really.

franchir *vt (fossé)* to jump (over), to clear; *(frontière etc)* to cross; *(porte)* to go through; *(distance)* to cover.

franchise *f* frankness.

francophone *mf* French speaker.

frange *f (de cheveux)* bangs.

frappant, -ante *adj* striking.

frapper 1 *vt* to hit, to strike; **f. qn** *(surprendre)* to strike sb. **2** *vi (à la porte etc)* to knock (**à** at); **f. du pied** to stamp (one's foot).

fraternel, -elle *adj* fraternal, brotherly.

fraude *f (à un examen)* cheating; *(crime)* fraud; **passer qch en f.** to smuggle sth.

frauder *vi (à un examen)* to cheat (**à** on).

frayer (se) *vpr* **se f. un passage** to clear a way (**à travers, dans** through).

frayeur *f* fright.

fredonner *vt* to hum.

freezer *m* freezer.

frein *m* brake; **donner un coup de f.** to brake.

freinage *m* braking.

freiner *vi* to brake.

frêle *adj* frail.

frémir *vi (trembler)* to shudder (**de** with).

fréquemment *adv* frequently.

fréquent, -ente *adj* frequent.

fréquenter *vt (école, église)* to attend; **f. qn** to see sb.

fréquenter (se) *vpr* to see each other.

frère *m* brother.

friandises *fpl* candy.

fric *m (argent) Fam* money.

frictionner *vt* to rub (down).

frigidaire® *m* refrigerator.

frigo *m* fridge.

frileux, -euse *adj* sensitive to cold.

frire* *vti* to fry; **faire f.** to fry.

frisé, -ée *adj* curly.

friser *vti (cheveux)* to curl.

frisson *m (de froid)* shiver; *(de peur etc)* shudder.

frissonner *vi (de froid)* to shiver; *(de peur etc)* to shudder (**de** with).

frit, frite *(pp of frire) adj* fried.

frites *fpl* French fries.

friteuse *f (deep)* fryer.

froid, froide 1 *adj* cold. **2** *m* cold; **avoir/prendre f.** to be/catch cold; **il fait f.** it's cold.

froisser (se) *vpr (tissu)* to crumple; *(personne)* to take offense (**de** at).

frôler *vt (toucher)* to brush against.

fromage *m* cheese; **f. blanc** soft white cheese.

fromagerie *f (magasin)* cheese shop.

froncer *vt* **f. les sourcils** to frown.

front *m* forehead, brow; *(de bataille)* front.

frontière *f* border.

frotter *vti* to rub; *(pour nettoyer)* to scrub.

frousse *f Fam* fear; **avoir la f.** to be scared.

fruit *m* fruit; **des fruits, les fruits** fruit; **fruits de mer** seafood.

fruitier *adj* **arbre f.** fruit tree.

frustré, -ée *adj* frustrated.

fuel *m (fuel)* oil.

fugitif, -ive *mf* fugitive.

fugue *f* **faire une f.** *(enfant)* to run away.

fuir* *vi* to run away; *(gaz, robinet etc)* to leak.

fuite *f* flight (**de** from); *(de gaz etc)* leak; **en f.** on the run; **prendre la f.** to run away *ou* off.

fulgurant, -ante *adj (progrès)* spectacular; *(douleur)* shooting.

fumé, -ée *adj* smoked.

fumée *f* smoke; *(vapeur)* fumes.

fumer 1 *vi* to smoke; *(liquide brûlant)* to steam. **2** *vt* to smoke.

fumeur, -euse *mf* smoker; **compartiment fumeurs** smoking compartment.

fumier *m* manure.

funérailles *fpl* funeral.

fur et à mesure (au) *adv* as one goes along; **au f. que** as.

fureur *f* fury; **faire f.** *(mode etc)* to be all the rage.

furie f fury.

furieux, -euse adj furious (**contre** with, at); (vent) raging.

furoncle m boil.

fuseau, -x m (pantalon) ski pants; **f. horaire** time zone.

fusée f rocket.

fusible m fuze.

fusil m rifle, gun; (de chasse) shotgun; **coup de f.** gunshot.

fusillade f (tirs) gunfire.

fusiller vt (exécuter) to shoot; **f. qn du regard** to glare at sb.

fusion f (de métal) melting; (en physique) fusion; **métal en f.** molten metal. ▪ (de sociétés) merger.

fusionner vti (sociétés) to merge.

fût m (tonneau) barrel, cask.

futé, -ée adj cunning.

futile adj (personne) frivolous; (prétexte) trivial.

futur, -ure adj & m future.

G

gâcher vt to spoil; (argent etc) to waste.

gâchette f trigger.

gâchis m (gaspillage) waste.

gadget m gadget.

gaffe f Fam (maladresse) gaffe; **faire une g.** to put one's foot in it. ▪ **faire g.** to be careful.

gag m gag.

gage m (garantie) security; **mettre en g.** to pawn.

gagnant, -ante 1 adj winning. **2** mf winner.

gagner 1 vt to earn; (par le jeu) to win; (atteindre) to reach; **g. une heure/etc** to save an hour/etc. **2** vi to win.

gai, -e adj cheerful.

gaiement adv cheerfully.

gaieté f cheerfulness.

gain m un **g. de temps** a saving of time; **gains** (salaire) earnings; (au jeu) winnings.

gaine f (sous-vêtement) girdle; (étui) sheath.

gala m gala.

galant, -ante adj gallant.

galerie f gallery; (porte-bagages) roof rack.

galet m pebble.

galette f (gâteau) butter cookie; (crêpe) buckwheat pancake; **g. des Rois** = Twelfth Night cake.

gallois, -oise 1 adj Welsh. **2** mf **G.** Welshman, Welshwoman. **3** m (langue) Welsh.

galon m (ruban) braid; (de soldat) stripe.

galop m gallop; **aller au g.** to gallop.

galoper vi to gallop.

gambade f leap.

gambader vi to leap around.

gamelle f Fam pan; (de chien) bowl; (d'ouvrier) lunch box.

gamin, -ine mf (enfant) kid.

gamme f (de notes) scale; (série) range.

gangster m gangster.

gant m glove; **g. de toilette** face-cloth; **boîte à gants** glove compartment.

ganté, -ée adj (main) gloved; (personne) wearing gloves.

garage m garage.

garagiste mf garage mechanic.

garantie f guarantee; **garantie(s)** (d'assurance) cover.

garantir vt to guarantee (**contre** against); **g. à qn que** to assure ou guarantee sb that.

garçon m boy; (jeune homme) young man; (de café) waiter.

garde 1 m guard; **g. du corps** bodyguard. **2** f (d'enfants, de bagages etc) care (**de** of); **avoir la g. de** to be in charge of; **prendre g.** to pay attention (**à qch** to sth); **prendre g.**

de ne pas faire to be careful not to do; **mettre en g.** to warn (**contre** against); **mise en g.** warning; **de g.** on duty; **monter la g.** to stand guard; **sur ses gardes** on one's guard; **chien de g.** watchdog.

garde-chasse, pl **gardes-chasses** m gamekeeper.

garder vt to keep; (vêtement) to keep on; (surveiller) to watch (over); (enfant) to take care of; **g. la chambre** to stay in one's room.

garder (se) upr (aliment) to keep.

garderie f daycare center.

garde-robe, pl **garde-robes** f wardrobe.

gardien, -ienne mf (d'immeuble etc) caretaker, janitor; (de prison) (prison) guard; (de zoo, parc) keeper; (de musée) attendant, guard; **g. de but** goalkeeper.

gare f station; **g. routière** bus station.

garer vt to park; (au garage) to put in the garage.

garer (se) upr to park.

garnement m rascal.

garnir vt (équiper) to outfit, to equip (**de** with); (magasin) to stock; (orner) to trim (**de** with).

garniture f (de légumes) garnish.

gars m fellow, guy.

gas-oil m diesel (oil).

gaspillage m waste.

gaspiller vt to waste.

gâté, -ée adj (dent etc) bad.

gâteau, -x m cake; **g. de riz** rice pudding; **g. sec** cookie.

gâter vt to spoil.

gâter (se) upr (aliment, dent) to go bad; (temps, situation) to get worse.

gâteux, -euse adj senile.

gauche 1 adj left. **2** f la g. (côté) the left (side); **à g.** (tourner) to (the) left; (marcher etc) on the left; **de g.** (fenêtre etc) left-hand; **à g. de** on ou to the left of.

gaucher, -ère adj & mf left-handed (person).

gaufre f waffle.

gaufrette f wafer.

Gaulois mpl les G. the Gauls.

gaver (se) upr to stuff oneself (**de** with).

gaz m inv gas; **réchaud à g.** gas stove.

gaze f gauze.

gazeux, -euse adj (boisson, eau) fizzy, carbonated.

gazinière f gas stove.

gazole m diesel (oil).

gazon m grass, lawn.

géant, -ante adj & mf giant.

gel m frost.

gelée f frost; **g. blanche** ground frost. ▪ (de fruits) jelly.

geler vti to freeze; **il gèle** it's freezing.

gémir vi to groan.

gémissement m groan.

gênant, -ante adj (objet) cumbersome; (situation) awkward; (bruit) annoying.

gencive f gum.

gendarme m gendarme.

gendarmerie f (local) police headquarters.

gendre m son-in-law.

gêne f (trouble physique) discomfort; (confusion) embarrassment.

gêné, -ée adj (mal à l'aise) awkward.

gêner vt to bother; (troubler) to embarrass; (mouvement) to hamper; (circulation) to hold up; **g. qn** (par sa présence) to be in sb's way.

général, -e, -aux 1 adj general; **en g.** in general. **2** m (officier) general.

généralement adv generally.

généraliste mf (médecin) family doctor.

génération f generation.

généreusement adv generously.

généreux, -euse adj generous (**de** with).

générique m (de film) credits.

générosité f generosity.

génial, -e, -aux *adj* brilliant.

génie *m* genius.

genou, -x *m* knee; **à genoux** kneeling (down); **se mettre à genoux** to kneel (down); **sur ses genoux** on one's lap.

genre *m* (*espèce*) kind, sort; (*d'un nom*) gender.

gens *mpl* people; **jeunes g.** young people; (*hommes*) young men.

gentil, -ille *adj* nice; **g. avec qn** nice *ou* kind to sb; **sois g.** (*sage*) be good.

gentillesse *f* kindness.

gentiment *adv* kindly; (*sagement*) nicely.

géographie *f* geography.

géographique *adj* geographical.

géomètre *m* surveyor.

géométrie *f* geometry.

géométrique *adj* geometric(al).

gerbe *f* (*de blé*) sheaf; (*de fleurs*) bunch.

gercer *vti*, **se gercer** *vpr* to chap.

gerçure *f* **avoir des gerçures aux mains/lèvres** to have chapped hands/lips.

gérer *vt* to manage.

germe *m* (*microbe*) germ; (*de plante*) shoot.

germer *vi* (*graine*) to start to grow; (*pomme de terre*) to sprout.

geste *m* gesture; **ne pas faire un g.** not to make a move.

gesticuler *vi* to gesticulate.

gestion *f* (*action*) management.

gibier *m* (*animaux etc*) game.

giboulée *f* shower.

gicler *vi* (*liquide*) to spurt; **faire g.** to spurt.

gifle *f* slap (in the face).

gifler *vt* **g. qn** to slap sb.

gigantesque *adj* gigantic.

gigot *m* leg of mutton *ou* lamb.

gigoter *vi* to wriggle, to fidget.

gilet *m* cardigan; (*de costume*) vest; **g. de sauvetage** life jacket.

girafe *f* giraffe.

giratoire *adj* **sens g.** traffic circle.

girouette *f* weather vane.

gitan, -ane *mf* (Spanish) gipsy.

gîte *m* (*abri*) resting place; **g. rural** gîte, = self-catering holiday cottage or apartment.

givre *m* frost.

givré, -ée *adj* frost-covered.

glace *f* (*eau gelée*) ice; (*crème glacée*) ice cream; (*vitre*) window; (*miroir*) mirror.

glacé, -ée *adj* (*eau, main etc*) icy.

glacer *vt* to chill.

glacial, -e, -aux *adj* icy.

glacier *m* (*vendeur*) ice-cream seller.

glacière *f* icebox.

glaçon *m* ice cube.

gland *m* acorn.

glande *f* gland.

glissant, -ante *adj* slippery.

glisser 1 *vi* (*involontairement*) to slip; (*volontairement*) (*sur la glace etc*) to slide; (*coulisser*) (*tiroir etc*) to slide; **ça glisse** it's slippery. **2** *vt* to slip (*dans into*).

glissière *f* **porte à g.** sliding door.

global, -e, -aux *adj* total, global.

globe *m* globe.

gloire *f* glory.

glorieux, -euse *adj* glorious.

gloussement *m* cluck(ing).

glousser *vi* to cluck.

glouton, -onne 1 *adj* greedy. **2** *mf* glutton.

gluant, -ante *adj* sticky.

goal *m* goalkeeper.

gobelet *m* (*de plastique, papier*) cup.

godet *m* pot.

golf *m* golf; (*terrain*) golf course.

golfe *m* gulf, bay.

golfeur, -euse *mf* golfer.

gomme *f* (*à effacer*) eraser.

gommer *vt* (*effacer*) to rub out, to erase.

gond *m* hinge.

gonflable *adj* inflatable.

gonflé, -ée *adj* swollen.

gonfler 1 *vt* (*pneu*) to pump up; (*en*

soufflant) to blow up. **2** *vi, se gonfler* *vpr* to swell.

gonfleur *m* (air) pump.

gorge *f* throat; (*vallée*) gorge.

gorgée *f* mouthful (*of wine etc*); **petite g.** sip.

gorille *m* gorilla.

gosier *m* throat.

gosse *mf* (*enfant*) *Fam* kid.

gouache *f* gouache.

goudron *m* tar.

goudronner *vt* to tar.

goulot *m* (*de bouteille*) neck; **boire au g.** to drink from the bottle.

gourde *f* water bottle.

gourdin *m* club, cudgel.

gourmand, -ande 1 *adj* (over)-fond of food; **g. de** fond of. **2** *mf* hearty eater.

gourmandise *f* (over)fondness for food.

gourmet *m* gourmet.

gourmette *f* identity bracelet.

gousse *f* **g. d'ail** clove of garlic.

goût *m* taste; **de bon g.** in good taste; **sans g.** tasteless.

goûter 1 *vt* to taste; **g. à qch** to taste (a little of) sth. **2** *vi* to have an afternoon snack. **3** *m* afternoon snack.

goutte *f* drop.

gouttelette *f* droplet.

goutter *vi* to drip (**de** from).

gouttière *f* (*d'un toit*) gutter.

gouvernail *m* rudder; (*barre*) helm.

gouvernement *m* government.

gouverner *vti* to govern.

grâce 1 *f* grace; (*avantage*) favor. **2** *prép* **g. à** thanks to.

gracieux, -euse *adj* (*élégant*) graceful.

grade *m* rank.

gradin *m* tier (of seats).

graffiti *mpl* graffiti.

grain *m* grain; (*de café*) bean; (*de poussière*) speck; **g. de beauté** mole; (*sur le visage*) beauty spot.

graine *f* seed.

graisse *f* fat; (*pour machine*) grease.

graisser *vt* to grease.

graisseux, -euse *adj* (*vêtement etc*) greasy.

grammaire *f* grammar; **livre de g.** grammar (book).

gramme *m* gram.

grand, grande 1 *adj* big, large; (*en hauteur*) tall; (*chaleur, découverte etc*) great; (*bruit*) loud; (*différence*) big, great; **g. frère/etc** (*plus âgé*) big brother/*etc*; **il est g. temps** it's high time (**que** that). **2** *adv* **g. ouvert** wide-open; **ouvrir g.** to open wide.

grand-chose *pron* **pas g.** not much.

grandeur *f* (*importance*) greatness; (*dimension*) size; **g. nature** life-size.

grandiose *adj* imposing.

grandir *vi* to grow.

grand-mère, *pl* **grands-mères** *f* grandmother.

grand-père, *pl* **grands-pères** *m* grandfather.

grand-route, *pl* **grands-routes** *f* main road.

grands-parents *mpl* grandparents.

grange *f* barn.

graphique *m* graph.

grappe *f* cluster; **g. de raisin** bunch of grapes.

gras, grasse 1 *adj* fat; (*aliment*) fatty; (*graisseux*) greasy; **matières grasses** fat. **2** *m* (*de viande*) fat.

gratin *m* **macaronis/chou-fleur au g.** macaroni and/cauliflower with cheese.

gratitude *f* gratitude.

gratte-ciel *m inv* skyscraper.

gratter *vt* to scrape; (*avec les ongles etc*) to scratch; **ça me gratte** it itches.

gratter (se) *vpr* to scratch oneself.

gratuit, -uite *adj* free.

gratuitement *adv* free (of charge).

gravats *mpl* rubble.

grave *adj* serious; *(voix)* deep; **ce n'est pas g.!** it's not important!; **accent g.** grave accent.

gravement *adv* seriously.

graver *vt (sur métal etc)* to engrave; *(sur bois)* to carve.

graveur *m* engraver.

gravier *m* gravel.

gravillons *mpl* gravel.

gravir *vt* to climb *(with effort)*.

gravité *f (de situation etc)* seriousness.

gravure *f (image)* print.

grec, grecque 1 *adj* Greek. **2** *mf* **G.** Greek. **3** *m (langue)* Greek.

greffe *f (de peau, d'arbre)* graft; *(d'organe)* transplant.

greffer *vt (peau etc)* to graft (**à** on to); *(organe)* to transplant.

grêle *f* hail.

grêler *vi* to hail.

grêlon *m* hailstone.

grelot *m (small round)* bell *(that jingles)*.

grelotter *vi* to shiver (**de** with).

grenade *f (fruit)* pomegranate; *(projectile)* grenade.

grenadine *f* pomegranate syrup, grenadine.

grenier *m* attic.

grenouille *f* frog.

grève *f* strike; **g. de la faim** hunger strike; **se mettre en g.** to go (out) on strike.

gréviste *mf* striker.

gribouiller *vti* to scribble.

gribouillis *m* scribble.

grièvement *adv* **g. blessé** seriously injured.

griffe *f (ongle)* claw; *(de couturier)* (designer) label.

griffer *vt* to scratch.

griffonner *vt* to scribble.

grignoter *vti* to nibble.

gril *m* grill.

grillade *f (viande)* grill.

grillage *m* window screen, chicken wire.

grille *f (clôture)* railing.

grille-pain *m inv* toaster.

griller 1 *vt (viande)* to grill; *(pain)* to toast; **g. un feu rouge** to run a red light. **2** *vi* **mettre à g.** to put on the grill.

grillon *m (insecte)* cricket.

grimace *f* **faire des grimaces/la g.** to make faces/a face.

grimacer *vi* to make faces *ou* a face.

grimpant, -ante *adj* climbing.

grimper 1 *vi* to climb (**à qch** up sth). **2** *vt* to climb.

grincement *m* creaking; *(des dents)* grinding.

grincer *vi* to creak; **g. des dents** to grind one's teeth.

grincheux, -euse *adj* grumpy.

grippe *f* flu.

grippé, -ée *adj* **être g.** to have (the) flu.

gris, grise 1 *adj* gray. **2** *m* gray.

grisaille *f* grayness.

grisâtre *adj* grayish.

grisonnant, -ante *adj (cheveux, personne)* graying.

grognement *m* growl; *(d'un cochon)* grunt.

grogner *vi* to growl (**contre** at); *(cochon)* to grunt.

grognon, -onne *adj* grumpy.

grommeler *vti* to mutter.

grondement *m* growl; *(de tonnerre)* rumble.

gronder 1 *vi* to growl; *(tonnerre)* to rumble. **2** *vt* to scold, to tell off.

groom *m* bellboy.

gros, grosse 1 *adj* big; *(gras)* fat; *(épais)* thick; *(effort, progrès)* great; *(somme)* large; *(averse, rhume)* heavy; **g. mot** swear word. **2** *adv* **en g.** roughly; *(écrire)* in big letters; *(vendre)* wholesale.

groseille *f (white ou red)* currant.

grossesse *f* pregnancy.

grosseur *f* size; *(tumeur)* lump.

grossier, -ière adj rough; (personne) rude (**envers** to).
grossièrement adv roughly; (répondre) rudely.
grossièreté f roughness; (insolence) rudeness; (mot) rude word.
grossir vi to put on weight.
grossiste mf wholesaler.
grotte f cave, grotto.
grouiller vi to be swarming (**de** with).
groupe m group.
grouper vt, **se grouper** vpr to group (together).
grue f crane.
grumeau, -x m lump.
gruyère m gruyère (cheese).
guenilles fpl rags (and tatters).
guenon f female monkey.
guêpe f wasp.
guère adv (ne)...g. hardly; **il ne sort g.** he hardly goes out.
guéri, -ie adj cured, better.
guérir 1 vt to cure (**de** of). **2** vi to recover (**de** from).
guérison f recovery.
guerre f war; **en g.** at war (**avec** with).
guerrier, -ière mf warrior.
guet m **faire le g.** to be on the lookout.
guetter vt to be on the lookout for.
gueule f mouth.
gui m mistletoe.
guichet m ticket office; (de banque etc) window.
guichetier, -ière mf (de banque etc) teller; (à la gare) ticket agent.
guide m (personne, livre) guide.
guider vt to guide.
guidon m handlebar(s).
guignol m (spectacle) = Punch and Judy show.
guillemets mpl quotation marks; **entre g.** in quotation marks.
guirlande f garland.
guitare f guitar.
guitariste mf guitarist.
gymnase m gymnasium.

gymnastique f gymnastics.
gynécologue mf gynecologist.

H

habile adj skillful (**à qch** at sth; **à faire** at doing).
habileté f skill.
habillé, -ée adj dressed (**de** in; **en** as a).
habiller vt to dress (**de** in).
habiller (s') vpr to dress, to get dressed; (avec élégance) to dress up.
habitable adj (maison) fit to live in.
habitant, -ante mf (de pays etc) inhabitant; (de maison) occupant.
habitation f house.
habité, -ée adj (région) inhabited; (maison) occupied.
habiter 1 vi to live (**à, en, dans** in). **2** vt (maison etc) to live in.
habits mpl (vêtements) clothes.
habitude f habit; **avoir l'h. de qch/faire** to be used to sth/doing; **d'h.** usually; **comme d'h.** as usual.
habitué, -ée mf regular.
habituel, -elle adj usual.
habituellement adv usually.
habituer vt h. qn à to accustom sb to.
habituer (s') vpr to get accustomed (**à** to).
hache f ax.
hacher vt to chop (up); (avec un appareil) to grind.
hachis m ground meat.
haie f (clôture) hedge; **course de haies** (coureurs) hurdle race.
haine f hatred.
haïr vt to hate.
haleine f breath; **hors d'h.** out of breath.

haleter *vi* to pant.

hall *m* (*de gare*) main hall; (*de maison*) hall(way).

halle *f* (covered) market; **les halles** the central food market.

hallucinant, -ante *adj* extraordinary.

halte 1 *f* (*arrêt*) stop. **2** *int* stop!

haltères *mpl* weights.

hamac *m* hammock.

hameçon *m* (fish) hook.

hamster *m* hamster.

hanche *f* hip.

handicap *m* (*physique, mental*) disability, handicap.

handicapé, -ée 1 *adj* disabled, handicapped. **2** *mf* disabled person, handicapped person.

hangar *m* shed; (*pour avions*) hangar.

hanté, -ée *adj* haunted.

harassé, -ée *adj* (*fatigué*) exhausted.

harceler *vt* (*importuner*) to harass; (*insister auprès de*) to pester.

hardi, -ie *adj* bold.

hareng *m* herring.

hargneux, -euse *adj* bad-tempered.

haricot *m* (*blanc*) (haricot) bean; (*vert*) green bean.

harmonica *m* harmonica.

harmonie *f* harmony.

harmonieux, -euse *adj* harmonious.

harnais *m* harness.

harpe *f* harp.

hasard *m* **le h. chance; un h.** a coincidence; **par h.** by chance; **au h.** at random; **à tout h.** just in case.

hasardeux, -euse *adj* risky.

hâte *f* haste; **à la h.** in a hurry; **avoir h. de faire** to be eager to do.

hâter (se) *vpr* to hurry (**de faire** to do).

hausse *f* rise (**de** in); **en h.** rising.

haut, haute 1 *adj* high; (*de taille*) tall; **à haute voix** aloud; **h. de 5 mètres** 16 feet high *ou* tall. **2** *adv* (*voler*

etc) high (up); (*parler*) loud; **tout h.** (*lire etc*) aloud; **h. placé** (*personne*) in a high position. **3** *m* top; **en h. de** at the top of; **en h.** (*loger*) upstairs; (*regarder*) up; (*mettre*) on (the) top; **avoir 5 mètres de h.** to be 16 feet high *ou* tall.

hautain, -aine *adj* haughty.

hauteur *f* height.

haut-parleur *m* loudspeaker.

hayon *m* (*porte*) hatchback.

hé! *int* (*appel*) hey!

hebdomadaire *adj & m* weekly.

héberger *vt* to put up.

hectare *m* hectare (= 2,47 acres).

hein! *int Fam* eh!

hélas! *int* unfortunately.

hélice *f* propeller.

hélicoptère *m* helicopter.

helvétique *adj* Swiss.

hémorragie *f* hemorrhage; **h. cérébrale** stroke.

hennir *vi* to neigh.

hépatite *f* hepatitis.

herbe *f* grass; (*pour soigner etc*) herb; **mauvaise h.** weed; **fines herbes** herbs.

hérisser (se) *vpr* (*poils*) to bristle (up).

hérisson *m* hedgehog.

héritage *m* (*biens*) inheritance.

hériter *vti* to inherit (**qch de qn** sth from sb); **h. de qch** to inherit sth.

héritier *m* heir.

héritière *f* heiress.

hermétique *adj* airtight.

héroïne *f* (*femme*) heroine; (*drogue*) heroin.

héroïque *adj* heroic.

héros *m* hero.

hésitant, -ante *adj* hesitant; (*pas, voix*) unsteady.

hésitation *f* hesitation; **avec h.** hesitantly.

hésiter *vi* to hesitate (**sur** over, about; **à faire** to do).

hêtre *m* (*arbre, bois*) beech.

heu! *int* er!

heure *f* hour; (*moment*) time;

quelle h. est-il? what time is it?; **il est six heures** it's six (o'clock); **six heures moins cinq** five to six; **six heures cinq** five after *ou* past six; **à l'h.** *(arriver)* on time; **dix kilomètres à l'h.** six miles an hour; **de bonne h.** early; **tout à l'h.** *(futur)* later; *(passé)* a moment ago; **heures supplémentaires** overtime; **l'h. de pointe** *(circulation etc)* rush hour.

heureusement *adv (par chance)* fortunately (**pour** for).

heureux, -euse 1 *adj* happy; *(chanceux)* lucky; **h. de qch/de voir qn** happy *ou* glad about sth/to see sb. **2** *adv (vivre etc)* happily.

heurter *vt* to hit.

heurter (se) *vpr* **se h. à** to bump into, to hit.

hexagone *m* hexagon; **l'H.** France.

hibou, -x *m* owl.

hier *adv & m* yesterday; **h. soir** last night.

hi-fi *adj inv & f inv* hi-fi.

hilarant, -ante *adj* hilarious.

hippodrome *m* racetrack.

hippopotame *m* hippopotamus.

hirondelle *f* swallow.

hisser (se) *vpr* to heave oneself up.

histoire *f* history; *(récit, mensonge)* story; **des histoires** *(ennuis)* trouble; **sans histoires** *(voyage etc)* uneventful.

historique *adj* historical; *(lieu, événement)* historic.

hiver *m* winter.

HLM *m ou f abrév (habitation à loyer modéré)* = low-income housing.

hocher *vt* **h. la tête** *(pour dire oui)* to nod one's head; *(pour dire non)* to shake one's head.

hochet *m (jouet)* rattle.

hockey *m* hockey; **h. sur glace** ice hockey.

hold-up *m inv (attaque)* holdup.

hollandais, -aise 1 *adj* Dutch. **2**
mf **H.** Dutchman, Dutchwoman; **les H.** the Dutch. **3** *m (langue)* Dutch.

homard *m* lobster.

homme *m* man *(pl* men); **l'h.** *(espèce)* man(kind); **des vêtements d'h.** men's clothes; **h. d'affaires** businessman.

homosexuel, -elle *adj & mf* homosexual.

honnête *adj* honest; *(satisfaisant)* decent.

honnêtement *adv* honestly; decently.

honnêteté *f* honesty.

honneur *m* honor; **en l'h. de** in honor of; **faire h. à** *(sa famille etc)* to be a credit to; *(repas)* to do justice to.

honorable *adj* honorable; *(convenable)* respectable.

honoraires *mpl* fees.

honte *f* shame; **avoir h.** to be *ou* feel ashamed (**de qch** of sth; **de faire** to do, of doing).

honteux, -euse *adj* ashamed; *(scandaleux)* shameful.

hôpital, -aux *m* hospital; **à l'h.** in the hospital.

hoquet *m* **avoir le h.** to have (the) hiccups.

horaire *m* timetable.

horizon *m* horizon; **à l'h.** on the horizon.

horizontal, -e, -aux *adj* horizontal.

horloge *f* clock.

horreur *f* horror; **faire h. à** to disgust; **avoir h. de** to hate.

horrible *adj* horrible.

horriblement *adv* horribly.

horrifiant, -ante *adj* horrifying.

horrifié, -ée *adj* horrified.

hors *prép* **h. service** out of order; **h. de** out of.

hors-bord *m inv* speedboat.

hors-d'œuvre *m inv (à table)* hors d'oeuvre, appetizer.

hors-taxe *adj inv* duty-free.

hospitaliser *vt* to hospitalize.

hospitalité *f* hospitality.

hostile *adj* hostile (**à** to, towards).

hostilité *f* hostility (**envers** to, towards).

hôte 1 *m (qui reçoit)* host. **2** *mf (invité)* guest.

hôtel *m* hotel; **h. de ville** city hall.

hôtesse *f* hostess; **h. (de l'air)** flight attendant.

hotte *f* basket *(carried on back)*.

houleux, -euse *adj (mer)* rough; *(réunion)* stormy.

hourra! *int* hurray!

housse *f* (protective) cover.

HT *abrév (hors taxe)* before tax, exclusive of tax.

hublot *m* porthole.

huées *fpl* boos.

huile *f* oil.

huit *adj & m* eight; **h. jours** a week.

huitième *adj & mf* eighth.

huître *f* oyster.

humain, -aine *adj* human.

humanité *f* humanity.

humble *adj* humble.

humblement *adv* humbly.

humecter *vt* to moisten.

humeur *f* mood; *(caractère)* temperament; **bonne h.** *(gaieté)* good humor; **de bonne/mauvaise h.** in a good/bad mood.

humide *adj* damp.

humidité *f* humidity; *(plutôt froide)* damp(ness).

humiliation *f* humiliation.

humilier *vt* to humiliate.

humoristique *adj* humorous.

humour *m* humor; **avoir de l'h.** to have a sense of humor.

hurlement *m (d'un loup, du vent)* howl; *(d'une personne)* scream.

hurler 1 *vi (loup, vent)* to howl; *(personne)* to scream. **2** *vt* to scream.

hydrater *vt (peau)* to moisturize.

hygiène *f* hygiene.

hygiénique *adj* hygienic; **papier h.** toilet paper.

hymne *m* **h. national** national anthem.

hypermarché *m* hypermarket.

hypocrisie *f* hypocrisy.

hypocrite 1 *adj* hypocritical. **2** *mf* hypocrite.

hypothèse *f (supposition)* assumption.

I

iceberg *m* iceberg.

ici *adv* here; **par i.** *(passer)* this way; *(habiter)* around here; **jusqu'i.** *(temps)* up to now; *(lieu)* as far as this *ou* here; **d'i. peu** before long.

idéal, -e, -aux *ou* **-als** *adj & m* ideal.

idée *f* idea; **changer d'i.** to change one's mind.

identifier *vt* to identify.

identifier (s') *vpr* **s'i. à** *ou* **avec** to identify (oneself) with.

identique *adj* identical (**à** to, with).

identité *f* identity; **carte d'i.** identity card, ID card.

idiot, -ote 1 *adj* silly. **2** *mf* idiot.

idiotie *f* **une i.** a silly thing.

idole *m* idol.

igloo *m* igloo.

ignifugé, -ée *adj* fireproof(ed).

ignoble *adj* vile.

ignorance *f* ignorance.

ignorant, -ante *adj* ignorant (**de** of).

ignorer *vt* not to know; **i. qn** to ignore sb.

il *pron (personne)* he; *(chose, animal)* it; **il pleut** it's raining; **il y a** there is; *pl* there are; **il y a six ans** six years ago; **il y a une heure qu'il travaille** he's been working for an hour; **qu'est-ce qu'il y a?** what's the matter?

île *f* island.

illégal, -e, -aux *adj* illegal.

illettré, -ée *adj* illiterate.

illisible *adj (écriture)* illegible.

illuminer *vt*, **s'illuminer** *vpr* to light up.

illusion *f* illusion; **se faire des illusions** to delude oneself (**sur** about).

illustration *f* illustration.

illustré *m* comic.

illustrer *vt* to illustrate (**de** with).

ils *pron* they.

image *f* picture; *(dans une glace)* reflection.

imaginaire *adj* imaginary.

imagination *f* imagination.

imaginer *vt*, **s'imaginer** *vpr* to imagine (**que** that).

imbattable *adj* unbeatable.

imbécile *mf* idiot.

imbécilité *f (état)* imbecility; **une i.** *(action, parole)* an idiotic thing.

imbuvable *adj* undrinkable.

imitateur, -trice *mf (artiste)* impersonator.

imitation *f* imitation.

imiter *vt* to imitate; **i. qn** *(pour rire)* to mimic sb; *(faire comme)* to do the same as sb.

immangeable *adj* inedible.

immatriculation *f* registration.

immédiat, -ate *adj* immediate.

immédiatement *adv* immediately.

immense *adj* immense.

immeuble *m* building; *(d'habitation)* apartment building; *(de bureaux)* office building.

immigration *f* immigration.

immigré, -ée *adj & mf* immigrant.

immobile *adj* still.

immobilier, -ère 1 *adj* marché i. property market. **2** *m* l'i. real estate.

immobiliser *vt* to bring to a stop.

immobiliser (s') *vpr* to come to a stop.

immonde *adj (sale)* foul; *(ignoble, laid)* vile.

immortel, -elle *adj* immortal.

immuable *adj* immutable, unchanging.

impair, -e *adj (nombre)* odd.

impardonnable *adj* unforgivable.

imparfait *m (temps) Grammaire* imperfect.

impartial, -e, -aux *adj* fair, unbiased.

impasse *f* dead end.

impassible *adj* impassive.

impatience *f* impatience.

impatient, -ente *adj* impatient (**de faire** to do).

impatienter (s') *vpr* to get impatient.

impeccable *adj (propre)* immaculate.

impératif *m Grammaire* imperative.

imperméable 1 *adj (tissu)* waterproof. **2** *m* raincoat.

impitoyable *adj* ruthless.

implanter (s') *vpr* to become established.

impoli, -ie *adj* rude.

impolitesse *f* rudeness.

importance *f* importance; **ça n'a pas d'i.** it doesn't matter.

important, -ante 1 *adj* important; *(quantité etc)* big. **2** *m* l'i., c'est **de** the important thing is to.

importateur, -trice 1 *adj* importing. **2** *mf* importer.

importation *f* import; **d'i.** *(article)* imported.

importer 1 *vi* n'importe qui/ quoi/où/quand/comment anyone/anything/anywhere/anytime/ anyhow. **2** *vt* to import (**de** from).

imposer *vt* to impose (**à** on).

impossibilité *f* impossibility.

impossible *adj* impossible (**à faire** to do); **il (nous) est i. de le faire** it is impossible (for us) to do it.

impôt *m* tax; **i. sur le revenu** income tax; **(service des) impôts** tax authorities.

impression *f* impression.

impressionnant, -ante *adj* impressive.

impressionner *vt (émouvoir)* to make a strong impression on.

imprévisible *adj* unforeseeable.

imprévu, -ue *adj* unexpected.

imprimante *f (d'ordinateur)* printer.

imprimé *m* printed form.

imprimer *vt (livre etc)* to print.

imprimerie *f* printing plant.

improviser *vti* to improvize.

improviste (à l') *adv* unexpectedly.

imprudence *f* carelessness, foolishness; **commettre une i.** to do something foolish.

imprudent, -ente *adj* careless, foolish.

impuissant, -ante *adj* helpless.

impulsif, -ive *adj* impulsive.

inabordable *adj (prix)* prohibitive.

inacceptable *adj* unacceptable.

inachevé, -ée *adj* unfinished.

inadapté, -ée *adj (socialement)* maladjusted; *(physiquement, mentalement)* handicapped; *(matériel)* unsuitable (**à** for).

inadmissible *adj* unacceptable, inadmissible.

inanimé, -ée *adj (mort)* lifeless; *(évanoui)* unconscious.

inaperçu, -ue *adj* **passer i.** to go unnoticed.

inapte *adj (intellectuellement)* unsuited (**à** for); *(médicalement)* unfit (**à** for).

inattendu, -ue *adj* unexpected.

inattention *f* lack of attention; **un moment d'i.** a moment of distraction.

inauguration *f* inauguration.

inaugurer *vt* to inaugurate.

incapable *adj* **i. de faire qch** unable to do sth.

incapacité *f (impossibilité)* inability (**de faire** to do); *(invalidité)* disability; **être dans l'i. de faire qch** to be unable to do sth.

incarner *vt* to embody.

incassable *adj* unbreakable.

incendie *m* fire.

incendier *vt* to set fire to.

incertain, -aine *adj* uncertain; *(temps)* unsettled.

incertitude *f* uncertainty.

incessamment *adv* very soon.

incessant, -ante *adj* continual.

inchangé, -ée *adj* unchanged.

incident *m* incident.

incisive *f* incisor (tooth).

inciter *vt* to encourage (**à faire** to do).

incliner *vt (courber)* to bend; *(pencher)* to tilt.

incliner (s') *vpr (se courber)* to bow (down).

inclure *vt* to include; *(dans un courrier)* to enclose (**dans** with).

inclus, -use *adj* inclusive; **jusqu'à lundi i.** up to and including Monday.

incohérent, -ente *adj (propos)* incoherent; *(histoire)* inconsistent.

incolore *adj* colorless; *(vernis)* clear.

incommoder *vt* to bother.

incomparable *adj* matchless.

incompatible *adj* incompatible.

incompétent, -ente *adj* incompetent.

incomplet, -ète *adj* incomplete.

incompréhensible *adj* incomprehensible.

inconnu, -ue 1 *adj* unknown (**à** to). **2** *mf (étranger)* stranger.

inconscient, -ente *adj* unconscious (**de** of); *(imprudent)* thoughtless.

inconsolable *adj* heartbroken, cut up.

incontestable *adj* undeniable.

inconvenant, -ante *adj* improper.

inconvénient *m* drawback.

incorrect, -e *adj (grossier)* impolite.

incroyable *adj* incredible.

inculpé, -ée *mf* **l'i.** the accused.

inculper *vt* to charge (**de** with).
inculte *adj (terre, personne)* uncultivated.
incurable *adj* incurable.
indécis, -ise *adj (hésitant)* undecided.
indéfini, -ie *adj* indefinite.
indéfiniment *adv* indefinitely.
indemne *adj* unhurt.
indemnisation *f* compensation.
indemnité *f* compensation; *(allocation)* allowance.
indépendance *f* independence.
indépendant, -ante *adj* independent (**de** of).
indescriptible *adj* indescribable.
indéterminé, -ée *adj (date, heure)* unspecified; *(raison)* unknown.
index *m (doigt)* index finger, forefinger.
indicatif *m (à la radio)* theme song *ou* music; *(téléphonique)* area code; *Grammaire* indicative.
indication *f (piece of)* information; **indications** *(pour aller quelque part)* directions.
indice *m (dans une enquête)* clue.
indien, -ienne 1 *adj* Indian. **2** *mf* I. Indian.
indifférence *f* indifference (**à** to).
indifférent, -ente *adj* indifferent (**à** to).
indigestion *f (attack of)* indigestion.
indignation *f* indignation.
indigne *adj (personne)* unworthy; *(conduite)* shameful; **i. de qn/qch** unworthy of sb/sth.
indigner (s') *vpr* to be *ou* become indignant (**de** at).
indiquer *vt (montrer)* to show; *(dire)* to tell; **i. du doigt** to point to *ou* at.
indirect, -e *adj* indirect.
indirectement *adv* indirectly.
indiscipliné, -ée *adj* unruly.
indiscret, -ète *adj* inquisitive.
indiscrétion *f* indiscretion.

indispensable *adj* essential.
indisponible *adj* unavailable.
indistinct, -incte *adj* unclear.
individu *m* individual.
individuel, -elle *adj* individual.
indolore *adj* painless.
indulgent, -ente *adj* indulgent (**envers** to).
industrialisé, -ée *adj* industrialized.
industrie *f* industry.
industriel, -elle *adj* industrial.
inédit, -ite *adj (texte)* unpublished.
inefficace *adj (mesure etc)* ineffective; *(personne)* inefficient.
inégal, -e, -aux *adj (parts, lutte)* unequal; *(sol, humeur)* uneven; *(travail)* inconsistent.
inépuisable *adj* inexhaustible.
inespéré, -ée *adj* unhoped-for.
inestimable *adj* priceless.
inévitable *adj* inevitable, unavoidable.
inexact, -e *adj* inaccurate.
inexcusable *adj* inexcusable.
inexplicable *adj* inexplicable.
inexpliqué, -ée *adj* unexplained.
infaillible *adj* infallible.
infarctus *m* **un i.** a coronary.
infatigable *adj* tireless.
infect, -e *adj (odeur)* foul; *(café etc)* vile.
infecter (s') *vpr* to get infected.
infection *f (odeur)* stench.
inférieur, -e *adj* lower; *(qualité etc)* inferior (**à** to); **l'étage i.** the floor below.
infériorité *f* inferiority.
infernal, -e, -aux *adj* infernal.
infesté, -ée *adj* **i. de requins**/*etc* shark/*etc*-infested.
infidèle *adj* unfaithful (**à** to).
infiltrer (s') *vpr (liquide)* to seep (through) (**dans** into).
infini, -ie 1 *adj* infinite. **2** *m* infinity.
infiniment *adv (regretter, remercier)* very much.

infinitif m Grammaire infinitive.
infirme adj & mf disabled (person).
infirmerie f sick room, sickbay.
infirmier m male nurse.
infirmière f nurse.
inflammable adj (in)flammable.
inflammation f inflammation.
inflation f inflation.
inflexible adj inflexible.
influence f influence.
influencer vt to influence.
informaticien, -enne mf computer scientist.
information f information; (nouvelle) piece of news; **les informations** the news.
informatique f (science) computer science; (technique) data processing.
informatisé, -ée adj computerized.
informer vt to inform (**de** of, about; **que** that).
informer (s') vpr to inquire (**de** about; **si** if, whether).
infraction f offense.
infusion f herbal ou herb tea.
ingénieur m engineer.
ingénieux, -euse adj ingenious.
ingrat, -ate adj ungrateful (**envers** to).
ingratitude f ingratitude.
ingrédient m ingredient.
inhabitable adj uninhabitable.
inhabité, -ée adj uninhabited.
inhabituel, -elle adj unusual.
inhumain, -aine adj inhuman.
inimaginable adj unimaginable.
ininflammable adj non-flammable.
ininterrompu, -ue adj continuous.
initiale f (lettre) initial.
initier (s') vpr s'i. à qch to start learning sth.
injecter vt to inject.
injection f injection.
injure f insult.
injurier vt to insult.

injuste adj (contraire à la justice) unjust; (non équitable) unfair.
injustice f injustice.
inlassable adj untiring.
innocence f innocence.
innocent, -ente 1 adj innocent (**de** of). **2** mf innocent person.
innombrable adj countless.
inoccupé, -ée adj unoccupied.
inoffensif, -ive adj harmless.
inondation f flood.
inonder vt to flood.
inoubliable adj unforgettable.
inouï, -ïe adj incredible.
inox® m stainless steel.
inoxydable adj acier i. stainless steel.
inqualifiable adj unspeakable.
inquiet, -iète adj worried (**de** about).
inquiétant, -ante adj worrying.
inquiéter vt to worry.
inquiéter (s') vpr s'i. (**de**) to worry (about).
inquiétude f worry.
insatisfait, -aite adj (personne) dissatisfied.
inscription f registration; (sur écriteau etc) inscription; **frais d'i.** (à l'université) tuition fees.
inscrire* vt to write ou put down; **i. qn** to enroll sb.
inscrire (s') vpr to put one's name down; **s'i. à** (club) to join; (examen) to enroll for, to register for.
insecte m insect.
insecticide m insecticide.
insécurité f insecurity.
insensé, -ée adj (projet, idée) crazy; (espoir) wild.
insensible adj insensitive (**à** to).
inséparable adj inseparable (**de** from).
insigne m badge.
insignifiant, -ante adj insignificant.
insistance f insistence.
insister vt to insist (**pour faire** on doing); **i. sur** (détail etc) to stress.

insolation f sunstroke.
insolence f insolence.
insolent, -ente adj insolent.
insomnie f insomnia.
insonoriser vt to soundproof.
insouciant, -ante adj carefree.
inspecter vt to inspect.
inspecteur, -trice mf inspector.
inspection f inspection.
inspiration f inspiration.
inspirer vt to inspire (**qch à qn** sb with sth).
instable adj (meuble) shaky.
installation f putting in; (dans une maison) moving in.
installer vt (appareil etc) to install, to put in; (étagère) to put up.
installer (s') vpr (s'asseoir, s'établir) to settle (down); **s'i. dans** (maison) to move into.
instant m moment; **à l'i.** a moment ago; **pour l'i.** for the moment.
instaurer vt to establish.
instinct m instinct.
instinctif, -ive adj instinctive.
instituteur, -trice mf elementary school teacher.
institution f (organisation, structure) institution.
instructif, -ive adj instructive.
instruction f education; instructions (ordres) instructions.
instruire* vt to teach, to educate.
instruire (s') vpr to educate oneself.
instrument m instrument; (outil) implement.
insuffisant, -ante adj inadequate.
insulte f insult (**à** to).
insulter vt to insult.
insupportable adj unbearable.
intact, -e adj intact.
intégral, -e, -aux adj (paiement) full; (édition) unabridged; **version intégrale** (de film) uncut version.
intégralement adv in full.
intégrer (s') vpr to become integrated.

intellectuel, -elle adj & mf intellectual.
intelligemment adv intelligently.
intelligence f intelligence.
intelligent, -ente adj intelligent.
intempéries fpl **les i.** bad weather.
intense adj intense; (circulation) heavy.
intensifier vt, **s'intensifier** vpr to intensify.
intensité f intensity.
intention f intention; **avoir l'i. de faire** to intend to do.
interchangeable adj interchangeable.
interdiction f ban (**de** on); 'i. de fumer' 'no smoking'.
interdire* vt to forbid, not to allow (**qch à qn** sb sth); **i. à qn de faire** not to allow sb to do.
interdit, -ite adj forbidden; 'stationnement i.' 'no parking'.
intéressant, -ante adj interesting; (prix etc) attractive.
intéresser vt to interest.
intéresser (s') vpr **s'i. à** to take an interest in.
intérêt m interest; **intérêts** (argent) interest; **tu as i. à faire** you'd do well to do.
intérieur, -e adj inner; (poche) inside; (politique) domestic. **2** m inside (**de** of); **à l'i. (de)** inside.
intérim m (travail temporaire) temporary work; **président par i.** acting president.
intérimaire 1 adj (fonction, employé) temporary. **2** mf (travailleur) temporary worker; (secrétaire) temp.
interlocuteur, -trice mf **mon i.** the person I am/was/etc speaking to.
intermédiaire mf **par l'i. de** through (the medium of).
interminable adj endless.

international, -e, -aux *adj* international.

internaute *mf* Internet surfer.

interne *mf (élève)* boarder.

interpeller *vt (appeler)* to shout at.

interphone *m* intercom.

interposer (s') *vpr* to intervene (**dans**).

interprète *mf* interpreter; *(chanteur)* singer.

interpréter *vt (expliquer)* to interpret; *(chanter)* to sing.

interrogatif, -ive *adj & m Grammaire* interrogative.

interrogation *f* question; *(à l'école)* test.

interrogatoire *m* interrogation.

interroger *vt* to question.

interrompre* *vt* to interrupt.

interrupteur *m (électrique)* switch.

interruption *f* interruption.

intersection *f* intersection.

intervalle *m (écart)* gap; *(temps)* interval.

intervenir* *vi* to intervene; *(survenir)* to occur.

intervention *f* intervention; **i. (chirurgicale)** operation.

interview *f* interview.

interviewer *vt* to interview.

intestin *m* bowel.

intime *adj* intimate; *(journal, mariage)* private.

intimider *vt* to intimidate.

intimité *f (familiarité)* intimacy; *(vie privée)* privacy; **dans l'i.** in private.

intituler (s') *vpr* to be entitled.

intolérable *adj* intolerable (**que** (+ *subjonctif*) that).

intoxication *f (empoisonnement)* poisoning; **i. alimentaire** food poisoning.

intraduisible *adj* impossible to translate.

intransitif, -ive *adj Grammaire* intransitive.

intrépide *adj* fearless.

intrigue *f* intrigue; *(de film, roman)* plot.

introduction *f* introduction.

introduire* *vt (insérer)* to put in (**dans** to); *(faire entrer)* to show in.

introduire (s') *vpr* **s'i. dans** to get into.

introuvable *adj* nowhere to be found.

intrus, -use *mf* intruder.

inusable *adj* durable.

inutile *adj* useless.

inutilement *adv* needlessly.

inutilisable *adj* unusable.

invalide 1 *adj* disabled. **2** *mf* disabled person.

invariable *adj* invariable.

invasion *f* invasion.

inventer *vt* to invent; *(imaginer)* to make up.

inventeur, -trice *mf* inventor.

invention *f* invention.

inverse *adj (sens)* opposite; *(ordre)* reverse.

inverser *vt (ordre)* to reverse.

investir *vti* to invest (**dans** in).

investissement *m* investment.

invisible *adj* invisible.

invitation *f* invitation.

invité, -ée *mf* guest.

inviter *vt* to invite.

inviter (s') *vpr* **s'i. (chez qn)** to (gate)crash (sb's house/*etc*).

involontaire *adj (geste etc)* unintentional.

invraisemblable *adj (extraordinaire)* incredible; *(alibi)* implausible.

ira, irai(t) *voir* **aller¹**.

irlandais, -aise 1 *adj* Irish. **2** *mf* **I.** Irishman, Irishwoman; **les I.** the Irish. **3** *m (langue)* Irish.

ironie *f* irony.

ironique *adj* ironic(al).

iront *voir* **aller¹**.

irréel, -elle *adj* unreal.

irrégulier, -ière *adj* irregular.

irremplaçable *adj* irreplaceable.

irréparable adj (véhicule etc) beyond repair.

irréprochable adj irreproachable.

irrésistible adj irresistible.

irriguer vt to irrigate.

irritable adj irritable.

irritation f irritation.

irriter vt to irritate.

irruption f faire i. dans to burst into.

islamique adj Islamic.

isolant m insulation (material).

isolé, -ée adj isolated (de from).

isolement m (de personne) isolation.

isoler vt to isolate (de from); (du froid etc) to insulate.

issu, -ue adj être i. de to come from.

issue f exit; rue/etc sans i. dead end.

italien, -ienne 1 adj Italian. **2** mf I. Italian. **3** m (langue) Italian.

italique m italics.

itinéraire m route.

IUT m abrév (institut universitaire de technologie) = vocational higher education college.

ivoire m ivory.

ivre adj drunk.

ivresse f drunkenness.

ivrogne mf drunk, drunkard.

J

jaillir vi (liquide) to spurt (out); (lumière) to beam out, to shine (forth).

jalousie f jealousy.

jaloux, -ouse adj jealous (de of).

jamais adv never; elle ne sort j. she never goes out; j. de la vie! (absolutely) never!; si j. if ever.

jambe f leg.

jambon m ham.

janvier m January.

japonais, -aise 1 adj Japanese. **2** mf J. Japanese man ou woman, Japanese inv; les J. the Japanese. **3** m (langue) Japanese.

jardin m garden; j. public park.

jardinage m gardening.

jardinier m gardener.

jardinière f (caisse à fleurs) window box.

jaune 1 adj yellow. **2** m yellow; j. d'œuf (egg) yolk.

jaunir vti to turn yellow.

jaunisse f jaundice.

Javel (eau de) f bleach.

jazz m jazz.

je pron (j' before vowel or mute h) I.

jean m (pair of) jeans.

jeep® f jeep®.

jerrycan m gasoline can; (pour l'eau) water can.

jet m (de vapeur) burst; (de tuyau d'arrosage) nozzle; j. d'eau fountain.

jetable adj disposable.

jetée f pier.

jeter vt to throw (à to; dans into); (à la poubelle) to throw away.

jeter (se) vpr se j. sur to pounce on; le fleuve se jette dans la mer the river flows into the sea.

jeton m (pièce) token; (de jeu) chip.

jeu, -x m game; (amusement) play; (d'argent) gambling; (série complète) set; (de cartes) deck; j. de mots play on words; jeux de société parlor ou indoor games; j. télévisé (television) quiz show.

jeudi m Thursday.

jeun (à) adv être à j. to have eaten no food.

jeune 1 adj young. **2** mf young person; les jeunes young people.

jeûner vi to fast.

jeunesse f youth; la j. (jeunes) the young.

jockey m jockey.

jogging m jogging; faire du j. to jog.

joie *f* joy.

joindre* *vt* to join; *(envoyer avec)* to enclose (**à** with); **j. qn** to get in touch with sb.

joindre (se) *vpr* **se j. à** *(un groupe etc)* to join.

joint, -ointe 1 *adj* **à pieds joints** with feet together; **pièces jointes** *(de lettre)* enclosures. **2** *m* joint; *(d'étanchéité)* seal; *(de robinet)* washer; **j. de culasse** gasket.

joker *m Cartes* joker.

joli, -ie *adj* nice; *(femme, enfant)* pretty.

jongler *vi* to juggle (**avec** with).

jongleur, -euse *mf* juggler.

jonquille *f* daffodil.

joue *f* cheek.

jouer 1 *vi* to play; *(acteur)* to act; *(au tiercé etc)* to gamble, to bet; **j. au tennis/aux cartes/etc** to play tennis/cards/*etc*; **j. du piano/***etc* to play the piano/*etc*. **2** *vt* to play; *(risquer)* to bet (**sur** on); *(pièce, film)* to put on.

jouet *m* toy.

joueur, -euse *mf* player; *(au tiercé etc)* gambler; **bon j.** good loser.

jour *m* day; *(lumière)* (day)light; **il fait j.** it's light; **en plein j.** in broad daylight; **de nos jours** nowadays; **du j. au lendemain** overnight; **le j. de l'An** New Year's Day.

journal, -aux *m* (news)paper; *(intime)* diary; **j. (télévisé)** television news.

journaliste *mf* journalist.

journée *f* day; **toute la j.** all day (long).

joyeux, -euse *adj* merry, happy; **j. Noël!** merry Christmas!; **j. anniversaire!** happy birthday!

jubiler *vi* to be jubilant.

judo *m* judo.

juge *m* judge.

jugement *m* judgment; *(verdict)* sentence; **passer en j.** to stand trial.

juger *vt* to judge; *(au tribunal)* to try; *(estimer)* to consider (**que** that).

juif, juive 1 *adj* Jewish. **2** *mf* Jew.

juillet *m* July.

juin *m* June.

jumeau, -elle, *pl* **-eaux, -elles** *mf & adj* twin; **frère j.** twin brother; **sœur jumelle** twin sister; **lits jumeaux** twin beds.

jumelles *fpl* *(pour regarder)* binoculars.

jument *f* mare.

jungle *f* jungle.

jupe *f* skirt.

jupon *m* slip, petticoat.

juré, -ée *mf* juror.

jurer 1 *vi* *(dire un gros mot)* to swear (**contre** at). **2** *vt* *(promettre)* to swear (**que** that; **de faire** to do).

juron *m* swearword.

jury *m* jury.

jus *m* juice; *(de viande)* gravy.

jusque 1 *prép* **jusqu'à** *(espace)* as far as; *(temps)* until; **jusqu'à cinquante euros** *(limite)* up to fifty euros; **jusqu'en mai** until May; **jusqu'où?** how far?; **jusqu'ici** *(temps)* up till now. **2** *conj* **jusqu'à ce qu'il vienne** until he comes.

juste 1 *adj* *(équitable)* fair; *(légitime)* just; *(exact)* right; *(étroit)* tight. **2** *adv* *(deviner etc)* right; *(chanter)* in tune; *(seulement)* just.

justement *adv* exactly.

justesse *f* *(exactitude)* accuracy; **de j.** *(éviter, gagner)* just.

justice *f* justice; *(autorités)* law.

justifier *vt* to justify.

juteux, -euse *adj* juicy.

K

kangourou *m* kangaroo.

karaté *m* karate.

képi *m* cap, kepi.

kidnapper *vt* to kidnap.

kilo *m* kilo.

kilogramme *m* kilogram.

kilométrage *m* = mileage.

kilomètre *m* kilometer.

kilo-octet, *pl* **kilo-octets** *m* kilobyte.

kinésithérapeute *mf* physical therapist.

kiosque *m (à journaux)* kiosk.

kit *m* **meuble en k.** (piece of) flat-pack furniture.

klaxon® *m* horn.

klaxonner *vi* to honk.

k.-o. *adj inv* **mettre k.** to knock out.

L

l', la *voir* le.

là *adv* (lieu) there; (chez soi) in; (temps) then; **je reste là** I'll stay here; **c'est là que** that's where; **à cinq mètres de là** 16 feet away; **jusque-là** (lieu) as far as that; (temps) up till then. **2** *int* **oh là là!** oh my goodness!

là-bas *adv* over there.

laboratoire *m* laboratory.

labourer *vt* to plow.

labyrinthe *m* maze.

lac *m* lake.

lacet *m* (shoe-)lace; (de route) twist.

lâche 1 *adj* cowardly. **2** *mf* coward.

lâcher 1 *vt* to let go of; (bombe) to drop. **2** *vi* (corde) to give way.

lâcheté *f* cowardice.

là-dedans *adv* in there.

là-dessous *adv* underneath.

là-dessus *adv* on there.

là-haut *adv* up there; (à l'étage) upstairs.

laid, laide *adj* ugly.

laideur *f* ugliness.

lainage *m* woolen garment.

laine *f* wool; **en l.** woolen.

laisse *f* lead, leash.

laisser *vt* to leave; **l. qn partir/etc** to let sb go/etc; **l. qch à qn** to let sb have sth.

lait *m* milk.

laitier *adj* **produit l.** dairy product.

laitue *f* lettuce.

lambeau, -x *m* shred, bit.

lame *f* (de couteau etc) blade; (vague) wave.

lamentable *adj* (mauvais) terrible.

lamenter (se) *vpr* to moan.

lampadaire *m* floor lamp; (de rue) street lamp.

lampe *f* lamp; (au néon) light; **l. de poche** flashlight.

lance *f* spear; (extrémité de tuyau) nozzle; **l. d'incendie** fire hose.

lancement *m* (de fusée etc) launch(ing).

lancer *vt* to throw (à to); (avec force) to hurl; (fusée, produit etc) to launch; (appel etc) to issue.

lancer (se) *vpr* (se précipiter) to rush.

landau, *pl* **-aus** *m* baby carriage.

langage *m* language.

langouste *f* (spiny) lobster.

langue *f* tongue; (langage) language; **l. maternelle** mother tongue; **langues vivantes** modern languages.

lanière *f* strap.

lanterne *f* lantern; **lanternes** (de véhicule) parking lights.

lapin *m* rabbit.

laque *f* lacquer.

lard *m* (fumé) bacon; (gras) (pig's) fat.

large 1 *adj* wide, broad; (vêtement) loose; **l. de six mètres** 20 feet wide. **2** *m* breadth, width; **avoir six mètres de l.** to be 20 feet wide; **le l.** (mer) the open sea; **au l. de Cherbourg** off Cherbourg.

largement *adv* (ouvrir) wide; (au moins) easily; **avoir l. le temps** to have plenty of time.

largeur f width, breadth.

larme f tear; **en larmes** in tears.

laser m laser.

lasser vt, **se lasser** vpr to tire (**de** of).

latéral, -e, -aux adj side.

latin m (langue) Latin.

lavabo m washbasin, sink.

lave-auto, pl lave-autos m car wash.

lave-linge m inv washing machine.

laver vt to wash.

laver (se) vpr to wash up; **se l. les mains** to wash one's hands.

laverie f (automatique) laundromat.

lavette f dishcloth.

lave-vaisselle m inv dishwasher.

layette f baby clothes.

le, la, pl **les** (le and la become **l'** before a vowel or mute h) **1** art déf (à + le = au, à + les = aux; de + le = du, de + les = des). ▪ (généralisation) **la beauté** beauty; **la France** France; **les hommes** men; **aimer le café** to like coffee. ▪ (possession) **il ouvrit la bouche** he opened his mouth; **avoir les cheveux blonds** to have blond hair. ▪ (mesure) **dix dollars la livre** ten dollars a pound. ▪ (temps) **ell vient le lundi** she comes on Monday(s); **l'an prochain** next year; **une fois l'an** once a year. **2** pron (homme) him; (femme) her; (chose, animal) it; pl them; **es-tu fatigué?– je le suis** are you tired?– I am; **je le crois** I think so.

lécher vt to lick.

lécher (se) vpr **se l. les doigts** to lick one's fingers.

leçon f lesson.

lecteur, -trice mf reader; **l. de cassettes/CD/DVD** cassette/CD/DVD player.

lecture f reading; **lectures** (livres) books.

légal, -e, -aux adj legal.

légende f (histoire) legend; (de plan) key; (de photo) caption.

léger, -ère adj light; (bruit, fièvre etc) slight; (café, thé) weak; (bière, tabac) mild.

légèrement adv (un peu) slightly.

légèreté f lightness.

légitime adj **être en état de l. défense** to act in self-defense.

légume m vegetable.

lendemain m **le l.** the next day; **le l. de** the day after; **le l. matin** the next morning.

lent, lente adj slow.

lentement adv slowly.

lenteur f slowness.

lentille f (graine) lentil; (verre) lens.

léopard m leopard.

lequel, laquelle, pl **lesquels, lesquelles** (+ à = auquel, à laquelle, auxquel(le)s; + de = duquel, de laquelle, desquel(le)s) pron (chose, animal) which; (personne) who, (indirect) whom; (interrogatif) which (one); **dans l.** in which; **parmi lesquels** (choses, animaux) among which; (personnes) among whom.

les voir **le**.

lessive f (laundry) detergent; (linge) laundry; **faire la l.** to do the laundry.

lettre f letter; **en toutes lettres** (mot) in full.

leur 1 adj poss their. **2** pron poss **le l., la l., les leurs** theirs. **3** pron inv (indirect) (to) them; **il l. est facile de** it's easy for them to.

levé, -ée adj **être l.** (debout) to be up.

lever 1 vt to lift (up); **l. les yeux** to look up. **2** m **l. du soleil** sunrise.

lever (se) vpr to get up; (soleil, rideau) to rise; (jour) to break.

levier m lever; (pour soulever) crowbar.

lèvre f lip.

lézard m lizard.

liaison f (routière etc) link; (entre mots) liaison.

liasse f bundle.

libération f freeing, release.

libérer vt to (set) free, to release (de from).

libérer (se) vpr to free oneself (de from).

liberté f freedom; **en l. provisoire** on bail; **mettre en l.** to free.

libraire mf bookseller.

librairie f bookshop.

libre adj free (de qch from sth; de faire to do); (voie) clear.

libre-échange m free trade.

librement adv freely.

libre-service, pl **libres-services** m self-service.

licence f (diplôme) (Bachelor's) degree; (sportive) license.

licencié, -ée adj & mf graduate; **l. ès lettres/sciences** Bachelor of Arts/Science.

licenciement m dismissal.

licencier vt (ouvrier) to lay off, to dismiss.

liège m (matériau) cork.

lien m (rapport) link; (ficelle) tie; **l. de parenté** family tie.

lier vt (attacher) to tie (up); (relier) to link (up).

lierre m ivy.

lieu, -x m place; (d'un accident) scene; **les lieux** (locaux) the premises; **avoir l.** to take place; **au l. de** instead of.

lièvre m hare.

ligne f line; (belle silhouette) figure; **(se) mettre en l.** to line up; **en l.** (au téléphone) connected; **grandes lignes** (de train) main line (services); **à la l.** new paragraph; **l. d'arrivée** finish line.

ligoter vt to tie up.

lilas m lilac.

limace f slug.

lime f file.

limer vt to file.

limitation f (de vitesse, poids) limit.

limite 1 f limit (à to); (frontière) boundary. **2** adj (cas) extreme; (vi-tesse etc) maximum; **date l.** latest date; **date l. de vente** sell-by date.

limiter vt to limit (à to).

limoger vt to dismiss.

limonade f lemon-lime soda.

limpide adj (crystal) clear.

lin m (tissu) linen.

linge m linen; (à laver) laundry.

lingerie f underwear.

lion m lion.

lionne f lioness.

liqueur f liqueur.

liquide 1 adj liquid; **argent l.** ready cash. **2** m liquid; **du l.** (argent) ready cash.

lire* vti to read.

lis m lily.

lis, lisant, lise(nt) etc voir **lire**.

lisible adj (écriture) legible.

lisse adj smooth.

lisser vt to smooth.

liste f list; **sur l. rouge** (numéro de téléphone) unlisted.

lit¹ m bed; **l. d'enfant** crib; **lits superposés** bunk beds.

lit² voir **lire**.

literie f bedding.

litre m liter.

littéraire adj literary.

littérature f literature.

littoral m coast(line).

livraison f delivery.

livre¹ m book; **l. de poche** paperback (book).

livre² f (monnaie, poids) pound.

livrer vt to deliver (à qn); **l. qn à** (la police etc) to give sb over to.

livret m **l.** scolaire report card; **l. de caisse d'épargne** bankbook, passbook.

livreur, -euse mf delivery man, delivery woman.

local, -ale, -aux adj local.

local, -aux m room; **locaux** premises.

locataire mf tenant.

location f (de maison, voiture) rental; (par propriétaire) renting (out), letting; (loyer) rental.

locomotive f (de train) engine.

locution f phrase.

loge f (de concierge) lodge; (d'acteur) dressing room; (de spectateur) box.

logement m accommodations; (appartement) apartment; (maison) house; **le l.** housing.

loger 1 vt to accommodate; (héberger) to put up. **2** vi (à l'hôtel etc) to put up; (habiter) to live.

logiciel m software inv.

logique adj logical.

logiquement adv logically.

loi f law; (du Parlement) act; **projet de l.** bill.

loin adv far (away ou off); **Boston est l. (de Paris)** Boston is a long way away (from Paris); **plus l.** further, farther; **de l.** from a distance.

lointain, -aine adj distant.

loisirs mpl spare time, leisure (time); (distractions) leisure activities.

long, longue 1 adj long; **être l. (à faire)** to be a long time ou slow (in doing); **l. de deux mètres** seven feet long. **2** m **avoir deux mètres de l.** to be seven feet long; **(tout) le l. de** (espace) (all) along; **de l. en large** (marcher) up and down; **à la longue** in the long run.

longer vt to go along; (forêt, mer) to skirt; (mur) to hug.

longtemps adv (for) a long time; **trop l.** too long.

longuement adv (expliquer) at length; (réfléchir) for a long time.

longueur f length; **à l. de journée** all day long; **l. d'ondes** wavelength.

lors adv **l. de** at the time of.

lorsque conj when.

losange m (forme) diamond.

lot m (de loterie) prize; **gros l.** grand prize, jackpot.

loterie f lottery.

lotion f lotion.

lotissement m (habitations) housing development.

louche f ladle.

loucher vi to squint.

louer vt (prendre en location) to rent; (donner en location) to rent (out), to let; **maison à l.** house to let.

loup m wolf; **avoir une faim de l.** to be ravenous.

loupe f magnifying glass.

lourd, lourde 1 adj heavy; (temps) close; (faute) gross. **2** adv **peser l.** to be heavy.

loyal, -e, -aux adj (honnête) fair (envers).

loyauté f fairness.

loyer m rent.

lu, lue pp of **lire**.

lucarne f (fenêtre) skylight.

lueur f glimmer.

luge f sled, toboggan.

lui 1 pron mf (complément indirect) (to) him; (femme) (to) her; (chose, animal) (to) it; **il lui est facile de** it's easy for him ou her to. **2** pron m (complément direct) him; (chose, animal) it; (sujet emphatique) he.

lui-même pron himself; (chose, animal) itself.

luisant, -ante adj shiny.

lumière f light.

lumineux, -euse adj (idée, ciel etc) bright.

lundi m Monday.

lune f moon; **l. de miel** honeymoon.

lunettes fpl glasses, spectacles; (de protection, de plongée) goggles; **l. de soleil** sunglasses.

lustre m (éclairage) chandelier.

lutte f fight, struggle; (sport) wrestling.

lutter vi to fight, to struggle.

luxe m luxury; **article de l.** luxury article.

luxueux, -euse adj luxurious.

lycée m = high school.

lycéen, -enne mf = high school student.

M

ma *voir* **mon.**

macaroni(s) *m(pl)* macaroni.

macédoine *f* m. (de légumes) mixed vegetables.

mâcher *vt* to chew.

machin *m Fam (chose)* whatchamacallit.

machinalement *adv* instinctively.

machine *f* machine; **m. à coudre** sewing machine; **m. à écrire** typewriter; **m. à laver** washing machine.

mâchoire *f* jaw.

maçon *m* bricklayer.

madame, *pl* **mesdames** *f* madam; **bonjour mesdames** good morning (ladies); **Madame** *ou* **Mme Legras** Mrs Legras; **Madame** *(dans une lettre)* Dear Madam.

madeleine *f* (small) sponge cake.

mademoiselle, *pl* **mesdemoiselles** *f* miss; **bonjour mesdemoiselles** good morning (ladies); **Mademoiselle** *ou* **Mlle Legras** Miss Legras; **Mademoiselle** *(dans une lettre)* Dear Madam.

magasin *m* store; **grand m.** department store; **en m.** in stock.

magazine *m* magazine.

magicien, -ienne *mf* magician.

magie *f* magic.

magique *adj (baguette etc)* magic; *(mystérieux)* magical.

magnétophone *(Fam* **magnéto)** *m* tape recorder; **m. à cassettes** cassette recorder.

magnétoscope *m* VCR, video (recorder).

magnifique *adj* magnificent.

mai *m* May.

maigre *adj (personne)* thin; *(viande)* lean.

maigrir *vi* to get thin(ner).

maille *f* (de tricot) stitch; (de filet) mesh.

maillon *m* (de chaîne) link.

maillot *m* (de sportif) jersey, shirt; **m. (de corps)** undershirt; **m. (de bain)** (de femme) swimsuit; (d'homme) (swim)trunks.

main *f* hand; **tenir à la m.** to hold in one's hand; **à la m.** (faire, coudre etc) by hand; **haut les mains!** hands up!; **donner un coup de m. à qn** to lend sb a (helping) hand; **sous la m.** handy.

main-d'œuvre, *pl* **mains-d'œuvre** *f* labor.

maintenant *adv* now; **m. que** now that.

maintenir* *vt (conserver)* to keep; *(retenir)* to hold.

maire *m* mayor.

mairie *f* city hall.

mais *conj* but; **m. oui, m. si** yes of course; **m. non** definitely not.

maïs *m* (céréale) corn.

maison *f* (bâtiment) house; (chez-soi) home; (entreprise) firm; **à la m.** at home; **aller à la m.** to go home; **m. de la culture** arts center; **m. des jeunes** youth center.

maître *m* (d'un chien etc) master; **m. d'école** teacher; **m. d'hôtel** (restaurant) head waiter; **m. nageur** swimming instructor (and lifeguard).

maîtresse *f* mistress; **m. d'école** teacher.

maîtrise *f* (diplôme) Master's degree (**de** in).

maîtriser *vt (incendie)* to (bring under) control; **m. qn** to overpower sb.

majesté *f* **Votre M.** (titre) Your Majesty.

majeur, -e 1 *adj* **être m.** to be of age. **2** *m* (doigt) middle finger.

majorette *f* majorette.

majoritaire *adj* majority; **être m.** to be in the majority.

majorité *f* majority (**de** of); (âge) coming of age.

majuscule f capital letter.
mal, maux 1 m (douleur) pain; **dire du m. de qn** to say bad things about sb; **m. de dents** toothache; **m. de gorge** sore throat; **m. de tête** headache; **m. de ventre** stomachache; **avoir le m. de mer** to be seasick; **avoir m. à la tête/gorge/etc** to have a headache/sore throat/etc; **ça (me) fait m., j'ai m.** it hurts (me); **faire du m. à** to hurt; **avoir du m. à faire** to have trouble doing; **le bien et le m.** good and evil. **2** adv (travailler etc) badly; (entendre, comprendre) not too well; **pas m.!** not bad!; **c'est m. de mentir** it's wrong to lie.
malade 1 adj ill, sick; **être m. du cœur** to have a bad heart. **2** mf sick person; (d'un médecin) patient.
maladie f illness.
maladresse f clumsiness.
maladroit, -droite adj clumsy.
malaise m **avoir un m.** to feel dizzy.
malaria f malaria.
malchance f bad luck.
malchanceux, -euse adj unlucky.
mâle adj & m male.
malentendant, -ante 1 adj hearing-impaired. **2** mf person who is hard of hearing.
malentendu m misunderstanding.
malfaiteur m criminal.
malgré prép in spite of; **m. tout** after all.
malheur m (événement, malchance) misfortune.
malheureusement adv unfortunately.
malheureux, -euse 1 adj (triste) miserable. **2** mf (pauvre) poor man ou woman.
malhonnête adj dishonest.
malice f mischievousness.
malicieux, -euse adj mischievous.
malin, -igne adj (astucieux) clever.

malle f (coffre) trunk; (de véhicule) trunk.
mallette f small suitcase; (pour documents) attaché case.
malmener vt to manhandle, to treat badly.
malpoli, -ie adj rude.
malsain, -saine adj unhealthy.
maltraiter vt to ill-treat.
malveillant, -ante adj malevolent.
maman f mom(my).
mamie f Fam grandma.
mammifère m mammal.
manche¹ f (de vêtement) sleeve; (d'un match) round; **la M.** the English Channel.
manche² m (d'outil) handle; **m. à balai** broomstick; (d'avion etc) joystick.
manchette f (de chemise) cuff.
manchot m (oiseau) penguin.
mandarine f tangerine.
mandat m (postal) money order.
manège m (à la foire) merry-go-round.
manette f lever.
mangeable adj (médiocre) eatable.
mangeoire f (feeding) trough.
manger vti to eat; **donner à m. à** to feed.
maniable adj easy to handle.
maniaque 1 adj fussy. **2** mf fussbudget.
manie f craze.
manier vt to handle.
manière f way; **de toute m.** anyway; **à ma m.** (in) my own way; **la m. dont elle parle** the way (in which) she talks; **faire des manières** (chichis) to make a fuss.
maniéré, -ée adj affected.
manifestant, -ante mf demonstrator.
manifestation f (défilé) demonstration.
manifester 1 vt (sa colère etc) to show. **2** vi (dans la rue) to demonstrate.

manifester (se) *vpr (maladie)* to show itself.

manipulation *f (d'appareils, de produits)* handling; **manipulations génétiques** genetic engineering.

manipuler *vt (manier)* to handle.

mannequin *m (personne)* (fashion) model; *(statue)* dummy, mannequin.

manœuvre 1 *m (ouvrier)* laborer. **2** *f (action)* maneuver.

manœuvrer *vti (véhicule)* to maneuver.

manque *m* lack (of).

manquer 1 *vt (cible, train etc)* to miss. **2** *vi (faire défaut)* to be short; *(être absent)* to be absent (**à** from); **m. de** *(pain, argent etc)* to be short of; *(attention)* to lack; **ça manque de sel** there isn't enough salt; **elle/cela lui manque** he misses her/that; **elle a manqué (de) tomber** she nearly fell; **il manque/il nous manque dix tasses** there are/we are ten cups short.

mansarde *f* attic.

manteau, -x *m* coat.

manuel, -elle 1 *adj (travail)* manual. **2** *m* handbook, manual; *(scolaire)* textbook.

mappemonde *f* map of the world; *(sphère)* globe.

maquereau, -x *m (poisson)* mackerel.

maquette *f* (scale) model.

maquillage *m (fard)* make-up.

maquiller *vt (visage)* to make up.

maquiller (se) *vpr* to put one's make-up on.

marais *m* marsh.

marathon *m* marathon.

marbre *m* marble.

marchand, -ande *mf* storekeeper; *(de voitures, meubles)* dealer; **m. de journaux** *(dans un magasin)* newspaper vendor; **m. de légumes** grocer.

marchander *vi* to haggle.

marchandise(s) *f(pl)* goods.

marche *f (d'escalier)* step; *(trajet)* walk; **la m.** *(sport)* walking; **faire m. arrière** *(en voiture)* to reverse; **un train en m.** a moving train; **mettre qch en m.** to start sth (up).

marché *m (lieu)* market; **faire son** *ou* **le m.** to do one's shopping *(in the market)*; **bon m.** cheap.

marcher *vi (à pied)* to walk; *(poser le pied)* to step (**dans** in); *(fonctionner)* to work; **faire m.** *(machine)* to work; **ça marche?** *Fam* how's it going?

mardi *m* Tuesday; **M. gras** Shrove Tuesday, Mardi Gras.

mare *f (étang)* pond.

marécage *m* swamp.

marécageux, -euse *adj* swampy.

marée *f* tide; **m. noire** oil slick.

marelle *f* hopscotch.

margarine *f* margarine.

marge *f (de cahier etc)* margin.

marginal, -e, aux 1 *adj (secondaire)* marginal; *(personne)* on the fringes of society. **2** *mf* dropout.

marguerite *f* daisy.

mari *m* husband.

mariage *m* marriage; *(cérémonie)* wedding.

marié, -ée 1 *adj* married. **2** *m* (bride)groom; **les mariés** the bride and (bride)groom. **3** *f* bride.

marier *vt* **m. qn** *(prêtre etc)* to marry sb.

marier (se) *vpr* to get married *(avec qn* to sb).

marin, -ine 1 *adj* air/*etc* **m.** sea air/*etc.* **2** *m* sailor.

marine 1 *f* **m.** *(de guerre)* navy. **2** *m & adj inv (couleur)* **(bleu) m.** navy (blue).

marionnette *f* puppet.

marmelade *f* **m. (de fruits)** stewed fruit.

marmite *f* (cooking) pot.

marmonner *vti* to mutter.

maroquinerie *f (magasin)* leather goods store.

marquant, -ante *adj (remarquable)* outstanding; *(épisode)* significant.

marque *f (trace)* mark; *(de produit)* make, brand; *(points)* score; **m. de fabrique** trademark; **m. déposée** (registered) trademark.

marquer 1 *vt (par une marque)* to mark; *(écrire)* to note down; *(but)* to score; **m. les points** to keep (the) score. **2** *vi (trace)* to leave a mark; *(joueur)* to score.

marqueur *m (crayon)* marker.

marraine *f* godmother.

marrant, -ante *adj Fam* funny.

marre *f* en avoir m. *Fam* to be fed up (**de** with).

marron 1 *m* chestnut. **2** *m & adj inv (couleur)* brown.

mars *m* March.

marteau, -x *m* hammer; **m. piqueur** jackhammer.

martien, -ienne *mf & adj* Martian.

martyriser *vt (enfant)* to batter, to abuse.

mascara *m* mascara.

mascotte *f* mascot.

masculin, -ine 1 *adj* male. **2** *adj & m Grammaire* masculine.

masque *m* mask.

massacre *m* slaughter.

massacrer *vt* to slaughter.

massage *m* massage.

masse *f (volume)* mass; **en m.** in large numbers.

masser *vt (frotter)* to massage.

masser (se) *vpr (gens)* to (form a) crowd.

masseur *m* masseur.

masseuse *f* masseuse.

massif, -ive 1 *adj (or, bois etc)* solid. **2** *m (de fleurs)* clump; *(de montagnes)* massif.

mastic *m (pour vitres)* putty.

mastiquer *vt (vitre)* to putty; *(mâcher)* to chew.

mat, mate *adj (papier, couleur)* mat(t).

mât *m (de navire)* mast; *(poteau)* pole.

match *m Sport* match, game.

matelas *m* mattress; **m. pneumatique** air mattress.

matelot *m* sailor.

matériaux *mpl* (building) materials.

matériel, -ielle 1 *adj (dégâts)* material. **2** *m (de camping etc)* equipment; *(d'ordinateur)* hardware *inv*.

maternel, -elle 1 *adj (amour, femme etc)* maternal. **2** *f (école)* **maternelle** kindergarten.

maternité *f (hôpital)* labor ward.

mathématiques *fpl* mathematics.

maths *fpl* math.

matière *f (à l'école)* subject; *(substance)* material; **m. première** raw material.

matin *m* morning; **le m.** *(chaque matin)* in the morning; **à sept heures du m.** at seven in the morning.

matinal, -e, -aux *adj* être m. to be an early riser.

matinée *f* morning; **faire la grasse m.** to sleep late.

matraque *f (de policier)* billy club; *(de malfaiteur)* club.

maussade *adj (personne)* bad-tempered, moody; *(temps)* gloomy.

mauvais, -aise *adj* bad; *(méchant)* wicked; *(mal choisi)* wrong; *(mer)* rough; **plus m.** worse; **le plus m.** the worst; **il fait m.** the weather's bad; **m. en** *(anglais etc)* bad at.

mauve *adj & m (couleur)* mauve.

maximal, -e *adj* maximum.

maximum *m* maximum; **le m. de** *(force etc)* the maximum (amount of); **au m.** *(tout au plus)* at most.

mayonnaise *f* mayonnaise.

mazout *m (fuel)* oil.

me (**m'** *before vowel or mute h*) *pron (complément direct)* me; *(indirect)* (to) me; *(réfléchi)* myself.

mécanicien *m* mechanic; *(de train)* engineer.

mécanique *adj* mechanical; **jouet** m. wind-up toy.

mécanisme m mechanism.

méchanceté f malice; **une m.** *(parole)* a malicious word.

méchant, -ante *adj (cruel)* wicked; *(enfant)* naughty.

mèche f *(de cheveux)* lock; *(de bougie)* wick; *(de pétard)* fuse.

méconnaissable *adj* unrecognizable.

mécontent, -ente *adj* dissatisfied **(de** with).

mécontentement m dissatisfaction.

mécontenter *vt* to displease.

médaille f *(décoration)* medal; *(bijou)* medallion; **être m. d'or** to be a gold medalist.

médecin m doctor.

médecine f medicine; **étudiant en m.** medical student.

médias *mpl* (mass) media.

médical, -e, -aux *adj* medical.

médicament m medicine.

médiéval, -e, -aux *adj* medieval.

médiocre *adj* second-rate.

médisance(s) f(pl) malicious gossip.

Méditerranée f **la M.** the Mediterranean.

méditerranéen, -enne *adj* Mediterranean.

méduse f jellyfish.

meeting m meeting.

méfiance f distrust.

méfiant, -ante *adj* suspicious.

méfier (se) *vpr* **se m. de** to distrust; *(faire attention à)* to watch out for; **méfie-toi!** watch out!; **je me méfie** I'm suspicious.

mégarde (par) *adv* inadvertently.

mégot m cigarette butt.

meilleur, -e 1 *adj* better **(que** than); **le m. résultat** /etc the best result /etc. **2** *mf* **le m., la meilleure** the best (one).

mélange m mixture.

mélanger *vt*, **se mélanger** *vpr (mêler)* to mix.

mêlée f fight, scuffle; *Rugby* scrum.

mêler *vt* to mix **(à** with).

mêler (se) *vpr* to mix **(à** with); **se m. à** *(la foule)* to join; **mêle-toi de ce qui te regarde!** mind your own business!

mélodie f melody.

melon m *(fruit)* melon; *(chapeau)* **m.** derby.

membre m *(bras, jambe)* limb; *(d'un groupe)* member.

même 1 *adj* same; **en m. temps** at the same time **(que** as). **2** *pron* **le m., la m.** the same (one); **les mêmes** the same (ones). **3** *adv* even; **m. si** even if; **ici m.** in this very place.

mémoire f memory; **à la m. de** in memory of.

mémorable *adj* memorable.

menaçant, -ante *adj* threatening.

menace f threat.

menacer *vt* to threaten **(de faire** to do).

ménage m housekeeping; *(couple)* couple; **faire le m.** to do the housework.

ménager, -ère *adj (appareil)* domestic; **travaux ménagers** housework.

ménagère f housewife.

mendiant, -ante *mf* beggar.

mendier 1 *vt (personne, vie etc)* to lead; *(enquête etc)* to carry out; **m. qn à** to take sb to. **2** *vi (en sport)* to lead.

menottes *fpl* handcuffs.

mensonge m lie.

mensuel, -elle *adj* monthly.

mensurations *fpl* measurements.

mental, -e, -aux *adj* mental.

menteur, -euse *mf* liar.

menthe f mint.

mention f *(à un examen)* distinction.

mentir* *vi* to lie **(à** to).

menton *m* chin.

menu *m* menu.

menuiserie *f* carpentry.

menuisier *m* carpenter.

mépris *m* contempt (**pour** for).

méprisant, -ante *adj* contemptuous.

méprise *f* mistake.

mépriser *vt* to despise.

mer *f* sea; **en m.** at sea; **aller à la m.** to go to the seaside.

mercerie *f* (*magasin*) notions store.

merci *int & m* thank you (**de, pour** for).

mercredi *m* Wednesday.

merde! *int Fam* shit!

mère *f* mother; **m. de famille** mother (of a family).

mérite *m* merit; (*honneur*) credit; **avoir du m. à faire qch** to deserve credit for doing sth.

mériter *vt* (*être digne de*) to deserve.

merle *m* blackbird.

merveille *f* wonder.

merveilleux, -euse *adj* wonderful.

mes *voir* **mon**.

mésaventure *f* slight mishap.

mesdames *voir* **madame**.

mesdemoiselles *voir* **mademoiselle**.

mesquin, -ine *adj* mean, petty.

message *m* message.

messager *m* messenger.

messagerie *f* courier company; **m. électronique** electronic mail service; **m. vocale** voice mail.

messe *f* mass (*church service*).

messieurs *voir* **monsieur**.

mesure *f* (*dimension*) measurement; (*action*) measure; (*cadence*) time.

mesurer *vt* to measure; **m. 1 mètre 83** (*personne*) to be six feet tall; (*objet*) to measure six feet.

métal, -aux *m* metal.

métallique *adj* échelle/*etc* **m.** metal ladder/*etc*.

métallurgie *f* (*industrie*) steel industry.

météo *f* (*bulletin*) weather forecast.

météorologique *adj* bulletin/*etc* **m.** weather report/*etc*.

méthode *f* (*manière, soin*) method.

méthodique *adj* methodical.

métier *m* (*travail*) job.

mètre *m* (*mesure*) meter; (*règle*) (meter) stick; **m. carré** square meter; **m. (à ruban)** tape measure.

métrique *adj* metric.

métro *m* subway.

metteur *m* **m. en scène** (*de cinéma*) director.

mettre* *vt* to put; (*table*) to set, to lay; (*vêtement*) to put on; (*chauffage etc*) to switch on; (*réveil*) to set (à for); **j'ai mis une heure** it took me an hour; **m. en colère** to make angry.

mettre (se) *vpr* to put oneself; (*debout*) to stand; (*assis*) to sit; (*objet*) to go; **se m. en short/*etc*** to put on one's shorts/*etc*; **se m. à faire** to start doing; **se m. à table** to sit (down) at the table.

meuble *m* piece of furniture; **meubles** furniture.

meublé *m* furnished apartment.

meubler *vt* to furnish.

meugler *vi* (*vache*) to moo.

meule *f* (*de foin*) haystack.

meurtre *m* murder.

meurtrier, -ière *mf* murderer.

mi- *préfixe* **la mi-mars/*etc*** mid March/*etc*.

miauler *vt* to miaow.

miche *f* round loaf.

mi-chemin (à) *adv* halfway.

mi-côte (à) *adv* halfway up *ou* down (the hill).

micro *m* microphone.

microbe *m* germ.

micro-ondes *m inv* microwave; **four à m.** microwave (oven).

micro-ordinateur, *pl* **micro-ordinateurs** *m* microcomputer.

microscope *m* microscope.

midi *m (heure)* twelve o'clock, noon; *(heure du déjeuner)* lunchtime.

mie *f* la m. the soft part of the bread; **pain de m.** sandwich loaf.

miel *m* honey.

mien, mienne *pron poss* le m., la mienne, les miens, les miennes mine; les deux miens my two.

miette *f (de pain)* crumb.

mieux *adv & adj inv* better (que than); le m., la m., les m. the best; *(de deux)* the better; **tu ferais m. de partir** you had better leave.

mignon, -onne *adj (joli)* cute; *(agréable)* nice.

migraine *f* headache.

mijoter 1 *vt (lentement)* to simmer. **2** *vi* to simmer.

mil *m inv (dans les dates)* l'an deux m. the year two thousand.

milieu, -x *m (centre)* middle; **au m. de** in the middle of.

militaire 1 *adj* military. **2** *m* soldier.

mille *adj & m inv* thousand; **m. hommes/etc** a ou one thousand men/etc.

mille-pattes *m inv* centipede.

milliard *m* billion.

millième *adj & mf* thousandth.

millier *m* thousand; **un m. (de)** a thousand or so.

millimètre *m* millimeter.

million *m* million; **un m. d'euros/etc** a million euros/etc; **deux millions** two million.

millionnaire *mf* millionaire.

mime *mf (acteur)* mime.

mimer *vti* to mime.

minable *adj* shabby.

mince *adj* thin; *(élancé)* slim.

mincir *vi* to get thin.

mine[1] *f* appearance; **avoir bonne m.** to look well.

mine[2] *f (de charbon etc)* mine; *(de crayon)* lead; *(engin explosif)* mine.

miner *vt (terrain)* to mine.

minerai *m* ore.

minéral, -e, -aux *adj & m* mineral.

mineur *m (ouvrier)* miner.

miniature *adj inv (train etc)* miniature.

minimal, -e *adj* minimum.

minimum *m* minimum; **le m. de** *(force etc)* the minimum (amount of); **au (grand) m.** at the very least.

ministère *m* ministry.

ministre *m* minister.

minorité *f* minority.

minou *m (chat)* kitty.

minuit *m* midnight.

minuscule *adj (petit)* tiny.

minute *f* minute.

minuterie *f* timer *(for lighting in a stairway)*.

minuteur *m* timer.

minutieux, -euse *adj* meticulous.

miracle *m* miracle; **par m.** miraculously.

miraculeux, -euse *adj* miraculous.

miroir *m* mirror.

mis, mise *pp of* mettre.

mise[1] *f (action)* putting; **m. en marche** starting up; **m. en scène** *(de film)* direction.

mise[2] *(argent)* stake.

misérable 1 *adj (très pauvre)* destitute. **2** *mf (personne pauvre)* pauper.

misère *f* (grinding) poverty.

missile *m (fusée)* missile.

mission *f* mission.

mite *f* (clothes) moth.

mi-temps *f (pause) (en sport)* half-time; *(période) (en sport)* half; **à m.** *(travailler)* part-time.

mitigé, -ée *adj (accueil)* lukewarm; *(sentiments, impressions)* mixed.

mitraillette *f* machinegun *(portable)*.

mitrailleuse *f* machinegun *(heavy)*.

mi-voix (à) *adv* in a low voice.

mixe(u)r *m* *(pour mélanger)* (food) mixer.

mixte *adj (école)* co-educational, mixed.

mobile *adj (pièce)* moving; *(personne)* mobile.

mobilier *m* furniture.

mobylette® *f* moped.

moche *adj (laid)* ugly.

mode 1 *f* fashion; **à la m.** fashionable. **2** *m* Grammaire mood; **m. d'emploi** directions (for use).

modèle *m* model; **m. (réduit)** (scale) model.

modération *f* moderation.

modéré, -ée *adj* moderate.

modérer *vt (vitesse, chaleur etc)* to reduce.

moderne *adj* modern.

moderniser *vt*, **se moderniser** *vpr* to modernize.

modeste *adj* modest.

modestie *f* modesty.

modification *f* alteration.

modifier *vt* to alter.

moelle *f (d'os)* marrow; **m. épinière** spinal cord.

moelleux, -euse *adj (lit, tissu)* soft.

mœurs *fpl (morale)* morals; *(habitudes)* customs; **entrer dans les m.** to become part of everyday life.

moi *pron (complément direct)* me; *(indirect)* (to) me; *(sujet emphatique)* I.

moi-même *pron* myself.

moindre *adj* **la m. erreur/***etc* the slightest mistake/*etc*; **le m.** *(de mes problèmes etc)* the least (**de** of).

moine *m* monk.

moineau, -x *m* sparrow.

moins 1 *adv* less (**que** than); **m. de** *(temps, travail)* less (**que** than); *(gens, livres)* fewer (**que** than); *(cent euros)* less than; **m. grand** not as big (**que** as); **de m. en m.** less and less; **le m.** *(travailler)* the least; **le m. grand, la m. grande,** *etc* the grand(e)s the smallest; **au m., du**

m. at least; **de m., en m.** *(qui manque)* missing; **dix ans de m.** ten years less; **en m.** *(personne, objet)* less; *(personnes, objets)* fewer; **à m. que** (+ *subjonctif*) unless. **2** *prép (en calcul)* minus; **deux heures m. cinq** five to two; **il fait m. dix (degrés)** it's minus ten (degrees).

mois *m* month; **au m. de juin** in (the month of) June.

moisi, -ie 1 *adj* moldy. **2** *m* mold; **sentir le m.** to smell musty.

moisir *vi* to get moldy.

moisson *f* harvest.

moissonner *vt* to harvest.

moite *adj* sticky.

moitié *f* half; **la m. de la pomme** half (of) the apple; **à m. fermé** half closed; **à m. prix** (at) half-price; **de m.** by half.

mol *voir* **mou**.

molaire *f* back tooth.

molette *f* **clé à m.** adjustable wrench.

molle *voir* **mou**.

mollet *m (de jambe)* calf.

moment *m (instant)* moment; *(période)* time; **en ce m.** at the moment; **par moments** at times; **au m. de partir** when just about to leave; **au m. où** just as; **du m. que** *(puisque)* seeing that.

momentanément *adv (temporairement)* temporarily; *(brièvement)* briefly.

mon, ma, *pl* **mes** (ma becomes mon before a vowel or mute h) *adj poss* my; **m. père** my father; **ma mère** my mother; **m. ami(e)** my friend.

monde *m* world; **du m.** *(beaucoup de gens)* a lot of people; **le m. entier** the whole world; **tout le m.** everybody.

mondial, -e, -aux *adj (crise etc)* worldwide; **guerre mondiale** world war.

mondialisation *f* globalization.

moniteur, -trice *mf* instructor; *(de colonie de vacances)* camp counselor.

monnaie *f (devise)* currency; *(pièces)* change; **faire de la m.** to get change; **faire de la m. à qn** to give sb change (**sur un billet** for a bill).

monopoliser *vt* to monopolize.

monotone *adj* monotonous.

monotonie *f* monotony.

monsieur, *pl* **messieurs** *m (homme)* man, gentleman; **oui m.** yes sir; **oui messieurs** yes gentlemen; **M. Legras** Mr Legras; **Monsieur** *(dans une lettre)* Dear Sir.

monstre *m* monster.

monstrueux, -euse *adj (abominable)* hideous.

mont *m (montagne)* mount.

montage *m (d'un appareil)* assembling; *(d'un film)* editing; *(image truquée)* montage.

montagnard, -arde *mf* mountain dweller.

montagne *f* mountain; **la m.** *(zone)* the mountains.

montagneux, -euse *adj* mountainous.

montant *m (somme)* amount; *(de barrière)* post.

montée *f (ascension)* climb; *(chemin)* slope.

monter 1 *vi (aux* **être)** *(personne)* to go up *ou* come up; *(s'élever) (ballon, prix etc)* to go up; *(grimper)* to climb (up) (**sur** onto); *(marée)* to come in; **m. dans un véhicule** to get in(to) a vehicle; **m. dans un train** to get on(to) a train; **m. sur** *ou* **à** *(échelle)* to climb up; **m. en courant/etc** to run/ *etc* up; **m. (à cheval)** to ride (a horse). **2** *vt (aux* **avoir)** *(côte)* to climb (up); *(objet)* to bring *ou* take up; *(cheval)* to ride; *(tente)* to set up; **m. l'escalier** to go *ou* come up the stairs.

montre *f* watch.

montrer *vt* to show (**à** to); **m. du doigt** to point to.

montrer (se) *vpr* to show oneself.

monture *f (de lunettes)* frame.

monument *m* monument; **m. aux morts** war memorial.

moquer (se) *vpr* **se m. de** to make fun of; **je m'en moque!** I couldn't care less!

moquette *f* wall-to-wall carpeting.

moqueur, -euse *adj* mocking.

moral *m* spirits, morale.

morale *f (d'histoire)* moral.

morceau, -x *m* piece; *(de sucre)* lump.

morceler *vt (terrain)* to divide up.

mordiller *vt* to nibble.

mordre *vt* to bite.

morne *adj (temps)* dismal; *(silence)* gloomy; *(personne)* glum.

morse *m (animal)* walrus.

morsure *f* bite.

mort *f* death.

mort, morte *(pp of* **mourir)** **1** *adj (personne, plante etc)* dead. **2** *mf* dead man, dead woman; **les morts** the dead; **de nombreux morts** *(victimes)* many casualties *ou* dead.

mortel, -elle *adj (hommes, ennemi etc)* mortal; *(accident)* fatal.

morue *f* cod.

mosquée *f* mosque.

mot *m* word; **envoyer un m. à** to drop a line to; **mots croisés** crossword (puzzle); **m. de passe** password.

motard *m* motorcyclist.

moteur *(de véhicule etc)* engine, motor.

motif *m (raison)* reason (**de** for).

motivé, -ée *adj* motivated.

motiver *vt (inciter, causer)* to motivate; *(justifier)* to justify.

moto *f* motorcycle.

motocycliste *mf* motorcyclist.

motte *f (de terre)* lump.

mou *(or* **mol** before vowel or mute h), **molle** *adj* soft; *(sans énergie)* feeble.

mouche *f (insecte)* fly.

moucher (se) *vpr* to blow one's nose.

moucheron *m* midge.

mouchoir *m* handkerchief; *(en papier)* tissue.

moudre* *vt (café)* to grind.

moue *f* long face; **faire la m.** to pull a (long) face.

mouette *f* (sea)gull.

moufle *f* mitten.

mouillé, -ée *adj* wet (**de** with).

mouiller *vt* to (make) wet; **se faire m.** to get wet.

mouiller (se) *vpr* to get (oneself) wet.

moulant, -ante *adj (vêtement)* tight-fitting.

moule¹ *m* mold; **m. à gâteaux** cake pan.

moule² *f (animal)* mussel.

moulder *vt* to mold; **m. qn** *(vêtement)* to fit sb tightly.

moulin *m* mill; **m. à vent** windmill; **m. à café** coffee grinder.

moulu *(pp of* **moudre***) adj (café)* ground.

mourir* *vi (aux* **être***)* to die (**de** of, from); **m. de froid** to die of exposure; **je meurs de faim!** I'm starving!

mousse *f (plante)* moss; *(écume)* foam; *(de bière)* froth; *(de savon)* lather; *(dessert)* mousse.

mousser *vi (bière)* to froth; *(savon)* to lather; *(eau)* to foam.

mousseux 1 *adj (vin)* sparkling. **2** *m* sparkling wine.

moustache *f* mustache; **moustaches** *(de chat)* whiskers.

moustachu, -ue *adj* wearing a mustache.

moustique *m* mosquito.

moutarde *f* mustard.

mouton *m* sheep *inv*; *(viande)* mutton.

mouvement *m (geste, groupe etc)* movement; *(de colère)* outburst.

mouvementé, -ée *adj (vie, voyage etc)* eventful.

moyen, -enne 1 *adj* average; *(format etc)* medium(-sized); **classe moyenne** middle class. **2** *f* average; *(dans un examen, un devoir)* passing grade; **en moyenne** on average.

moyen *m (procédé, façon)* means, way (**de faire** of doing, to do); **il n'y a pas m. de faire** it's not possible to do; **je n'ai pas les moyens** *(argent)* I can't afford it.

muer *vi (animal)* to molt; *(voix)* to break.

muet, -ette 1 *adj (infirme)* mute; *(film, voyelle)* silent. **2** *mf* mute person.

mufle *m (d'animal)* muzzle.

mugir *vi (bœuf)* to bellow.

mugissement(s) *m(pl)* bellow(-ing).

muguet *m* lily of the valley.

mule *f (pantoufle)* mule; *(animal)* (she-)mule.

multicolore *adj* multicolored.

multiple *m (nombre)* multiple.

multiplication *f* multiplication.

multiplier *vt* to multiply.

municipal, -e, -aux *adj* municipal; **conseil m.** city council.

municipalité *f (maires et conseillers)* city council; *(commune)* municipality.

munir *vt* **m. de** to equip with.

muner (se) *vpr* **se m. de** to provide oneself with.

munitions *fpl* ammunition.

mur *m* wall; **m. du son** sound barrier.

mûr, mûre *adj (fruit)* ripe.

muraille *f* (high) wall.

mûre *f (baie)* blackberry.

mûrir *vti (fruit)* to ripen.

murmure *m* murmur.

murmurer *vti* to murmur.

muscle *m* muscle.

musclé, -ée *adj (bras)* muscular.

museau, -x *m (de chien, chat)* nose, muzzle.

musée *m* museum.

museler *vt (animal, presse)* to muzzle.

muselière f (appareil) muzzle.
musical, -e, -aux adj musical.
musicien, -ienne mf musician.
musique f music.
musulman, -ane adj & mf Muslim.
muter vt to transfer.
mutuel, -elle adj (réciproque) mutual.
myope adj & mf shortsighted (person).
myrtille f (baie) bilberry.
mystère m mystery.
mystérieux, -euse adj mysterious.

N

nage f (swimming) stroke; **traverser à la n.** to swim across; **en n.** sweating.
nageoire f (de poisson) fin.
nager 1 vi to swim. **2** vt (crawl etc) to swim.
nageur, -euse mf swimmer.
naïf, -ïve adj naïve.
nain, naine mf dwarf.
naissance f (de personne, animal) birth.
naître* vi to be born.
nappe f (sur une table) table cloth.
napperon m (pour vase etc) (cloth) mat, doily.
narguer vt to taunt.
narine f nostril.
naseau, -x m (de cheval) nostril.
natal, -e, -als adj (pays) native; **sa maison natale** the house where he ou she was born.
natation f swimming.
nation f nation.
national, -e, -aux adj national; **(route) nationale** highway.
nationalité f nationality.

natte f (de cheveux) braid; (tapis) mat.
nature 1 f (monde naturel, caractère) nature. **2** adj inv (omelette, yaourt etc) plain; (café) black.
naturel, -elle adj natural.
naufrage m (ship)wreck; **faire n.** to be (ship)wrecked.
naufragé, -ée adj & mf shipwrecked (person).
nausée f nausea, sickness; **avoir la n.** to feel nauseous.
nautique adj ski/etc n. water skiing/etc.
naval, -e, -als adj naval.
navet m (plante) turnip.
navette f **faire la n.** to shuttle back and forth (**entre** between); **n. spatiale** space shuttle.
navigateur, -trice mf (marin) navigator.
navigation f (trafic de bateaux) shipping.
naviguer vi (bateau) to sail.
navire m ship.
navrant, -ante adj appalling.
navré, -ée adj **je suis n.** I'm (terribly) sorry (**de faire** to do).
ne (n' before vowel or mute h; used to form negative verb with **pas, jamais, personne, rien, que** etc) adv (+ pas) not; **il ne boit pas** he does not ou doesn't drink.
né, -ée adj (pp of **naître**) born; **elle est née** she was born.
néanmoins adv nevertheless.
nécessaire 1 adj necessary. **2** m **n. de toilette** (d'homme) shaving kit; (de femme) cosmetic case; **faire le n.** to do what's necessary.
nécessité f necessity.
nécessiter vt to require.
nectarine f nectarine.
néerlandais, -aise 1 adj Dutch. **2** mf **N.** Dutchman, Dutchwoman; **les N.** the Dutch. **3** m (langue) Dutch.
néfaste adj harmful (**à** to).
négatif, -ive 1 adj negative. **2** m (de photo) negative.

négation f Grammaire negation; (mot) negative.

négligence f (défaut) carelessness.

négligent, -ente adj careless.

négliger vt (personne, travail etc) to neglect; **n. de faire** to neglect to do.

négociant, -ante mf merchant, dealer.

négociation f negotiation.

négocier vti to negotiate.

neige f snow; **n. fondue** sleet.

neiger vi to snow.

nénuphar m water lily.

néon m éclairage au n. neon lighting.

nerf m nerve; **du n.!** buck up!; **ça me tape sur les nerfs** it gets on my nerves.

nerveux, -euse adj (agité) nervous.

nescafé® m instant coffee.

n'est-ce pas? adv isn't he?/don't you?/etc; **tu l'as, n?** you've got it, haven't you?; **elle vient, n.?** she's coming, isn't she?

net, nette 1 adj (image, refus) clear; (coupure, linge) clean; (soigné) neat; (poids, prix) net. 2 adv (s'arrêter) dead; (casser, couper) clean.

nettement adv (bien plus) definitely.

nettoyage m cleaning; **n. à sec** dry cleaning.

nettoyer vt to clean (up).

neuf, neuve 1 adj new; **quoi de n.?** what's new(s)? 2 m **remettre à n.** to make as good as new.

neuf adj & m nine.

neutre adj (pays) neutral.

neuvième adj & mf ninth.

neveu, -x m nephew.

nez m nose; **n. à n.** face to face (**avec** with).

ni conj **ni...ni** (+ ne) neither...nor; **il n'a ni faim ni soif** he's neither hungry nor thirsty; **sans manger ni**

boire without eating or drinking; **ni l'un(e) ni l'autre** neither (of them).

niche f (de chien) doghouse.

nicher vi, **se nicher** vpr (oiseau) to nest.

nid m nest.

nièce f niece.

nier vt to deny (**que** that).

niveau, -x m level; **au n. de qn** (élève etc) up to sb's standard.

noble 1 adj noble. 2 mf nobleman, noblewoman.

noce(s) f(pl) wedding.

nocif, -ive adj harmful.

Noël m Christmas; **le père N.** Father Christmas, Santa Claus.

nœud m knot; (ruban) bow; **n. coulant** slipknot, noose; **n. papillon** bow tie.

noir, noire 1 adj black; (nuit, lunettes etc) dark; **il fait n.** it's dark. 2 m (couleur) black; (obscurité) dark; **N.** (homme) black. 3 f **Noire** (femme) black.

noircir 1 vt to make black. 2 vi, **se noircir** vpr to turn black.

noisetier m hazel (tree).

noisette f hazelnut.

noix f (du noyer) walnut; **n. de coco** coconut.

nom m name; Grammaire noun; **n. de famille** last name, surname; **n. propre** Grammaire proper noun.

nombre m number.

nombreux, -euse adj (amis, livres) numerous, many; (famille) large; **peu n.** few; **venir n.** to come in large numbers.

nombril m navel.

nommer vt (appeler) to name; **n. qn** (désigner) to appoint sb (**à un poste** to a post).

nommer (se) vpr to be called.

non adv & m inv no; **tu viens ou n.?** are you coming or not?; **n. seulement** not only; **je crois que n.** I don't think so; **(ni) moi n. plus** neither do/am/can/etc I.

nonante *adj (en Belgique, en Suisse)* ninety.

non-fumeur, -euse *mf* non-smoker.

non-voyants *mpl* **les n.** the unsighted.

nord *m* north; **au n. de** north of; **du n.** *(vent)* northerly; *(ville)* northern.

nord-africain, -aine 1 *adj* North African. **2** *mf* **N.-A.** North African.

nord-américain, -aine 1 *adj* North American. **2** *mf* **N.-A.** North American.

nord-est *m & adj inv* northeast.

nord-ouest *m & adj inv* northwest.

normal, -e, -aux *adj* normal.

normale *f* **au-dessus/au-dessous de la n.** above/below normal.

normalement *adv* normally.

norvégien, -ienne 1 *adj* Norwegian. **2** *mf* **N.** Norwegian. **3** *m (langue)* Norwegian.

nos *voir* **notre**.

notaire *m* lawyer.

notamment *adv* particularly.

note *f (de musique, remarque)* note; *(à l'école)* grade; *(facture)* bill; **prendre n. de** to make a note of.

noter *vt* to note; *(un devoir)* to grade.

notice *f (mode d'emploi)* instructions.

notoriété *f (renom)* fame; **il est de n. publique que…** it's common knowledge that…

notre, *pl* **nos** *adj poss* our.

nôtre, *pron poss* **le** *ou* **la n., les nôtres** ours.

nouer *vt (chaussure etc)* to tie.

nouilles *fpl* noodles.

nounours *m* teddy bear.

nourrice *f (assistante maternelle)* nanny.

nourrir *vt* to feed.

nourrissant, -ante *adj* nourishing.

nourrisson *m* infant.

nourriture *f* food.

nous *pron (sujet)* we; *(complément direct)* us; *(indirect)* (to) us; *(réfléchi)* ourselves; *(réciproque)* each other.

nous-mêmes *pron* ourselves.

nouveau (*or* **nouvel** *before vowel or mute* h*)*, **nouvelle,** *pl* **nouveaux, nouvelles 1** *adj* new. **2** *mf (dans une classe)* new boy, new girl. **3 m de n., à n.** again.

nouveau-né, -née *mf* new-born baby.

nouveauté *f* novelty; **nouveautés** *(livres)* new books; *(disques)* new releases.

nouvelle *f (information)* nouvelle(s) news; **une n.** a piece of news.

novembre *m* November.

noyade *f* drowning.

noyau, -x *f (fruit)* pit.

noyé, -ée *mf* drowned man *ou* woman.

noyer[1] *vt*, **se noyer** *vpr* to drown.

noyer[2] *m (arbre)* walnut tree.

nu, nue *adj (personne)* naked; *(mains)* bare; **tout nu** (stark) naked; **tête nue, nu-tête** bareheaded.

nuage *m* cloud.

nuageux, -euse *adj* cloudy.

nuance *f (de couleurs)* shade.

nucléaire *adj* nuclear.

nuire* *vi* **n. à qn** to harm sb.

nuisible *adj* harmful.

nuit *f* night; *(obscurité)* dark(ness); **il fait n.** it's dark; **la n.** *(se promener etc)* at night; *(aujourd'hui)* tonight; *(hier)* last night; **bonne n.** *(au coucher)* good night.

nul, nulle *adj (médiocre)* hopeless; **faire match n.** to tie; **nulle part** nowhere.

numérique *adj* numerical; *(montre, clavier, données)* digital.

numéro *m* number; *(de journal)* issue; *(au cirque)* act; **un n. de danse** a dance number; **n. vert** *(au téléphone)* = tollfree number.

numéroter vt (page etc) to number.

nuque f back of the neck.

nylon® m nylon; **chemise**/etc **en n.** nylon shirt/etc.

O

obéir vi to obey; **o. à qn** to obey sb.

obéissance f obedience.

obéissant, -ante adj obedient.

objectif m (but) objective; (d'appareil photo) lens.

objet m (chose) object; **objets trouvés** (bureau) lost and found.

obligation f obligation.

obligatoire adj compulsory.

obliger vt to force, to compel (**à faire** to do); **être obligé de faire** to have to do.

oblique adj oblique.

obscène adj obscene.

obscur, -e adj (noir) dark.

obscurcir vt (pièce) to make dark(er).

obscurcir (s') vpr (ciel) to get dark(er).

obscurité f dark(ness).

obséder vt to obsess.

obsèques fpl funeral.

observation f (étude) observation; (reproche) (critical) remark.

observatoire m (endroit élevé) lookout (post).

observer vt (regarder) to watch; (remarquer, respecter) to observe.

obstacle m obstacle.

obstiné, -ée adj stubborn, obstinate.

obstiner (s') vpr s'o. à faire to persist in doing.

obstruer vt to obstruct.

obtenir* vt to get, to obtain.

obus m (arme) shell.

occasion f chance (**de faire** to do); (prix avantageux) bargain; **d'o.** second-hand, used.

occasionner vt to cause.

Occident m l'O. the West.

occidental, -e, -aux adj western.

occupation f (activité etc) occupation.

occupé, -ée adj busy (**à faire** doing); (place, maison etc) occupied; (téléphone) busy; (taxi) hired.

occuper vt (maison, pays etc) to occupy; (place, temps) to take up; **o. qn** (travail, jeu) to keep sb busy.

occuper (s') vpr to keep (oneself) busy (**à faire** doing); **s'o. de** (affaire, problème) to deal with; **s'o. de qn** (malade etc) to take care of sb; **occupe-toi de tes affaires!** mind your own business!

océan m ocean.

octet m byte; **milliard d'octets** gigabyte.

octobre m October.

oculiste mf eye specialist.

odeur f smell.

odieux, -euse adj horrible.

odorat m sense of smell.

œil, pl yeux m eye; **lever/baisser les yeux** to look up/down; **coup d'o.** look, glance; **jeter un coup d'o. sur** to (have a) look at; **o. poché, o. au beurre noir** black eye.

œillet m (fleur) carnation.

œuf, pl œufs m egg; **o. sur le plat** fried egg.

œuvre f (travail, livre etc) work.

offenser vt to offend.

office m (messe) service.

officiel, -ielle adj official.

officier m (dans l'armée etc) officer.

offre f offer; **l'o. et la demande** supply and demand; **offres d'emploi** job vacancies, positions vacant.

offrir* vt to offer (**de faire** to do); (cadeau) to give.

offrir (s') vpr s'o. qch to treat oneself to sth.

oh! *int* oh!

oie *f* goose (*pl* geese).

oignon *m* (*légume*) onion; (*de fleur*) bulb.

oiseau, -x *m* bird.

oisif, -ive *adj* (*inactif*) idle.

oisiveté *f* idleness.

olive *f* olive; **huile d'o.** olive oil.

olivier *m* olive tree.

olympique *adj* (*jeux*) Olympic.

ombragé, -ée *adj* shady.

ombre *f* (*d'arbre etc*) shade; (*de personne, objet*) shadow; **à l'o.** in the shade.

omelette *f* omelet(te); **o. au fromage/etc** cheese/*etc* omelet(te).

omettre* *vt* to omit (**de faire** to do).

omnibus *adj & m* (*train*) **o.** slow *ou* local train.

omoplate *f* shoulder blade.

on *pron* (*les gens*) they, people; (*nous*) we; (*vous*) you; **on frappe** someone's knocking; **on m'a dit que** I was told that.

oncle *m* uncle.

onde (*de radio*) wave; **grandes ondes** long wave; **ondes courtes** short wave.

ondulation *f* (*de cheveux*) wave.

onduler *vi* (*cheveux*) to be wavy.

ongle *m* (*finger*) nail.

ont *voir* avoir.

ONU *f abrév* (Organisation des Nations Unies) UN.

onze *adj & m* eleven.

onzième *adj & mf* eleventh.

opaque *adj* opaque.

opéra *m* (*musique*) opera; (*édifice*) opera house.

opération *f* operation.

opérer *vt* (*en chirurgie*) to operate on (**de** for); **se faire o.** to have an operation.

opinion *f* opinion (**sur** about, on).

opportun, -une *adj* opportune, timely.

opposé, -ée 1 *adj* (*direction, opinion etc*) opposite; (*équipe*) oppos-

ing; **o. à** opposed to. **2** *m* **l'o.** the opposite (**de** of); **à l'o.** (*côté*) on the opposite side (**de** from, to).

opposer *vt* (*résistance*) to put up (**à** against); (*équipes*) to bring together; **o. qn à qn** to set sb against sb.

opposer (s') *upr* (*équipes*) to play against each other; **s'o. à** (*mesure, personne*) to be opposed to, to oppose.

opposition *f* opposition (**à** to).

oppressant, -ante *adj* oppressive.

opticien, -ienne *mf* optician.

optimiste *adj* optimistic.

optique 1 *adj* (*nerf*) optic; (*verre, fibres*) optical. **2** *f* optics; **d'o.** (*instrument*) optical. ▪ (*point de vue*) perspective.

or 1 *m* gold; **montre/etc en or** gold watch/*etc*, **d'or** (*règle*) golden; **mine d'or** goldmine. **2** *conj* (*cependant*) now, well.

orage *m* (*thunder*)storm.

orageux, -euse *adj* stormy.

oral, -e, -aux 1 *adj* oral. **2** *m* (*examen*) oral.

orange 1 *f* (*fruit*) orange. **2** *adj & m inv* (*couleur*) orange.

orangeade *f* orangeade.

orbite *f* (*d'astre*) orbit; (*d'œil*) socket.

orchestre *m* (*classique*) orchestra; (*jazz, pop*) band; (*places*) orchestra.

ordinaire *adj* (*habituel, normal*) ordinary, regular; (*médiocre*) ordinary; **d'o.** usually.

ordinateur *m* computer.

ordonnance *f* (*de médecin*) prescription.

ordonné, -ée *adj* tidy.

ordonner *vt* to order (**que** (+ *subjonctif*) that); (*médicament etc*) to prescribe; **o. à qn de faire** to order sb to do.

ordre *m* (*commandement, classement*) order; (*absence de désordre, tidiness* (*of room, person etc*)

o. (chambre etc) tidy; **mettre en o.,
mettre de l'o. dans** to tidy (up);
jusqu'à nouvel o. until further
notice.

ordures fpl (débris) garbage.

oreille f ear; **faire la sourde o.** to
take no notice, to refuse to listen.

oreiller m pillow.

oreillons mpl mumps.

organe m (de corps) organ.

organisateur, -trice mf organizer.

organisation f organization.

organiser vt to organize.

organiser (s') vpr to get organized.

organisme m (corps) body; (bureaux etc) organization.

orge f barley.

orgue 1 m (instrument) organ. **2** fpl
grandes orgues great organ.

orgueil m pride.

orgueilleux, -euse adj proud.

oriental, -e, -aux adj (côte, pays
etc) eastern; (du Japon, de la Chine)
far-eastern, oriental.

orientation f direction; (de maison) orientation; **o. professionnelle**
career counseling.

orienté, -ée adj (appartement
etc) **o. à l'ouest** facing west.

orienter vt (lampe etc) to position;
(voyageur, élève) to direct.

orienter (s') vpr to find one's bearings ou direction.

originaire adj **être o. de** (natif) to
be a native of.

original, -e, -aux 1 adj (idée, artiste etc) original. **2** m (texte)
original.

originalité f originality.

origine f origin; **à l'o.** originally;
d'o. (pneu etc) original; **pays d'o.**
country of origin.

...ment m ornament.

... vt to decorate (**de** with).

...lin, -ine mf orphan.

...linat m orphanage.

... m toe; **gros o.** big toe.

orthographe f spelling.

ortie f nettle.

os m bone; **trempé jusqu'aux os**
soaked to the skin.

osé, -ée adj daring.

oser vti to dare; **o. faire** to dare (to)
do.

osier m wicker; **panier d'o.** wicker
basket.

otage m hostage; **prendre qn en o.**
to take sb hostage.

OTAN f abrév (Organisation du
traité de l'Atlantique Nord) NATO.

otarie f (animal) sea lion.

ôter vt to take away (**à qn** from sb);
(vêtement) to take off; (déduire) to
take away.

otite f ear infection.

ou conj or; **ou bien** or else; **ou elle
ou moi** either her or me.

où adv & pron where; **le jour où** the
day when; **la table où** the table on
which; **par où?** which way?; **d'où?**
where from?; **le pays d'où** the country from which.

oubli m **l'o. de** qch forgetting sth;
un o. (dans une liste etc) an oversight.

oublier vt to forget (**de faire** to do).

ouest m & adj inv west; **d'o.** (vent)
west(erly); **à l'o.** western.

ouf! int (whew,) what a relief!

oui adv & m inv yes; **tu viens, o. ou
non?** are you coming or aren't you?;
je crois que o. I think so.

ouïe f hearing.

ouïes fpl (de poisson) gills.

ouille! int ouch!

ouragan m hurricane.

ourlet m hem.

ours m bear; **o. blanc** polar bear.

outil m tool.

outillage m tools.

outre 1 prép besides. **2** adv en o.
besides.

outre-mer adv overseas; **d'o.**
(marché) overseas; **territoires d'o.**
overseas territories.

outré, -ée adj (révolté) outraged.

ouvert, -erte (*pp of* **ouvrir**) *adj* open; (*robinet, gaz*) on.

ouvertement *adv* openly.

ouverture *f* opening; (*trou*) hole.

ouvrage *m* (*travail, livre*) work; (*couture*) (needle)work; **un o.** (*travail*) a piece of work.

ouvre-boîtes *m inv* can opener.

ouvre-bouteilles *m inv* bottle opener.

ouvreuse *f* usherette.

ouvrier, -ière 1 *mf* worker; **o. qualifié/spécialisé** skilled/unskilled worker. **2** *adj* (*quartier*) working-class; **classe ouvrière** working class.

ouvrir* **1** *vt* to open (up); (*gaz, radio etc*) to turn on, to switch on. **2** *vi* to open; (*ouvrir la porte*) to open (up).

ouvrir (s') *vpr* (*porte, boîte etc*) to open (up).

ovale *adj & m* oval.

OVNI *m abrév* (*objet volant non identifié*) UFO.

oxygène *m* oxygen.

P

pacifique 1 *adj* (*manifestation etc*) peaceful; (*côte etc*) Pacific. **2** *m* **le P.** the Pacific.

pagaie *f* paddle.

pagaille *f* (*désordre*) mess; **en p.** in a mess.

pagayer *vi* to paddle.

page *f* (*de livre etc*) page.

paie *f* pay, wages.

paiement *m* payment.

paillasson *m* (door)mat.

paille *f* straw; (*pour boire*) (drinking) straw; **tirer à la courte p.** to draw lots ou straws.

paillette *f* (*d'habit*) sequin; **paillettes** (*de savon*) flakes.

pain *m* bread; **un p.** a loaf (of bread); **p. grillé** toast; **p. complet** whole-wheat bread; **p. d'épice** gingerbread; **p. de seigle** rye bread; **petit p.** roll.

pair, -e *adj* (*numéro*) even.

paire *f* pair (**de** of).

paisible *adj* (*vie, endroit*) peaceful.

paître* *vi* to graze.

paix *f* peace; (*traité*) peace treaty; **en p.** in peace; **avoir la p.** to have (some) peace and quiet.

palais¹ *m* (*château*) palace; **P. de justice** courthouse; **p. des sports** sports stadium.

palais² *m* (*dans la bouche*) palate.

pâle *adj* pale.

paletot *m* (knitted) cardigan.

palette *f* (*de peintre*) palette.

pâleur *f* paleness.

palier *m* (*descalier*) landing; **être voisins de p.** to live on the same floor.

pâlir *vi* to turn pale (**de** with).

palissade *f* fence (*of stakes*).

palmarès *m* prize list; (*de chansons*) charts.

palme *f* palm (leaf); (*de nageur*) flipper.

palmier *m* palm (tree).

palper *vt* to feel.

palpitant, -ante *adj* thrilling.

palpiter *vi* (*cœur*) to throb.

pamplemousse *m* grapefruit.

pan! *int* bang!

panaché *adj & m* **(demi) p.** shandy (*beer and lemonade*).

pancarte *f* sign; (*de manifestant*) placard.

pané, -ée *adj* breaded.

panier *m* basket; **p. à salade** (*ustensile*) salad basket.

panique *f* panic.

paniqué, -ée *adj* panic-stricken.

paniquer *vi* to panic.

panne *f* breakdown; **tomber en** to break down; **être en p.** to b broken down; **p. d'électricité** h out, power outage.

panneau, -x m (écriteau) sign; (de porte etc) panel; **p.** (de signalisation) road sign; **p.** (d'affichage) billboard.

panoplie f (jouet) outfit.

panorama m view.

pansement m dressing, bandage; **p. adhésif** Band-Aid®.

panser vt (main etc) to dress, to bandage.

pantalon m (pair of pants); **en p.** in pants.

pantin m puppet, jumping jack.

pantoufle f slipper.

paon m peacock.

papa m dad(dy).

pape m pope.

papeterie f (magasin) stationery store.

papi m Fam grand(d)ad.

papier m (matière) paper; **un p.** (feuille) a sheet of paper; (formulaire) a form; **sac/etc en p.** paper bag/etc; **papiers (d'identité)** (identity) papers; **p. hygiénique** toilet paper; **p. à lettres** writing paper; **du p. journal** (some) newspaper; **p. peint** wallpaper; **p. de verre** sandpaper.

papillon m butterfly; **p.** (de nuit) moth.

paquebot m (ocean) liner.

pâquerette f daisy.

Pâques m sing & fpl Easter.

paquet m (de bonbons etc) packet; (colis) package; (de cigarettes) pack; (de cartes) pack, deck.

par prép (agent, manière, moyen) by; **choisi p.** chosen by; **p. le train** by train; **p. le travail** by ou through work; **apprendre p. un ami** to learn ‸om ou through a friend; **commen**‸ **. qch** to begin with sth. ▪ (lieu) ‸gh; **p. la porte** through ou by ‸loor; **jeter p. la fenêtre** ‸ out (of) the window; **p. ici/là** ‸ this/that way; (habiter) ‸ here/there. ▪ (motif) out o‸ **p. pitié** out of ou from pity.

▪ (temps) on; **p. un jour d'hiver** on a winter day; **p. ce froid** in this cold. ▪ (distributif) **dix fois p. an** ten times a year; **deux p. deux** two by two.

parachute m parachute.

parachutisme m parachute jumping.

paradis m heaven, paradise.

paragraphe m paragraph.

paraître* vi (sembler) to seem; (livre) to come out; **il paraît qu'il va partir** it appears ou seems he's leaving.

parallèle adj parallel (à with, to).

paralyser vt to paralyze.

parapente m (activité) paragliding; **faire du p.** to go paragliding.

parapluie m umbrella.

parasite m parasite; **parasites** (à la radio) interference.

parasol m sunshade.

paravent m (folding) screen.

parc m park; (de château) grounds; (de bébé) playpen; **p. (de stationnement)** parking lot.

parce que conj because.

parcelle f fragment; (terrain) plot.

par-ci par-là adv here, there and everywhere.

parcmètre m parking meter.

parcourir* vt (region) to travel all over; (distance) to cover; (texte) to glance through.

parcours m (itinéraire) route; (distance) distance.

par-dessous prép & adv under(neath).

pardessus m overcoat.

par-dessus prép & adv over (the top of); **p. tout** above all.

pardon m p.! (excusez-moi) sorry!; **demander p.** to apologize (à to).

pardonner vt to forgive; **p. qch à qn/à qn d'avoir fait qch** to forgive sb for sth/for doing sth.

pare-brise m inv windshield.

pare-chocs m inv bumper.

pareil, -eille 1 adj similar; **p. à the**

same as; **être pareils** to be the same; **un p. désordre/etc** such a mess/etc. **2** adv Fam the same.

parent, -ente 1 mf relative. **2** mpl (père et mère) parents. **3** adj related (**de** to).

parenté f relationship; **avoir un lien de p.** to be related.

parenthèse f (signe) bracket.

paresse f laziness.

paresseux, -euse adj & mf lazy (person). .

parfait, -aite adj perfect; **p.!** excellent!

parfaitement adv perfectly; (certainement) certainly.

parfois adv sometimes.

parfum m (odeur) fragrance; (goût) flavor; (liquide) perfume.

parfumé, -ée adj (savon, fleur) scented; **p. au café/etc** coffee/etc-flavored.

parfumer vt to perfume; (glace, crème) to flavor (**à** with).

parfumer (se) vpr to put on perfume.

parfumerie f perfume shop.

pari m bet; **p. mutuel urbain** = pari-mutuel.

parier vti to bet (**sur** on; **que** that).

parisien, -ienne 1 adj Parisian; **la banlieue parisienne** the outskirts of Paris. **2** mf P. Parisian.

parking m parking lot.

parlement m parliament.

parlementaire mf member of parliament, = Congressman.

parler 1 vi to talk, to speak (**de** about, of; **à** to). **2** vt (langue) to speak.

parler (se) vpr (langue) to be spoken.

parmi prép among(st).

paroi f (inside) wall; (de rocher) (rock) face.

paroisse f parish.

paroissial, -e, -aux adj église/etc paroissiale parish church/etc.

parole f (mot, promesse) word;

adresser la p. à to speak to; **prendre la p.** to speak; **demander la p.** to ask to speak.

parquet m (parquet) floor.

parrain m godfather.

parrainer vt (course etc) to sponsor.

parsemé, -ée adj **p. de** (sol) strewn (all over) with.

part f (portion) share; (de gâteau) portion; **prendre p. à** (activité) to take part in; (la joie etc de qn) to share; **de toutes parts** from ou on all sides; **de p. et d'autre** on both sides; **d'autre p.** (d'ailleurs) moreover; **de la p. de** (provenance) from; **quelque p.** somewhere; **nulle p.** nowhere; **autre p.** somewhere else; **à p.** (mettre) aside; (excepté) apart from; (personne) different.

partage m (de gâteau, trésor etc) sharing.

partagé, -ée adj (amour) mutual; **les avis sont partagés** opinions are divided.

partager vt (repas, joie etc) to share (**avec** with).

partance (en) adj (train) about to depart; **en p. pour...** for...

partenaire mf partner.

partenariat m partnership.

parterre m (de jardin) flower bed.

parti m (politique) party.

partial, -e, -aux adj biased.

participant, -ante mf participant.

participation f participation; **p. (aux frais)** contribution (towards expenses).

participe m Grammaire participle.

participer vi **p. à** (jeu etc) to take part in; (frais, joie) to share (in).

particularité f peculiarity.

particulier, -ière adj (spécial) particular; (privé) private; (bizarre) peculiar; **en p.** (surtout) in particular.

particulièrement adv particularly.

partie f part; (de cartes, tennis etc) game; **en p.** partly; **faire de p.** to be a part of; (club etc) to belong to.

partiel, -elle adj partial.

partir* vi (aux **être**) (aller) to go; (s'en aller) to go, to leave; (coup de feu) to go off; (tache) to come out; **à p. de** (date, prix) from.

partisan m supporter; **être p. de qch/de faire** to be in favor of sth/of doing.

partition f (musique) score.

partout adv everywhere; **p. où tu vas** ou **iras** everywhere ou wherever you go.

parvenir* vi (aux **être**) **p. à** (lieu) to reach; **p. à faire** to manage to do.

pas¹ adv (négatif) not; (**ne**)...**p.** not; **je ne sais p.** I don't know; **p. de pain**/etc no bread/etc; **p. encore** not yet; **p. du tout** not at all.

pas² m step; (allure) pace; (bruit) footstep; (trace) footprint; **rouler au p.** (véhicule) to go dead slow; **au p.** (cadencé) in step; **faire les cent p.** to walk up and down, to pace; **faux p.** (en marchant) stumble; (erreur) blunder; **le p. de la porte** the doorstep.

passable adj (travail, résultat) (just) average.

passage m passing; (traversée en bateau) crossing; (extrait, couloir) passage; (droit) right of way; (chemin) path; **p. clouté** ou **pour piétons** (pedestrian) crosswalk; **p. souterrain** underground passage (for pedestrians); **p. à niveau** grade crossing; **'p. interdit'** 'no through traffic'; **'cédez le p.'** (au carrefour) 'yield'.

passager, -ère mf passenger.

passant, -ante mf passer-by.

passe f Sport pass.

passé, -ée 1 adj (temps) past; (couleur) faded; **la semaine passée** last week; **dix heures passées** after ten (o'clock); **être passé** (personne) to have been here/there; (orage) to

be over; **avoir vingt ans passés** to be over twenty. **2** m past; Grammaire past (tense).

passe-passe m inv **tour de p.** magic trick.

passeport m passport.

passer 1 vi (aux **être** ou **avoir**) to pass (**à** to; **de** from); (traverser) to go through ou over; (facteur) to come; (temps) to pass, to go by; (film) to be shown; (douleur) to pass; (couleur) to fade; **p. devant** (maison etc) to go past, to pass (by); **p. à la boulangerie** ou **chez le boulanger** to go to ou by the bakery; **laisser p.** (personne, lumière) to let through; **p. prendre** to pick up; **p. voir qn** to drop in on sb; **p. pour** (riche etc) to be taken for; **p. en** (seconde etc) (à l'école) to advance to; (en voiture) to shift into. **2** vt (aux **avoir**) (frontière etc) to cross; (donner) to pass, to hand (**à** to); (temps) to spend (**à faire** doing); (CD, chemise, film) to put on; (examen) to take; (thé) to strain; (café) to filter; (limites) to go beyond; (visite médicale) to have; **p. qch à qn** (caprice etc) to grant sb sth; **p. un coup d'éponge**/etc **à qch** to go over sth with a sponge/etc.

passer (se) vpr to take place, to happen; (douleur) to go (away); **se p. de** to do ou go without; **ça s'est bien passé** it went off well.

passerelle f footbridge; (d'avion, de bateau) gangway.

passe-temps m inv pastime.

passif, -ive 1 adj passive. **2** m Grammaire passive.

passion f passion; **avoir la p. des voitures/d'écrire** to have a passion for cars/writing.

passionnant, -ante adj thrilling.

passionné, -ée adj passionate; **p. de qch** passionately fond of sth.

passionner vt to thrill.

passionner (se) vpr **se p. pour** to have a passion for.

passoire f (à thé) strainer; (à légumes) colander.

pastèque f watermelon.

pasteurisé, -ée pasteurized.

pastille f pastille, lozenge.

patauger vi (dans la mue) (in the mud etc), (barboter) to splash around.

pâte f paste; (à pain) dough; (à tarte) pastry; **pâtes (alimentaires)** pasta; **p. à modeler** modeling clay.

pâté m (charcuterie) pâté; **p. (en croûte)** meat pie; **p. (de sable)** sand castle; **p. de maisons** block of houses.

pâtée f (pour chien, chat) pet food.

paternel, -elle adj paternal.

pathétique adj moving.

patiemment adv patiently.

patience f patience.

patient, -ente 1 adj patient. 2 mf (malade) patient.

patienter vi to wait.

patin m p. (à glace) (ice) skate; **p. à roulettes** roller skate.

patinage m skating; **p. artistique** figure skating.

patiner vi (en sport) to skate; (roue) to spin round.

patineur, -euse mf skater.

patinoire f skating rink.

pâtisserie f pastry; (magasin) pastry shop.

pâtissier, -ière mf pastry cook.

patrie f (native) country.

patrimoine m heritage; (biens) property.

patriote 1 mf patriot. 2 adj patriotic.

patriotique adj (chant etc) patriotic.

patron, -onne 1 mf (chef) boss. 2 m (modèle de papier) pattern.

patronat m employers.

patrouille f patrol.

patrouiller vi to patrol.

patte f leg; (de chat, chien) paw; **marcher à quatre pattes** to crawl.

pâturage m pasture.

paume f (de main) palm.

paupière f eyelid.

pause f (arrêt) break.

pauvre 1 adj poor. 2 mf poor man ou woman; **les pauvres** the poor.

pauvreté f (besoin) poverty.

pavé m (de rue) paving stone.

paver vt to pave.

pavillon m (maison) (detached) house; (drapeau) flag.

payant, -ante adj (hôte, spectateur) paying; (place, entrée) that one has to pay for.

paye f pay, wages.

payer 1 vt (personne, somme) to pay; (service, objet) to pay for; **p. qn pour faire** to pay sb to do ou for doing. 2 vi (personne, métier) to pay.

pays m country; **du p.** (vin, gens) local.

paysage m landscape.

paysan, -anne mf (small) farmer.

PCV abrév (paiement contre vérification) **téléphoner en P.** to reverse the charges, to call collect.

PDG m abrév (président directeur général) CEO.

péage m (droit) toll; (lieu) tollbooth.

peau, -x f skin; (de fruit) peel, skin; (cuir) hide.

pêche¹ f fishing; (poissons) catch; **p. (à la ligne)** angling; **aller à la p.** to go fishing.

pêche² f (fruit) peach.

péché m sin.

pêcher¹ 1 vi to fish. 2 vt (attraper) to catch.

pêcher² m peach tree.

pêcheur m fisherman; (à la ligne) angler.

pédale f pedal; **p. de frein** footbrake (pedal).

pédaler vi to pedal.

pédalo m paddle boat.

pédiatre mf children's doctor.

pédicure mf chiropodist.

peigne m comb; **se donner un coup de p.** to give one's hair a comb.

peigner *vt (cheveux)* to comb; **p. qn** to comb sb's hair.

peigner (se) *vpr* to comb one's hair.

peignoir *m* bathrobe; **p. (de bain)** bathrobe.

peindre* *vti* to paint; **p. en bleu/** *etc* to paint blue/*etc.*

peine (à) *adv* hardly.

peine *f (châtiment)* **la p. de mort** the death penalty; **p. de prison** prison sentence. ▪ *(chagrin)* sorrow; **avoir de la p.** to be upset; **faire de la p. à** to upset. ▪ *(effort, difficulté)* trouble; **se donner de la p.** to go to a lot of trouble (**pour faire** to do); **avec p.** with difficulty; **ça vaut la p. d'attendre/***etc* it's worth (while) waiting/*etc*; **ce n'est pas** *ou* **ça ne vaut pas la p.** it's not worth it.

peintre *m* painter; **p. (en bâtiment)** (house) painter.

peinture *f (tableau, activité)* painting; *(matière)* paint; **'p. fraîche'** 'wet paint'.

pelage *m (d'animal)* coat, fur.

peler 1 *vt (fruit)* to peel. **2** *vi (peau bronzée)* to peel.

pelle *f* shovel; *(d'enfant)* spade; **p. à poussière** dustpan.

pelleteuse *f* steam shovel.

pellicule *f (pour photos)* film; *(couche)* layer; **pellicules** *(dans les cheveux)* dandruff.

pelote *f (de laine)* ball.

peloton *m (cyclistes)* pack.

pelotonner (se) *vpr* to curl up (into a ball).

pelouse *f* lawn.

peluche *f* **peluches** *(flocons)* fluff; **jouet en p.** = stuffed animal; **chien en p.** *(jouet)* stuffed dog; **ours en p.** teddy bear.

penalty *m Football* penalty.

penchant *m (préférence)* penchant (**pour** for); *(tendance)* propensity (**pour** for).

penché, -ée *adj* leaning.

pencher 1 *vt (objet)* to tilt; *(tête)* to lean. **2** *vi (arbre etc)* to lean (over).

pencher (se) *vpr* to lean (over *ou* forward); **se p. par** *(fenêtre)* to lean out of.

pendant *prép* during; **p. la nuit** during the night; **p. deux mois** for two months; **p. que** while.

penderie *f* closet.

pendre *vti* to hang (**à** from); **p. qn** to hang sb (**pour** for).

pendre (se) *vpr* to hang (**à** from).

pendu, -ue *adj (objet)* hanging (**à** from).

pendule *f* clock.

pénétrer *vi* **p. dans** to enter; *(profondément)* to penetrate (into).

pénible *adj* difficult; *(douloureux)* painful.

péniblement *adv* with difficulty.

péniche *f* barge.

pénicilline *f* penicillin.

pensée *f (idée)* thought.

penser 1 *vi* to think (**à** of, about); **p. à qch/à faire qch** *(ne pas oublier)* to remember sth/to do sth. **2** *vt* to think (**que** that); **je pensais rester** I was thinking of staying; **je pense réussir** I hope to succeed; **que pensez-vous de?** what do you think of *ou* about?

pensif, -ive *adj* thoughtful, pensive.

pension¹ *f (élève)* boarding school; *(somme à payer)* board; **être en p.** to board (**chez** with); **p. complète** full board.

pension² *f (de retraite etc)* pension.

pensionnaire *mf (élève)* boarder; *(d'hôtel)* resident; *(de famille)* lodger.

pensionnat *m* boarding school.

pente *f* slope; **en p.** sloping.

Pentecôte *f* Pentecost.

pénurie *f* shortage (**de** of).

pépin *m (de fruit)* seed, pit.

perçant, -ante *adj (cri, froid)* piercing; *(yeux)* sharp.

percepteur *m* tax collector.

percer 1 *vt* to pierce; *(avec une per-*

ceuse) to drill (a hole in); *(ouverture)* to make. **2** *vi (avec un outil)* to drill.

perceuse *f (outil)* drill.

percevoir* *vt (sensation)* to perceive; *(son)* to hear. ▪ *(impôt)* to collect.

perche *f (bâton)* pole.

percher (se) *vpr (oiseau)* to perch.

perchoir *m* perch.

percuter *vt (véhicule)* to crash into.

perdant, -ante *mf* loser.

perdre 1 *vt* to lose; *(gaspiller)* to waste; **p. de vue** to lose sight of. **2** *vi* to lose.

perdre (se) *vpr (s'égarer)* to get lost; **je m'y perds** I'm lost *ou* confused.

perdrix *f* partridge.

perdu, -ue *adj* lost; *(gaspillé)* wasted; **c'est du temps p.** it's a waste of time.

père *m* father.

perfection *f* perfection; **à la p.** perfectly.

perfectionné, -ée *adj (machine)* advanced.

perfectionnement *m* improvement *(de* in; *par rapport à* on); **cours de p.** proficiency course.

perfectionner *vt* to improve.

perfectionner (se) *vpr* **se p. en anglais/etc** to improve one's English/etc.

perforeuse *f (paper)* punch.

performance *f* performance.

performant, -ante *adj* highly efficient.

péril *m* danger, peril.

périlleux, -euse *adj* dangerous.

périmé, -ée *adj (billet)* expired.

période *f* period.

périphérique *adj & m (boulevard)* **p.** beltway.

perle *f (bijou)* pearl; *(de bois, verre)* bead.

permanence *f (salle d'étude)* stu-

dy hall; **être de p.** to be on duty; **en p.** permanently.

permanent, -ente 1 *adj* permanent; *(spectacle)* continuous. **2** *f (coiffure)* perm.

permettre* *vt* to allow; **p. à qn de faire** to allow sb to do; **vous permettez?** may I?; **je ne peux pas me p. de l'acheter** I can't afford (to buy) it.

permis, -ise 1 *adj* allowed. **2** *m* license; **p. de conduire** driver's license; **passer son p. de conduire** to take one's driving test.

permission *f* permission; *(congé de soldat)* leave; **demander la p.** to ask permission *(de* faire to do).

perpendiculaire *adj* perpendicular *(à* to).

perpétuel, -elle *adj (incessant)* continual, non-stop.

perplexe *adj* perplexed, puzzled.

perquisitionner *vi* to make a search.

perron *m (front)* steps.

perroquet *m* parrot.

perruche *f* parakeet.

perruque *f* wig.

persécuter *vt* to persecute.

persécution *f* persecution.

persévérance *f* perseverance.

persévérer *vi* to persevere *(dans* in).

persil *m* parsley.

persister *vi* to persist *(à* faire in doing; **dans qch** in sth).

personnage *m (important)* person; *(de livre, film)* character.

personnalité *f* personality.

personne 1 *f* person; **personnes** people; **grande p.** grown-up; **en p.** in person. **2** *pron (négatif)* nobody; **je ne vois p.** I don't see anybody; **mieux que p.** better than anybody.

personnel, -elle 1 *adj* personal. **2** *m* staff.

personnellement *adv* personally.

perspective *f (idée, possibilité)* prospect *(de* of).

perspicace *adj* shrewd.

persuader *vt* to persuade (**qn de faire qch** to do); **être persuadé que** to be convinced that.

persuasion *f* persuasion.

perte *f* loss; (*gaspillage*) waste (**de temps/d'argent** of time/money).

pertinemment *adv* **savoir qch p.** to know sth for a fact.

perturbation *f* disruption.

perturber *vt* (*trafic etc*) to disrupt; (*personne*) to disturb.

pervers, -erse 1 *adj* perverse. **2** *mf* pervert.

pesant, -ante *adj* heavy.

pesanteur *f* (*force*) gravity.

pèse-personne, *pl* **pèse-personne(s)** *m* (bathroom) scales.

peser *vti* to weigh; **p. lourd** to be heavy.

pessimiste *adj* pessimistic.

peste *f* (*maladie*) plague.

pétale *m* petal.

pétanque *f* (French) bowling game.

pétard *m* firecracker.

pétillant, -ante *adj* fizzy; (*vin, yeux*) sparkling.

pétiller *vi* (*champagne*) to fizz; (*yeux*) to sparkle.

petit, -ite 1 *adj* small, little; (*de taille*) short; (*bruit, coup*) slight; (*jeune*) little; **tout p.** tiny; **un p. Français** a (little) French boy. **2** *mf* (little) boy *ou* girl; (*personne*) small person; **petits** (*d'animal*) young. **3** *adv* **p. à p.** little by little.

petite-fille, *pl* **petites-filles** *f* granddaughter.

petit-fils, *pl* **petits-fils** *m* grandson.

petits-enfants *mpl* grandchildren.

petit-suisse *m* soft cheese (*for dessert*).

pétrole *m* oil.

pétrolier *m* (*navire*) (oil) tanker.

peu *adv* (*manger etc*) not much, little; **un p.** a little, a bit; **p. de sel/ de temps/etc** not much salt/time/ *etc*; **un p. de fromage/etc** a little cheese/*etc*; **p. de gens/etc** few people/*etc*; **un (tout) petit p.** a (tiny) little bit; **p. intéressant/etc** not very interesting/*etc*; **p. de chose** not much; **p. à p.** little by little; **à p. près** more or less; **p. après** shortly after.

peuple *m* people.

peuplé, -ée *adj* **très/peu/etc p.** highly/sparsely/*etc* populated; **p. de** populated by.

peur *f* fear; **avoir p.** to be afraid *ou* frightened (**de qch/qn** of sth/sb; **de faire** to do, of doing); **faire p. à** to frighten; **de p. que** (+ *subjonctif*) for fear that.

peureux, -euse *adj* easily frightened.

peut, peuvent, peux *voir* **pouvoir.**

peut-être *adv* perhaps, maybe; **p. qu'il viendra** perhaps *ou* maybe he'll come.

phare *m* (*pour bateaux*) lighthouse; (*de véhicule*) headlight; **faire un appel de phares** to flash one's lights.

pharmacie *f* drugstore, pharmacy; (*armoire*) medicine cabinet.

pharmacien, -ienne *mf* pharmacist.

philatélie *f* stamp collecting.

philatéliste *mf* stamp collector.

philosophe 1 *mf* philosopher. **2** *adj* (*résigné*) philosophical.

philosophie *f* philosophy.

phonétique *adj* phonetic.

phoque *m* (*animal*) seal.

photo *f* photo; (*art*) photography; **prendre une p. de** to take a photo of; **se faire prendre en p.** to have one's photo taken.

photocopie *f* photocopy.

photocopier *vt* to photocopy.

photocopieuse *f* (*machine*) photocopier.

photographe *mf* photographer.

photographier *vt* to photograph.

photographique adj photographic.

photomaton® m photo booth.

phrase f sentence.

physique 1 adj physical. 2 m (corps, aspect) physique; (science) physics.

physiquement adv physically.

pianiste mf pianist.

piano m piano.

pic m (cime) peak.

pic (à) adv couler à p. to sink to the bottom.

pichet m jug.

pickpocket m pickpocket.

picorer vti to peck.

picoter vt (yeux) to make sting; **les yeux me picotent** my eyes are stinging.

pièce f (de maison etc) room; (de pantalon) patch; **p. (de monnaie)** coin; **p. (de théâtre)** play; **p. d'identité** identity card; **pièces détachées** (de véhicule etc) spare parts; **cinq dollars p.** five dollars each.

pied m foot (pl feet); (de meuble) leg; (de verre, lampe) base; **à p.** on foot; **au p. de** at the foot of; **coup de p.** kick; **donner un coup de p.** to kick (**à qn** sb).

piège m trap.

piéger vt (animal) to trap; (voiture) to booby-trap.

pierre f stone; (précieuse) gem; **p. (à briquet)** flint.

piétiner 1 vt to trample (on). 2 vi to stamp (one's) feet.

piéton m pedestrian.

piétonne adj **rue p.** pedestrian street.

pieu, -x m post, stake.

pieuvre f octopus.

pigeon m pigeon.

pile 1 vt (électrique) battery; (tas) pile; **radio à piles** battery radio; **en p.** in a pile; **p. (ou face)?** heads (or tails)? 2 adv **s'arrêter p.** to stop short; **à deux heures p.** at two o'clock sharp ou on the dot.

pilier m pillar.

pillage m looting.

piller vti to loot.

pilotage m **poste de p.** cockpit.

pilote m (d'avion) pilot; (de voiture) driver.

piloter vt (avion) to fly; (voiture) to drive.

pilule f pill; **prendre la p.** to be on the pill.

piment m (chili) pepper.

pimenté, -ée adj spicy.

pin m (arbre) pine; **pomme de p.** pine cone.

pince f (outil) pliers; (de cycliste) clip; (de crabe) pincer; **p. (à linge)** (clothes) peg; **p. (à épiler)** tweezers; **p. (à sucre)** (sugar) tongs; **p. à cheveux** bobby pin.

pinceau, -x m (paint)brush.

pincée f (de sel etc) pinch (**de** of).

pincer vt to pinch.

pincer (se) upr **se p. le doigt** to get one's finger caught (**dans** in).

pingouin m penguin.

ping-pong m table tennis.

pin's m inv button, lapel pin.

pintade f guinea fowl.

pioche f pick(ax).

piocher vti to dig (with a pick).

pion m (au jeu de dames) piece; Échecs pawn.

pipe f pipe; **fumer la p.** to smoke a pipe.

pipi m **faire p.** Fam to take a pee.

piquant, -ante adj (plante, barbe) prickly.

pique m (couleur) Cartes spades.

pique-nique, pl **pique-niques** m picnic.

pique-niquer vi to picnic.

piquer 1 vt (percer) to prick; (langue, yeux) to sting; (coudre) to (machine-)stitch; **p. qn** (abeille) to sting sb; **p. qch dans** (enfoncer) to stick sth into; **p. une colère** to fly into a rage. 2 vi (avion) to dive; (moutarde etc) to be hot.

piquet m (pieu) stake; (de tente) peg.

piqûre f (d'abeille) sting; (avec un seringue) injection, shot.

pirate m pirate; **p. de l'air** hijacker; **p. informatique** (computer) hacker.

pire 1 adj worse (**que** than); **le p. moment**/etc the worst moment/ etc. **2** mf **le** ou **la p.** the worst.

piscine f swimming pool.

pissenlit m dandelion.

pistache f pistachio.

piste f (traces) trail; (de course) racetrack; (de cirque) ring; (de patinage) rink; **p. (d'envoi)** runway; **p. cyclable** bicycle path; **p. de danse** dance floor; **p. de ski** ski run ou slope.

pistolet m gun; **p. à eau** water pistol.

pitié f pity; **j'ai p. de lui** I feel sorry for him.

pitoyable adj pitiful.

pittoresque adj picturesque.

pivoter vi (personne) to swing round; (fauteuil) to swivel.

pizza f pizza.

pizzeria f pizzeria.

placard m (dans la cuisine) cupboard, cabinet; (pour linge, vêtements etc) closet.

place f (endroit, rang) place; (espace) room; (lieu public) square; (siège) seat, place; (emploi) job; **p. de parking** parking place ou space; **à la p. (de)** instead (of); **à votre p.** in your place; **sur p.** on the spot; **en p.** in place; **mettre en p.** (installer) to set up; **changer de p.** to change places; **changer qch de p.** to move sth.

placement m (d'argent) investment.

placer vt to place; (invité, spectateur) to seat; (argent) to invest (**dans** in).

placer (se) vpr (debout) to (go and) stand; (s'asseoir) to (go and) sit; **se troisième**/etc (en sport) to come third/etc.

plafond m ceiling.

plage f beach; **p. arrière** (de voiture) (back) window shelf.

plaider vti (défendre) to plead; **p. coupable** to plead guilty.

plaie f wound; (coupure) cut.

plaindre* vt to feel sorry for.

plaindre (se) vpr to complain (**de** about; **que** that); **se p. de** (douleur) to complain of.

plaine f plain.

plainte f complaint; (cri) moan.

plaire* vi **p. à qn** to please sb; **elle lui plaît** he likes her; **ça me plaît** I like it; **s'il vous** ou **te plaît** please.

plaire (se) vpr (dans un endroit) to like ou enjoy it.

plaisanter vi to joke (**sur** about).

plaisanterie f joke; **par p.** as a joke.

plaisir m pleasure; **faire p. à** to please; **pour le p.** for fun.

plan m (projet, dessin) plan; (de ville) map; **au premier p.** in the foreground.

planche f board; **p. à repasser** ironing board; **p. (à roulettes)** skateboard; **p. (à voile)** sailboard; **faire de la p.** to go windsurfing.

plancher m floor.

planer vi (oiseau, avion) to glide.

planète f planet.

planeur m (avion) glider.

planifier vt to plan.

plante¹ f plant; **p. verte** house plant.

plante² f **p. du pied** sole (of the foot).

planter vt (fleur etc) to plant; (clou, couteau) to drive in.

planter (se) vpr **se p. devant** to come ou go and stand in front of, to plant oneself in front of.

plaque f plate; (de verre, métal, verglas) sheet; (de chocolat) bar; **p. chauffante** hotplate; **p. d'immatriculation** license plate.

plaqué, -ée adj **p. or** gold-plated.

plaquer vt Sport to tackle; (aplatir) to flatten (**contre** against).

plastique *adj & m* (*matière*) p. plastic; **en p.** (*bouteille etc*) plastic.

plat, plate 1 *adj* flat; **à p. ventre** flat on one's face; **à p.** (*pneu, batterie*) flat; **poser à p.** to put down flat; **assiette plate** dinner plate; **eau plate** still water. **2** *m* (*récipient, nourriture*) dish; (*partie du repas*) course; **'p. du jour'** today's special.'

platane *m* plane tree.

plateau, -x *m* (*pour servir*) tray; **p. à fromages** cheeseboard.

plate-forme, *pl* **plates-formes** *f* platform; **p. pétrolière** oil rig.

plâtre *m* (*matière*) plaster; **un p. a** (plaster) cast; **dans le p.** in plaster.

plâtrer *vt* (*bras, jambe*) to put a cast on.

plein, pleine 1 *adj* full (**de** of); **en pleine mer** out at sea; **en pleine figure** right in the face. **2** *prép & adv* **des bonbons p. les poches** pockets full of candy; **du chocolat p. la figure** chocolate all over one's face; **p. de lettres/d'argent/***etc Fam* lots of letters/money/*etc.* **3** *m* **faire le p.** (*d'essence*) to fill up (the tank).

pleurer *vi* to cry.

pleuvoir* *vi* to rain; **il pleut** it's raining.

pli *m* (*de papier*) fold; (*de jupe*) pleat; (*de pantalon*) crease; (**faux**) **p.** crease; **mise en plis** (*coiffure*) set.

pliable *adj* foldable.

pliant, -ante *adj* (*chaise etc*) folding.

plier 1 *vt* to fold; (*courber*) to bend. **2** *vi* (*branche*) to bend.

plier (se) *vpr* (*lit, chaise etc*) to fold (up).

plissé, -ée *adj* (*tissu, jupe*) pleated.

plisser *vt* (*front*) to wrinkle; to crease, to fold; **p. les yeux** to squint.

plomb *m* (*métal*) lead; (*fusible*) fuze; **plombs** (*de chasse*) lead shot.

plombage *m* (*de dent*) filling.

plomber *vt* (*dent*) to fill.

plomberie *f* plumbing.

plombier *m* plumber.

plongée *f* (*sport*) diving.

plongeoir *m* diving board.

plongeon *m* dive.

plonger 1 *vi* (*personne*) to dive. **2** *vt* (*mettre*) to plunge (**dans** into).

plongeur, -euse *mf* diver.

plu *voir* **plaire, pleuvoir.**

pluie *f* rain; **sous la p.** in the rain.

plume *f* (*d'oiseau*) feather; (*de stylo*) (pen) nib; **stylo à p.** (fountain) pen.

plumer *vt* (*volaille*) to pluck.

plupart (la) *f* most; **la p. des cas** most cases; **la p. du temps** most of the time; **la p. d'entre eux** most of them; **pour la p.** mostly.

pluriel, -ielle *adj & m* plural; **au p.** in the plural.

plus¹ *adv comparatif* (*travailler etc*) more (**que** than); **p. d'une livre/de dix** more than a pound/ten; **p. de thé** more tea; **p. beau** more beautiful (**que** than); **p. tard** later; **p. petit** smaller; **de p. en p.** more and more; **p. ou moins** more or less; **en p.** in addition (**de** to); **de p. more** (**que** than); (*en outre*) moreover; (*âgé*) **de p. de dix ans** over ten; **j'ai dix ans de p. qu'elle** I'm ten years older than she is; **il est p. de cinq heures** it's after five. **2** *adv superlatif* **le p.** (*travailler etc*) (the) most; **le p. beau** the most beautiful (**de** in); **le p. grand** the biggest (**de** in); **j'ai le p. de livres** I have (the) most books.

plus² *adv de négation* **(de** (*pain, argent*) no more; **il n'a p. de pain** he has no more bread, he doesn't have any more bread; **tu n'es p. jeune** you're not young any more; **je ne la reverrai p.** I won't see her again.

plus³ *prép* plus; **deux p. deux** two plus two; **il fait p. deux (degrés)** it's two degrees above freezing.

plusieurs *adj & pron* several.

plutôt *adv* rather (**que** than).

pluvieux, -euse *adj* rainy.

pneu *m* (*pl* **-s**) tire.

pneumatique *adj* **matelas p.** air mattress; **canot p.** rubber dinghy.

poche *f* pocket; *(de kangourou)* pouch.

pocher *vt (œufs)* to poach; **p. l'œil à qn** to give sb a black eye.

pochette *f (sac)* bag; *(d'allumettes)* book; *(de disque)* sleeve; *(sac à main)* (clutch) bag.

poêle 1 *m* stove. **2** *f* p. (**à frire**) frying pan.

poème *m* poem.

poésie *f (art)* poetry; *(poème)* poem.

poète *m* poet.

poétique *adj* poetic.

poids *m* weight; **au p.** by weight.

poids lourd *m* (heavy) truck.

poignard *m* dagger.

poignarder *vt* to stab.

poignée *f (quantité)* handful (**de** of); *(de porte etc)* handle; **p. de main** handshake; **donner une p. de main à** to shake hands with.

poignet *m* wrist; *(de chemise)* cuff.

poil *m* hair; *(pelage)* fur.

poilu, -ue *adj* hairy.

poinçonner *vt (billet)* to punch.

poing *m* fist; **coup de p.** punch.

point *m (lieu, score etc)* point; *(sur i, à l'horizon)* dot; *(tache)* spot; *(de couture)* stitch; **sur le p. de faire** about to do; **p. (final)** period; **p. d'exclamation** exclamation point; **p. d'interrogation** question mark; **points de suspension** ellipsis; **p. de vue** *(opinion)* point of view; **à p.** *(steak)* medium rare; **au p. mort** *(véhicule)* in neutral; **p. de côté** *(douleur)* stitch (in one's side).

pointe *f (extrémité)* tip; *(clou)* nail; **sur la p. des pieds** on tiptoe; **en p.** pointed.

pointer 1 *vt (cocher)* to check (off); *(braquer)* to point (**sur** at). **2** *vi* **p. vers** to point (upwards) towards.

pointillé *m* dotted line.

pointu, -ue *adj (en pointe)* pointed.

pointure *f (de chaussure, gant)* size.

point-virgule, *pl* **points-virgules** *m* semicolon.

poire *f* pear.

poireau, -x *m* leek.

poirier *m* pear tree.

pois *m* pea; **petits p.** peas; **p. chiche** garbanzo, chickpea.

poison *m* poison.

poisseux, -euse *adj* sticky.

poisson *m* fish; **p. rouge** goldfish.

poissonnerie *f* fish market.

poissonnier, -ière *mf* fish merchant.

poitrine *f* chest; *(de femme)* bust.

poivre *m* pepper.

poivré, -ée *adj (piquant)* peppery.

poivrer *vt* to pepper.

poivrière *f* peppershaker.

poivron *m (légume)* pepper.

pôle *m* **p. Nord/Sud** North/South Pole.

polémique 1 *adj* polemical. **2** *f* heated debate.

poli, -ie *adj (courtois)* polite (**avec** to, with); *(lisse)* polished.

police¹ *f* police; **p. secours** police emergency services.

police² *f* **p.** *(d'assurance)* (insurance) policy.

policier, -ière 1 *adj* **enquête/etc policière** police investigation/*etc*; **roman p.** mystery novel. **2** *m* policeman, detective.

poliment *adv* politely.

polio 1 *f (maladie)* polio. **2** *mf (personne)* polio victim.

polir *vt* to polish.

politesse *f* politeness.

politique 1 *adj* political; **homme p.** politician. **2** *f (activité)* politics; **une p.** a policy.

pollen *m* pollen.

polluer *vt* to pollute.

pollution *f* pollution.

polo *m (chemise)* polo shirt.

polochon *m* bolster.

polonais, -aise 1 *adj* Polish. **2** *mf* P. Pole. **3** *m* (*langue*) Polish.

polycopié *m* duplicated course notes.

polyester *m* polyester; **chemise/** *etc* **en p.** polyester shirt/*etc*.

polyvalent, -ente *adj* (*salle*) multi-purpose; (*personne*) versatile.

pommade *f* ointment.

pomme *f* apple; **p. de terre** potato; **pommes frites** French fries; **pommes chips** potato chips.

pommier *m* apple tree.

pompe *f* pump; **p. à essence** gas station; **pompes funèbres** undertaker's; **entrepreneur de pompes funèbres** undertaker.

pomper *vt* (*eau*) to pump out (**de** of).

pompier *m* fireman; **voiture des pompiers** fire engine.

pompiste *mf* gas station attendant.

pompon *m* pompon.

poncer *vt* to rub down, to sand.

ponctuation *f* punctuation.

ponctuel, -elle *adj* (*à l'heure*) punctual.

pondre 1 *vt* (*œuf*) to lay. **2** *vi* (*poule*) to lay (eggs *ou* an egg).

poney *m* pony.

pont *m* bridge; (*de bateau*) deck.

pop *m & adj inv* (*musique*) pop.

populaire *adj* (*qui plaît*) popular; (*quartier*) working-class; (*expression*) colloquial.

population *f* population.

porc *m* pig; (*viande*) pork.

porcelaine *f* china.

porche *m* porch.

porcherie *f* (pig)sty.

port *m* port, harbor.

portable 1 *adj* (*portatif*) portable. **2** *m* (*ordinateur*) laptop; (*téléphone*) cellphone.

portail *m* (*de jardin*) gate(way).

portant, -ante *adj* **bien p.** in good health.

portatif, -ive *adj* portable.

porte *f* door; (*de jardin*) gate; (*de ville*) entrance; **p. (d'embarquement)** (*d'aéroport*) (departure) gate; **p. d'entrée** front door; **p. coulissante** sliding door; **mettre à la p.** to throw out.

porte-avions *m inv* aircraft carrier.

porte-bagages *m inv* luggage rack.

porte-bonheur *m inv* (lucky) charm.

porte-clefs *m inv* key ring.

porte-documents *m inv* briefcase.

portée *f* (*de fusil etc*) range; (*animaux*) litter; **à p. de la main** within (easy) reach; **à p. de voix** within earshot; **hors de p.** out of reach.

porte-fenêtre, *pl* **portes-fenêtres** *f* French door *ou* window.

portefeuille *m* wallet.

portemanteau, -x *m* coatrack; (*crochet*) coat hook.

porte-monnaie *m inv* purse.

porte-parole *m inv* spokesman; (*femme*) spokeswoman.

porter 1 *vt* to carry; (*vêtement, lunettes, barbe etc*) to wear; **p. qch à** (*apporter*) to take sth to; **p. bonheur/malheur** to bring good/bad luck. **2** *vi* (*voix*) to carry.

porter (se) *vpr* (*vêtement*) to be worn; **se p. bien/mal** to be well/ill; **comment te portes-tu?** how are you?

porte-revues *m inv* newspaper rack.

porte-savon *m inv* soapdish.

porte-serviettes *m inv* towel rack.

porteur *m* (*à la gare*) porter.

porte-voix *m inv* loudspeaker, megaphone.

portier *m* doorman.

portière *f* (*de véhicule, train*) door.

portion *f* (*partie*) portion; (*de nourriture*) helping.

portique m (de balançoire etc) crossbar.

portrait m portrait.

portrait-robot, pl **portraits-robots** m composite picture.

portugais, -aise 1 adj Portuguese. **2** mf **P.** Portuguese man, Portuguese woman, Portuguese inv; **les P.** the Portuguese. **3** m (langue) Portuguese.

pose f (installation) putting up; putting in; laying; (attitude de modèle) pose.

posé, -ée adj (calme) composed.

poser 1 vt to put (down); (papier peint, rideaux) to put up; (sonnette, chauffage) to put in; (moquette) to lay; (question) to ask (**à qn** sb). **2** vi (modèle) to pose (**pour** for).

poser (se) vpr (oiseau, avion) to land.

positif, -ive adj positive.

position f position.

posséder vt to possess; (maison etc) to own.

possessif, -ive adj & m Grammaire possessive.

possibilité f possibility.

possible 1 adj possible (**à faire** to do); **il (nous) est p. de le faire** it is possible (for us) to do it; **il est p. que** (+ subjonctif) it is possible that; **si p.** if possible; **le plus tôt p.** as soon as possible; **autant que p.** as far as possible; **le plus p.** as much ou as many as possible. **2** m faire **son p.** to do one's best (**pour faire** to do).

postal, -e, -aux adj postal; **boîte postale** PO Box; **code p.** zip code.

poste 1 f (service) post; (bureau de) **p.** post office; **la P.** the Post Office; **par la p.** by post; **p. aérienne** airmail. **2** m (lieu, emploi) post; (radio, télévision) set; **p. de secours** first aid station; **p. de police** police station.

poster vt (lettre) to mail.

postier, -ière mf postal worker.

postuler vi **p. à un emploi** to apply for a job.

pot m pot; (à confiture) jar; (à lait) jug; (à bière) mug; (de crème, yaourt) carton; (de bébé) potty; **p. de fleurs** flower pot.

potable adj drinkable; **'eau p.'** 'drinking water'.

potage m soup.

potager adj & m **(jardin) p.** vegetable garden.

pot-au-feu m inv beef stew.

pot-de-vin, pl **pots-de-vin** m bribe.

poteau, -x m post; **p. indicateur** signpost; **p. d'arrivée** winning post; **p. télégraphique** telegraph pole.

poterie f (art) pottery; **une p.** a piece of pottery; **des poteries** (objets) pottery.

potier m potter.

potiron m pumpkin.

pou, -x m louse; **poux** lice.

poubelle f garbage can.

pouce m thumb; (mesure) inch.

poudre f powder; (explosif) gunpowder; **en p.** (lait) powdered; **chocolat en p.** cocoa powder.

poudrer (se) vpr (femme) to powder one's face.

poudrier m (powder) compact.

pouf m (siège) (cushioned) ottoman ou footstool.

poulailler m henhouse.

poulain m (cheval) foal.

poule f hen.

poulet m chicken.

poulie f pulley.

pouls m pulse.

poumon m lung; **à pleins poumons** (respirer) deeply; (crier) loudly.

poupée f doll.

pour 1 prép for; **p. toi/etc** for you/etc; **partir p.** (Paris, cinq ans) to leave for; **elle est p.** she's in favor; **p. faire** (in order) to do; **p. que tu saches** so (that) you know; **p. quoi faire?** what for?; **trop petit/etc p.**

faire too small/*etc* to do; **assez grand**/*etc* **p. faire** big/*etc* enough to do. **2** *m* **le p. et le contre** the pros and cons.

pourboire *m* (*argent*) tip.

pourcentage *m* percentage.

pourchasser *vt* to pursue.

pourparlers *mpl* negotiations, talks.

pourquoi *adv & conj* why; **p. pas?** why not?

pourra, pourrai(t) *etc voir* **pouvoir**.

pourri, -ie *adj* (*fruit, temps etc*) rotten.

pourrir *vi* to rot.

poursuite *f* chase; **se mettre à la p. de** to go after, to chase (after).

poursuivant, -ante *mf* pursuer.

poursuivre* *vt* to chase, to go after; (*lecture, voyage etc*) to continue (with).

poursuivre (se) *vpr* to continue, to go on.

pourtant *adv* yet.

pourvu que *conj* (*condition*) provided *ou* providing (that); (*souhait*) **p. qu'elle soit là!** I only hope (that) she's there!

pousser 1 *vt* to push; (*cri*) to utter; (*soupir*) to heave; **p. qn à faire** to urge sb to do. **2** *vi* (*croître*) to grow; **faire p.** (*plante etc*) to grow.

poussette *f* stroller.

poussière *f* dust.

poussiéreux, -euse *adj* dusty.

poussin *m* (*poulet*) chick.

poutre *f* (*en bois*) beam; (*en acier*) girder.

pouvoir* 1 *v aux* (*capacité*) can, to be able to; (*permission, éventualité*) may, can; **je peux deviner** I can guess; **tu peux entrer** you may *ou* can come in; **il peut être sorti** he may *ou* might be out; **elle pourrait/pouvait venir** she might/could come; **j'ai pu l'obtenir** I managed to get it; **j'aurais pu l'obtenir** I could have gotten it; **je n'en peux plus** I'm utterly exhausted. **2** *m* (*capacité, autorité*) power; **les pouvoirs publics** the authorities; **au p.** in power.

pouvoir (se) *vpr* **il se peut qu'elle parte** (it's possible that) she might leave.

prairie *f* meadow.

pratique 1 *adj* practical. **2** *f* (*exercice, procédé*) practice; **la p. de la natation/du golf** swimming/golfing.

pratiquement *adv* (*presque*) practically.

pratiquer *vt* (*sport, art etc*) to practice.

pré *m* meadow.

préalable 1 *adj* prior, previous; **p. à** prior to. **2** *m* precondition, prerequisite; **au p.** beforehand.

préau, -x *m* (*d'école*) covered playground.

préavis *m* (advance) notice (**de** of); **p. de grève** strike notice; **p. de licenciement** notice of dismissal.

précarité *f* precariousness; **p. de l'emploi** lack of job security.

précaution *f* precaution (**de faire** of doing); (*prudence*) caution.

précédent, -ente 1 *adj* previous. **2** *mf* previous one.

précéder *vti* to precede.

précieux, -euse *adj* precious.

précipice *m* chasm, precipice.

précipitamment *adv* hastily.

précipitation *f* haste.

précipiter *vt* (*hâter*) to rush.

précipiter (se) *vpr* to throw oneself; (*foncer*) to rush (**à, sur** on to); (*s'accélérer*) to speed up.

précis, -ise *adj* precise; **à deux heures précises** at two o'clock sharp.

préciser *vt* to specify (**que** that).

préciser (se) *vpr* to become clear(er).

précision *f* precision; (*explication*) explanation.

précoce *adj* (*fruit etc*) early; (*enfant*) precocious.

prédécesseur *m* predecessor.

prédiction *f* prediction.

prédire* *vt* to predict (**que** that).

préfabriqué, -ée *adj* prefabricated.

préface *f* preface.

préfecture *f* prefecture; **la P. de police** police headquarters.

préféré, -ée *adj & mf* favorite.

préférence *f* preference (**pour** for); **de p.** preferably.

préférer *vt* to prefer (**à** to); **p. faire** to prefer to do.

préfet *m* prefect *(chief administrator in a department)*.

préfixe *m* prefix.

préhistorique *adj* prehistoric.

préjudice *m (à une cause)* prejudice; *(à une personne)* harm; **porter p. à qn** to do sb harm.

préjugé *m* prejudice; **être plein de préjugés** to be full of prejudice.

prélèvement *m (d'échantillon)* taking; *(de somme)* deduction; **p. automatique** automatic deduction.

premier, -ière 1 *adj* first; *(étage)* second; **nombre p.** prime number; **le p. rang** the front row; **P. ministre** Prime Minister. **2** *mf* first (one); **arriver le p.** to arrive first; **être le p. de la classe** to be (at) the head of the class. **3** *m (date)* first; **le p. de l'an** New Year's Day. **4** *f (wagon, billet)* first class; *(au lycée)* = junior year; *(de véhicule)* first (gear).

premièrement *adv* firstly.

prendre* 1 *vt* to take (**à qn** from sb); *(attraper)* to catch; *(voyager par)* to take *(train etc)*; *(douche, bain)* to take, to have; *(repas)* to have; *(photo)* to take, to have; *(temps)* to take (up); **p. qn pour** *(un autre)* to mistake sb for; *(considérer)* to take sb for; **p. feu** to catch fire; **p. de la place** to take up room; **p. du poids** to put on weight. **2** *vi (feu)* to catch; *(ciment)* to set; *(vaccin)* to take.

prendre (se) *vpr (objet)* to be taken; *(s'accrocher)* to get caught; **se p. pour un génie** to think one is a genius; **s'y p.** to go about it; **s'en p. à** to attack; *(accuser)* to blame.

prénom *m* first name.

prénommer *vt* to name.

prénommer (se) *vpr* to be called; **il se prénomme Daniel** his first name is Daniel.

préoccupation *f* worry.

préoccupé, -ée *adj* worried.

préoccuper *vt (inquiéter)* to worry.

préoccuper (se) *vpr* **se p. de** to be worried about.

préparatifs preparations (**de** for).

préparation *f* preparation.

préparer *vt* to prepare (**qch pour** sth for; **qn à** sb for); *(examen)* to prepare for.

préparer (se) *vpr* to get (oneself) ready (**à, pour qch** for sth); **se p. à faire** to prepare to do.

préposition *f Grammaire* preposition.

préretraite *f* early retirement.

près *adv* **p. de** *(qn, qch)* near (to); **p. de deux ans/etc** nearly two years/*etc*; **tout p.** nearby (**de qn/qch** sb/sth); **de p.** *(lire, suivre)* closely.

presbyte *adj* long-sighted.

prescrire* *vt (médicament)* to prescribe.

présence *f* presence; *(à l'école etc)* attendance (**à** at); **feuille de p.** attendance sheet; **en p. de** in the presence of.

présent, -ente 1 *adj (non absent)* present (**à** at; **dans** in); *(actuel)* present. **2** *m Grammaire* present (tense); **à p.** at present.

présentateur, -trice *mf* announcer.

présentation *f* presentation; *(d'une personne à une autre)* introduction.

présenter *vt* to present; **p. qn à qn** to introduce sb to sb.

présenter (se) *vpr* to introduce

oneself (**à** to); **se p. à** *(examen)* to take; *(élections)* to run in.

préservatif *m* condom.

préserver *vt* to protect (**de, contre** from).

présidence *f (de nation)* presidency; *(de firme)* chairmanship.

président, -ente *mf (de nation)* president; *(de réunion, firme)* chairman, chairwoman; **p. directeur général** chief executive officer.

présidentiel, -ielle *adj* presidential.

presque *adv* almost.

presqu'île *f* peninsula.

presse *f (journaux, appareil)* press; **conférence/etc de p.** press conference/*etc.*

presse-citron *m inv* lemon juicer.

pressé, -ée *adj (personne)* in a hurry; *(travail)* urgent.

pressentir* *vt* to sense (**que** that).

presser 1 *vt (serrer)* to squeeze; *(bouton)* to press; *(fruit)* to squeeze, to juice. **2** *vi (temps)* to press; **rien ne presse** there's no hurry.

presser (se) *vpr (se serrer)* to squeeze (together); *(se hâter)* to hurry (**de faire** to do).

pressing *m (magasin)* dry cleaner's.

pression *f* pressure.

prestation *f (allocation)* benefit; **prestations** *(services)* services; **prestations sociales** welfare payments. ■ *(de comédien)* performance.

prestidigitateur, -trice *mf* magician.

prestidigitation *f* tour de p. magic trick.

prêt *m (emprunt)* loan.

prêt, prête *adj (préparé)* ready (**à faire** to do; **à qch** for sth).

prêt-à-porter *m inv* ready-to-wear clothes.

prétendre *vt* to claim (**que** that; **être** to be).

prétendre (se) *vpr* elle se prétend riche she claims to be rich.

prétendu, -ue *adj* so-called.

prétentieux, -euse *adj & mf* conceited (person).

prêter *vt (argent, objet)* to lend (**à** to); **p. attention** to pay attention (**à** to).

prétexte *m* excuse; **sous p. de/que** on the pretext of/that.

prêtre *m* priest.

preuve *f (preuve(s))* proof, evidence; **faire p. de** to show.

prévenir *vt (avertir)* to warn (**que** that); *(aviser)* to inform (**que** that).

prévention *f* prevention; **p. routière** road safety.

prévisible *adj* foreseeable.

prévision *f* forecast.

prévoir* *vt (anticiper)* to foresee (**que** that); *(prédire)* to forecast (**que** that); *(temps)* to forecast; *(organiser)* to plan; *(préparer)* to provide, to make provision for.

prévoyant, -ante *adj* far-sighted.

prévu, -ue *adj* **un repas est p.** a meal is provided; **au moment p.** at the appointed time; **comme p.** as expected; **p. pour** *(véhicule, appareil)* designed for.

prier 1 *vti* to pray (**pour** for). **2** *vt* **p. qn de faire** to ask sb to do; **je vous en prie** *(faites donc)* please; *(en réponse à 'merci')* don't mention it, you're welcome.

prière *f* prayer; **p. de répondre/etc** please answer/*etc.*

primaire *adj* primary.

prime *f (d'employé)* bonus; **en p.** *(cadeau)* as a free gift; **p. (d'assurance)** (insurance) premium.

primevère *f* primrose.

primitif, -ive *adj (société etc)* primitive.

primordial, -e, -aux *adj* vital (**de faire** to do).

prince *m* prince.

princesse *f* princess.

principal, -e, -aux 1 *adj* main. **2** *m (de collège)* principal; **le p.** *(essentiel)* the main thing.

principe *m* principle; **en p.** theoretically; *(normalement)* as a rule.

printemps *m (saison)* spring.

prioritaire *adj* **être p.** to have priority; *(en voiture)* to have the right of way.

priorité *f* priority (**sur** over); **la p.** *(sur la route)* the right of way; **la p. à droite** right of way to traffic coming from the right; **'cédez la p.'** 'yield'.

pris, prise *(pp of* **prendre**) *adj (place)* taken; *(crème, ciment)* set; *(nez)* congested; **être (très) p.** to be (very) busy; **p. de** *(peur, panique)* stricken with.

prise *f (de judo etc)* hold; *(objet saisi)* catch; **p. (de courant)** *(mâle)* plug; *(femelle)* outlet, socket; **p. multiple** *(électrique)* adaptor; **p. de sang** blood test.

prison *f* prison, jail; **en p.** in prison *ou* jail.

prisonnier, -ière *mf* prisoner; **faire qn p.** to take sb prisoner.

privé, -ée *adj* private.

priver *vt* to deprive (**de** of).

priver (se) *vpr* **se p. de** to do without.

prix¹ *m (d'un objet etc)* price; **à tout p.** at all costs; **à aucun p.** on no account.

prix² *m (récompense)* prize.

probable *adj* likely, probable (**que** that); **peu p.** unlikely.

probablement *adv* probably.

problème *m* problem.

procédé *m* process.

procéder *vi (agir)* to proceed; **p. à** *(enquête, arrestation)* to carry out; **p. par élimination** to follow a process of elimination.

procès *m (criminel)* trial; *(civil)* lawsuit; **faire un p. à** to take to court.

procès-verbal, -aux *m (contravention)* (traffic) ticket.

prochain, -aine *adj* next.

prochainement *adv* shortly.

proche *adj (espace)* near, close; *(temps)* close (at hand); *(parent, ami)* close; **p. de** near (to), close to.

procuration *f* power of attorney; **par p.** by proxy.

procurer *vt* **p. qch à qn** *(personne)* to obtain sth for sb.

procurer (se) *vpr* **se p. qch** to obtain sth.

prodigieux, -euse *adj* extraordinary.

producteur, -trice 1 *mf* producer. **2** *adj* **pays p. de pétrole** oil-producing country.

production *f* production.

produire* *vt (fabriquer, causer etc)* to produce.

produire (se) *vpr (événement etc)* to happen.

produit *m (article etc)* product; *(pour la vaisselle)* liquid; **produits** *(de la terre)* produce; **p. (chimique)** chemical; **p. de beauté** cosmetic.

prof *mf Fam* teacher; *(à l'université)* professor.

proférer *vt* to utter.

professeur *m* teacher; *(à l'université)* professor.

profession *f* occupation; *(de médecin etc)* profession; *(manuelle)* trade.

professionnel, -elle 1 *adj* professional; *(école)* vocational. **2** *mf* professional.

profil *m* **de p.** (viewed) from the side, in profile.

profit *m* profit; **tirer p. de** to benefit from *ou* by.

profitable *adj (utile)* beneficial (**à** to).

profiter *vi* **p. de** to take advantage of; **p. à qn** to profit sb.

profond, -onde 1 *adj* deep; **p. de deux mètres** seven feet deep. **2** *adv (pénétrer etc)* deep.

profondément *adv* deeply; *(dormir)* soundly.

profondeur f depth; **à six mètres de p.** at a depth of 20 feet.

progiciel m (software) package.

programmateur m (de four etc) timer.

programme m program; (scolaire) syllabus; (d'ordinateur) program.

programmer vt (ordinateur) to program.

progrès m & mpl progress; **faire des p.** to make progress.

progresser vi to progress.

progressif, -ive adj gradual.

progressivement adv gradually.

proie f prey.

projecteur m (de monument) floodlight; (de film etc) projector.

projectile m missile.

projection f (de film) projection; (séance) showing.

projet m plan.

projeter vt (lancer) to hurl; (film) to project; (voyage, fête etc) to plan; **p. de faire** to plan to do.

prolonger vt to extend.

prolonger (se) vpr (séance, rue) to continue.

promenade f (à pied) walk; (en voiture) drive; (en vélo, à cheval) ride; **faire une p.** to (go for a) walk; (en voiture) to (go for a) drive.

promener vt to take for a walk ou drive.

promener (se) vpr to (go for a) walk; (en voiture) to (go for a) drive.

promeneur, -euse mf stroller.

promesse f promise.

promettre* vt to promise (**qch à qn** sb sth; **que** that); **p. de faire** to promise to do; **c'est promis** it's a promise.

promotion f **en p.** (produit) on (special) offer.

pronom m pronoun.

prononcer vt (articuler) to pronounce; (dire) to utter; (discours) to deliver.

prononcer (se) vpr (mot) to be pronounced.

prononciation f pronunciation.

pronostic m forecast; (d'un médecin) prognosis.

propager vt, **se propager** vpr to spread.

propice adj favorable (**à** to); **le moment p.** the right moment.

proportion f proportion; (rapport) ratio.

propos 1 mpl (paroles) remarks. **2** prép **à p. de** about. **3** adv **à p.!** by the way!

proposer vt to suggest, to propose (**qch à qn** sth to sb; **que** (+ subjonctif) that); (offrir) to offer (**qch à qn** sb sth; **de faire** to do); **je te propose de rester** I suggest you stay.

proposer (se) vpr **se p. pour faire** to offer to do.

proposition f Grammaire clause.

propre¹ adj clean; (soigné) neat. **2** m **mettre qch au p.** to make a clean copy of sth.

propre² adj own; **mon p. argent** my own money.

proprement adv cleanly; (avec netteté) neatly.

propreté f cleanliness; (netteté) neatness.

propriétaire mf owner; (qui loue) landlord, landlady.

propriété f (bien, maison) property.

prose f prose.

prospectus m leaflet.

prospère adj thriving.

protecteur, -trice 1 mf protector. **2** adj (geste etc) protective.

protection f protection; **de p.** (écran etc) protective.

protège-cahier, pl **protège-cahiers** m note book cover.

protéger vt to protect (**de** from; **contre** against).

protestant, -ante adj & mf Protestant.

protestataire mf protester.

protestation f protest (**contre** against).

protester *vi* to protest (**contre** against).

prothèse *f* prosthesis; **p. auditive** hearing aid; **p. dentaire** false teeth.

prouver *vt* to prove (**que** that).

provenance *f* origin; **en p. de** from.

provenir* *vi* **p. de** to come from.

proverbe *m* proverb.

province *f* province; **la p.** the provinces; **en p.** in the provinces; **de p.** *(ville etc)* provincial.

provincial, -e, -aux *adj & mf* provincial.

proviseur *m* *(de lycée)* principal.

provision *f* supply; **provisions** *(achats)* shopping; *(nourriture)* food; **sac à provisions** shopping bag; **chèque sans p.** bad check.

provisoire *adj* temporary.

provisoirement *adv* temporarily.

provoquer *vt* *(causer)* to bring (sth) about; *(défier)* to provoke (sb).

proximité *f* closeness; **à p.** close by; **à p. de** close to.

prudemment *adv* cautiously, carefully.

prudence *f* caution, care.

prudent, -ente *adj* cautious, careful.

prune *f* *(fruit)* plum.

pruneau, -x *m* prune.

prunier *m* plum tree.

psychiatre *mf* psychiatrist.

psychologique *adj* psychological.

psychologue *mf* psychologist.

PTT *fpl abrév (Postes, Télégraphes, Téléphones)* Post Office.

pu *voir* **pouvoir.**

puanteur *f* stink.

public, -ique 1 *adj* public. **2** *m* public; *(de spectacle)* audience; **en p.** in public.

publication *f* publication.

publicité *f* advertising, publicity; *(annonce)* advertisement; *(filmée)* commercial.

publier *vt* to publish.

puce *f* flea; *(d'ordinateur)* chip; **marché aux puces** flea market.

pudeur *f* modesty; **par p.** out of a sense of decency.

pudique *adj* modest.

puer 1 *vi* to stink. **2** *vt* to stink of.

puéricultrice *f* pediatric nurse.

puis *adv* then.

puiser *vt* to draw (**dans** from).

puisque *conj* since, as.

puissance *f* *(force, nation)* power.

puissant, -ante *adj* powerful.

puisse(s), puissent *etc voir* **pouvoir.**

puits *m* well; *(de mine)* shaft.

pull(-over) *m* sweater.

pulluler *vi* *(abonder)* to swarm.

pulvérisateur *m* spray.

pulvériser *vt* *(liquide)* to spray.

punaise *f* *(insecte)* bug; *(clou)* thumbtack.

punir *vt* to punish (**de qch** for sth; **pour avoir fait** for doing).

punition *f* punishment.

pupille *f* *(d'œil)* pupil.

pupitre *m* *(d'écolier)* desk; *(d'orateur)* lectern.

pur, -e *adj* pure.

purée *f* purée; **p. (de pommes de terre)** mashed potatoes.

pureté *f* purity.

pus *m* *(liquide)* pus.

puzzle *m* *(jigsaw)* puzzle.

p.-v. *m inv abrév (procès-verbal)* (traffic) ticket.

pyjama *m* pajamas; **un p.** a pair of pajamas.

pylône *m* pylon.

pyramide *f* pyramid.

Q

QI *m inv abrév (quotient intellectuel)* IQ.

quadrillé, -ée *adj* *(papier)* squared.

quai *m* (*de port*) (*pour passagers*) quay; (*pour marchandises*) wharf; (*de fleuve*) embankment; (*de gare*) platform.

qualifié, -ée *adj* (*équipe etc*) that has qualified; (*ouvrier*) skilled.

qualifier *vt* (*équipe*) to qualify (**pour qch** for sth; **pour faire** to do); (*décrire*) to describe (**de** as).

qualifier (se) *vpr* (*en sport*) to qualify (**pour** for).

qualité *f* quality.

quand *conj & adv* when; **q. je viendrai** when I come; **q. même** all the same.

quant à *prép* as for.

quantité *f* quantity; **une q.** (*beaucoup*) a lot (**de** of).

quarantaine *f* une q. (de) about forty.

quarante *adj & m* forty.

quarantième *adj & mf* fortieth.

quart *m* quarter; **q. (de litre)** quarter liter (= *one cup*); **q. d'heure** quarter of an hour; **une heure et q.** an hour and a quarter; **il est une heure et q.** it's a quarter after one; **une heure moins le q.** quarter to one.

quartier¹ *m* (*de ville*) neighborhood, district; (*chinois etc*) quarter; **de q.** (*cinéma etc*) local.

quartier² *m* (*de pomme*) quarter; (*d'orange*) segment.

quartz *m* montre/*etc* **à q.** quartz watch/*etc*.

quasiment *adv* almost.

quatorze *adj & m* fourteen.

quatre *adj & m* four; **q. heures** (*goûter*) afternoon snack.

quatre-vingt(s) *adj & m* eighty; **q.-vingts ans** eighty years; **q.-vingt-un** eighty-one; **page quatre-vingt** page eighty.

quatre-vingt-dix *adj & m* ninety.

quatrième *adj & mf* fourth.

que (**qu'** *before a vowel or mute h*) **1** *conj* that; **je pense qu'elle restera** I think (that) she'll stay; **qu'elle**

vienne ou non whether she comes or not; **qu'il s'en aille!** let him leave! **qu'il n'a...q.** only; **tu n'as qu'un euro** you only have one euro. ■ (*comparaison*) than; (*avec aussi, même, tel, autant*) as; **plus âgé q.** older than; **aussi sage q.** as wise as; **le même q.** the same as. **2** *adv* (**ce**) **qu'il est bête!** how silly he is! **3** *pron rel* (*chose*) that, which; (*personne*) that; (*temps*) when; **le livre q. j'ai** the book (that *ou* which) I have; **l'ami q. j'ai** the friend (that) I have; **un jour q.** one day when. **4** *pron interrogatif* what; **q. fait-il?**, **qu'est-ce qu'il fait?** what is he doing?; **qu'est-ce qui est dans ta poche?** what's in your pocket?

quel, quelle 1 *adj interrogatif* what, which; (*qui*) who; **q. livre/acteur?** what *ou* which book/actor?; **je sais q. est ton but** I know what your aim is. **2** *pron interrogatif* which (one); **q. est le meilleur?** which (one) is the best? **3** *adj exclamatif* **q. idiot!** what a fool!

quelconque *adj* any (whatever); **une raison q.** any reason (whatever).

quelque 1 *adj* **quelques femmes/livres**/*etc* some *ou* a few women/books/*etc*; **les quelques amies qu'elle a** the few friends she has. **2** *pron* **q. chose** something; (*interrogation*) anything, something; **il y a q. chose** (*un problème*) there's something the matter with him; **q. chose d'autre/de grand**/*etc* something else/big/*etc*. **3** *adv* **q. part** somewhere; (*interrogation*) anywhere, somewhere.

quelquefois *adv* sometimes.

quelques-uns, -unes *pron pl* some.

quelqu'un *pron* someone; (*interrogation*) anyone, someone; **q. d'intelligent**/*etc* someone smart/*etc*.

question *f* question; (*problème*)

matter; **il est q. de** there's some talk about (**faire** doing); **il a été q. de vous** we ou they talked about you; **il n'en est pas q.** it's out of the question.

questionner vt to question (**sur** about).

quête f (collecte) collection; **faire la q.** to collect money.

quêter vi to collect money.

queue[1] f (d'animal etc) tail; (de fleur) stem; (de fruit) stalk; (de poêle) handle; (de train) rear; **q. de cheval** (coiffure) ponytail; **à la q. leu leu** in single file.

queue[2] f (file) line; **faire la q.** to line up.

qui pron (personne) who, that; (interrogatif) who; (chose) which, that; **l'homme q.** the man who ou that; **la maison q.** the house which ou that; **q. est là?** who's there?; **q. désirez-vous voir?, q. est-ce que vous désirez voir?** who do you want to see?; **la femme de q. je parle** the woman I'm talking about; **l'ami sur l'aide de q. je compte** the friend on whose help I rely; **à q. est ce livre?** whose book is this?

quiche f quiche.

quiconque pron (sujet) whoever; (complément) anyone.

quille f (de jeu) (bowling) pin; **jouer aux quilles** to bowl.

quincaillerie f hardware store.

quincaillier, -ière mf hardware store owner.

quinzaine f **une q. (de)** about fifteen; **q. (de jours)** two weeks.

quinze adj & m fifteen; **q. jours** two weeks.

quinzième adj & mf fifteenth.

quittance f (reçu) receipt.

quitte adj even (**envers** with).

quitter **1** vt to leave; **q. qn des yeux** to take one's eyes off sb. **2** vi **ne quittez pas!** (au téléphone) hold on!

quitter (se) vpr (se séparer) to part, to say goodbye.

quoi pron what; (après prép) which; **à q. penses-tu?** what are you thinking about?; **de q. manger** something to eat; **de q. couper/écrire** something to cut/write with; **il n'y a pas de q.!** (en réponse à 'merci') don't mention it!

quoique conj (al)though; **q. je le sache déjà** (al)though I already know.

quotidien, -ienne 1 adj daily. **2** m daily (paper).

R

rabâcher 1 vt to repeat endlessly. **2** vi to say the same thing over and over again.

rabais m reduction, discount.

rabattre* vt to pull down; (refermer) to close (down).

rabattre (se) vpr (barrière) to come down; (après avoir doublé un véhicule) to cut in.

rabbin m rabbi.

rabot m (outil) plane.

raboter vt to plane.

raccommodage m mending; (de chaussette) darning.

raccommoder vt to mend; (chaussette) to darn.

raccompagner vt to see ou accompany back (home); **r. à la porte** to see to the door.

raccord m (dispositif) connection, connector; (de papier peint) seam.

raccourci m (chemin) short cut.

raccourcir 1 vt to shorten. **2** vi to get shorter.

raccrocher 1 vt (objet tombé) to hang back up; (téléphone) to put down. **2** vi (au téléphone) to hang up.

race f (groupe ethnique) race; (d'animal) breed.

rachat m (de voiture, d'appartement) repurchase; (de firme) buyout.

racheter vt r. un manteau/une voiture/etc to buy another coat/car/etc; r. des chaussettes/du pain/etc to buy some more socks/bread/etc.

racial, -e, -aux adj racial.

racine f root; **prendre r.** (plante) to take root.

racisme m racism.

raciste adj & mf racist.

racler vt to scrape; (enlever) to scrape off.

racler (se) vpr se r. la gorge to clear one's throat.

racontars mpl gossip.

raconter vt (histoire) to tell; r. qch à qn (vacances etc) to tell sb about sth; r. à qn que to tell sb that.

radar m radar.

radeau, -x m raft.

radiateur m heater; (de chauffage central, voiture) radiator.

radieux, -euse adj (personne, visage) beaming; (soleil) brilliant; (temps) glorious.

radio[1] f radio; (poste) radio (set); **à la r.** on the radio.

radio[2] f (examen, photo) X-ray; **passer une r.** to have an X-ray.

radioactif, -ive adj radioactive.

radiodiffuser vt to broadcast (on the radio).

radiographier vt to X-ray.

radis m radish.

radoucir (se) vpr (temps) to become milder.

radoucissement m r. (du temps) milder weather.

rafale f (vent) gust.

raffiné, -ée adj refined.

raffoler vi r. de (aimer) to be crazy about.

rafistoler vt Fam to patch up.

rafraîchir vt to cool (down).

rafraîchir (se) vpr (boire) to refresh oneself; (temps) to get cooler.

rafraîchissant, -ante adj refreshing.

rafraîchissement m (de température) cooling; (boisson) cold drink; **rafraîchissements** (glaces etc) refreshments.

rage f (colère) rage; (maladie) rabies; **r. de dents** violent toothache.

ragoût m stew.

raid m raid.

raide adj (rigide) stiff; (côte) steep; (cheveux) straight; (corde) tight.

raidir vt, **se raidir** vpr to stiffen; (corde) to tighten.

raie f (trait) line; (de tissu, zèbre) stripe; (de cheveux) part.

rail m (barre) rail (for train).

rainure f groove.

raisin m (grain de) r. grape; **du r., des raisins** grapes; **r. sec** raisin.

raison f reason; **la r. de/pour laquelle...** the reason for/why...; **en r. de** on account of; **avoir r.** to be right (**de faire** to do).

raisonnable adj reasonable.

raisonnement m reasoning.

raisonner 1 vi (penser) to reason. **2** vt r. qn to reason with sb.

rajeunir vt to make (sb) feel ou look) younger.

rajouter vt to add (à to).

ralenti m au r. (filmer) in slow motion; **tourner au r.** (moteur) to turn over.

ralentir vti to slow down.

ralentissement m slowing down; (embouteillage) hold-up.

rallonge f (de table) extension; (électrique) extension cord.

rallonger vti to lengthen.

rallumer vt (feu, pipe) to light again; (lampe) to switch on again.

rallye m (automobile) rally.

ramassage m (de par terre) picking up; (d'ordures, de copies) collection; *(de fruits, de coquillages)* gathering; **r. scolaire** school bus service.

ramasser *vt (prendre par terre, réunir)* to pick up; *(ordures, copies)* to collect; *(fruits, coquillages)* to gather.

rame *f (aviron)* oar; *(de métro)* train.

ramener *vt* to bring *ou* take *(sb)* back.

ramer *vi* to row.

ramollir *vt*, **se ramollir** *vpr* to soften.

ramoner *vt (cheminée)* to sweep.

rampe *f (d'escalier)* banister(s); **r. (d'accès)** ramp; **r. de lancement** *(de fusées)* launching pad.

ramper *vi* to crawl.

ranch *m* ranch.

rançon *f (argent)* ransom.

rancune *f* grudge; **garder r. à qn** to bear sb a grudge.

rancunier, -ière *adj* spiteful.

randonnée *f (à pied)* hike; *(en voiture)* drive; *(en vélo)* ride.

rang *m (rangée)* row, line; *(classement)* rank; **se mettre en rang(s)** to line up *(par trois/etc* in threes/ *etc)*.

rangé, -ée *adj (chambre etc)* tidy.

rangée *f* row, line.

rangements *mpl (placards)* storage space.

ranger *vt (papiers etc)* to put away; *(chambre etc)* to tidy (up); *(chiffres, mots)* to arrange; *(voiture)* to park.

ranger (se) *vpr (élèves etc)* to line up; *(s'écarter)* to stand aside; *(voiture)* to pull over.

ranimer *vt (réanimer)* to revive *(sb)*, *(feu)* to poke, to stir.

rapace *m* bird of prey.

râpe *f (à fromage etc)* grater.

râper *vt (fromage, carottes)* to grate.

rapetisser *vi* to get smaller.

rapide 1 *adj* fast, quick. **2** *m (train)* express (train).

rapidement *adv* fast, quickly.

rapidité *f* speed.

rapiécer *vt* to patch (up).

rappeler *vt* to call back; *(souvenir)* to recall; **r. qch à qn** to remind sb of sth.

rappeler (se) *vpr* to remember *(que* that).

rapport *m (lien)* connection; *(récit)* report; **rapports** *(entre personnes)* relations; **par r. à** compared to; **ça n'a aucun r.!** it has nothing to do with it!

rapporter 1 *vt* to bring *ou* take back; *(profit)* to bring in. **2** *vi (dénoncer) Fam* to tell tales; *(investissement)* to bring in a good return.

rapporter (se) *vpr* **se r. à** to relate to.

rapporteur, -euse 1 *mf* telltale. **2** *m (en géométrie)* protractor.

rapprocher *vt* to bring closer *(de* to); *(chaise)* to pull up *(de* to).

rapprocher (se) *vpr* to come *ou* get closer *(de* to).

raquette *f (de tennis)* racket; *(de ping-pong)* paddle.

rare *adj* rare; **il est r. que** (+ *subjonctif)* it's rare that.

rarement *adv* rarely, seldom.

ras, rase *adj (cheveux)* close-cropped; *(herbe, poil)* short; **en rase campagne** in the open country; **à r. bord** *(remplir)* to the brim.

rasé, -ée *adj* **être bien r.** to have shaved; **mal r.** unshaven.

raser *vt (menton, personne)* to shave; *(barbe, moustache)* to shave off; *(démolir)* to knock down; *(frôler)* to skim.

raser (se) *vpr* to (have a) shave.

rasoir *m* razor; *(électrique)* shaver.

rassemblement *m* gathering.

rassembler *vt (gens, objets)* to gather (together).

rassembler (se) *vpr* to gather.

rassis, *f* **rassie** *adj (pain etc)* stale.

rassurant, -ante *adj* reassuring.

rassurer vt to reassure; **rassure-toi** don't worry.

rat m rat.

ratatiner (se) vpr to shrivel up.

râteau, -x (outil) rake.

rater vt (bus, cible etc) to miss; (travail, gâteau etc) to ruin; (examen) to fail.

ration f ration.

rationnement m rationing.

rationner vt to ration.

ratisser vt (allée etc) to rake; (feuilles etc) to rake up.

rattacher vt (lacets etc) to tie up again.

rattrapage m cours de r. remedial class.

rattraper vt to catch; (prisonnier) to recapture; (temps perdu) to make up for; **r. qn** (rejoindre) to catch up with sb.

rature f crossing out.

raturer vt to cross out.

rauque adj (voix) hoarse.

ravager vt to devastate.

ravages mpl havoc; **faire des r.** to cause havoc ou widespread damage.

ravaler vt (façade etc) to clean (and restore).

ravi, -ie adj delighted (**de** with; **de faire** to do).

ravin m ravine.

ravioli(s) mpl ravioli.

ravir vt (plaire) to delight.

raviser (se) vpr to change one's mind.

ravissant, -ante adj beautiful.

ravisseur, -euse mf kidnapper.

ravitaillement m supplying; (denrées) supplies.

ravitailler vt to supply (**en** with).

ravitailler (se) vpr to stock up (with supplies).

rayé, -ée adj scratched; (tissu) striped.

rayer vt (érafler) to scratch; (mot etc) to cross out.

rayon m (de lumière, soleil) ray; (de cercle) radius; (de roue) spoke; (planche) shelf; (de magasin) department.

rayonnant, -ante adj (visage etc) beaming (**de** with).

rayure f scratch; (bande) stripe; **à rayures** striped.

raz-de-marée m inv tidal wave.

re-, ré- préfixe re-.

réacteur m (d'avion) jet engine; (nucléaire) reactor.

réaction f reaction; **avion à r.** jet (aircraft).

réagir vi to react (**contre** against; **à** to).

réalisateur, -trice mf (de film) director.

réaliser vt (projet etc) to carry out; (rêve) to fulfill; (fabriquer) to make; (film) to direct.

réaliser (se) vpr (vœu) to come true; (projet) to materialize.

réaliste adj realistic.

réalité f reality; **en r.** in fact.

réanimation f **en r.** in intensive care.

réanimer vt to revive, to resuscitate.

rebond m bounce.

rebondir vi to bounce.

rebord m **r. de (la) fenêtre** windowsill.

reboucher vt (flacon) to put the top back on; (trou) to fill in again.

rébus m inv rebus (word guessing game).

récemment adv recently.

récent, -ente adj recent.

réception f (réunion, de radio etc) reception; (d'hôtel) reception (desk); **dès r. de** on receipt of.

recette f (de cuisine) recipe (**de** for); (argent, bénéfice) takings.

recevoir* 1 vt to receive; (accueillir) to welcome; **être reçu (à)** (examen) to pass. **2** vi to have guests.

rechange (de) adj (outil etc) spare; **vêtements de r.** a change of clothes.

recharge f (de stylo) refill.
recharger vt (fusil, appareil photo) to reload; (briquet, stylo) to refill; (batterie) to recharge.
réchaud m (portable) stove.
réchauffement m (de température) rise (de in).
réchauffer vt to warm up.
réchauffer (se) vpr se r. to warm oneself up; (temps) to get warmer.
recherche f la r., des recherches (scientifique etc) research (sur on, into); faire des recherches to (do) research; (enquêter) to investigate.
recherché, -ée adj r. pour meurtre wanted for murder.
rechercher vt (personne, objet) to search for.
rechute f relapse.
récif m reef.
récipient m container.
réciproque adj mutual.
récit m (histoire) story.
récitation f (poème) poem (learned by heart and recited aloud).
réciter vt to recite.
réclamation f complaint.
réclame f advertising; (annonce) advertisement; en r. on (special) offer.
réclamer 1 vt (demander) to ask for (sth) back. **2** vi to complain.
recoin m nook.
recoller vt (objet cassé) to stick back together; (enveloppe) to reseal.
récolte f (action) harvest; (produits) crop.
récolter vt to harvest.
recommandation f recommendation.
recommander vt to recommend (à to; pour for); r. à qn de faire to recommend to sb to do; lettre recommandée certified letter; en recommandé (envoyer) by certified mail.
recommencer vti to start again.

récompense f reward (pour for).
récompenser vt to reward (de, pour for).
réconciliation f reconciliation.
réconcilier (se) vpr to settle one's differences, to make it up (avec with).
reconduire* vt r. qn to see sb back.
réconfort m comfort.
réconfortant, -ante adj comforting.
réconforter vt to comfort.
reconnaissance f (gratitude) gratitude.
reconnaissant, -ante adj grateful (à qn de qch to sb for sth).
reconnaître vt to recognize (à qch by sth); (admettre) to admit (que that); reconnu coupable found guilty.
reconstruire* vt (ville) to rebuild.
reconvertir (se) vpr (personne) to retrain.
recopier vt to copy out.
record m & adj inv (en sport etc) record.
recoudre* vt (bouton) to sew (back) on; (vêtement) to stitch (up).
recourbé, -ée adj (clou etc) bent; (nez) hooked.
recourir* vi r. à (moyen, violence) to resort to; (personne) to turn to.
recours m recourse; avoir r. à (chose) to resort to; (personne) to turn to; en dernier r. as a last resort.
recouvrir* vt (livre, meuble etc) to cover.
récréation f (à l'école) recess.
recroquevillé, -ée adj (personne, papier etc) curled up.
recrue f recruit.
rectangle m rectangle.
rectangulaire adj rectangular.
rectification f correction.
rectifier vt to correct.
recto m front (of the page).
reçu, reçue 1 pp of **recevoir**. **2** m (écrit) receipt.

recueil m anthology, collection (**de** of).

recueillir* vt to collect; (prendre chez soi) to take (sb) in.

recul m (d'armée, de négociateur, de maladie) retreat; (de canon) recoil; (déclin) decline; **avoir un mouvement de r.** to recoil; **manquer de r.** to be too closely involved; **prendre du r.** to stand back from things.

reculer 1 vi to move back; (véhicule) to reverse. **2** vt to push back.

reculons (à) adv backwards.

récupérer 1 vt (objet prêté) to get back. **2** vi to get one's strength back.

récurer vt (casserole etc) to scrub.

recyclage m (de matériaux) recycling; (de personne) retraining.

recycler vt (matériaux) to recycle.

rédacteur, -trice mf (de journal) editor; **r. en chef** editor(-in-chief).

rédaction f (devoir de français) essay, composition.

redescendre 1 vi (aux être) to come ou go back down. **2** vt (aux avoir) to bring ou take back down.

rediffusion f (de film etc) repeat, rerun.

rédiger vt to write.

redire* vt to repeat.

redonner vt (donner plus) to give more; **r. un euro/etc** to give another euro/etc.

redoublant, -ante mf student repeating a grade.

redoublement m repeating a grade.

redoubler vti **r. (une classe)** to repeat a grade.

redoutable adj formidable.

redouter vt to dread (**de faire** doing).

redresser vt (objet tordu etc) to straighten (out).

redresser (se) vpr to sit up; (debout) to stand up.

réduction f reduction (**de** in); (prix réduit) discount; **en r.** (copie, modèle) small-scale.

réduire* vt to reduce (**à** to; **de** by); **r. en cendres** to reduce to ashes.

réduit, -uite adj (prix, vitesse) reduced; (modèle) small-scale.

rééducation f (de personne) rehabilitation; **faire de la r.** to have physical therapy.

réel, -elle adj real.

réellement adv really.

réexpédier vt (faire suivre) to forward (letter).

refaire* vt (exercice, travail) to do again, to redo; (chambre etc) to redecorate.

réfectoire m refectory.

référence f reference.

refermer vt, **se refermer** vpr to close (again).

réfléchir 1 vt (image) to reflect; **verbe réfléchi** reflexive verb. **2** vi (penser) to think (**à** about).

réfléchir (se) vpr to be reflected.

reflet m (image) reflection; **reflets** (couleurs) highlights.

refléter vt (image etc) to reflect.

refléter (se) vpr to be reflected.

réflexe m reflex.

réflexion f (méditation) thought; (remarque) remark.

réforme f (changement) reform.

refrain m (de chanson) chorus.

réfrigérateur m refrigerator.

refroidir vti to cool (down).

refroidir (se) vpr (prendre froid) to catch cold; (temps) to get cold.

refroidissement m (rhume) chill; **r. de la température** fall in the temperature.

refuge m refuge; (pour piétons) median; (de montagne) (mountain) hut.

réfugié, -ée mf refugee.

réfugier (se) vpr to take refuge.

refus m refusal.

refuser 1 vt to refuse (**qch à qn** sb sth; **de faire** to do); (candidat) to fail. **2** vi to refuse.

regagner vt to regain, to get back; (revenir à) to get back to.

régaler (se) *vpr* to have a feast.

regard *m* look; *(fixe)* stare; **jeter un r. sur** to glance at.

regarder[1] *vt* to look at; *(fixement)* to stare at; *(observer)* to watch; **r. qn faire** to watch sb do. **2** *vi* to look; to stare; to watch.

regarder[2] *vt* *(concerner)* to concern; **ça ne te regarde pas!** it's none of your business!

régime[1] *m* *(politique)* (form of) government; *(alimentaire)* diet; **se mettre au r.** to go on a diet; **suivre un r.** to be on a diet.

régime[2] *m* *(de bananes, dattes)* bunch.

régiment *m* *(soldats)* regiment.

région *f* region, area.

régional, -e, -aux *adj* regional.

registre *m* register.

réglable *adj* *(siège)* adjustable.

réglage *m* adjustment; *(de moteur)* tuning.

règle *f* rule; *(instrument)* ruler; **en r. générale** as a rule; **règles** *(de femme)* (monthly) period.

règlement *m* *(règles)* regulations; *(paiement)* payment; **contraire au r.** against the rules.

réglementation *f* *(règles)* regulations.

régler 1 *vt* *(problème etc)* to settle; *(mécanisme)* to adjust; *(moteur)* to tune. **2** *vti* *(payer)* to pay; **r. qn** to settle up with sb.

réglisse *f* licorice.

règne *m* *(de roi)* reign.

régner *vi* *(roi, silence)* to reign (**sur** over).

regret *m* regret; **à r.** with regret.

regrettable *adj* unfortunate, regrettable.

regretter *vt* to regret; **r. qn** to miss sb; **r. que** (+ *subjonctif*) to be sorry that; **je (le) regrette** I'm sorry.

regrouper *vt*, **se regrouper** *vpr* to gather together.

régularité *f* regularity; *(de progrès, vitesse)* steadiness.

régulier, -ière *adj* regular; *(progrès, vitesse)* steady.

régulièrement *adv* regularly.

réhabituer (se) *vpr* **se r. à qch/à faire qch** to get used to sth/to doing sth again.

rein *m* kidney; **les reins** *(dos)* the (small of the) back.

reine *f* queen.

réinsertion *f* reintegration; **r. sociale** rehabilitation.

rejeter *vt* to throw back; *(refuser)* to reject.

rejoindre* *vt* *(famille, lieu etc)* to get back to; **r. qn** *(se joindre à)* to join sb; *(rattraper)* to catch up with sb.

rejoindre (se) *vpr* *(personnes, routes)* to meet.

réjouir (se) *vpr* to be delighted (**de** at, about; **de faire** to do).

réjouissances *fpl* festivities.

relâcher *vt* *(corde etc)* to slacken; **r. qn** to release sb.

relais *m* **prendre le r.** to take over (**de** from).

relancer *vt* *(lancer à nouveau)* to throw again; *(rendre)* to throw back; *(production)* to boost; *(moteur)* to restart.

relatif, -ive *adj* relative.

relation *f* relation(ship); *(ami)* acquaintance; **entrer en relations avec** to come into contact with.

relativement *adv* *(assez)* relatively.

relayer *vt* to take over from *(sb)*.

relayer (se) *vpr* to take (it in) turns (**pour faire** to do).

relevé *m* *(de compteur)* reading; **r. de compte** (bank) statement.

relever *vt* to raise; *(personne tombée)* to help up; *(col)* to turn up; *(manches)* to roll up; *(compteur)* to read.

relever (se) *vpr* *(personne tombée)* to get up.

relief *m* *(forme)* relief; **en r.** *(cinéma)* 3-D.

relier *vt* to connect (**à** to); *(livre)* to bind.

religieux, -euse 1 *adj* religious. **2** *f* nun.

religion *f* religion.

relire* *vt* to read again, to reread.

reliure *f (de livre)* binding.

reluire* *vi* to shine.

remarquable *adj* remarkable (**par** for).

remarquablement *adv* remarkably.

remarque *f* remark; *(écrite)* note.

remarquer *vt* to notice (**que** that); **faire r.** to point out (**à** to; **que** that); **se faire r.** to attract attention; **remarque!** mind you!, you know!

rembobiner *vt*, **se rembobiner** *(bande)* to rewind.

rembourré, -ée *adj (fauteuil etc)* padded.

remboursement *m* repayment; *(dans un magasin etc)* refund.

rembourser *vt* to pay back, to repay; *(billet)* to refund.

remède *m* cure; *(médicament)* medicine.

remédier *vi* **r. à qch** to remedy sth.

remémorer (se) *vpr* to remember.

remerciements *mpl* thanks.

remercier *vt* to thank (**de qch, pour qch** for sth); **je vous remercie d'être venu** thank you for coming.

remettre* *vt* to put back; *(vêtement)* to put back on; *(donner)* to hand over (**à** to); *(démission, devoir)* to hand in; *(différer)* to postpone (**à** until); **r. en question** to call into question; **r. en état** to repair.

remettre (se) *vpr* **se r. à** *(activité)* to go back to; **se r. à faire** to start to do again; **se r. de** *(chagrin, maladie)* to get over.

remise *f (rabais)* discount.

remonte-pente, *pl* **remonte-pentes** *m* ski lift.

remonter 1 *vi (aux* **être)** to come

ou go back up; **r. dans** *(voiture)* to get back in(to); *(bus, train)* to get back on(to); **r. sur** *(cheval, vélo)* to get back on(to). **2** *vt (aux* **avoir)** *(escalier, pente)* to come ou go back up; *(porter)* to bring ou take back up; *(montre)* to wind; *(relever)* to raise; *(col)* to turn up; *(objet démonté)* to put back together.

remords *m & mpl* remorse; **avoir des r.** to feel remorse.

remorque *f (de voiture etc)* trailer; **prendre en r.** to tow; **en r.** in tow.

remorquer *vt* to tow.

remorqueur *m* tug(boat).

remplaçant, -ante *mf (personne)* replacement; *(enseignant)* substitute teacher; *(en sport)* reserve.

remplacement *m* replacement; **assurer le r. de qn** to stand in for sb.

remplacer *vt* to replace (**par** with, by); *(succéder)* to take over from.

rempli, -ie *adj* full (**de** of).

remplir *vt* to fill (up) *(de* with); *(fiche etc)* to fill in ou out.

remplir (se) *vpr* to fill (up).

remporter *vi (objet)* to take back; *(prix, victoire)* to win.

remuant, -ante *adj (enfant)* restless.

remuer 1 *vt* to move; *(café etc)* to stir; *(salade)* to toss. **2** *vi* to move; *(gigoter)* to fidget.

renard *m* fox.

rencontre *f* meeting; *(en sport)* game; **aller à la r. de qn** to go to meet sb.

rencontrer *vt* to meet; *(équipe)* to play.

rencontrer (se) *vpr* to meet.

rendez-vous *m inv* appointment; *(d'amoureux)* date; *(lieu)* meeting place; **donner r. à qn** to make an appointment with sb.

rendormir* (se) *vpr* to go back to sleep.

rendre 1 *vt* to give back; *(monnaie)* to give; *(vomir)* to bring up; **r. célè-**

bre/plus grand/*etc* to make famous/bigger/*etc*. **2** *vti* (*vomir*) to throw up.

rendre (se) *vpr* to surrender (**à qn** to sb); (*aller*) to go (**à** to); **se r. utile/** *etc* to make oneself useful/*etc*.

rênes *fpl* reins.

renfermé *m* sentir le r. (*chambre etc*) to smell stuffy.

renfermer *vt* to contain.

renflement *m* bulge.

renforcer *vt* to strengthen.

renforts *mpl* (*troupes*) reinforcements.

renier *vt* (*ami, pays*) to disown; (*foi*) to deny.

renifler *vti* to sniff.

renne *m* reindeer.

renommé, -ée *adj* famous (**pour** for).

renommée *f* fame.

renoncer *vi* **r. à qch/à faire** to give up sth/doing.

renouvelable *adj* renewable.

renouveler *vt* to renew; (*erreur, question*) to repeat.

renouveler (se) *vpr* (*incident*) to happen again.

renseignement *m* (piece of) information; **des renseignements** information; **les renseignements** (*au téléphone*) directory assistance, information.

renseigner *vt* to inform, to give some information to (**sur** about).

renseigner (se) *vpr* to find out, to inquire (**sur** about).

rentable *adj* profitable.

rentrée *f* return; **r. (des classes)** beginning of the school year.

rentrer 1 *vi* (*aux être*) to go *ou* come back; (*chez soi*) to come (back) home; (*entrer de nouveau*) to go *ou* come back in; (*élèves*) to go back to school; **r. dans** to go *ou* come back into; (*pays*) to return to; (*heurter*) to crash into; (*s'emboîter dans*) to fit into. **2** *vt* (*aux avoir*) to bring *ou* take in; (*voiture*) to put

away; (*chemise*) to tuck in; (*griffes*) to draw in.

renverse (à la) *adv* (*tomber*) backwards.

renverser *vt* (*mettre à l'envers*) to turn upside down; (*faire tomber*) to knock over; (*piéton*) to knock down; (*liquide*) to spill.

renverser (se) *vpr* (*vase etc*) to fall over; (*liquide*) to spill.

renvoi *m* (*d'un employé*) dismissal; (*rot*) burp.

renvoyer* *vt* to send back; (*employé*) to dismiss; (*élève*) to expel; (*balle etc*) to throw back.

réorganiser *vt* to reorganize.

repaire *m* den.

répandre *vt* (*liquide*) to spill; (*nouvelle*) to spread.

répandre (se) *vpr* **se r. dans** (*fumée, odeur*) to spread through.

répandu, -ue *adj* (*opinion etc*) widespread.

reparaître *vi* to reappear.

réparateur, -trice *mf* repairer.

réparation *f* repair; **en r.** under repair.

réparer *vt* to repair, to mend; (*erreur*) to correct.

repartir* *vi* (*aux être*) to set off again; (*s'en retourner*) to go back.

répartir *vt* (*partager*) to share (out).

repas *m* meal; **prendre un r.** to have a meal.

repassage *m* ironing.

repasser 1 *vi* to come *ou* go back. **2** *vt* (*traverser*) to go back over; (*leçon*) to go over; (*film*) to show again; (*linge*) to iron.

repêcher *vt* (*objet*) to fish out.

repentir* (se) *vpr* to be sorry (**de** for).

repère *m* (*guide*) mark; **point de r.** (*espace, temps*) landmark.

repérer *vt* to locate.

repérer (se) *vpr* to get one's bearings.

répertoire *m* **r. d'adresses** address book.

répéter *vti* to repeat; *(pièce de théâtre)* to rehearse.

répéter (se) *vpr (événement)* to happen again.

répétitif, -ive *adj* repetitive.

répétition *f* repetition; *(au théâtre)* rehearsal.

répit *m* rest, respite; **sans r.** ceaselessly.

replacer *vt* to put back.

repli *m* fold.

replier *vt* to fold (up); *(couverture)* to fold back; *(ailes, jambes)* to tuck in.

replier (se) *vpr (siège)* to fold up; *(couverture)* to fold back.

réplique *f* (sharp) reply; *(au théâtre)* lines.

répliquer 1 *vt* to reply (sharply) (**que** that). **2** *vi* to answer back.

répondeur *m (téléphonique)* answering machine.

répondre 1 *vi* to answer; *(être impertinent)* to answer back; *(réagir)* to respond (**à** to); **r. à qn** to answer sb; *(avec impertinence)* to answer sb back; **r. à** *(lettre, question)* to answer. **2** *vt* **r. que** to answer that.

réponse *f* answer.

reportage *m* (news) report; *(en direct)* (live) commentary.

reporter[1] *vt* to take back; *(différer)* to put off (**à** until).

reporter[2] *m* reporter.

repos *m* rest; *(tranquillité)* peace (and quiet); **jour de r.** day off.

reposant, -ante *adj* restful.

reposer *vt (objet)* to put back down; *(délasser)* to relax.

reposer (se) *vpr* to rest.

repousser 1 *vt* to push back; *(écarter)* to push away; *(différer)* to put off. **2** *vi (cheveux, feuilles)* to grow again.

reprendre* 1 *vt (objet)* to take back; *(évadé)* to recapture; *(souffle, forces)* to get back; *(activité)* to take up again; *(refrain)* to take up; **r. de la viande/un œuf/etc** to take (some) more meat/another egg/*etc.* **2** *vi (recommencer)* to start (up) (again); *(affaires)* to pick up; *(dire)* to go on.

reprendre (se) *vpr* to correct oneself; **s'y r. à deux fois** to give it another try.

représentant, -ante *mf* representative; **r. de commerce** (traveling) salesman *ou* saleswoman.

représentation *f (au théâtre)* performance.

représenter *vt* to represent; *(pièce de théâtre)* to peform.

réprimander *vt* to reprimand.

reprise *f (démission de télévision)* rerun, repeat; *(de tissu)* mend; *Boxe* round; *(économique)* recovery; *(pour nouvel achat)* trade-in; **à plusieurs reprises** on several occasions.

repriser *vt (chaussette etc)* to mend.

reproche *m* criticism; **faire des reproches à qn** to criticize sb.

reprocher *vt* **r. qch à qn** to criticize sb for sth.

reproduction *f* breeding; *(copie)* copy.

reproduire* *vt (modèle etc)* to copy.

reproduire (se) *vpr (animaux)* to breed; *(incident etc)* to happen again.

reptile *m* reptile.

républicain, -aine *adj & mf* republican.

république *f* republic.

réputation *f* reputation; **avoir la r. d'être** to have a reputation for being.

requin *m (poisson)* shark.

rescapé, -ée *mf* survivor.

réseau, -x *m* network.

réservation *f* reservation, booking.

réserve *f (provision)* stock, reserve; *(entrepôt)* storeroom; **en r.** in reserve; **r. naturelle** nature reserve.

réservé, -ée *adj (personne, place)* reserved.

réserver *vt (garder)* to save, to reserve (**à** for); *(place, table)* to book, to reserve.

réserver (se) *vpr* se r. pour to save oneself for.

réservoir *m (citerne)* tank; **r. d'essence** gas tank.

résidence *f* residence; **r. secondaire** second home.

résidentiel, -ielle *adj (quartier)* residential.

résider *vi* to be resident (**à, en, dans** in).

résigner (se) *vpr* to resign oneself (**à qch** to sth; **à faire** to doing).

résistance *f* resistance (**à** to); *(électrique)* (heating) element; **plat de r.** main dish.

résistant, -ante *adj* tough; **r. à la chaleur** heat-resistant; **r. au choc** shockproof.

résister *vi* r. à to resist; *(chaleur, fatigue)* to withstand.

résolu, -ue *adj* determined (**à faire** to do).

résolution *f (décision)* decision.

résonner *vi (cris etc)* to ring out; *(salle)* to echo (**de** with).

résoudre* *vt (problème)* to solve; *(difficulté)* to clear up.

respect *m* respect (**pour, de** for).

respecter *vt* to respect.

respectueux, -euse *adj* respectful (**envers** to).

respiration *f* breathing; *(haleine)* breath.

respirer 1 *vi* to breathe; *(reprendre haleine)* to get one's breath back. **2** *vt* to breathe (in).

resplendissant, -ante *adj (visage)* glowing (**de** with).

responsabilité *f* responsibility.

responsable 1 *adj* responsible (**de qch** for sth; **devant qn** to sb). **2** *mf (chef)* person in charge; *(coupable)* person responsible (**de** for).

ressaisir (se) *vpr* to pull oneself together.

ressemblance *f* likeness (**avec** to).

ressembler *vi* r. à to look *ou* be like.

ressembler (se) *vpr* to look *ou* be alike.

ressentir* *vt* to feel.

resserrer *vt*, **se resserrer** *vpr (nœud etc)* to tighten.

resservir* *vi (outil etc)* to come in useful (again).

resservir (se) *vpr* se r. de *(plat)* to have another helping of.

ressort *m (objet)* spring.

ressortir* *vi (aux être)* to go *ou* come back out; *(se voir)* to stand out.

ressources *fpl (moyens, argent)* resources.

restaurant *m* restaurant.

restauration *f (hôtellerie)* catering; *(de tableau)* restoration.

restaurer *vt (réparer)* to restore.

reste *m* rest (**de** of); **restes** *(de repas)* leftovers; **un r. de fromage/** *etc* some leftover cheese/etc.

rester *vi (aux être)* to stay; *(calme etc)* to keep, to stay; *(subsister)* to be left; **il reste du pain/etc** there's some bread/etc left (over); **il me reste une minute** I have one minute left; **l'argent qui lui reste** the money he *ou* she has left.

restreindre* *vt* to limit (**à** to).

résultat *m (score, d'examen etc)* results; *(conséquence)* outcome, result.

résumé *m* summary.

résumer *vt* to summarize; *(situation)* to sum up.

rétablir *vt* to restore.

rétablir (se) *vpr (malade)* to recover.

rétablissement *m (de malade)* recovery.

retard *m (sur un programme etc)* delay; **en r.** late; **en r. dans qch** behind in sth; **en r. sur qn/qch** behind sb/sth; **rattraper son r.** to catch up; **avoir du r.** to be late; *(sur un programme)* to be behind; *(montre)* to be slow; **avoir une heure de r.** to be an hour late.

retardataire *mf* latecomer.

retarder 1 *vt* to delay; *(date, montre)* to put back; **r. qn** *(dans une activité)* to put sb back. **2** *vi* *(montre)* to be slow; **r. de cinq minutes** to be five minutes slow.

retenir* *vt* *(empêcher d'agir)* to hold back; *(souffle)* to hold; *(réserver)* to book; *(se souvenir de)* to remember; *(fixer)* to hold (in place); *(chiffre)* to carry; *(chaleur, odeur)* to retain; **r. qn prisonnier** to keep sb prisoner.

retenir (se) *vpr* *(se contenir)* to restrain oneself; **se r. de faire** to stop oneself (from) doing; **se r. à** to cling to.

retentir *vi* to ring (out) (**de** with).

retenue *f* *(punition)* detention.

retirer *vt* *(sortir)* to take out; *(ôter)* to take off; *(éloigner)* to take away; **r. qch à qn** *(permis etc)* to take sth away from sb.

retomber *vi* to fall (again); *(pendre)* to hang (down); *(après un saut etc)* to land.

retouche *f* *(de vêtement)* alteration.

retoucher *vt* *(vêtement)* to alter.

retour *m* return; **être de r.** to be back (**de** from); **à mon r.** when I get *ou* got back.

retourner 1 *vt* *(aux avoir)* *(matelas, steak etc)* to turn over; *(terre etc)* to turn; *(vêtement, sac etc)* to turn inside out. **2** *vi* *(aux être)* to go back, to return.

retourner (se) *vpr* to turn around, to look around; *(sur le dos)* to turn over; *(voiture)* to overturn.

retrait *m* withdrawal; *(de bagages, de billets)* collection; *(des eaux)* receding; **en r.** *(maison)* set back; **rester en r.** to stay in the background.

retraite *f* *(d'employé)* retirement; *(pension)* (retirement) pension; **prendre sa r.** to retire; **à la r.** retired.

retraité, -ée 1 *adj* retired. **2** *mf* senior citizen, pensioner.

retransmettre *vt* to broadcast.

retransmission *f* broadcast.

rétrécir *vi* *(au lavage)* to shrink.

rétrécir (se) *vpr* *(rue etc)* to narrow.

rétro *adj inv* *(personne, idée etc)* old-fashioned.

rétrograder *vi* *(automobiliste)* to change down.

retrousser *vt* *(manches)* to roll up.

retrouver *vt* to find (again); *(rejoindre)* to meet (again); *(forces, santé)* to get back; *(se rappeler)* to recall.

retrouver (se) *vpr* to find oneself (back); *(se rencontrer)* to meet (again); **s'y r.** to find one's way.

rétroviseur *m* *(de véhicule)* rearview mirror.

réunion *f* *(séance)* meeting.

réunir *vt* *(objets)* to gather; *(convoquer)* to call together.

réunir (se) *vpr* to meet, to get together.

réussi, -ie *adj* successful.

réussir 1 *vi* to succeed (**à faire** in doing); **r. à** *(examen)* to pass; **r. à qn** *(aliment, climat)* to agree with sb. **2** *vt* to make a success of.

réussite *f* success.

revanche *f* *(en sport)* rematch; **en r.** on the other hand.

rêve *m* dream; **faire un r.** to have a dream (**de** about); **maison/etc de r.** dream house/etc.

réveil *m* *(pendule)* alarm (clock); **à son r.** when he wakes (up) *ou* woke (up).

réveillé, -ée *adj* awake.

réveiller *vt*, **se réveiller** *vpr* to wake (up).

réveillon *m* midnight supper *(on Christmas Eve or New Year's Eve)*.

réveillonner *vi* to see in Christmas/the New Year (with a midnight supper and party).

révéler vt to reveal (**que** that).

revenant m ghost.

revendication f claim; (exigence) demand.

revendiquer vt to claim; (exiger) to demand.

revenir* vi (aux être) to come back; (coûter) to cost (**à qn** sb); **r. à** (activité, sujet) to go back to; **r. à qn** (forces, mémoire) to come back to sb; **r. à soi** to come to; **r. de** (surprise) to get over; **r. sur** (décision, promesse) to go back on.

revenu m income (**de** from).

rêver 1 vi to dream (**de** of; **de faire** of doing). **2** vt to dream (**que** that).

rêverie f daydream.

revers m (de veste) lapel; (de pantalon) cuff.

revêtement m (de route etc) surface.

rêveur, -euse mf dreamer.

revient m prix de r. (production) cost.

réviser vt (leçon) to revise; (machine, voiture) to service.

révision f (de leçon) revision; (de machine, voiture) service.

revoir* vt to see (again); (texte, leçon) to revise; **au r.** goodbye.

révoltant, -ante adj revolting.

révolte f rebellion, revolt.

révolté, -ée mf rebel.

révolter vt to sicken.

révolter (se) vpr to rebel (**contre** against).

révolution f revolution.

révolutionnaire adj & mf revolutionary.

revolver m gun.

revue f (magazine) magazine.

rez-de-chaussée m inv first floor.

rhabiller (se) vpr to get dressed again.

rhinocéros m rhinoceros.

rhubarbe f rhubarb.

rhum m rum.

rhumatisme m rheumatism; **avoir des rhumatismes** to have rheumatism.

rhume m cold; **r. des foins** hay fever.

ri, riant pp & pres p of rire.

ricaner vi to snicker.

riche 1 adj rich. **2** mf rich person; **les riches** the rich.

richesse f wealth; **richesses** (trésor) riches.

ricocher vi to ricochet.

ricochet m (de pierre) ricochet.

ride f wrinkle.

ridé, -ée adj wrinkled.

rideau, -x m curtain; (de magasin) shutter.

ridicule adj ridiculous.

ridiculiser (se) vpr to make a fool of oneself.

rien 1 pron nothing; **il ne sait r.** he knows nothing, he doesn't know anything; **r. du tout** nothing at all; **r. d'autre/de bon/etc** nothing else/good/etc; **de r.!** (je vous en prie) don't mention it!; **ça ne fait r.** it doesn't matter; **r. que** just. **2** m (mere) nothing.

rigide adj rigid; (carton, muscle) stiff.

rigoler vi Fam to laugh; (s'amuser) to have fun.

rigolo, -ote adj Fam funny.

rigoureux, -euse adj (analyse) rigorous; (climat, punition) harsh; (personne, morale, neutralité) strict.

rigueur f (d'analyse) rigor; (de climat) harshness; (de personne) strictness; **être de r.** to be the rule; **à la r.** if need be.

rillettes fpl potted ground pork.

rime f rhyme.

rimer vi to rhyme (**avec** with).

rinçage m rinsing.

rincer vt to rinse; (verre) to rinse (out).

ring m (boxing) ring.

riposter 1 *vt* **r. que...** to retort that... **2** *vi* to counterattack; **r. à** (*attaque*) to counter; (*insulte*) to reply to.

rire* 1 *vi* to laugh (**de** at); (*s'amuser*) to have a good time; (*plaisanter*) to joke; **pour r.** as a joke. **2** *m* laugh; **rires** laughter; **le fou r.** the giggles.

risque *m* risk (**de faire** of doing; **à faire** in doing); **assurance tous risques** comprehensive insurance.

risqué, -ée *adj* risky.

risquer *vt* to risk; **r. de faire** to stand a good chance of doing.

rivage *m* shore.

rival, -e, -aux *adj & mf* rival.

rivaliser *vi* to compete (**avec** with; **de** in).

rive *f* (*de fleuve*) bank; (*de lac*) shore.

riverain, -aine *mf* (*près d'une rivière*) riverside resident; (*près d'un lac*) lakeside resident; (*de rue*) resident.

rivière *f* river.

riz *m* rice; **r. au lait** rice pudding.

RN *abrév* = **route nationale**.

robe *f* (*de femme*) dress; **r. du soir/de mariée** evening/wedding dress; **r. de chambre** bathrobe.

robinet *m* tap, faucet; **eau du r.** tap water.

robot *m* robot.

robuste *adj* sturdy.

roche *f*, **rocher** *m* rock.

rocheux, -euse *adj* rocky.

rock *m* (*musique*) rock.

roder *vt* (*moteur, voiture*) to break in.

rôder *vi* to prowl (about).

rôdeur, -euse *mf* prowler.

rognon *m* (*d'animal*) kidney.

roi *m* king.

rôle *m* (*au théâtre*) role, part; (*d'un père etc*) job; **à tour de r.** in turn.

romain, -aine *adj & mf* Roman.

roman *m* novel; **r. d'aventures** adventure story.

romancier, -ière *mf* novelist.

romantique *adj* romantic.

romarin *m* rosemary.

rompre* (se) *vpr* (*corde etc*) to break; (*digue*) to burst.

ronces *fpl* brambles.

ronchonner *vi* Fam to grumble.

rond, ronde 1 *adj* round; **dix euros tout r.** ten euros exactly. **2** *m* (*cercle*) circle, ring; **en r.** (*s'asseoir etc*) in a ring *ou* circle; **tourner en r.** to go round and round.

ronde *f* (*de soldat*) round; (*de policier*) beat, round.

rondelle *f* (*tranche*) slice.

rondin *m* log.

rond-point, *pl* **ronds-points** *m* traffic circle.

ronflement *m* snore; **ronflements** snoring.

ronfler *vi* to snore.

ronger *vt* to gnaw (at); (*ver, mer, rouille*) to eat into.

ronger (se) *vpr* **se r. les ongles** to bite one's nails.

ronronnement *m* purr(ing).

ronronner *vi* to purr.

rosbif *m* du **r.** roast beef; (*à rôtir*) (beef) roast; **un r.** (beef) roast.

rose 1 *f* (*fleur*) rose. **2** *adj & m* (*couleur*) pink.

rosé *adj & m* (*vin*) rosé.

roseau, -x *m* (*plante*) reed.

rosée *f* dew.

rosier *m* rose bush.

rossignol *m* nightingale.

rot *m* Fam burp.

roter *vi* Fam to burp.

rôti *m* du **r.** roast; (*cuit*) meat roast; **un r.** a roast; **r. de porc** pork roast.

rotin *m* cane.

rôtir *vti*, **se rôtir** *vpr* to roast; **faire r.** to roast.

roue *f* wheel.

rouge 1 *adj* red; (*fer*) red-hot. **2** *m* (*couleur*) red; **r. (à lèvres)** lipstick; **le feu est au r.** the (traffic) light is red.

rouge-gorge, *pl* **rouges-gorges** *m* robin.

rougeole f measles.

rougir vi (de honte) to blush; (de colère) to flush (**de** with).

rouille f rust.

rouillé, -ée adj rusty.

rouiller vi, **se rouiller** vpr to rust.

roulant, -ante adj (escalier) moving; (meuble) on wheels.

rouleau, -x m (outil) roller; (de papier etc) roll; **r. à pâtisserie** rolling pin; **r. compresseur** steamroller.

rouler 1 vt to roll; (brouette) to push; (crêpe, ficelle etc) to roll up. **2** vi to roll; (train, voiture) to go; (conducteur) to drive.

rouler (se) vpr to roll; **se r. dans** (couverture etc) to roll oneself (up) in.

roulette f (de meuble) castor; (de dentiste) drill.

roulotte f (de gitan) caravan.

round m Boxe round.

rouspéter vi Fam to complain.

rousse voir **roux**.

rousseur f **tache de r.** freckle.

roussir vt (brûler) to scorch.

route f road (**de** to); (itinéraire) way; **r. nationale/départementale** main/secondary road; **en r.!** let's go!; **par la r.** by road; **mettre en r.** (voiture etc) to start (up); **se mettre en r.** to set out (**pour** for); **une heure de r.** an hour's drive; **bonne r.!** have a good trip!

routier, -ière 1 adj **carte/sécurité routière** road map/safety. **2** mf (long-distance) truck driver.

roux, rousse 1 adj (cheveux) red; (personne) red-haired. **2** mf redhead.

royal, -e, -aux adj (famille, palais) royal.

royaume m kingdom.

ruban m ribbon; **r. adhésif** (adhesive) tape.

rubéole f German measles.

rubis m ruby; (montre) jewel.

rubrique f (article de journal) column; (catégorie, titre) heading.

ruche f (bee)hive.

rude adj (pénible) tough; (hiver, voix) harsh; (grossier) crude; (rêche) rough.

rudement adv (parler, traiter) harshly; (très) Fam awfully.

rue f street; **à la r.** (sans domicile) on the streets.

ruelle f alley(way).

ruer vi (cheval) to kick (out).

ruer (se) vpr to rush (**sur** at).

rugby m rugby.

rugbyman, pl **-men** m rugby player.

rugir vi to roar.

rugissement m roar.

rugueux, -euse adj rough.

ruine f ruin; **en r.** in ruins; **tomber en r.** (bâtiment) to become a ruin, to crumble; (mur) to crumble.

ruiner vt (personne, santé etc) to ruin.

ruiner (se) vpr **se r.** to be(come) ruined.

ruisseau, -x m stream.

ruisseler vi to stream (**de** with).

rumeur f (murmure) murmur; (nouvelle) rumor.

rupture f breaking; (de fiançailles, de relations) breaking off; (de pourparlers) breakdown (**de** in); (dispute) break-up; **être en r. de stock** to be out of stock.

rural, -e, -aux adj **vie/école**/etc **rurale** country life/school/etc.

ruse f (subterfuge) trick; **la r.** (habileté) cunning.

rusé, -ée adj & mf cunning (person).

russe 1 adj Russian. **2** mf **R.** Russian. **3** m (langue) Russian.

rythme m rhythm; (de travail) rate; **au r. de trois par jour** at a rate of three a day.

rythmé, -ée adj rhythmical.

S

sa *voir* **son.**

sable *m* sand.

sabler *vt (rue)* to sand.

sablier *m (de cuisine)* egg timer.

sablonneux, -euse *adj* sandy.

sabot *m (de cheval etc)* hoof; *(chaussure)* clog; **s. (de Denver)** (Denver) boot.

sac *m* bag; *(grand et en toile)* sack, tote; **s. (à main)** purse; **s. à dos** backpack.

saccadé, -ée *adj* jerky.

saccager *vt (détruire)* to wreck.

sachant, sache(s), sachent *etc voir* **savoir.**

sachet *m* (small) bag; **s. de thé** teabag.

sacoche *f* bag; *(de vélo)* saddlebag.

sacré, -ée *adj (saint)* sacred; **un s. menteur**/*etc Fam* a damned liar/*etc*.

sacrifice *m* sacrifice.

sacrifier *vt* to sacrifice (**à** to; **pour** for).

sacrifier (se) *vpr* to sacrifice oneself.

sage *adj* wise; *(enfant)* good.

sage-femme, *pl* **sages-femmes** *f* midwife.

sagement *adv* wisely; *(avec calme)* quietly.

sagesse *f (philosophie)* wisdom; *(calme)* good behavior.

saignant, -ante *adj (viande)* rare.

saignement *m* bleeding; **s. de nez** nosebleed.

saigner *vti* to bleed.

sain, saine *adj* healthy; **s. et sauf** safe and sound.

saint, sainte 1 *adj* holy; **s. Jean** Saint John; **la Sainte Vierge** the Blessed Virgin. **2** *mf* saint.

Saint-Sylvestre *f* New Year's Eve.

sais, sait *voir* **savoir.**

saisir *vt* to grab (hold of); *(occasion)* to jump at; *(comprendre)* to understand.

saisir (se) *vpr* **se s. de** to grab (hold of).

saison *f* season.

salade *f (laitue)* lettuce; **s. (verte)** (green) salad; **s. de fruits**/*etc* fruit/*etc* salad.

saladier *m* salad bowl.

salaire *m* wage(s).

salarié, -ée *mf* wage earner.

sale *adj* dirty; *(dégoûtant)* filthy.

salé, -ée *adj (goût, plat)* salty; *(aliment)* salted.

saler *vt* to salt.

saleté *f* dirtiness; filthiness; *(crasse)* dirt, filth; **saletés** *(détritus)* garbage.

salière *f* saltshaker.

salir *vt* to (make) dirty.

salir (se) *vpr* to get dirty.

salissant, -ante *adj* dirty; *(étoffe)* that shows the dirt.

salive *f* saliva.

salle *f* room; *(très grande)* hall; *(de théâtre)* theater, auditorium; *(de cinéma)* cinema; *(d'hôpital)* ward; **s. à manger** dining room; **s. de bain(s)** bathroom; **s. d'opération** operating room.

salon *m* sitting room, lounge; *(exposition)* show.

salopette *f (d'enfant, d'ouvrier)* overalls.

saluer *vt* to greet; *(de la main)* to wave to; *(de la tête)* to nod to.

salut 1 *m* greeting; *(de la main)* wave; *(de la tête)* nod. **2** *int* hi!; *(au revoir)* bye!

samedi *m* Saturday.

SAMU *m abrév (service d'aide médicale d'urgence)* emergency medical service.

sanctionner *vt (approuver)* to sanction; *(punir)* to punish.

sandale *f* sandal.

sandwich *m* sandwich; **s. au fromage**/*etc* cheese/*etc* sandwich.

sandwicherie f sandwich shop.

sang m blood.

sang-froid m self-control; **garder son s.** to keep calm; **avec s.** calmly.

sanglant, -ante adj bloody.

sangle f strap.

sanglier m wild boar.

sanglot m sob.

sangloter vi to sob.

sanguin adj **groupe s.** blood group.

sans prép without; **s. faire** without doing; **s. qu'il le sache** without him ou his knowing; **s. cela** otherwise; **s. importance** unimportant.

sans-abri mf inv homeless person.

sans-gêne 1 adj inv ill-mannered. **2** m inv ill manners.

sans-papiers mf inv illegal immigrant.

santé f health; **(à votre) s.!** your (good) health!, cheers!

sapeur-pompier, pl **sapeurs-pompiers** m fireman, firefighter.

sapin m (arbre, bois) fir; **s. de Noël** Christmas tree.

sardine f sardine.

satellite m satellite.

satin m satin.

satisfaction f satisfaction.

satisfaire* vt to satisfy (sb); **satisfait (de)** satisfied (with).

satisfaisant, -ante adj satisfactory.

sauce f sauce; (jus de viande) gravy; **s. tomate** tomato sauce.

saucisse f sausage.

saucisson m (cold) sausage.

sauf prép except (**que** that).

saule m willow.

saumon m salmon.

sauna m sauna.

saupoudrer vt to sprinkle (**de** with).

saura, saurai(t) etc voir **savoir**.

saut m jump, leap; **faire un s.** to jump, to leap; **faire un s. chez qn** to drop in on sb, to pop over to see sb.

sauter 1 vi to jump, to leap; **faire s.** (détruire) to blow up; **s. à la corde** jump rope; **ça saute aux yeux** it's obvious. **2** vt to jump (over); (mot, repas) to skip.

sauterelle f grasshopper.

sauvage adj (animal, plante) wild; (tribu, homme) primitive.

sauvegarder vt to safeguard; (fichier) to save.

sauver vt to save; (d'un danger) to rescue (from); **s. la vie à qn** to save sb's life.

sauver (se) vpr to run away ou off.

sauvetage m rescue.

sauveteur m rescuer.

sauveur m savior.

savant m scientist.

savate f old slipper.

saveur f flavor.

savoir* vt to know; **s. lire/nager/** etc to be able to read/swim/etc; **faire s. à qn que** to inform sb that; **je n'en sais rien** I have no idea.

savon m soap; (morceau) (bar of) soap.

savonner vt to wash with soap.

savonnette f bar of soap.

savonneux, -euse adj soapy.

savourer vt to enjoy.

savoureux, -euse adj tasty.

saxophone m saxophone.

scandale m scandal; **faire un s.** to make a scene.

scandaleux, -euse adj shocking.

scandaliser vt to shock.

scandinave 1 adj Scandinavian. **2** mf **S.** Scandinavian.

scanner m (appareil) scanner.

scarlatine f scarlet fever.

scénario m (dialogues etc) movie script.

scénariste mf scriptwriter.

scène f (plateau) stage; (décors, partie de pièce, dispute) scene; **mettre en s.** to direct.

sceptique 1 adj skeptical. **2** mf skeptic.

schéma m diagram.

scie f saw.

science f science; **étudier les sciences** to study science.

science-fiction f science fiction.

scientifique 1 adj scientific. **2** mf scientist.

scier vt to saw.

scintiller vi to sparkle; (étoiles) to twinkle.

scission f (de parti) split (de in).

scolaire adj année/etc s. school year/etc.

scolarité f schooling; **pendant ma s.** during my school years.

score m (de match) score.

scotch® m (ruban) scotch tape®.

scrutin m voting, ballot.

sculpter vt to carve, to sculpt.

sculpteur m sculptor.

sculpture f (art, œuvre) sculpture.

SDF mf abrév (sans domicile fixe) homeless person.

se (**s'** before vowel or mute h) pron (complément direct) himself; (féminin) herself; (non humain) itself; (indéfini) oneself, pl themselves. ■ (indirect) to himself; (féminin) to herself; (non humain) to itself; (indéfini) to oneself. ■ (réciproque) each other, one another; (indirect) to each other, to one another. ■ (possessif) **il se lave les mains** he washes his hands.

séance f (au cinéma) screening.

seau, -x m bucket.

sec, sèche 1 adj dry; (légumes) dried; (ton) harsh; **coup s.** (sharp) knock, bang; **frapper un coup s.** to knock (sharply), to bang; **bruit s.** (rupture) snap. **2 m à s.** (rivière) dried up; **au s.** in a dry place.

sécateur m pruning shears.

sèche-cheveux m inv hair dryer.

sèche-linge m inv tumble dryer.

sécher 1 vti to dry. **2** vt (cours) to skip.

sécheresse f (période) drought.

séchoir m **s. à linge** drying rack.

second, -onde 1 adj second; (étage) third. **2** mf second (one) **3** m (étage) third floor. **4** f (de lycée) = sophomore year; (vitesse) second (gear).

secondaire adj secondary.

seconde f (instant) second.

secouer vt to shake.

secourir vt to assist.

secouriste mf first-aid worker.

secours m assistance, help; (premiers) **s.** first aid; **au s.!** help!; **sortie de s.** emergency exit; **roue de s.** spare tire.

secousse f jolt.

secret, -ète 1 adj secret. **2 m** secret; **en s.** in secret.

secrétaire 1 mf secretary; (de médecin etc) receptionist. **2 m** (meuble) writing desk.

secrétariat m (bureau) secretary's office.

secteur m (électricité) mains.

sectionner vt (couper) to sever.

sécurité f safety; **en s.** safe; **S. sociale** = Social security.

séduire* vt to charm; (plaire à) to appeal to; (abuser de) to seduce.

séduisant, -ante adj attractive.

segment m segment.

seigneur m lord.

sein m breast.

séisme m earthquake.

seize adj & m sixteen.

seizième adj & mf sixteenth.

séjour m stay; (salle de) **s.** living room.

séjourner vi to stay.

sel m salt; **sels de bain** bath salts.

sélection f selection.

sélectionner vt to select.

self(-service) m self-service restaurant ou store.

selle f saddle.

selon prép according to (**que** whether).

semaine f week; **en s.** during the week.

semblable adj similar (**à** to).

semblant *m* **faire s.** to pretend (**de faire** to do).

sembler *vi* to seem (**à** to); **il (me) semble vieux** he seems *ou* looks old (to me); **il me semble que** (+ *indicatif*) I think that, it seems to me that.

semelle *f* (*de chaussure*) sole.

semer *vt* (*graines*) to sow.

semestre *m* half(year); (*scolaire*) semester.

semi-remorque *m* semi(trailer).

semoule *f* semolina.

sénat *m* senate.

sens¹ *m* (*signification*) meaning, sense; **avoir du bon s.** to have sense, to be sensible; **avoir un s.** to make sense; **ça n'a pas de s.** that doesn't make sense.

sens² *m* (*direction*) direction; **s. giratoire** traffic circle; **s. interdit** *ou* **unique** (*rue*) one-way street; **'s. interdit'** 'no entry'; **s. dessus dessous** upside down; **dans le s./le s. inverse des aiguilles d'une montre** clockwise/counterclockwise.

sensation *f* feeling.

sensationnel, -elle *adj* sensational.

sensé, -ée *adj* sensible.

sensibilité *f* sensitivity.

sensible *adj* sensitive (**à** to); (*douloureux*) tender; (*progrès etc*) noticeable.

sentier *m* path.

sentiment *m* feeling.

sentimental, -e, -aux *adj* sentimental; **vie sentimentale** love life.

sentir* *vt* to feel; (*odeur*) to smell; (*goût*) to taste; **s. le parfum/etc** to smell of perfume/*etc*; **s. le poisson/ etc** (*avoir le goût de*) to taste of fish/ *etc*; *Fam* **je ne peux pas le s.** (*supporter*) I can't stand him.

sentir (se) *vpr* **se s. fatigué/etc** to feel tired/*etc*.

séparément *adv* separately.

séparer *vt* to separate (**de** from).

séparer (se) *vpr* (*se quitter*) to

part; (*couple*) to separate; **se s. de** (*chien etc*) to part with.

sept *adj & m* seven.

septante *adj* (*en Belgique, Suisse*) seventy.

septembre *m* September.

septième *adj & mf* seventh.

sera, serai(t) *etc voir* **être**.

serein, -eine *adj* serene.

série *f* series; (*ensemble*) set.

sérieusement *adv* seriously; (*travailler*) conscientiously.

sérieux, -euse *adj* serious. **2** *m* **prendre au s.** to take seriously; **garder son s.** to keep a straight face.

seringue *f* syringe.

serment *m* oath; **faire le s. de faire** to promise to do.

sermonner *vt* (*faire la morale à*) to lecture.

séropositif, -ive *adj* HIV positive.

serpent *m* snake.

serpillière *f* floor cloth.

serre *f* greenhouse; **effet de s.** greenhouse effect.

serré, -ée *adj* (*nœud etc*) tight; (*gens*) packed (together).

serrer 1 *vt* (*tenir*) to grip; (*presser*) to squeeze; (*nœud, vis*) to tighten; (*poing*) to clench; (*frein*) to apply; **s. la main à qn** to shake hands with sb; **s. qn** (*embrasser*) to hug sb. **2** *vi* **s. à droite** to keep (to the) right.

serrer (se) *vpr* to squeeze up *ou* together; **se s. contre** to squeeze up against.

serrure *f* lock.

serveur, -euse *mf* waiter, waitress; (*au bar*) bartender, barmaid.

serviable *adj* helpful.

service *m* service; (*pourboire*) service (charge); (*dans une entreprise*) department; **un s.** (*aide*) a favor; **rendre s.** to be of service (**à qn** to sb); **s. (non) compris** service (not) included; **s. après-vente** aftersales service; **être de s.** to be on duty.

serviette *f* towel; (*sac*) briefcase;

s. hygiénique sanitary napkin; **s. (de table)** napkin, serviette.

servir* 1 vt to serve (**qch à qn** sb with sth, sth to sb). **2** vi (être utile) to be useful; **s. à qch/à faire** (objet) to be used for sth/to do; **ça ne sert à rien** it's useless (**de faire** doing); **ça me sert à faire/de qch** l use it to do/as sth.

servir (se) vpr (à table) to help oneself (**de** to); **se s. de** (utiliser) to use.

ses voir **son**.

set m Tennis set; **s. (de table)** place mat.

seuil m doorstep.

seul¹, -e 1 adj alone; **tout s.** by oneself, on one's own; **se sentir s.** to feel lonely. **2** adv (tout) **s.** (rentrer, vivre etc) by oneself, on one's own, alone; (parler) to oneself.

seul², -e adj (unique) only; **la seule femme**/etc the only woman/etc; **un s. chat**/etc only one cat/etc; **pas un s. livre**/etc not a single book/etc. **2** mf le s., la seule the only one; **un s., une seule** only one; **pas un s.** not (a single) one.

seulement adv only.

sévère adj severe; (parents etc) strict.

sévérité f severeness, severity; (de parents etc) strictness.

sévices mpl ill-treatment; **s. à enfant** child abuse.

sexe m sex.

sexuel, -elle adj sexual; **éducation/vie sexuelle** sex education/life.

shampooing m shampoo; **faire un s. à qn** to shampoo sb's hair.

short m (pair of) shorts.

si¹ 1 (s' before il, ils) conj if; **je me demande si** l wonder whether ou if; **si on restait?** what if we stayed? **2** adv (tellement) so; **pas si riche que toi** not as rich as you; **un si bon dîner** such a good dinner; **si bien que** (+ indicatif) with the result that.

si² adv (après négative) yes; **tu ne viens pas? – si!** you're not coming? – yes (I am!).

SIDA m abrév (syndrome immuno-déficitaire acquis) AIDS.

sidérurgie f iron and steel industry.

siècle m century; (époque) age.

siège m seat; (de parti etc) headquarters; **s. (social)** head office.

sien, sienne pron poss le s., la sienne, les sien(ne)s his; (de femme) hers; (de chose) its; **les deux siens** his ou her two.

sieste f faire la s. to take a nap.

sifflement m whistling; (de gaz, serpent) hiss(ing).

siffler 1 vi to whistle; (avec un sifflet) to blow one's whistle; (gaz, serpent) to hiss. **2** vt (chanson) to whistle; (chien) to whistle to; (acteur) to boo.

sifflet m whistle; (coup de) **s.** (son) whistle; **sifflets** (des spectateurs) boos.

sigle m acronym.

signal, -aux m signal; **s. d'alarme** (de train) alarm.

signaler vt to point out (**à qn** to sb; **que** that); (à la police etc) to report (**à** to).

signature f signature.

signe m sign; **faire s. à qn** (geste) to motion (to) sb (**de faire** to do).

signer vt to sign.

signification f meaning.

signifier vt to mean (**que** that).

silence m silence; **en s.** in silence; **garder le s.** to keep silent (**sur** about).

silencieusement adv silently.

silencieux, -euse adj silent.

silhouette f outline; (ligne du corps) figure.

sillonner vt (parcourir) to criss-cross.

similitude f similarity.

simple adj simple.

simplement adv simply.

simplifier *vt* to simplify.

simultané, -ée *adj* simultaneous.

simultanément *adv* simultaneously.

sincère *adj* sincere.

sincèrement *adv* sincerely.

sincérité *f* sincerity.

singe *m* monkey, ape.

singeries *fpl* antics.

singulier, -ière *adj & m (non pluriel)* singular; **au s.** in the singular.

sinistre 1 *adj* sinister. **2** *m* disaster.

sinon *conj (autrement)* otherwise, or else.

sirène *f (d'usine etc)* siren.

sirop *m* syrup; **s. contre la toux** cough medicine *ou* syrup.

site *m (endroit)* site; *(pittoresque)* beauty spot; **s. touristique** place of interest; **s. classé** conservation area; **s. Web** website.

situation *f* situation.

situé, -ée *adj* situated, located.

situer (se) *vpr* to be situated, to be located.

six *adj & m* six.

sixième *adj & mf* sixth.

sketch, *pl* **sketches** *m (de théâtre)* sketch.

ski *m* ski; *(sport)* skiing; **faire du s.** to ski; **s. nautique** water skiing.

skier *vi* to ski.

skieur, -euse *mf* skier.

slip *m (d'homme)* briefs, underwear; *(de femme)* panties, underwear; **s. de bain** (swimming) trunks.

slogan *m* slogan.

SMIC *m abrév (salaire minimum interprofessionnel de croissance)* guaranteed minimum wage.

smoking *m (veston, costume)* tuxedo.

SNCF *f abrév (Société nationale des chemins de fer français)* = French railroad system.

social, -e, -aux *adj* social.

socialiste *adj & mf* socialist.

société *f* society; *(compagnie)* company.

socquette *f* anklet.

sœur *f* sister.

soi *pron* oneself; **cela va de soi** it's evident *(que* that).

soi-disant 1 *adj inv* so-called. **2** *adv* supposedly.

soie *f* silk.

soient *voir* **être**.

soif *f* thirst; **avoir s.** to be thirsty; **donner s. à qn** to make sb thirsty.

soigné, -ée *adj (vêtement)* neat; *(travail)* careful.

soigner *vt* to look after, to take care of; *(maladie)* to treat; **se faire s.** to get (medical) treatment, to be treated.

soigneusement *adv* carefully.

soigneux, -euse *adj* careful (**de** with); *(propre)* neat.

soi-même *pron* oneself.

soin *m* care; *(à un malade)* treatment, care; **avec s.** carefully; **prendre s. de qch** to take care of sth; **les premiers soins** first aid.

soir *m* evening; **le s.** *(chaque soir)* in the evening; **à neuf heures du s.** at nine in the evening.

soirée *f* evening; *(réunion)* party.

sois, soit *voir* **être**.

soit *conj* **s.... s....** either... or...

soixantaine *f* **une s. (de)** about sixty.

soixante *adj & m* sixty.

soixante-dix *adj & m* seventy.

soixante-dixième *adj & mf* seventieth.

soixantième *adj & mf* sixtieth.

soja *m (plante)* soya; **germes** *ou* **pousses de s.** beanshoots.

sol *m* ground; *(plancher)* floor.

solaire *adj* solar; **crème/huile s.** sun(tan) lotion/oil.

soldat *m* soldier.

solde *m (de compte)* balance; **en s.** *(acheter)* on sale; **soldes** *(marchandises)* sale goods; *(vente)* (clearance) sale(s).

soldé, -ée adj (article etc) reduced.

solder vt (articles) to put on sale.

sole f (poisson) sole.

soleil m sun; (chaleur, lumière) sunshine; **au s.** in the sun; **il fait (du) s.** it's sunny; **coup de s.** sunburn.

solennel, -elle adj solemn.

solidarité f (de personnes) solidarity.

solide adj & m solid.

solidement adv solidly.

solitaire adj (tout seul) all alone.

solitude f aimer la s. to like being alone.

solliciter vt (audience) to request; (emploi) to apply for; **s. qn** (faire appel à) to appeal to sb (**de faire** to do).

sombre adj dark; **il fait s.** it's dark.

sombrer vi (bateau) to sink; **s. dans** (folie, sommeil) to sink into.

sommaire 1 adj summary; (repas) basic. **2** m (table des matières) contents.

somme 1 f sum; **faire la s. de** to add up. **2** m (sommeil) nap; **faire un s.** to take a nap.

sommeil m sleep; **avoir s.** to be ou feel sleepy.

sommes voir **être**.

sommet m top.

sommier m (de lit) base.

somnifère m sleeping pill.

somnoler vi to doze.

son m (bruit) sound.

son, sa, pl **ses** (sa becomes son before a vowel or mute h) adj poss his; (de femme) her; (de chose) its; (indéfini) one's; **s. père** his ou her ou one's father; **sa mère** his ou her ou one's mother; **son ami(e)** his ou her ou one's friend; **sa durée** its duration.

sondage m s. (d'opinion) opinion poll.

songer vi s. à qch/à faire to think of sth/of doing.

songeur, -euse adj thoughtful, pensive.

sonner vi to ring; **on a sonné** (à la porte) someone's at the door.

sonnerie f (son) ring(ing); (appareil) bell; (au téléphone) ring; **s. 'occupé'** busy signal.

sonnette f bell; **coup de s.** ring.

sonore adj (rire) loud; (salle) resonant.

sont voir **être**.

sorcière f witch.

sort m (destin, hasard) fate; (condition) lot.

sorte f sort, kind (**de** of); **toutes sortes de** all sorts ou kinds of; **de (telle) s. que** (+ subjonctif) so that; **faire en s. que** (+ subjonctif) to see to it that.

sortie f (promenade à pied) walk; (en voiture) drive; (excursion) outing; (porte) exit, way out; (de disque, film) release; **à la s. de l'école** when the children get out of school.

sortir* 1 vi (aux être) to go out, to leave; (venir) to come out; (pour s'amuser, danser etc) to go out; (film etc) to come out; **s. de table** to leave the table; **s'en s.** to pull ou come through. **2** vt (aux avoir) to take out (**de** of).

sottise f (action, parole) foolish thing; **faire des sottises** (enfant) to misbehave.

sou m sous (argent) money; **elle n'a pas un s.** she doesn't have a bean; **appareil** ou **machine à sous** slot machine.

souche f (d'arbre) stump.

souci m worry; (préoccupation) concern (**de** for); **se faire du s.** to worry; **ça lui donne du s.** it worries him ou her.

soucier (se) vpr se s. de to be worried about.

soucieux, -euse adj worried (**de qch** about sth).

soucoupe f saucer; **s. volante** flying saucer.

soudain *adv* suddenly.
souder *vt* to weld.
souffle *m* puff; *(haleine)* breath; *(respiration)* breathing; *(de bombe etc)* blast.
souffler 1 *vi* to blow. **2** *vt (bougie)* to blow out; *(chuchoter)* to whisper.
souffrance(s) *f(pl)* suffering.
souffrant, -ante *adj* unwell.
souffrir* *vi* to suffer *(de* from); **faire s. qn** to hurt sb.
souhait *m* wish; **à vos souhaits!** *(après un éternuement)* bless you!, gesundheit!
souhaitable *adj* desirable.
souhaiter *vt* to wish for; **s. qch à qn** to wish sb sth; **s. faire** to hope to do; **s. que** *(+ subjonctif)* to hope that.
soûl, soûle *adj* drunk.
soulagement *m* relief.
soulager *vt* to relieve *(de* of).
soulever *vt* to lift (up); *(poussière, question)* to raise.
soulier *m* shoe.
souligner *vt* to underline; *(faire remarquer)* to emphasize.
soumettre *vt (pays, rebelles)* to subdue; *(rapport, demande)* to submit *(à* to); **s. qn à** *(assujettir)* to subject sb to.
soumis, -ise *adj (docile)* submissive; **s. à** subject to.
soupçon *m* suspicion.
soupçonner *vt* to suspect *(de* of; **d'avoir fait** of doing; **que** that).
soupe *f* soup.
souper 1 *m* supper. **2** *vi* to have supper.
soupir *m* sigh.
soupirer *vi* to sigh.
souple *adj* supple; *(tolérant)* flexible.
souplesse *f* suppleness; *(tolérance)* flexibility.
source *f (point d'eau)* spring; *(origine)* source; **eau de s.** spring water.
sourcil *m* eyebrow.
sourd, sourde 1 *adj* deaf; *(dou-*

leur) dull; **bruit s.** thump. **2** *mf* deaf person.
sourd-muet, sourde-muette, *pl* **sourds-muets, sourdes-muettes** *adj & mf* deaf-mute.
sourire* 1 *vi* to smile *(à qn* at sb). **2** *m* smile; **faire un s. à qn** to give sb a smile.
souris *f* mouse *(pl* mice).
sournois, -oise *adj* sly, underhand.
sous *prép (position)* under(neath), beneath; **s. la pluie** in the rain; **s. Charles X** under Charles X; **s. peu** *(bientôt)* shortly.
sous-développé, -ée *adj (pays)* underdeveloped.
sous-entendre *vt* to imply.
sous-entendu, *pl* **sous-entendus** *m* insinuation.
sous-estimer *vt* to underestimate.
sous-marin, *pl* **sous-marins** *m* submarine.
sous-sol, *pl* **sous-sols** *m (d'immeuble)* basement.
sous-titre, *pl* **sous-titres** *m* subtitle.
soustraction *f* subtraction.
soustraire* *vt (nombre)* to take away, to subtract *(de* from).
sous-traitant, *pl* **sous-traitants** *m* subcontractor.
sous-vêtements *mpl* underwear.
soutenir* *vt* to support; **s. que** to maintain that.
soutenir (se) *vpr (blessé etc)* to hold oneself up.
souterrain, -aine 1 *adj* underground. **2** *m* underground passage.
soutien *m* support; *(personne)* supporter.
soutien-gorge, *pl* **soutiens-gorge** *m* bra.
souvenir *m* memory; *(objet)* memento; *(cadeau)* keepsake; *(pour touristes)* souvenir.
souvenir* (se) *vpr* **se s. de** to re-

member; **se s. que** to remember that.

souvent *adv* often; **peu s.** seldom; **le plus s.** usually.

soyeux, -euse *adj* silky.

soyez, soyons *voir* **être.**

spacieux, -euse *adj* spacious.

spaghetti(s) *mpl* spaghetti.

sparadrap *m* Band-Aid®.

speaker, speakerine *mf (à la radio etc)* announcer.

spécial, -e, -aux *adj* special.

spécialement *adv* specially.

spécialiste *mf* specialist.

spécialité *f* specialty.

spécimen *m* specimen.

spectacle *m (vue)* sight; *(représentation)* show.

spectaculaire *adj* spectacular.

spectateur, -trice *mf* spectator; *(témoin)* onlooker; **les spectateurs** *(le public)* the audience.

sphère *f* sphere.

spirale *f* spiral.

spirituel, -elle *adj (amusant)* witty.

splendide *adj* splendid.

spontané, -ée *adj* spontaneous.

sport *m* sport; **faire du s.** to play sports; **voiture/veste/terrain de s.** sports car/jacket/ground.

sportif, -ive 1 *adj (personne)* fond of sports. **2** *mf* sportsman, sportswoman, athlete.

spot *m (lampe)* spotlight; **s. (publicitaire)** commercial.

squash *m (jeu)* squash.

squelette *m* skeleton.

stable *adj* stable.

stade *m* stadium.

stage *m (cours)* (training) course; *(en entreprise)* internship.

stagiaire *mf* intern.

stand *m (d'exposition etc)* stand.

standard 1 *m (téléphonique)* switchboard. **2** *adj inv (modèle etc)* standard.

station *f* station; *(de ski etc)* resort; *(d'autobus)* stop; **s. de taxis** taxi stand.

stationnement *m* parking.

stationner *vi (se garer)* to park; *(être garé)* to be parked.

station-service, *pl* **stations-service** *f* service station, gas station.

statistique *f (donnée)* statistic.

statue *f* statue.

steak *m* steak.

stéréo *adj inv* stereo.

stériliser *vt* to sterilize.

stock *m* stock, supply (**de** of); **en s.** in stock.

stocker *vt (provisions etc)* to store.

stop 1 *int* stop. **2** *m (panneau)* stop sign; *(feu arrière)* brake light; **faire du s.** to hitchhike.

stopper *vti* to stop.

store *m (window)* shade.

stress *m inv* stress.

stressant, -ante *adj* stressful.

stressé, -ée *adj* under stress.

strict, -e *adj* strict.

strictement *adv* strictly.

structure *f* structure.

studieux, -euse *adj* studious; *(vacances)* devoted to study.

studio *m* studio; *(logement)* studio apartment.

stupéfaction *f* amazement.

stupéfait, -faite *adj* amazed (**de** at, by).

stupéfiant, -ante 1 *adj* amazing. **2** *m* drug, narcotic.

stupide *adj* stupid.

stupidité *f* stupidity; *(action, parole)* stupid thing.

style *m* style.

stylo *m* pen; **s. à bille** ballpoint (pen); **s.-plume** fountain pen.

su, sue *pp of* **savoir.**

subir *vt* to undergo; *(conséquences, défaite)* to suffer; *(influence)* to be under.

subit, -ite *adj* sudden.

subitement *adv* suddenly.

subjonctif *m* Grammaire subjunctive.

submergé, -ée *adj* flooded (**de** with); **s. de travail** overwhelmed with work.

substance f substance.

subtil, -e adj subtle.

subvention f subsidy.

succéder vi s. à qch to follow sth.

succéder (se) vpr to follow one another.

succès m success; **avoir du s.** to be successful.

successif, -ive adj successive.

succession f (série) sequence (**de** of).

succursale f (de magasin) branch; **magasin à succursales multiples** chain store.

sucer vt to suck.

sucette f lollipop; (tétine) pacifier.

sucre m sugar; (morceau) sugar lump; **s. cristallisé** granulated sugar; **s. en morceaux** lump sugar; **s. en poudre, s. semoule** fine sugar.

sucré, -ée adj sweet.

sucrer vt to sugar.

sucreries fpl candy.

sucrier m sugar bowl.

sud m south; **au s. de** south of; **du s.** (vent) southerly; (ville) southern.

sud-est m & adj inv southeast.

sud-ouest m & adj inv southwest.

suédois, -oise 1 adj Swedish. **2** mf S. Swede. **3** m (langue) Swedish.

suer vi to sweat; **faire s. qn** Fam to get on sb's nerves.

sueur f sweat; **en s.** sweating.

suffire* vi to be enough (**à** for); **ça suffit!** that's enough!; **il suffit d'une goutte**/etc **pour faire** a drop/etc is enough to do.

suffisamment adv sufficiently; **s. de** enough.

suffisant, -ante adj sufficient.

suffocant, -ante adj stifling.

suggérer vt to suggest (**à** to; **de faire** doing; **que** (+ subjonctif) that).

suggestion f suggestion.

suicide m suicide.

suicider (se) vpr to commit suicide.

suis voir **être, suivre**.

suisse 1 adj Swiss. **2** mf S. Swiss inv; **les Suisses** the Swiss.

Suissesse f Swiss woman ou girl, Swiss inv

suite f (reste) rest; (de film, roman) sequel; (série) series; **faire s. (à)** to follow; **par la s.** afterwards; **à la s.** one after another; **à la s. de** (événement etc) as a result of; **de s.** (deux jours etc) in a row.

suivant, -ante 1 adj next, following. **2** mf next (one); **au s.!** next!

suivre* **1** vt to follow; (accompagner) to go with; (classe) to attend, to go to; **s. (des yeux** ou **du regard)** to watch. **2** vi to follow; **faire s.** (courrier) to forward; **'à s.'** 'to be continued'.

suivre (se) vpr to follow each other.

sujet m (question) Grammaire subject; (d'examen) question; **au s. de** about; **à quel s.?** about what?

super 1 adj inv (bon) great. **2** m (essence) premium gas.

superbe adj superb.

supercherie f deception.

supérette f convenience store.

superficie f surface.

superficiel, -ielle adj superficial.

supérieur, -e adj upper; (qualité etc) superior (**à** to); (études) higher; **l'étage s.** the floor above.

supériorité f superiority.

supermarché m supermarket.

superposer vt (objets) to put on top of each other.

superstitieux, -euse adj superstitious.

superstition f superstition.

supplément m (argent) extra charge; **en s.** extra.

supplémentaire adj extra.

supplier vt s. qn de faire to beg sb to do.

support m support; (d'instrument etc) stand.

supporter¹ vt to bear; (résister à) to withstand; (soutenir) to support.

supporter² *m* supporter.
supposer *vti* to suppose (**que** that).
supposition *f* assumption.
suppositoire *m* suppository.
suppression *f* removal; *(de train)* cancellation.
supprimer *vt* to get rid of; *(mot)* to cut out; *(train)* to cancel.
sur *prép* on, upon; *(par-dessus)* over; *(au sujet de)* on, about; **six s. dix** six out of ten; **un jour s. deux** every other day; **six mètres s. dix** 20 by 33 feet.
sûr, sûre *adj* sure, certain (**de** of; **que** that); *(digne de confiance)* reliable; *(lieu)* safe; **c'est s. que** (+ *indicatif*) it's certain that; **s. de soi** self-assured; **bien s.!** of course!
sûrement *adv* certainly.
sûreté *f* safety; **être en s.** to be safe; **mettre en s.** to put in a safe place.
surexcité, -ée *adj* overexcited.
surf *m* surfing; **faire du s.** to go surfing.
surface *f* surface; *(dimensions)* (surface) area; **(magasin à) grande s.** hypermarket.
surgelé, -ée *adj (viande etc)* frozen.
surgelés *mpl* frozen foods.
surgir *vi* to appear suddenly *(de* from*)*; *(problème)* to arise.
sur-le-champ *adv* immediately.
surlendemain *m* **le s.** two days later; **le s. de** two days after.
surligneur *m* highlighter (pen).
surmener (se) *vpr* to overwork.
surmonter *vt (obstacle etc)* to get over.
surnom *m* nickname.
surnommer *vt* to nickname.
surpasser (se) *vpr* to surpass oneself.
surprenant, -ante *adj* surprising.
surprendre* *vt (étonner)* to surprise; *(prendre sur le fait)* to catch; *(conversation)* to overhear.

surpris, -ise *adj* surprised (**de** at; **que** (+ *subjonctif*) that); **je suis surpris de te voir** I'm surprised to see you.
surprise *f* surprise.
sursauter *vi* to jump, to start.
surtout *adv* especially; *(avant tout)* above all; **s. pas** certainly not; **s. que** especially since.
surveillant, -ante *mf (au lycée)* monitor; *(au prison)* (prison) guard.
surveiller *vt* to watch; *(contrôler)* to supervise.
survêtement *m* tracksuit.
survivant, -ante *mf* survivor.
survivre* *vi* to survive (**à qch** sth).
survoler *vt* to fly over.
susceptibilité *f* touchiness, sensitivity.
susceptible *adj* touchy, sensitive.
susciter *vt (sentiment)* to arouse; *(ennuis, obstacles)* to create.
suspect, -ecte 1 *adj* suspicious. **2** *mf* suspect.
suspendre *vt (accrocher)* to hang (up) (**à** on).
suspendre (se) *vpr* **se s. à** to hang from.
suspendu, -ue *adj* **s. à** hanging from.
suspense *m* suspense.
suspension *f (de véhicule)* suspension.
suture *f* **point de s.** stitch *(in wound)*.
SVP *abrév (s'il vous plaît)* please.
syllabe *f* syllable.
symbole *m* symbol.
symbolique *adj* symbolic.
sympa *adj inv Fam =* **sympathique**.
sympathie *f* liking; **avoir de la s. pour qn** to be fond of sb.
sympathique *adj* nice, pleasant.
sympathiser *vi* to get along well (**avec** with).
symphonie *f* symphony.
symptôme *m* symptom.
synagogue *f* synagogue.

syndicat m (d'ouvriers) (labor) union; **s. d'initiative** tourist (information) office.

syndiqué, -ée mf union member.

synonyme 1 adj synonymous (**de** with). **2** m synonym.

système m system.

T

ta voir **ton**.

tabac m tobacco; (magasin) tobacco store.

table f table; (d'école) desk; **t. de nuit** bedside table; **t. basse** coffee table; **t. à repasser** ironing board; **t. roulante** (serving) cart; **t. des matières** table of (contents); **à t.** sitting at the table; **à t.!** (food's) ready!

tableau, -x m (image) picture; (panneau) board; (liste) list; (graphique) chart; **t. (noir)** (black) board; **t. d'affichage** bulletin board; **t. de bord** dashboard.

tablette f (de chocolat) bar; (de lavabo etc) shelf.

tablier m apron; (d'écolier) smock.

tabouret m stool.

tache f spot; (salissure) stain.

tâche f task, job; **tâches ménagères** housework.

tacher vti, **se tacher** vpr to stain.

tâcher vi **t. de faire** to try to do.

tact m tact; **avoir du t.** to be tactful.

tactique f **la t.** tactics; **une t.** a tactic.

tag m spray-painted graffiti.

taie d'oreiller f pillowcase.

taille f (hauteur) height; (dimension, mesure) size; (ceinture) waist; **tour de t.** waist measurement.

taille-crayon, pl **taille-crayons** m pencil sharpener.

tailler vt to cut; (haie, barbe) to trim; (arbre) to prune; (crayon) to sharpen.

tailleur m (personne) tailor; (vêtement) suit.

taire* (se) vpr (ne rien dire) to keep quiet (**sur qch** about sth); (cesser de parler) to stop talking; **tais-toi!** be quiet!

talent m talent; **avoir du t. pour** to have a talent for.

talentueux, -euse adj talented.

talon m heel; (de chèque, carnet) stub.

talus m slope, embankment.

tambour m drum; (personne) drummer.

tambourin m tambourine.

tamis m sieve.

tamiser vt (farine) to sift.

tampon m (marque, instrument) stamp; (de coton) wad; **t. hygiénique** tampon; **t. à récurer** scrubbing pad.

tamponner vt (lettre, document) to stamp; (visage) to dab; (plaie) to swab; (train, voiture) to crash into.

tandis que conj while.

tant adv (travailler etc) so much (**que** that); **t. de** (temps etc) so much (**que** that); (gens etc) so many (**que** that); **t. que** (aussi longtemps que) as long as; **t. mieux!** good!; **t. pis!** too bad!

tante f aunt.

tantôt adv **t.... t....** sometimes… sometimes…

tapage m din, uproar.

tape f slap.

taper¹ 1 vt (enfant, cuisse) to slap; (table) to bang. **2** vi **t. sur qch** to bang on sth; **t. du pied** to stamp one's foot.

taper² vti **t. (à la machine)** to type.

tapis m carpet; **t. roulant** (pour marchandises) conveyor belt.

tapisser vt (mur) to (wall)paper.

tapisserie f (papier peint) wallpaper; (broderie) tapestry.

tapoter *vt* to tap; *(joue)* to pat.

taquiner *vt* to tease.

tard *adv* late; **plus t.** later (on); **au plus t.** at the latest.

tarder *vi* **t. à faire** to take one's time doing; **elle ne va pas t.** she won't be long; **sans t.** without delay.

tardif, -ive *adj* late; *(regrets)* belated.

tarif *m (prix)* rate; *(de train)* fare; *(tableau)* price list.

tarte *f* (open) pie, tart.

tartine *f* slice of bread; **t. (de beurre/de confiture)** slice of bread and butter/jam.

tartiner *vt (beurre etc)* to spread.

tas *m* pile, heap; **un** *ou* **des t. de** *(beaucoup) Fam* lots of; **mettre en t.** to pile *ou* heap up.

tasse *f* cup; **t. à café** coffee cup; **t. à thé** teacup.

tasser *vt* to pack, to squeeze (**dans** into).

tasser (se) *vpr (se serrer)* to squeeze together.

tâter *vt* to feel.

tâtonner *vi* to grope around.

tâtons (à) *adv* **avancer à t.** to feel one's way (along); **chercher à t.** to grope for.

tatouage *m (dessin)* tattoo.

tatouer *vt* to tattoo.

taudis *m* slum.

taupe *f* mole.

taureau, -x *m* bull.

taux *m* rate; **t. d'alcool** alcohol level.

taxe *f (impôt)* tax; *(de douane)* duty; **t. à la valeur ajoutée** sales tax.

taxé, -ée *adj* taxed.

taxi *m* taxi.

te (t' *before vowel or mute h) pron (complément direct)* you; *(indirect)* (to) you; *(réfléchi)* yourself.

technicien, -ienne *mf* technician.

technique 1 *adj* technical. **2** *f* technique.

technologie *f* technology.

tee-shirt *m* tee-shirt.

teindre* *vt* to dye; **t. en rouge** to dye red.

teindre (se) *vpr* to dye one's hair.

teint *m* complexion.

teinte *f* shade.

teinture *f (produit)* dye.

teinturerie *f (boutique)* (dry) cleaner's.

teinturier, -ière *mf* (dry) cleaner.

tel, telle *adj* such; **un t. livre/***etc* such a book/*etc*; **un t. intérêt/***etc* such interest/*etc*; **de tels mots/***etc* such words/*etc*; **rien de t. que** (there's) nothing like.

télé *f* TV; **à la t.** on TV.

télécommande *f* remote control.

télécopie *f* fax.

télécopieur *m* fax (machine).

téléfilm *m* TV movie.

télégramme *m* telegram.

téléphérique *m* cable car.

téléphone *m* (tele)phone; **coup de t.** (phone) call; **passer un coup de t. à qn** to give sb a call; **au t.** on the (tele)phone.

téléphoner 1 *vt (nouvelle etc)* to (tele)phone (**à** to). **2** *vi* to (tele)-phone; **t. à qn** to (tele)phone sb.

téléphonique *adj* **appel/***etc* **t.** (tele)phone call/*etc*.

télescope *m* telescope.

télésiège *m* chair lift.

téléspectateur, -trice *mf* (television) viewer.

télévisé *adj* **journal t.** television news.

téléviseur *m* television (set).

télévision *f* television; **à la t.** on (the) television.

telle *voir* **tel**.

tellement *adv (si)* so; *(tant)* so much; **t. de** *(travail etc)* so much; *(soucis etc)* so many; **pas t.!** not much!

téméraire *adj* reckless.

témoignage *m* evidence; *(récit)* account.

témoigner *vi* to give evidence (**contre** against).

témoin m witness; **être t. de** to witness.

température f temperature; **avoir de la t.** to have a fever.

tempête f storm; **t. de neige** snowstorm.

temple m (romain, grec) temple.

temporaire adj temporary.

temps¹ m time; (de verbe) tense; **il est t. (de faire)** it's time (to do); **ces derniers t.** lately; **de t. en t.** from time to time; **à plein t.** (travailler) full-time; **à temps partiel** (travailler) part-time; **dans le t.** (autrefois) once.

temps² m (climat) weather; **quel t. fait-il?** what's the weather like?

tenailles fpl (outil) pincers.

tendance f tendency; **avoir t. à faire** to tend to do.

tendeur m (à bagages) bungee (cord).

tendre¹ vt to stretch; (main) to hold out (**à qn** to sb); (bras, jambe) to stretch out; (piège) to set, to lay; **t. qch à qn** to hold out sth to sb; **t. l'oreille** to prick up one's ears.

tendre² adj (viande etc) tender; (personne) affectionate (**avec** to).

tendrement adv tenderly.

tendresse f affection.

tendu, -ue adj (corde) tight; (personne, situation, muscle) tense; (main) held out.

tenir* vt to hold; (promesse, comptes, hôtel) to keep; (rôle) to play; **t. sa droite** (conducteur) to keep to the right. 2 vi to hold; (résister) to hold out; **t. à** (personne, jouet etc) to be attached to; **t. à faire** to be anxious to do; **t. dans qch** (être contenu) to fit into sth; **tenez!** (prenez) here (you are)!; **tiens!** (surprise) well!

tenir (se) vpr (avoir lieu) to be held; **se t. (debout)** to stand (up); **se t. droit** to stand up ou sit up straight; **se t. par la main** to hold hands; **se t. bien** to behave oneself.

tennis m tennis; (terrain) (tennis) court; (chaussure) sneaker; **t. de table** table tennis.

tension f tension; **t. (artérielle)** blood pressure; **avoir de la t.** to have high blood pressure.

tentant, -ante adj tempting.

tentation f temptation.

tentative f attempt.

tente f tent.

tenter¹ vt to try (**de faire** to do).

tenter² vt (faire envie à) to tempt.

tenue f (vêtements) clothes; (conduite) (good) behavior; **t. de soirée** evening dress.

tergal® m Dacron®.

terme m (mot) term; (fin) end; **mettre un t. à** to put an end to; **à court/long t.** (conséquences) short-/long-term; **en bons/mauvais termes** on good/bad terms (**avec** with).

terminaison f (de mot) ending.

terminal, -e, -aux 1 adj & f (classe) **terminale** = senior year. **2** m **t. (d'ordinateur)** (computer) terminal.

terminer vt to end.

terminer (se) vpr to end (**par** with; **en** in).

terne adj dull.

terrain m ground; (étendue) land; (à bâtir) plot; Football etc field; **t. de camping** campsite; **t. de jeux** (pour enfants) playground; (stade) playing field; **t. vague** vacant lot.

terrasse f terrace; (de café) sidewalk area.

terre f (matière, monde) earth; (sol) ground; (opposé à mer) land; **par t.** (poser, tomber) to the ground; (assis, couché) on the ground; **sous t.** underground.

terre-à-terre adj inv down-to-earth.

terrestre adj **la surface t.** the earth's surface; **globe t.** globe (model).

terreur f terror.

terrible *adj* awful, terrible; *(formidable) Fam* terrific.

terrifiant, -ante *adj* terrifying.

terrifier *vt* to terrify.

territoire *m* territory.

terroir *m (sol)* soil; *(région)* region.

terroriser *vt* to terrorize.

terroriste *adj & mf* terrorist.

tes *voir* **ton**.

test *m* test.

testament *m (en droit)* will.

tester *vt* to test.

tête *f* head; *(visage)* face; *(d'arbre)* top; **tenir t. à** to stand up to; **faire la t.** to sulk; **à la t. de** *(entreprise)* at the head of; *(classe)* at the top *ou* head of; **en t.** *(sportif)* in the lead.

tête-à-tête *adv* **(en) t.** alone together.

téter 1 *vt* to suck. **2** *vi* **le bébé tète** the baby is feeding; **donner à t. à** to feed.

tétine *f (de biberon)* nipple; *(sucette)* pacifier.

têtu, -ue *adj* stubborn.

texte *m* text.

textile *adj & m* textile.

TGV *m abrév* = **train à grande vitesse**.

thé *m* tea.

théâtre *m* theater; *(œuvres)* drama; **faire du t.** to act.

théière *f* teapot.

théorie *f* theory; **en t.** in theory.

thermomètre *m* thermometer.

thermos® *m ou f* Thermos®.

thermostat *m* thermostat.

thèse *f (proposition, ouvrage)* thesis.

thon *m* tuna (fish).

tibia *m* shin (bone).

ticket *m* ticket.

tiède *adj (luke)* warm.

tien, tienne *pron poss* **le t., la tienne, les tien(ne)s** yours; **les deux tiens** your two.

tiens, tient *voir* **tenir**.

tiercé *m* **jouer/gagner au t.** = to bet/win on the horses.

tiers *m (fraction)* third.

tiers-monde *m* **le t.** the Third World.

tige *f (de plante)* stem; *(barre)* rod.

tigre *m* tiger.

tilleul *m (arbre)* lime tree; *(infusion)* lime blossom tea.

timbre *m* stamp.

timbre-poste, *pl* **timbres-poste** *m (postage)* stamp.

timbrer *vt (lettre)* to stamp.

timide *adj* shy.

timidement *adv* shyly.

timidité *f* shyness.

tinter *vi (cloche)* to ring; *(clefs)* to jingle.

tir *m* shooting; *Sport* shot; **t. à arc** archery.

tirage *m (de journal)* circulation; *(de loterie)* draw; **t. au sort** drawing of lots.

tire-bouchon, *pl* **tire-bouchons** *m* corkscrew.

tirelire *f* coin bank.

tirer 1 *vt* to pull; *(langue)* to stick out; *(trait, rideaux)* to draw; *(balle, canon)* to shoot; **t. de** *(sortir)* to pull *ou* draw out of; *(obtenir)* to get from; **t. qn de** *(danger, lit)* to get sb out of. **2** *vi* to pull *(sur* on, at); *(faire feu)* to shoot *(sur* at); *Sport* to shoot; **t. au sort** to draw lots; **t. à sa fin** to draw to a close.

tirer (se) *vpr* **se t. de** *(travail)* to cope with; *(situation)* to get out of; **se t. d'affaire** to get out of trouble.

tiret *m (trait)* dash.

tireur *m (au fusil)* gunman.

tiroir *m* drawer.

tisane *f* herbal tea.

tisonnier *m* poker.

tisser *vt* to weave.

tissu *m* material, cloth; **du t.-éponge** toweling.

titre *m* title; **(gros) t.** *(de journal)* headline; **à t. d'exemple** as an example; **à juste t.** rightly.

tituber *vi* to stagger.

titulaire 1 *adj (enseignant)* tenured; **être t. de** *(permis)* to be the holder of; *(poste)* to hold. **2** *mf (de permis, de poste)* holder (**de** of).

toast *m (pain grillé)* piece *ou* slice of toast.

toboggan *m* slide; *(pour voitures)* overpass.

toc *int* **t. t.!** knock knock!

toi *pron (complément, sujet)* you; *(réfléchi)* **assieds-t.** sit (yourself) down; **dépêche-t.** hurry up.

toile *f* cloth; *(à voile, sac etc)* canvas; *(tableau)* painting; **t. d'araignée** spider's web.

toilette *f (action)* wash(ing); *(vêtements)* clothes; **eau de t.** eau de toilette; **faire sa t.** to wash (and dress); **les toilettes** the bathroom, the men's *ou* ladies' room; **aller aux toilettes** to go to the bathroom *ou* to the men's *ou* ladies' room.

toi-même *pron* yourself.

toit *m* roof; **t. ouvrant** *(de voiture)* sunroof.

tôle *f* une **t.** a piece of sheet metal; **t. ondulée** corrugated iron.

tolérant, -ante *adj* tolerant (**à l'égard de** of).

tolérer *vt* to tolerate.

tomate *f* tomato.

tombe *f* grave.

tombeau, -x *m* tomb.

tombée *f* **t. de la nuit** nightfall.

tomber *vi (aux* être*)* to fall; **t. malade** to fall ill; **t. (par terre)** to fall (down); **faire t.** *(personne)* to knock over; **laisser t.** to drop; **tu tombes bien/mal** you've come at the right/wrong time; **t. sur** *(trouver)* to come across.

tombola *f* raffle.

ton, ta, *pl* **tes** (**ta** becomes **ton** before a vowel or mute h) *adj poss* your; **t. père** your father; **ta mère** your mother; **t. ami(e)** your friend.

ton *m (de voix etc)* tone.

tonalité *f (téléphonique)* dial tone.

tondeuse *f* **t. (à gazon)** (lawn)-mower.

tondre *vt (gazon)* to mow.

tonne *f* metric ton; **des tonnes de** *(beaucoup)* Fam tons of.

tonneau, -x *m* barrel.

tonner *vi* **il tonne** it's thundering.

tonnerre *m* thunder; **coup de t.** burst of thunder.

tonton *m* Fam uncle.

torche *f (flamme)* torch; **t. électrique** flashlight.

torchon *m (à vaisselle)* dish towel; *(de ménage)* dust cloth.

tordre *vt* to twist; *(linge)* to wring (out); *(barre)* to bend.

tordre (se) *vpr* to twist; *(barre)* to bend; **se t. la cheville** to twist *ou* sprain one's ankle. **se t. de douleur** to be doubled up with pain; **se t. (de rire)** to split one's sides (laughing).

tordu, -ue *adj* twisted; *(esprit)* warped.

torrent *m* (mountain) stream; **il pleut à torrents** it's pouring (down).

torse *m* chest; **t. nu** stripped to the waist.

tort *m* **avoir t.** to be wrong (**de faire** to do, in doing); **être dans son t.** to be in the wrong; **donner t. à qn** *(accuser)* to blame sb; **à t.** wrongly; **parler à t. et à travers** to talk nonsense.

torticolis *m* **avoir le t.** to have a stiff neck.

tortiller *vt* to twist, to twirl.

tortue *f* turtle.

torture *f* torture.

torturer *vt* to torture.

tôt *adv* early; **le plus t. possible** as soon as possible; **t. ou tard** sooner or later; **je n'étais pas plus t. sorti que** no sooner had I gone out than.

total, -e, -aux *adj & m* total.

totalement *adv* totally.

totaliser *vt* to total.

totalité *f* **en t.** *(détruit etc)* entirely; *(payé)* fully.

touchant, -ante *adj* moving; touching.

touche f (de clavier) key; (de téléphone) (push-)button; **téléphone à touches** touch-tone phone.

toucher 1 vt to touch; (paie) to draw; (chèque) to cash; (cible) to hit; (émouvoir) to touch, to move. **2** vi **t. à** to touch. **3** m (sens) touch.

toucher (se) vpr (lignes, mains etc) to touch.

touffe f (de cheveux, d'herbe) tuft.

toujours adv always; (encore) still; **pour t.** for ever.

tour¹ f tower; (immeuble) high-rise; Echecs castle, rook.

tour² m turn; (de magie etc) trick; **t. de poitrine/etc** chest/etc measurement; **faire le t. de** to go around; **faire un t.** to go for a walk; (en voiture) to go for a drive; (voyage) to go on a trip; **jouer un t. à qn** to play a trick on s.o.; **c'est mon t.** it's my turn; **à t. de rôle** in turn.

tourbillon m (de vent) whirlwind; (d'eau) whirlpool; (de sable) swirl.

tourisme m tourism; **faire du t.** to go sightseeing.

touriste mf tourist.

touristique adj guide/etc **t.** tourist guide/etc.

tourmenter (se) vpr to worry.

tournage m (de film) shooting.

tournant m (de route) bend.

tourne-disque m record player.

tournée f (de livreur, boissons) round; (de spectacle) tour.

tourner 1 vt to turn; (film) to shoot. **2** vi to turn; (tête) to spin; (moteur) to run; (lait) to go off; **t. autour de** (objet) to go around.

tourner (se) vpr to turn (vers to).

tournesol m sunflower.

tournevis m screwdriver.

tournoi m tournament.

Toussaint f All Saints' Day.

tousser vi to cough.

tout, toute, pl **tous, toutes 1** adj all; **tous les livres** all the books; **t. l'argent/le temps** all the money/ time; **t. le village** the whole village;

toute la nuit all night; **tous (les) deux** both; **tous les trois** all three. ■ (chaque) every; **tous les ans** every ou each year; **tous les cinq mois/ mètres** every five months/16 feet. **2** pron pl all; **ils sont tous là** they're all there. **3** pron m sing everything; **t. ce que** everything that, all that; **en t.** (au total) in all. **4** adv (tout à fait) quite, very; **t. simplement** quite simply; **t. petit** very small; **t. neuf** brand new; **t. seul** all alone; **t. autour** all around; **t. en chantant/ etc** while singing/etc, **t. à coup** suddenly; **t. à fait** completely; **t. de même** all the same; **t. de suite** at once. **5** m le **t.** everything; **pas du t.** not at all; **rien du t.** nothing at all.

toutefois adv nevertheless, however.

toux f cough.

toxique adj poisonous.

trac m avoir le **t.** to be ou become nervous.

tracasser vt, **se tracasser** vpr to worry.

trace f trace (de of); (marque) mark; **traces** (de bête, pneus) tracks; **traces de pas** footprints.

tracer vt (dessiner) to draw.

tracteur m tractor.

tradition f tradition.

traditionnel, -elle adj traditional.

traducteur, -trice mf translator.

traduction f translation.

traduire* vt to translate (de from; en into).

trafic m traffic.

trafiquant, -ante mf trafficker, dealer.

tragédie f tragedy.

tragique adj tragic.

trahir vt to betray.

trahir (se) vpr to give oneself away.

trahison f betrayal.

train¹ m train; **t. à grande vitesse** high-speed train; **t. couchettes** sleeper.

train² *m* être en t. de faire to be (busy) doing.

traîneau, -x *m* sled.

traînée *f (de peinture etc)* streak.

traîner 1 *vt* to drag. **2** *vi (jouets etc)* to lie around; *(s'attarder)* to lag behind; **t. (par terre)** *(robe etc)* to trail (on the ground).

traîner (se) *vpr (par terre)* to crawl.

train-train *m* routine.

traire* *vt* to milk.

trait *m* line; *(en dessinant)* stroke; *(caractéristique)* feature; **t. d'union** hyphen.

traité *m (accord)* treaty; *(ouvrage)* treatise (**sur** on); **t. de paix** peace treaty.

traitement *m* treatment; *(salaire)* salary; **t. de texte** word processing; **machine de t. de texte** word processor.

traiter 1 *vt* to treat; *(problème)* to deal with; **t. qn de lâche**/*etc* to call sb a coward/*etc.* **2** *vi* **t. de** *(sujet)* to deal with.

traiteur *m* **chez le t.** at the delicatessen.

traître *m* traitor.

trajectoire *f* path.

trajet *m* trip; *(distance)* distance; *(itinéraire)* route.

tramway *m* streetcar, trolley.

tranchant, -ante *adj (couteau, voix)* sharp.

tranche *f (morceau)* slice.

tranchée *f* trench.

trancher *vt* to cut.

tranquille *adj* quiet; *(mer)* calm; *(conscience)* clear; **laisser t.** to leave alone.

tranquillement *adv* calmly.

tranquillisant *m* tranquilizer.

tranquilliser *vt* to reassure.

tranquillité *f* (peace and) quiet.

transat *m (chaise)* deckchair.

transférer *vt* to transfer (**à** to).

transfert *m* transfer.

transformation *f* change.

transformer *vt* to change; *(maison)* to remodel; **t. en** to turn into.

transfusion *f* **t. (sanguine)** (blood) transfusion.

transgresser *vt (ordres)* to disobey; *(loi)* to infringe.

transistor *m* transistor (radio).

transitif, -ive *adj* Grammaire transitive.

transmettre* *vt (message etc)* to pass on (**à** to).

transparent, -ente *adj* clear, transparent.

transpercer *vt* to pierce.

transpiration *f* sweat.

transpirer *vi* to sweat.

transport *m* transportation (**de** of); **moyen de t.** means of transportation; **les transports en commun** public transportation.

transporter *vt* to transport; *(à la main)* to carry; **t. d'urgence à l'hôpital** to rush to the hospital.

trappe *f* trap door.

trapu, -ue *adj (personne)* stocky, thickset.

traquer *vt* to hunt (down).

traumatisant, -ante *adj* traumatic.

traumatisme *m (choc)* trauma.

travail, -aux *m (activité, lieu)* work; *(à effectuer)* job, task; *(emploi)* job; **travaux** *(dans la rue)* roadwork, construction; *(aménagement)* alterations; **travaux pratiques** *(à l'école etc)* practical work.

travailler *vi* to work (**à qch** at *ou* on sth).

travailleur, -euse 1 *adj* hard-working. **2** *mf* worker.

travers 1 *prép & adv* **à t.** through; **en t. (de)** across. **2** *adv* **de t.** *(chapeau etc)* crooked; *(comprendre)* badly; **j'ai avalé de t.** it went down the wrong way.

traversée *f* crossing.

traverser *vt* to cross, to go across; *(foule, période)* to go through.

traversin *m* bolster.

trébucher *vi* to stumble (**sur** over); **faire t. qn** to trip sb (up).

trèfle *m Cartes* clubs.

treize *adj & m inv* thirteen.

treizième *adj & mf* thirteenth.

tréma *m* dieresis.

tremblement *m* shaking, trembling; **t. de terre** earthquake.

trembler *vi* to shake, to tremble (**de** with).

tremper 1 *vt* to soak; (*plonger*) to dip (**dans** in). **2** *vi* to soak; **faire t. qch** to soak sth.

tremplin *m* springboard.

trentaine *f* une **t. (de)** about thirty.

trente *adj & m* thirty; **un t.-trois tours** an album.

trentième *adj & mf* thirtieth.

très *adv* very; **t. aimé**/*etc* (*with past participle*) much *ou* greatly liked/ *etc*.

trésor *m* treasure.

tresse *f* (*cheveux*) braid.

tresser *vt* to braid.

tri *m* sorting (out); **faire le t. de** to sort (out); **centre de t.** (*des postes*) sorting office.

triangle *m* triangle.

triangulaire *adj* triangular.

tribu *f* tribe.

tribunal, -aux *m* court.

tribune *f* (*de stade*) (grand)stand.

tricher *vi* to cheat.

tricheur, -euse *mf* cheater.

tricolore *adj* red, white and blue; **feu t.** traffic light.

tricot *m* (*activité*) knitting; (*chandail*) sweater.

tricoter *vti* to knit.

tricycle *m* tricycle.

trier *vt* to sort (out).

trimestre *m* (*période*) quarter; (*scolaire*) term.

trimestriel, -ielle *adj* (*revue*) quarterly; **bulletin t.** (quarter) report card.

tringle *f* rail, rod.

trinquer *vi* to clink glasses; **t. à la santé de qn** to drink to sb's health.

triomphe *m* triumph (**sur** over).

triompher *vi* to triumph (**de** over).

triple *m* **le t.** three times as much (**de** as).

tripler *vti* to treble, to triple.

tripoter *vt* to fiddle around with.

triste *adj* sad; (*couleur, temps*) gloomy.

tristement *adv* sadly.

tristesse *f* sadness; (*du temps*) gloom(iness).

trivial, -e, -aux *adj* coarse, vulgar.

trognon *m* (*de fruit*) core.

trois *adj & m* three.

troisième *adj & mf* third.

troisièmement *adv* thirdly.

trombone *m* trombone; (*agrafe*) paper clip.

trompe *f* (*d'éléphant*) trunk.

tromper *vt* to deceive; (*être infidèle à*) to be unfaithful to.

tromper (se) *vpr* to be mistaken; **se t. de route**/*etc* to take the wrong road/*etc*; **se t. de date**/*etc* to get the date/*etc* wrong.

trompette *f* trumpet.

trompeur, -euse *adj* (*apparences*) deceptive, misleading; (*personne*) deceitful.

tronc *m* trunk.

tronçonneuse *f* chain saw.

trône *m* throne.

trop *adv* too; too much; **t. dur**/*etc* too hard/*etc*; **t. fatigué pour jouer** too tired to play; **boire**/*etc* **t.** to drink/*etc* too much; **t. de sel**/*etc* (*quantité*) too much salt/*etc*; **t. de gens**/*etc* (*nombre*) too many people/*etc*; **un euro**/*etc* **de t.** *ou* **en t.** one euro/*etc* too many.

tropical, -e, -aux *adj* tropical.

trot *m* trot; **aller au t.** to trot.

trotter *vi* (*cheval*) to trot.

trottinette *f* (*jouet*) scooter.

trottoir *m* sidewalk.

trou *m* hole; **t. de (la) serrure** keyhole; **t. (de mémoire)** lapse (of memory).

troublant, -ante *adj (détail)* disturbing, disquieting.

trouble *adj (liquide)* cloudy; *(image)* blurred; **voir t.** to see things blurred.

troubler *vt* to disturb; *(vue)* to blur.

troubles *mpl (de santé)* trouble; *(désordres)* disturbances.

trouer *vt* to make a hole *ou* holes in.

troupe *f (groupe)* group; *(de théâtre)* company; **troupes** *(armée)* troops.

troupeau, -x *m (vaches)* herd; *(moutons, oies)* flock.

trousse *f (étui)* case, kit; *(d'écolier)* pencil case; **t. à outils** toolkit; **t. à pharmacie** first-aid kit; **t. de toilette** *(de femme)* cosmetic case; *(d'homme)* shaving kit.

trousseau, -x *m (de clefs)* bunch.

trouver *vt* to find; **aller/venir t. qn** to go/come and see sb; **je trouve que** I think that.

trouver (se) *vpr* to be; *(être situé)* to be located; *(se sentir)* to feel; *(dans une situation)* to find oneself.

truc *m (astuce)* trick; *(moyen)* way; *(chose) Fam* thing.

truite *f* trout.

truquer *vt (photo)* to fake; *(élections, match)* to rig.

TTC *abrév (toutes taxes comprises)* inclusive of tax.

tu *pron* you *(familiar form of address)*.

tu, tue *voir* **taire**.

tuba *m (instrument de musique)* tuba; *(de plongée)* snorkel.

tube *m* tube; *(chanson) Fam* hit.

tuberculose *f* TB.

tue-tête (à) *adv* at the top of one's voice.

tuer *vti* to kill.

tuer (se) *vpr* to kill oneself; *(dans un accident)* to be killed.

tuile *f* tile.

tulipe *f* tulip.

tunisien, -ienne 1 *adj* Tunisian. **2** *mf* T. Tunisian.

tunnel *m* tunnel.

turbulent, -ente *adj (enfant)* disruptive.

tutoyer *vt* **t. qn** to use the familiar *tu* form with sb.

tutu *m* ballet skirt.

tuyau, -x *m* pipe; **t. d'arrosage** hose(pipe); **t. d'échappement** tailpipe.

TVA *f abrév (taxe à la valeur ajoutée)* sales tax.

type *m* type; *(individu)* fellow, guy.

typique *adj* typical (**de** of).

tzigane 1 *adj* gipsy. **2** *mf* T. gipsy.

U

UE *f abrév (Union Européenne)* EU.

ulcère *m* ulcer.

ULM *m inv abrév (ultraléger motorisé)* microlight.

ultérieurement *adv* later (on), subsequently.

ultime *adj* last; *(préparatifs)* final.

ultramoderne *adj* ultramodern.

ultra-secret, -ète *adj* top-secret.

un, une 1 *art indéf* a; *(devant voyelle)* an; **une page** a page; **un ange** an angel. **2** *adj* one; **la page un** page one; **un mètre** one metre. **3** *pron & mf* one; **l'un** one; **les uns some**; **j'en ai un** I have one; **l'un d'eux, l'une d'elles** one of them; **la une** *(de journal)* the front page.

unanime *adj* unanimous.

unanimité *f* **à l'u.** unanimously.

uni, -ie *adj* united; *(famille)* close; *(surface)* smooth; *(couleur)* plain.

unième *adj (after a number)* (-)first; **trente et u.** thirty-first; **cent u.** hundred and first.

uniforme *m* uniform.
union *f* union.
Union Européenne *f* European Union.
unique *adj (fille, espoir etc)* only; *(prix, marché)* single; *(exceptionnel)* unique.
uniquement *adv* only.
unir *vt (efforts, forces)* to combine; *(deux pays etc)* to unite, to join together; **u. deux personnes** *(amitié)* to unite two people.
unir (s') *vpr (étudiants etc)* to unite.
unité *f (mesure, élément)* unit.
univers *m* universe.
universel, -elle *adj* universal.
universitaire *adj* ville/*etc* u. university town/*etc*.
université *f* university; **à l'u.** at college, at school.
urgence *f (cas)* emergency; *(de décision etc)* urgency; **faire qch d'u.** to do sth urgently; **(service des) urgences** *(d'hôpital)* emergency room.
urgent, -ente *adj* urgent.
urne *f* ballot box; **aller aux urnes** to go to the polls, to vote.
usage *m* use; *(habitude)* custom; **faire u. de** to make use of; **hors d'u.** not in service.
usagé, -ée *adj* worn.
usager *m* user.
usé, -ée *adj (tissu etc)* worn (out).
user *vt*, **s'user** *vpr (vêtement)* to wear out.
usine *f* factory.
ustensile *m* utensil.
usuel, -elle *adj* everyday.
usure *f* wear (and tear).
utile *adj* useful (à to).
utilisateur, -trice *mf* user.
utilisation *f* use.
utiliser *vt* to use.
utilité *f* use(fulness); **d'une grande u.** very useful.

V

va *voir* aller[1].
vacances *fpl* vacation; **en v.** on vacation; **les grandes v.** the summer vacation.
vacancier, -ière *mf* vacationer.
vacarme *m* din, uproar.
vaccin *m* vaccine; **faire un v. à** to vaccinate.
vaccination *f* vaccination.
vacciner *vt* to vaccinate.
vache *f* 1 cow. 2 *adj (méchant) Fam* mean.
vachement *adv Fam (très)* damned; *(beaucoup)* a hell of a lot.
vaciller *vi* to sway; *(flamme, lumière)* to flicker.
vagabond, -onde *mf* tramp, hobo.
vague 1 *adj* vague; *(regard)* vacant. 2 *f* wave; **v. de chaleur** heat wave; **v. de froid** cold spell.
vaguement *adv* vaguely.
vain (en) *adv* in vain.
vaincre* *vt* to beat.
vaincu, -ue *mf (sportif)* loser.
vainqueur *m (sportif)* winner.
vais *voir* aller[1].
vaisselle *f* dishes; *(à laver)* dirty dishes; **faire la v.** to wash the dishes.
valable *adj (billet etc)* valid.
valet *m Cartes* jack.
valeur *f* value; **avoir de la v.** to be valuable; **objets de v.** valuables.
valide *adj (personne)* fit, able-bodied; *(billet)* valid.
valise *f (suit)case*; **faire ses valises** to pack (one's bags).
vallée *f* valley.
valoir* *vi* to be worth; **v. cher** to be worth a lot; **un vélo vaut bien une auto** a bicycle is just as good as a car; **il vaut mieux rester** it's better

to stay; **il vaut mieux que j'attende** I'd better wait; **ça ne vaut rien** it's no good; **ça vaut le coup** it's worth it (**de faire** to do).

valoir (se) *vpr* to be as good as each other; **ça se vaut** it's all the same.

valse *f* waltz.

vandale *mf* vandal.

vanille *f* vanilla; **glace à la v.** vanilla ice cream.

vaniteux, -euse *adj* conceited.

vantard, -arde *mf* braggart.

vanter (se) *vpr* to boast (**de** about, of).

vapeur *f* v. (**d'eau**) steam.

vaporisateur *m* (*appareil*) spray.

variable *adj* (*humeur, temps*) changeable.

varicelle *f* chicken pox.

varié, -ée *adj* varied; (*divers*) various.

varier *vti* to vary.

variété *f* variety; **spectacle de variétés** variety show.

vas *voir* **aller**[1].

vase *m* vase.

vaste *adj* vast, huge.

vaut *voir* **valoir**.

veau, -x *m* calf; (*viande*) veal; (*cuir*) calfskin, (calf) leather.

vécu, -ue (*pp of* **vivre**) *adj* (*histoire etc*) true.

vedette *f* (*de cinéma etc*) star.

végétarien, -ienne *adj & mf* vegetarian.

végétation *f* vegetation.

véhicule *m* vehicle; **v. tout terrain** all-terrain *ou* four-wheel drive vehicle.

veille *f* **la v. (de)** the day before; **la v. de Noël** Christmas Eve.

veiller *vi* to stay up; (*sentinelle*) to keep watch; **v. à qch** to see to sth; **v. sur qn** to watch over sb.

veilleur *m* **v. de nuit** night watchman.

veilleuse *f* (*de voiture*) parking light; (*de cuisinière*) pilot light; (*lampe allumée la nuit*) nightlight.

veine *f* vein; (*chance*) *Fam* luck.

vélo *m* bike, bicycle; (*activité*) cycling; **faire du v.** to cycle; **v. tout terrain** mountain bike.

vélomoteur *m* motorcycle.

velours *m* velvet; **v. côtelé** corduroy.

velu, -ue *adj* hairy.

vendange *f* (*récolte*) grape harvest; (*raisin récolté*) grapes (harvested); **vendanges** (*période*) grape-harvesting time; **faire les vendanges** to pick the grapes.

vendeur, -euse *mf* sales clerk; (*de voitures etc*) salesman, saleswoman.

vendre *vt* to sell (**qch à qn** sb sth, sth to sb); **à v.** for sale.

vendre (se) *vpr* to sell; **ça se vend bien** it sells well.

vendredi *m* Friday; **V. saint** Good Friday.

vénéneux, -euse *adj* poisonous.

vengeance *f* revenge.

venger (se) *vpr* to get one's revenge, to get one's own back (**de qn** on sb; **de qch** for sth).

venimeux, -euse *adj* poisonous.

venin *m* poison.

venir* *vi* (*aux* **être**) to come (**de** from); **v. faire** to come to do; **viens me voir** come and see me; **je viens/venais d'arriver** I've/I'd just arrived; **où veux-tu en v.?** what are you getting at?; **faire v.** to send for, to get.

vent *m* wind; **il y a du v.** it's windy; **coup de v.** gust of wind.

vente *f* sale; **v. (aux enchères)** auction; **en v.** on sale; **prix de v.** selling price.

ventilateur *m* fan.

ventre *m* stomach; **avoir mal au v.** to have a stomachache.

venu, -ue *mf* **nouveau v., nouvelle venue** newcomer; **le premier v.** anyone.

ver *m* worm; (*de fruits etc*) maggot; **v. de terre** (earth)worm.

véranda f *(en verre)* sunroom *(attached to house).*

verbe m verb.

verdict m verdict.

verdure f *(végétation)* greenery.

verger m orchard.

verglas m (black) ice.

véridique adj truthful.

vérification f check(ing).

vérifier vt to check.

véritable adj true, real; *(non imité)* real.

véritablement adv really.

vérité f truth.

vernir vt to varnish.

vernis m varnish; **v. à ongles** nail polish.

verra, verrai(t) etc voir **voir**.

verre m glass; **boire** ou **prendre un v.** to have a drink; **v. de bière** glass of beer; **v. à bière** beer glass.

verrou m bolt; **fermer au v.** to bolt.

verrouiller vt *(porte)* to bolt; *(quartier)* to seal off.

verrue f wart.

vers[1] prép *(direction)* toward(s).

vers[2] m *(de poème)* line.

verse (à) adv **pleuvoir à v.** to pour (down).

versement m payment.

verser vt to pour; *(larmes)* to shed; *(argent)* to pay.

version f *(de film, d'incident etc)* version.

verso m 'voir au v.' see over.'

vert, verte 1 adj green; *(pas mûr)* unripe. **2** m green.

vertical, -e, -aux adj vertical.

vertige m **avoir le v.** to be ou feel dizzy; **donner le v. à qn** to make sb (feel) dizzy.

vessie f bladder.

veste f jacket.

vestiaire m locker room.

veston m (suit) jacket.

vêtement m garment; **vêtements** clothes; **vêtements de sport** sportswear.

vétérinaire f vet.

vêtu, -ue adj dressed *(de in).*

vétuste adj dilapidated.

veuf, veuve 1 adj widowed. **2** mf widower, widow.

veuille(s), veuillent etc voir **vouloir**.

veulent, veut, veux voir **vouloir**.

vexant, -ante adj upsetting.

vexer vt to upset.

VF f abrév *(version française)* film en VF film dubbed into French.

viande f meat.

vibration f vibration.

vibrer vi to vibrate.

vice m vice.

vicieux, -euse adj *(pervers)* depraved; *(perfide)* underhand.

victime f victim; *(d'un accident)* casualty; **être v. de** to be the victim of.

victoire f victory; *(en sports)* win.

victorieux, -euse adj victorious; *(équipe)* winning.

vidange f *(de véhicule)* oil change.

vide 1 adj empty. **2** m emptiness; *(trou)* gap.

vidéo adj inv video.

vidéocassette f video cassette.

vide-ordures m inv garbage chute.

vide-poches m inv glove compartment.

vider vt, **se vider** vpr to empty.

vie f life; *(durée)* lifetime; **le coût de la v.** the cost of living; **gagner sa v.** to earn one's living; **en v.** living.

vieil voir **vieux**.

vieillard m old man.

vieille voir **vieux**.

vieillesse f old age.

vieillir 1 vi to get old; *(changer)* to age. **2** vt **v. qn** *(vêtement etc)* to make sb look old(er).

vierge 1 adj *(femme, neige)* virgin; *(feuille de papier, film)* blank; **être v.** *(femme, homme)* to be a virgin. **2** f virginity.

vieux *(or* **vieil** *before vowel or*

mute h), **vieille,** *pl* **vieux, vieilles 1** *adj* old. **2** *m* old man; **les vieux** old people; **mon v.!** *(mon ami)* buddy!, pal! **3** *f* old woman; **ma vieille!** *(ma chère)* dear!

vif, vive *adj (enfant)* lively; *(couleur, lumière)* bright; *(froid)* biting; **brûlé v.** burned alive.

vignette *f (de véhicule)* road tax sticker.

vignoble *m* vineyard.

vilain, -aine *adj (laid)* ugly; *(enfant)* bad; *(impoli)* rude.

villa *f* (detached) house.

village *m* village.

villageois, -oise *mf* villager.

ville *f* town; *(grande)* city; **aller/être en v.** to go (in)to/be in town.

vin *m* wine.

vinaigre *m* vinegar.

vinaigrette *f* oil-and-vinegar dressing, vinaigrette.

vingt *adj & m* twenty. **v. et un** twenty-one.

vingtaine *f* **une v. (de)** about twenty.

vingtième *adj & mf* twentieth.

viol *m* rape.

violemment *adv* violently.

violence *f* violence.

violent, -ente *adj* violent.

violer *vt* to rape.

violet, -ette *adj & m* purple.

violeur *m* rapist.

violon *m* violin.

violoncelle *m* cello.

vipère *f* adder.

virage *m (de route)* bend; *(de véhicule)* turn.

virement *m* transfer.

virgule *f* comma; *(de nombre)* (decimal) point; **2 v. 5** 2 point 5.

virus *m* virus.

vis¹ *voir* **vivre, voir.**

vis² *f* screw.

visa *m (de passeport)* visa.

visage *m* face.

viser 1 *vi* to aim (**à** to). **2** *vt (cible)* to aim at.

visible *adj* visible.

visite *f* visit; **rendre v. à** to visit; **v. (médicale)** medical examination; **v. guidée** guided tour.

visiter *vt* to visit.

visiteur, -euse *mf* visitor.

visser *vt* to screw on.

vit *voir* **vivre, voir.**

vitamine *f* vitamin.

vite *adv* quickly.

vitesse *f* speed; *(sur un véhicule)* gear; **boîte de vitesses** transmission; **à toute v.** at full speed.

viticulteur, -trice *mf* wine grower.

vitrail, -aux *m* stained-glass window.

vitre *f* (window)pane; *(de véhicule, train)* window.

vitrine *f* (shop) window; *(meuble)* display cabinet.

vivace *adj (plante)* perennial; *(tradition, sentiment)* deep-rooted; *(souvenir)* vivid.

vivant, -ante *adj* living; *(récit, rue)* lively.

vive *int* **v. le roi!/etc!** long live the king!/etc!; **v. les vacances!** hurray for vacation!

vivement *adv* quickly; *(répliquer)* sharply; *(regretter)* deeply.

vivre* **1** *vi* to live; **v. vieux** to live to be old; **v. de** *(fruits etc)* to live on; *(travail etc)* to live by. **2** *vt (vie)* to live; *(aventure)* to live through.

VO *f abrév (version originale)* **film en VO** film in the original language.

vocabulaire *m* vocabulary.

vodka *f* vodka.

vœu, -x *m* wish.

voici *prép* here is, this is, *pl* here are, these are; **me v.** here I am; **v. dix ans que** it's ten years since.

voie *f* road; *(rails)* track; *(partie de route)* lane; *(chemin)* way; *(de gare)* platform; **v. sans issue** dead end; **sur la bonne v.** on the right track.

voilà *prép* there is, that is, *pl* there are, those are; **les v.** there they are; **v., j'arrive!** all right, I'm coming!; **v. dix ans que** it's ten years since.

voile[1] *m (tissu)* veil.

voile[2] *f (de bateau)* sail; *(sport)* sailing; **faire de la v.** to sail.

voilier *m (de plaisance)* sailboat.

voir* *vti* to see; **faire v. qch** to show sth; **fais v.** let me see; **je ne peux pas la v.** *Fam* I can't stand (the sight of) her; **ça n'a rien à v. avec** that's got nothing to do with.

voir (se) *vpr (se fréquenter)* to see each other; **ça se voit** that's obvious.

voisin, -ine 1 *adj* neighboring; *(maison, pièce)* next (**de** to). **2** *mf* neighbor.

voisinage *m* neighborhood.

voiture *f* car.

voix *f* voice; *(d'électeur)* vote; **à v. basse** in a whisper.

vol[1] *m (d'avion, d'oiseau)* flight.

vol[2] *m (délit)* theft; *(hold-up)* robbery.

volaille *f* une v. a fowl.

volant *m (steering)* wheel.

volcan *m* volcano.

voler[1] *vi (oiseau, avion etc)* to fly.

voler[2] *vti (prendre)* to steal (**à** from).

volet *m (de fenêtre)* shutter.

voleur, -euse *mf* thief; **au v.!** stop thief!

volontaire 1 *adj (voulu) (geste etc)* deliberate. **2** *mf* volunteer.

volontairement *adv (exprès)* deliberately.

volontariat *m* voluntary work.

volonté *f* will; **bonne v.** goodwill; **mauvaise v.** ill will.

volontiers *adv* gladly.

volume *m (de boîte, de son, livre)* volume.

volumineux, -euse *adj* bulky.

vomir 1 *vt* to bring up. **2** *vi* to be sick, to vomit.

vomissements *mpl* **avoir des** to vomit.

vont *voir* **aller**[1].

vos *voir* **votre**.

vote *m* vote; *(de loi)* passing; **bureau de v.** polling place.

voter *vi* to vote. **2** *vt (loi)* to pass.

votre, pl vos *adj poss* your.

vôtre *pron poss* **le** *ou* **la v., les vôtres** yours; **à la v.!** cheers!

voudra, voudrai(t) *etc voir* **vouloir**.

vouloir* *vt* to want (**faire** to do); **je veux qu'il parte** I want him to go; **v. dire** to mean (**que** that); **je voudrais rester** I'd like to stay; **je voudrais un pain** I'd like a loaf of bread; **voulez-vous me suivre** will you follow me; **si tu veux** if you like *ou* wish; **en v. à qn d'avoir fait qch** to be angry with sb for doing sth; **je veux bien (attendre)** I don't mind (waiting); **sans le v.** unintentionally.

vous *pron (sujet, complément direct)* you; *(complément indirect)* (to) you; *(réfléchi)* yourself, *pl* yourselves; *(réciproque)* each other.

vous-même *pron* yourself.

vous-mêmes *pron pl* yourselves.

vouvoyer *vt* **v. qn** to use the formal *vous* form with sb.

voyage *m* trip, journey; **aimer les voyages** to like traveling; **faire un v., partir en v.** to go on a trip; **bon v.!** have a pleasant trip!; **v. organisé** *(package)* tour; **agent/agence de voyages** travel agent/agency.

voyager *vi* to travel.

voyageur, -euse *mf* traveler; *(passager)* passenger.

voyant, -ante 1 *adj (couleur)* gaudy, loud. **2** *m (signal) (warning)* light; *(d'appareil électrique)* pilot light.

voyelle *f* vowel.

voyou *m* hooligan.

vrac (en) *adv (en désordre)* in a muddle, haphazardly.

vrac /

vra... adj true; (réel) real; (...ue) genuine.

...t adv really.

vra...nblable adj (probable) likely.

VTT m inv abrév (vélo tout terrain) mountain bike.

vu, vue pp of **voir**.

vue f (spectacle) sight; (sens) (eye)sight; (panorama, photo) view; **en v.** (proche) in sight; **de v.** (connaître) by sight.

vulgaire adj vulgar.

Y

y 1 adv there; **allons-y** let's go; **j'y suis!** now I get it!; **je n'y suis pour rien** I have nothing to do with it. **2** pron (= à cela) **je m'y attendais** I was expecting it; **ça y est!** that's it!

yacht m yacht.

yaourt m yogurt.

yeux voir **œil**.

W

wagon m (de voyageurs) car; (de marchandises) freight car.

wagon-lit, pl **wagons-lits** m sleeping car.

wagon-restaurant, pl **wagons-restaurants** m dining car.

waters mpl bathroom, men's ou ladies' room.

w-c mpl bathroom, men's ou ladies' room.

week-end m weekend.

western m (film) western.

whisky, pl **-ies** m whiskey.

Z

zèbre m zebra.

zéro m zero; **deux buts à z.** two nothing.

zeste m **un z. de citron** a piece of lemon peel.

zigzag m zigzag; **en z.** (route etc) zigzag(ging).

zigzaguer vi to zigzag.

zone f zone, area; **z. bleue** restricted parking area; **z. industrielle** industrial park.

zoo m zoo.

zut! int oh dear!